Learn TypeScript 3 by Building Web Applications

Gain a solid understanding of TypeScript, Angular, Vue, React, and NestJS

Sebastien Dubois
Alexis Georges

BIRMINGHAM - MUMBAI

Learn TypeScript 3 by Building Web Applications

Copyright © 2019 Packt Publishing

Commissioning Editor: Aaron Lazar
Acquisition Editor: Alok Dhuri
Content Development Editor: Pathikrit Roy
Senior Editor: Afshaan Khan
Technical Editor: Gaurav Gala
Copy Editor: Safis Editing
Project Coordinator: Francy Puthiry
Proofreader: Safis Editing
Indexer: Manju Arasan
Production Designer: Arvindkumar Gupta

First published: November 2019

Production reference: 1221119

Published by Packt Publishing Ltd.
Livery Place
35 Livery Street
Birmingham
B3 2PB, UK.

ISBN 978-1-78961-586-9

www.packtpub.com

To my beloved family, who have supported me more than I could ever hope for. I couldn't have made it without them!

– Sebastien Dubois

To my girlfriend, who has supported me during this challenge.

– Alexis Georges

Packt.com

Subscribe to our online digital library for full access to over 7,000 books and videos, as well as industry leading tools to help you plan your personal development and advance your career. For more information, please visit our website.

Why subscribe?

- Spend less time learning and more time coding with practical eBooks and Videos from over 4,000 industry professionals

- Improve your learning with Skill Plans built especially for you

- Get a free eBook or video every month

- Fully searchable for easy access to vital information

- Copy and paste, print, and bookmark content

Did you know that Packt offers eBook versions of every book published, with PDF and ePub files available? You can upgrade to the eBook version at www.packt.com and as a print book customer, you are entitled to a discount on the eBook copy. Get in touch with us at customercare@packtpub.com for more details.

At www.packt.com, you can also read a collection of free technical articles, sign up for a range of free newsletters, and receive exclusive discounts and offers on Packt books and eBooks.

Foreword

TypeScript was unleashed into the world on October 1, 2012. At the time of writing, that makes it 7 years old. I was fortunate enough at that time to be allowed to use it from the get-go and spend time helping others with it via Stack Overflow. Sebastien has been part of the TypeScript journey with me since before it was popular. It was only later (circa 2016) that TypeScript blew up in popularity and now, in 2019, it is quickly becoming the de facto way to create web applications. Two key popular web UI frameworks, Angular and Vue, are both being written in TypeScript. The React team keeps a close eye on TypeScript, ensuring that new APIs are typesafe and that the TypeScript team supports React and JSX out of the box.

That brings us to this book. There are few books out there that tackle the topic of building web applications with TypeScript head-on in the way that Sebastien's book does. One of the great things about this book is the expansive coverage of the best of what the JavaScript and TypeScript ecosystem has to offer. All major UI frameworks (React, Angular, and Vue) are covered. My personal recommendation of unit test framework (Jest) is in there. And even the backend portion of the ecosystems (GraphQL, Apollo, and Nest) is covered, providing a full picture on how to create modern web applications. In all honesty, I cannot think of a better resource that provides such a complete picture for developing web applications today with TypeScript in one place. And what better author than Sebastien, someone who has been such a helpful part of the TypeScript community.

Basarat Ali Syed

Basarat is a Microsoft MVP for TypeScript, an OSS fanatic, a book author, an egghead, and a Youtuber. He is a top contributor for TypeScript on Stack Overflow and, by day, he is a frontend practice lead. Find out more at http://basarat.com.

Contributors

About the authors

Sebastien Dubois is a passionate software craftsman and FOSS contributor with many years of experience as a senior developer and technical team leader.

He is an entrepreneur, IT consultant/coach, and owner of DeveloPassion, a Belgian IT firm.

Over the years, Sebastien has worked on backend systems, web applications, architecture, and IT security for various organizations. He has used different programming languages, which gives him a broad perspective on modern software development. He has also been using, teaching, and advocating TypeScript since 2015.

You can find him on Twitter as `@dSebastien`, on Medium as `@dSebastien`, or on his personal blog: dsebastien.

Alexis Georges is a developer who is passionate about software development, but also about everything related to IT: open source, system administration, respect for privacy, and many others.

During his studies in programming and networking, he learned the basics of programming and system administration.

Alexis has some experience in JavaScript, PHP, Java, C, and (obviously) TypeScript. He discovered the TypeScript programming language when he began his career as a software engineer in Sebastien's team. Later, he participated in the migration of the Stark framework from AngularJS to Angular.

You can find him on Twitter as `@Super_ITMan` and on his blog: SuperITMan.

About the reviewers

Christopher Allán Cortés Ruiz is a skilled developer and experienced frontend architect with a deep knowledge of JavaScript and TypeScript. He can grasp their new features rapidly to get the most out of them. He has mastered several of the latest frontend technologies, such as AngularJS, Angular, Redux, and NPM, which he has used in several recent projects. Moreover, he has made an outstanding contribution to advertising and financial companies in Mexico, Spain, and Belgium by revamping their frontend applications with the most cutting-edge standards and technologies, from contributing to architectural design and coaching junior developers, through putting in place solid and stable coding, right to the implementation of the user interface.

> *I want to thank Sebastien Dubois for allowing me to be part of his excellent book about TypeScript as a reviewer. I'm also grateful to my former colleagues, Jurgen and Hendrik, who have taught me a lot professionally and personally. Finally, I also want to thank my wife, Rosa, because without her patience and understanding, all those long nights of learning and reading about the latest technologies wouldn't have been so rewarding.*

Martin Jurča works as a tech leader and developer for Seznam.cz. He is passionate about TypeScript, frontend technologies, and pushing the limits of what is possible. Martin was a reviewer of *Hands-On RESTful APIs with TypeScript 3*, gave a speech at JSConf Iceland, is a regular speaker at tech conferences in Brno, and is a regular tutor at the Seznam IT academy.

Martin likes to relax with a good book, a hike, or his friends over a bottle of wine or a cup of tea. He lives in Brno with his wife and baby daughter.

> *I would like to thank my amazing wife for all the support she gives me and for every day I get to spend with her. I would also like to thank my daughter for motivating me to be a better person every day.*

Packt is searching for authors like you

If you're interested in becoming an author for Packt, please visit `authors.packtpub.com` and apply today. We have worked with thousands of developers and tech professionals, just like you, to help them share their insight with the global tech community. You can make a general application, apply for a specific hot topic that we are recruiting an author for, or submit your own idea.

Table of Contents

Preface

Dear reader,

Thank you for joining us on this learning journey!

As we will discover together throughout the book, the TypeScript programming language can be used to write awesome applications and greatly enhance the developer experience and code quality/safety. TypeScript can be used wherever JavaScript can be, which means *practically everywhere*. Moreover, TypeScript works wonderfully well with all major libraries and frameworks. Last but not least, it also has a large, vibrant, and enthusiastic community.

With this book, our hope is that we will be able to convince you that TypeScript is a great programming language and that it is relevant whether you are writing frontend applications, backend systems – or whatever else, actually.

Throughout the book, we will give you everything you need in order to acquire a good understanding of how powerful TypeScript really is, how versatile it can be, and how it fits into the modern development puzzle.

But don't take our word for it – we'll show you!

This is a practical book, not a reference guide. We will hold your hand through the journey, but you'll have to roll up your sleeves and get your hands dirty. We strongly believe that learning by doing is the most time-efficient approach to mastering new subjects and this is exactly why we have created this book regarding the TypeScript programming language. In addition, we also *love* to share our passion for technology and we really hope that you'll enjoy reading this book.

In the first half, we will introduce you to many important features of the TypeScript programming language through exercises and by helping you to create multiple applications. While creating those first applications, you will also learn about many important APIs of the modern web as well as many useful design patterns, techniques, libraries, and tools.

By reading through the chapters and, most importantly, by coding these applications, you'll gain a really good understanding of how TypeScript works and how it fits into the modern software ecosystem.

In the second half of the book, we will continue to teach you about TypeScript features, but our focus will shift to discovering how TypeScript can be combined with some of the most popular libraries and frameworks out there today: Angular, Vue.js, and React. Not only that, but we will also show you how to write backend applications using NestJS, GraphQL, and Apollo.

All of those frameworks and libraries will be explained in the book in enough detail to give you a real taste of how they actually work and without requiring you to do a lot of side research. You'll go from zero to hero in no time!

This book is truly unique; you won't find many others covering so many subjects in a simple, approachable, and cohesive way. Step by step, you'll go from the basics to the more advanced concepts and you'll create cool applications along the way!

Who this book is for

This book is for software developers looking to discover the following:

- What TypeScript is
- What TypeScript brings to the table
- Why TypeScript adds value for both small and large software development teams
- How to leverage TypeScript to write great quality software

This book is also relevant for developers already familiar with TypeScript who wish to know how the language has evolved over time or get a refresh, including what has been introduced by the most recent releases and how best to leverage the language with various modern web frameworks.

In any case, this book is for developers who want to learn by doing rather than by reading a thousand pages of language specifications. This book is also relevant/useful for both backend and frontend software engineers.

What this book covers

Chapter 1, *Introduction to TypeScript,* presents the current frontend development landscape and explains why TypeScript comes into the picture. It illustrates the problems of vanilla JavaScript and goes on to present TypeScript and show how it can improve code quality, improve the developer's life, and help larger teams. Then, it shows you how to install everything you'll need to work on the projects covered in the book.

Chapter 2, *Building TodoIt – Your Own Todo Management Web Application with TypeScript,* guides you in building a first concrete project using TypeScript: a simple todo management web application. This application will make use of npm, TypeScript, HTML, and a bit of CSS for good measure. This project is a great introduction to the TypeScript language, tsc (the TypeScript compiler), its configuration file (tsconfig.json), npm, and some other valuable tools. By going through this chapter, you will learn about TypeScript basics by creating some TypeScript files, defining variables of different (basic) types, functions, and compiling code before checking the results.

Chapter 3, *Improving TodoIt with Classes and Interfaces,* revisits the TodoIt application by making use of classes and interfaces. This will drastically improve code quality by going from a purely imperative programming approach to a more object-oriented one. This will help code convey more meaning and isolate concerns more properly. This chapter covers **Object-Oriented Programming (OOP)** basic concepts and nomenclature: encapsulation, abstraction, inheritance, polymorphism, interfaces and classes, composition over inheritance, and more. The chapter then helps you define the domain model of the application using **Unified Modeling Language** (**UML**). That model is then implemented using TypeScript. While doing so, you will create some classes, and you will discover how to define constructors, how to set default values, how to use accessors, and more. Inheritance will also be covered as well as interfaces. You will learn about structural typing as well as how TypeScript classes and interfaces, and JavaScript objects and classes, relate to one another.

Chapter 4, *Leveraging Generics and Enums,* guides you through building a media management web application. Along the way, you will learn about generics and enums and you will leverage them to write better code. The application's data will also be persisted in the web browser's local storage, which will teach you about its existence and the corresponding APIs used to store/retrieve data from local storage. While implementing the application, you will discover how to use third-party libraries with TypeScript, what type definitions are, and how to retrieve them.

Chapter 5, *Coding WorldExplorer to Explore the Population of the World*, helps you to create an application that gets data from a RESTful web API of the World Bank using the `Fetch` and `Promise` APIs available in all modern web browsers. With this project, you'll dive deeper into TypeScript concepts such as modules, module resolution, and barrels. You will also learn about using `async` and `await` to make asynchronous code look synchronous. While covering these subjects, we will take some time to discuss REST, RESTful, and web APIs. The project code will be organized so as to facilitate testing, which will again put emphasis on the importance of testing and good isolation between parts of the code base. Finally, the project will make use of Chart.js (`https://www.chartjs.org/`) to create interactive visualizations of the data. Again, this will familiarize you with the usage of third-party libraries in TypeScript.

Chapter 6, *Introduction to Testing*, covers some important ideas around code quality and software testing. The focus of the chapter will be on how to ensure that an application behaves in the intended manner, both from a functional and non-functional point of view. You'll discover, or re-discover, the different types of tests that can be written, the different testing techniques, and the tools of the trade in the JavaScript and TypeScript ecosystem. Finally, you will also learn how to write tests using the Jest (`https://jestjs.io/`) library.

Chapter 7, *Discovering Angular, Angular Material, and RxJS*, explains what modern web applications are all about. It then goes on to introduce the Angular (`https://angular.io/`) framework, as well as Material Design (`https://material.io/design/`) and Angular Material (`https://material.angular.io/`). In addition, it will also teach you about Reactive Programming and the RxJS (`https://rxjs-dev.firebaseapp.com/`) library.

Chapter 8, *Rewriting MediaMan Using Angular and Angular Material*, helps you to create your first Angular application using TypeScript, Angular Material, and RxJS.

Chapter 9, *Introducing Vue.js*, introduces Vue.js (`https://vuejs.org/`), its major concepts, as well as the surrounding tools (such as Vue CLI). This will provide you with a broader point of view as it shows a different and lighter way of creating modern web applications. While introducing Vue.js, we will also explain how to leverage TypeScript to write better code. This chapter also covers the dependency injection pattern and explains how to use InversifyJS (`http://inversify.io/`) to implement this pattern within Vue.js applications.

Chapter 10, *Creating LyricsFinder with Vue.js*, helps you create yet another application, this time using Vue.js, Vue CLI, and the Element (https://element.eleme.io/#/en-us) UI toolkit. This application will be more complex, as it will need to interact with multiple web APIs in order to fetch the required information. This will help us demonstrate how to properly handle asynchronous processing using modern libraries.

Chapter 11, *Diving into React, NestJS, GraphQL, and Apollo*, introduces one more way to create modern web applications, using React (https://reactjs.org/), a tremendously popular library. This chapter also introduces NestJS (https://nestjs.com/), a backend application framework, as well as GraphQL (https://graphql.org/) and Apollo (https://www.apollographql.com/), which can be leveraged to create modern APIs. Of course, you'll also see how to best leverage TypeScript with each of those!

Chapter 12, *Revisiting LyricsFinder*, revisits the LyricsFinder application using React and React Bootstrap (https://react-bootstrap.github.io/). In this chapter, you'll also build a backend application using the NestJS framework. On the backend side, you will create a simple GraphQL API using the Apollo framework. After completing this project, you will have seen three different approaches to create modern web applications and will have integrated multiple libraries, clearly showing the benefits and complexities that arise along the way. Also, you will have used TypeScript to implement a backend system using NestJS, a modern framework inspired by Angular.

What's Next?, concludes the book, but only marks the beginning of your own learning journey.

To get the most out of this book

Basic knowledge of the web platform, web browsers, HTML, and JavaScript is expected. Knowledge of CSS would be nice to have but is not mandatory. Basic familiarity with OOP concepts is also expected.

This book will introduce the most important concepts in any case to make sure that more beginner readers can follow along and gain additional knowledge.

Download the example code files

You can download the example code files for this book from your account at `www.packt.com`. If you purchased this book elsewhere, you can visit `www.packt.com/support` and register to have the files emailed directly to you.

You can download the code files by following these steps:

1. Log in or register at `www.packt.com`.
2. Select the **SUPPORT** tab.
3. Click on **Code Downloads & Errata**.
4. Enter the name of the book in the **Search** box and follow the onscreen instructions.

Once the file is downloaded, please make sure that you unzip or extract the folder using the latest version of:

- WinRAR/7-Zip for Windows
- Zipeg/iZip/UnRarX for Mac
- 7-Zip/PeaZip for Linux

The code bundle for the book is also hosted on GitHub at `https://github.com/PacktPublishing/Learn-TypeScript-3-by-Building-Web-Applications`. In case there's an update to the code, it will be updated on the existing GitHub repository.

We also have other code bundles from our rich catalog of books and videos available at `https://github.com/PacktPublishing/`. Check them out!

Download the color images

We also provide a PDF file that has color images of the screenshots/diagrams used in this book. You can download it here: `https://static.packt-cdn.com/downloads/9781789615869_ColorImages.pdf`.

Conventions used

There are a number of text conventions used throughout this book.

`CodeInText`: Indicates code words in text, database table names, folder names, filenames, file extensions, pathnames, dummy URLs, user input, and Twitter handles. Here is an example: "As you can see, with the `package.json` file, you can do much more than just manage your dependencies."

A block of code is set as follows:

```
import React from 'react';
export const Home = () => {
    return <h2>Home</h2>;
};
```

When we wish to draw your attention to a particular part of a code block, the relevant lines or items are set in bold:

```
let x = 13;
let y = 37;
[x, y] = [y, x];
console.log(`${x} - ${y}`); // 37 - 13
```

Any command-line input or output is written as follows:

```
npm install --global npm@latest
```

Bold: Indicates a new term, an important word, or words that you see on screen. For example, words in menus or dialog boxes appear in the text like this. Here is an example: "Click on **Download for Windows**."

Warnings or important notes appear like this.

Tips and tricks appear like this.

Get in touch

Feedback from our readers is always welcome.

General feedback: If you have questions about any aspect of this book, mention the book title in the subject of your message and email us at `customercare@packtpub.com`.

Errata: Although we have taken every care to ensure the accuracy of our content, mistakes do happen. If you have found a mistake in this book, we would be grateful if you would report this to us. Please visit www.packt.com/submit-errata, selecting your book, clicking on the Errata Submission Form link, and entering the details.

Piracy: If you come across any illegal copies of our works in any form on the internet, we would be grateful if you would provide us with the location address or website name. Please contact us at copyright@packt.com with a link to the material.

If you are interested in becoming an author: If there is a topic that you have expertise in, and you are interested in either writing or contributing to a book, please visit authors.packtpub.com.

Reviews

Please leave a review. Once you have read and used this book, why not leave a review on the site that you purchased it from? Potential readers can then see and use your unbiased opinion to make purchase decisions, we at Packt can understand what you think about our products, and our authors can see your feedback on their book. Thank you!

For more information about Packt, please visit packt.com.

Introduction to TypeScript

1

In this first chapter, we start by looking back in time in order to explain how the JavaScript language has evolved since its creation. This will help us to better understand why/where TypeScript comes into the picture.

We begin by illustrating the problems of vanilla JavaScript. Then, we will turn our attention to TypeScript.

This chapter also states how TypeScript can improve code quality and a developer's life, and help larger teams, by making it possible to create solid and easier-to-maintain code bases.

After that, we review some of the tools that you will need to work on the projects provided in the book and cover how to install each of them. This includes the code editor, the JavaScript runtime, the package manager, a source control management system, TypeScript, and more.

We will also see how to write the famous `Hello World` program with TypeScript and you'll learn a few things about variable declarations and basic TypeScript types.

In this chapter, we will cover the following topics:

- Overview of the current frontend software development landscape
- What is TypeScript and how does it help to improve code quality?
- Similarities between .NET (C#), Java, and TypeScript
- The minimum level of toolkit necessary for frontend development
- How to install Visual Studio Code

- How to install Git
- How to install Node.js and `npm`
- How to update `npm`
- Where are `npm` packages installed?
- How to install TypeScript
- Introduction to basic TypeScript types (`boolean`, `number`, `string`, **string literals**)
- Variable declarations: `var` versus `let` versus `const`
- Basic functions
- How to write the `Hello World` program in TypeScript

TypeScript in a few words

The TypeScript programming language (`http://www.typescriptlang.org`) was created by Microsoft and was later open sourced under the Apache 2.0 license. The source code of the language is available on GitHub over at `https://github.com/Microsoft/TypeScript`. At the time of writing, TypeScript now has 51,705 stars and 7,116 forks on GitHub and its popularity continues to rise.

The first thing to realize is that TypeScript compiles to JavaScript. This means that the output of the TypeScript compiler can run wherever JavaScript code can run, which actually means, nowadays, basically everywhere, since JavaScript can run in the following:

- Web browser
- Backend (for example, with Node.js)
- Desktop (for example, with Electron)
- Mobile, with frameworks such as React Native, NativeScript, Ionic, and many others
- The cloud, with platforms such as Azure Functions, Google Cloud Functions, and Firebase

As stated earlier, TypeScript is *compiled* and not interpreted like JavaScript is. Actually, people often talk about *transpilation* rather than compilation in the case of TypeScript, since the TypeScript compiler actually does source-to-source transformation.

The second key point is that **TypeScript** is a superset of **JavaScript** as shown in the following diagram:

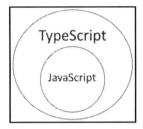

This means that any valid JavaScript code is also valid TypeScript code. This is great because it means that it is very easy to introduce TypeScript into an existing JavaScript code base. It does not stop there, though! As you'll see throughout the book, TypeScript adds a lot over vanilla JavaScript.

A third takeaway is that TypeScript is (optionally) typed. If you're familiar with JavaScript, then you probably know that it is a dynamically and weakly typed language. As any JavaScript code is also valid TypeScript code, it also means that you can declare variables without specifying their type and later assign different types to them (for example, numbers, strings, and more).

Although the fact that defining types is optional by default in TypeScript does not mean that you should avoid defining types. Instead, TypeScript shines when you make clever use of its type system.

TypeScript allows you to clearly specify the type of your variables and functions. In addition, it also has very powerful type inference, support for classes, generics, enums, mixins, and many other cool things that we'll see throughout the book.

We'll see later in the book how to configure the TypeScript compiler to be stricter and we'll also learn the benefits of enforcing and leveraging strong typing at work, as well as for personal projects.

This quick introduction to TypeScript is useful for you to grasp what it is, but it does not explain *why* it exists and why it makes sense for you to use it.

JavaScript

Before we begin our TypeScript journey, it is useful to take a look back at JavaScript and where it comes from.

JavaScript's history in a nutshell

Before we go any further, we should take some time to briefly discuss the history of JavaScript and how it has evolved in recent years. You probably know that JavaScript is the core language of the web. It's actually a very versatile language that supports different programming paradigms such as imperative, object-oriented, functional, and event-driven programming.

As mentioned in the previous section, JavaScript can now be used almost everywhere, but that was not always the case. The language was initially designed by Brendan Eich (`https://brendaneich.com`) around 1995 (more than 20 years ago!) for the Mosaic web browser. The first version of the language was written in 10 days (!) and was called **Mocha**, and was later renamed to **LiveScript**. The whole story is very interesting and well worth reading.

It is important to realize that JavaScript has been here for a very long time and has also evolved a lot, especially since 2005, and more than ever since 2015.

ECMAScript

Another important thing to understand is that behind JavaScript, there is actually a language specification called **ECMAScript**, standardized by Ecma International in ECMA-262 since 1996. Though reading about it will be time consuming for now and not mandatory in order to understand further topics, you should know that this specification governs what JavaScript is and how it evolves. New language features and API proposals all go through the Ecma TC39 technical committee, which decides which ones are mature enough to make it into the specification. This all happens in the open, so don't hesitate to go and check it out.

ECMAScript evolution and support

The version of JavaScript that most developers around the world are familiar with is ES5, which was released in 2009. It included strict mode, accessors, syntax changes, meta-programming, and, most importantly, support for JSON.

Since 2015, ECMAScript, and thus JavaScript, has rapidly evolved. The specification now has a yearly release schedule, meaning that a new version is released each year. Thanks to this evolution, each year, all of the language change proposals that are mature enough get included in the new version of the specification. This follows a trend that we can see throughout the industry to increase the pace at which things evolve. It is very disruptive for large enterprises but is great for innovation.

In 2015, ECMAScript 6 was released and was later renamed ES2015. Since then, ES2016, ES2017, ES2018, and ES2019 have been released in the respective years.

 Note that **ESNext** will always refer to the next version with the proposals that have not been finalized yet.

Make sure to stop by Dr. Axel Rauschmayer's blog (`http://2ality.com`) to learn more. Comparatively, ES2015 was incredibly big compared to the following iterations.

As you can imagine, it takes time for browser vendors and JavaScript engine developers to integrate newly standardized elements of the language. With ES2015, this meant that things such as `let`, `const`, `classes`, and many other features could not be used directly. This led to the increase in popularity of transpilation using tools such as **Babel** or **TypeScript**. Basically, the idea is to be able to use the newest features of the specification in your code right now and to transpile it so that it can run in environments that don't support those features just yet.

JavaScript gotchas

Now that you know a bit more about the history of JavaScript, and before we finally dive into TypeScript, we need to learn about the importance of knowing JavaScript, with its good and bad parts.

As you now know, JavaScript was initially created in 10 days, so it had issues, some of which are, unfortunately, still here today. The TypeScript compiler will protect you from some of these issues but it can't change things that are fundamental in JavaScript such as how numbers are represented.

Here are a few examples of things that are surprising (to say the least) in JavaScript:

- JavaScript variables declared with `var` are function-scoped. For example, if you declare a variable in a `for` loop, then that variable declaration actually gets **hoisted** (that is, moved) to the top of the enclosing function. Block scoping is only possible since **ES2015** with the `let` and `const` keywords (which you should always use instead of `var`!).
- JavaScript's `number` type supports only 64-bit doubles (IEEE 754 double precision standard). Integers are represented as floating point variables; that is, some precision is lost once numbers get too large. Here's an example where it breaks: `9999999999999999` `===` `10000000000000000` evaluates to `true`!
- `typeof(NaN)` evaluates to `number`.
- `true == 1` evaluates to `true` because `==` does type coercion (that is, converts the type).
- `null == undefined` evaluates to `true`.
- `42 == [42]` evaluates to `true`: in conclusion, always prefer `===` and `!==` over `==` and `!=`.
- `0 == ''` evaluates to `true`.
- `null == undefined` evaluates to `true`.
- `alert((![]+[])[+[]]+(![]+[])[+!+[]]+([![]]+[][[]])[+!+[]+[+[]]]+(![]+[])[!+[]+!+[]]);`: Displays an alert box with the message *fail*. Check out the JSF*ck website to know more about this one. Needless to say, hackers love these kinds of things!

The list could go on and on but we will leave it here. As mentioned earlier, *TypeScript transpiles into JavaScript, which means that you need to have a good understanding of JavaScript, even if you program in TypeScript, and have knowledge about its good and bad parts.*

Douglas Crockford has written a lot and given many talks about JavaScript. He has covered at great length JavaScript's weaknesses and strengths and we really recommend you watch some of his talks and read his book. You'll have fun while doing so and you'll discover many things that you should avoid at all costs in JavaScript as well as some that are really worth using. For a quick review, you can also check out the following summary: `https://github.com/dwyl/Javascript-the-Good-Parts-notes`.

Mr. Crockford has also created JSLint, a JavaScript linter (that is, a code quality checker) that helps to avoid dangerous syntax and detect possible mistakes before it is too late. A similar tool exists for TypeScript and is called **TSLint**.

How can TypeScript help?

Now that we've introduced TypeScript and have briefly covered JavaScript's history, evolution, and gotchas, we can finally discuss why TypeScript is relevant and why you should use it.

Enhanced JavaScript

First and foremost, TypeScript does not aim to replace JavaScript; instead, it aims to improve the lives of developers by providing a more powerful language that generates clean and simple JavaScript code. In a way, you could consider TypeScript as a code quality checker for JavaScript on steroids.

Future JavaScript today

A second big benefit is that TypeScript allows you to use the newest ECMAScript features right now, whether you're targeting the latest version of Node.js or Internet Explorer 11 (poor soul!). This is great because it means that you don't need to wait until everything is supported in the target environment.

You can very easily configure the TypeScript compiler to generate ES3-, ES5-, ES2015-, ES2016-, ES2017-, ES2018-, ES2019-, or ESNext-compatible code.

To make this clearer, let's take an example. In TypeScript, you can create classes while transpiling your code to ES3-compliant code, even though classes were only introduced in ES2015. The TypeScript compiler **only** performs transformations to use language constructs that existed in that version of ECMAScript. When TypeScript does this, we often talk about *down-level emit*. There are many features of most recent ECMAScript versions that you can use with TypeScript while targeting ES5.

Static typing

One of the best features of TypeScript is its powerful type system added on top of JavaScript. This alone should appeal to any developer who is used to working with strongly typed languages, and thus, used to benefiting from great IDE support.

When you develop using C# or Java with a solid editor/IDE, you get powerful auto-completion, refactoring support, access to the documentation, in-context hints, and warnings and errors, all **for free**. TypeScript provides the same developer experience for the JavaScript ecosystem and allows developers to benefit from a highly productive development environment. This is great for all developers, not only larger teams.

Whether you're a fan of static or dynamic typing, TypeScript will make you happy as types in TypeScript are *optional* and TypeScript has very powerful type inference capabilities. Moreover, type inference improves with each new release of the compiler.

Put simply TypeScript definitely will help you discover bugs earlier and it will help you to better organize and structure your code, whether you're working on a small application or a large project.

Structural typing

In TypeScript, usually, if things quack like ducks, then TypeScript assumes that they're ducks. **Duck typing** as it is called is baked into the language. We can say that TypeScript considers the compatibility of types. We'll leverage this great feature in the projects to make things clear.

To give you an idea, if some function expects to receive an object of a Foo type and is instead called with an object of a Bar type, then TypeScript will not complain as long as Bar has the same structure as Foo. That is to say, a Bar object can be considered to be Foo if it exposes at least the expected properties/methods.

 This is an oversimplification as there are actually many rules at play, depending on the considered types.

Structural typing is very useful as it helps avoid writing quite some boilerplate code; one example is when you have two equivalent data structures. In programming languages that don't support structural typing, you have to manually convert from one type to the other, just because the compiler doesn't recognize the *structural compatibility* of the types.

TypeScript does also supports some **nominal typing** (that is, non-structural). Nominal typing is interesting for cases where you want to distinguish objects with different types, even if their structure is identical.

We won't be covering nominal typing specifically in this book as it is more advanced, but do check out the following link if you're curious: `https://basarat.gitbooks.io/typescript/docs/tips/nominalTyping.html.`

Types for JavaScript libraries

Having auto-completion and type information for third-party libraries that you use is a huge time saver and it can also help you avoid many bugs. Now, you might wonder how TypeScript can provide you with type information for third-party libraries when they are not written themselves in TypeScript. Well, the TypeScript team and the community have got you covered!

TypeScript supports type definitions, also known as **typings**. Type definitions are sets of declarations that provide additional information to the compiler (somewhat similar to header files in C). You'll discover how this works while working on the projects of this book.

Type definitions are maintained for most major libraries and are maintained either by the community or the library developers themselves. In most cases, typings are available on **DefinitelyTyped**, a community-driven repository of type definitions available on GitHub, over at `https://github.com/DefinitelyTyped/DefinitelyTyped.`

 In the following article, you can find the history of DefinitelyTyped, explaining how it came to be and how it has evolved to become so central in the TypeScript ecosystem: `https://blog.johnnyreilly.com/2019/10/definitely-typed-movie.html.`

This isn't perfect because, sometimes, type definitions fall out of sync with the corresponding library (for example, after a new release) or are flat-out wrong but, most of the time, they definitely improve the developer experience and code quality.

As a matter of fact, type definitions are also useful for JavaScript developers as they provide information about the library APIs that might not even be documented otherwise.

.NET and Java developers will feel at home

TypeScript will feel natural for any Java or .NET developer as it supports many of the concepts that developers with that background should be familiar with.

Career-wise, learning TypeScript is beneficial for any backend developer as more and more code is written using JavaScript and TypeScript nowadays.

TypeScript supports **object-oriented programming** (OOP) concepts through classes, inheritance, constructors, property accessors, methods, and interfaces. It also supports enums, generics, iterators, generators, modules, decorators (also known as annotations), and many others.

If you only consider the OOP and modularity features of TypeScript, you can easily understand that it makes it much simpler to structure and organize your code base while defining your domain model using familiar concepts.

Also, since it is a superset of JavaScript, it also has great support for functional programming.

Having prior experience with all these concepts certainly gives you an edge to quickly get up to speed with TypeScript.

 If you're coming from Java, .NET, or a similar language, do not underestimate the differences between the language(s) you are familiar with and TypeScript; some are quite profound. For example, the `this` keyword exists both in JavaScript and TypeScript, but it behaves differently in both, which can be very surprising.

That being said, one of the reasons for me (Sébastien) to introduce TypeScript at work a few years back (2016), was to allow our Java development teams to participate in the development and maintenance of frontend applications. At the time, we were developing **JavaServer Faces** (JSF)-based web applications almost completely in Java, so the introduction of RESTful web services and single page applications was quite a revolution. The fact that we have chosen to use TypeScript really helped the teams to quickly get on board and, in hindsight, it was a really good choice.

Of course, the matter is more complex than this; it isn't because our developers could contribute to the elaboration of frontend application code that they became frontend developers overnight. In our humble opinion, frontend and backend developers usually have a fundamentally different focus during their work. Some have a good feeling for user experience and user interface development and some others just don't.

By now, you have enough background information about JavaScript, TypeScript, how they fit together, and why you have chosen the right language to learn at the right time.

So, let's get started, shall we?

What you'll need to install

In order to implement the different projects of this book, and in order to work with TypeScript, you'll need a few tools. In this section, we'll go through the list together to briefly explain what those tools are and why you're going to need those. Bear in mind that these are merely the strict minimum. In practice, you'll need more than these to build real-world applications.

Text editor

First of all, you'll need a code editor. For this book, we'll be using **Visual Studio Code** (also known as **VS Code** or **VSCode**), an excellent tool created by Microsoft that is free and open source. VS Code provides great editing and debugging support as well as many extensions. It works on Windows, macOS, and Linux. As a bonus, VS Code is also written in TypeScript!

One of the great strengths of VS Code is its extensibility through plugins that are available on the VS Code Marketplace (`https://marketplace.visualstudio.com/VSCode`). The Marketplace contains thousands of extensions.

As an alternative, you may also use a full-blown **Integrated Development Environment** (**IDE**) of your choice, such as WebStorm (`https://www.jetbrains.com/webstorm`) or IntelliJ (`https://www.jetbrains.com/idea`), which both closely follow the TypeScript releases and quickly deliver improvements and support for newer versions.

There are, of course, other ones such as Eclipse (`https://www.eclipse.org`), NetBeans (`https://netbeans.org`), or Visual Studio (`https://visualstudio.microsoft.com`) from Microsoft.

In any case, choose well, because the editor is your main weapon and it can have a dramatic impact on your productivity.

Version control system

The second tool that we will use is a version control (VCS or SCM) system. Git (`https://git-scm.com`) is the de facto standard, so we'll use that. You will mainly use Git to retrieve the book's code samples, but you can also use it to keep track of your own modifications to the projects. We won't cover Git at great length since it is out of the scope of this book, but if you're not familiar with it yet, you should take a look at the official book, which is fantastic to quickly get started. You can find it here: `https://git-scm.com/book/en/v2`.

Shell

Another tool that we will use heavily with this book is the shell. You can do many things through the command line and it can really have an important impact on your productivity as a developer. With modern shells, you can script many operations and automate a lot of the tasks that you perform many times each day.

On Linux and macOS, using **Bash** is recommended. There might be some minor differences on macOS because it uses FreeBSD-based utilities, while usually on Linux, you'll have the GNU project ones, but nothing relevant for the purposes of this book.

If you're working in Windows, you can use **Git BASH**. Git BASH is a Bash shell emulation that is provided along with the Git installer on Windows. There are multiple reasons for this (opinionated) choice, but the main ones are simplicity and homogeneity across platforms. For example, if you need to remove a folder on Windows and Linux, then the commands will differ if you use `cmd` on one side and `bash` or `sh` on the other, while you'll be able to use the exact same command on both Windows and Linux if you're using Bash.

As an alternative on Windows 10 and newer, you may also use **Windows Subsystem for Linux (WSL)**, in which case you'll have access to a standard Bash shell. If you really prefer, you may also use a standard `cmd.exe` shell or a PowerShell one, but in this book, we'll use Bash for simplicity.

JavaScript runtime

In order to execute TypeScript and many other tools in the JavaScript ecosystem, you'll need a JavaScript runtime. The default option here is **Node.js** (`https://nodejs.org`).

Node.js provides multiple things when you install it:

- A JavaScript runtime available via the node command-line interface: `https://nodejs.org/api/cli.html`
- An SDK: `https://nodejs.org/en/docs`
- A package manager called `npm`—see next point for details

Node.js can actually be used to develop full-blown applications, but in this book, we will mainly use its runtime and package manager. We will only use the Node SDK indirectly.

For the purposes of this book, though, the necessary knowledge of Node.js will be quite limited, as you'll see shortly.

Package manager

The second-to-last tool is also one that you will use most of the time; `npm` (`https://www.npmjs.com`) is the official package manager for Node.js. With `npm`, and through the official `npm` registry, you will have access to more than 1,000,000 packages, and the numbers keep rising. Hopefully, though, you'll probably need a bit less than that to create your applications!

So why would you need a package manager? If you have experience with any widespread ecosystem, then you'll probably be familiar with a few already: NuGet for .NET, Groovy and Maven for Java, Composer for PHP, and `pip` for Python. You name it. If not, then here's a short introduction. The basic idea of package management is very straightforward; your projects have dependencies and you need a clean and easy way to get them on your machine, update them to newer releases, and many others.

No matter the size of the project you'll work on in the future, you should consider package management (and actually configuration management in general) as a must. It streamlines your workflow (it's better to have a single, standard way to manage the project), it stabilizes your application if properly used, and can actually help you avoid or detect security issues. For example, npm can detect outdated and/or vulnerable dependencies and warn you. You certainly don't want to have to find/download/extract your dependencies manually.

There are actually three things that we call npm:

- The **command-line interface (CLI)**
- The official npm registry: `https://www.npmjs.com`
- The website of the official npm registry

For now, you just need to know that you'll use npm to install dependencies easily and execute scripts. In addition, note that in the npm jargon, the dependencies that npm will manage for you will come in the form of npm packages, which will be downloaded from the official npm registry. Just for completeness, you should also know that there is a popular alternative to the npm CLI called **Yarn** (`https://yarnpkg.com`). Yarn was created at Facebook and published as open source in 2016.

TypeScript

Finally, as obvious as it may be, yes, you will also need to install TypeScript.

If you install VS Code, Visual Studio, WebStorm, IntelliJ, or another IDE that supports TypeScript natively, then you already have TypeScript on your machine. Anyway, you'll still need to install it separately from the IDE for reasons that we'll cover in the next sections.

Regardless of how you install it, once TypeScript is installed on your machine, you will get access to the TypeScript compiler, which is called `tsc`. TypeScript is distributed as an npm package and it can easily be installed using npm. As you will soon see, there are different ways to install npm packages. Some make more or less sense depending on the use case and some others may cause actual issues for development teams.

Installing VS Code

In this section, let's install the VS Code together.

Note that we will only cover the installation in Windows and Linux, as we don't own a Mac. Don't worry, though, the procedure is quite similar on macOS.

Windows

Let us assume that you have administrator privileges on your machine, but if you don't, note that you can also download a portable version, as shown in the following steps:

1. Go to the official website of VS Code and download the installer: `https://code.visualstudio.com`:

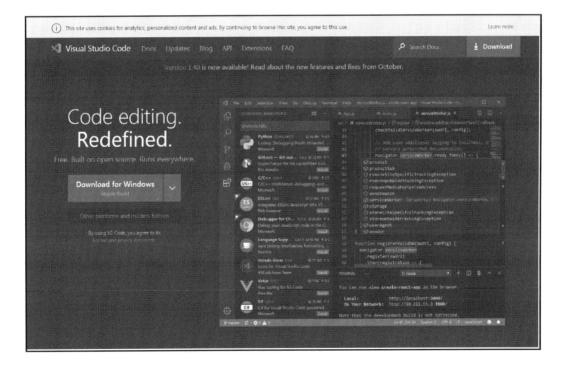

2. Click on **Download for Windows**:

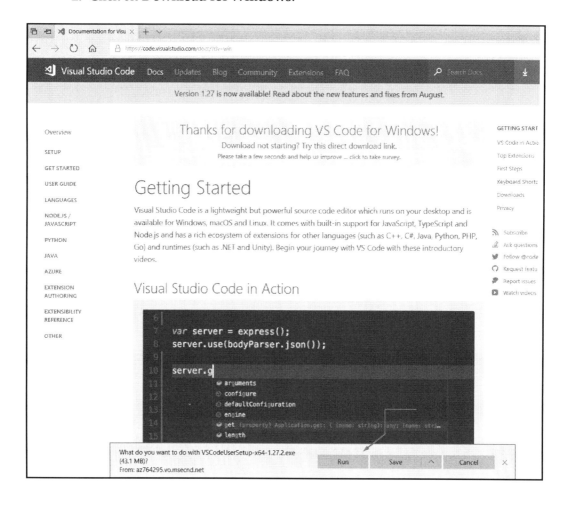

3. Once the installer has been downloaded, click on **Run** to start it:

4. Click on **Next >**.
5. Make sure to read the license agreement and get it reviewed by your favorite lawyer. Once you're fully aware of what it all means, click on the **Next >** button:

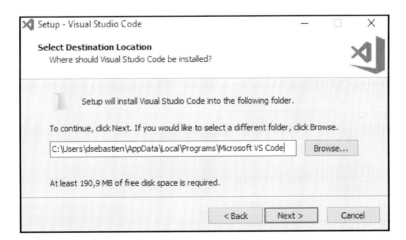

6. Change the target location if needed, then click on **Next >**:

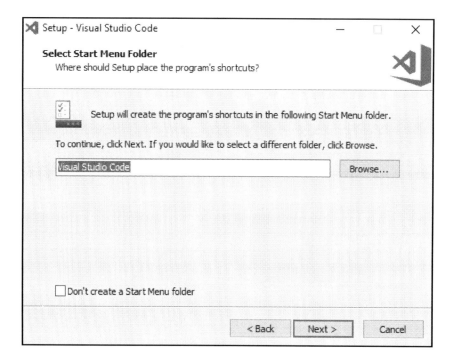

7. Click on **Next >**.
8. On the next screen, make sure to check the **Add to PATH** (available after restart) option. This is for ease of use only. Then, click on **Next >** and **Install** in the next screen.
9. Once completed, click on **Finish**:

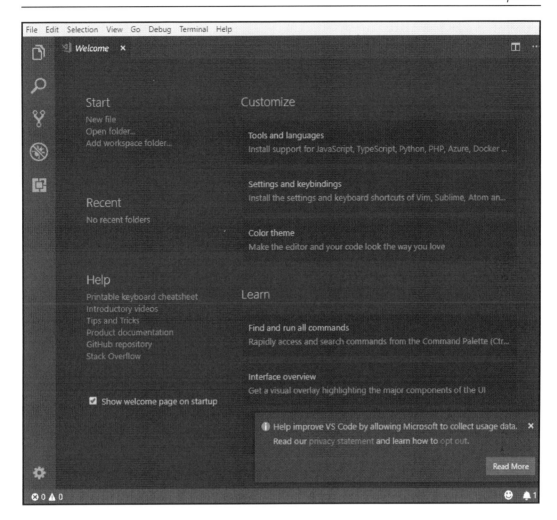

Congratulations, you're now officially among the cool kids with the `code` command on their machine.

Windows (shell)

On Windows, you can also easily install VS Code directly from the command line, for example using Chocolatey (`https://chocolatey.org`).

Linux (GUI)

For Linux, if you're using Ubuntu, you can really easily install VS Code using the native package manager of Ubuntu called **Ubuntu Software**:

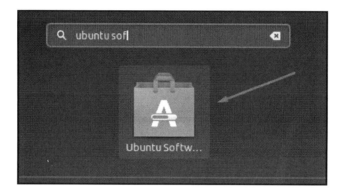

Let's perform the steps as follows:

1. Open Ubuntu Software.
2. Then, search for `Visual Studio Code` and install it:

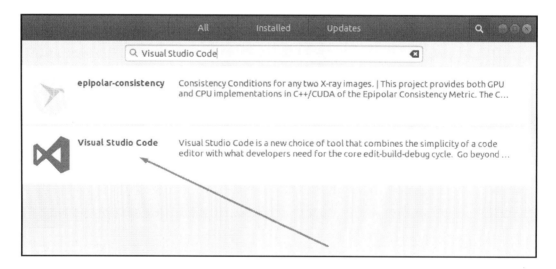

3. Once you have found it, click on **Install**:

Installation should be pretty quick:

4. Once completed, you should be able to start it:

The following screenshot shows that you are all ready to go:

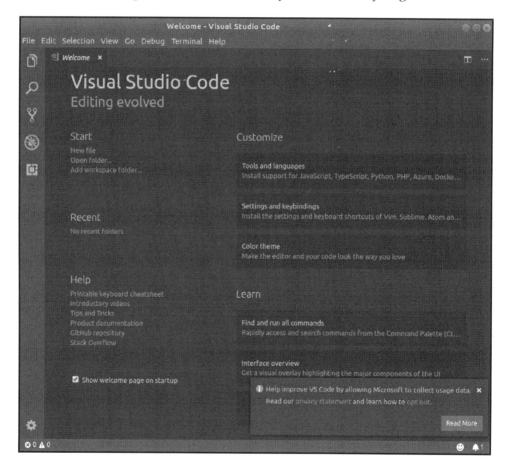

Let's see how to do the same on Linux.

Linux (shell)

Now, if you're anything like us, at this point you are probably feeling nauseous already. You might not like installing software using a GUI.

Indeed, things have changed, it seems. However, rejoice because if you prefer the command line, then you can still do it (phew!). Microsoft loves open source, so they have great documentation: `https://code.visualstudio.com/docs/setup/linux`.

For Debian/Ubuntu-based distributions, follow these steps:

1. Open the Terminal.
2. Download the latest `.deb` package from the official website: `https://code.visualstudio.com/docs/?dv=linux64_deb`.
3. Execute the following commands:
    *   `sudo dpkg -i <file>.deb`
    *   `sudo apt-get install -f`

Extensions

In order to install extensions for VS Code, you have two options:

1. First, you can visit the Visual Studio Marketplace and install extensions from there through the **Install** links, which will open up in VS Code (that is, `vscode://` links):

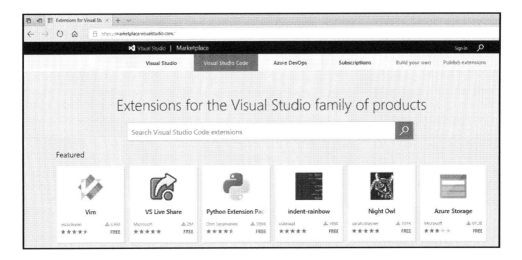

2. Once you're on an extension's page, click on **Install**:

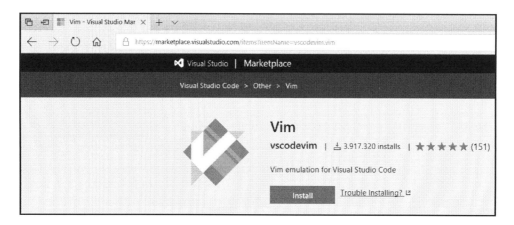

And if all goes well, VS Code should be opened and it should ask whether you would like to install the extension:

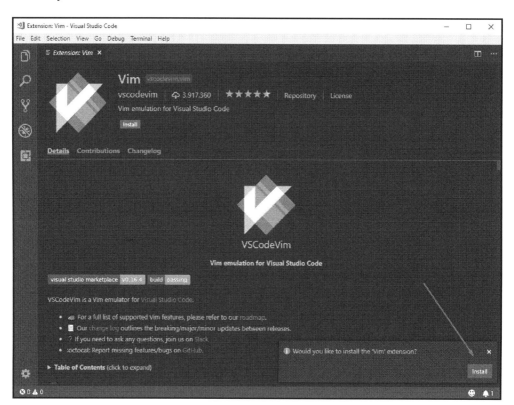

This approach is nice because it allows you to easily browse the catalog of extensions. As an alternative, you can use *Ctrl + Shift + X* (Windows and Linux) in order to install extensions directly from within VS Code:

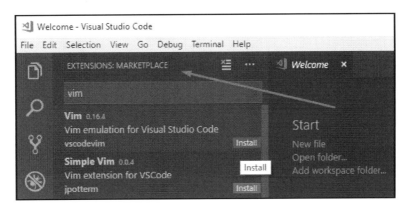

Here's a small list of nice-to-have extensions (in no particular order). You will not need to have any of these for the purposes of this book, but they'll probably help you, should you decide to install them:

- **Latest TypeScript and JavaScript Grammar:** `https://marketplace.visualstudio.com/items?itemName=ms-vscode.typescript-javascript-grammar`
- **Auto close tag:** `https://marketplace.visualstudio.com/items?itemName=formulahendry.auto-close-tag`
- **Code Runner:** `https://marketplace.visualstudio.com/items?itemName=formulahendry.code-runner`
- **Debugger for Chrome:** `https://marketplace.visualstudio.com/items?itemName=msjsdiag.debugger-for-chrome`
- **TSLint:** `https://marketplace.visualstudio.com/items?itemName=eg2.tslint`
- **vs-code icons:** `https://marketplace.visualstudio.com/items?itemName=robertohuertasm.vscode-icons`
- **GitLens:** `https://marketplace.visualstudio.com/items?itemName=eamodio.gitlens`
- **Prettier:** `https://marketplace.visualstudio.com/items?itemName=esbenp.prettier-vscode`
- **npm:** `https://marketplace.visualstudio.com/items?itemName=eg2.vscode-npm-script`
- **npm intellisense:** `https://marketplace.visualstudio.com/items?itemName=christian-kohler.npm-intellisense`

- TS hero: `https://marketplace.visualstudio.com/items?itemName=rbbit.typescript-hero`
- Import Cost: `https://marketplace.visualstudio.com/items?itemName=wix.vscode-import-cost`
- TS Auto Import: `https://marketplace.visualstudio.com/items?itemName=steoates.autoimport`
- TypeScript Importer: `https://marketplace.visualstudio.com/items?itemName=pmneo.tsimporter`
- Paste JSON as code: `https://marketplace.visualstudio.com/items?itemName=quicktype.quicktype`
- IntelliSense for CSS class names in HTML: `https://marketplace.visualstudio.com/items?itemName=Zignd.html-css-class-completion`
- TODO Highlight: `https://marketplace.visualstudio.com/items?itemName=wayou.vscode-todo-highlight`
- Open in Browser: `https://marketplace.visualstudio.com/items?itemName=techer.open-in-browser`
- Move TypeScript files and update relative imports: `https://marketplace.visualstudio.com/items?itemName=stringham.move-ts`
- EditorConfig for VS Code: `https://marketplace.visualstudio.com/items?itemName=EditorConfig.EditorConfig`

You can find a ton more on the official Marketplace website: `https://marketplace.visualstudio.com/vscode`.

Installing and configuring Git

Now let's install Git, a tool that you will actually use for many years to come.

Windows

Here are the steps to follow in order to install Git on Windows:

1. Go to the official site for Git and download the binaries: `https://gitforwindows.org`.
2. Once downloaded, click on **Run**. Again, make sure that you don't sell your soul, although this time, we're in safer GNU territory:

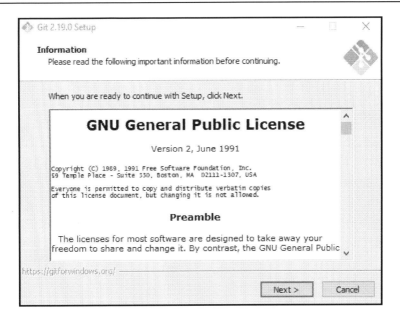

3. On the next screen, make sure to add the **Windows Explorer integration
   (Git Bash Here)** and to check the **Use a TrueType font in all console
   windows** (your eyes will thank us):

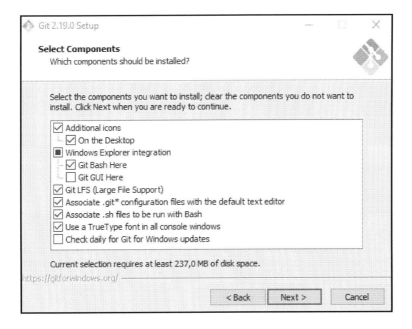

4. Select your text editor of choice (are you a `nano` or a `vim` person? That actually says a lot about you!):

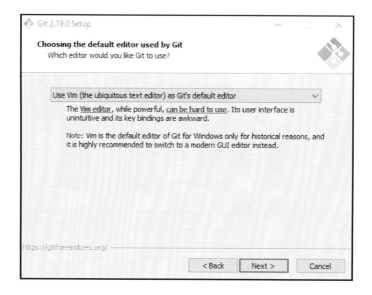

On the next screen, decide how you prefer to work. The default is to **Use Git from the Windows Command Prompt**, which is a safe choice. The last option is interesting for those among you that would want to use the same *nix tools whether you work in Git BASH, `cmd`, or another shell:

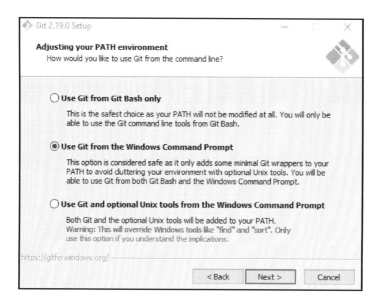

5. Choose your preferred transport backend for HTTPS. This is usually relevant for enterprises:

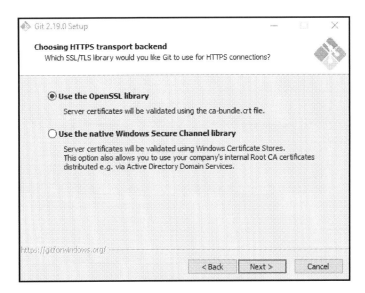

6. When you reach the following screen, read carefully. This is where many hair loss issues begin and end. The last option is recommended (setting `core.autocrlf` to false):

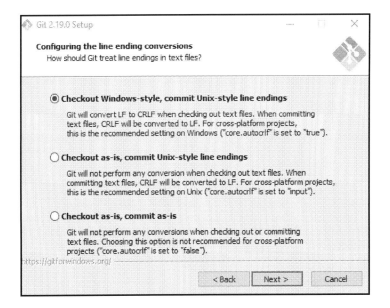

7. Click on **Next >**:

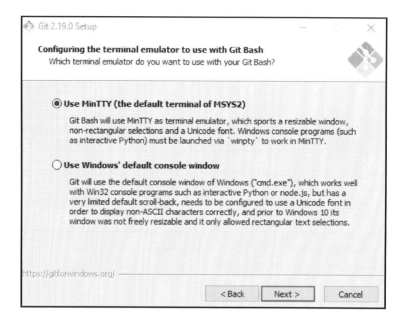

8. Click on **Next >**:

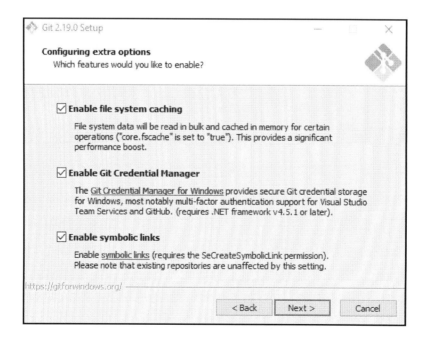

There you go! Now you've got access to Git BASH, your new best friend, right next to PowerShell:

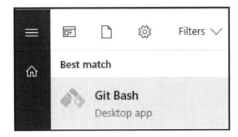

Look how beautiful that prompt looks in the following screenshot:

```
MINGW64:/c/dev/wks                                      —    □    ×

trankill@trankillux MINGW64 /c/dev/wks
$
```

Once again, let's see how this is done with Linux.

Linux (shell)

On Linux, simply fire up your Terminal and use `apt-get`, `pacman`, `yum`, `dpkg`, `portage`, and friends to install Git. Here's how simple the installation looks on Ubuntu when running the `sudo apt install git` command:

```
                            dsebastien@vm: ~

File  Edit  View  Search  Terminal  Help
dsebastien@vm:~$ git

Command 'git' not found, but can be installed with:

sudo apt install git

dsebastien@vm:~$ sudo apt install git
[sudo] password for dsebastien:
Reading package lists... Done
Building dependency tree
Reading state information... Done
The following packages were automatically installed and are no longer required:
  app-install-data apt-clone archdetect-deb btrfs-tools cryptsetup-bin
  dmeventd dmraid dpkg-repack gir1.2-timezonemap-1.0 gir1.2-xkl-1.0
  grub-pc-bin kpartx kpartx-boot libdebian-installer4 libdevmapper-event1.02.1
  libdmraid1.0.0.rc16 libido3-0.1-0 liblvm2app2.2 liblvm2cmd2.02 libreadline5
  libtimezonemap-data libtimezonemap1 lvm2 python3-icu python3-pam rdate
  u-boot-tools
Use 'sudo apt autoremove' to remove them.
The following additional packages will be installed:
  git-man liberror-perl
Suggested packages:
  git-daemon-run | git-daemon-sysvinit git-doc git-el git-email git-gui gitk
  gitweb git-cvs git-mediawiki git-svn
The following NEW packages will be installed:
  git git-man liberror-perl
0 upgraded, 3 newly installed, 0 to remove and 76 not upgraded.
Need to get 4.731 kB of archives.
After this operation, 33,9 MB of additional disk space will be used.
Do you want to continue? [Y/n]
```

Once you have accepted, `apt` will install everything you need. After that, the `git` command will be available for use.

Configuring git

Once `git` is installed, you can configure it as you see fit. This is out of the scope of this book, so please refer to the official documentation: `https://git-scm.com/book/en/v2/Customizing-Git-Git-Configuration`.

Downloading the book samples

Now that you have Git on your machine, you can use the following command to download the latest version of the book's samples on your machine:

```
git clone --depth 1 -b
master https://github.com/PacktPublishing/-Typescript-3.0-Projects
---Learn-Typescript-by-Building-Web-Applications typescript-book
```
You can do it now, as we will use them throughout the book.

Once the command has been executed, you'll find the code samples in the TypeScript book folder.

Code samples are arranged by chapter.

Installing Node.js and npm

In this section, we'll explain how to install both Node.js and `npm` on your machine.

Windows

Go to the official website of Node.js: `https://nodejs.org` and download the latest **LTS** (short for **Long Term Support**) release; you'll find the download links directly on the home page. This is preferred at work, but you may also install the latest and greatest.

 For this book, we will be using 8.12.0 LTS, but newer versions should be okay.

Once downloaded, run the installer as follows:

1. On the first screen, select where to install and click on **Next**:

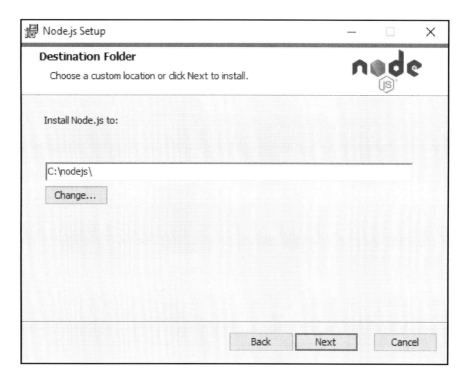

On the next screen, make sure that **npm package manager** is selected so that npm gets installed as well.

2. Also, check that **Add to PATH** is selected:

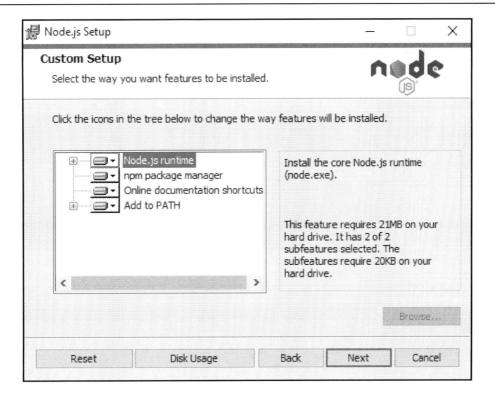

3. On the next screen, click on **Install**:

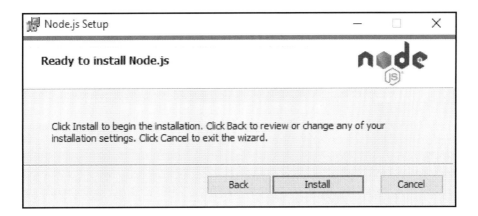

The installation should then get going:

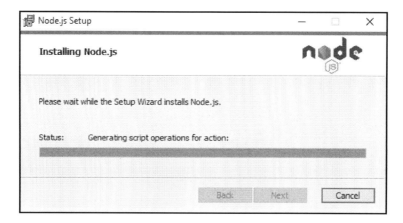

4. Once completed, click on **Finish**:

Congratulations, you now have both `node` and `npm` on your machine.
In addition, Node.js also comes with a pre-configured shell called **Node.js**:

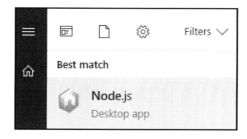

If you open up Command Prompt (for example, with `cmd.exe`), then you should be able to execute `node` and `npm` and retrieve their respective versions:

```
C:\Users\username>node --version
v8.12.0

C:\Users\username>npm
5.8.0
```

It should also work fine within PowerShell if you prefer that:

```
PS C:\Users\username>node --version
v8.12.0

PS C:\Users\username>npm --version
5.8.0
```

The exact version numbers don't matter that much as this evolves all the time, but if you want to be sure to have the exact same behavior, then you can try to match ours.

Git BASH

If you follow our advice and try to use Git BASH, then you might be disappointed at first.

Execute the following command:

```
$ node --version
```

When you do so, you should get back the following error: `bash: node: command not found`.

Changes to the Windows path are not immediately picked up by Git BASH; for this to happen, sometimes a reboot is necessary (Windows, eh?). If rebooting the operating system doesn't solve the issue, then you can also edit your user profile through the `.bash_rc` file and modify the path manually. For example, if you've installed Node.js under `C:/nodejs`, then you can add this to your Bash profile: `PATH=$PATH:/c/nodejs`. Once done, you should be able to execute both `node` and `npm`.

Linux (shell)

On Linux, the installation can easily be done using the Terminal with the following steps:

1. First of all, open up the Terminal.
2. Next, install `curl` as you'll need it to install Node.js: `sudo apt install curl`
3. Then, install Node.js from the NodeSource (`https://nodesource.com`) repository:

   ```
   curl -sL https://deb.nodesource.com/setup_8.x | sudo -E bash -
   sudo apt-get install -y nodejs
   ```

4. You should now have both `node` and `npm` installed. Here's a link to the reference installation guide for Debian-and Ubuntu-based distributions: `https://nodejs.org/en/download/package-manager/#debian-and-ubuntu-based-linux-distributions`.

 `nvm` (`https://github.com/nvm-sh/nvm`) is also a popular option to manage multiple `node`/`npm` installations.

Let's now see how to update `npm`.

Updating npm

Updating `npm` is not always as straightforward as it should be, so let us cover this subject, at least for Windows and Linux.

Linux

On Linux, updating `npm` is very straightforward; just execute the following command:

```
npm install --global npm@latest
```

This single command will update npm for you.

Windows

On Windows, updating npm is trickier. The issue on Windows is that npm is installed along with Node.js and if you simply try the same approach as for Linux, the new version of npm that you download will always be shadowed by the one coming with node itself. This is due to the order of the entries in your PATH environment variables.

One workaround consists in changing the order of the path entries. Another one is to avoid installing npm when you install node. This lets you install and upgrade npm separately. That also comes with its hassles, though.

Instead, here's a simple solution, using the npm-windows-upgrade (https:// github.com/felixrieseberg/npm-windows-upgrade) utility. To use it, open up a Windows shell (that is, cmd.exe) as administrator then execute the following commands:

- npm install -g npm-windows-upgrade
- npm-windows-upgrade

You'll be asked to select the version of npm that you want to install. In the proposed list, select a version that is greater than and equal to 6.4.1. Once the upgrade is completed, you should be able to use the new npm version directly! If you're curious about what changed in the npm cli, check out the official release notes: https:// github.com/npm/cli/releases.

Note that there are other solutions such as nvm-windows (https://github.com/ coreybutler/nvm-windows) that we won't be covering here.

Installing TypeScript

TypeScript is distributed as an npm package, and thus, it can easily be installed using npm.

Here's how to install TypeScript globally:

```
npm install --global typescript
```

If all goes well, you should be able to execute the compiler from anywhere:

```
$ tsc --version
Version 3.1.1
```

As you can see from the preceding command, we could invoke the compiler without prefixing it by its path.

 An alternative to the `typescript` package is the `npx` command, which comes along with `npm`. `npx` allows you to use commands easily without having to go through the hassle of installing packages globally. Note that `npx` also works for locally installed packages, but we'll learn about that later on!

Let's now start using TypeScript!

Hello world with TypeScript

Now that you have all the tools at your disposal, let's write the ceremonial `Hello World` in TypeScript.

Creating the project

Open your favorite Terminal (again, we will assume Bash here). Create a new folder called `hello-world`:

```
$ mkdir hello-world
```

After the previous command, you can go into the newly created folder:

```
$ cd hello-world
```

Now open VS Code in the current folder using the `code .` command.

Hello (Type/Java)Script!

So, TypeScript is a superset of JavaScript, right? Let's see what that actually means by following these steps:

1. Create a new file called `hello-world.ts`:

 The `.ts` file extension stands for TypeScript.

You can do it from within VS Code:

As you can see, VS Code directly recognizes TypeScript files:

2. Now add the following code to your newly created file:

```
var hello = "Hello world";

function say(something) {
 console.log(something);
}

say(hello);
```

Now let's do a silly thing: let's ask Node (our JavaScript interpreter) to execute our TypeScript code:

```
$ node hello-world.ts
```

The output will be as follows:

```
$ node hello-world.ts
Hello world
```

That worked? Well, as you have probably guessed, this first example only contains JavaScript, which is why `node` doesn't have any issue.

Compiling manually using the TypeScript compiler

Now let's try to use `tsc` (the TypeScript compiler) to manually compile our code. Go back to the Terminal and run `tsc`:

```
$ tsc
Version 3.7.2
Syntax:   tsc [options] [file...]

Examples: tsc hello.ts
          tsc --outFile file.js file.ts
          tsc @args.txt
          tsc --build tsconfig.json

Options:
 -h, --help                               Print this message.
 -w, --watch                              Watch input files.
 --pretty                                 Stylize errors and messages using color and context (experimental).
 --all                                    Show all compiler options.
 -v, --version                            Print the compiler's version.
 --init                                   Initializes a TypeScript project and creates a tsconfig.json file.
 -p FILE OR DIRECTORY, --project FILE OR DIRECTORY  Compile the project given the path to its configuration file, or to a folder with
 a 'tsconfig.json'.
 -b, --build                              Build one or more projects and their dependencies, if out of date
 -t VERSION, --target VERSION             Specify ECMAScript target version: 'ES3' (default), 'ES5', 'ES2015', 'ES2016', 'E
 S2017', 'ES2018', 'ES2019' or 'ESNEXT'.
 -m KIND, --module KIND                   Specify module code generation: 'none', 'commonjs', 'amd', 'system', 'umd', 'es20
 15', or 'ESNext'.
 --lib                                    Specify library files to be included in the compilation.
                                            'es5' 'es6' 'es2015' 'es7' 'es2016' 'es2017' 'es2018' 'es2019' 'es2020' 'esnext
 ' 'dom' 'dom.iterable' 'webworker' 'webworker.importscripts' 'scripthost' 'es2015.core' 'es2015.collection' 'es2015.generator' 'es201
 5.iterable' 'es2015.promise' 'es2015.proxy' 'es2015.reflect' 'es2015.symbol' 'es2015.symbol.wellknown' 'es2016.array.include' 'es2017
 .object' 'es2017.sharedmemory' 'es2017.string' 'es2017.intl' 'es2017.typedarrays' 'es2018.asyncgenerator' 'es2018.asynciterable' 'es2
 018.intl' 'es2018.promise' 'es2018.regexp' 'es2019.array' 'es2019.object' 'es2019.string' 'es2019.symbol' 'es2020.string' 'es2020.sym
 bol.wellknown' 'esnext.array' 'esnext.symbol' 'esnext.asynciterable' 'esnext.intl' 'esnext.bigint'
 --allowJs                                Allow javascript files to be compiled.
 --jsx KIND                               Specify JSX code generation: 'preserve', 'react-native', or 'react'.
 -d, --declaration                        Generates corresponding '.d.ts' file.
 --declarationMap                         Generates a sourcemap for each corresponding '.d.ts' file.
 --sourceMap                              Generates corresponding '.map' file.
 --outFile FILE                           Concatenate and emit output to single file.
 --outDir DIRECTORY                       Redirect output structure to the directory.
 --removeComments                         Do not emit comments to output.
 --noEmit                                 Do not emit outputs.
 --strict                                 Enable all strict type-checking options.
 --noImplicitAny                          Raise error on expressions and declarations with an implied 'any' type.
 --strictNullChecks                       Enable strict null checks.
 --strictFunctionTypes                    Enable strict checking of function types.
 --strictBindCallApply                    Enable strict 'bind', 'call', and 'apply' methods on functions.
 --strictPropertyInitialization           Enable strict checking of property initialization in classes.
 --noImplicitThis                         Raise error on 'this' expressions with an implied 'any' type.
 --alwaysStrict                           Parse in strict mode and emit "use strict" for each source file.
 --noUnusedLocals                         Report errors on unused locals.
 --noUnusedParameters                     Report errors on unused parameters.
 --noImplicitReturns                      Report error when not all code paths in function return a value.
```

As you can see, there are many options. You can list all the available options using `tsc --all`. We'll discover some of those as we go about building cool applications together but, for now, let's focus on the task at hand: compiling a single file. You can do this by executing `tsc hello-world.ts`.

If all goes well, you should see nothing. But TypeScript should have transpiled your code to JavaScript.

By convention, TypeScript generates a `.js` file with the same name as the input file, right next to it. If you list the directory contents, you should see the newly added file:

```
$ ls
total 2.0K
 drwxr-xr-x 1 dsebastien 197121   0 Sep 25 15:42 .
 drwxr-xr-x 1 dsebastien 197121   0 Sep 25 14:07 ..
 drwxr-xr-x 1 dsebastien 197121   0 Sep 25 14:16 .vscode
 -rw-r--r-- 1 dsebastien 197121 100 Sep 25 15:42 hello-world.js <-----
 -rw-r--r-- 1 dsebastien 197121 104 Sep 25 15:29 hello-world.ts
```

Let's see what TypeScript has generated for us:

```
var hello = "Hello world";
function say(something) {
console.log(something);
}
say(hello);
```

This is, apart from whitespace, the exact same code. Captain Obvious again here, but indeed, since we have given JavaScript code as input to TypeScript's compiler, it didn't have much to do for us. This was just a tease; now let's make use of the TypeScript type system!

Variables declaration

In the previous code sample, we used the familiar `var` keyword of JavaScript to declare our variable.

Before we code anything else together, you really need to know that `var` is a keyword that you should forget about and never use again.

Why? The issue is that `var` does not support block scope. Instead, variables declared with `var` are function-scoped and any variable declarations in a block will get *hoisted* to the surrounding function.

Hoisting is a weird JavaScript concept. In JavaScript, variable declarations (and declarations in general) are treated first, before anything else is executed. This means that declaring a variable anywhere is exactly the same as declaring it at the top. This also means that a variable can be used before it is declared, which is counter-intuitive, to say the least.

This might sound unclear, so let us give you an example:

```
var a = 12;
var result = a + b;
var b = 30;
console.log("Result: ",result);
```

The previous code is a perfectly valid JavaScript code (but is certainly not recommended).

Up until ES5, `var` was the only way to declare variables, but this has changed with ES2015, which has introduced two new keywords: `let` and `const`. Both of these keywords do support block scope.

The `let` keyword is the safer alternative to `var`, while `const` allows you to define **constants**.

We are putting constants between quotes because the `const` keyword does not make objects immutable; it only ensures that the variable cannot be reassigned, but the contents of the object it points to *can* be modified.

Here is the recommended order of preference: `const` > `let` > `var`.

Why? As you'll see throughout the book, defensive programming has many merits and can help you write better and safer code. While programming defensively, you'll notice that immutability has many benefits, for example, to avoid side effects and surprises.

In practice, even if `const` does not guarantee immutability, it is still a step in the right direction and it clearly conveys the intent of your code, which is very important. Hence, our recommendation is to use `const` whenever possible and to only use `let` when you need to be able to assign different values.

Basic TypeScript types

Before we go on, let's see what basic types are supported by TypeScript:

- `boolean`: `true` or `false`.
- `number`: Floating point values. Those can be expressed in hexadecimal, decimal, binary, and octal forms.
- `string`: can be delimited by single quotes (`'`), double quotes (`"`), or back-ticks (`` ` ``) to define template literals (also known as **template strings**).

Here are some examples of numbers:

- `let decimal: number = 42`
- `let hexadecimal: number = 0x42`
- `let binary: number = 0b101010`
- `let octal: number = 0o52`

Here are some string examples:

- `let hello: string = 'Hello'`
- `let world: string = "World" // same as above`
- `` let cool: string = `${hello} ${world}!` ``

Template strings are very useful—they make it really easy to embed expressions. In the preceding example, we've just included another string, but in a template string expression, you could also invoke functions, perform calculations, and so on. Template strings usually help improve code readability. Note that string templates are actually a feature of ES2015 (that TypeScript supports by default).

 You can also define multiline template literals!

TypeScript also supports other basic types that we will cover later on: arrays, tuples, enums, `any`, `void`, `null`, `undefined`, `never`, and object.

A tiny bit of type safety can't hurt

To wrap this chapter up, let's write another example. This time, we will write an unsafe program and then we will see how we can make it safer using TypeScript.

Our program will be a simple calculator. For the sake of the example, our calculator will only be able to multiply values together, but don't hesitate to extend the example to include other operations as well.

Create a new file and call it `calculator.ts`. In that file, add the following code:

```
function multiply(a, b) {
  const result = a * b;
  console.log("The multiplication of "+a+"*"+b+" equals to :
   "+result);
  return result;
}

multiply(1, 2);
multiply(2,2);
multiply(-10,10);
//multiply('foo', "bar");
```

We've used `const` this time because the calculation result should never be changed.

If you now compile and execute this calculator (using `tsc calculator.ts`, remember?), you'll see the results of our calls to the `multiply` function.

Everything seems fine so far, as shown here:

```
$ node calculator-unsafe.js
The multiplication of 1*2 equals to : 2
The multiplication of 2*2 equals to : 4
The multiplication of -10*10 equals to : -100
```

However, that code isn't very safe. What if you uncomment the last line? Do you think it makes sense to multiply strings together when doing calculations?

Now, indeed, the output is more problematic:

```
$ node calculator-safer.js
The multiplication of 1*2 equals to : 2
The multiplication of 2*2 equals to : 4
The multiplication of -10*10 equals to : -100
The multiplication of foo*bar equals to : NaN
```

Is this a behavior that you had intended? Probably not! The main problem that you have here, since that code is actually again mostly JavaScript, is one of expressiveness; you cannot easily/clearly state which types you expect as an input of the function. This is really unsafe because you could pass just about anything to your function.

You can, of course, write safer code in JavaScript, but at the expense of readability and conciseness.

Now, let's see how TypeScript can help. Actually, without you knowing, it already does!

Try to add this line to the code: `multiply(1)`. This lacks an expected parameter. In pure JavaScript code, this would be alright, but TypeScript's compiler does complain now: `TS2554: Expected 2 arguments, but got 1`.

Let's go further now. Adapt the code as follows to specify the types that you expect:

```
function multiply(a: number, b: number) {
    const result: number = a * b;
    console.log(`The multiplication of ${a}*${b} equals to
     ${result}`);
    return result;
}

multiply(1, 2);
multiply(2,2);
multiply(-10,10);
multiply("foo", 'bar');
```

We now have changed the `console.log` call to make use of a template string. Doesn't this make the code more readable? Also, take a look at the generated JavaScript code for this line: `console.log("The multiplication of " + a + "*" + b + " equals to " + result);`. As you can see, TypeScript has replaced our template string, making the code compatible with ES3.

As you can see, we can easily specify variable types using the `:` `type` notation, including for function parameters.

If you try to compile the program again, you'll see that TypeScript now helps us to avoid more mistakes:

```
$ tsc calculator-safer.ts
calculator.ts:10:10 - error TS2345: Argument of type '"foo"' is not
assignable to parameter of type 'number'.
10 multiply("foo", "bar");
            ~~~~~
```

Isn't this wonderful? But wait, there's so much more yet to discover!

Summary

In this chapter, you have discovered the current frontend development landscape and seen why/where TypeScript comes into the picture.

We have illustrated the issues with vanilla JavaScript and shown how TypeScript can help to improve code quality.

We have presented the different tools that you'll use on a day-to-day basis, including how to install them. Now, you know about VS Code, Node.js, npm, Git, and Git BASH. There are more tools that you should add to your toolbox, but we will discover them together later on.

Finally, you have written your first pieces of code using TypeScript, compiled them using tsc, and discovered how to improve your code using basic types and safer variable declarations.

In the next chapter, we'll create our first real application. It won't take over the world (yet), but it will certainly help you to learn more about TypeScript's basic features!

Further reading about ECMAScript

- ES2015: http://es6-features.org
- ES2016: http://2ality.com/2016/01/ecmascript-2016.html
- ES2017: http://2ality.com/2016/02/ecmascript-2017.html
- ES2018: http://2ality.com/2017/02/ecmascript-2018.html
- ES2019: https://2ality.com/2018/02/ecmascript-2019.html
- Tools to check compatibility with ES features from the following links:
    - http://kangax.github.io
    - https://caniuse.com
- Other books written about JavaScript by Dr. Axel Rauschmayer: http://exploringjs.com

2
Building TodoIt - Your Own Web Application with TypeScript

In this chapter, we are going to build our first application together. It won't take over the world (yet), but it will certainly help you to become more familiar with TypeScript's basic features.

Building this first concrete application will give us the chance to look at many TypeScript concepts.

We'll also take the opportunity to learn about `npm` with its `package.json` configuration file, as well as `tsc` (the TypeScript compiler) and the `tsconfig.json` configuration file.

What will you build?

It has now become a rite of passage for developers learning new programming languages and frameworks, so we will abide and build a todo (that is, task) management web application that we'll call `TodoIt`.

`TodoIt` will have the following features:

- Add a new todo item
- List existing todo items
- Filter the list of existing todo items
- Remove a single todo item
- Remove all todo items

Creating the project using npm

First things first, let's create the project as follows:

1. Open your favorite shell.
2. Create a new folder called `todoit-v1`.
3. Go into the newly created folder.
4. Create the project using the `npm init` command.

When you execute the following `npm init` command, `npm` will request some input to properly configure the project:

```
$ npm init
This utility will walk you through creating a package.json file.
It only covers the most common items, and tries to guess sensible
defaults.

Execute `npm help json` to get a more comprehensive description of
these fields.

Use `npm install <pkg>` afterwards to install a package and
save it as a dependency in the package.json file.

Press ^C at any time to quit.
...
```

The following are the different inputs that `npm` will request. Just press the *Enter* key multiple times as we will not need to change the defaults:

```
package name: (todoit-v1)
version: (1.0.0)
description:
entry point: (index.js)
test command:
git repository:
keywords:
author:
license: (ISC)
About to write to C:\dev\wks\tsbook\assets\2\todoit-v1\package.json:

{
  "name": "todoit-v1",
  "version": "1.0.0",
  "description": "",
  "main": "index.js",
  "scripts": {
```

```
    "test": "echo \"Error: no test specified\" && exit 1"
  },
  "author": "dSebastien <seb@dsebastien.net>
   (https://www.dsebastien.net)",
  "license": "ISC"
}

Is this OK? (yes)
```

Once done, you should have a `package.json` file in the folder with the following content:

```
{
  "name": "todoit-v1",
  "version": "1.0.0",
  "description": "",
  "main": "index.js",
  "scripts": {
    "test": "echo \"Error: no test specified\" && exit 1"
  },
  "author": "dSebastien <seb@dsebastien.net>
   (https://www.dsebastien.net)",
  "license": "ISC"
}
```

There's not much to it for now, but let's see what it is and what we can do with it before we continue.

Introducing npm

As we saw in the first chapter, `npm` (or `yarn` if you prefer that alternative package manager) will become one of your best friends. With it, you will be able to manage the dependencies of your projects, install and update them, and execute scripts as well.

package.json

When you work on a project, usually, you simply don't want to create a long document explaining how to download/install each and every dependency. Instead, you want to have a simple way to install everything at once.

As explained in the official documentation
(`https://docs.npmjs.com/getting-started/using-a-package.json`), a
`package.json` file does the following:

- Lists the packages that your project depends on
- Allows you to specify the versions of all dependencies required by the project using semantic versioning rules (that is, `major.minor.patch`)
- Makes your build reproducible, and therefore **much** easier to share with other developers

> If you want to know more about **semantic versioning** (also known as **semver**), check out the following website: `https://semver.org`.

We'll add to that list; the file also allows you to do the following:

- Define scripts. (We will use that feature soon to improve our application's build, that is, the set of scripts that will construct our application, by the way.)
- Document metadata about your project in a central location (for example, name, version, description, author, contributors, bug tracker, repository, and much more).
- Store the configuration for specific tools.

As you can see, with the `package.json` file, you can do much more than just manage your dependencies.

Regarding dependencies, those are mainly defined in two different sections, depending on the needs:

- `dependencies`: For all the things that your program requires at runtime.
- `devDependencies`: For all the rest; for example, transpilers, testing tools, and so on.

> There's also an `optionalDependencies` section that can sometimes prove useful: `http://npm.github.io/using-pkgs-docs/package-json/types/optionaldependencies.html`.

You can find everything there is to know about the `package.json` file here:
`https://docs.npmjs.com/files/package.json`.

Installing dependencies with npm

You can install any npm package in any folder containing a package.json file, using
npm install <options> <package_name>.

After executing npm install a few times, you might wonder where those packages
might be getting installed. First off, you need to know that npm packages can be
installed in two different ways:

- **Locally**: By default, npm packages are installed in the current folder, under
  node_modules/. For example, if you execute npm install lodash in the
  current folder, then npm will create the following folder structure for you:
  ./node_modules/lodash. Usually, you'll install most, if not all, of your
  project dependencies locally.
- **Globally**: If you pass the --global or –g flag to npm install, then the
  package will get installed globally. Normally, only utilities should be
  installed globally. When a package is installed globally, it can be used from
  anywhere on your machine. This is, of course, very useful for utilities, but it
  should be used sparingly as it can cause issues for teams. For instance, how
  do you make sure that everyone uses the same version?

On Windows, global packages are installed by default under:
%APPDATA%/npm.

You can find the official documentation of npm install here: https://docs.npmjs.
com/cli/install.

Here are some examples of packages that you might consider installing globally:

- caniuse: https://www.npmjs.com/package/caniuse
- webpack: https://www.npmjs.com/package/webpack
- yarn: https://www.npmjs.com/package/yarn
- prettier: https://www.npmjs.com/package/prettier
- typescript: https://www.npmjs.com/package/typescript

By default, npm will fetch packages from the official npm registry. The registry is basically the package hosting service. Enterprises can also deploy internal registries for security, proxying, and caching. The registry/registries to use can be configured through the local or global npm configuration files, but this is out of the scope of this book. To learn more about this, check out the following link: https://docs.npmjs.com/files/npmrc.

There are actually hundreds of thousands of packages! Always be careful when choosing, as there are many potential pitfalls: abandoned ones, malicious ones, bogus ones, and many others.

 You should also know that npm maintains a local cache. Sometimes, it might cause surprises. In those cases, refer to the official troubleshooting guide: https://docs.npmjs.com/troubleshooting/try-clearing-the-npm -cache.

Let's now discover the purpose of the package.json file.

Installing dependencies with npm and package.json

As we have explained, if you have package.json, then you can define both dependencies and devDependencies. Here's an example:

```
{
  "name": "npm-install-example",
  "version": "1.0.0",
  "description": "",
  "main": "index.js",
  "scripts": {
    "test": "echo \"Error: no test specified\" && exit 1"
  },
  "author": "dSebastien <seb@dsebastien.net>
   (https://www.dsebastien.net)",
  "dependencies": {
    "lodash": "4.17.11"
  },
  "devDependencies": {
    "karma": "3.0.0"
  }
}
```

In this example, we have defined the dependencies section and we have added a dependency in relation to the 4.17.11 version of the lodash (https://lodash.com) library. In devDependencies, we have defined a dependency in relation to the karma (https://karma-runner.github.io) test runner.

 In both dependencies and devDependencies, you can specify the versions using semantic versioning (https://semver.org). Check out the following link for details: https://docs.npmjs.com/files/package.json#dependencies. Note that, usually, you should be careful about approximately equivalent and compatible version definitions.

Once your dependencies are configured, you can invoke npm install to install them. Here's the output of that command for the preceding example:

```
$ npm install
...
npm WARN npm-install-example@1.0.0 No description
npm WARN npm-install-example@1.0.0 No repository field.
npm WARN npm-install-example@1.0.0 No license field.
npm WARN optional SKIPPING OPTIONAL DEPENDENCY: fsevents@1.2.4
(node_modules\fsevents):
npm WARN notsup SKIPPING OPTIONAL DEPENDENCY: Unsupported platform for
fsevents@1.2.4: wanted
{"os":"darwin","arch":"any"} (current: {"os":"win32","arch":"x64"})


added 257 packages from 502 contributors and audited 2342 packages in
14.476s

found 0 vulnerabilities
```

Ignore the warnings for now and concentrate on the last two lines as those are the interesting bits:

- The installer has installed our dependencies.
- The installer did not find any known security vulnerabilities.

If you try this out, you'll see that you now have a new folder called node_modules. Go ahead and give it a look; verify that you do find lodash and karma in it, along with many other dependencies.

You might be surprised to see so many packages (257, in this example) being installed while our example only has two dependencies. This is simply the way Node.js and npm work. Your direct dependencies have transitive dependencies themselves, and all of these need to be installed.

One huge benefit of this approach is that you can, of course, version the package.json file with the rest of your project. Along with that, you can also be sure that the other developers working on the same project will easily be able to install everything they need to start working on it.

The node_modules folder content

As we saw, if you install the npm packages in a folder, they end up in the node_modules folder. If you list its contents, you'll see that each package is placed in a separate directory (let's keep it like that for simplicity, although the reality is more complex):

```
drwxr-xr-x 1 dsebastien 197121 0 Sep 28 19:07 .
drwxr-xr-x 1 dsebastien 197121 0 Sep 28 19:07 ..
drwxr-xr-x 1 dsebastien 197121 0 Sep 28 19:07 .bin
drwxr-xr-x 1 dsebastien 197121 0 Sep 28 19:07 accepts
drwxr-xr-x 1 dsebastien 197121 0 Sep 28 19:07 after
drwxr-xr-x 1 dsebastien 197121 0 Sep 28 19:07 anymatch
drwxr-xr-x 1 dsebastien 197121 0 Sep 28 19:07 arraybuffer.slice
...
drwxr-xr-x 1 dsebastien 197121 0 Sep 28 19:07 karma
...
drwxr-xr-x 1 dsebastien 197121 0 Sep 28 19:07 lodash
```

We have omitted the 200 plus other ones for clarity. Notice that both devDependencies and dependencies end up installed in the same base folder. This is done to avoid duplication, which is great since there are already a lot of files and folders inside node_modules. Some even go as far as calling that folder a black hole deeper than /dev/null.

Also, there is an interesting .bin folder. This is where npm places the **binaries** that come along with some packages such as karma:

```
drwxr-xr-x 1 dsebastien 197121   0 Sep 28 19:07 .
drwxr-xr-x 1 dsebastien 197121   0 Sep 28 19:07 ..
-rwxr-xr-x 1 dsebastien 197121 303 Sep 28 19:07 atob
-rw-r--r-- 1 dsebastien 197121 180 Sep 28 19:07 atob.cmd
```

```
-rwxr-xr-x 1 dsebastien 197121 301 Sep 28 19:07 karma
-rw-r--r-- 1 dsebastien 197121 178 Sep 28 19:07 karma.cmd
-rwxr-xr-x 1 dsebastien 197121 293 Sep 28 19:07 mime
-rw-r--r-- 1 dsebastien 197121 170 Sep 28 19:07 mime.cmd
-rwxr-xr-x 1 dsebastien 197121 305 Sep 28 19:07 mkdirp
-rw-r--r-- 1 dsebastien 197121 182 Sep 28 19:07 mkdirp.cmd
-rwxr-xr-x 1 dsebastien 197121 297 Sep 28 19:07 rimraf
-rw-r--r-- 1 dsebastien 197121 174 Sep 28 19:07 rimraf.cmd
```

We'll see how we can execute those programs next.

Updating dependencies with npm

Updating project dependencies is very easy with npm; there's no need to fiddle with the package.json content manually all the time.

You can use npm update to install the available updates, and npm outdated to get a list of packages that need to be updated.

Of course, you can still edit the package.json file manually if you prefer.

 Some IDEs such as IntelliJ will provide autocompletion for the package names and package versions when editing the file.

For more information, have a look at the following links:

- https://docs.npmjs.com/cli/update
- https://docs.npmjs.com/cli/outdated

package-lock.json

Whenever npm modifies the content of your node_modules folder or package.json (for example, when using npm install), it will also automatically create or update a file called package-lock.json.

That file describes the exact filesystem tree that was generated by npm while installing the dependencies. Basically, it includes the complete list of dependencies and exact versions that were installed, both for your direct dependencies and the transitive ones.

When that file is present, subsequent installs will leverage it to install the exact same versions of the dependencies, regardless of any dependency updates that could've occurred.

This is great because it ensures that anyone installing your project will get the exact same versions of all dependencies (direct and transitive ones).

We don't have time to dive into the details about `package-lock.json`, so please refer to the official documentation to find out more:
`https://docs.npmjs.com/files/package-lock.json`.

Defining and executing npm scripts

Scripts are an awesome feature of npm that we will use throughout the book and that we heavily recommend not overlooking.

Scripts are sets of commands that you can include in the `package.json` file of your projects in order to automate various tasks. An example of a task that you could automate using scripts is the compilation of your project (for example, in our case, the transpilation from TypeScript to JavaScript).

Using scripts, you can define fairly complex build systems for your applications. If you want a real-world example, check this `package.json` file out: `https://github.com/NationalBankBelgium/stark/blob/master/package.json`.

With a newly initialized `npm` project, you usually only have the following:

```
"scripts": {
 "test": "echo \"Error: no test specified\" && exit 1"
},
```

Inside the `scripts` block, you can actually define as many scripts as you'd like. Each entry has a name (the one you'll use to execute the script) and a body containing the command(s) to execute when invoking the script.

In those scripts, you can use any command available in your current path (for example, `bash`, `npm`, `ls`, `mkdir`, and many others), as well as any binary located under `node_modules/.bin`.

Here's an example to invoke `karma` as part of the `test` script:

```
"scripts": {
 "test": "karma"
},
```

 We don't need to prefix the `karma` command with `node_modules/.bin` in this case because `npm` adds those binaries to `script path`, thus the command will be found.

To invoke a script, you simply have to execute `npm run <script name>`. You can try it out with the previous example.

For some special scripts such as `test`, you may also use shorthand: `npm test`. Here's an example of the output:

```
$ npm test

> npm-install-example@1.0.0 test C:\dev\wks\tsbook\assets\2\npm-
install-example
> karma

Command not specified.
Karma - Spectacular Test Runner for JavaScript.
...

Commands:
  start [<configFile>] [<options>] Start the server / do single run.
  init [<configFile>] Initialize a config file.
  run [<options>] [ -- <clientArgs>] Trigger a test run.
  completion Shell completion for karma.

Run --help with particular command to see its description and
available options.

Options:
  --help     Print usage and options.
  --version  Print current version.

npm ERR! Test failed.  See above for more details.
```

Executing a binary installed locally through npm using scripts is equivalent to (but simpler than) executing it via $ ./node_modules/.bin/karma, with the added benefit that it uses the expected folder as the current working directory.

We'll look at more examples throughout the book.

 You can pass parameters to scripts using the following notation: npm run <script_name> -- <params>. Notice the double dash between the script's name and the parameters to pass.

Check out the official documentation if you want to know more about npm scripts: https://docs.npmjs.com/misc/scripts.

When not to install packages globally

One last note before we dive into TypeScript.

In the first chapter, we installed the npm package for TypeScript globally. Actually, it is not something that we recommend, apart from for demonstration purposes; we only did this to quickly get started.

Now that we are going to create actual projects, we should use a cleaner and safer alternative. Having TypeScript installed globally is useful for small tests, but can cause harm in real projects. If each developer in a team installs TypeScript globally and you rely on that, what guarantee do you have that each and every developer in your team will still have the same version of TypeScript installed in a month? Here's a hint: **none**.

In most cases, you should prefer to install npm packages locally by listing them in package.json, whether that package is a library, a framework, or a tool used in your build chain. By doing so, npm can take care of installing everything at once, which is already nice, but more importantly, it also ensures that anyone working on the project will get the exact same set of dependencies as you do (assuming that your dependency versions are correctly defined and that you use a package-lock.json file or similar).

For tools such as TypeScript, `webpack`, and the like, what you should do is leverage the `scripts` section of `package.json` in order to make sure to invoke the version that you expect and not another one. We'll do exactly that for our project in a second.

Adding TypeScript to the project

Now that you're more familiar with `npm`, let's add TypeScript to our project. As discussed in the last section, we'll add it to the `package.json` file and then we will also add a script to invoke it easily.

First, add the `devDependencies` section and add TypeScript to those dependencies (since TypeScript is a tool and is only necessary at build time):

```
"devDependencies": {
    "typescript": "3.4.4"
},
```

 As we've already mentioned before, you can search for `npm` packages on the official website: `https://www.npmjs.com`. In the case of TypeScript, the package is located here: `https://www.npmjs.com/package/typescript`.

Next, replace the `scripts` section with the following:

```
"scripts": {
    "compile": "tsc"
},
```

With this script, we will be able to easily invoke the TypeScript version that we have now added to our project. This will avoid issues in case you (or someone else working on the project) have another version of TypeScript installed globally.

Now that your `package.json` file is ready, you can go ahead and install the project dependencies using `npm install`:

```
$ npm install

npm notice created a lockfile as package-lock.json. You should commit
this file.
npm WARN todoit-v1@1.0.0 No description
npm WARN todoit-v1@1.0.0 No repository field.

added 1 package from 1 contributor and audited 1 package in 1.213s
found 0 vulnerabilities
```

Now you should have a `node_modules` folder with TypeScript inside as well as `tsc binary` under `node_modules/.bin`. You should also have the `package-lock.json` file.

If you look into it, you'll see that it lists all of the dependencies (including transitive ones), along with an exact version:

```
{
  "name": "todoit-v1",
  "version": "1.0.0",
  "lockfileVersion": 1,
  "requires": true,
  "dependencies": {
    "typescript": {
      "version": "3.4.4",
      "resolved": "https://registry.npmjs.org/typescript/-/typescript-
        3.4.4.tgz",
      "integrity": "sha512-xt5RsIRCEaf6+j9AyOBgvVuAec0i92rgCaS3S+UVf5Z
        /vF2Hvtsw08wtUTJqp4djwznoAgjSxeCcU4r+CcDBJA==",
      "dev": true
    }
  }
}
```

As you can see, npm keeps tracks of the exact version that it has installed for us.

You can actually get the same result with `npm install typescript --save-dev`. That command will add the dependency to the `devDependencies` section for you automatically and then install the package directly.

At this point, you should be able to execute the TypeScript compiler by running the `tsc` script, using `npm run compile`:

```
$ npm run compile

> todoit-v1@1.0.0 tsc C:\dev\wks\tsbook\assets\2\todoit-v1
> tsc

Version 3.4.4
Syntax:    tsc [options] [file...]
...
```

For now, TypeScript doesn't yet know what to do for us, which brings us to the next point: `tsconfig.json`.

Configuring the TypeScript compiler

Now that everything is set up with `npm`, we can turn our focus to TypeScript.

Typically, the first thing to do in any TypeScript project is to create the compiler configuration file. So, indeed, at this point, you need to be aware of the fact that the TypeScript compiler can be configured through a file called `tsconfig.json`. The presence of a `tsconfig.json` file in a folder tells TypeScript that the folder is the root of a TypeScript project.

Through `tsconfig.json`, you can precisely configure the compiler, adapting it to your project and its specific needs.

To get started, create a default configuration file using `npm run compile -- --init`.

 Do you remember `npm <script_name> -- <arguments>`? This is how you can pass arguments to the programs executed by your `npm` scripts. If you don't like that approach, then you can also invoke `npx tsc <arguments>`. That is a lighter option that doesn't require scripts. Usually, though, you should prefer using scripts as they make sure that the build is fully part of the code base.

There are many options to choose from, and we won't go over them all, but we will cover some more as we progress through the chapters. For now, let's review some of the defaults together:

- `"target": "es5"`: TypeScript will convert everything it can down to ES5 compliant code. This is still a great default in 2019. In the future, we should be able to target newer versions safely (if you're creating web applications, then that will most probably be as soon as Internet Explorer is out of the picture).

- "module": "commonjs": CommonJS is the de facto module specification used with Node.js (http://www.commonjs.org/specs/modules/1.0). We'll tell you more about modules in the next chapters.
- "strict": true: TypeScript is strict by default (which is great!). This setting actually enables multiple other options (listed in the default configuration file). Those defaults do wonders to keep your code bug free. We'll briefly explain those to clarify, but things will get much clearer later on, especially once we have covered special types.
- "esModuleInterop": true: As the name indicates, this one is very useful for interoperability between different module types and how they can be imported (we'll learn more about modules later in the book).

Here's a brief explanation of the options hidden behind strict: true:

Option	Explanation
noImplicitAny	TypeScript will complain if you forget to specify the type for an expression or declaration. This way, you'll know for sure that your code base is using types as it should.
strictNullChecks	With this option enabled, TypeScript will protect you against invalid assignments by forcing you to declare when something may be assigned undefined or null. You can learn more about it here: https://www.typescriptlang.org/docs/handbook/release-notes/typescript-2-0.html.
strictFunctionTypes	This option is actually hard to explain with a one-liner, especially at this stage in the book. We recommend that you keep the following link aside and check it out once you're familiar with the language: https://www.typescriptlang.org/docs/handbook/release-notes/typescript-2-6.html.
strictPropertyInitialization	With this option enabled, TypeScript will make sure that class properties that are non-undefined are initialized next to their declaration or in the constructor.

noImplicitThis	With this option enabled, TypeScript will raise an error if you try to write expressions using the `this` keyword with an implied `any` type. As we mentioned in the first chapter, `this` behaves very surprisingly in JavaScript, where it is actually lexically scoped. This option can help you to avoid issues where `this` would be used unsafely. Check out the following blog article for a more detailed explanation: `https://www.logicbig.com/tutorials/misc/typescript/no-implicit-this.html`.
alwaysStrict	With this option enabled, TypeScript will parse all of your code in strict mode, and will also emit the `"use strict";` directive in the output files. Strict mode is actually a notion of ECMAScript/JavaScript that is an absolute must. It simply eliminates many quirks of the language, so why not use it? Refer to this Mozilla Developer Network article for details: `https://developer.mozilla.org/en-US/docs/Web/JavaScript/Reference/Strict_mode.`. You can also refer to this related StackOverflow question: `https://stackoverflow.com/questions/1335851/what-does-use-strict-do-in-javascript-and-what-is-the-reasoning-behind-it`.

 You can opt out of any of the options by setting the values to `false` while keeping `"strict": true`, even though we do not recommend it.

For now, you only have a `compilerOptions` section in your `tsconfig.json` configuration file, but you can actually have additional ones, such as the following:

- `files`: Allows you to list all the files to include when compiling.
- `include` and `exclude`: Respectively includes or excludes specific paths from the compilation. Both of these support **glob patterns**.

VS Code, IntelliJ, and other IDEs will provide autocompletion when you edit `tsconfig.json`, which is very useful:

Here are some useful links about `tsconfig.json` and the compiler configuration:

- Official documentation for
  `tsconfig.json`: `https://www.typescriptlang.org/docs/handbook/tsconfig-json.html`
- Official documentation listing all the options:
  `https://www.typescriptlang.org/docs/handbook/compiler-options.html`
- JSON Schema of
  `tsconfig.json`: `http://json.schemastore.org/tsconfig`

Creating the TodoIt application

You should now have a good starting point with both `npm` and TypeScript configured. If you're not sure or something went wrong, then you can start here with the initial code that we have provided with the book's sample code. You can find it in the `Chapter02` folder (corresponding to the second chapter) and in the `todoit-v1-initial` folder.

In the initial project, we've called the `compile` script `tsc` for simplicity, but you can name it as you prefer. This is why we use `npm run tsc` in the following examples instead of `npm run compile`.

Ready? Great, let's write our application and learn some more together!

Opening the project in VS Code

Go to the project's folder and open VS Code (or another editor if you prefer). If `code` is in your path, then you can simply execute this (assuming you're in the right folder in your shell): `code  .`

Now is a great time for you to install the VS Code extensions that we mentioned in the previous chapter as they'll prove useful soon, when editing both HTML and TypeScript code.

Defining the basic application structure

In this first project, we will create a fairly simple web application. Usually, web applications start and end with HTML. Here's what we will do:

- We will create the user interface of our application using a single HTML file called `index.html`.

- We will put as much logic as we can in TypeScript code, in a single file called `todo-it.ts`.

- We will make sure that our HTML file loads the compiled version of our code (that is, JavaScript code).

Go ahead and create an `index.html` file at the root of the project. This will be the entry point for our application. For now, just add the following to it:

```
<!DOCTYPE html>
<html lang="en">
<head>
    <meta charset="UTF-8">
    <title>TodoIt</title>
</head>

<body id="todoIt" style="text-align: center">
    <h1>TodoIt</h1>
```

```
    <p>TODO</p>
</body>
</html>
```

This is a simple HTML5 starting point, nothing fancy. For now, this doesn't do much, but we'll come back to it soon.

Next, create a TypeScript file called `todo-it.ts`, and add the following code to it:

```
console.log("TodoIt");
```

This will help us validate that we've got the setup right.

Leveraging VS Code support for TypeScript

Now that the application structure is in place, let's see how we can build the JavaScript version of our code directly from VS Code.

To manually compile the TypeScript code, go to **Terminal | Run Build Task...** (*Ctrl + Shift + B* on Windows or *cmd + Shift + B* on macOS) and select **tsc: build - tsconfig.json**:

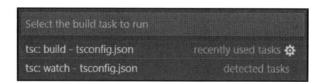

When executed, this will compile all the TypeScript code detected by `tsc`, based on the `tsconfig.json` configuration. By default, any `.ts` file in the project folder or subfolders will be picked up. Note that `node_modules` is obviously ignored by default. After the build has completed, you should find the expected `todo-it.js` file right next to `todo-it.ts`.

 For a more elaborate example, we would actually generate the JavaScript file in a build directory such as **dist** (common practice), but for simplicity's sake, we'll skip that this time.

It is usually best to have the IDE automatically compile the project all the time. The good news is that you can also start the TypeScript build in watch mode from VS Code. To do so, go back to the **Run Build Task...** menu and, this time, select `tsc: watch - tsconfig.json`. This will start the incremental compilation:

```
PROBLEMS    OUTPUT    DEBUG CONSOLE    TERMINAL         1: Task - watch - tsconfi ▼

[18:33:15] File change detected. Starting incremental compilation...

[18:33:15] Found 0 errors. Watching for file changes.
```

In VS Code, you can press *Ctrl + Shift + M* to show or hide the **PROBLEMS** view. It is very useful to quickly have an overview of all the issues in the project.

You now know enough to get started. There is actually a whole lot more to say about what VS Code can do, but we will let you discover the rest on your own. Here is a great resource that you can check out: `https://vscodecandothat.com`.

Here's the reference documentation for TypeScript support in VS Code: `https://code.visualstudio.com/docs/languages/typescript`.

Building from the Terminal

As you might guess, you can also easily build your project both in *one-shot* and in watch mode from the Terminal.

To build the project once, simply execute `npm run tsc`, as we saw before.

To build the project in watch mode, you can run `npm run tsc -- --watch`. Again, alternatively, you can execute `npx tsc --watch`. Actually, automating things will make your life easier, so why not add a new script to `package.json`?

Your script block should now look like this:

```
"scripts": {
    "tsc": "tsc",
    "watch": "tsc --watch"

},
```

With that in place, you should be able to start `tsc` in watch mode and get the compilation results right from the Terminal:

```
[20:41:20] Starting compilation in watch mode...
[20:41:21] Found 0 errors. Watching for file changes.
...
```

If you modify the code and break it, then you'll directly see the results in the console:

```
[20:41:31] File change detected. Starting incremental compilation...

todo-it.ts:2:17 - error TS1136: Property assignment expected.
2 let todoList = {;                        ~
```

Now, you have seen two ways to continuously compile your code. It's up to you to decide which approach you prefer.

Using Browsersync to refresh automatically

At this point, our application's page is pretty much empty. Before we go about adding some things to it, we'll present you with one more tool that'll be of use.

Browsersync (`https://browsersync.io`) is a very cool utility for web development. Using Browsersync, you'll get live reloading without much effort.

Live reloading simply means that the web page will get refreshed automatically whenever you modify the source code.

In brief, once Browsersync is installed, your workflow will be as follows:

- Start Browsersync through `npm`.
- Browsersync will start a web server serving your content, and once ready, it will open `index.html` in your default web browser.
- Modify `index.html` in VS Code (or using any other code editor).
- Immediately see the updated version in your web browser.

Installing Browsersync is very easy. Execute the following command to add it to the project and install it: `npm install browser-sync --save-dev`.

 Again, we are using `--save-dev` since Browsersync is a tool and not a library that we will need in production.

Now that Browsersync is there, go ahead and add a new script to `package.json`:

```
"serve": "browser-sync start --server --watch"
```

Execute it with `npm run serve`. Wait a bit and once the page is opened in your web browser, go ahead and change `index.html`.

 Browsersync can actually do a whole lot more than this. If you want to find out a bit more about its capabilities, you can go to `http://localhost:3001` and have a look at the control panel.

Implementing the user interface

Now let's modify the `index.html` page to add the basic user interface structure; we'll add the behavior later:

```html
<!DOCTYPE html>
<html lang="en">
<head>
    <meta charset="UTF-8">
    <title>TodoIt</title>
</head>

<body id="todoIt" style="text-align: center">

<h1>TodoIt</h1>
<h2>Add new items</h2>
<p>
    What needs to be done?
    <input type="text" id="todoInput" title="What should be added to
     the todo list?" />
    <input type="button" value="Add todo" />
</p>

<h2>Current todo list</h2>
<p>Filter: <input type="text" id="todoFilter" title="Filter for the
todo list" /></p>

<div id="todoListContainer">Nothing to do, hurray!</div>
</body>
</html>
```

Our page contains the following:

- An input box called `todoInput`, which will be used to describe the new todo item.
- A button to add the new todo item.
- Another input box called `todoFilter`, which will be used to filter the list of todo items.
- A `div` called `todoListContainer`, which is empty for now, but will later contain the (filtered) list of todo items.

 Granted, the `TodoIt` **user interface (UI)** is basic, but we'll see how to create much better-looking web applications in later chapters.

Right now, you can't do anything with the page as there's no logic behind it yet. Let's fix that with TypeScript's help.

Loading the TodoIt code and checking the browser console

For now, our `todo-it.ts` program only has a log statement: `console.log("TodoIt");`.

Keep it like that for a minute and compile the file using your preferred approach; you should now have a `todo-it.js` file available.

Now, open the `index.html` file and add a `script` tag inside it, right before the closing `</body>` tag:`<script type="text/javascript" src="todo-it.js"></script>`.

This is the classic way to load scripts within a web page. Once this script is in place, refresh the page in your web browser.

Did you notice anything? That's normal—it's all under the hood!

Press *F12* in the web browser to open up the developer tools. If you then go to the **Console** tab, you should see the **TodoIt** message that we've added in our TypeScript code.

Here's what it looks like in Google Chrome:

We'll discover a bit more about the Chrome Developer Tools throughout the book as we'll be using those as a reference, but note that Mozilla Firefox, Microsoft Edge, and other modern web browsers also offer great developer tools.

From now on, make sure that you have `tsc` running in watch mode; that way, you'll only have to refresh the page in your web browser to see the results of your changes. And if you have Browsersync (or a similar tool) taking care of live reloading, then you can concentrate on writing TypeScript code and contemplating the updated results.

Creating the todo list with TypeScript arrays

Now we'll create our todo list in TypeScript, and then we'll implement a way to add new items to that list.

To model our todo list, we will make use of a TypeScript array.

Open `todo-it.ts`, then, after the `console.log` statement, add a new constant: `const todoList: string[] = [];`.

Arrays can also be created using the generic `Array` type as follows: `const todoList: Array<string> = [];`. This is equivalent to what we did earlier, but the TypeScript community usually uses the other form for readability. Note that there are other ways still to declare arrays.

If you log the array object at this point, you'll see that the web browser console can help you peek into the values: `console.log("Current todo list: ", todoList);`.

Here's the corresponding output in the Chrome Developer Tools:

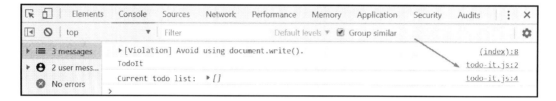

In TypeScript, our array is type safe because we have defined the type of data that it will hold. If you try to add another type of data into the array, for example, `todoList.push(1);`, then TypeScript will complain: `Argument of type '1' is not assignable to parameter of type 'string'.`

It is really important to understand that this safety only exists at compile time. Once the JavaScript version of the code executes in the web browser, those restrictions don't apply anymore, and TypeScript can't help you there. You can easily verify this now in your browser. In the console, type the following: `todoList.push(1);`. Did that fail? Of course not! If you look at the content of the `todoList` array now, you'll see that it contains the item, even though it isn't a string. Here's an example:

```
>  todoList
⊲  ▼[]
       0: 1
       length: 1
     ▶ __proto__: Array(0)
>  todoList.push(1);
⊲  1
>  todoList
⊲  ▼[1]
       0: 1
       length: 1
     ▶ __proto__: Array(0)
>  todoList.push("ohoh");
⊲  2
>  todoList
⊲  ▼(2) [1, "ohoh"]
       0: 1
       1: "ohoh"
       length: 2
     ▶ __proto__: Array(0)
```

Getting hold of inputs and casting using the *as* operator

In `todo-it.ts`, add the following line: `const todoInput: HTMLInputElement = document.getElementById('todoInput') as HTMLInputElement;`.

This allows us to retrieve the `todoInput` input object from the DOM. We'll use that to get the value of the input.

 The **Document Object Model (DOM)** is the in-memory representation of a page that web browsers create once they have loaded your page. The DOM evolves while users interact with the page, usually through event handlers that modify its structure. Web browsers include an API to interact with the DOM, just like we did previously. Through that API, you can easily query and modify the DOM. DOM manipulation is actually the bread and butter of all web frameworks. If you want to know more, have a look here: `https://developer.mozilla.org/en-US/docs/Web/API/Document_Object_Model/Introduction`

This allows us to mention a few more things about TypeScript.

TypeScript includes type definitions for some standard libraries, including the DOM API. As you saw before, we did not declare `HTMLInputElement,` but TypeScript already knows about it.

 Check out `https://github.com/Microsoft/TypeScript/blob/master/src/lib/dom.generated.d.ts` and try to find the definition of `HTMLInputElement` in it. This file (and others) is included automatically when you compile using `tsc`.

In the preceding code, did you notice the `as` keyword? Note that `as` is the **cast operator**; it simply lets you tell TypeScript to consider a type as if it was another one. In this example, we did it because `document.getElementById(...)` returns a generic `HTMLElement` element while we know for a fact that our element should be an `HTMLElement` one.

Adding todo items to the list

In order to allow the users to add items to the todo list, you need to add event handlers to the `todoInput` input and to the `Add` button.

Go back to `index.html` and replace the `todoInput` input with the following code:

```
<input type="text" id="todoInput" title="What should be added to the
todo list?" onblur="addTodo()" />
```

Then, replace the `button` input with the following:

```
<input type="button" value="Add todo" onclick="addTodo()" />
```

In the case of `todoInput`, we have added an `onblur` event handler; it will be called whenever the user leaves the field. In the case of the button, we have added an `onclick` handler.

> Note that `onclick` and `onblur` are just two of many standard browser events. You can find a list of those here:
> `https://developer.mozilla.org/en-US/docs/Web/Events#Standar d_events`.

In both cases, we simply invoke the `addTodo` function. Let's implement that one now:

```
function addTodo(): void {
    // if we don't have the todo input
    if(todoInput == null) {
        console.error('The todo input is missing from the page!');
        return;
    }

    // get the value from the input
    const newTodo: string = todoInput.value;

    // verify that there is text
    if ('' !== newTodo.trim()) {
        console.log('Adding todo: ', newTodo);

        // add the new item to the list
        todoList.push(newTodo);
        console.log('New todo list: ', todoList);

        // clear the input
        todoInput.value = '';
    }
}
```

Notice that our function's return type is `void`. This is how you tell TypeScript not to expect anything in return from the function. With that defined, TypeScript will complain if you do return a value. Defining the return type of your functions is very important, as that will help you avoid many bugs.

 Did you notice the `'' !== newTodo.trim()` check? Always put the **safe** part of the check on the left (that is, the two single quotes). In this case, the empty string, `''`, is safe, while calling `trim()` on `newTodo` could trigger an error (for example, if it was `null`). This is just one of many defensive programming tricks.

Did you notice how VS Code helps with autocompletion as seen in the following screenshot:

This is really where TypeScript shines.

 The TypeScript architecture was designed to allow any editor/IDE to leverage easily the same capabilities (type checking, statement completion, signature help, code formatting, and so on). This is why you can have a great editing experience with VS Code, Sublime Text, IntelliJ, or any other environment supporting TypeScript. Check out the following page to learn more: `https://github.com/Microsoft/TypeScript/wiki/Architectural-Overview`.

Listing existing todo items using lambda expressions

Speaking about the user experience, so far, we can add things to our todo list, but the only way to see the results is to open the web browser's console. We could certainly improve the user experience; let's give it a try!

In `todo-it.ts`, add a variable for the `todoListContainer` div element:

```
const todoListDiv: HTMLDivElement =
document.getElementById('todoListContainer') as HTMLDivElement;
```

Add the following function:

```
function updateTodoList(): void {
    console.log("Updating the rendered todo list");
    todoListDiv.innerHTML = '';
    todoListDiv.textContent = ''; // Edge, ...

    const ul = document.createElement('ul');
    ul.setAttribute('id', 'todoList');
    todoListDiv.appendChild(ul);

    todoList.forEach(item => {
        const li = document.createElement('li');
        li.setAttribute('class','todo-list-item');
        li.innerText = item;
        ul.appendChild(li);
    });
}
```

This function first clears the content of the `todoListContainer` div. Then, it loops over the content of the `todoList` array, using the standard `forEach` function. Here is the reference for this function: `https://developer.mozilla.org/en-US/docs/Web/JavaScript/Reference/Global_Objects/Array/forEach`.

If you're familiar with other programming languages that support **functional programming (FP)** concepts, such as C#, Java, Python, Ruby, and so on, then you won't be surprised by the notation. Basically, what we pass to the `forEach` function is a function.

In ECMAScript 2015 and TypeScript jargon, people talk about **arrow functions** or **fat-arrow functions**. More generally, these are called **lambda functions** or **lambda expressions**. Let's call them **lambdas** for simplicity. In JavaScript and TypeScript, functions are first-class citizens—they can be treated like other types: passed as arguments to other functions and stored in variables.

The general syntax for lambdas in TypeScript is simple: `(arguments)` ⇒ `{ function body }`.

By the way, take a look at the generated JavaScript code for the lambda: `todoList.forEach(function (item) {...})`.

TypeScript has converted our lambda expression to an anonymous function declaration; that way, our code is compatible with older environments, which is great. This is the beauty of TypeScript!

Lambdas can be written in a lighter form, as we did before—since there is only one function argument, we can omit the parentheses: `()`. If there was a single expression in the body of the function, then we could also omit the brackets as that expression would become the implicit return value of the function. Check out the reference guide for functions for all the details: `https://www.typescriptlang.org/docs/handbook/functions.html` .

Let's continue.

We didn't have to specify the type of the `item` function argument because TypeScript infers it for us automatically.

Next, add the following code at the end of the `if` block (inside it) within the `addTodo` function, in order to update the todo list when new items are added:

```
// keep the list sorted
todoList.sort();

// update the todo list
updateTodoList();
```

Now give it a try. Add some tasks to your list, and you should see them appear on the screen (while remaining sorted). Yes, indeed, this is awesome!

Jokes apart, you can probably feel how painful it would be to maintain a complex user interface using only the DOM API. Others have felt that too, and that has led to the creation of libraries such as jQuery and, later, to the creation of frameworks such as Angular, React, and many others.

Listing existing todo items using loops

Just so you know, TypeScript does indeed support loops. You could rewrite the previous example with classic loops. Although, we do not recommend it, since `forEach` and lambdas, in general, are very expressive, concise, and readable (after a bit of getting used to).

In TypeScript, objects are considered to be **iterable** if they have an implementation for the `Symbol.iterator` property. This probably isn't very clear, but the following built-in types do have that implementation: `Array`, `Map`, `Set`, `String`, `Int32Array`, and `UInt32Array`. The `Symbol.iterator` function is called by loops to get the list of values to iterate on.

TypeScript supports two interesting `for` loop forms:

- `for..of`: Loops over the values of an iterable object, invoking the `Symbol.iterator` property on it to get those values
- `for..in`: Loops over a list of keys on the object

An important distinction between `for..of` and `for..in` is also that `for..in` works with any object while `for..of` only works with iterables.

Here's an example:

```
const todoList: string[] = ["A", "B", "C"];
for (let item in todoList) {
    console.log(item); // 0, 1, 2 // keys
}

for (let item of todoList) {
    console.log(item); // "A", "B", "C" // values
}
```

In addition, TypeScript also supports classic `for` loops:

```
const numbers = [1, 2, 3];
for (let val = 0; val < numbers.length; val++) {
    const number = numbers[val];
    console.log(number); // 1 2 3
}
```

This last form is what the TypeScript compiler transforms `for..of` loops into when it targets ES5 and ES3. This is explained here in detail: https://www.typescriptlang.org/docs/handbook/iterators-and-generators.html.

If you need to make performance improvements in your code, then you might want to consider using `for..of` loops, as they're converted to simple `for` loops, which have better performance compared to `Array.forEach`. However, take this advice with a grain of salt; it is true while we continue to target ES5, but runtime performance and TypeScript type inference both evolve over time.

Based on this information, you should be able to easily rewrite the `updateTodoList` function to use a `for..of` loop.

Finally, note that TypeScript also supports the `while` and `do..while` loops, even if they are seldom used:

```
let count = 5;
while (count > 0) {
    console.log("Counting downwards: ", count);
    count--;
}

do {
    console.log("Counting upwards: ", count);
    count++;
} while (count <= 5);
```

Filtering existing todo items using the ES2015 TypeScript support

It's time to take care of filtering.

Open `index.html` and modify the `todoFilter` input as follows:

```html
<input type="text" id="todoFilter" title="Filter for the todo list"
onkeyup="filterTodoList()" onblur="filterTodoList()" />
```

As you might guess, the next step is to implement the `filterTodoList` function in TypeScript.

Here's an implementation of that function:

```typescript
function filterTodoList(): void {
    console.log("Filtering the rendered todo list");

    const todoListHtml: HTMLUListElement =
     document.getElementById('todoList') as HTMLUListElement;

    if (todoListHtml === null) {
        console.log("Nothing to filter");
        return;
    }

    const todoListFilter = document.getElementById('todoFilter') as
     HTMLInputElement;
    const todoListFilterText = todoListFilter.value.toUpperCase();

    todoListHtml.childNodes.forEach((item) => {
        let itemText: string | null = item.textContent;
        if (itemText !== null) {
            itemText = itemText.toUpperCase();

            if (itemText.startsWith(todoListFilterText)) {
                (item as HTMLLIElement).style.display = "list-item";
            } else {
                (item as HTMLLIElement).style.display = "none";
            }
        }
    });
}
```

There are a few interesting things to explain about that code, but first, you also need to modify the `addTodo` function to invoke `filterTodoList` right after `updateTodoList`:

```
if ('' !== newTodo.trim()) {

    ...

    // update the todo list
    updateTodoList();

    // apply the todo list filter
    filterTodoList();
}
```

First of all, if you simply add it to `todo-it.ts` and compile it, note that you'll make TypeScript angry:

```
todo-it.ts:97:25 - error TS2339: Property 'startsWith' does not exist
on type 'string'.
97 if(itemText.startsWith(todoListFilterText)) {
```

Can you guess why you're getting this compilation error?

`startsWith(...)` is a function that was introduced in ES2015, but so far, in our project, we have targeted ES5. TypeScript can help us because, as we said earlier, it includes a set of libraries/type definitions for the DOM and some other things. One of these libraries is the ES2015 library.

The set of libraries that are included by default are defined by the `target` option in `tsconfig.json`. In our case, with ES5, the following libraries are included: DOM, ES5, and ScriptHost.

To fix the compilation issue, edit the `tsconfig.json` file of your project, uncomment the `lib` option, and set its value as follows: `"lib": ["es2015", "dom", "scripthost"],`.

As soon as you do so, the compiler should stop complaining. Now, we need to take a step back and clarify what we have done.

The `target` option in `tsconfig.json` basically tells TypeScript which language features should be down-level emitted, while the `lib` option tells TypeScript what is supported by the target environment. Thus, it is logical that if we are targeting ES5, ES2015 features such as the `startsWith` method will not be available.

By modifying the `lib` property, we have told TypeScript that it is okay to let us use some of the ES2015 features directly. But doing so means that the compiled code will not be changed. If you look at the generated JS code, you'll see that, indeed, the `startsWith` call remains there.

This should be safe as most modern web browsers already support ES2015 to a very large extent. Although, if you want to maintain compatibility with older execution environments, then you need to learn about **shims** and **polyfills**. They are libraries that you can add to your project in order to really have access to newer features in an environment that does not provide them by default. We might touch on this again later in the book, but probably not in detail.

Make sure to check out the home page of the `core-js` project (`https://github.com/zloirock/core-js`), as it provides polyfills for many features. If you want a good exercise for later, then try the following:

1. Add `core-js` to your project dependencies.
2. Import the `starts-with` feature using `import 'core-js/features/string/starts-with'`.
3. Compile and test it in an old browser.

Another interesting point about the `filterTodoList` function is that it explicitly marks the `itemText` variable as **nullable** using `let itemText: string | null`. Without this, TypeScript wouldn't let you compile the code since the value could indeed be `null`.

Once this is done though, it is impossible to simply call methods such as `toUpperCase()` on the `itemText` variable. Before doing so, a null check is required for type safety. Again, TypeScript type inference helps a lot since, within the `if (itemText !== null) { ... }` block, TypeScript *knows* that `itemText` is not `null`.

If we focus on what the code actually does, then it can be summarized as follows:

- Loops over each entry (`li`) in the displayed list (`ul`)
- For each item, it does the following:
    - Gets its text and changes it to uppercase
    - Checks whether the item text starts with the uppercase filter text:
        - If it does, then it sets the default `list-item` style on it
        - Otherwise, it hides the item using the `none` display style

While you're still looking at that piece of code, notice how we've used `!==` instead of `!=`. We have mentioned the good parts of JavaScript. Essentially, `===` and `!==` should always be preferred to their less safe counterparts (`==` and `!=`). See `https://stackoverflow.com/questions/359494/which-equals-ope rator-vs-should-be-used-in-javascript-comparisons` (and many other articles on the web!) for details.

Removing a single todo item

For now, you can only add things to the todo list, but it would certainly be better to be able to remove tasks once they've been completed.

In `todo-it.ts`, replace the following `li.innerText = item;` line with `li.innerHTML = <a href='#' onclick='removeTodoListItem("${item}")'>${item}</a>;`.

With this, we simply generate dummy HTML links that we use to highlight the fact that we can click on each of the items in the todo list. With the `onclick` event, we simply call a `removeTodoListItem` function, passing it the item to remove.

Again, using template strings allows us to write more readable code.

Let's implement that function now:

```typescript
function removeTodoListItem(itemToRemove: string): void {
    console.log("item to remove: ",itemToRemove);

    todoList = todoList.filter((value: string, _index, _array) =>{
        if(value === itemToRemove) {
            return false;
        }
        return true;
    });
    // unsafe alternative: todoList.splice(...)

    // update the todo list
    updateTodoList();

    // apply the todo list filter
    filterTodoList();
}
```

For this to compile, you'll need to modify the `todoList` declaration to switch it from `const` to `let`. This is because we need to reassign the object when we filter it.

As you can see in the preceding code snippet, we are using the `filter` method on the array to create a new one excluding the value we wish to remove. We heavily recommend this approach as it is much safer to create a brand new array than to mutate an existing one.

This might feel counterintuitive if you have an object-oriented background, where mutation is the norm, but, as you'll see with experience, immutability truly helps to avoid surprises and side effects from your code, and is a core functional programming principle.

The main (unsafe) alternative to using `filter` is to use `splice` (https://developer.mozilla.org/en-US/docs/Web/JavaScript/Reference/Global_Objects/Array/splice) instead, but, as we mentioned, it really is unsafe. Basically, `splice` is also slower, creates garbage and is error-prone. More than enough reasons to simply forget about it!

Another even more dangerous alternative is to use `delete` to remove items from the array. Again that is a mutation, hence is not recommended. In addition, it'll just poke holes in the array, which you simply don't want to have.

By creating a new array instead of mutating the existing one, we could very easily implement an `undo` functionality! This is how patterns/tools such as Redux work. We won't be able to dive into Redux in this book, but it is definitely something to take a look at `https://redux.js.org`.

 Check out this great article to learn about common pitfalls when working with arrays in JavaScript:
`https://www.thecodeship.com/web-development/common-pitfalls-when-working-with-javascript-arrays`.

In the lambda declaration for the filter, we have used `_index` and `_array` as variable names to indicate that we don't care about some of the parameters. **Prefixing a parameter name with an underscore is a TypeScript coding convention** (also seen in languages such as Kotlin). If we had used another name, then the compiler would've complained about the presence of unused variables in our code. Alternatively, in this case, you could also remove those parameters and TypeScript wouldn't mind. Check out this issue to learn more: `https://github.com/Microsoft/TypeScript/issues/9458`.

 You can find the full list of possible TypeScript compiler errors here:
`https://github.com/microsoft/TypeScript/blob/v3.4.1/src/compiler/diagnosticMessages.json`. Just adapt the version number to see those of newer releases. There is also an excellent write-up of the errors that you will most commonly encounter:
`https://www.sitepen.com/blog/2017/11/01/common-typescript-error-messages`.

Debugging your code in the web browser

Usually, you shouldn't get into a lot of trouble while coding the examples in this book. But, of course, in the typical day of any software developer, there will be *many* times where things go awry and where a good debugging session will help.

Let's see how you can debug web applications. This is a *must-have* skill for any developer out there, and there are many tools and solutions to help you figure out what your programs are doing.

The most basic debugging tool at your disposal is simply the `console.log` function, which you can use to log variables while your program executes. Although, it clearly isn't a panacea and far from a best practice, so you should use it sparingly for small checks. When your code reaches production, you don't want it to be cluttered with `console.log` statements. Debugging and logging are two separate concerns that should each be treated in an appropriate way.

Debugging is something that you should normally do using a debugger such as the ones that web browser developer tools offer out of the box.

Let's see how to use those included with Google Chrome. Press *F12* to display them, then go to the **Console** tab. If you look on the right, you'll see that each time a log entry is added, you have the corresponding file and line where the statement came from. Click on one of those:

Once you do so, you should be brought to the **Sources** tab, which should look like this:

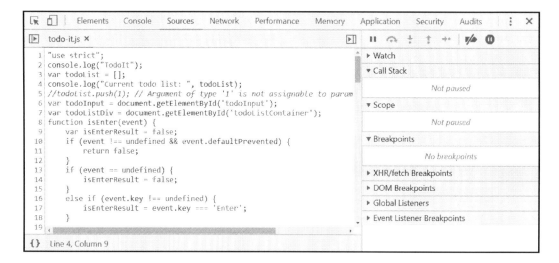

At the top, you will see the currently opened file(s). If you click on the icon on the left, you can display the navigator and open additional files.

In the next screenshot, you can see the file content with the line numbers. If you click on a line number, for example, on line 10 in this example, then you'll add a **breakpoint**:

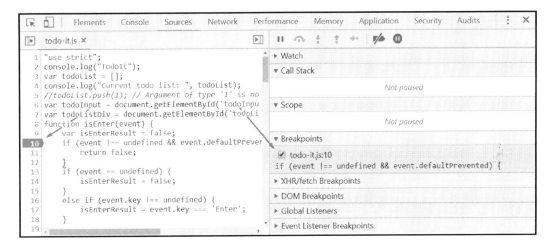

If you click on that line again, you'll remove the breakpoint. On the right, you can see the list of breakpoints under **Breakpoints,** and you can enable/disable each of them.

Whenever a breakpoint is hit (that is, when the runtime is about to execute the line where the breakpoint is located), the debugger will pause the application and will let you inspect the state of the program.

Since we have added a breakpoint in the isEnter function, go ahead and press *Enter* in the **Add todo** input:

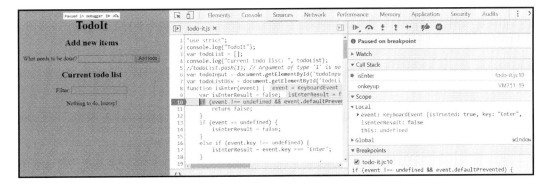

As you can see, the program is now paused. On the left, you can see that it is, and you can resume it if you want. On the right, you can see that the breakpoint that was hit is highlighted. Also, under the **Scope** section on the right, you can now see the current stack and inspect the state of the variables, such as the event that was just passed to the `isEnter` function.

On the left, you can see exactly where the debugger has paused the program.

Finally, on the right, you should learn to master the different buttons:

- Resume (*F8*): Let the program continue.
- Step over next function call (*F10*): Continue the execution of the next function without going into it.
- Step into next function call (*F11*): Continue the execution of the next function and go into it.
- Step out of current function (*Shift + F11*): Get out of the current function.
- Step (*F9*): Continue to the next statement.

These functions allow you to step through the code, going as deep as you need to understand everything that is going on. Usually, you should get into the function calls that you care about (for example, the `addTodo` function) and step over the functions that you are not interested in. If you simply step into everything, then you could easily spend days debugging and be drowned by the excruciating amount of information.

In the debugger, you can also use the **Watch** section to define expressions to keep an eye on.

The debugger is your best weapon for troubleshooting issues, so take your time to learn and master it. Check out the official documentation to learn more: `https://developers.google.com/web/tools/chrome-devtools`.

Debugging your code in VS Code

Another interesting alternative to debug your code is to make use of the VS Code debugger.

As with Chrome, you can define breakpoints by clicking next to a line:

```
12    function isEnter(event: KeyboardEvent): boolean {
13        let isEnterResult = false;
14
15        if(event !== undefined && event.defaultPrevented) {
```

Once done, you can start debugging by going to **Debug** | **Start Debugging** or by pressing *F5*:

The first time that you do so, VS Code will create a `.vscode/launch.json` file for you. This file tells VS Code what to do when it starts a debugging session. In our case, we can leverage the fact that we have Browsersync running in the background and adapt the configuration to let VS Code open Chrome (or another browser) and go to `http://localhost:3000` instead of the default `8080` port. Once adapted, the file should look as follows:

```
{
    // Use IntelliSense to learn about possible attributes.
    // Hover to view descriptions of existing attributes.
    // For more information, visit: https://go.microsoft.com/fwlink/?
    // linkid=830387
```

```
    "version": "0.2.0",
    "configurations": [
        {
            "type": "chrome",
            "request": "launch",
            "name": "Launch Chrome against localhost",
            "url": "http://localhost:3000",
            "webRoot": "${workspaceFolder}"
        }
    ]
}
```

In VS Code, you can easily switch between views from the **View** menu:

Now go ahead and put a breakpoint on the first line of the `isEnter` function in `todo-it.ts`. Once done, press *F5* in VS Code to start debugging. It will open a new web browser window and will switch to the **Debug** view. In Chrome, press *Enter* in the add todo input field to trigger the breakpoint. Now, in VS Code, you should be able to debug your code, just like you did before from the Chrome developer tools:

If you're like us, you'll prefer staying as much as possible in your IDE of choice as that's where you'll be the most productive. A nice side effect of debugging through VS Code is that you directly debug from your sources, which is great!

Check out the following link to learn more about the VS Code debugger: `https://code.visualstudio.com/docs/editor/debugging`.

Generating source maps for easier debugging

One thing that you might have noticed while we were using the debugging in the web browser before is that we only had access to the JavaScript code (as opposed to the TypeScript code when debugging with VS Code directly). In our case, with `TodoIt`, it is okay because the program is very simple, and so it remains intuitive. But in larger applications, this will simply not be usable.

This is why a feature called **source maps** is really, really valuable. Source maps are mapping files that create the link between lines in the JavaScript sources and the corresponding ones in the original source code (TypeScript source code, in our case).

Source maps can either be stored in the JavaScript files themselves, in which case, they are called **inline source maps** or in the separate (that is, external) .map files.

We won't dive much more into the details of how source maps work, but you should simply know that web browsers and their debuggers will automatically detect and load source maps if they're available or reachable. You can check out the following links if you want to know more about source maps:

- https://www.html5rocks.com/en/tutorials/developertools/sourcemaps
- https://developer.mozilla.org/en-US/docs/Tools/Debugger/How_to/Use_a_source_map

TypeScript supports generating source maps easily (whether inline or external).

In order to enable the generation of source maps in TypeScript, edit the tsconfig.json file and add the "sourceMap": true, option.

Once done, you should restart the compiler so that you can see a new file: todo-it.js.map.

If you now reload the page in your web browser and check out the **Console** tab, you'll see that the .ts files are mentioned:

From now on, you can define breakpoints in the original source code, which, as you'll see in later chapters, will become really useful as we build more complex applications:

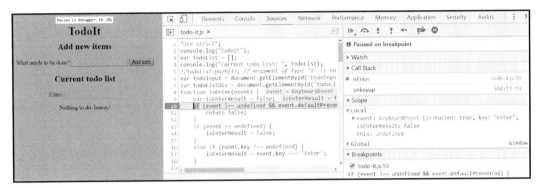

If you look at the generated `todo-it.js` file, you'll notice this at the end: `//#sourceMappingURL=todo-it.js.map`.

This is what tells the web browsers where to find the source map file.

For the sake of completeness, you should also know that `sourceMap` is not the only option that TypeScript supports. You can also configure the compiler to generate inline source maps using the `inlineSourceMap` option.

You can also force TypeScript to include the original sources in the source map files. This can be useful for cases where the original source files are not readily available or when your application or build configuration becomes too complex. Refer to the compiler options for more information: `https://www.typescriptlang.org/docs/handbook/compiler-options.html`.

Summary

In this chapter, you have built your very first web application with TypeScript.

`TodoIt` is quite basic, but by building it you should now have a better understanding of how useful TypeScript is during development and how easy it is to configure its compiler through `tsconfig.json`. Along the way, you have learned about some additional TypeScript concepts, such as type declarations, type annotations, arrays handling, the `null` special type, the `as` cast operator, lambda expressions, and the different types of loops supported in TypeScript.

Also, you should now have a good understanding of `npm`, `package.json`, dependency management, and defining and executing scripts with `npm`.

We have explained what Browsersync is and how to integrate it into your project to get live reloading during development.

In addition, we have seen how to use VS Code to develop with TypeScript and how to use it to debug your applications easily. You have also discovered how to leverage the web browser console, the debugger, and what source maps are and how to generate them using TypeScript.

In the next chapter, we will revisit the `TodoIt` application to improve it using classes and interfaces.

3
Improving TodoIt with Classes and Interfaces

In this chapter, we will improve our `TodoIt` application by making use of classes and interfaces, which will improve the code quality and make the application easily extendable and more maintainable.

By going from an almost purely imperative programming approach to a more object-oriented one, our code will convey more meaning, and we will be able to isolate specific concerns better.

First of all, we will briefly review the major object-oriented programming principles, including what classes and interfaces are and why they're beneficial when building applications, from the smallest to the largest ones.

We will go on to define the domain model of the `TodoIt` application using **UML** (short for **Unified Modeling Language**, for more information, see `https://www.uml.org`).

Then, we'll implement the code of our domain model, when you will be able to write your first classes and discover how to define constructors, accessors, default values, and so on. By introducing interfaces in the code base, we will be able to touch on why they're important and why composition is generally preferred over inheritance.

Through practice, you will also see how TypeScript classes/interfaces and JavaScript classes/objects relate to each other. Finally, we will also see how to leverage structural typing to improve our code.

Let's have a look at the important topics we are going to cover in this chapter:

- Basic **object-oriented programming (OOP)** concepts and nomenclature
- TypeScript concepts

- The relation between TypeScript classes, interfaces, and JavaScript objects/classes
- The UML and class diagrams
- Object-oriented design
- The **single responsibility principle** (**SRP**) and SOLID design concepts
- The **Law of Demeter** (**LoD**)
- Open/closed principle
- Fluent API

About programming paradigms

Before we dive into this chapter, let's discuss a bit about **programming paradigms**.

Bluntly put, programming paradigms are different ways to express what a program should do. Paradigms have a very important influence over many aspects of the code you write, regarding maintainability, readability, performance, and so on.

The classic paradigms are the imperative/procedural ones that focus purely on the logical sequence of operations to perform and organize the code in groups of procedures that modify the state. The C programming language is a great example of a procedural/imperative programming language.

Another hugely popular programming paradigm in the industry nowadays is the **functional programming** (**FP**) one, which is declarative and focuses on the desired outcomes. With FP, you declare a series of functions to apply in order to reach the results.

Finally, the programming paradigm that we will explore a bit in this chapter is the OOP one. With the OOP paradigm, you focus mainly on how the code is organized and structured, regrouping code into logical units. With OOP, the state and the code, which influences the state, are both grouped together. OOP helps to create more understandable code by abstracting elements and by clearly defining the business domain concepts. Java, C#, C++, TypeScript, Python, and others support this approach.

 Most **object-oriented** (**OO**) programming languages also support other programming paradigms. For example, in TypeScript, C#, and Java, it is possible to use and mix OOP, imperative, and functional programming styles.

Check out the following article if you want to read more about programming paradigms: `http://cs.lmu.edu/~ray/notes/paradigms`.

In the previous chapter, we mainly used imperative programming and a tiny bit of functional programming (for example, the `forEach` and `filter` functions combined with lambda expressions). In the rest of this book, we will continually mix paradigms, depending on the context. Each paradigm has its own benefits, depending on the situation.

Finally, as we will see in this chapter, the best way to define the domain model of your applications is to use OOP, as this is where it can bring the most value, by making the code clearer and more readable.

Basic OOP principles and nomenclature

Let's quickly review the basic OOP principles:

- Encapsulation
- Abstraction
- Inheritance
- Interfaces
- Polymorphism
- Composition

Encapsulation and classes

The idea of encapsulation is to create objects that hold a private state and that *keep control* over it. Keeping control means that other objects may not modify the private state directly. Instead, they have to call specific functions called methods to be able to make those changes. Encapsulation is a core idea of OOP; it helps to ensure that mutations (that is, modifications) cannot be made without control/oversight of the owner of the relevant data. Also, encapsulation helps in *hiding* complexity.

To support encapsulation, OOP languages have the notion of **classes**. A class is a logical unit that describes a single concept with all its fields (that is, the properties representing the state) and methods (the operations that can be performed on it).

For example, you could create a `Car` class describing what a car is, how many wheels it has, its color, and so on. In addition, you could define methods such as `startEngine`, `stopEngine`, and many others to describe its behavior. Along with this, you could write specific functions called **accessors** to give read/write access to the encapsulated information (for example, `getColor`, `getEngineType`, and so on).

While a class describes a concept, class instances are objects created based on the class definition, which all have the same set of fields and methods. Hence, classes serve as **templates** or **recipes** for new objects. For example, you could create 1,000 `Car` **instances** (that is, objects) in your program. Classes have constructors, which are functions that are called when an object of a given class needs to be created. Constructors are responsible for initializing the new object as required. Inside constructors, you can put initialization logic, require some parameters to be provided, validate those, and so on.

Abstraction

Abstraction is a key concept of OOP that builds upon the idea of encapsulation by allowing you to hide/remove superfluous details and inner workings of elements in the system. Abstraction is central to being able to tame the complexity of building large systems and to decompose them into manageable subsystems. Classes are merely abstractions of real-world concepts, limited to the set of fields and methods that are relevant for the application.

If you were building a garage management application, then you might need to model things such as the following:

- The date of the last repairs for a given car
- The date when the filters were last changed
- How many kilometers were on the counter
- The license plate number

The inner workings of the car wouldn't matter in this case.

If you were rather building an application for a car manufacturer, then you might instead want to maintain information about the following:

- The car types
- Their bill of materials
- The associated costs
- The materials and their resistance

These two examples merely aim to express how different your abstractions may be, depending on the application you are building.

Classes have control over the visibility of their fields and methods:

- **Private** fields and methods are not accessible from the outside.
- **Protected** fields and methods are not accessible from the outside, but are accessible by descendants.
- **Public** fields and methods are accessible by everyone.

Inheritance and abstract classes

Inheritance is another important OOP concept. It allows you to abstract things away by reusing definitions. Let's take an analogy with the real world: cats and dogs are both animals. In an OO system, you can use inheritance to model the relationship between a given concept and its generalizations (that is, ancestors). When using inheritance, we define **is-a** relationships: a dog is an animal, a cat is an animal, and so on.

By using inheritance, you can regroup fields and methods that are common to a set of closely related classes in a common ancestor class. For example, in an `Animal` class, you could define fields such as `Sex` and `Age`, as well as methods such as `breathe`, `move`, and many others.

In OO terms, we say that a class **extends** another one and **inherits** from its parent. A class that extends another one inherits its fields and methods. We can also say that a base class or superclass is extended or derived by a subclass.

Some programming languages such as C++ support multiple inheritance, while others such as TypeScript, C#, and Java don't (at least not through classes). Multiple inheritance is known to be problematic because of the **diamond problem**. You can learn more about this here: `http://www.lambdafaq.org/what-about-the-diamond-problem`.

Usually, in OO languages, classes can be **concrete**, which means that you can create instances of those or they can be abstract, meaning that you cannot do so.

An **abstract** class may include abstract methods, which are method signatures without an implementation. Abstract methods should be implemented by concrete classes extending from them. Also, a class extending another one (whether abstract or concrete) is usually able to override the methods of its ancestor(s); that is, it can provide another implementation for a function defined in an ancestor class.

A class may also include **static fields** and **static methods**. Static members are elements that are unique for the class and not specific to each instance. Static elements can be accessed through the class itself and not necessarily via an instance of the class.

Here's an example:

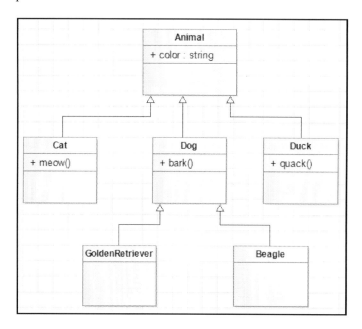

 Inheritance can indeed have multiple levels (for example, `Beagle` inherits from `Dog`, which itself inherits from `Animal`).

Interfaces

Besides inheritance, through which you can create *is-a* relationships, there is another way to define abstractions. You can also create and implement interfaces that define **has-a** relationships. Interfaces are most commonly described as **contracts**.

They only contain (public) method signatures (that is, method names, inputs, and outputs) and (public) constants. When a piece of code **implements** an interface, it is forced to respect the contract and to implement each and every method of the interface. Otherwise, the contract is not properly implemented (and the compiler will not be happy), unless it is an abstract class.

If we continue with our `Car` analogy, you could define an `Engine` interface with the `startEngine` and `stopEngine` methods. If the `Car` class implements the `Engine` interface, then it must provide an implementation for both methods.

Polymorphism

Polymorphism is the last important concept of OOP that you need to understand. Polymorphism basically means *many forms/shapes*, and it actually exists at different levels in OO languages.

First, functions can be polymorphic: you can create multiple variants of a given function that all accept arguments of different types. This is generally known as **function overloading**.

Another type of polymorphism is called **parametric polymorphism**, or generics, as we will see in the case of TypeScript. We will learn more about generics later in the book.

Another form of polymorphism is subtyping. For example, some programming languages allow you to define functions taking an object of the `Animal` type, but still work fine if passed an object that belongs to a subtype, like `Dog`. This type of polymorphism is usually referred to as the **Liskov Substitution Principle**.

The **Liskov Substitution Principle (LSP)** is part of the **SOLID** design principles. We'll explore these as we progress through the book. Check out this article to learn more about them: `https://stackify.com/solid-design-principles`.

A final form of polymorphism that we will consider is generally called **duck typing**, or structural typing. Structural typing is a concept that we already discussed in the first chapter and, as mentioned, is supported by TypeScript.

Composition

When a field within a class has the type of a class or interface, objects of that class will be able to hold a reference to objects of another class. This is called an **association**.

There are multiple types of associations (for example, one-to-one, one-to-many, many-to-one, many-to-many) as well as some nuances. For example, when a class fully owns/controls the life cycle of one of its associations, then we talk about an **aggregation**.

As soon as you create such associations, you are composing OO elements together. Effectively, when you do so, you are reusing other elements to provide some or all of the functionality that you need.

Composition is, of course, central to OO code since it is natural to decompose complex systems into smaller parts and make those parts collaborate by composing them together.

We'll see how composition relates and compares to inheritance.

Composition over inheritance

One last point that we should touch on before we continue is the idea of composition over inheritance. It is generally useful and also very relevant for the domain model of the applications that we will implement in the next chapters.

While designing the domain model of applications, you will often have the choice between relying on *is-a* relationships (that is, inheritance) or *has-a* relationships through composition and interfaces.

 Creating good domain models is both challenging and fun. It takes experience to create solid ones with the right amount of abstraction and that can evolve while remaining maintainable over time. It is definitely a skill well worth acquiring for any software developer.

Inheritance is most useful for grouping related concepts together, but the problem with it is that it encourages you to create a hierarchy of classes very early during the development of your application, and often things change (a lot) over time. This is why you will probably make design mistakes at an early stage, leading to important maintenance problems later on (especially if you are working on a large project).

For this reason, unless you are able to predict the future somehow, you will probably be better off with composition.

Composition is generally a more flexible approach, through which you compose elements in your system and split the responsibilities more logically. Instead of trying to fit everything into some logical hierarchy of classes, you define contracts through interfaces and reuse implementations in order to implement the functionality.

With composition, your applications should better stand the test of time and will be easier to adapt.

You can check the following article for more in-depth advice:
`https://www.thoughtworks.com/insights/blog/composition-vs-inheritance-how-choose`.

 If you already know UML, you can safely skip over this section.

Bonus: UML

Have you noticed that the example diagrams that we have shown so far in this chapter are all based on the same notation? It is called UML.

UML is a standard notation that defines a set of diagram types and visual elements that can be used to model systems and their different facets. Using UML, you can clearly model/document your systems and their structure/relationships. It can be used for both small and very large projects. The value of UML lies in standardization. Once you know it, you can more efficiently share your designs with other developers and analysts. Also, since it is a visual notation, it is also understood by business users.

In this book, we will only use the most common diagram type, which is called the **class diagram** (CD). There are many other types of diagrams that are definitely worth learning about, such as use case diagrams, sequence diagrams, state diagrams, and many more. Refer to the official UML website to learn more: `https://www.uml.org`.

Class diagrams

Class diagrams are used to model classes with their fields and methods as well as their relationships with other elements. Class diagrams can also include interfaces and elements such as packages, which are used to group elements together.

Here's a really short and non-exhaustive summary of what you can define using class diagrams.

For classes, it is possible to define field and method visibility, which is interesting in terms of clearly describing what **private**, **protected**, or **public** is (that is, related to the encapsulation and abstraction concepts that we discussed previously). Public elements are prefixed with +, protected ones with #, and private ones with −.

Here's an example of how this looks:

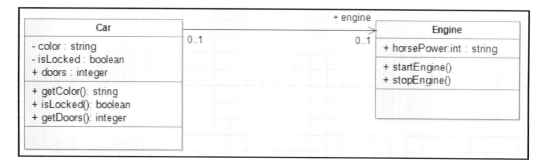

As you can see from the preceding diagram, it is also possible to specify the data types for fields and methods.

You can indeed model the inputs of methods along with their data types. Here's an example with the addPassenger method:

Car
- color : string - isLocked : boolean + doors : integer
+ getColor(): string + isLocked(): boolean + getDoors(): integer + addPassenger(in name: string)

Relationships between classes are defined with a line, and annotations can be added to it to describe those relationships. The cardinality can also be indicated on both sides to clearly specify whether the association is a *one-to-one, one-to-many, many-to-one*, or *many-to-many* type.

For example in the first schema, the Car class has an association with the Engine class.

If a class extends another (that is, an *is-a* relationship), then a specific arrow type needs to be used. Here's an example where the Car class extends from a MotorizedVehicle class:

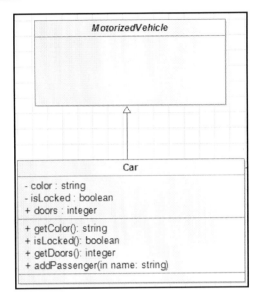

 `MotorizedVehicle` is written in *italics*, to indicate that it is **abstract**.

If a class or interface implements another interface, then a dashed line with an arrow can be used to make the *has-a* relationship visible:

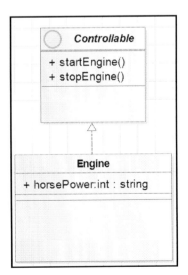

Again, this is only a short summary of elements relevant to this book, and it should not be considered as an exhaustive description of class diagrams. There's a lot more to know about class diagrams and UML, but we'll stick to the basics here.

JavaScript and OOP

In JavaScript, the concept of classes did not exist before ES2015. Inheritance in JavaScript is based on the **prototype chain**; we say that JavaScript uses **prototypal inheritance**.

Also, the `class` keyword added by ES2015 is actually only **syntactic sugar** around the usage of prototypes—it does not really introduce a new inheritance mechanism!

JavaScript has no notion of interfaces, and, as a matter of fact, TypeScript interfaces are actually never converted to JavaScript—they simply disappear.

Overview of the TypeScript support for OOP

TypeScript has great support for OOP. With TypeScript, you can define the following:

- Classes
- Interfaces
- Mixins

Specifically for classes, you can define the following:

- Fields and methods
- Constructors and parameter properties
- Field/method visibility using the `public` (default), `protected`, and `private` keywords
- Static fields and methods
- Read-only properties
- Accessors using the `get` and `set` keywords

In addition, TypeScript supports inheritance through the `extends` keyword, and you can override methods in descendants.

Mixins are supported in TypeScript and provide an alternative way to build classes by combining other ones. You can learn more about mixins here: `https://www.typescriptlang.org/docs/handbook/mixins.html`.

Classes and interfaces are not only great OO concepts, but they're also very useful for type checking in TypeScript, as we will see together.

TypeScript classes

Now, let's dive into how you can implement classes in TypeScript.

Basics

Creating a class in TypeScript is really straightforward:

```
class Car {
}
```

As we have mentioned before, classes were only officially introduced in the JavaScript ecosystem with ES2015. Luckily for us, TypeScript can down-level emit classes if you target ES5 or earlier versions; thus, it allows you to use classes in your TypeScript code even if you are targeting older versions of the specification. This is great for maintaining compatibility while still being able to use new features.

The preceding example gets translated to the following ES5 code:

```
"use strict";

var Car = /** @class */ (function () {
    function Car() {
    }
    return Car;
}());
```

As you can see, TypeScript classes are transpiled into a variable named after the class associated with the constructor function.

Creating an instance of a class is straightforward using the `new` keyword:

```
let car: Car = new Car();
```

As you might have guessed, the constructor function gets invoked, initializing the new object, and returning it so that we can store it in the variable.

 If you are not interested in lower-level details, then you can skip this section.

Bonus: How TypeScript converts classes to JavaScript

The JavaScript code that TypeScript generates when it down-level emits classes is actually very interesting. Here is a bit of information that should help you to understand what the TypeScript compiler does there.

When TypeScript down-level emits a TypeScript class to ES5 or older, it creates an **Immediately Invoked Function Expression (IIFE)** in which the class is defined (as a simple function) and returned. The result of the execution of that IIFE is stored in a variable and used when the class is later referenced (for example, to create a new instance or to access a static field or static method). Inside the IIFE, a function is defined with the name of the `class` and constructor arguments handled in that function.

As the name clearly indicates, an IIFE is a function definition that is invoked *immediately*. Here's an example:

```
function() {
    var secret = "I am private";

    function privateFunction() {
        console.log("Hello world from the private function");
    };

    console.log("Hello world: ",secret);
    privateFunction();
}();
```

One benefit of using IIFEs is that they prevent the global scope from being cluttered with functions and variables, and, as you probably know, polluting the global scope is not something you should do happily unless you enjoy endless debugging sessions. We will discuss this idea again when we introduce modules later in the book.

Within the function definition, it is, of course, possible to define variables (whose scope, if you remember, is limited to the function) and also nested functions.

If you want to learn more about how classes are converted to TypeScript code, you can check out the following page:
`https://basarat.gitbooks.io/typescript/docs/classes-emit.html`.

Fields, methods, visibility, and constructors

Here's how you can define fields, methods, visibility, and constructors in your TypeScript classes:

```
class ColoredCar {
    private _color: string;
    private static DEFAULT_COLOR = "Red";

    constructor(color: string) {
        this._color = color;
    }

    displayColor() {
        console.log(`Color of this car: ${this.color}`);
    }

    public get color(): string {
        return this._color;
    }

    public set color(color: string) {
        this._color = color
    }

    private resetColor() {
        this._color = ColoredCar.DEFAULT_COLOR;
    }
}
```

As you saw earlier, methods are not prefixed by the `function` keyword.

TypeScript provides a shorthand for defining properties through the constructor function. For example, the `constructor(private foo: string) { }` notation may be surprising for .NET and Java developers, but that is usually recommended as it is more concise and clear.

Here is the corresponding JavaScript (ES5) code. Notice how the `displayColor` method is added to the prototype of the class:

```
"use strict";

var ColoredCar = /** @class */ (function () {
    function ColoredCar(color) {
        this._color = color;
    }

    ColoredCar.prototype.displayColor = function () {
        console.log("Color of this car: ", this.color);
    };

    Object.defineProperty(ColoredCar.prototype, "color", {
        get: function () {
            return this._color;
        },

        set: function (color) {
            this._color = color;
        },

        enumerable: true,
        configurable: true
    });

    ColoredCar.prototype.resetColor = function () {
        this._color = ColoredCar.DEFAULT_COLOR;
    };

    ColoredCar.DEFAULT_COLOR = "Red";
    return ColoredCar;
}());
```

The `this` keyword is used to refer to the specific instance of the class.

 You need to be aware that the `this` keyword does not always behave as you would expect in other languages.

Check out these articles to learn more about `this` in TypeScript and JavaScript:

- `https://github.com/Microsoft/TypeScript/wiki/'this'-in-TypeScript`. This article also gives recommendations to avoid surprises when using the `this` keyword in TypeScript.
- `https://developer.mozilla.org/en-US/docs/Web/JavaScript/Reference/Operators/this`.

TypeScript goes further and improves JavaScript classes by adding support for field/method visibility, static properties, and type checking.

In the previous example, the `color` field is marked as `private`, and is thereby encapsulated and not directly accessible from the outside. The default visibility in TypeScript is public, which is logical since there is no notion of visibility in JavaScript (that is, everything is public). Nevertheless, it is a good practice, as we did earlier, to use encapsulation and mark elements as `private` when possible (or `protected`) so as to ensure a better cohesion of our code and to limit possible side effects.

 Visibility can also be defined for methods, as we did with the `resetColor` method in the example. The default visibility for methods is also `public`.

By convention, we have also prefixed the private `color` field with an underscore. Then, we have created accessor methods using the `get` and `set` keywords. The former allows you to get data, while the latter allows you to modify the state of the `color` field. If you look at the generated JavaScript code, you'll see that this translates into actual property definitions in JavaScript.

 Using the `private` and `protected` keywords has an impact on the type compatibility. We'll soon learn more about that. Meanwhile, you can check out this part of the official handbook if you can't wait: `https://www.typescriptlang.org/docs/handbook/type-compatibility.html`.

Finally, in the example, note that we have defined a static field called `DEFAULT_COLOR` using the `static` keyword. As we explained earlier in the chapter, static elements (fields/methods) are shared by all instances of the class. So, in this example, `DEFAULT_COLOR` is only defined once and shared by all instances of the `ColoredCar` class. In the `resetColor` method, you can also see how static elements are used.

Inheritance

The last point that we need to cover for classes is indeed inheritance. As you might guess, TypeScript does indeed support it.

In the following code snippet, we are defining an abstract Shape class:

```
abstract class Shape {
    constructor(private readonly _shapeName: string) {
        this.displayInformation();
    }

    abstract displayArea(): void;
    abstract displayPerimeter(): void;

    protected get shapeName(): string {
        return this._shapeName
    }
    public displayInformation(): void {
        console.log(`This shape is a ${this._shapeName}`);
    }
    public doSomething(): void {
        console.log("Not interesting");
    }
}
```

And here, we create a Square class extending the abstract base class:

```
class Square extends Shape {
    constructor(private _width: number) {
        super("Square");
    }

    displayArea(): void {
        const area = this._width * this._width;
        console.log(`This ${this.shapeName} has an area of: ${area}`);
    }

    displayPerimeter(): void {
        const perimeter = 2 * (this._width + this._width);
        console.log(`This ${this.shapeName} has a perimeter of :
         ${perimeter}`)
    }

    public doSomething(): void {
        console.log("Something more interesting");
    }
}
```

This example alone covers most of what you can do with inheritance in TypeScript:

- `Shape` is abstract, meaning that you cannot instantiate it.
- Because `Shape` is abstract, it can have abstract methods that are methods marked with the `abstract` keyword and without an implementation (for example, `getArea`).
- All concrete (as opposed to abstract) descendants such as `Square` must implement abstract methods to make them concrete as well.
- `Shape` has a constructor that all descendants **must** call first (if they have a constructor themselves) using the `super` keyword.
- `Shape` has defined a _shapeName private field through the constructor (useful shorthand, as noted earlier).
- `Shape` has marked its _shapeName private property as `readonly`, which means that it won't be possible to assign another value to it after the constructor has been invoked.
- `Square` extends `Shape` and inherits the methods and fields defined on `Shape`.
- `Square` can override methods defined in `Shape`. For example, we have done so with `doSomething`.
- `Square` does not have direct access to the _shapeName private property of `Shape` (that is, private means for your eyes only, not even descendants). `Square` can only access it through the `protected` accessor that has been defined on `Shape` (that is, protected means for you and your deriving classes).

When overriding a method, a subclass cannot change its visibility. For example, if you try to override `doSomething` and mark it as `private` instead of `public`, then you'll get an error like the following:

```
[ts]
Class 'Square' incorrectly extends base class 'Shape'.
Property 'doSomething' is private in type 'Square' but not in type
'Shape'.
```

As you can see, the compiler is not happy.

 There is one notable exception though: a subclass can change the visibility of a parent field/method from `protected` to `public`, as explained here: https://stackoverflow.com/questions/43084483/why-protected-members-can-be-overridden-by-public-members-in-typescript.

Another thing to know is that you cannot define multiple constructors on a class in TypeScript.

 Take good note of the pattern that we have used to keep control/protect the encapsulation by marking fields as `private` and implementing accessors. This can seem useless, but it goes a long way to making a code base more reliable. Note that using accessors forces you to transpile to ES5 or higher.

Using our `Square` class is easy:

```
let square:Square = new Square(5);
square.displayArea();
square.displayPerimeter();
square.displayPerimeter();
square.doSomething();

let shape:Shape = new Square(10);
shape.doSomething();
```

We can assign a `Square` object to a `Shape` variable. The compiler doesn't mind because both have the same shape (remember what we discussed in `Chapter 1`, *Introduction to TypeScript and Preparing Your Development Environment*, about structural typing).

 In TypeScript, we'll see that you can actually use a class as if it was an interface. We won't cover this here simply because it is something that you should really avoid.

TypeScript does not allow multiple inheritance, but you can implement multiple interfaces perfectly well. You can also use mixins, which are a way to mix partial classes: `https://www.typescriptlang.org/docs/handbook/mixins.html`.

Great, now we have covered most of what TypeScript offers around classes and inheritance!

Fluent APIs

Now that you're familiar with classes, we can present a very useful idiom called **fluent APIs**. Using a fluent API feels natural because it allows you to chain method calls without having to create intermediary variables.

Fluent APIs are often used with the builder design pattern, where you configure an object to create by calling different methods one after another, before triggering the effective construction using a `build()` method.

Here's an example to make this clear:

```
class Calculator {
    constructor(private _currentValue: number = 0) { }

    add(a: number): this {
        this._currentValue += a;
        return this;
    }

    substract(a: number): this {
        this._currentValue -= a;
        return this;
    }

    multiply(a: number): this {
        this._currentValue *= a;
        return this;
    }

    divide(a: number): this {
        this._currentValue /= a;
        return this;
    }

    get value(): number {
        return this._currentValue;
    }
}

let result: number = new Calculator(0)
    .add(5) // returns this
    .multiply(2) // returns this
    .add(10) // we can keep chaining method calls
    .divide(4)
    .substract(2)
    .value; // returns the value

console.log(`Result: ${result}`); // 3
```

In this example, we have re-implemented our calculator from Chapter 1, *Introduction to TypeScript and Preparing Your Development Environment*, using a fluent API. As you can see, the principle is simply that each of the method calls returns this, thus, the class instance. This allows us to call other methods directly afterward. Finally, we retrieve the current value using the accessor.

 When you return this, with a method, you actually use a feature of TypeScript called **polymorphic this**, which corresponds to the type or subtype of the containing class/interface. Another name for this feature is F-bounded polymorphism. You can, of course, still extend a class that uses this feature.

Building fluent APIs is great for code readability, and it should definitely be part of your arsenal.

Custom types

One thing that we haven't shown yet is that in TypeScript, you can define **custom types**.

In TypeScript, as we have already mentioned a few times, type checking is structural; it is strongly tied with the *shape* of the objects that are considered. When you define the type of an element (for example, variable, field/property, function argument, or function return type), you can use primitive types, classes, interfaces, or **custom types**.

Inline types

Custom types can also be defined inline.

Here is an example of a variable type:

```
const plane: {
    name: string,
    description: string
} = {
    name: "Plane",
    description: "Something that flies"
};
```

In this example, we have defined a custom shape. Any value assigned to the `plane` variable **must** have a `name` property of the `string` type, as well as a `description` property of the `string` type.

And here's another one for a function argument:

```
function foo(bar: { firstName: string, lastName: string}): void {
    console.log(`Hello ${bar.firstName}.. or should I call you Mr
    ${bar.lastName}?`);
}

foo({
    firstName: "Sebastien",
    lastName: "Dubois"
});
```

In this last example, we defined a `foo` function requiring a single `bar` argument with another custom inline type.

When TypeScript compiles the code, its type checker enforces those shape constraints. As a result, when we invoke the `foo` function or assign a value to the `plane` variable, we must indeed respect the type contracts and pass an object with the required shape.

 A key point to understand here is that *any* object or class will do, as long as it exposes the required properties with the expected type!

Inline types are great because they allow you to clearly specify the type requirements and get the help of the compiler to detect mistakes.

In addition, since functions are first-order elements in TypeScript, you can also define function types:

```
function performCalculation(
    a: number,
    b: number,
    calculationFn: (x: number, y: number) => number
): void {
    console.log(`The result is ${calculationFn(a, b)}`);
}
performCalculation(
    5,
    10,
    (x: number, y: number) => x + y
);
```

This time, the `performCalculation` function expects to receive two values as well as a function accepting two numbers and returning a number.

 You can mark elements in a type as optional using the ? character. For example, you could write something like `function foo({firstName: string, lastName: string, title?: string}) { ... }`, and, in that case, the `title` argument would be optional. The same is true for properties.

This way of defining custom types can be surprising at first. It takes some time to get used to it, but it is really powerful. There is a lot more to say about custom types, but we will stop here for now.

Type aliases

Type aliases are custom types defined using the `type` keyword:

```
type Thing = {
    name: string
    description: string
};

// usage:
const myThing: Thing = {
    name: "Computer",
    description: "A thing that can perform calculations"
};
```

As you saw earlier, the `Thing` type can be used easily to enforce the presence of specific properties/functions on an object.

TypeScript interfaces

Let's now see how you can use interfaces in TypeScript.

Defining contracts

In terms of OO design, we have seen that interfaces play a big role as they allow us to define and enforce contracts in a code base, whether for internal or external (that is, client) code.

First of all, of course, TypeScript interfaces allow you to define such contracts. Here's a simple example:

```
interface MusicPlayer {
    play(): void;
    pause(): void;
    stop(): void;
    rewind(seconds: number): void;
    fastForward(seconds: number): void;
}
```

As you can see, we just need to use the `interface` keyword and list the method signatures. Any element realizing (that is, implementing) this interface will have to implement those methods.

Here's how a class could implement the interface of the previous example:

```
class BasicMusicPlayer implements MusicPlayer {
    fastForward(seconds: number): void {
        console.log(`Moving forward ${seconds} seconds`);
    }

    pause(): void {
        console.log("Pausing");
    }

    play(): void {
        console.log("Playing")
    }

    rewind(seconds: number): void {
        console.log(`Rewinding ${seconds}`);
    }

    stop(): void {
        console.log("Stopping");
    }
}
```

But TypeScript interfaces are actually much more powerful!

Naming custom types using interfaces

TypeScript interfaces allow us to define contracts and also to give names to specific types/shapes.

When you need to use a custom type somewhere in your code, you should always consider creating an interface and/or a class for it. We'll soon see what to take into consideration in order to decide whether a class or interface makes more sense.

For now, let's concentrate on the number of times that a given custom type will need to be used. If you only need it in one place, then maybe a custom type is fine. If, on the other hand the custom type is going to be used at multiple locations, then it probably makes more sense to create an interface or a class for it.

Using an interface or class rather than a custom type means that you define the first-level *concept* for your application, which can tremendously improve the readability of your code.

Let's revisit our previous example:

```
interface Person {
    firstName: string,
    lastName: string,
    age: number
}

function sayHelloTo(bar: Person): void {
    console.log(`Hello ${bar.firstName}.. or should I call you Mr
    ${bar.lastName}?`);
}

let persjohnDoeon: Person = {
    firstName: "John",
    lastName: "Doe",
    age: 42
};

sayHelloTo(johnDoe);
```

Isn't it clearer when using interfaces, as we did previously?

 Don't prefix your interface names with I (for example, IService, and IController); this isn't useful in modern languages and hinders readability. If you use good editors, then the fact that your code is using interfaces should be obvious.

Let's see what else we can do using interfaces.

> You can also mark some interface properties with `readonly`, just like with classes.

Extending interfaces

Just like classes, you can use the `extends` keyword to extend an existing interface, adding method signatures and properties to it. This is, of course, interesting when creating higher-level abstractions and specialized interfaces for your APIs.

Here's an example:

```
interface Club {
    name: string;
    logoLocation: string;

    isActive(): boolean;
}

interface SoccerClub extends Club {
    league: string;
}
```

> It is actually possible for interfaces to extend classes, but it is really something that you should avoid doing at all costs. There might be valid use cases, but, generally speaking, you should consider that an anti-pattern.

Interfaces only exist at compile time

One thing to keep in mind is that TypeScript interfaces only exist at compile time. If you try to compile the previous examples, you'll see that the interfaces completely disappear in generated JavaScript code!

Because of type erasure, the type checking that you enforce on your code base through the usage of TypeScript, its type checker, and constructs (such as types, custom types, and interfaces) has zero impact on what happens at runtime. This is simply because all the type information disappears at runtime, so the JavaScript interpreters won't know about them. This means that even if your code compiles without any issues, it might still be misused at runtime. The lesson here is that you should not rely too much on the compiler. If you care about runtime safety, then you should add safety/defensive checks in your code.

The fact that interfaces disappear once compiled is positive in the sense that they do not add **weight** to the code that you generate. For this reason, you should never **avoid** creating interfaces because you fear the size impact.

Interfaces versus type aliases and inline types

Interfaces are more powerful than type aliases since they can be extended using the `extends` keyword.

In general, our advice is to prefer interfaces over type aliases. Although using the `type` keyword, you can sometimes create useful composed types.

Similarly, you should generally prefer interfaces and keep inline types for exceptional cases (for example, one-time needs).

Interfaces versus classes

So now that you have seen both classes and interfaces/custom types, one question that you might ask yourself is how to choose between the two? When does it make sense to create one rather than the other?

As with many design choices, the general answer is it depends, but here are a few points that you should consider to help you decide.

Consider defining a class when you need to do any of the following:

- You need to create multiple new instances at different locations of your code base. Using a class, you can centralize the logic for doing so and adapt it easily in one place.
- You need to validate things when creating new instances (for example, ensure that a date has been provided, is valid, and so on). With a class, you can put the initialization logic and validations inside the constructor.
- You need to keep control over the data. With classes, you can have private/protected fields (that is, encapsulation) and define accessors.

Consider defining an interface when you want or need to do any of the following:

- You want to enforce a contract (that is, methods that should be implemented).
- You want to create simple **data transfer objects** (**DTOs**) that you can easily convert to/from JSON, for example (at least as long as there is no complex (de)serialization logic).
- You want to describe a type shape (that is, properties that passed objects should have) and give a name to it.
- You don't need encapsulation.
- You don't need initialization/validation logic.

Starting point

We hope that you share our feeling that this theoretical detour was useful for us to get started. Now, let's proceed and improve our `TodoIt` application.

The starting point for this new version is the code of `TodoIt` that we have built together in the previous chapter (version 1). If you don't have it anymore, you can get it from the sample code in `Chapter 2`, *Building TodoIt - Your Own Todo Management Web Application with TypeScript* (the Chapter`todoit-v1` folder). Create a copy of the project and rename it `todoit-v2`.

Designing the domain model of TodoIt v2

In the first version of `TodoIt`, the model was almost non-existent:

- There were no classes or interfaces.
- All the logic was held in functions within `todo-it.ts`.
- The state was stored in a global variable.

Also, the todo items only had a description.

Now that we have reviewed the major OO building blocks, the UML, and the class diagrams, let's use our newly acquired skills to help us visualize our target domain model. Let's imagine how we could leverage classes and interfaces to organize things a bit better and improve the quality of our application code.

First proposal

Here is a first proposal:

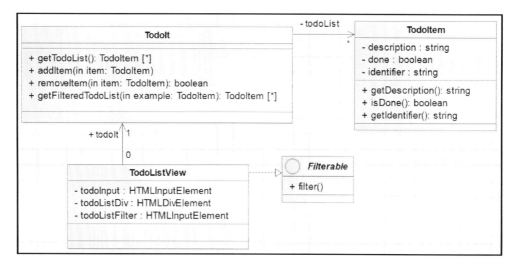

The first obvious benefit of this first approach is that we would have a clear model for items in our todo list. With that in place, it would become easy to come back and modify the data model in order to add new elements to it (for example, due date, assignee, and many others). This means that we would increase the clarity, readability, and maintainability of our code.

Also, since `TodoItem` objects would have a unique identifier, then it would be easy to manipulate them properly. In the first version of `TodoIt`, when we wanted to remove an item, we did so using only `name`, which simply removed any matching entry in the array. In our case, it wasn't a big issue, but for other use cases, you can imagine that it would not be ideal.

The `TodoIt` class would be the owner of the todo list and would expose methods to manipulate it: `addItem` and `removeItem`. In addition, it would also allow its clients to retrieve the full list of todo items through the `getTodoList` method, and to get a filtered version using an example object with the `getFilteredTodoList` method. With this defined, the application would expose a clear API to manipulate the todo list.

Moreover, thanks to the `TodoIt` class, we would be able to encapsulate all the logic related to the manipulation of the todo list.

Finally, the `TodoListView` would be the one responsible for handling all the DOM-related operations, such as retrieving the field values, and for updating the DOM to reflect the new content of the todo list.

Unfortunately, this first proposal has some major flaws. For instance, what is the entry point of the application? Is it `TodoIt` or `TodoListView`? Actually, with this first design, the view would be in charge of everything, which is far from ideal because it would have more responsibilities than it needs. The view should only ever be responsible for the user interface; it shouldn't control the flow of the application or its data model.

Single responsibility principle (SRP)

To improve our design, we actually need to apply the SRP.

The SRP is a very important and useful design principle for ensuring code quality, maintainability, and separation of concerns. It is actually the first of the SOLID design principles.

SRP states that a class should have *one*, and *only one*, responsibility.

The main benefit of applying the SRP is that when changes need to be applied, they should have a limited impact on the code base.

As we all know, requirements evolve and change over time. Each of those changes also impacts the responsibilities of some parts of the system. If specific parts of your code have many responsibilities, then it increases the chance of those being impacted when something changes. Moreover, having a component with many responsibilities also implies that there is a stronger coupling with other parts of the system, meaning a larger potential impact down the line for your overall code base.

Separation of concerns is important for maintainability, and our goal throughout this book is not only to show you the TypeScript syntax, but also to guide you toward creating better applications with the language, and others for that matter.

Law of Demeter (LoD)

Another interesting object-oriented design guideline is called the LoD, or the principle of least knowledge.

It states that the less different parts of your system know about each other, the better. By limiting the amount of required knowledge, you make sure that different parts can evolve without incurring large adaptations to other parts.

The LoD can be summarized as follows:

- Each subsystem should only have limited knowledge of other subsystems that are closely related.
- Each subsystem should only talk to friends, usually not to strangers.
- Each subsystem should only talk to its close friends.

These rules are, of course, all in favor of a good functional decomposition and loose coupling, limiting the impact and cost of changes. The LoD is closely related and complementary to the SRP and OO principles, such as encapsulation.

Open/closed principle

One last principle that we can quickly discuss is the **open/closed principle**. It states that you should write your code and functionality so as to limit the number of changes necessary to add new functionality. Your OO designs should be open for extension but closed for modifications. Note that this principle is not only applicable to classes.

Using the Model View Controller (MVC) design pattern

Let's try another approach:

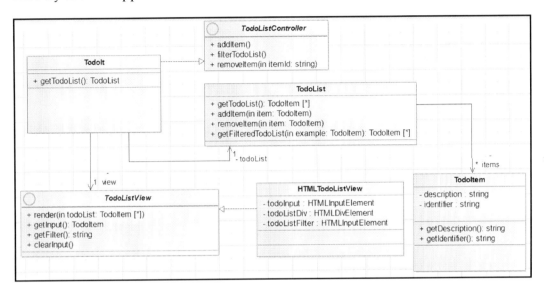

This time around, we have applied the **Model View Controller (MVC)** design pattern. MVC is a very popular way of isolating responsibilities:

- The **Model** contains the data.
- The **View** is responsible for the user interface.
- The **Controller** contains the logic to handle user actions and to update the system.

Refer to this article for more details about the MVC design pattern: `https://developer.mozilla.org/en-US/docs/Glossary/MVC`.

With the MVC pattern applied, our application will have a better structure:

- `TodoList` will be the model of the application and will take care of maintaining the list of todo items.
- `TodoListView` will be responsible for the view of the application.
- `TodoIt` will be the controller of the application and will implement the `TodoListController` interface. It will thus expose the methods to add, filter, and remove items. When those methods get called, `TodoIt` will update the model with the new information and will request an update of the view.

With this new design, we keep the main advantages of the first proposal, but some interesting improvements can be observed. For example, `TodoIt` will use composition to handle the view; it will know and use the `TodoListView` interface, but will not need to know about the HTML implementation that will be used (`HTMLTodoListView`). This means that it will be easy to plug other types of views into the application.

Another interesting point is the fact that `TodoList` and `TodoItem` use encapsulation, so they can take care of the integrity of the data. Also if you were to implement a persistence mechanism, it would be easy to make that change transparent.

Implementing the new domain model

Let's start with the domain model, as it will become the core of our application.

Creating the TodoItem class

Remove everything from the `todo-it.ts` file. Then, add the definition of the `TodoItem` class:

```
class TodoItem {
    private readonly _creationTimestamp: number;
    private readonly _identifier: string;

    constructor(private _description: string, identifier?: string) {
        this._creationTimestamp = new Date().getTime();

        if (identifier) {
            this._identifier = identifier;
        } else {
```

```
            // this is just for the example; for any real project, use
            // UUIDs instead: https://www.npmjs.com/package/uuid
            this._identifier = Math.random().toString(36).substr(2,
              9);
        }
    }

    get creationTimestamp(): number {
        return this._creationTimestamp;
    }

    get identifier(): string {
        return this._identifier;
    }

    get description(): string {
        return this._description;
    }
}
```

We are using encapsulation in order to protect the integrity of our data model (by making the different fields `private`), and we only create accessors for the fields that we want to expose to the outside. Notice that in the constructor of the class, we initialize a creation timestamp and an identifier (if it wasn't provided).

Creating a `TodoItem` instance is easy: `const todo: TodoItem = new TodoItem("Do the laundry");`

If you implement the `TodoItem` class as we propose, instances of the class will be immutable: **Once an instance has been created, you cannot modify it, whether from the inside or from the outside**. This is guaranteed because the fields are private and only expose a getter that protects the field from external modifications. In addition, the fields are also read-only, which prevents internal modifications as well. This is a practice that we heavily recommend.

Another common name for such an immutable class is a **data class**.

Creating the TodoList class

Now, you can also implement the `TodoList` class:

```
class TodoList {
    private _todoList: ReadonlyArray<TodoItem> = [];

    constructor(todoList?: TodoItem[]) {
        // first we make sure that we have received a valid array
        // reference: https://developer.mozilla.org/en-
        // US/docs/Web/JavaScript/Reference/Global_Objects
        // /Array/isArray
        if(Array.isArray(todoList) && todoList.length) {
            this._todoList = this._todoList.concat(todoList);
        }
    }

    get todoList(): ReadonlyArray<TodoItem> {
        return this._todoList
    }

    addTodo(todoItem: TodoItem) {
        if(todoItem) {
            // the value is "truthy":
            // not null, not undefined, not NaN, not an empty string,
            // not 0, not false
            this._todoList = this._todoList.concat(todoItem);
        }
    }

    removeTodo(itemId: string) {
        if(itemId) {
            this._todoList = this._todoList.filter(item => {
                if(item.identifier === itemId) {
                    return false; // drop
                } else {
                    return true; // keep
                }
            });
        }
    }
}
```

Here, we again favor immutability to use a more functional approach.

A note about TypeScript's ReadonlyArray

Internally, the `_todoList` field is defined as `ReadonlyArray<TodoItem>`. Don't worry too much about the angle brackets for now; instead, focus on the type. This is a read-only array of the `TodoItem` objects. Using `ReadonlyArray` is very beneficial because it ensures that the array content cannot be changed directly. All mutating methods are gone; thus, for example, you cannot re-assign elements in the array or use methods such as `push` to add items to it.

This might be counterintuitive for programmers with a strong OO background, but it will actually increase the safety of our code. For example, in the constructor, we accept an optional argument called `todoList`. If the given argument is defined and is a valid array, then we create a new internal representation by concatenating the existing array with the provided one. This creates a new array that we keep internally.

Why does it add safety to the code? Because we are sure that we are the only ones with a reference toward the internal array. If we had instead directly assigned the array like this—`this._todoList = todoList;`—then the calling code would still have a valid reference towards that array and could modify it at will, breaking the encapsulation!

 This code is safe because the array items (the `TodoItem` instances) are also immutable, meaning that even if external code has a reference toward one of those, it will not be able to change things.

To continue with this trail of thought, notice how we have implemented the `addTodo` and `removeTodo` methods: both create new instances instead of trying to mutate the existing array. We do this for the very same safety reasons.

 `ReadonlyArray` is not the only immutable type that you can use in TypeScript. TypeScript actually also provides `Readonly<T>`, which you can use to define a read-only type, based on another existing type. For example, if you have a mutable `Person` class, then you can simply create a read-only version of the type using `Readonly<Person>`. This is very useful for defensive programming.

Implementing the view

Now that we have defined our domain model, let's implement the view layer.

Creating the TodoListView interface

We'll start with the `TodoListView` interface:

```
interface TodoListView {
    render(todoList: ReadonlyArray<TodoItem>): void;
    getInput(): TodoItem;
    getFilter(): string;
    clearInput(): void;
    filter(): void;
}
```

Next, we will create an HTML-based implementation of this interface.

Implementing the TodoListView interface

Then, of course, we can implement this interface:

```
class HTMLTodoListView implements TodoListView {
    constructor() {
        // TODO
    }

    clearInput(): void {
        // TODO
    }

    getFilter(): string {
        // TODO
    }

    getInput(): TodoItem {
        // TODO
    }

    render(todoList: ReadonlyArray<TodoItem>): void {
        // TODO
    }

    filter(): void {
```

```
            // TODO
        }
    }
```

This is the base structure. Now, we need to start refactoring/integrating our previous code to this new class while implementing the interface methods.

First, add `private` fields to the class for the different HTML elements that we know for sure should be available. Then, make sure to initialize them in the constructor:

```
private readonly todoInput: HTMLInputElement;
private readonly todoListDiv: HTMLDivElement;
private readonly todoListFilter: HTMLInputElement;

constructor() {
    this.todoInput = document.getElementById('todoInput') as
     HTMLInputElement;
    this.todoListDiv = document.getElementById
     ('todoListContainer') as HTMLDivElement;
    this.todoListFilter = document.getElementById
     ('todoFilter') as HTMLInputElement;

    // defensive checks
    if(!this.todoInput) {
        throw new Error("Could not find the todoInput HTML input
         element. Is the HTML correct?");
    }

    if(!this.todoListDiv) {
        throw new Error("Could not find the todoListContainer HTML
         div. Is the HTML correct?");
    }

    if(!this.todoListFilter) {
        throw new Error("Could not find the todoFilter HTML input
         element. Is the HTML correct?");
    }
}
```

With this, we know that when the class is instantiated, it will retrieve the necessary HTML elements from the DOM. If that fails, then errors will be thrown to help us identify what went wrong.

Such validations are usually referred to as **defensive programming** checks. Oftentimes, defensive checks incur *wasted* CPU cycles checking elements that should be invariants, but in practice, those checks actually help avoid a lot of troubleshooting to identify where bugs have been introduced.

In our case, if the HTML template gets modified in a way that prevents our code from getting the elements that we expected to be available, then errors will be thrown right away.

Perform defensive checks as soon as possible and make your code fail fast. The sooner you let errors surface, the easier it becomes to identify and fix problems.

Next up, let's add the implementation of the `clearInput` method:

```
clearInput(): void {
    this.todoInput.value = '';
}
```

The `getFilter` method is also straightforward to implement:

```
getFilter(): string {
    return this.todoListFilter.value.toUpperCase();
}
```

Now, implement the `getInput` method:

```
getInput(): TodoItem {
    const todoInputValue: string = this.todoInput.value.trim();
    const retVal: TodoItem = new TodoItem(todoInputValue);
    return retVal;
}
```

We have created a superfluous constant called `retVal` simply to ease debugging later on.

For the `render` function, we simply need to integrate/refactor the code of the `updateTodoList` function:

```
render(todoList: ReadonlyArray<TodoItem>): void {
    console.log("Updating the rendered todo list");
    this.todoListDiv.innerHTML = '';
    this.todoListDiv.textContent = ''; // Edge, ...

    const ul = document.createElement('ul');
    ul.setAttribute('id', 'todoList');
    this.todoListDiv.appendChild(ul);

    todoList.forEach(item => {
```

```
        const li = document.createElement('li');
        li.setAttribute('class','todo-list-item');
        li.innerHTML = `<a href='#'
         onclick='todoIt.removeTodo("${item.identifier}")
         '>${item.description}</a>`;
        ul.appendChild(li);
    });
}
```

Notice that we have modified the link to remove a todo item. As you can see, we invoke the `removeTodo` function on a `todoIt` object. We will define this later on.

Finally, we need to implement the `filter` function, which will simply show/hide elements in the view depending on the filter value:

```
filter(): void {
    console.log("Filtering the rendered todo list");
    const todoListHtml: HTMLULIistElement =
     document.getElementById('todoList') as HTMLULIistElement
    if (todoListHtml == null) {
        console.log("Nothing to filter");
        return;
    }

    const todoListFilterText = this.getFilter();
    todoListHtml.childNodes.forEach((item) => {
        let itemText: string | null = item.textContent;
        if (itemText !== null) {
            itemText = itemText.toUpperCase();

            if (itemText.startsWith(todoListFilterText)) {
                (item as HTMLLIElement).style.display = "list-
                  item";
            } else {
                (item as HTMLLIElement).style.display = "none";
            }
        }
    });
}
```

At this point, our view implementation is almost done, but the puzzle remains incomplete. We now need to turn our attention to the controller layer.

Implementing the controller layer

The biggest part of our refactoring revolves around the introduction of the controller layer, the orchestrator of our new version.

Creating the TodoListController interface

First, let's define our controller interface, `TodoListController`. Add it underneath the `HTMLTodoListView` class:

```
interface TodoListController {
    addTodo(): void;
    filterTodoList(): void;
    removeTodo(identifier: string): void;
}
```

This interface might surprise you because, apart from the `removeTodo` method, the methods don't accept parameters. The reason for this is that our view will interact with the controller layer by passing signals to it.

To give you an example, when you click on the **Add** button or press *Enter* to add an item to the list, then it will simply invoke the `addTodo` method on the controller. Then, the controller's implementation will ask its view (more precisely, its view model) to get the input value from the DOM. Once it has the value, the controller will update the model and then it will ask the view to update itself. As you can see, the controller is the orchestrator of the whole process.

Implementing the TodoIt controller class

Now, start with the base skeleton of the controller implementation:

```
class TodoIt implements TodoListController {
    private readonly _todoList: TodoList = new TodoList();

    constructor(private _todoListView: TodoListView) {
        console.log("TodoIt");

        if(!_todoListView) {
            throw new Error("The todo list view implementation is
                required to properly initialize TodoIt!");
        }
    }
```

```
addTodo(): void {
    // TODO
}

filterTodoList(): void {
    // TODO
}

removeTodo(identifier: string): void {
    // TODO
}
}
```

As you can see earlier, our controller implementation requires `TodoListView` to be provided, but it does not care about which specific implementation. This is how you usually want to work with interfaces: by programming against them rather than against implementations. This decouples your code.

 Again, we have added a defensive check in the constructor.

Implement the `addTodo` method as follows:

```
addTodo(): void {
    // get the value from the view
    const newTodo = this._todoListView.getInput();

    // verify that there is something to add
    if ('' !== newTodo.description) {
        console.log("Adding todo: ", newTodo);

        // add the new item to the list (i.e., update the model)
        this._todoList.addTodo(newTodo);
        console.log("New todo list: ", this._todoList.todoList);

        // clear the input
        this._todoListView.clearInput();

        // update the rendered todo list
        this._todoListView.render(this._todoList.todoList);

        // filter the list if needed
        this.filterTodoList();
    }
}
```

This is where the code begins to get interesting. As you can see, our controller retrieves information from the view and does not care about its exact subtype; all it cares about is the interface.

Also, our controller is responsible for the orchestration:

- Performing the necessary validations
- Updating the model
- Asking the view to clear the input field
- Asking the view to render the updated todo list

The next method is much simpler:

```
filterTodoList(): void {
    this._todoListView.filter();
}
```

Filtering the todo list on screen is now just a matter of giving the order to the view; we do not need to know how it gets done.

Finally, add the removeTodo method:

```
removeTodo(identifier: string): void {
    if(identifier) {
        console.log("item to remove: ", identifier);
        this._todoList.removeTodo(identifier);
        this._todoListView.render(this._todoList.todoList);
        this.filterTodoList();
    }
}
```

Again, the implementation is straightforward. The controller receives the identifier of the item to remove, asks the model to remove that entry, and requests a view update.

Initializing TodoIt

Now that we have created our implementations, we need to leverage those.

We first need to instantiate the view:

```
const view = new HTMLTodoListView();
```

Then, we also need to create an instance of our controller, `TodoIt`:

```
const todoIt = new TodoIt(view);
```

Here, we pass a concrete implementation of the view interface, but our controller doesn't know and doesn't care. All it cares about is that it gets something that is compatible with the interface.

Isolating the utility function

A small detail that we have left aside is the `isEnter` function. To have cleaner code, we can isolate it in a class and define it as a static member:

```
class EventUtils {
    static isEnter(event: KeyboardEvent): boolean {
        let isEnterResult = false;

        if(event !== undefined && event.defaultPrevented) {
            return false;
        }

        if (event == undefined) {
            isEnterResult = false;
        } else if (event.key !== undefined) {
            isEnterResult = event.key === 'Enter';
        } else if (event.keyCode !== undefined) {
            isEnterResult = event.keyCode === 13;
        }

        return isEnterResult;
    }
}
```

We can invoke it as easily as before, using `EventUtils.isEnter(...)`. This doesn't change much, but is cleaner and conveys more meaning. One important rule, whenever you develop software, is to keep in mind that your code will be read many more times than it is written or changed.

 However, do also consider how easy it will be to test the code. Generally speaking, static elements are harder to test.

Let's now turn our attention to the HTML page.

Updating the HTML page

At this point, if you open the `index.html` page and take a look at the console, you'll see the `TodoIt` message being logged, indicating that our code works as expected.

The final step in our refactoring is to adapt `index.html` in order to call the methods of our instance of `TodoIt`, which we have called `todoIt`.

Adapt the file as follows:

```html
<!DOCTYPE html>
<html lang="en">
<head>
    <meta charset="UTF-8">
    <title>TodoIt</title>
</head>
<body id="todoIt" style="text-align: center">

<h1>TodoIt</h1>
<h2>Add new items</h2>

<p>
    What needs to be done?
    <input type="text" id="todoInput" title="What should be added to
        the todo list?"
        onkeyup="if(EventUtils.isEnter(event)) { todoIt.addTodo() }"
        onblur="todoIt.addTodo()" />
    <input type="button" value="Add todo" onclick="todoIt.addTodo()"
/>
</p>

<h2>Current todo list</h2>
<p>Filter: <input type="text" id="todoFilter" title="Filter for the
    todo list"
    onkeyup="todoIt.filterTodoList()" onblur="todoIt.filterTodoList()"
    />
</p>

<div id="todoListContainer">Nothing to do, hurray!</div>

<script type="text/javascript" src="todo-it.js"></script>

</body>
</html>
```

All the function calls that we had previously are now replaced by method calls on our instance of `TodoIt` (our controller). This is lighter and much clearer.

Job done, congratulations!

At this point, your refactoring of `TodoIt` should be fully functional. Go ahead and give it a try.

Also, take some time to observe the console output and explore the objects.

If we look at the application from a functional point of view, we haven't changed anything. But we have actually drastically improved the code quality, even if it has doubled the number of lines of code:

- We now have a solid domain model that uses encapsulation.
- We have applied the SRP to isolate responsibilities and avoid mixing concerns.
- We have applied the MVC design pattern to isolate parts of our code, which has helped us respect the LoD.
- We have applied composition (for example, coding the controller against the view interface).

With this structure in place, it actually becomes very easy to modify or extend our application. For instance, if you later decide to add new fields to `TodoItem`, then you know where to start: adapt the domain model. Then, you can adapt the view and the controller layer. Most importantly, those changes won't require you to change everything again because the structure is SOLID!

Summary

In this chapter, we quickly reviewed programming paradigms, including imperative, procedural, functional, and OO.

Then, we presented OOP principles, such as encapsulation, abstraction, classes and inheritance, interfaces, polymorphism, and composition. We also discussed the choice between composition and inheritance.

After that, we discussed UML and OO domain modeling. We saw what class diagrams look like and how they can easily present a design and help to prepare, discuss, and document domain models.

We also briefly reviewed how JavaScript inheritance works.

Afterward, we covered how TypeScript supports OO programming concepts and how to implement classes and interfaces in TypeScript.

We also saw how to define custom types and explained that interfaces have major advantages over custom types.

We learned that TypeScript interfaces only exist at compile time and also how to choose between classes and interfaces when programming using TypeScript. In addition, we saw how TypeScript classes and interfaces relate to JavaScript classes and objects, as well as how structural typing and duck typing help us.

Then, we designed the domain model of the `TodoIt` application using classes and interfaces, allowing us to dramatically improve the design through applying the SRP, the LoD, the open/closed principle, and the MVC design pattern.

Once we achieved a good model, we implemented the different interfaces and classes together and migrated/refactored our existing code.

By going from an almost purely imperative programming approach to a more OO one, we saw that our code conveys more meaning and is more readable. Our `TodoIt` application became much more maintainable and easily extensible.

Finally, while explaining the theory and coding in the new version of `TodoIt`, we discovered many more TypeScript concepts in practice.

In the next chapter, we will learn about generics and enums and we will see how we can take advantage of those to write more reusable code.

4
Leveraging Generics and Enums

In this chapter, we will build on the concepts and patterns that we have discussed so far in this book. We will guide you on how to create a media management web application named **MediaMan**. This new application will be a simple **CRUD** (short for **Create**, **Read**, **Update**, and **Delete**) system for managing collections of media (for example, books, movies, and more).

While building MediaMan, we will learn about **generics** and **enums** in TypeScript and demonstrate how you can leverage them to write better code. While coding, we will also discover new elements of the TypeScript language.

Additionally, we will persist data in the web browser's local storage. This will allow you to discover related APIs that are part of modern web browsers. We will make use of those APIs to persist and retrieve data on the client side. To do so, we will use `localForage`, which is a third-party open source library.

This will be the perfect opportunity for you to understand how to use third-party libraries with TypeScript; learn what **type definitions** (also known as **typing** and referred to as `@types` or `.d.ts` files) are; and understand how to retrieve them.

In this chapter, we will cover the following topics:

- TypeScript concepts: Generics, enums, string literal types, union and intersection types, type definitions (or typings) and `@types`, decorators, the `any` and `never` special types, the `keyof` index type query operator, and mapped types
- The service layer design pattern
- The `LocalStorage` and `SessionStorage` APIs
- The `IndexedDB` API

- The `Promise` API
- The `localForage` library
- The `class-transformer` library

What will you build?

As explained in the introduction to this chapter, we will build a media management web application together. There are many types of media that we could consider managing; for example, books, comic books, mangas, movies, TV shows, anime, and much more. These types of media usually exist in different forms/formats, such as on paper, digitally, or disks.

Our application will be useful for people who are looking to manage their personal collections.

Through our application, it will be possible to manage lists of media of different types. For simplicity, we will limit ourselves to books, but we will try to create a solid foundation, so that the application can be easily extended to support new media types.

We'll explore the features of our application in detail while looking at its domain model.

In order to write better code for this application, we will first learn about **generics** and **enumerations**, which are two major features of TypeScript.

Generics

There are numerous ways to make your code more extensible, maintainable, and, most importantly, reusable. One such way, which we will discuss now, is through the usage of **generic**, or **parameterized**, **types**. Simply put, as their name suggests, they allow you to write more generic code. Generic code is great because it can help you to avoid duplication and increase reusability.

Generics allow you to write code that works with a variety of types instead of just a single type. They allow you to *abstract over types* by enabling classes, types, and interfaces to act as *parameters*. In practice, using generics means that you can pass different types as parameters, making your types and functions more open and reusable.

Generics are supported in many languages such as C++, Java, C#, and Haskell. And, last but not least, TypeScript, of course, also supports generics! This is great because it means that once you are familiar with the concept, you'll be able to leverage that knowledge in TypeScript and in any other language.

The benefits of using generics

By using generics you can do the following:

- Improve the type safety of your code; for example, in TypeScript, you can accept generic types instead of having to rely on the any keyword.
- Avoid unnecessary type casts.
- Define generic algorithms that are applicable to different data types.
- Define generic data structures that can manipulate different data types.
- Create a link between the input and output types of your functions (for example, define a function that returns a Person type if it receives a Person type as input).

An example without generics

The most straightforward examples are lists and arrays—two incredibly useful data structures that you'll find in most programming languages. Generally speaking, you do not want to have to reimplement such data structures for each specific data type. Instead, you want to have a single, canonical, and generic implementation that can work with different types.

In TypeScript, we can use the any keyword as a type to allows us to pass any type to our functions. However, as we have just mentioned, this would imply having to use type casts all the time, which is far from convenient.

 any is actually the type that is used by default in TypeScript when no type is specified for a variable or function argument.

Let's imagine what the `Array` interface would look like if it used `any`:

```
interface Array {
    ...
    push(...items: any[]): number;
    ...
    pop(): any;
    ...
}
```

This interface is OK for JavaScript, but it is far from ideal in TypeScript. This is because it forces us to use type casts all the time when accessing data, as shown in the following example:

```
const myArray: any[] = [];
myArray.push(new Person("John", "Doe"));
const person: Person = <Person> myArray.pop();
```

Of course, this works, but it means a lot of added ceremony around data retrieval. In addition, this code is unsafe because you have no guarantees that what you get out of the array will be of the type you expect when performing the type cast.

An example with generics

Because TypeScript supports generics, it can actually leverage them for its own libraries.

If you look at the `lib.es5.d.ts` (https://github.com/Microsoft/TypeScript/blob/master/lib/lib.es5.d.ts) file (which is part of TypeScript) and search for `Array<T>`, you'll stumble upon this definition:

```
interface Array<T> {
    ...
    push(...items: T[]): number;
    pop(): T;
    ...
}
```

As you can see, the `Array` interface accepts a generic parameter (inside the angle brackets: `<>`) named `T`. This `T` is actually just *a label used to refer to a type that will be defined/given at runtime*. That same label is then used in function definitions.

If we observe the `push` method, we can see that it accepts an array of T elements. The `pop` method returns T.

The following is how you can use this:

```
let persons: Array<Person> = [];
```

This syntax is the clearest because you are using angle brackets, which clearly indicate that you're passing a type parameter when creating the `Array` instance. However, note that the equivalent shorthand notation is generally recommended, as we discussed earlier in Chapter 2, *Building TodoIt - Your Own Web Application with TypeScript*:

```
let persons: Person[] = [];
```

By passing in our `Person` type, we are allowing the `Array` function to accept and return our generic type:

```
let persons: Array<Person> = [];

// <1> add a single person
persons.push(new Person("John", "Doe"));

// <2> add multiple persons
persons.push(
    new Person("John", "McClane"),
    new Person("John", "Smith"),
    new Person("John", "Dunbar")
);

// <3> retrieve a single person
const person:Person = persons.pop() as NonNullable<Person>;

// <4> loop over all entries
persons.forEach(person => { console.log(`Hello ${person.firstName}
${person.lastName}`); });

// <5> classic for loop over all entries
for(let person: Person, i:number=0; i < persons.length; i++) {
    person = persons[i];
    console.log(`Hello ${person.firstName} ${person.lastName}`);
}

// <6> for..of loop to also loop over all the entries
for(const person of persons) {
    console.log(`Hello ${person.firstName`);
}
```

In the preceding example, there are multiple things to point out:

In <1>, you can see that we can pass a `Person` object. Actually, here, we can only pass `Person` instances:

```
push(...items: Person[])
```

In <2>, we can pass multiple items if we wish to.

In <3>, note that we need to do a type cast even though we have passed a generic type in. The reason for this is that the `pop()` method returns `Person |` `Undefined` simply because the array might be empty when we call `pop`, and therefore could return `undefined`. The `NonNullable` type that we use here is part of the standard TypeScript library and is defined as `type NonNullable<T> = T` `extends null | undefined ? never : T;`. It simply removes `null` and `undefined` from the given type; so, in our case, it tells TypeScript *don't worry, it won't be null or undefined here*. Of course, you should still use this carefully! The `|` and `?` characters in the type definition of `NonNullable` are two advanced concepts of the type system that we haven't discussed yet, that is, **union types** and **conditional types**, respectively. We will review these in more detail shortly.

In <4>, we simply loop over all the entries in the array. We don't need to use type casts since the `forEach` loop gives us `Person` objects.

In <5>, we do the same using a classic `for` loop, which you won't see many occurrences of in this book.

Finally, in <6>, we do the same using a `for..of` loop, which we don't use much in this book either.

As you can see, thanks to the fact that the `Array` type is generic (that is, it accepts type parameters to be passed in), we can avoid type casts in most cases and we can also benefit from an increase in type safety.

An example with generic functions and interfaces

Let's go through one more example to show how we can link the input and output types of a function thanks to generics.

Suppose that we want to write a function that accepts different types as input and returns the same types as output. Without generics, we would need to rely on any, which would mean losing valuable type information. With generics, we can define the function as follows:

```
function log<T>(arg: T): T {
    console.log("Log entry: ", arg);
    return arg;
}

class Person {
    constructor(private name: string){}
}

const person: Person = log(new Person("foo"));
```

In this case, the log function's return type will always match the argument type.

 It is also possible to explicitly define the generic type when calling the function, although this is less common: log<string>(""). **It is usually preferable to let the compiler infer the types for us**. Sometimes, though, the compiler fails to infer the type and you need to be more explicit.

Of course, you can also use generics when defining interfaces:

```
interface Logger<T> {
    debug(arg: T): T
    info(arg: T): T
    warn(arg: T): T
    error(arg: T): T
    fatal(arg: T): T
}

interface BasicLogger {
    log<T>(arg: T): T
}
```

In the preceding code, you can see two ways of achieving the same result. The first form, shown in the Logger interface, is preferred if the generic argument can be reused for multiple elements of the definition (as illustrated in the example). The second form, in the BasicLogger interface, is only relevant if there's only a single place where a generic type needs to be used.

An example with classes

You can, of course, also use generics in your class definitions:

```
class NaiveMap<Key, Value> {
    private _keys: Key[] = [];
    private _values: Value[] = [];

    constructor(){}

    contains(key: Key): boolean {
        const result = this._keys.indexOf(key);
        return result !== -1;
    }

    put(key: Key, value: Value): void {
        if(!this.contains(key)) {
            this._keys.push(key);
            this._values.push(value);
        }
    }

    get(key: Key): Value | undefined {
        if(this.contains(key)) {
            return this._values[this._keys.indexOf(key)];
        } else{
            return undefined;
        }
    }
}


class Thing {
    constructor(public name: string){}
}

const naiveMap = new NaiveMap<string, Thing>();

naiveMap.put("foo", new Thing("The thing"));
console.log(naiveMap.contains("foo")); // true
console.log(naiveMap.get("foo")); // Thing { name: 'The thing' }
```

In this example, we have defined two generic parameters that we use to create generic arrays and define the input and output types of our functions.

Avoid implementing such general-purpose data structures yourself. `Map` and `Set` are actually supported natively in JavaScript and TypeScript:

`https://codecraft.tv/courses/angular/es6-typescript/mapset`.

As you can see, thanks to generics, this very naive implementation of a `Map` data structure can be used with many different types and is therefore highly reusable. This also highlights the fact that, in a generic class, you may define generic members as we did previously (that is, the `_keys` and `_values` arrays).

As demonstrated earlier, you can define and use multiple generic parameters by separating them with a comma, as follows:

One more thing to note is that you can define default generic types for both interfaces and classes. This is especially useful for interfaces because it can allow you to omit generic types. The following is an example:

```
interface InterfaceWithDefaultGenericType<T=string> {
    doSomething(arg: T): T
}

class ClassWithDefaultGenericType<T=string> {
    constructor(public something: T) {}
}

interface InterfaceWithSpecializedGenericType<T = Person & {age:
number}> {
    doSomethingElse(arg: T): T
}
```

The previous example shows an even more advanced trick: defining custom types as the default generic type. It's good to know that this is possible, but it should certainly not be abused as it makes the code harder to understand and reason about.

Next, let's look at generic constraints.

Generic constraints

One last point that we would like to raise about generics is the fact that you can define **generic constraints** to narrow down the set of generic types that you accept. This is done by using the `extends` keyword (for example, `T extends SomeType`).

This is useful when you only want to allow a specific subset of types to be passed as generic arguments. Thanks to generic constraints, you can be sure that the properties/methods you expect will be available.

The following is an example:

```
abstract class Recipe {
    constructor(public name: string, public ingredients: string[]) {
    }
}

class ItalianRecipe extends Recipe {
}

class FrenchRecipe extends Recipe {
    constructor(name: string, ingredients: string[], public chef:
    string) {
        super(name, ingredients);
    }
}

class BrittanyRecipe extends FrenchRecipe {
}

// generic constraint
function displayRecipe<T extends FrenchRecipe>(recipe: T): void {
    console.log(`This is a french recipe conceived by the following
    chef: ${recipe.chef}`); // we know that it has the 'chef' property
}

const brittanyRecipe = new BrittanyRecipe("Crèpe Bretonne", ["Eggs",
"Flour", "Salt", "..."], "Bertrand Denis");
const italianRecipe = new ItalianRecipe("Spaghetti Bolognese",
["Pasta", "Tomatoes", "Garlic", "Onions", "..."]);

// displayRecipe(italianRecipe); // If you uncomment this line you'll
get the following error: property 'chef' is missing
displayRecipe(brittanyRecipe); // This is a french recipe conceived by
the following chef: Bertrand Denis
```

In the preceding example, our generic `displayRecipe` function only accepts an argument that is **of** or **extends** the `BrittanyRecipe` type. Thanks to this constraint, we know that the `chef` property will be available on the given object.

You can actually go even further and define type parameters in your generic constraints; refer to the official handbook to find out more:
`https://www.typescriptlang.org/docs/handbook/generics.html`.

If you want to learn more advanced concepts, you can check out the following article about **covariance** and **contravariance**:
`https://www.stephanboyer.com/post/132/what-are-covariance-and-contravariance`.

Enums

Enums or **enumerations** provide a way to give labels to a set of related concepts/values.

 This section only provides a high-level overview of enums. You can learn more about TypeScript enums in the official handbook:
`https://www.typescriptlang.org/docs/handbook/enums.html`.

Numerical enums

Numerical enums are the simplest way to define enumerations (or enums) in TypeScript. Each entry in such an enum simply associates a logical name with a numerical value.

The following is a basic example of a numerical enum:

```
enum VehicleType {
    Car,
    Bus,
    Train
}

let myVehicleType = VehicleType.Car;
console.log("My vehicle type: ", myVehicleType);
```

And the following is the corresponding output:

```
$ node ts-enums-01.js
My vehicle type:   0
```

As you can see, in their basic form, enum entries map to unsigned integer values that start at 0.

 As you can guess, **reordering entries in a numerical enum has an immediate impact on the associated values**. This matters **a lot** if you persist those values somehow, as you will get different results later if you have changed the enum after having persisted the data. If you perform **safe** modifications, such as adding new entries at the end, then it's okay; otherwise, you will have issues.

If you need to, you can actually define the starting value of your enum, as illustrated in the following example:

```
enum VehicleType {
    Car = 1,
    Bus,
    Train
}
```

Of course, the next values increment from the starting value. In this example, the Bus enum entry will be associated with the number 2.

TypeScript also supports **reverse mapping** for numerical enums; that is, when you have an enum value, you can retrieve the name of the corresponding enum entry:

```
enum Month {
    January,
    February,
    March,
    April,
    May,
    June,
    July,
    August,
    September,
    October,
    November,
    December,
}
const june: Month = Month.June;
const nameOfJuneEntry: string = Month[june];
console.log(nameOfJuneEntry); // June
```

You can use bitwise numbers in enums to store more than one value per entry. The following is an explanation of how to do this: https://patrickdesjardins.com/blog/how-to-set-and-read-bitwise-enum-values-in-typescript. While this is not recommended, it can be useful in some situations.

String enums

In TypeScript, it is also possible to define **string enums**. The following is an example:

```
enum TShirtType {
    CrewNeck = "Crew Neck", // must be initialized with a constant
    VNeck = "V Neck",
    Henley = "Henley",
    Polo = "Polo",
    SpecialPolo = Polo, // may be initialized with another entry
    ScoopNeck = "Scoop Neck"
}

let myTShirtType = TShirtType.CrewNeck;

console.log("My T-Shirt type: ", myTShirtType);
```

And again, the corresponding output, is as follows:

```
$ node ts-enums-02-string-enum.js
My T-Shirt type:  Crew Neck
```

String enums do not have the same numerical index value as numerical enums. The constants associated with the enum entry names are the values.

One direct benefit is that you can serialize/persist these values without worrying too much about their retrieval/interpretation later on. Of course, if you modify the string value associated with an enum entry, then you might break your application, but not as badly as with numerical values (since there are no issues with the order of the entries).

A second benefit is that string enum entries are associated with meaningful values as opposed to numerical values that don't necessarily convey any meaning for numerical enums.

You can actually mix numerical and string enums together, but it should really be avoided in practice.

Enums are converted to JavaScript when your code is transpiled, so they still exist (though in another form) at runtime. The following is what our string enum example looks like in JavaScript:

```
"use strict";
var TShirtType;
(function (TShirtType) {
    TShirtType["CrewNeck"] = "Crew Neck";
    TShirtType["VNeck"] = "V Neck";
    TShirtType["Henley"] = "Henley";
    TShirtType["Polo"] = "Polo";
    TShirtType["SpecialPolo"] = "Polo";
    TShirtType["ScoopNeck"] = "Scoop Neck";
})(TShirtType || (TShirtType = {}));
var myTShirtType = TShirtType.CrewNeck;
console.log("My T-Shirt type: ", myTShirtType);
```

const enums

Another useful thing to know is that it is possible to define enums that do not subsist after transpilation by using the `const` keyword. When doing so, the compiler inlines the values and doesn't transpile the enum at all. This can be useful for reducing the size of the generated JavaScript code. This must only be used as an optimization technique because it hinders the readability of the generated code, so it shouldn't be your default choice.

The following is an example:

```
const enum TransientEnum {
    A,
    B
}

console.log(TransientEnum.A); // 0
```

As you can see, const enums are defined using `const enum` but are then used normally.

The corresponding JavaScript code is as follows:

```
"use strict";
console.log(0 /* A */); // 0
```

Note that the enum has completely disappeared in the transpiled code! The enum value has simply been `replaced` (inlined) directly where it was used.

The never keyword

In TypeScript, `never` is a **bottom type** (that is, primitive) that you can use to indicate the type of values that never happen. This type **represents the absence of type**; you can see it as the exact opposite of `any`. When TypeScript performs code flow analysis, it identifies sections of code that are unreachable; when it discovers one, it uses the `never` type.

You can also use the `never` type yourself in the following cases:

- As the return type of a function that will never return
- As the type for variables under type guards that are never `true`

If you don't specify the `never` type yourself, TypeScript will use it when it detects a situation where something can never occur. For example, `never` will be inferred as the return type of the following function:

```
function doSomethingForever() {
    while(true) {
        console.log("Still busy...");
    }
}
```

The preceding function will never stop, hence the function will never return. For that reason, the return type of that function is inferred to as `never`.

Similarly, the following function's return type will be inferred to as `never`:

```
function failure(msg: string) {
    console.error(msg);
    throw new Error(msg);
}
```

In this case, again the function doesn't have a reachable endpoint.

Let's now discuss a concrete case where you can leverage the `never` type to improve compile time safety.

Sometimes, you might need to write `switch` statements that check values against the entries of an enum:

```
enum Color {
    Red,
    Green,
    Blue
    //, Orange
}

function displayColor(color: Color): Color  {
    switch (color) {
        case Color.Red:
            return color;
        case Color.Green:
            return color;
        case Color.Blue:
            return color;
        default:
            throw new Error(`Unknown color: ${color}`);
    }
}
```

In this example, if new entries get added to the `Color` enum (for example, if you uncomment `Orange`) and you forget to adapt the `displayColor` function to handle the new cases, then the code will fail at runtime. To avoid this pitfall, you can actually leverage the `never` type. The following is how to do this:

```
class UnreachableCaseError extends Error {
    constructor(val: never) {
        super(`Unreachable case: ${val}`);
    }
}

enum Color {
    Red,
    Green,
    Blue
    //, Orange
}

function displayColor(color: Color): Color  {
```

```
switch (color) {
    case Color.Red:
        return color;
    case Color.Green:
        return color;
    case Color.Blue:
        return color;
    default:
        throw new UnreachableCaseError(color);
    }
}
```

This time, if you uncomment `Orange` in the enum, then the compiler will complain with the following error: `TS2345: Argument of type 'Color.Orange' is not assignable to parameter of type 'never.'`. This is great because you'll know when something is off when using this enum. This is a trick that Tomas Brambora shared and allowed us to reuse in this book. You can find his article here: `http://ideasintosoftware.com/exhaustive-switch-in-typescript`.

You can learn more about `never` here:

- `https://www.typescriptlang.org/docs/handbook/basic-types.html`
- `https://basarat.gitbooks.io/typescript/docs/types/never.html`

String literal types

A nice alternative to enums and string enums in TypeScript is **string literal types**. They provide a way to specify the value that a string must have and can actually provide the same kind of behavior as enums. One benefit of string literal types is that you can also combine them with type guards, type aliases, and unions.

The following is an example:

```
type Mood = "Great" | "Good" | "Bad" | "Awful";
const myCurrentMood: Mood = "Great"; // may only be assigned values
that are part of the Mood union!
```

With the `Mood` type defined, we can get auto-completion, as shown in the following screenshot:

```
type Mood = "Great" | "Good" | "Bad" | "Awful";

const myCurrentMood: Mood =
        "Awful"
        "Bad"
        "Good"
        "Great"
        undefined
Use Ctrl+Shift+Enter to syntactically correct your code after completing (balance parentheses etc.) >> π
```

While using this type, you are, of course, not allowed to pass a value that is not part of the type, hence the similarity with enums.

String literal types are also inlined. If you look at the generated code for the previous example, you'll also see that no specific code is generated for the type itself:

```
"use strict";
var myCurrentMood = "Great"; // may only be assigned values part of
the Mood union!
```

We won't be using those in this chapter, but it's good to know that they exist.

Union and intersection types

In the previous section, we mentioned **union types** but haven't covered them as yet. Let's fix that right away – it will only be a small detour and will prove very useful later on!

Union types allow us to define new types by joining existing ones together using the | (pipe) character. When you use a union type, you can only access the members that are common to all those types in the union.

A great example is that you can use a union instead of `any` to indicate that you accept either one type or the other:

```
interface BoardGame {
    name: string;
    description: string;
    minimalAge: number;
    players: string;
    duration: string;
}

interface VideoGame {
    name: string;
    description: string;
    minimalAge: number;
    players: string;
    online: boolean;
}

function displayGame(game: VideoGame | BoardGame) {
    console.log(`Game name: ${game.name}`);
}
```

Here, our `displayGame` function allows either a `VideoGame` or a `BoardGame` object to be passed in. This is cleaner than allowing `any`, don't you think? If we use autocompletion, we can only see the members that are available in both types:

Another closely related concept is **intersection types**, which allow you to **combine** types (such as interfaces, classes, and custom types/aliases) so that you have all the properties and members of both types at your disposal.

This is an example of how to **mix** concepts with TypeScript, without relying on object-oriented principles such as inheritance. Using intersections, you can create new types that combine interfaces, classes, and custom types that are not related to each other at all.

The following is an example:

```
interface Person {
    name: string;
    age: number;
}

interface Address {
    street: string;
    streetNumber: number;
    town: string;
    postalCode: number;
    country: string;
}

type PersonWithAddress = Person & Address;

function displayPerson(person: PersonWithAddress) {
    console.log(`${person.name} lives in ${person.country}`);
}

let person: PersonWithAddress = {
    name: "Foo",
    age: 42,
    street: "UnknownStreet",
    streetNumber: 1,
    postalCode: 1337,
    town: "UnknownTown",
    country: "Bar"
};

displayPerson(person); // Foo lives in Bar
```

Here, the `PersonWithAddress` type is an intersection of the `Person` and `Address` interfaces. The `person` object that we create must have the properties of both.

If you want to mix unrelated classes together, then you should be using mixins:

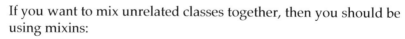

`https://www.typescriptlang.org/docs/handbook/mixins.html`. You can actually create an intersection with a class and interface but it doesn't make much sense to do this as it will only take the properties of both types into consideration, which is probably not what you want.

Type guards

TypeScript's main power comes from its strong static analysis capabilities. However, at runtime, as we previously noted, types are mostly gone. Type guards actually provide the means to perform type checks at runtime.

TypeScript supports different **type guards**. Let's discover those next.

The typeof keyword

In TypeScript, you can use the typeof keyword to check for basic types (that is, number, string, boolean, and more). If you perform such a check in an if statement, then, inside the block, TypeScript will know whether the type matches and will consider the variable to be of that type. The following example will make this clearer:

```
let hello = "Hello";

function saySomething(something: any): void {
    if(typeof something === "string") {
        console.log(`You passed in a string; its first character is:
        ${something.charAt(0)}`);
    } else if(typeof something === "number") {
        console.log(`You passed in a number: ${something}`);
    } else{
        console.log(`You didn't pass in a string or number. Type of
         the given element: ${typeof something}`);
    }
}

saySomething("Hello");
saySomething(42);
saySomething({foo: "Bar"});
```

As you can see in the preceding example, once we're in a block where the type has been checked, although any was passed in, TypeScript then knows the exact type and treats the object accordingly. In the preceding code, it allows us to use the charAt string method directly.

`typeof` is especially useful for strings and numbers.

 Checks that you perform are also valid at runtime since `typeof` is a JavaScript operator.

You can learn more about `typeof` here:
`https://developer.mozilla.org/en-US/docs/Web/JavaScript/Reference/Operators/typeof`.

The instanceof keyword and the Visitor pattern

The `instanceof` keyword can be used to check whether a given object is an instance of a given class. The keyword is not TypeScript-specific; it actually is part of ECMAScript, and therefore JavaScript, and checks the prototype chain of a type for the existence of the given type. You can learn more about `instanceof` here:
`https://developer.mozilla.org/en-US/docs/Web/JavaScript/Reference/Operators/instanceof`.

The following are a few examples to illustrate how it works:

```
class Animal {
    constructor(public name: string) {}
}

class Dog extends Animal {}

class Cat extends Animal {}

class Human {}

const johnDoe: Human = new Human();

// johnDoe instanceof Human // true
// johnDoe instanceof Animal // false

const animals: Animal[] = [];

animals.push(new Cat("O'Malley"));
animals.push(new Dog("Dingo"));

animals.forEach(animal ⇒ {
```

```
    if (animal instanceof Cat) {
        console.log(`${animal.name} is a famous Cat!`);
    } else if (animal instanceof Dog) {
        console.log(`${animal.name} is a famous Dog!`);
    } else {
        console.log(`${animal.name} is another type of animal!`);
        console.log(`type: ${typeof animal}`);
    }
});
```

The TypeScript compiler is very smart because, each time you perform an `instanceof` check, if it doesn't match, then TypeScript can narrow down the set of possible types. For instance, if you are in a situation where a type could either be A or B and you perform an `instanceof` check that doesn't match A, then in the `else` branch, TypeScript knows that the type is B and you won't need to perform additional checks or type casts to use it as such.

Even though `instanceof` can sometimes be useful, it is usually an indication of object-oriented design issues. The main issue when using `instanceof` checks is that, if new types appear in your hierarchies, then you need to revisit the places where `instanceof` was used (this is obvious in the last example!). This is error-prone as you might easily forget to add checks at some locations.

Using polymorphism usually helps to reduce or eliminate the need for using `instanceof`. The **Visitor** design pattern (`https://sourcemaking.com/design_patterns/visitor`) can also help. Check out the following article if you want to dig deeper into such design issues: `https://sites.google.com/site/steveyegge2/when-polymorphism-fails`.

User-defined type guards and the is operator

When you manipulate simple JavaScript objects (also known as **Plain Old JavaScript Objects**, or **POJOs**), you can't use `typeof` or `instanceof`, as you will only match the `object` type. Still, sometimes you might want to perform some type checks. In those cases, you can define user-defined type guard functions with the `is` operator.

The following is an example:

```
type Dog = {
    name: string;
    race: string;
};
```

```
function isDog(arg: any): arg is Dog {
    return arg.race !== undefined;
}

console.log(isDog({name: "Pluto", race: "Saint-Hubert"})); // returns
true
```

As you can see here, we have defined an `isDog` function that returns `true` if the given argument has the properties we expect. Of course, the function can perform more advanced checks if needed.

And more on type guards

There is actually more to learn about type guards. Take a look at the *Advanced Types* section in the official TypeScript handbook:

`https://www.typescriptlang.org/docs/handbook/advanced-types.html`.

But that's enough theory for now; let's get started with our new application!

Creating the project

We have prepared the base skeleton of this new project for you. You can find it in the code samples folder, under `Chapter04/mediaman-v1-initial`. Copy that folder and open it in your favorite editor.

Next, install the necessary dependencies using `npm install`.

 If you look at the `package.json` and `index.html` files, you'll notice some changes compared to what we did for `TodoIt`. You don't need to worry about those for now, as we will cover related subjects in later chapters. If you're really curious and/or impatient though, you can take a look at the documentation for Parcel.js (`https://parceljs.org`), which is the **bundler** and **module loader** that we have added to the project and with which we will now build it.

The scripts are mostly the same as before:

- `npm install` will install everything you need.
- `npm run tsc` will compile the code.

- `npm run build` will generate a `dist` folder with the compiled version.
- `npm start` and `npm run serve` will both build and start a web server to serve the files and make them available over at `http://localhost:3000`.

We'll keep the same high-level code organization as we did for the last project, that is, a single folder with a single TypeScript file and a single HTML file.

At this point, you might feel that putting everything into a single TypeScript file is far from ideal and you'd be totally right. As a matter of fact, in later chapters, we will learn about **modules** and other features of TypeScript that will help us to **modularize** our code.

For now, bear with us as we want to keep our attention on generics and enums.

Designing the model

We will again start our project with a brief analysis of the domain model.

The core domain model

In this application, we want to manage **collections of media** of different types:

- Books
- Movies
- More, if you want

Each media type will have specific characteristics. For example, movies will have the following:

- A duration
- A director

Whereas books will have the following:

- The number of pages
- An author

Next to that, all media types will also have common characteristics such as the following:

- A unique identifier
- A name
- A description
- A picture location
- A genre

For genres, we can make use of an enum because there will be a fairly limited set of entries in our case and that set will mostly remain static. With an enum, we will be able to easily provide an autocompletion feature later on if we wish to.

The following is how we could design the base concepts of our core domain model:

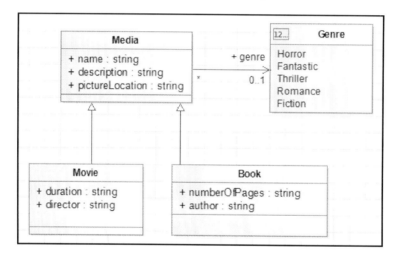

High-level design – first proposal

Beyond our base concepts, we also need to think about the design of the other elements of the application. For simplicity, we won't consider multiple users; we'll just have a single one, the *active* user. This user should be able to do the following:

- Create media collections of a certain type.
- Manage existing collections.
- Display the contents of existing collections.
- Manage the contents of displayed collection.

Most importantly, this time, we would like to *persist* our data (that is, the collections and their contents) and be able to restore the data when we come back to the application. We'll worry about the *how* later on.

With this in mind, we can start thinking about MVC again and learn how to distribute/delimit the responsibilities, for example, by using the MVC pattern as we did in the last chapter.

The following is our first proposal:

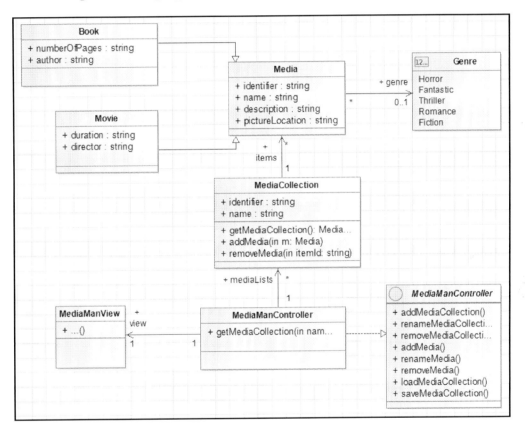

 We have left the view layer in abeyance for now. We will come back to it later.

There are good and bad things about this first approach. First of all, we have applied the MVC pattern again. As we saw in the previous chapter, this helps us to keep a clear separation of concerns between the model, the view, and the controller layers.

The main problem we see with this approach is that our controller will have to handle persisting media collections on its own. This is bad because it gives it too many responsibilities.

The service layer design pattern

One way to improve our design is to introduce a new layer in order to limit the responsibilities of our controller layer. We need something to handle the persistence of our media collections and our controller should be able to *delegate* those operations.

This new layer can apply the **service layer design pattern**, which is at the heart of **service-oriented design**.

The idea is that the service layer contains **services** that handle specific parts of the functionality of an application. For instance, services can take care of data retrieval (for example, fetching data from a remote location), data persistence, data manipulation/transformation, and more.

As applications grow in size and complexity, having a service layer quickly becomes very beneficial as it limits the mental overhead. Additionally, in larger applications, you can even decompose things further by splitting the service layer into two, as follows:

- So-called **business** services that own the business logic
- Repositories that take care of data persistence/retrieval

We won't go this far for our current application.

You can learn more about the service layer design pattern here:
`https://martinfowler.com/eaaCatalog/serviceLayer.html`.

High-level design – second proposal

Let's introduce a **media service** that will take care of loading/persisting media collections, removing that burden from the controller layer:

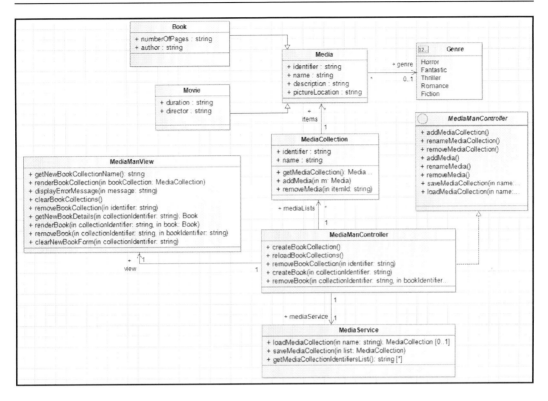

With this new design, our controller has fewer responsibilities. As an added benefit, this design also allows us to develop the service layer independently.

We have also added details for the view layer. This interface is the basis for the implementation as it already defines which operations our controller will be able to perform via the view.

For now, all of the code will still be co-located in the same TypeScript file; however, later on, we will see how we can better isolate things using TypeScript modules. For the time being, we only gain in terms of logical design and the distribution of responsibilities, but this is already a big improvement on what we did earlier.

Implementing the domain model

First of all, let's define our `Genre` enum. We'll use a string enum since this will be the easiest to understand:

```
enum Genre {
    Horror = "Horror",
    Fantastic = "Fantastic",
    Thriller = "Thriller",
    Romance = "Romance",
    Fiction = "Fiction"
}
```

Next, we can implement the base `Media` class:

```
abstract class Media {
    private _identifier: string;

    protected constructor(
        private _name: string,
        private _description: string,
        private _pictureLocation: string,
        private _genre: Genre,
        identifier?: string,
    ) {
        if (identifier) {
            this._identifier = identifier;
        } else {
            // this is just for the example; for any real project, use
            // UUIDs instead: https://www.npmjs.com/package/uuid
            this._identifier = Math.random().toString(36).
              substr(2,9);
        }
    }

    get identifier(): string {
        return this._identifier;
    }

    set identifier(identifier: string) {
        this._identifier = identifier;
    }

    get name(): string {
        return this._name;
    }
```

```
set name(name: string) {
    this._name = name;
}

get description(): string {
    return this._description;
}

set description(description: string) {
    this._description = description;
}

get pictureLocation(): string {
    return this._pictureLocation;
}

set pictureLocation(pictureLocation: string) {
    this._pictureLocation = pictureLocation;
}

get genre(): Genre {
    return this._genre;
}

set genre(genre: Genre) {
    this._genre = genre;
}
}
```

Once again, we are using encapsulation. Additionally, we have marked this class as `abstract` since it doesn't make sense to be able to instantiate it.

 The `_identifier` member will be used to acquire a somewhat unique technical key for each media instance. Note that you should use **Universally Unique Identifiers (UUIDs)** for this purpose in real applications instead, as the preceding approach is unsafe. We will do so in later chapters using the UUID library: `https://www.npmjs.com/package/uuid`.

Now we can implement the `Book` and `Movie` classes.

The following is the code for the `Book` class:

```
class Book extends Media {
    private _author: string;
    private _numberOfPages: number;
```

```
    constructor(
        name: string,
        description: string,
        pictureLocation: string,
        genre: Genre,
        author: string,
        numberOfPages: number,
        identifier?: string
    ) {
        super(name, description, pictureLocation, genre, identifier);
        this._numberOfPages = numberOfPages;
        this._author = author;
    }

    get author(): string {
        return this._author;
    }

    set author(author: string) {
        this._author = author;
    }

    get numberOfPages(): number {
        return this._numberOfPages;
    }

    set numberOfPages(numberOfPages: number) {
        this._numberOfPages = numberOfPages;
    }
}
```

And the following is the `Movie` class:

```
class Movie extends Media {
    private _duration: string;
    private _director: string;

    constructor(
        name: string,
        description: string,
        pictureLocation: string,
        genre: Genre,
        duration: string,
        director: string,
        identifier?: string
    ) {
        super(name, description, pictureLocation, genre, identifier);
        this._duration = duration;
```

```
        this._director = director;
    }

    get director(): string {
        return this._director;
    }

    set director(director: string) {
        this._director = director;
    }

    get duration(): string {
        return this._duration;
    }

    set duration(duration: string) {
        this._duration = duration;
    }
}
```

Note that we optionally allow forcing an identifier. This will be useful when we retrieve persisted data, as we want those keys to remain stable (that is, they don't change).

Finally, we can also implement our `MediaCollection` class.

First of all, you need to add the class, private fields, and the constructor:

```
class MediaCollection<T extends Media> {      private _identifier:
string;
    private _name: string = "";
    private _collection: ReadonlyArray<T> = [];
    private readonly _type: Function;

    constructor(
        type: Function,
        name?: string,
        identifier?: string
    ) {
        this._type = type;

        if(name) {
            this._name = name;
        }

        if (identifier) {
            this._identifier = identifier;
        } else {
```

```
                    // this is just for the example; for any real project, use
                    // UUIDs instead: https://www.npmjs.com/package/uuid
                    this._identifier = Math.random().toString(36).
                     substr(2, 9);
                }
            }

    }
```

Then add the methods:

```
        get identifier(): string {
            return this._identifier;
        }

        set identifier(identifier: string) {
            this._identifier = identifier;
        }

        get name(): string {
            return this._name;
        }

        set name(name: string) {
            this._name = name;
        }

        get collection(): ReadonlyArray<T> {
            return this._collection;
        }

        set collection(collection: ReadonlyArray<T>) {
            this._collection = collection;
        }

        addMedia(media: Readonly<T>): void {
            if (media) {
                this._collection = this._collection.concat(media);
            }
        }

        removeMedia(itemId: string) {
            if (itemId) {
                this._collection = this._collection.filter(item => {
                    return item.identifier !== itemId;
                });
            }
        }
```

As with the `TodoIt` application, we are using optional properties as well as read-only arrays with the `ReadonlyArray` type and generics. This code should already feel familiar to you.

 We haven't marked properties as `readonly` for simplicity in terms of serialization/deserialization; `readonly` properties would have made the code more complex. For the same reason, we have also added setters for the different properties in all classes.

The idea with this design is that we will manipulate collections of different media types and the changes that the user makes will be transient, until they decide to hit the **Save** button. At that point, the collection will be persisted.

You should also note that this class accepts a generic type: `<T extends Media>`. This clearly states that instances of this class will hold instances of a class that extends from our abstract `Media` class. Thanks to that definition, both the `collection` array and the `addMedia` method can be made generic.

Defining the media service interface

As we explained earlier, we will isolate persistence concerns in the service layer. Let's implement the service interface now!

One great thing about functionally decomposing our application like this is that we can focus on specific parts of the system without necessarily thinking about the rest too much. In this case, we will focus on how we can persist and load data, as this will be the main responsibility of our media service.

The following is the service interface that we will later code **against**:

```
interface MediaService<T extends Media> {
    loadMediaCollection(identifier: string):
    Promise<MediaCollection<T>>;
    saveMediaCollection(collection: Readonly<MediaCollection<T>>):
    Promise<void>;
    getMediaCollectionIdentifiersList(): Promise<string[]>;
    removeMediaCollection(identifier: string): Promise<void>;
}
```

This interface doesn't say anything about *how* the lists will be loaded or persisted. An implementation of this interface might save the lists to disk, over the network through a REST API. As a matter of fact, clients of this interface (such as our controller) do not care about the *how*; it is none of their concern. What they do care about is that it gets done; the how is entirely the responsibility of the service implementation.

This way of isolating concerns is very beneficial because we could later swap one implementation for another without impacting those parts of the system that rely on the interface.

For now, don't worry about the return types; we'll explain those shortly.

Storing data on the client side

Before we implement our media service, let's first explore different ways of storing data on the client side, that is, on users' machines when they access our web applications.

We'll use of one these mechanisms in this chapter to store application data and provide the illusion of having a database and allowing our application to persist data. To do so, we will actually create what is known as an **offline-first web application**.

LocalStorage and SessionStorage

LocalStorage and SessionStorage are two different mechanisms that are both part of modern web browsers. Through these, you can easily store key/value pairs in the user's web browser storage space. That space is limited in size, but you can normally store around 10 MB on desktops and around 5 MB on mobile devices; this will be more than enough for our small application.

 The storage space is user-configurable and can also be 0 if the browser is in private or incognito mode.

`LocalStorage` and `SessionStorage` both expose the same APIs and capabilities, but differ in persistence. While `LocalStorage` survives page reloads, `SessionStorage` does not. Also, each browser session has a separate `SessionStorage` instance: if the browser tab or window is closed, then the data will be lost.

The data that you store is only accessible to the **document origin**, which is determined by the combination of a domain, subdomain, and port. This means that a web application hosted at a different origin should not be able to access the data.

 Both of these APIs are very useful for storing non-sensitive data, but **they should never be used to store confidential information** since they were not designed for that. Any JavaScript code executing on your page has full access to the storage space. Additionally, because the data is stored on the client's computer, it is at risk from that fact alone. You can learn more about the security of these APIs here: `https://www.rdegges.com/2018/please-stop-using-local-storage`.

The API is very simple to use:

```
// persisting:
let key = 'Foo';
localStorage.setItem(key, 'Bar');

// retrieving
let value = localStorage.getItem(key);

// updating
localStorage.setItem(key, 'Bar2');

// removing
localStorage.removeItem(key);

// removing everything
localStorage.clear();
```

As you can see, the API is **synchronous**. The same is true for `sessionStorage`.

One drawback of these two APIs is that *they can only store string values*. This means that, if you have another type of data, then you need to convert them back and forth, for example, using `JSON.stringify(data)` and `JSON.parse(jsonData)`.

Before using these APIs, you need to make sure that they are actually available, using a check such as
if(!window.localStorage) { ... } or
if(!window.sessionStorage) { ... }.

You can find everything there is to know about these APIs here:

* https://developer.mozilla.org/en-US/docs/Web/API/Storage/LocalStorage
* https://developer.mozilla.org/fr/docs/Web/API/Window/sessionStorage

IndexedDB

IndexedDB is another API supported by most modern web browsers for storing data on the client side.

IndexedDB provides a database-like API to store objects (that is, not mere strings like LocalStorage and SessionStorage). As with LocalStorage and SessionStorage, it lets you store, retrieve, update, and delete data. IndexedDB actually goes further and allows you to define primary keys and indexes, and use transactions to protect data integrity.

IndexedDB lets you store just about anything and provides a SQL-like syntax. It is similar to classical **relational database management systems** (**RDBMSes**) but works with JavaScript objects. You can actually define complex database schemas and even update/upgrade them when your application evolves.

IndexedDB is an asynchronous API. As such, it is non-blocking, which is great for performance and for delivering great user experiences. Initially, IndexedDB also had a synchronous API, but this was removed from the specification at some point.

The following is the general workflow when using IndexedDB:

1. Check whether the API is available using a command such as if(!window.indexedDB) { ... }.
2. Open a database.
3. Create an object store in the database (that is, define the database schema).
4. Start a transaction and make requests (for example, add/retrieve data).
5. Wait for the operations to complete and handle the results.

Just like `LocalStorage` and `SessionStorage`, IndexedDB has space limitations. You can learn more about these here: `https://developer.mozilla.org/en-US/docs/Web/API/IndexedDB_API/Browser_storage_limits_and_eviction_criteria`.

To structure the database, `IndexedDB` uses object stores (as opposed to tables in classic relational databases). A given database can contain as many object stores as you want. Each value that you put in an object store is associated with a key. Finally, those keys can either be automatically generated or defined manually.

One downside of `IndexedDB` is that it is more complex and less **approachable** than `LocalStorage/SessionStorage`; this is the price you pay for the added functionality.

 You can view and access local storage, session storage, and `IndexedDB` through browser developer tools. Open Chrome's developer tools using *F12*, and then go to the **Application** tab. You can find more information in the official Chrome DevTools documentation at `https://developers.google.com/web/tools/chrome-devtools`.

We'll see how to use `IndexedDB` while implementing our application later on in this chapter.

You can learn more about `IndexedDB` here:

- `https://developer.mozilla.org/en-US/docs/Web/API/IndexedDB_API`
- `https://developer.mozilla.org/en-US/docs/Web/API/IndexedDB_API/Basic_Concepts_Behind_IndexedDB`
- `https://developer.mozilla.org/en-US/docs/Web/API/IndexedDB_API/Using_IndexedDB`

Implementing the media service

Now that we know about the different APIs that we can use to manage data locally, let's implement our media service.

Library choice

As we've already seen, `LocalStorage` and `IndexedDB` are standard APIs available in modern web browsers. However, there are always small discrepancies between implementations (for example, around error handling), and it is usually simpler to rely on a library, both for homogeneity and simplicity.

In our case, we will use the `localForage` library, which provides an easy-to-use API on top of both `IndexedDB` and `LocalStorage`. By default, it will try to use `IndexedDB` and will fall back to `LocalStorage` if it isn't available. You can find the documentation for `localForage` here:
`https://github.com/localForage/localForage`.

Introduction to the Promise API

`localForage` exposes a `Promise`-based API. The `Promise` API is another modern web standard. `Promise` provides a good solution for implementing asynchronous code without ending up with the famous **pyramid of doom**, also known as **callback hell**. Take a look at this website to learn more: `http://callbackhell.com`.

We won't be able to explore how they work in any detail, but here's a quick summary to give you an idea so that the rest of the code doesn't scare you too much.

As its name implies, a promise represents a vow to deliver *something* at a later point in time, unless something goes wrong, thereby making the promise impossible to respect. There are two basic possible outcomes for a promise:

- The promise can be kept and the *something* can be delivered.
- The promise cannot be held and an error is returned.

Promises can be in three different states:

- **Pending**: Not resolved yet
- **Fulfilled**: Resolved
- **Rejected**: Failed

You should also know that there are two functions that we can call on a `Promise` object:

- `then(result ⇒ { ... })`: The `then` function can be used to define a success callback function. That callback function will be invoked if/when the promise is resolved successfully. In this example, the `result` argument of the lambda will be the outcome of the promise.
- `catch(error ⇒ { ... })`: The `catch` function can be used to define a failure callback function. That callback function will be invoked if/when the promise is broken. In this example, the `error` argument of the lambda will be the error raised if the promise is broken.

Earlier, when we've created our `MediaService` interface, we defined the `loadMediaCollection` method as `loadMediaCollection(name: string): Promise<MediaCollection<T>>`. Based on what we've just explained, you should have an idea of what this declaration means. Just in case, here it goes: when this method is called, it will immediately (that is, synchronously) return a `Promise<MediaCollection<T>>` object. This `Promise` object will later receive the result or an error.

Since TypeScript has excellent support for promises and also generics, you can see that our promises have a generic type. Check out Basarat's book if you want to learn more: `https://basarat.gitbooks.io/typescript/docs/promise.html`.

We will stop here with promises, but there's much more to learn! For more information, you can refer to this article: `https://developer.mozilla.org/en-US/docs/Web/JavaScript/Reference/Global_Objects/Promise`.

 In later chapters, we will learn about observables, which are like promises on steroids. If you're curious already, then check out the official website at `https://rxjs-dev.firebaseapp.com`.

TypeScript type definitions (typings)

In TypeScript, most of the time, we also need to install **type definitions** (also called **typings**) separately for the JavaScript libraries that we use. Type definitions are files used by the TypeScript compiler to help us out while coding and compiling. They contain all the information about types that are used in a library: interfaces, classes, module declarations, custom types, and more.

When the TypeScript compiler finds type definition files, they're included in the compilation scope and the definitions are **ambient**. You can learn more about that here: `https://medium.com/@mikenorth/guide-to-typescript-ambient-d eclarations-717ef6da6514`.

Without type definitions, the TypeScript compiler wouldn't know much about the types used in third-party JavaScript libraries that you may want to use. Without that information, TypeScript loses a lot of its appeal because you have to rely on the `any` keyword everywhere.

Type definitions are stored in `.d.ts` files. They are only needed for JavaScript libraries but, of course, as soon you transpile TypeScript code to JavaScript, all the type information is lost.

For TypeScript-based projects, generating type definition files is very easy: you only need to set the `declaration` compiler option to `true` in the `tsconfig.json` file (or enable it by passing the `--declaration` argument directly when invoking `tsc`). Go ahead and change that option now for MediaMan. If you build the application after that, you'll see that TypeScript generates an additional `mediaman.d.ts` file for you, containing all the type information.

As you know, there are hundreds of thousands of JavaScript libraries and, of course, only a small subset of those libraries are written in TypeScript. For all the other ones, type definitions have to be created by hand or using other tools such as `dts-gen`: `https://github.com/Microsoft/dts-gen`.

As the TypeScript community grew, the need to centralize type definition files arose and, at some point, a project called DefinitelyTyped (`http://definitelytyped.org`) was created to regroup as many type definitions as possible. Today, DefinitelyTyped hosts type definitions for *thousands* of libraries.

Initially, installing type definitions in your project required manual work, but nowadays it has become very straightforward. The TypeScript team has automated the process of creating `npm` packages out of the type definitions hosted on DefinitelyTyped. Thanks to this, you can simply use `npm` to install type definitions, knowing that the following naming convention is used for typings: `@types/<library_name>` (`@types` being the name of the **namespace** under which all type definition packages are published).

For example, type definitions for the very popular `lodash` (`https://github.com/lodash/lodash`) library are available at `https://www.npmjs.com/package/@types/lodash` and can be installed easily using `npm install @types/lodash`.

> Sometimes, you might need to create type definitions by hand, for example, if no typings exist for a library or if they are outdated/broken. When doing so, you'll need to use triple-slash directives to load them: `https://www.typescriptlang.org/docs/handbook/triple-slash-directives.html`.

Whenever you add a library to your projects, check whether the typings are provided along with the library, or whether they are on DefinitelyTyped and accessible through `@types/<library_name>`.

> In the compiler configuration, you can customize locations where TypeScript will look for type definitions using the `typeRoots` option. You can learn more about it here: `https://www.typescriptlang.org/docs/handbook/tsconfig-json.html#types-typeroots-and-types`.

You can learn more about type definitions here:

- `https://blog.angular-university.io/typescript-2-type-system-how-do-type-definitions-work-in-npm-when-to-use-types-and-why-what-are-compiler-opt-in-types`
- `https://basarat.gitbooks.io/typescript/docs/types/@types.html`

Adding localForage to the project

First of all, we need to add `localForage` to our project. We can do so using `npm`:

```
npm install localforage --save
```

Luckily for us, some libraries such as `localForage` include type definitions directly and so they're even easier to use with TypeScript!

We don't need to do anything more to get started with `localForage` in our project!

Service implementation

First of all, we need to import `localForage` in our code:

1. Add the following statement at the top of the file in order to import `localForage`: `import localForage from "localforage";`. Without this, you will not be able to use the library. By doing this, we will actually trigger loading `localForage` when our JavaScript code gets loaded by the `index.html` file.

2. Now that we have added `localForage` and have loaded it, we can create an implementation of the `MediaService` interface:

```
class MediaServiceImpl<T extends Media> implements
MediaService<T>
{
    loadMediaCollection(identifier: string):
    Promise<MediaCollection<T>> { ... }
    saveMediaCollection(collection: MediaCollection<T>):
        Promise<void>
    { ... }
    getMediaCollectionIdentifiersList(): Promise<string[]> {
... }
    removeMediaCollection(identifier: string): Promise<void> {
... }
}
```

Notice how we have made our service implementation generic by requiring a type argument extending from our `Media` abstract class and how this `T` generic type is also used on the right side of the `implements` keyword.

 We have added the `Impl` suffix to the class name to indicate that this is an implementation of an interface. This is a common naming convention. Opt for this approach instead of prefixing interfaces with an `I` character.

The first thing that we need to do is configure `localForage` properly. In order to keep things simple, we will create a separate instance of the `MediaServiceImpl` class for each media type that we will manage. We could actually make our code smarter and even more generic, but it would hinder readability. For this reason, we will use a specific object store for each type of media. Let's see how!

Add the following code to the class:

```
private readonly _store: LocalForage;

constructor(private _type: Function) {
    console.log(`Initializing media service for ${_type.name}`);

    // each instance of the media service has its own data store:
    https://github.com/localForage/localForage
    // the initialization options are described here:
    https://localforage.github.io/localForage/#settings-api-config
    this._store = localForage.createInstance({
        name: 'mediaMan',
        version: 1.0,
        storeName: `media-man-${_type.name}`, // we add the type name
        to the object store name!
        description: 'MediaMan data store'
    });
}
```

First of all, we have declared a `_store` field. This is what our service will use to load/persist data using `localForage`. The `_store` field gets initialized in the constructor, where we used the `createInstance` function, allowing us to create a dedicated store instance. This is explained in the official `localForage` documentation at https://localforage.github.io/localForage/#multiple-instances-createinstance.

Notice the `-<name>` suffix that we have added to the `storeName` property with `-${_type.name}`. This suffix will help us to differentiate between collections of media (for example, between collections of `Book` objects, collections of `Movie` objects, and so on). The `_type.name` property will give us the name of the type that this specific service instance will take care of (for example, `Book`).

If you pay close attention to the constructor of our class, you'll note that the type is passed through there as `Function`. Actually, when creating an instance of the `MediaServiceImpl` class, we can pass it a type by name. The following is an example of what this looks like: `const bookService = new MediaServiceImpl<Book>(Book);`. When you pass the **name** of a class as an argument, you actually pass its **constructor function**. The reality is more complicated than this; take a look at the TypeScript handbook (`https://www.typescriptlang.org/docs/handbook/classes.html`) for details. Classes actually have a *static* and a *non-static* (or instance) side. Here, we took advantage of the static side to get the class name.

Next, we will implement the `saveMediaCollection` method. This method needs to invoke `localForage` to **serialize** and **persist** the given `MediaCollection` object. As this operation will be asynchronous, our method will have to return a `Promise` object. Before we can do so, we need to take care of two important issues.

Handling serialization/deserialization

When `localForage` persists objects, it first serializes them to JSON. Since we are using TypeScript classes for our data model, one issue that we have to tackle right away is *How can we serialize TypeScript class instances to JSON?*

There are actually many answers to this question. The most obvious one is to use `JSON.stringify` (`https://developer.mozilla.org/en-US/docs/Web/JavaScript/Reference/Global_Objects/JSON/stringify`), a standard API that converts JavaScript objects to a JSON string. However that solution is hard to implement, if you try it out you'll see that private fields will be serialized without taking getters into account. Hence, the JSON objects will have keys such as _name, which is far from ideal.

Other answers include the following:

- Implementing base classes to handle serialization: This is not great and there is a big risk of introducing subtle bugs.
- Implementing a `toJSON` function on the prototype, which should be called by `JSON.stringify`: This is far from straightforward, especially for more advanced cases (complex data structures, circular references, and much more); again there is a risk of introducing bugs.

There is also a second closely related issue that we need to solve: **How can we deserialize a JSON object back into a class instance?**

There are actually even harder problems to consider (for example, how to properly handle versioning), but we'll only focus on those two issues for now.

To ease our lives and reduce the risk of introducing bugs, we will use the `class-transformer` (`https://github.com/typestack/class-transformer`) library. This library can handle both the serialization and deserialization of classes from/to POJOs or literal objects.

Using `class-transformer`, we will add **decorators** such as `@Expose()` to our classes in order to guide `class-transformer` when it performs serialization/deserialization.

 Decorators are a fairly advanced feature of TypeScript, somewhat akin to *attributes* in C# and *annotations* in Java. We'll cover decorators in greater detail when we implement our first Angular application together. For now, just know that they are actually functions that can be used to add metadata and/or processing to different kinds of element. Decorators still exist at runtime. As we saw earlier, decorator support is enabled through the `experimentalDecorators` flag in `tsconfig.json`.

Installing class-transformer and reflect-metadata

Now that you understand why we need this library, let's install `class-transformer`. Install the dependency using `npm install class-transformer --save`.

Once again we're in luck: since `class-transformer` is written in TypeScript, its npm package includes type definitions so we don't need to install them separately.

You also need to install `reflect-metadata` (`https://www.npmjs.com/package/reflect-metadata`), which is a library that `class-transformer` requires to perform runtime reflection on types. You can learn more about it here: `http://blog.wolksoftware.com/decorators-metadata-reflection-in-typescript-from-novice-to-expert-part-4`. Install `reflect-metadata` using `npm install reflect-metadata --save`.

Again, the type definitions for this are included in the npm package.

Adding class-transformer decorators to domain classes

First of all, since we are going to use decorators, we need to adapt the tsconfig.json file to add support for them (actually, to remove warnings):

1. Edit the file and set the experimentalDecorators option to true.

   Next, import the decorators from class-transformer.

2. Add the following import statement at the top of the mediaman.ts file:
   ```
   import {classToPlain, plainToClassFromExist, Expose, Type}
   from "class-transformer";.
   ```

   Finally, you also need to import reflect-metadata.

3. Add the import statement, import "reflect-metadata";, at the top of the file (that is, before the class-transformer imports).

4. Now, adapt the MediaCollection class as follows:
   ```
   class MediaCollection<T extends Media> {
       ...
       @Expose()
       get identifier(): string {
           return this._identifier;
       }

       ...

       @Expose()
       get name(): string {
           return this._name;
       }

       ...

       @Expose()
       @Type(options => {
           if(options) {
               return (options.newObject as
               MediaCollection<T>)._type;
           } else {
   ```

```
                    throw new Error("Cannot not determine the type
                    because the options object is null or undefined");
                }
            })
            get collection(): ReadonlyArray<T> {
                return this._collection;
            }

            ...

    }
```

The `@Expose()` decorators instruct `class-transformer` to serialize the corresponding properties when converting an object to JSON. In the preceding example, `class-transformer` will thus serialize the identifier, the name, and the collection properties for us.

The `@Type(...)` decorator is required in order to help `class-transformer` know how to serialize the collection. Without it, `class-transformer` will just convert array entries into raw objects instead of instances of the generic type (that is, `Book` or `Movie`, in our case).

 If you want to know more about using `@Type` decorator for generics, refer to this issue:
`https://github.com/typestack/class-transformer/issues/14`.
There is also a code sample that you can check out:
`https://github.com/typestack/class-transformer/tree/develop`
`/sample/sample4-generics`.

Next, you need to do the same for the `Media` class:

```
abstract class Media {
    ...
    @Expose()
    get identifier(): string {
        return this._identifier;
    }

    ...

    @Expose()
    get name(): string {
        return this._name;
    }

    ...
```

```
    @Expose()
    get description(): string {
        return this._description;
    }

    ...

    @Expose()
    get pictureLocation(): string {
        return this._pictureLocation;
    }

    ...

    @Expose()
    get genre(): Genre {
        return this._genre;
    }
}
```

And the Book class:

```
class Book extends Media {
    ...

    @Expose()
    get author(): string {
        return this._author;
    }

    ...

    @Expose()
    @Type(() => Number)
    get numberOfPages(): number {
        return this._numberOfPages;
    }
}

class Movie extends Media {
    ...

    @Expose()
    get director(): string {
        return this._director;
    }

    ...
```

```
@Expose()
get duration(): string {
    return this._duration;
}
}
```

With this done, `class-transformer` knows everything it needs: it will expose all of our properties properly.

The last thing that we need to take care of is actually serializing information. To do so, we need to use the `classToPlain(...)` function provided by `class-transformer`. This function takes two arguments:

1. The object to serialize (ideally containing the `class-transformer` decorators).
2. An `options` object: through this object, it is possible to alter the serialization process.

The following is an example:

```
const serializedVersion = classToPlain(someObject, { excludePrefixes:
["_"] });
```

This example highlights how easy it is to serialize class instances using this library!

Doing the opposite transformation (from JSON back to class instances) is also doable now that we've annotated our domain model. Because we are using generics, we will need to use the `plainToClassFromExist(...)` function, which will **populate** an existing object with the provided data.

The following is an example:

```
const instance = plainToClassFromExist<Something, any>(new
Something(), value);
```

This line of code requires a few explanations:

*   With `plainToClassFromExist<Something, any>`, we pass the type to convert to as a *generic type argument* to the function; thanks to this, we don't need to use an explicit type cast (that is, `as ...`).
*   The first argument of the function is an instance that we create and that `class-transformer` will populate for us.
*   The last argument is the value to convert (that is, the raw JavaScript object).

Implementing the saveMediaCollection method

Now we know everything we need to serialize our media collections!

Go ahead and rewrite the saveMediaCollection method as follows:

```
saveMediaCollection(collection: Readonly<MediaCollection<T>>):
Promise<void> { // 1
    return new Promise<void>((resolve, reject) => { // 2
        if (!collection) { // 3
            reject(new Error("The list cannot be null or
            undefined!"));
        }

        console.log(`Saving media collection with the following name
        ${collection.name}`);

        const serializedVersion = classToPlain(collection, {
        excludePrefixes: ["_"] }); // 4
        console.log("Serialized version: ", serializedVersion);

        this._store.setItem(collection.identifier, serializedVersion)
        // 5
            .then(value => { // 6
                console.log(`Saved the ${collection.name} collection
                successfully! Saved value: ${value}`);
                resolve();
            })
            .catch(err => {
                console.error(`Failed to save the ${collection.name}
                collection with identifier
                ${collection.identifier}. Error: ${err}`);
                reject(err);
            });
    });
}
```

If you are not familiar with the Promise API, this will take some time to digest. However, once you understand it, you'll see that this code is quite simple. Let's analyze this piece of code together:

1. Our method accepts MediaCollection<T> as input and returns Promise<void>, which simply indicates that there won't be a value coming out of the promise upon resolution (that is, it will just be a signal).

2. We immediately return a new `Promise` object.

3. The first thing we do in the promise definition is to check whether the expected argument was provided. If not, we use the `reject` callback to directly return an error.

4. We use `classToPlain` to serialize the `MediaCollection` object:
   - Note that we use the `excludePrefixes` option in order to exclude all properties whose name starts with an underscore in order to avoid exposing our private properties directly (for example, `_name` in the `Media` class).

5. We invoke the `setItem` function on our store (that is, `localForage`) to persist the serialized version of the `MediaCollection` object, using the collection's identifier as a key.

6. Since the `setItem` function returns a promise, we use `.then` to define what to do when it resolves:
   - In this case, we simply call `resolve()` on the promise that we have returned at the beginning.

7. We also use `.catch` to catch and pass any errors through using the `reject(...)` function on our promise.

 By marking the `saveMediaCollection` argument as read-only, we make sure that we don't modify the object by mistake.

Next, let's take care of the `loadMediaCollection` method.

Implementing the loadMediaCollection method

Persisting data is nice but, of course, it's even nicer if it can be retrieved later.

Let's implement the load method as follows:

```
loadMediaCollection(identifier: string): Promise<MediaCollection<T>> {
    console.log(`Trying to load media collection with the following
    identifier: ${identifier}`);
    return new Promise<MediaCollection<T>>((resolve, reject) => {
        this._store.getItem(identifier)
            .then(value => {
                console.log("Found the collection: ", value);

                const retrievedCollection =
```

```
            plainToClassFromExist<MediaCollection<T>,
            any>(new MediaCollection<T>(this._type), value);

            console.log("Retrieved collection: ",
            retrievedCollection);
            resolve(retrievedCollection);
        })
        .catch(err => {
            reject(err); // let the error through
        });
    });
}
```

The following are some explanations of the preceding code:

- This time, the method accepts a string identifier as input and returns `Promise<MediaCollection<T>>`, which means that we promise to try and deliver an instance of the `MediaCollection` subsequently.
- We use the `getItem` function of the store, which returns `Promise`.
- In the `then` callback function, we use the `plainToClassFromExist` function that we mentioned earlier to deserialize the value into an instance of our `MediaCollection` class:
    - Note that we pass `this._type` as an argument to the constructor, which will then allow `class-transformer` to get access to the type through the `@Type` decorator that we defined earlier.
- Finally, we use the `resolve(...)` function to return the object.

Implementing the getMediaCollectionIdentifiersList method

This method will simply return an array containing all the keys in the store. This will come in handy later when we work on the UI, in order to allow us to load the existing collections.

The following is the relevant code:

```
getMediaCollectionIdentifiersList(): Promise<string[]> {
    return new Promise<string[]>((resolve, reject) => {
        console.log("Retrieving the list of media collection
        identifiers");
        this._store.keys().then(keys => {
```

```
            console.log(`Retrieved the of media collection
             identifiers:
            ${keys}`);
            resolve(keys);
        })
        .catch(err => {
            console.error(`Failed to retrieve the list of media
            collection identifiers. Error: ${err}`);
            reject(err);
        })
    });
}
```

This is, of course, very similar to what we've just done in the preceding section. The main difference the following is that we use the `keys()` method, which returns the list of keys, as described in the `localForage` documentation:

`https://localforage.github.io/localForage/#data-api-keys`.

Implementing the removeMediaCollection method

This is the final method for our service. Its code shouldn't require any more explanations:

```
removeMediaCollection(identifier: string): Promise<void> {
    return new Promise<void>((resolve, reject) => {
        if (!identifier || '' === identifier.trim()) {
            reject(new Error("The identifier must be provided!"));
        }
        console.log(`Removing media collection with the following
        identifier ${identifier}`);

        this._store.removeItem(identifier)
            .then(() => {
                console.log(`Removed the ${identifier} collection
                successfully!`);
                resolve();
            })
            .catch(err => {
                console.error(`Failed to removed the ${identifier}
                collection`);
                reject(err);
            });
    });
}
```

Great! Our service is now fully implemented. We'll see how it is used later.

Implementing the view

As with `TodoIt`, our view layer will be composed of an HTML page, a view interface, and an HTML-aware implementation of that interface.

CSS

For this project, we have provided you with a default style sheet called `mediaman.css`; you can find it at the root of the initial project. This is by no means expert-level CSS code, but it provides a nice improvement on what we did in our first project and it should be enough for our purposes. If you're curious, the CSS code uses Flexbox Layout, which is a very powerful API available in modern web browsers for creating flexible UI layouts. You can learn more about Flexbox here: `https://css-tricks.com/snippets/css/a-guide-to-flexbox`.

HTML page

Open the `index.html` file and replace the default content with the following:

```
<!DOCTYPE html>
<html lang="en">
<head>
    <meta charset="UTF-8">
    <title>MediaMan</title>
    <link rel="stylesheet" type="text/css" href="mediaman.css">
</head>
<body id="mediaMan">

<h1>MediaMan</h1>

<h2>Book collections</h2>

<div class="collectionContainerGroup">
    <div class="containerGroup">
        <div class="container">
            <h3>New collection</h3>
            <form id="newBookCollection" action="#">
                <input id="newBookCollectionName" type="text"
                title="Name" placeholder="Name" required>
```

```
                    <input type="button" value="Create"
                        onclick="mediaManController.
                        createBookCollection();" />
                </form>
            </div>
            <div class="container">
                <h3>Tools</h3>
                <form action="#">
                    <input type="button" value="Reload collections"
                    onclick="mediaManController.
                    reloadBookCollections();" />
                </form>
            </div>
        </div>

        <div id="bookCollections" class="containerGroup">
        </div>
    </div>

    <hr>

    <h2>Movie collections</h2>

    Bonus exercise!

    <script src="./mediaman.ts"></script>

</body>
</html>
```

This will be our base structure for the page. In this chapter, we will not modify it any further. We will make all the necessary modifications programmatically in TypeScript.

Note that we can only refer to the mediaman.ts file in the index.html file because we are using the Parcel bundler in the base project!

 The preceding identifiers do matter! As you'll see throughout the chapter, we will refer to these in our code, so make sure that you do not change them for now. The CSS class names also matter as the default style sheet won't work if you change these class names.

The following is how the page should initially look:

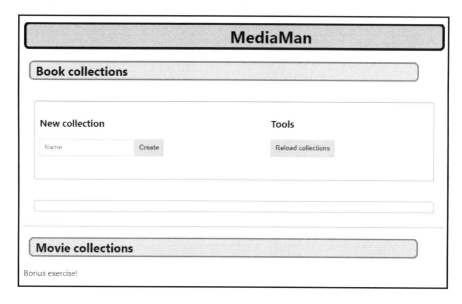

Still not too fancy, but be patient; later in the book, we will use much better-looking widgets.

Defining the view interface

Add the following interface to mediaman.ts:

```
interface MediaManView {
    getNewBookCollectionName(): string;
    renderBookCollection(bookCollection:
    Readonly<MediaCollection<Book>>): void;
    displayErrorMessage(message: string): void;
    clearBookCollections(): void;
    removeBookCollection(identifier: string): void;
    getNewBookDetails(collectionIdentifier: string): { error?: string,
    book?: Readonly<Book> };
    renderBook(collectionIdentifier: string, book: Readonly<Book>):
    void;
    removeBook(collectionIdentifier: string, bookIdentifier: string):
    void;
    clearNewBookCollectionForm(collectionIdentifier: string): void;
}
```

As in the previous chapter, the different view methods will hide internal details for the controller, which will simply use the view implementation as a black box. Again, the less the components know about each other, the better.

Implementing the HTMLMediaManView class

Let's now create our HTML-based view implementation. As we did with `TodoIt`, we will manipulate the DOM through TypeScript.

The base structure

First, add the base structure of the class to `mediaman.ts`:

```
class HTMLMediaManView implements MediaManView {
    private readonly _newBookCollectionForm: HTMLFormElement;
    private readonly _newBookCollectionName: HTMLInputElement;
    private readonly _bookCollectionsContainer: HTMLDivElement;

    private readonly _genreOptions: string = "";

    constructor() {
        this._newBookCollectionForm =
        document.getElementById('newBookCollection')
         as HTMLFormElement;
        this._newBookCollectionName =
        document.getElementById('newBookCollectionName') as
        HTMLInputElement;
        this._bookCollectionsContainer =
        document.getElementById("bookCollections")
         as HTMLDivElement;

        if (!this._newBookCollectionForm) {
            throw new Error("Could not initialize the view. The
             'newBookCollection' element id was not found. Was the
             template changed?");
        }

        if (!this._newBookCollectionName) {
            throw new Error("Could not initialize the view. The
             'newBookCollectionName' element id was not found. Was the
             template changed?");
```

```
        }

    if (!this._bookCollectionsContainer) {
        throw new Error("Could not initialize the view. The
        'bookCollections' element id was not found. Was the
        template changed?");
    }

    for (let genreKey in Genre) {
        this._genreOptions += `<option
        value="${genreKey}">${Genre[genreKey]}</option>">`;
    }
}

// Add the methods here
}
```

In the constructor, we directly retrieve some DOM elements that we will use later:

- The form used to create new book collections
- The input field used for the name of new book collections
- The container for book collections through which we will be able to add new book collections later on

If those cannot be found, then there's probably a bug to fix; so, again, the sooner we know, the better.

Finally, we also generate a list of `<option>` elements corresponding to the entries in our `Genre` enum. We'll use this when we generate the form used to create new books in the `renderBookCollection` method.

You can also add method skeletons for now:

```
getNewBookCollectionName(): string {
    ...
}

clearNewBookCollectionForm(): void {
    ...
}

renderBookCollection(bookCollection:
Readonly<MediaCollection<Book>>): void {
    ...
}

displayErrorMessage(message: string): void {
```

```
    ...
}

clearBookCollections(): void {
    ...
}

removeBookCollection(identifier: string): void {
    ...
}

getNewBookDetails(collectionIdentifier: string): { error?:
    string, book?: Book } {
    ...
}

renderBook(collectionIdentifier: string, book: Readonly<Book>):
void {
    ...
}

removeBook(collectionIdentifier: string, bookIdentifier: string):
void {
    ...
}

clearNewBookForm(collectionIdentifier: string): void {
    ...
}
```

Next, we will implement those methods one by one.

Implementing basic validation using the HTML Form Validation API

Let's start by implementing the getNewBookCollectionName method. Its goal is simply to return the name of the book collection that needs to be created. It will be called whenever the user asks you to create a collection:

```
getNewBookCollectionName(): string {
    // build upon standard HTML DOM validation
    if (this._newBookCollectionName.checkValidity() === false) {
        this._newBookCollectionName.reportValidity();
        throw new Error("Invalid collection name!");
    }
```

```
        return this._newBookCollectionName.value;
    }
```

When this method executes, it first checks whether the field is currently *valid* or not. To do this, it relies on native HTML form validation support (https://developer.mozilla.org/en-US/docs/Learn/HTML/Forms/Form_val idation) and the corresponding JavaScript DOM APIs. If you look at the index.html template, you'll see that the newBookCollectionName input field has been marked as mandatory using the required attribute:

```
<input id="newBookCollectionName" type="text" title="Name"
placeholder="Name" *required*>
```

The check is done using the checkValidity() method on the DOM input node. If the input is not valid (for example, no value has been given), then the method calls reportValidity(), which will let the user know that something is wrong. Then, the method throws an Error instance to let the calling code know that something went wrong. Actually, this is not the best practice, as it actually abuses exceptions. We will explain why in the next subsection.

Finally, the method returns the value of the input field.

The following is what the user will see when there are validation issues:

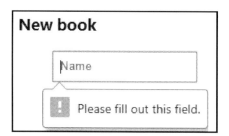

This is great because we get nice-looking error messages that work in all modern web browsers without any effort.

Why exceptions should not be used in this case

The problem with throwing an exception in the `getNewBookCollectionName` method is that **it changes the control flow** of the application. The calling code will have to explicitly catch this exception if it wants to be able to react to it. However, since there is no notion such as **checked exceptions** in JavaScript and TypeScript, the calling code might not even know that an exception could be raised when calling the method!

 Note that proper code documentation and tools can help with this issue. For instance, you can add JSDoc comments to the code to explicitly state that it might throw an error: `http://usejsdoc.org/ tags-throws.html`.

We say that throwing exceptions changes the control flow because, when we throw exceptions, it is practically the same as a `goto` statement, as you should know, `goto` is considered to be harmful: `http://wiki.c2.com/?GotoConsideredHarmful`. It makes the code harder to read/understand and can also cause bugs and unwanted behavior. This is related to the **principle of least astonishment** (`http://wiki.c2.com/?PrincipleOfLeastAstonishment`), which simply states that operations should act in an obvious, consistent, and predictable way.

You should bear in mind the following rule of thumb: **exceptions should only be used for exceptional occasions.**

You can learn more about this issue at `http://wiki.c2.com/?DontUseExceptionsForFlowControl`.

So, what is the alternative then? If you examine the `getNewBookDetails` method signature in the `MediaManView` interface, you'll note that it returns a custom object shape: `{ error?: string, book?: Readonly<Book> }`. The idea is to return a known data structure. This makes the fact that errors could be returned more explicit, hence making the code more predictable and understandable. This is a recommended approach to keep a logical control flow and avoid abusing exceptions, which should be exceptional. This is a pattern that should be familiar to JavaScript and Node.js developers.

Implementing the clearBookCollections method

The `clearBookCollections` method's goal is to remove all book collections from the document. You can easily implement it as follows:

```
clearBookCollections(): void {
    this._bookCollectionsContainer.innerHTML = "";
}
```

We do not need to make checks here since the DOM node was retrieved and checked in the constructor.

Implementing the displayErrorMessage method

This method will be a simple utility that displays messages to the end user. For simplicity, we will only use a basic alert box. In later projects, we will use so-called **toast** notifications instead, as it'll look better and will also provide a better user experience.

The following is the implementation:

```
displayErrorMessage(errorMessage: string): void {
    if (!errorMessage) {
        throw new Error("An error message must be provided!");
    }
    alert(errorMessage); // bad for user experience but ignore this
for
    now
}
```

 We have added a defensive check for the argument. In this case, using an exception makes sense because, if no message is passed, it is certainly due to a bug, so it should be discovered as soon as possible.

Next, let's look at how to render books.

Implementing the renderBookCollection method

The next method is also the longest. This method accepts `MediaCollection<Book>` as input and appends it to the DOM. By doing this, we can leverage template strings. These will allow us to write HTML code easily without requiring a lot of escape characters that would otherwise be needed if we used standard or single quotes instead.

The following is the code:

```
renderBookCollection(bookCollection: Readonly<MediaCollection<Book>>):
void {
    this._bookCollectionsContainer.innerHTML += `
    <div id="bookCollection-${bookCollection.identifier}"
    class="collection">
        <h3 class="collectionName">${bookCollection.name}</h3>

        <div class="containerGroup">
            <div class="container">
                <h3>New book</h3>

                <form id="newBook-${bookCollection.identifier}"
                action="#">
                    <ul>
                        <li>
                            <input
                            id="newBookName-$
                            {bookCollection.identifier}" type="text"
                            title="Name" placeholder="Name" required>
                            <input id="newBookAuthor-$
                            {bookCollection.identifier}"
                            type="text" placeholder="Author" required>
                        </li>
                        <li>
                            <select id="newBookGenre-
                            ${bookCollection.identifier}" required>
                            ${this._genreOptions}
                            </select>
                            <input id="newBookPages-$
                            {bookCollection.identifier}"
                            type="number" placeholder="Pages"
                             required>
                        </li>
                        <li>
                            <input id="newBookPicture-
```

```
                        ${bookCollection.identifier}" type="url"
                        title="Picture" placeholder="Picture URL">
                    </li>
                    <li>
                        <textarea id="newBookDescription-
                        ${bookCollection.identifier}"
                        placeholder="Description"></textarea>
                    </li>
                </ul>
                <input type="button" value="Create"
                onclick="mediaManController.
            createBook('${bookCollection.identifier}');" />
                </form>
            </div>
            <div class="collectionToolsContainer">
                <h3>Tools</h3>
                <form action="#">
                    <input type="button" value="Remove collection"
                    onclick="mediaManController.removeBookCollection
                ('${bookCollection.identifier}');" />
                </form>
            </div>
        </div>

        <div class="containerGroup">
            <div class="container">
                <table class="collectionTable">
                    <thead>
                    <tr>
                        <td>Picture</td>
                        <td>Name</td>
                        <td>Genre</td>
                        <td>Description</td>
                        <td>Author</td>
                        <td>Pages</td>
                        <td>Remove</td>
                    </tr>
                    </thead>
                    <tbody id="collectionTableBody-
                    ${bookCollection.identifier}"></tbody>
                </table>
            </div>
        </div>
    </div>
    `;

bookCollection.collection.forEach(book => {
    this.renderBook(bookCollection.identifier, book);
```

```
    });
}
```

The DOM structure is actually pretty simple. When a book collection is added, we add a `div` container for it inside the book collection's container (note that this has the `collection` class applied to it). Inside the book collection container, we display the collection name.

Below the name, we add a form for creating new books inside that specific collection. In addition to this, we add a container for `tools` related to this collection. For now, we will only provide a button for removing the collection, but we can easily come up with other options (for example, revert changes, rename collection, export, and more).

Finally, we add another container with a table inside. That table will be empty when a new collection is created, but if the collection contains media, then they will be added to it. This is handled by the code at the end of the method:

```
bookCollection.collection.forEach(book => {
    this.renderBook(bookCollection.identifier, book);
});
```

This simply invokes the `renderBook` method (which we will soon implement) for each and every book within the collection.

> The `Array.forEach(...)` method is actually not the fastest, but we do still recommend it for readability. It is slower because a lexical scope is created for each loop iteration; however, this is actually a good thing to have in many cases. You can learn more about this here: `https://coderwall.com/p/kvzbpa/don-t-use-array-foreach-use-for-instead`. There is also a nice performance analysis here: `https://github.com/dg92/Performance-Analysis-JS`. Take these with a pinch of salt though, since JavaScript engines keep getting faster!

We have also defined HTML identifiers for the most important elements. Those identifiers will make it easy to retrieve DOM nodes in our TypeScript code, as you'll see in the coming sections.

You can see that we have already added event handlers in order to call our controller. For example, on the **Remove collection** button, we invoke `mediaManController.removeCollection(...)`. We have already seen how this all works while working on `TodoIt`.

The following is what a newly created collection should look like, assuming that our default `mediaman.css` style sheet is applied:

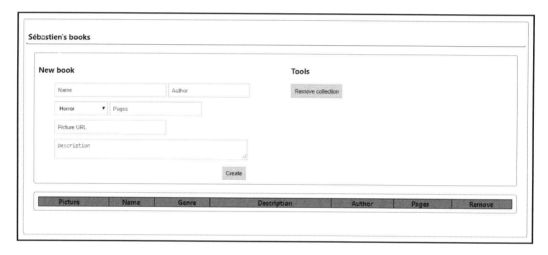

Thanks to Flexbox (used in our CSS code), when multiple collections are added, they can be put side by side if space allows:

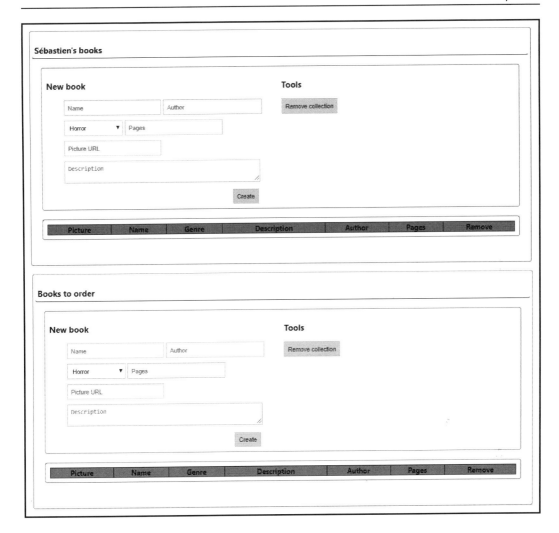

Modern CSS APIs do a lot to make our lives easier.

Implementing the clearNewBookCollectionForm method

This method will simply reset the new book collection form using the `reset()` method available on `HTMLFormElement` objects.

The following is the code:

```
clearNewBookCollectionForm(): void {
    this._newBookCollectionForm.reset();
}
```

 TypeScript class names for DOM elements correspond to the actual JavaScript class names.

Let's continue with the `renderBook` method.

Implementing the renderBook method

The `renderBook` method will add the given book to the DOM of the corresponding collection. This is done using the identifiers that we defined earlier. As you can see, they're necessary and central to application code:

```
renderBook(collectionIdentifier: string, book: Book): void {
    if (!book) {
        throw new Error("The book to render must be provided!");
    }

    const collectionTableBody = document.getElementById
    (`collectionTableBody-${collectionIdentifier}`) as
    HTMLTableSectionElement;

    if (!collectionTableBody) {
        throw new Error(`The table body for collection
        ${collectionIdentifier}
        could not be found! Was the template changed?`);
    }

    const tableRow: HTMLTableRowElement =
    collectionTableBody.insertRow();

    tableRow.id = `book-${collectionIdentifier}-${book.identifier}`;

    tableRow.innerHTML = `
        <td>
            <img class="mediaImage" src="${book.pictureLocation}">
        </td>
        <td>${book.name}</td>
        <td>${book.genre}</td>
        <td>${book.description}</td>
```

```
<td>${book.author}</td>
<td>${book.numberOfPages}</td>
<td>
    <a href="#" onclick="mediaManController.removeBook
  ('${collectionIdentifier}','${book.identifier}');">X</a>
</td>
`;

collectionTableBody.appendChild(tableRow);
}
```

Here, we again throw an exception if no book object is as given, simply because this will be a bug.

The rest of the code should be self-explanatory.

Once added, books will appear in the corresponding collection's table:

Picture	Name	Genre	Description	Author	Pages	Remove
	Dune	Science Fiction		Frank Herbert	832	X
	1984	Science Fiction		George Orwell	438	X

Now that we can add and display books, let's demonstrate how to remove them.

Implementing the removeBookCollection method

This method removes given book collection from the DOM. Again, collections have an identifier and this is what we'll use here, as those identifiers are also present in the DOM that we generate.

The following is the code for the method:

```
removeBookCollection(identifier: string) {
    const bookCollectionDOMNode: HTMLDivElement =
    document.getElementById(`bookCollection-${identifier}`) as
    HTMLDivElement;
    if (!bookCollectionDOMNode) {
```

```
        throw new Error("Could not remove the book collection from
        the DOM. Couldn't find the DOM node");
    } else {
        bookCollectionDOMNode.remove();
    }
}
```

As you can see, we simply use the `remove()` method present on DOM nodes. If the DOM node is not found, we again throw an exception as this should not happen.

Implementing the getNewBookDetails method using keyof and typeof

The `getNewBookDetails` method will simply retrieve values for the different fields in the new book creation form (in a specific book collection) and will create a `Book` object corresponding to those values.

Let's add the code for it.

First, add the method and some defensive checks:

```
getNewBookDetails(collectionIdentifier: string): { error?: string,
book?: Book } {
    if (!collectionIdentifier) {
        // we throw this one because it means that there is a bug!
        throw new Error("The collection identifier must be
        provided!");
    }
    // required
    const newBookForm = document.getElementById(`newBook-$
    {collectionIdentifier}`) as HTMLFormElement;

    if (!newBookForm) {
        throw new Error(`Could not find the new book form for
        collection ${collectionIdentifier}`);
    }
    // build upon standard HTML DOM validation
    if (newBookForm.checkValidity() === false) {
        newBookForm.reportValidity();
        return {
            error: "The new book form is invalid!"
        };
    }
    // Continue here
}
```

Then, retrieve the different DOM elements:

```
// from here on out, no need to check the validity of the specific
//form fields
// we just need to check if the fields can be found
const newBookNameField = document.getElementById(`newBookName-$
{collectionIdentifier}`) as HTMLInputElement;
if (!newBookNameField) {
    throw new Error("The new book form's name input was not found!
    Did the template change?");
}
const newBookAuthorField = document.getElementById
(`newBookAuthor-${collectionIdentifier}`) as HTMLInputElement;
if (!newBookAuthorField) {
    throw new Error("The new book form's author input was not
    found! Did the template change?");
}
const newBookGenreSelect = document.getElementById
(`newBookGenre-${collectionIdentifier}`) as HTMLSelectElement;
if (!newBookGenreSelect) {
    throw new Error("The new book form's genre select was not
    found! Did the template change?");
}
const newBookPagesField = document.getElementById(`newBookPages-
${collectionIdentifier}`) as HTMLInputElement;
if (!newBookPagesField) {
    throw new Error("The new book form's page input was not found!
    Did the template change?");
}

// optional
const newBookPictureField = document.getElementById
(`newBookPicture-${collectionIdentifier}`) as HTMLInputElement;
if (!newBookPictureField) {
    throw new Error("The new book form's picture input was not
    found! Did the template change?");
}
const newBookDescriptionField = document.getElementById
(`newBookDescription-${collectionIdentifier}`) as
HTMLTextAreaElement;
if (!newBookDescriptionField) {
    throw new Error("The new book form's description input was not
    found! Did the template change?");
}

// Continue here
```

Finally, create the object and return it:

```
const newBookGenre = Genre[newBookGenreSelect.value as keyof typeof
Genre];

const newBookNumberOfPages = Number.parseInt(newBookPagesField.value);

return {
    book: new Book(newBookNameField.value,
    newBookDescriptionField.value, newBookPictureField.value,
    newBookGenre, newBookAuthorField.value, newBookNumberOfPages)
};
```

First, we check the validity of the whole form and report to the user if something is wrong.

Note that we also return a new object including the optional `error` property that we defined in our custom return type. This is what we meant when we mentioned the Node.js way of handling exceptions earlier.

By doing this, the calling code will be able to easily check for the presence of an error and react accordingly. In this case, this is much cleaner and less surprising than throwing an exception.

Then the major part of the code simply retrieves the DOM nodes that we expect to find and raise exceptions if they're not there (as this would be due to bugs and/or major changes in our code).

The way we retrieve the book's genre is also interesting:

```
const newBookGenre = Genre[newBookGenreSelect.value as keyof typeof
Genre];
```

What we are doing with the preceding code is retrieving the `Genre` enum entry corresponding to the value selected by the user in the `<select>` element of the form.

In the code, you can see that we use both the `keyof` and `typeof` keywords. The reason for this is that, if we simply tried to use `Genre[newBookGenreSelect.value]`, the TypeScript compiler would raise an error (https://stackoverflow.com/questions/36316326/typescript-ts7015-error-when-accessing-an-enum-using-a-string-type-parameter) because the string is arbitrary and TypeScript cannot know for sure that it will correspond to an existing entry of the `Genre` enum.

For those familiar with C# or .NET, this will be disappointing because it isn't safe: we tell TypeScript that this should be okay so that it stops complaining, but we cannot be sure either!

You can find a great explanation of the `keyof typeof <type>` trick at `https://github.com/Microsoft/TypeScript/issues/14106#issuecomment-28025 3269`. The short version implies that, if we had only used `keyof Genre`, we would have obtained a union of the numeric values behind our enum entries, whereas we are rather interested in the string values.

Bonus – the keyof operator

The `keyof` operator is also called the *index type query* operator. It returns permitted property names for the given type. This operator is **useful when you want to make sure that a given name is actually a valid key of some type**.

This happens quite often in the JavaScript ecosystem, for example, when APIs accept property names as parameters and later access those properties using the `someObject[propertyName]` syntax.

Let's look at an example of how to use `keyof` in practice:

```
interface Game {
    name: string;
    players: number;
}

function displayGameProperty(game: Game, propertyName: keyof Game):
void {
    console.log(game[propertyName]);
}

const game: Game = {name: "Chess", players: 2};

displayGameProperty(game, "name");

//displayGameProperty(game, "foo"); // error TS2345: Argument of type
'"foo"' is not assignable to parameter of type '"name" | "players"'
```

In this example, the `displayGameProperty` function accepts a `game` object as a parameter as well as the name of a property to display. Using the `keyof` operator, we can make sure **at compile time** that the property name is a valid property name.

Thanks to this, we can again have powerful autocompletion in our editors:

You can learn more about
`keyof` at `https://www.typescriptlang.org/docs/handbook/advanced-types.html#index-types`.

Bonus – mapped types

The `Readonly<T>` type that we have used in our code is actually an example of a **mapped type**. Mapped types are derived types that we can define based on existing types. Mapped types apply **transformations** to each property of the existing type they are based on.

Take a look at the definition of the `Readonly<T>` type that you can find in standard TypeScript libraries
(`https://github.com/Microsoft/TypeScript/blob/master/lib/lib.es5.d.ts`):

```
type Readonly<T> = {
    readonly [P in keyof T]: T[P];
}
```

This mapped type is actually really straightforward once you know how to read it. It takes each and every property (called `P` here) and adds the `readonly` keyword to them, making the whole type read-only. Using `keyof` and mapped types, you can do a ton of fun things with the TypeScript type system.

 The `T[P]` return type is a lookup type; it corresponds to the type of the given property on the `T` type.

The following is how you could define and use a mapped type to indicate that its properties may be `null`:

```
type Nullable<T> = {
    [P in keyof T]: T[P] | null
};

interface Thing {
```

```
    name: string
}

const thing: Thing = {
    name: "The thing"
};

const thingName = thing.name;

const nullableThing: Nullable<Thing> = {
    name: "The thing"
};

const nullableThingName: string | null = nullableThing.name;
```

TypeScript includes a few other mapped types in its standard library:

- `Required<T>`: This makes all properties in `T` required.
- `Partial<T>`: This makes all properties in `T` optional.
- `Omit<T,K>`: This omits some properties from a type (that is, this is used to create derived types).
- `Pick<T, K extends keyof T>`: These pick a set of properties from a type.
- `Record<K extends string, T>`: These create a new type with a set of properties `K`, of the `T` type.

The following is another example of a useful trick that we can perform by combining mapped types, `keyof` and `typeof`:

```
type PartialBy<T, K extends keyof T> = Omit<T, K> & Partial<Pick<T,
K>>
```

The preceding example is not so easy to read, but it is interesting; it takes a `T` type and makes some of its properties optional. The nice thing here is the type safety that TypeScript allows.

You can learn more about mapped types here:

- https://www.typescriptlang.org/docs/handbook/advanced-types.html#mapped-types
- https://www.stevefenton.co.uk/2017/11/typescript-mighty-morphing-mapped-types
- https://blog.mariusschulz.com/2017/01/20/typescript-2-1-mapped-types

Implementing the clearNewBookForm method

This method is very straightforward. We retrieve the form element from the DOM and call `reset()` on it:

```
clearNewBookForm(collectionIdentifier: string): void {
    if (!collectionIdentifier) {
        throw new Error("The collection identifier must be
        provided!");
    }

    const newBookForm = document.getElementById
    (`newBook-${collectionIdentifier}`) as HTMLFormElement;

    if (!newBookForm) {
        throw new Error(`Could not find the new book form for
        collection ${collectionIdentifier}`);
    }

    newBookForm.reset();
}
```

Let's continue with the `removeBook` method.

Implementing the removeBook method

The last method that we need to implement is `removeBook`. Here, we'll simply retrieve the DOM node corresponding to the book (that is, the table row) and remove it:

```
removeBook(collectionIdentifier: string, bookIdentifier: string) {
    if (!collectionIdentifier) {
        throw new Error("The collection identifier must be
provided!");
    }

    if (!bookIdentifier) {
        throw new Error("The book identifier must be provided!");
    }

    const bookElement = document.getElementById
    (`book-${collectionIdentifier}-${bookIdentifier}`)
     as HTMLInputElement;
    if (!bookElement) {
        throw new Error("The element corresponding to the book to
        remove could not be found! Did the template change?");
```

```
    }

    bookElement.remove();
}
```

Voilà! Our view is now fully implemented – great!

Creating the controller layer

The last and most important piece of the puzzle is, of course, the controller layer. Let's implement it now.

Defining the interface

First, we define our interface:

```
interface MediaManController {
    createBookCollection(): void;
    reloadBookCollections(): void;
    removeBookCollection(identifier: string): void;
    createBook(collectionIdentifier: string): void;
    removeBook(collectionIdentifier: string, bookIdentifier: string):
    void;
}
```

Our controller is really simple at this point; it defines methods to manage book collections and books.

Implementing the MediaManController class

Go ahead and add the skeleton of the controller implementation:

```
class MediaManControllerImpl implements MediaManController {
    private readonly _view: MediaManView; // <1>
    private readonly _bookService: MediaService<Book>; // <2>
    private readonly _movieService: MediaService<Movie>;

    private _bookCollections: Map<string, MediaCollection<Book>> =
     new Map<string, MediaCollection<Book>>(); // <3>
    private _movieCollections: Map<string, MediaCollection<Movie>> =
     new Map<string, MediaCollection<Movie>>();
```

```
constructor(view: MediaManView, bookService: MediaService<Book>,
movieService: MediaService<Movie>) {
    if (!view) {
        throw new Error("The view is mandatory!");
    }
    if (!bookService) {
        throw new Error("The book service is mandatory!");
    }
    if (!movieService) {
        throw new Error("The movie service is mandatory!");
    }

    this._view = view;
    this._bookService = bookService;
    this._movieService = movieService;

    // <4>
    this.reloadBookCollections(); // reload saved data when the
    application starts
    }
}
```

There are a few things to mention here:

- As with `TodoIt`, our controller holds a reference to an instance of the view.
- Our controller also holds references to service implementations.
- We have defined maps for caching collections.
- In the constructor, we call the `reloadBookCollections()` method to directly load the data.

 Maps are very useful when it comes to having efficient lookup times. Maps have constant lookup times, so no matter how big the map becomes, finding an item by its key will remain efficient.

Then add method skeletons underneath the constructor:

```
reloadBookCollections(): void {
    console.log('Reloading the book collections');
    // TODO add implementation here
}

createBookCollection(): void {
    console.log('Creating a book collection');
    // TODO add implementation here
}
```

```
removeBookCollection(identifier: string): void {
    console.log(`Removing book collection with id:
    ${identifier}`);
    // TODO add implementation here
}

createBook(collectionIdentifier: string): void {
    console.log(`Creating book collection called:
    ${collectionIdentifier}`);
    // TODO add implementation here
}

removeBook(collectionIdentifier: string, bookIdentifier: string):
void {
    console.log(`Removing book [${bookIdentifier}] from collection
    [${collectionIdentifier}]`);
    // TODO add implementation here
}
```

We'll implement those methods next.

Implementing the reloadBookCollections method

Implement this method as follows:

```
reloadBookCollections(): void {
    this._bookService.getMediaCollectionIdentifiersList().then(keys =>
{
        this._bookCollections.clear(); // clear the current state
        this._view.clearBookCollections(); // remove the DOM nodes
        keys.forEach(key => {
            this._bookService.loadMediaCollection(key).then(collection
            => {
                this._bookCollections.set(key, collection);
                this._view.renderBookCollection(collection);
            });
        });
    });
}
```

This method relies on the book service to manage the collection and orchestrate the view.

Implementing the createBookCollection method

The following is the code for the next method:

```
createBookCollection(): void {
    const newBookCollectionName: string =
    this._view.getNewBookCollectionName();

    console.log("Creating a new book collection: ",
    newBookCollectionName);

    const newBookCollection: MediaCollection<Book> = new
    MediaCollection<Book>(Book, newBookCollectionName);
    this._bookCollections.set(newBookCollection.identifier,
    newBookCollection);

    this._bookService.saveMediaCollection(newBookCollection).then(()
     => {
        console.log(`New book collection called
        "${newBookCollection.name}"
        saved successfully. Identifier: `,
         newBookCollection.identifier);
        this._view.clearNewBookCollectionForm();
        this._view.renderBookCollection(newBookCollection);
    }).catch(_ => {
        this._view.displayErrorMessage(`Failed to save the new book
        collection called ${newBookCollectionName}`);
    });
}
```

Here, we get the information we need out of the view. We adapt our map by associating the collection identifier with the newly created media collection. Finally, we use the service to persist in our collection.

Implementing the removeBookCollection method

This next method is straightforward:

```
removeBookCollection(identifier: string): void {
    if (!identifier) {
        throw new Error("An identifier must be provided");
    }
```

```
    this._bookCollections.delete(identifier);
    this._view.removeBookCollection(identifier);
    this._bookService.removeMediaCollection(identifier).then(() => {
        console.log("Removed the collection with identifier: ",
        identifier);
    }).catch(_ => {
        this._view.displayErrorMessage("Failed to remove the
        collection!");
    });
}
```

This method first makes sure that an identifier is provided. Then, it deletes the corresponding key from the map, tells the view to remove it as well, and, finally, invokes the corresponding service method.

In the event of an error, the view is asked to display an error message.

Implementing the createBook method

Next up is the createBook method. This is the most complicated one.

First of all, implement all the required validations:

```
createBook(collectionIdentifier: string): void {
    if (!collectionIdentifier) {
        throw new Error("The collection identifier is required to
        create a new book!");
    }

    console.log("Retrieving the details about the new book to
    create...");

    const bookDetailsResult =
    this._view.getNewBookDetails(collectionIdentifier);

    if (bookDetailsResult.error) {
        console.error("Failed to retrieve the book details: ",
        bookDetailsResult.error);
        return;
    }

    if (!this._bookCollections.has(collectionIdentifier) ||
    !this._bookCollections.get(collectionIdentifier)) {
        console.error("Tried to add a book to an unknown collection.
        Identifier: ", collectionIdentifier);
        this._view.displayErrorMessage("Failed to create the new
```

```
            book!");
            return;
    }

    const existingCollection =
    this._bookCollections.get(collectionIdentifier);
    if (!existingCollection || !bookDetailsResult.book) {
        throw new Error("The collection couldn't be retrieved or we
        could not get the book details from the view!");
    }

    // add the rest of the code here
}
```

Then add the following:

```
const newBook: Readonly<Book> = bookDetailsResult.book;
existingCollection.addMedia(newBook);
this._bookService.saveMediaCollection(existingCollection)
    .then(() => {
        console.log(`Book collection called
        "${existingCollection.name}" updated successfully.`);
        this._view.clearNewBookForm(collectionIdentifier);
        this._view.renderBook(existingCollection.identifier, newBook);
// here we are sure that the book property is set
    })
    .catch(error => {
        console.error("Error while updating an existing book
        collection: ", error);
        this._view.displayErrorMessage(`Failed to update the existing
        book collection called ${existingCollection.name}`);
    });
```

In this second part of the method, we have added our new book to the existing collection and then asked the service to persist the updated collection.

Again, in the event of an error, the view is asked to display an error message.

Implementing the removeBook method

The last remaining method is easier to implement.

First, let's again add some validations:

```
removeBook(collectionIdentifier: string, bookIdentifier: string): void
{
```

```
    if (!collectionIdentifier) {
        throw new Error("The collection identifier is required to
        remove a book!");
    }

    if(!bookIdentifier) {
        throw new Error("The book identifier is required to remove a
        book");
    }

    console.log(`Removing book ${bookIdentifier} which should be part
    of collection ${collectionIdentifier}`);

    const existingCollection =
    this._bookCollections.get(collectionIdentifier);
    if (!existingCollection) {
        throw new Error("The collection couldn't be retrieved or we
        could not get the book details from the view!");
    }

    // Add the rest of the code here
}
```

Then add the following code:

```
existingCollection.removeMedia(bookIdentifier);
bookService.saveMediaCollection(existingCollection)
    .then(() => {
        console.log(`Book collection called
        "${existingCollection.name}" updated successfully.`);
        this._view.removeBook(collectionIdentifier, bookIdentifier);
    })
    .catch(error => {
        console.error("Error while updating an existing book
        collection: ", error);
        this._view.displayErrorMessage(`Failed to save the
        modifications made to the ${existingCollection.name}
        book collection (removal of the following book:
        ${bookIdentifier}`);
    });
```

Here, we have removed the book (by its identifier) from the collection and have again asked the service to persist the updated collection.

Job done – congratulations! The controller is now fully implemented.

Initializing the application

We are almost there! The last thing that we need to do is to instantiate our different classes.

Add the following code at the end of `mediaman.ts`.

First, create an instance of the view:

```
const view: HTMLMediaManView = new HTMLMediaManView();
```

Then instantiate the services:

```
const bookService = new MediaServiceImpl<Book>(Book);
console.log("Book service initialized: ", bookService);

const movieService = new MediaServiceImpl<Movie>(Movie);
console.log("Movie service initialized: ", movieService);
```

Now we can finally instantiate our controller and provided it with the view and service instances:

```
const mediaManController = new MediaManControllerImpl(view,
bookService, movieService);
```

Finally, because of the way our code is bundled and loaded in the browser using Parcel.js (`https://parceljs.org`), we need to add a global variable on the `Window` object. Without this, our event handlers will not be able to access the `mediaManController` object at runtime:

```
interface CustomWindow extends Window {
    mediaManController?: MediaManController
}

const customWindow: CustomWindow = window;
customWindow.mediaManController = mediaManController;

console.log("MediaMan ready!", customWindow.mediaManController);
```

Take note of how we have added the global variable. Since `Window` is a type included in the standard TypeScript library, you cannot change it easily. This is why we're creating a `CustomWindow` interface, extending from the one provided by TypeScript. In this way, we can properly declare our property. Once done, we assign the `window` object to a constant using our `CustomWindow` type, which allows us to bind the `mediaManController` property to it.

You can learn more about this trick here:
`https://stackoverflow.com/questions/12709074/how-do-you-explicitly-set-a-n ew-property-on-window-in-typescript`.

At this point, you should have a fully functional web application! Go ahead and create some collections/books, then hit the refresh button, and see that your data was not lost thanks to `IndexedDB`!

Summary

In this chapter, we learned about important features in TypeScript. Now that you know about generics and enums, you can write better code and eliminate a lot of duplication in your applications. While building MediaMan, we also had occasion to put those concepts to good use.

Building MediaMan has also allowed us to introduce many other TypeScript features, such as the following:

- Type definitions (typings)
- String literal types
- Union and intersection types
- Decorators
- The `any` special type
- The `keyof` index type query operator
- Mapped types

Since we wanted to build an offline web application, we also learned about standard web APIs such as `LocalStorage`, `SessionStorage`, and `IndexedDB`.

We then explored, in practice, how to leverage these using the open source `localForage` library. While doing so, we also introduced the `Promise` API, which helped us to easily deal with asynchronous operations in a clean manner. We also learned how to serialize and deserialize data using the `class-transformer` library and TypeScript decorators.

Finally, we presented the service layer design pattern and leveraged it to better separate concerns in our application.

At this point in our journey, you may feel that we still lack some important knowledge that is necessary for building larger applications. One big concern with the code of MediaMan is that it is all stored in a single file. This is, of course, far from ideal as it impacts readability and testability. In the next chapter, we will learn about **modules**, which will help us to *modularize* our code and make it easier to read, understand, navigate, and maintain.

Additionally, we haven't tested any of our code so far and it's normal to feel really bad about that! This means that there are probably bugs in our code that we could've detected and fixed. In the next chapter, we will also introduce you to libraries and tools that you can use to test your applications.

5
Coding WorldExplorer to Explore the Population of the World

In this chapter, we will build `WorldExplorer`, a web application that will retrieve and display information about the world population. The data will be obtained through a RESTful web service of the World Bank (`https://datahelpdesk.worldbank.org`). The application will display interactive charts using the Chart.js (`https://www.chartjs.org`) library.

We will introduce you to additional TypeScript concepts such as modules, module resolution, barrels, and some others. Thanks to modules, we will be able to drastically improve the organization of our code, as well as its readability and testability.

In order to get the data, we will use the Fetch (`https://developer.mozilla.org/en-US/docs/Web/API/Fetch_API`) and Promise (`https://developer.mozilla.org/en-US/docs/Web/JavaScript/Reference/Global_Objects/Promise`) APIs included in modern web browsers. We will also learn about `async` and `await` to make our asynchronous code look synchronous.

In this chapter, we are hence covering the following topics:

- Understanding modules
- Loading and bundling modules
- Exploring TypeScript modules
- Introducing module resolution
- Building the `WorldExplorer` application
- World Bank Open Data APIs
- Understanding the Fetch API

- Understanding `async`/`await` and generators
- Implementing the domain model
- Implementing the population service
- High-level design
- Implementing the view layer
- Implementing the controller layer

Understanding modules

Before we dive into code, we need to take a step back and discuss some theories.

We will first take a short detour through the history of JavaScript to better understand what modules are and where they come from, before looking at how they're defined in TypeScript.

Why do we need modules?

Modules are a design pattern used to improve the structure, readability, and testability of code. Many programming languages have some level of support for modules. Of course, TypeScript is one of them!

Modules are incredibly useful; thanks to them, you can do the following:

- Structure code in self-contained **blocks** (just like sections in a document or chapters in a book).
- Encapsulate code (since modules are self-contained).
- Define public APIs: Modules expose what they want to define their interface with the outside world.
- Create isolated namespaces: Modules have their own namespaces and they don't pollute other modules.
- Reuse existing code by loading and using third-party libraries, other modules, and much more.
- Define your dependencies: Explicitly define the list of modules that the current one requires to function.

Code is difficult to organize without the possibility to isolate parts of it in modules. By the way, this was one of the main issues with our `TodoIt` and MediaMan applications.

Note that, without modules, we would have to pollute the global scope a lot more. And, as you should know, **global state is considered evil and needs to be avoided whenever possible!** This reason alone should be enough to convince you to use modules.

In the next subsections, we will explore different types of modules that have been introduced into the JavaScript ecosystem over time and that are still being used today.

A bit of history about JavaScript modules

When JavaScript came out, it didn't provide any support for modularization. There was no specific feature that you could make use of to organize your code in logical groups, expose/hide parts of your code base and define your dependencies.

Given that JavaScript was initially intended to be a glue language rather than a language used to build fully-fledged applications, it wasn't too much of an issue. And of course, when the web was younger, web developers usually didn't do much using JavaScript apart from changing status bar messages, creating small animations, or displaying alert boxes (there were, indeed, exceptions).

Over time, more and more code got written in JavaScript and, of course, the lack of modularity became problematic. At the time, people would isolate their code in different JavaScript files and import them one by one along with their dependencies, hoping to do it in the correct order and with compatible versions.

Code also often defined global variables and it wasn't rare to get into **deadlock** situations where two different libraries wanted to use the same global variable names (for example, the $ global variable name used by jQuery).

The situation was actually worse since dependencies also had to be downloaded manually and loaded separately. Integrating code from different library authors was no fun.

JavaScript developers suffered a lot back then, which of course led to the introduction of clever workarounds (or hacks, as you might prefer to call them).

The Revealing Module pattern

To ease the pain, many developers started using object literals and naming conventions to try and avoid name clashes, but this wasn't so great. Others were more clever and leveraged JavaScript closures with IIFEs (we discussed those in `Chapter 3`, *Improving TodoIt with Classes and Interfaces*; IIFEs are anonymous, immediately invoked, function expressions) to encapsulate/isolate parts of their code and expose only the properties and functions that they wanted to.

This approach became known as the **Revealing Module pattern** (`http://jargon.js.org/_glossary/REVEALING_MODULE_PATTERN.md`). A popular example of this was jQuery, whose plugin system used this approach.

Here's a concrete example of a module using this pattern:

```
var myBooks = (function() {
    var collection = [
        {
            name: "Lord of the rings",
            author: "JRR Tolkien",
            rating: 10
        },
        {
            name: "1984",
            author: "George Orwell",
            rating: 9
        }
    ];
    function getCollection() {
        return collection;
    }
    function favoriteBook() {
        return collection[0];
    }
    function sortBooks() {
        // no-op
    }
    function addBook(book) {
        collection.push(book);
        sortBooks();
    }
    return {
        books: getCollection(),
        addBook: addBook,
        favoriteBook: favoriteBook()
    }
})(); // immediately invoked
```

```
myBooks.addBook({name: "foo", author: "bar"});
console.log(myBooks.books);
console.log("Favorite: ", myBooks.favoriteBook);
```

In this example, the only global variable is `myBooks`. In the `return` statement of its associated function, we define the public API of our module. This allows us to keep some parts private, such as the `sortBooks` function.

 These IIFE-based solutions can be considered basic modules even though they don't rely on a dedicated language keyword.

IIFEs and the Revealing Module pattern were only the first steps toward better code organization and other variations of module definitions were devised over time. Unfortunately, they only solved part of the modularization puzzle. They only helped with the isolation/encapsulation of code, not dealing with dependencies.

The AMD and CommonJS modules

As time went on, library authors joined forces and two de facto standards emerged in the JavaScript community: **Asynchronous Module Definition** (**AMD**) and **CommonJS (CJS)**. Both of these are specifications for module types that also **describe a way to load those modules and their dependencies**.

AMD modules were mainly used by RequireJS (`https://requirejs.org`) and Dojo Toolkit (`https://dojotoolkit.org`) while CJS modules were initially used by Node.js before it created its own derived module specification.

CommonJS modules allow you to export **symbols** (variables, functions, classes, and many more) using the `exports.<symbol>` syntax. Both CommonJS and AMD allow you to load other modules using a `require` function. The specification for `require` differs, but we won't dive into those details here.

The most important difference between AMD and CJS is that **AMD modules are loaded asynchronously while CommonJS ones are loaded synchronously**. CommonJS modules were not created with the web in mind but rather server-side development. However, nowadays, CommonJS has become the most popular format for the web thanks to tools such as Browserify (`http://browserify.org`) and webpack (`https://webpack.js.org`).

UMD modules

Later on, the **Universal Module Definition (UMD)** (`https://github.com/umdjs/umd`) specification was created, aiming to create a bridge between AMD and CJS. The idea of this specification was to create modules capable of being loaded everywhere (that is, on the client and the server-side).

Since both AMD and CommonJS were popular, it was difficult to choose only one and make it *the* official standard. Ultimately, all these specifications provided the JavaScript community with more choice and cleaner ways to modularize code and thus avoid global variables and the script tags nightmare.

Although, there was still no standard solution or official language support for modules at that point, there weren't many tools to ease the pain either, so dependency management was still a very manual, time-intensive, and error-prone task.

ES modules

With ES2015, ECMAScript introduced official language support for modules. Hence, it is now possible to define modules using a standard module format called **ES Modules (ESM)**.

This new standard is very well supported (`https://caniuse.com/#feat=es6-module`) by modern web browsers such as Google Chrome, Mozilla Firefox, Microsoft Edge, Safari, and Opera. Thanks to that support, it is now possible to load standard modules in the browser using the following syntax: `<script type="module">`. At the time of writing, support for ES modules is still experimental in Node.js: `https://nodejs.org/api/esm.html`.

ESM uses the `import` and `export` reserved keywords. Using the `export` keyword in a module allows you to make the corresponding symbol (that is, `var`, `let`, `const`, `function`, `class`, and many others) accessible from outside of your module. On the other hand, the `import` keyword allows you to *bind* (one or more) symbols from another module for use in the current one.

With ESM, imports and exports and defined per file. Each file is considered to be a module as soon as it imports or exports symbols.

Here's a simple example:

```
const myPrivateKey = "Secret";
export const myPublicKey = "Public";

// exported function
export function bar(message) {
    say(message);
}

// private function
function say(message) {
    console.log(message);
}
```

This first file is a module stored in a `my-utils-module.mjs` file. As you can see, it only exports a part of its definitions; for example, the `say` function and `myPrivateKey` constant are not exported and, thus, they will not be visible or accessible from the outside.

 The `.mjs` file extension is used to clearly indicate that the file contains an ES module. This extension is also supported by Node.js: `https://nodejs.org/api/esm.html`.

Importing the exported symbols from other modules is also easy:

```
import {bar, myPublicKey} from "./my-utils-module";

console.log("Public key: ", myPublicKey);
bar("foo!");
```

As you can see, we simply use the `import` keyword and put the list of symbols that we want to import within brackets.

 We don't need to specify the file extension when importing!

If you execute this code using Node.js, you'll see that we do indeed have access to what we have imported:

```
$ node my-module.js
Public key:  Public
foo!
```

It is also possible to import everything from a module using the `import * as newName from ...` syntax:

```
import * as utils from "./my-utils-module";

console.log("Public key: ", utils.myPublicKey);
utils.bar("foo!");
```

In this example, we have specified a relative path to the module, but it is also possible to use a URL. In the future, it will probably also be possible to use simple names such as `jquery`. Take a look at the following link if you're curious about this: `https://github.com/domenic/import-maps`.

The `import` and `export` statements must be located at the top level of the files. For example, it is forbidden to use them in an `if` block. Imports are hoisted (that is, moved to the top), so it doesn't matter if you put them at the end of a file, even though it is recommended to put them at the top for clarity and readability.

ESM actually supports two kinds of exports: `named` and `default`. You must use `named` exports when you want to export multiple symbols in a single module. When you only want to export one symbol, you can use the `export default ...` syntax instead.

Default exports can be imported using any name; you can choose the name to use when you import the module.

One big advantage of **ES modules** over CommonJS ones is that they **can be statically analyzed**, which means that tooling can eliminate dead code (that is, code that is known not to be used). This process is also known as **tree shaking**.

Files that contain at least one top-level import or export are considered as modules; otherwise, they're considered as scripts. The distinction is important because all modules are executed in strict mode (among other differences).

Yet another module specification worth mentioning here is `System.register`—also called `System` (`https://github.com/systemjs/systemjs/blob/mas ter/docs/system-register.md`). It was created to add support for ES2015 modules in ES5. But, as we'll see later on, there are other options to be able to work with modules in ES5.

There is actually a lot more to know but we cannot go further here. Check the *Further reading* section if you want to delve deeper.

Loading and bundling modules

As we've just seen, there are now quite a few module specifications. Not all of them can be loaded natively, depending on the target environment. Also, within a single application, you might have dependencies using different module types and this isn't easy to handle without getting into trouble.

Currently, to make this possible, we often need to use tools. There are two categories of tools that we should briefly discuss: module loaders and bundlers.

Module loaders

Module loaders take care of loading modules at runtime. Different loaders support different combinations of module formats. They are useful as soon as your target environment cannot load all the modules that you intend to make use of (for example, if you want to load AMD modules in a web browser).

However, bundlers provide a much more powerful and interesting alternative, as we'll see shortly!

Here are a few examples of module loaders:

- SystemJS: `https://github.com/systemjs/systemjs`
- jspm.io: `https://jspm.io`
- StealJS: `https://stealjs.com`
- RequireJS: `https://requirejs.org`

Bundlers

Bundlers take care of bundling or *grouping* assets together, including modules at build time. The main responsibility of bundlers is to understand the dependency graph of your code (whether that means links in an HTML file, imports in ES2015, or TypeScript code) and to bundle/group everything together.

That is the basis of all bundlers, but some of them can actually do a whole lot more:

- **Tree shaking**: Removing unused/dead code (also known as **dead code elimination**)
- **Splitting code**: Splitting your code into different bundles that you can load lazily (that is, on demand/when needed)
- **Transpiling code** (for example, TypeScript to JavaScript)
- **Inlining different types of resources** (for example, HTML, CSS, JSON, images, and many others)
- **Minification and uglification**: Compressing the code for production
- **Processing CSS** (for example, using SASS, Less, PostCSS, and many others)
- **Processing other types of resources**
- **Linting code**: Checking the code quality
- **Testing code**: Executing tests automatically
- **Generating source maps**
- **Copying and transforming assets**: Copying images, fonts, and much more and transforming them if needed (for example, compressing images)
- **Handling cache busting**: Adding suffixes to generated files (for example, hashes) to avoid caching issues
- **Running development web servers with hot reloading**: Just like browser-sync, which we used for `TodoIt`
- **Providing Hot Module Replacement (HMR) during development**: Automatically updating modules at runtime when code changes, without needed a full page refresh. You can learn more about HMR here: `https://parceljs.org/hmr.html`.

And this list could go on and on.

Here are a few examples of bundlers:

- Webpack: `https://webpack.js.org`
- Parcel: `https://parceljs.org`
- Rollup: `https://rollupjs.org/guide/en`
- StealJS: `https://stealjs.com`
- FuseBox: `https://fuse-box.org`
- Babel: `https://babeljs.io`
- Browserify: `http://browserify.org`

Webpack is one of the most popular bundlers at the moment. It has a vast ecosystem of plugins (`https://webpack.js.org/plugins`) and loaders (`https://webpack.js.org/loaders`), giving it an impressive feature set.

 You might not have realized it until now, but, in Chapter 4, *Leveraging Generics and Enums to Build a Media Management Web Application*, we already used the Parcel bundler! Thanks to that, we could directly link our `mediaman.ts` file in the HTML. Parcel took care of the whole of the processing for us, including the transpilation and bundling of our TypeScript code and the processing of the HTML/CSS files.

The key takeaway message here is that module bundlers are very important tools in today's JavaScript ecosystem. As platforms evolve (whether we consider the client/web or server side), some of their features get standardized/integrated. However, this standardization process takes time. So, for the time being, using bundlers has great benefits.

Exploring TypeScript modules

Now that we have a shared understanding of what modules are in the JavaScript ecosystem, we can take a look at what TypeScript offers.

Export and import syntax

As we have seen, since ES2015 was released, modules have been a part of the specification. Given that TypeScript is a superset of JavaScript, it, of course, supports them as well and uses the same keywords: `export` and `import`.

As with ESM, TypeScript modules have their own scope and thus they don't pollute the global scope. Unless you export a symbol, it remains internal to the module and is not visible to the outside world.

You'll certainly appreciate the similarity of this TypeScript example to the previous ESM one:

```
// my-utils-module.ts
const myPrivateKey: string = "Secret";
export const myPublicKey: string = "Public";

export enum MessageType {
```

```
        INFORMATION,
        WARNING,
        ERROR,
        DEBUG
    }

    // exported interface
    export interface Message {
        content: string;
        type: MessageType;
    }

    // private function
    function logToConsole(message: Message): void {
        switch (message.type) {
            case MessageType.INFORMATION:
                console.log(message.content);
            ...
            default:
                console.error(message.content);
        }
        console.log(message);
    }

    // exported function
    export function log(message: Message): void {
        logToConsole(message);
    }
```

Importing works in the same way too:

```
    // my-module.ts
    import {log, Message, MessageType, myPublicKey} from "./my-utils-
    module";

    console.log("Public key: ", myPublicKey);

    const infoMessage: Message = {
        content: "Hello world",
        type: MessageType.INFORMATION
    };

    const errorMessage: Message = {
        content: "Oopsie doopsie",
        type: MessageType.ERROR
    };
    log(infoMessage);
    log(errorMessage);
```

As demonstrated in the preceding example, we can not only export/import interfaces, but also classes, `var`/`let`/`const`, `type` aliases, and other symbols!

> It is possible to rename symbols when importing them using the following syntax: `import { Foo as Bar } from ....`

Just like with ES2015, you can also use `import * as newName from...` to import everything from a module and give it a name of your choice.

Finally, by setting the `esModuleInterop` option to `true` in `tsconfig.json`, it is also possible to import CommonJS modules using the `import foo from "someCommonJsModule";` syntax, which is compliant with the ECMAScript specifications.

Before TypeScript 2.7, such an import needed to be written like this instead: `import * as foo from "someCommonJsModule";`. The `esModuleInterop` setting is enabled automatically for new TypeScript 3+ projects.

You can learn more about this here:
`https://itnext.io/great-import-schism-typescript-confusion-around-imports-explained-d512fc6769c2`.

Export statements

In the previous example, we showed that the `export` keyword can be used inline to export a symbol. It is also possible to use `export` statements to export one or more symbols.

This can be useful to rename things, as shown:

```
interface Thing {
    name: string
}
// 1
export {
    Thing
}
// 2
export {
    Thing as RenamedThing
}
```

The first `export` simply exports the symbol with its original name, while the second one exports it under a different name, using the `as` keyword.

Also, just like with ES modules, each module can have a default export using the `export default foo` syntax. This is recommended by the TypeScript team if you only export one symbol, as it makes it easier on the consumer side.

Finally, in a module, it is possible to export a single object, as it is possible to do with both CommonJS and UMD. This is done using the `export = ...` syntax.

Here's an example:

```
function sayHi(message: string): void {
    console.log(message);
}

export = sayHi;
```

Given that we have exported the `sayHi` function with `export =`, it has to be imported using `import someName = require("moduleName");`. Here's how it looks for our example:

```
import sayHi = require("./single-export");

sayHi("foo");
```

This is not a recommended approach though. On the export side, you should only use this import style when you are forced to (that is when it is the only way to import some symbols from a module).

Re-exports and barrels

It is also possible to re-export symbols exported by other modules:

```
// my-module-with-reexports.ts
export {log, Message, MessageType} from "./my-utils-module";
```

In the preceding example, we did nothing in the module apart from re-exporting the symbols of another module. This is particularly useful when defining public APIs for parts of your applications.

Finally, it is also possible to re-export everything from a module using the following syntax: `export * from ....`

Barrels

Barrels are a technique used to **roll up** exports from different modules into a single one, usually called `index.ts`, to simplify the imports. Barrels thus simply combine the exports of one or more other modules. By making use of the re-export functionality, you can actually create barrels.

For example, if you create a library, then it is useful to expose a single module exposing the public API to the outside world. As a consumer, barrels are useful because they let you concentrate on what you want to use and not on where symbols are located.

Here's an example of a barrel in the Angular framework:
`https://github.com/angular/angular/blob/master/packages/core/src/core.ts`.
This barrel is re-exported by
`https://github.com/angular/angular/blob/master/packages/core/public_api.ts`
, which is itself re-exported one level above:
`https://github.com/angular/angular/blob/master/packages/core/index.ts`. This
allows developers to simply use the following to import symbols from Angular:
`import { ... } from "@angular/core";`.

 As an added benefit, if the library maintainers decide to move things around, then it won't impact the developers if they rely on the barrels and those continue to exist!

Barrels have one drawback: they make it easier to introduce circular dependencies in your projects, which are annoying to resolve. For this reason, barrels should not be overused; that is, not every folder should contain a barrel. On the contrary, barrels can be used tactically, for example, to ease the imports of a specific type of element (for example, all services in a module of the application). If you're in doubt, then check out the following
article: `https://medium.com/@adrianfaciu/barrel-files-to-use-or-not-to-use-75521cd18e65`.

You can learn more about barrels here:

- `https://basarat.gitbooks.io/typescript/docs/tips/barrel.html`
- `https://medium.com/@adrianfaciu/barrel-files-to-use-or-not-to-use-75521cd18e65`

Bonus: Leveraging modules in MediaMan

Just by knowing this much about how modules work in TypeScript, you can certainly already imagine how we could revisit and improve the structure of our `TodoIt` application. We could place each concept in its own file; for example:

- `mediaman-controller.intf.ts`
- `mediaman-controller-impl.ts`
- `mediaman-view.intf.ts`

This would immediately make our code much easier to read and navigate. As an added benefit, it would also make the dependencies between parts of the system much clearer.

Why don't you go ahead and give it a try?

Ambient modules

Ambient modules are modules defined as part of type definitions in order to provide information to TypeScript.

The `declare module "name"` syntax is used to define the name of the module that can be imported for those libraries (for example, `localForage`, which we used in Chapter 4, *Leveraging Generics and Enums to Build a Media Management Web Application*).

Here's a simple example:

```
// my-module-with-reexports.ts
export {log, Message, MessageType} from "./my-utils-module";
```

As a second example, here's how the `localForage` module is declared by its typings:

```
declare module "localforage" {
    let localforage: LocalForage;
    export = localforage;
}
```

When TypeScript finds those type declarations, it knows that you can import that module by its name. We'll learn a bit more about module resolution soon.

Type definitions are called **ambient** because they don't define an implementation; they just provide information about the API that will be loaded and available at runtime. So, actually, when you create type definitions, you make a sort of promise to the compiler, assuring it that the things you define will actually be present at runtime, with the shape that you've described.

Configuring module transpilation

Now we can discuss another great feature of TypeScript. As you know, at its heart, TypeScript is a transpiler that can do wonders with your code and can make it compatible with older runtime environments, even if you're using the newest ECMAScript features.

TypeScript can actually transpile your modules into different module types, depending on the compiler's configuration. By default, TypeScript generates CommonJS modules, but it also supports the following:

- AMD
- System
- UMD
- ESM
- ESNext: Future ES versions

You can modify the type of modules that you want your code to be transpiled to using the `module` option.

Advanced concepts

There are other more advanced features, such as **optional module loading, single-object export**, but we won't cover those in this book. Check out the official documentation if you want to dive deeper: `https://www.typescriptlang.org/docs/handbook/modules.html`.

Namespaces

Namespaces are another way to isolate elements in your TypeScript applications. Using the `namespace` keyword, you can define an isolated namespace to avoid name clashes.

In practice, **we don't recommend using namespaces**, which is why we won't cover them in any more detail here. Modules provide everything you need to properly isolate code. Modules are more interesting since they declare their dependencies, which allows bundlers to remove unused code.

At the end of the day, modules win in terms of isolation, code reuse, and tooling support. This is true for both web and server-side applications. Also, remember that modules are supported natively from ES2015 onward.

 One case where namespaces are very useful is when you are creating type definitions for JavaScript libraries.

There is one more point that we need to address before we start developing our new application together: How does TypeScript resolve imports?

Introducing module resolution

Module resolution is the process used to find the **definitions** of the modules that you want to use. Without module resolution, TypeScript wouldn't be able to provide you with useful suggestions regarding what can be imported and what can't. Also, it wouldn't be able to perform type checking for the code using those modules.

 Module loaders and bundlers (for example, `webpack`: `https://webpack.js.org/concepts/module-resolution`) also perform module resolution, but be careful not to mix that process with what we will describe here, as it is specific to how TypeScript works, even if the ideas are closely related.

Let's look at resolution strategies.

Resolution strategies

TypeScript has two built-in strategies for resolving modules: **classic** and **node**. The default is node, which corresponds to the Node.js style (`https://nodejs.org/api/modules.html`). You can change the default strategy through the `moduleResolution` compiler flag.

As its name suggests, the *node* strategy takes inspiration from the mechanism used by Node.js to resolve modules at runtime. It is described here:
`https://nodejs.org/api/modules.html`.

> We'll spare you the explanation of the *classic* mode as it not used much nowadays, apart from for backward compatibility.

Let's now look at relative imports.

Resolving relative imports

In most of our examples so far, we have used **relative imports** using relative paths (that is, `/`, `./`, and `../`) to indicate the location of the modules to load. The resolution of relative imports is straightforward: it is done based on the location of the importing file.

> You should generally use relative import paths only for your own code.

Next up are non-relative imports.

Resolving non-relative imports

It is also possible to import symbols from a module by giving a name instead of a relative path, as we saw in the Angular example before (`import { ... } from "@angular/core"`), and also in `Chapter 4`, *Leveraging Generics and Enums to Build a Media Management Web Application*, with `localForage`.

How does TypeScript know what to load when a module name is used? This question is important and certainly not trivial, so let's take some time to go through this. Understanding this process will allow you to avoid seeing module resolution as some kind of magical process.

If you import `import {foo} from "bar"` and if the **node** strategy is used by the compiler, then TypeScript will try to locate the `bar` module in folders called `node_modules`, starting from the current folder and going up folder by folder until it finds the module or reaches the root of the filesystem.

TypeScript will not only look for `.ts` files, but also for `.d.ts`, `.tsx`, and `package.json` files. If it finds a `package.json` file, then it will check whether it contains a `types` property pointing to a typings file (that is, ambient definitions). If TypeScript can't find any of those, it'll try looking for *index* files (that is, barrels) before moving on to the next folder.

Here is an overview of the lookup process for the `bar` module, assuming that you try to import it from a file located in `/projectRoot/src/`:

1. Does `/projectRoot/src/node_modules/bar.ts` exist?
2. Does `/projectRoot/src/node_modules/bar.tsx` exist?
3. Does `/projectRoot/src/node_modules/bar.d.ts` exist?
4. Does `/projectRoot/src/node_modules/bar/package.json` exist? Does it contain a `types` property?
5. Does `/projectRoot/src/node_modules/bar/index.ts` exist?
6. Does `/projectRoot/src/node_modules/bar/index.tsx` exist?
7. Does `/projectRoot/src/node_modules/bar/index.d.ts` exist?

At this point, if the module has not been found yet, the same process is repeated with the parent folder:

1. Does `/projectRoot/node_modules/bar.ts` exist?
2. Does `/projectRoot/node_modules/bar.tsx` exist?
3. Does `/projectRoot/node_modules/bar.d.ts` exist?
4. Does `/projectRoot/node_modules/bar/package.json` exist? Does it contain a `types` property?
5. Does `/projectRoot/node_modules/bar/index.ts` exist?
6. Does `/projectRoot/node_modules/bar/index.tsx` exist?
7. Does `/projectRoot/node_modules/bar/index.d.ts` exist?

The process goes on, level by level until the module is found or the root level is reached. At that point, if the module could not be found, then TypeScript will bail out.

Configuring module resolution

Build processes can be quite complex. TypeScript provides multiple compiler options that you can use to configure the module resolution process and adapt it to your project needs.

The first setting that you can use is `baseUrl`. It tells the compiler where to look for modules. **All non-relative module imports will be searched relative to** `baseUrl`.

Another useful setting is called `paths`. It allows you to configure path mappings. Such mappings can be used to override the module resolution process for a given name or pattern (including wildcards).

Check out the following article if you want to know more about path mappings: `https://netbasal.com/sexier-imports-in-typescript-e3c645bdd3c6`.

 Paths are resolved relative to the base path defined using the `baseUrl` property in `tsconfig.json`.

A final useful option is called `rootDirs`, which allows you to list all the directories that contain sources to include so that TypeScript treats them as a single logical unit. Also, `rootDirs` impacts module resolution since all directories listed there will be searched when a relative import needs to be resolved.

 You can trace module resolution using the `--traceResolution` compiler flag. This will always come in handy!

You can find all the details about those options here: `https://www.typescriptlang.org/docs/handbook/module-resolution.html`.

What will you build?

We are going to build the `WorldExplorer` application together.

Our application will make calls to a RESTful API to retrieve information about the world population. We'll then generate interactive charts to visualize the data.

To generate/render the charts, we will use the Chart.js (`https://www.chartjs.org`) library.

To make the API calls to the web service, we will use the Fetch API, yet another standard API available in modern runtime environments. Also, we will discover what hides behind the `async` and `await` keywords.

Since we have learned about modules in this chapter, we will leverage them to improve the structure of our application.

Finally, to further increase the readability and navigability of the code, we will organize it based on the logical layers (for example, services, domain, views, controllers, and many others). To do so, we'll create a folder per layer. These can also be called **packages**.

 In larger applications, it is beneficial to organize code around feature blocks instead, where all the code related to a specific set of features is grouped together.

Bonus: REST, RESTful and web APIs

Before we talk about the API that we are going to use, we'll very briefly review the main ideas behind the RESTful approach. Entire books are dedicated to this architectural style, but we will try to convey the essence of what it is in a few paragraphs. So, please, bear with us!

REpresentational State Transfer (REST) is an **architectural style for designing web services**, which is heavily centered on the notion of *resources* that is core to the **World Wide Web (WWW)**. The REST architectural style was defined by Roy Fielding in his Ph.D. dissertation (`https://www.ics.uci.edu/~fielding/pubs/dissertation/top.htm`). Interestingly, Mr. Fielding is also one of the main authors of the HTTP specifications.

The main goals of REST are to create **loosely coupled**, **scalable**, and **efficient** applications with simple, consistent, flexible, and easy-to-use interfaces.

To realize these goals, REST defines a set of principles and constraints:

- Client-server: Clients and servers are isolated.
- Stateless: The web service doesn't keep track of its client and each request contains all the information needed.
- Cacheable: Devices between the client and server can cache responses and there is a mechanism to control caching.
- Layered infrastructure: Devices can be placed between the client and server to improve scalability, provide load balancing, and so on.
- Clients and servers communicate through a **uniform interface:**
    - Individual resources are identified in requests (for example, using URIs with HTTP).
    - Every element in the API has an identifier (for example, each specific resource instance).
    - Resources are separated from the representations that are returned to the client: for example, the server may send data from its data store as JSON or XML, none of which is necessarily the internal representation on the server-side.
    - Resources are manipulated through their *representation*: clients get a representation of specific resources, manipulate those, and then send them back (either partially or fully) to the server so that their changes can be persisted. Those interactions are done via HTTP calls using specific HTTP methods such as PUT or POST and are sent to specific URLs.
- **Hypermedia as the Engine of Application State (HATEOAS)**.
- Resource representations come along with hyperlinks, making it easy for clients to identify possible actions.
- Clients should not assume that any particular action is available for any particular resource.

These are the main constraints that a REST API must adhere to. An API that does not respect all of these constraints is not a truly RESTful API, but rather a web API or REST-like API.

An important point to keep in mind, though, is that **REST is NOT a standard**. As a matter of fact, there are probably as many different variants of REST APIs as there are APIs. We won't enter into this debate here though; for the rest of this book, we'll talk about REST, RESTful, and web APIs interchangeably (apologies to the purists).

 RESTful APIs usually rely on the HTTP protocol and they try to make the best use of it. For the rest of our explanation, we'll assume HTTP-based REST APIs.

Resources are concrete, high-level concepts (for example, cars, employees, bills) using nouns and lower/kebab case (for example, `/api/v1/current-deals`). Each resource is associated with a specific URL (for example, `/api/v1/cars`). If you know how to access one resource type, then accessing another should be easy if the uniformity constraint is respected (for example, `/api/v1/employees`).

The plural form is used because, usually, resources are collections. For example, we could retrieve the first car in the preceding example at the following URL: `/v1/cars/1`.

Depending on the considered APIs and domain models, resources can have links to other resources and can have subresources, actions, and so on. For example, assuming that **cars** have passengers, we could retrieve those passengers via a call to `/api/v1/cars/1/passengers`. Again, in this case, **passengers** would be a collection.

URIs have the following structure: `URI = scheme "://" authority "/" path [ "? query ] [ "#" fragment ]`

Here's an example:
`https://www.foo.bar/hello-world?param1=value1&param2=value2#section1`

Here are the most important parts of URLs:

- Protocol/scheme: `https://`
- Subdomain: `www`
- Domain: `foo.bar`
- Path: `/hello-world`
- Query string: `?param1=value1`

- Query parameters (key-value pairs):
  - param1: `value1`
  - param2: `value2`
  - Separator: `&`
- Fragment: `section1`

In addition, here are some points to be aware of regarding resource URLs:

- The query string is used to pass options (for example, paging, filtering, sorting, fields to retrieve or exclude, and many more).
- The body is used for actual contents (for example, complex search criteria).

To manipulate resources, RESTful APIs make use of the different HTTP methods/verbs:

- `GET`: Retrieves resource representations. This operation is safe, idempotent, and cacheable.
- `HEAD`: Retrieves headers (no body in the response). This operation is safe, idempotent, and cacheable.
- `POST`: Creates or partially updates resources. This operation is not safe, nor idempotent.
- `PATCH`: Update existing resources by patching them. This operation is not safe, nor idempotent.
- `DELETE`: Deletes resources. This operation is not safe, but idempotent.
- `OPTIONS`: Gets the allowed options for the target resource. This operation is safe and idempotent.
- `PUT`: Fully updates a resource. This operation is not safe, but idempotent.

Usually, RESTful APIs expose data as JSON, less often so as XML, and sometimes even both (for example, using parameters to select the format).

HTTP status codes are used to indicate the result of the different operations. There are only a few categories:

- 2xx codes: Success; everything worked.
- 3xx codes: Redirection; no problem occurred, but further actions are required by the client.
- 4xx codes: Client error; the client did something wrong.
- 5xx codes: Server error; the server had a problem.

There are many HTTP status codes, so we can't go through them all. Still, here are a few important ones to know about:

- 200 (OK): Returned when a retrieval/update operation succeeds.
- 201 (Created): Returned after a successful `POST` creation request.
- 202 (Accepted): Returned when a request has been accepted for processing, but the processing has not completed yet.
- 204 (No content): Returned after a deletion, to indicate that it has succeeded, but that no content is being returned.
- 301 (Moved permanently): Returned when a resource has moved permanently and should be accessed through a different URI.
- 400 (Bad request): The server rejected the request (not understood, not compliant). The request must be modified by the client.
- 401 (Unauthorized): The server rejected the request because the user is not authenticated.
- 403 (Forbidden): The server rejected the request because the user is not authorized/allowed to perform the operation.
- 404 (Not found): The server did not find the requested resource.
- 500 (Internal server error): The server encountered an internal issue.

Finally, RESTful APIs also rely a lot on standard HTTP headers (for example, `Accept`, `Content-Type`, `Encoding`, `Cache-Control`, `ETag`, and many more).

There is really a lot more to know about REST APIs, but we'll stop here as it should be just about enough for our purposes.

World Bank Open Data APIs

We will use the freely available data offered by the World Bank Group as part of their open data initiative (`https://data.worldbank.org`). The World Bank provides many APIs (`http://databank.worldbank.org/data/Databases.aspx`) that can be used to access information about many subjects, such as countries, economic growth, education, environment, energy, population (which we will use), and many more!

You can find out more about those APIs here:
`https://datahelpdesk.worldbank.org/knowledgebase/articles/889386-developer -information-overview`.

Country information

Here is the URL for this API:

`https://api.worldbank.org/v2/countries?format=json.`

With this request, we can get the following:

- Countries
- Regions
- Capitals and their coordinates (latitude and longitude)
- Income levels

Here's an example response:

```
[
    {
        "page":1,
        "pages":7,
        "per_page":"50",
        "total":304
    },
    [
        {
            "id":"AFG",
            "iso2Code":"AF",
            "name":"Afghanistan",
            "region":{
                "id":"SAS",
                "iso2code":"8S",
                "value":"South Asia"
            },
            "incomeLevel":{
                "id":"LIC",
                "iso2code":"XM",
                "value":"Low income"
            },
            "capitalCity":"Kabul",
            "longitude":"69.1761",
            "latitude":"34.5228"
            ...
        }
        ...
    ]
]
```

Notice that the response contains an array with two objects. The first one contains **metadata** about the response such as the current page, the total number of pages, and much more. The second one contains the actual data.

It is also possible to retrieve information about a specific country directly by adding the country's ID to the URL:
`https://api.worldbank.org/v2/countries/be?format=json`. In this case, we'll retrieve information about Belgium (that is, `id: BE`).

Indicators

The Indicators API
(`https://datatopics.worldbank.org/world-development-indicators`) is one of the most interesting ones as it exposes data about hundreds of different indicators. With our project, we'll explore just a tiny fraction of the data accessible through these.

You can find the list of indicators here:

- Featured: `https://data.worldbank.org/indicator?tab=featured`
- Complete list: `https://data.worldbank.org/indicator?tab=all`

The basic call structure is
`http://api.worldbank.org/v2/countries/COUNTRIES/indicators/INDICATOR_NAME?PARAMS`:

- COUNTRIES: Can be a specific country ID (for example, `be`), all countries (that is, `all`), or a set of countries, separated by `;` (for example, `be;fr`):
    - Here's an example for France and Belgium: `https://api.worldbank.org/v2/countries/fr;be/indicators/DPANUSSPB?date=2012M01`
- INDICATOR_NAME: Can be one of the hundreds of indicators (we'll discover some in the next section).
- PARAMS: Different parameters can be passed through the query string (that is, after the `?` in the URL):
    - Date: `?date=2018`
    - Date range: `?date=2000:2010`
    - Year-to-date to get all the data since a given point in time: `?date=YTD:2015`
    - Format to select the output format: `?format=json` (or `xml`)

- Download format: `?downloadformat=csv` (or `xml` or `excel`)
- Page to retrieve: `?page=2`
- Items per page: `?per_page=25`

There are actually more options but we'll stop there.

You can find more details about this API here:

- `https://datahelpdesk.worldbank.org/knowledgebase/articles/898599-indicator-api-queries`
- `https://datahelpdesk.worldbank.org/knowledgebase/articles/898581-basic-api-call-structures`

Let's now discover some interesting queries that we could use in our application.

Population information

Given a country code, we can easily gather a lot of information about its population, using indicators such as the following:

- `SP.POP.TOTL`: Total population (`https://api.worldbank.org/v2/countries/BE/indicators/SP.POP.TOTL?per_page=100format=jsondate=2000:2018`)
- `SP.POP.TOTL.MA.IN`: Male population (`https://api.worldbank.org/v2/countries/BE/indicators/SP.POP.TOTL.MA.IN?per_page=100format=jsondate=2000:2018`)
- `SP.POP.TOTL.FE.IN`: Female population (`https://api.worldbank.org/v2/countries/BE/indicators/SP.POP.TOTL.FE.IN?per_page=100format=jsondate=2000:2018`)
- `SP.DYN.LE00.IN`: Life expectancy (`https://api.worldbank.org/v2/countries/BE/indicators/SP.DYN.LE00.IN?per_page=100format=jsondate=2000:2018`)
- `SP.DYN.TO65.FE.ZS`: Survival to age 65, female (`https://api.worldbank.org/v2/countries/BE/indicators/SP.DYN.TO65.FE.ZS?per_page=100format=jsondate=2000:2018`)
- `SP.DYN.TO65.MA.ZS`: Survival to age 65, male (`https://api.worldbank.org/v2/countries/BE/indicators/SP.DYN.TO65.MA.ZS?per_page=100format=jsondate=2000:2018`)

In the preceding examples, we've retrieved the available data points for Belgium between 2000 and 2018. As we saw in the previous section, there are actually many more indicators, but we'll play with only a few.

Understanding the Fetch API

In order to call the RESTful API, we will use the Fetch API (`https://developer.mozilla.org/en-US/docs/Web/API/Fetch_API`). It is a standard API of the web, supported by most modern browsers. Fetch defines an interface for fetching resources across the network that is similar to the one of `XMLHttpRequest` (also known as **XHR**):
`https://developer.mozilla.org/en-US/docs/Web/API/XMLHttpRequest`.

Fetch has a couple of main concepts:

- `Request` (`https://developer.mozilla.org/en-US/docs/Web/API/Request`) represents a request for a resource.
- `Response` (`https://developer.mozilla.org/en-US/docs/Web/API/Response`) represents the response and its metadata.

We can configure the request as needed, for example, by adding credentials, defining the HTTP method (for example, `GET`, `POST`, and many others), adding HTTP headers (for example, `Content-Type`), adding a body, and more.

On the other hand, we can extract information from the response object, such as the following:

- The HTTP headers
- The HTTP status code/text
- The response body

Here's a basic example of how to use Fetch with TypeScript:

```
const responsePromise: Promise<Response> =
    fetch('https://api.worldbank.org/v2/countries?format=json');

responsePromise
    .then((response: Response) => {
        if (response.status !== 200) {
            console.warn('Unexpected response status: ',
                response.statusText);
```

```
        return;
    }

    response.json()
        .then((jsonContent: unknown) => {
            console.log("Response content: ", jsonContent);
        }).catch((error: unknown) => {
            console.error("Failed to parse the response body as JSON:
            ", error);
        });
})

.catch((error: unknown) => {
    console.error("An error occurred while fetching the data: ",
    error);
});
```

Let's go through the code together. The `fetch` function takes the resource URL as a parameter and returns `Promise<Response>`. As we saw in Chapter 4, *Leveraging Generics and Enums to Build a Media Management Web Application,* handling promises is done using the callback functions passed to the `then` and `error` functions.

In the `then` callback function, we receive a `Response` object that we can use to check the HTTP status code of the response. Once we are sure that there was no problem with our request, we call the `json()` (`https://developer.mozilla.org/en-US/docs/Web/API/Body/json`) function. This function reads the whole response before returning `Promise`. The returned promise will later yield the body content, parsed as JSON. At that point, we can process the information.

Notice that we have also implemented the `.catch` callbacks in order to handle errors gracefully.

For the preceding code to work, you need to add the following entries to the `lib` setting of your `tsconfig.json` file:

- `es2015`: Makes the `Promise` API available for use.
- `dom`: Makes the `Request` and `Response` interfaces available for use.

You should only configure the above if you're sure that those APIs will be available at runtime. If you want to support legacy web browsers such as Internet Explorer 11, then you should also add/load the necessary polyfills to your application. For instance, you can use the following polyfill: `whatwg-fetch` (`https://www.npmjs.com/package/whatwg-fetch`). It is also possible to use the Fetch API with Node.js using this library: `https://www.npmjs.com/package/node-fetch`.

Finally, if you want to use another HTTP method (for example, `POST`), define headers, and so on, then you can use the following form to invoke `fetch`:

```
fetch('foo', {
    method: 'POST',
    headers: new Headers({
        'Content-Type': 'application/json',
        ...
    }),
    body: '{ foo: "bar" }',
    ...
});
```

The additional `options` object allows you to have full control over the call.

Let's move on.

Using the unknown keyword

Did you notice the `unknown` keyword used in the Fetch API example? Here's the code we are referring to: `.then((jsonContent: unknown) >= ....`

The `unknown` keyword was introduced with TypeScript 3.0. It is a type safe alternative to the `any` keyword that we have used so far in this book. With this keyword, we simply tell TypeScript that the type of the `jsonContent` object is not known at this point and that it should be checked before being manipulated. Basically, it means that the content should not be trusted and considered safe to use as is.

Anything can be assigned to a variable with the `unknown` type, but not the other way around. You cannot assign an object of type `unknown` to anything but itself and `any` unless you perform type checks to assert the type. Also, no operations can be applied to an `unknown` object without first performing type assertions.

Using `unknown` is heavily recommended over `any` when you want to **clearly convey that some type checks must be performed before doing anything else**. Using `any` doesn't enforce further type checks and thus, `unknown` is a safer option.

You can learn more and find many examples in the release notes of TypeScript 3.0: `https://www.typescriptlang.org/docs/handbook/release-notes/typescript-3-0.html#new-unknown-top-type`.

Chaining promises

One thing that we haven't touched on so far, which is interesting to consider, is the fact that **promises can be chained**. This is especially useful to avoid code duplication.

In our Fetch example, we have called an API, checked the status code, retrieved the body and parsed it as JSON. Here's another way to implement the same functionality but in a more reusable manner:

```typescript
function checkResponseStatus(response: Response): Promise<Response> {
    if (response.status >= 200 && response.status < 300) {
        return Promise.resolve(response);
    } else {
        return Promise.reject(new Error(response.statusText));
    }
}

function toJSON(response: Response): Promise<Response> {
    return response.json();
}

const responsePromise: Promise<Response> =
    fetch('https://api.worldbank.org/v2/countries?format=json');
    responsePromise
    .then(checkResponseStatus)
    .then(toJSON)
    .then((jsonContent: unknown) => {
        console.log("Response content: ", jsonContent);
    })
    .catch((error: unknown) => {
        console.error("An error occurred while fetching the data: ",
        error);
    });
```

This time, we've defined a function whose sole responsibility is to check whether the given response has a valid status; it uses the `Promise.resolve(...)` and `Promise.reject(...)` functions to return a promise and a result.

It is possible to wait for a set of promises to complete/resolve using `Promise.all(...)`.

We've also defined a simple function taking care of the `.json()` call, which also returns a promise. Our code handling the `Promise` response is now more concise and much clearer. Also, the functions that we have defined can be reused!

You can define a function that will be invoked whether a promise succeeds or fails using `.finally(() => { ... });`. This is now well supported by modern runtime environments. To be able to use this with TypeScript, you need to add `es2018.promise` to the `lib` array in `tsconfig.json`, as explained here: `https://blog.mariusschulz.com/2018/11/27/using-promise-finally-in-typescript`.

Chaining promises is really useful and will make your life easier. But we can do even better by leveraging `async` and `await`. Let's look at those next.

Understanding async/await and generators

While chaining promises helps to create cleaner and more readable code, there is actually still room for improvement. Let's learn about the `async` and `await` keywords!

Asynchronous code that looks synchronous

Since ES2015, ECMAScript has supported the creation of asynchronous functions. Asynchronous functions are marked as such using the `async` keyword and can be written as if they were synchronous. They make asynchronous code simpler to read and easier to reason about.

On the other hand, callers of asynchronous functions can *wait* for the result(s) of the calls instead of relying on separate event handlers and callback functions.

Async/await leverages promises and **generators** to avoid blocking your code while asynchronous operations are ongoing.

 Generators are special function types that return a generator object that implements the `Iterator` interface with methods such as `next()`. The interesting thing about **generator functions** is that they **can be paused and their execution can be controlled from the outside**. We will learn a bit more about generators later in this chapter. If you can't wait, then you can check out the following article:
`https://developer.mozilla.org/en-US/docs/Web/JavaScript/Guide/Iterators_and_Generators`.

Here's a simple example of `async/await` in action:

```
async function makeCoffee(): Promise<void> {
    return new Promise<void>(resolve => {
        setTimeout(() => {
            console.log("Coffee is ready");
            resolve();
        }, 1000);
    });
}

async function main(): Promise<void> {
    await makeCoffee();
    console.log("The coffee has been prepared!")
}

main().then(() => {
    console.log("All done!");
});
```

The `makeCoffee` function is marked as `async` and, as such, it **must** return a `Promise`. The function resolves the promise after 1 second has passed, thanks to the `setTimeout(...)` call.

Next, the `main` function, which is also marked as `async`, **awaits** the completion of `setCoffee` to display a message on the console. Finally, we call the `main` function and handle the promise.

If you execute this code using Node.js, you should see the following:

```
$ node asyncawait-01.js
Coffee is ready
The coffee has been prepared!
All done!
```

The output corresponds to our expectations and the code looks synchronous thanks to the `async` and `await` keywords.

Let's revisit our previous Fetch example using `async` and `await`:

```
async function checkResponseStatus(response: Response):
Promise<Response> {
    if (response.status >= 200 && response.status < 300) {
        return Promise.resolve(response);
    } else {
        return Promise.reject(new Error(response.statusText));
    }
}

async function toJSON(response: Response): Promise<Response> {
    return response.json();
}

async function loadData(): Promise<unknown> {
    const response = await fetch('https://api.worldbank.org
    /v2/countries?format=json');
    const checkedResponse = await checkResponseStatus(response);
    const jsonContent: unknown = await toJSON(checkedResponse);
    return Promise.resolve(jsonContent);
}

loadData()
    .then((jsonContent: unknown) => {
        console.log("Response content: ", jsonContent);
    })
    .catch((error: unknown) => {
        console.error("An error occurred while fetching the data: ",
        error);
    });
```

The most interesting part is the `loadData` function. Again, notice how readable it is!

When the code runs, the execution of the `loadData` function will be suspended each time the `await` keyword is used, until the corresponding `Promise` has settled.

> Just like `Promise.then(...)`, `await` allows us to use so-called **thenable** objects, which are objects with a `then(...)` function. This means that promises are not the only option here (even if they will be the most prevalent).

How cool is this? Synchronous-looking asynchronous code!

> It is useful to know that `await` can also be combined with `Promise.all(...)`.

But what about compatibility?

Compatibility

It took quite a while for web browsers to integrate support for `async` and `await`. In the meantime, polyfills could be used to fill the gap. In TypeScript, `async` and `await` have been supported since version 1.7. Until version 2.1, though, they were only supported with ES2015 as a target. Since then, TypeScript can down-level emit code that uses `async` and `await` to ES5 and even ES3. This is great, as it removes the need for polyfills.

Adding runtime type checks

We would like to touch on one more important subject: type safety at runtime. This knowledge will come in very handy when you need to deal with external data sources.

In the previous chapter, we used the `class-transformer` library in order to easily serialize/deserialize our objects. This time, we'll discover another way of doing things that will add more safety to our code.

TypeScript non-goals

As we've discussed before, once your code has been transpiled, most of the type information is gone. As a matter of fact, the TypeScript team has documented the goals but also some **non-goals** for the TypeScript programming language. You can find those here:
`https://github.com/Microsoft/TypeScript/wiki/TypeScript-Design-Goals`.

There are two explicit non-goals that are relevant to our discussion:

1. Add or rely on runtime type information in programs, or emit different code based on the results of the type system. Instead, encourage programming patterns that do not require runtime metadata.
2. Provide additional runtime functionality or libraries. Instead, use TypeScript to describe existing libraries.

This means that TypeScript will not include facilities to help us further at runtime! But don't despair just yet.

Use cases

There are actually quite a few valid use cases to consider for runtime type checks.

For instance, when the service layer of our `WorldExplorer` application makes calls to the REST API, it will get the data back as JSON. Once we get hold of the corresponding JSON, we will need to extract information from it in order to create instances of our own domain model types. Doing so requires attention to avoid runtime type safety issues.

One problem with web APIs is that their implementation can change over time. At some point, some fields that we expect to be present might be renamed or even disappear. APIs should, of course, be versioned, but theory and reality don't always agree. In addition, we might also make spelling mistakes on our side (for example, using an invalid name for a property).

On its own, the TypeScript compiler can't know for sure that the API responses will have the shape that we expect, that fields will have the expected types, and many more things.

The question when there are issues at runtime is: how will our code react? Will it fail in a predictable way or not? If not, then we risk impacting the users of our applications, which is far from ideal.

To avoid such pitfalls, we need to be able to validate that fields are present, with correct names and the expected types.

Here are a few additional use cases to consider:

- Sometimes, fields are optional and will not necessarily be present; how do we handle that?
- We might not want to create a one-to-one mapping between the structure of API responses and our own data model.
- We might want to perform transformations.
- We might want to fetch additional information to enrich our representation.

We would certainly benefit from having the possibility to perform runtime type checks and validations, as well as conversions without compromising type safety at runtime. This would enable us to react appropriately in the event of errors, thus failing faster if needed.

Now that you understand why having type safety at runtime is beneficial, let's discover a library that we can use to achieve precisely that.

io-ts

io-ts (https://github.com/gcanti/io-ts) is a library that can be used to define **runtime types**. Those runtime types will allow us to perform stricter type checks at runtime.

The io-ts library defines a Type class. We will use instances of that class as *validators*. At runtime, they'll be used to strictly validate that objects have the shape and types that we expect. That way, we will be able to use them safely.

Instances of the Type class can be created using utility functions provided by io-ts. Here's a basic example that creates and uses a string validator:

```
import * as t from "io-ts";
const nameValidator = t.string;
const validationResult = nameValidator.decode('foobar');
validationResult.isRight(); // true
```

In this example, we've created a string validator using t.string. We use that validator to ensure that the given value (that is, foobar) is indeed a string. The validation is performed at runtime using the decode(...) function.

The `decode` function of `io-ts` does not throw errors if validation fails. To throw errors, we can use `ThrowReporter` provided by `io-ts` as follows:

```
import {ThrowReporter} from "io-ts/lib/ThrowReporter";
...
const validationResult = someValidator.decode(foo);
ThrowReporter.report(validationResult); // throws if the input is
invalid
```

With the preceding code, `ThrowReporter` will throw an error if `foo` is not valid.

To retrieve the decoded value, we can use `.value` on the object returned by `decode`:

```
...
const validationResult = someValidator.decode(foo);
ThrowReporter.report(validationResult);
...
const myValue = validationResult.value as SomeType
```

What is great here is that, once `ThrowReporter` has been executed, we know for a fact that the value is exactly as we expect (shape and types), hence we can cast it to the target type safely!

It is also possible to combine validators and to compose definitions. Thanks to this feature, it is possible to create custom complex types. This is useful for validating more advanced data structures, such as API call responses. We can create such composite types using `t.type`, `t.interface`, `t.union`, and other methods provided by `io-ts`.

The `io-ts` library is not perfect, but it provides great benefits for type safety, both at compile time and at runtime. Next, we'll explore a few examples to make these ideas clearer.

 There's also a very interesting tool called `io-ts-codegen` (`https://github.com/gcanti/io-ts-codegen`), which you can use to generate `io-ts` types (both static and runtime ones) from schemas such as JSON Schema, Swagger, and others.

Last but not least, at compile time, we can generate types using `io-ts` based on the validator types. This means that we can limit code duplication in addition to adding type safety! Isn't that great?

Let's explore those features with a few examples.

io-ts examples

Here's a first example showing how to create a *composite* validator type:

```
import * as t from "io-ts";
...
const countryValidator = t.type({
    id: t.string,
    name: t.string,
    capitalCity: t.string

});
```

Here, we have used `t.type` to define a runtime type that combines different properties.

Now let's look at a more concrete example:

```
import * as t from "io-ts";

import {ThrowReporter} from "io-ts/lib/ThrowReporter";

const countryValidator = t.type({
    id: t.string,
    name: t.string,
    capitalCity: t.string,
});

// extract the corresponding static types
interface Country extends t.TypeOf<typeof countryValidator> {}

const validCountry:Country = {
    id: "BE",
    name: "Belgium",
    capitalCity: "Brussels"
};

const invalidCountry: unknown = {
    foo: "foo",
    name: "bar"
    // missing id
    // missing capitalCity
};
```

After the runtime type definition, notice that we have created an interface called `Country` that extends from the type created for `countryValidator`. This is made possible by the `t.TypeOf` function of `io-ts`. By doing so, we have effectively created an interface that we can use at compile time in our code.

With that defined, validating is easy:

```
// validate both the valid and the invalid objects
const validationResultForValidCountry =
countryValidator.decode(validCountry);
const validationResultForInvalidCountry =
countryValidator.decode(invalidCountry);

// check the validation result
ThrowReporter.report(validationResultForValidCountry); // would throw
                                          // if the object was invalid
const validCountryObject = validationResultForValidCountry.value as
Country;
console.log(`Valid country's name: ${validCountryObject.name}`);

try {
    ThrowReporter.report(validationResultForInvalidCountry); // will
                                          // throw an error
    console.log("Done!"); // will not be displayed!
} catch(error) {
    console.error("An error occurred: ", error);
}
```

In the preceding code, we have created two different objects. The first one is of type `Country` and is valid. Then, the second one lacks some properties. Using the `decode(...)` function of our validator, we can obtain the validation results both for the valid and the invalid object.

As we noted earlier, `decode(...)` calls don't throw errors directly. When `decode(...)` is called, it returns a `Validation<T>` instance, which is actually an `Either<Errors, T>` object. It corresponds to two possible types. The `io-ts` library simply uses the `Either` type to indicate that, when validation is done, either the operation succeeded and we have a valid object, or it failed and we have validation errors. `Either` is one of many more functional types in the `fp-ts` (https://github.com/gcanti/fp-ts) library, used by `io-ts` (from the same author). You can learn more about the `Either` type here: https://gcanti.github.io/fp-ts/modules/Either.ts.

Once we have the validation results, we use `ThrowReporter` to report errors found on the validated object. Since it is indeed valid in the first case, no error is thrown. After that point, we can safely cast the value held by the object to our `Country` class. We can do so because we know that the object is valid and that it has the shape that we expected. After doing so, we have both compile-time and runtime type safety and we can use the object as we wish, without any doubts about its structure.

We finally run the `ThrowReporter.report(...)` function for the invalid object. This time, it will throw an error since the object is invalid. If you execute the code, you'll get the following output:

```
$ node iotsexample.js

Valid country's name : Belgium
An error occurred:  Invalid value undefined supplied to : { id:
string, name: string, capitalCity: string }/id: string
Invalid value undefined supplied to : { id: string, name: string,
capitalCity: string }/capitalCity: string
```

The error describes precisely what was invalid, which is great for troubleshooting.

We'll leverage `io-ts` for `WorldExplorer` in order to validate the API responses.

Enough theory now; let's get started!

Creating the project

Once again, we have already prepared the base skeleton of the project. You can find it in the code samples folder, under `05/worldexplorer-initial`:

1. Copy that folder.
2. Install the necessary dependencies using `npm install`.

Now, open it in your favorite editor.

What's inside of the project skeleton?

We will again be using the Parcel bundler for this application. Now that you know a bit more about bundlers, you should be able to better appreciate how this helps us to build the application.

The output of the Parcel bundling process will be stored in the `dist` folder, which will thus contain the production version of the code. That way, we will not mix build-time elements and production ones.

Another change that we have made, compared to the previous applications, is that we will put our source code inside the `src` subfolder, instead of at the root level. This will introduce a cleaner separation of concerns as we'll avoid mixing configuration files with the application code.

The output of the TypeScript compiler will also be stored separately, under the `.tmp` folder. We did this in order to avoid mixing the source TypeScript files with the generated JavaScript code.

To do this, we have modified the `tsconfig.json` file as follows:

1. Set the `rootDir` property to `./src`: Specifies the root directory of input files
2. Set the `outDir` property to `./.tmp`: Specifies the output directory for generated code

With this in place, we have created a clean separation between project-level configuration files, application source code, generated code and production build output. We heavily recommend doing so for all of your projects.

Regarding the code itself, we still have an `index.html` file. This time, it loads `world-explorer.ts` as the main entry point. As we'll soon see, this file will contain much less code than the entry point of our previous applications, thanks to modules.

Finally, note that we have already added the `io-ts` library to the dependencies of the project as we'll be using it. Also, if you look under `src/services`, you'll see that there is already a file there called `world-bank-api.ts`. We've placed all the necessary validators and runtime types for the API parts that we'll use there.

Don't hesitate to take a look at those to see `io-ts` in action!

Designing the model

As usual, we will start our project with a brief analysis of the domain model.

Core domain

Since we'll exploit the World Bank APIs, we'll design our domain model based on the information we plan on using from the API responses. We'll simply omit all the objects and properties that we don't care about. Here's our initial domain design:

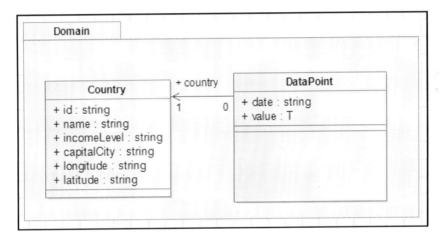

For starters, this will be enough as it will allow us to represent the countries we gather information for and the data points that we'll retrieve. Those will then be used to construct the charts.

Implementing the domain model

First of all, do the following:

1. Create a `domain` folder inside `src`. We'll put all of our domain-related modules inside of it.
2. Now, go ahead and create a `country.ts` file within the `src/domain` folder.

In that file, define the `Country` class:

```
export class Country {
    constructor(
        private _name: string,
        private _id: string,
        private _iso2Code: string,
        private _capitalCity: string,
        private _longitude: string,
        private _latitude: string
    ) {
    }
}
```

Inside the class, add the following accessors:

```
get name() {
    return this._name;
}
get id(): string {
    return this._id;
}
get iso2Code(): string {
    return this._iso2Code;
}
get capitalCity(): string {
    return this._capitalCity;
}
get longitude(): string {
    return this._longitude;
}
get latitude(): string {
    return this._latitude;
}
```

By exporting the `Country` class, we have just created our very first module together!

 If you go back to the countries API response example, you'll notice that we have omitted some fields (for example, `lendingType`, `adminregion`, and many others), and flattened others (for example, `incomeLevel`). We did this simply because we won't be using the rest of the data.

Now, create a file called `datapoint.ts` in the same folder and add the following content to it:

```
export class DataPoint {
    constructor(
        private _date: string,
        private _value: number
    ) { }

    get date() {
        return this._date;
    }

    get value(): number {
        return this._value;
    }
}
```

 We have used the `number` type for the `DataPoint` class for simplicity since we'll only exploit numerical data, but we could've used a generic type here.

Now that we have created our base classes, let's create a barrel for this layer.

Create a file called `index.ts` under `src/domain`. Inside, re-export the `Country` and `DataPoint` classes:

```
export * from "./country";
export * from "./datapoint";
```

As explained earlier, this barrel will help us to import our types more easily.

Implementing the population service

Now, we can implement the population service. This service will be responsible for handling the interactions with the World Bank APIs.

Here's how it should look:

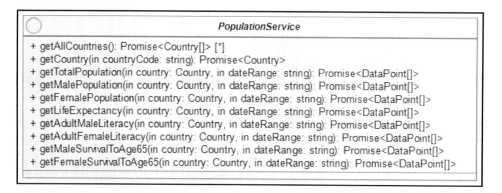

Since we will be calling an API, our method calls cannot immediately return the results. We'll thus use promises again to indicate that the methods are asynchronous.

Also, we are now going to use modules, so we might as well make that clear in our UML diagram. We can do so using **packages**, which are simply containers for design elements:

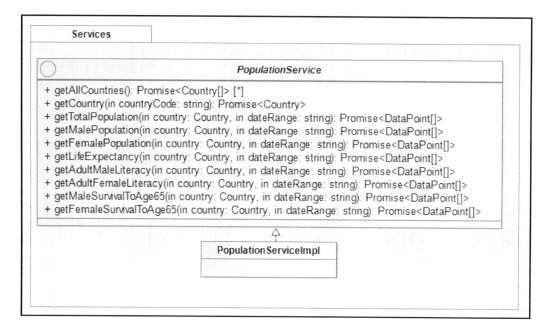

UML packages have a name, which defines a namespace for the components that they contain.

Let's now turn this UML diagram into actual code.

Defining the contract

As discussed earlier, we will isolate our services in a dedicated folder. The `src/services` folder already exists; we'll use it now.

Within that folder, create a new TypeScript file called `population-service.intf.ts`.

The name ends with the `.intf.ts` suffix to clearly indicate that the file contains an interface definition. Usually, you should define a single concept per file (that is, class, interface, type, and so on). The folder structure and file naming conventions help navigate around the code easily.

In this file, define the interface of the service as follows:

```typescript
import {Country, DataPoint} from "../domain";

export interface PopulationService {
    getAllCountries(): Promise<Country[]>;
    getCountry(countryCode: string): Promise<Country>;
    getTotalPopulation(country: Country, dateRange: string):
        Promise<DataPoint[]>;
    getMalePopulation(country: Country, dateRange: string):
        Promise<DataPoint[]>;
    getFemalePopulation(country: Country, dateRange: string):
    Promise<DataPoint[]>;
    getLifeExpectancy(country: Country, dateRange: string):
        Promise<DataPoint[]>;
    getAdultMaleLiteracy(country: Country, dateRange: string):
        Promise<DataPoint[]>;
    getAdultFemaleLiteracy(country: Country, dateRange: string):
        Promise<DataPoint[]>;
    getMaleSurvivalToAge65(country: Country, dateRange: string):
        Promise<DataPoint[]>;
    getFemaleSurvivalToAge65(country: Country, dateRange: string):
        Promise<DataPoint[]>;
}
```

If you want to impose more type safety in this interface, then you can change the return types to `Readonly<DataPoint[]>`, just as we did in the previous chapter.

Also, notice how we've imported the `Country` and `DataPoint` classes from our `domain` module; we can import those this way thanks to the barrel that we created before.

Creating the service implementation skeleton

Create a file called `population-service.ts` under `src/services` and add the skeleton to it:

```
import {PopulationService} from "./population-service.intf";
import {Country, DataPoint} from "../domain";
import {
    WorldBankApiV2,
} from "./world-bank-api";

export class PopulationServiceImpl implements PopulationService {
    private readonly countriesApiBaseUrl: string;

    constructor(baseUrl: string) {
        if (!baseUrl || baseUrl.trim().length === 0) {
            throw new Error("The base URL must be provided!");
        } else if (!baseUrl.toLocaleLowerCase().startsWith('https://')
        && !baseUrl.toLocaleLowerCase().startsWith('http://')) {
            throw new Error("The URL looks invalid. It should start
            with 'http://' or https://'");
        }

        let cleanBaseUrl = baseUrl.trim();
        if (cleanBaseUrl.endsWith('/')) {
            cleanBaseUrl = cleanBaseUrl.substr(0,
             cleanBaseUrl.lastIndexOf('/'));
        }
        this.countriesApiBaseUrl =
         `${cleanBaseUrl}/${WorldBankApiV2.VERSION}/
          ${WorldBankApiV2.COUNTRIES_API_PREFIX}`;
        console.log(`Population service initialized.\nCountries API
         URL: [${this.countriesApiBaseUrl}]`);
    }

    async getAllCountries(): Promise<Country[]> {
```

```
        // TODO implement
        throw new Error("Not implemented yet");
}

async getCountry(countryCode: string): Promise<Country> {
        // TODO implement
        throw new Error("Not implemented yet");
}

async getTotalPopulation(country: Country, dateRange: string):
 Promise<DataPoint[]> {
        // TODO implement
        throw new Error("Not implemented yet");
}

async getFemalePopulation(country: Country, dateRange: string):
 Promise<DataPoint[]> {
        // TODO implement
        throw new Error("Not implemented yet");
}

async getMalePopulation(country: Country, dateRange: string):
Promise<DataPoint[]> {
        // TODO implement
        throw new Error("Not implemented yet");
}

async getAdultFemaleLiteracy(country: Country, dateRange: string):
 Promise<DataPoint[]> {
        // TODO implement
        throw new Error("Not implemented yet");
}

async getAdultMaleLiteracy(country: Country, dateRange: string):
 Promise<DataPoint[]> {
        // TODO implement
        throw new Error("Not implemented yet");
}

async getFemaleSurvivalToAge65(country: Country, dateRange:
 string): Promise<DataPoint[]> {
        // TODO implement
        throw new Error("Not implemented yet");
}

async getLifeExpectancy(country: Country, dateRange: string):
 Promise<DataPoint[]> {
        // TODO implement
```

```
            throw new Error("Not implemented yet");
        }
    async getMaleSurvivalToAge65(country: Country, dateRange: string):
     Promise<DataPoint[]> {
            // TODO implement
            throw new Error("Not implemented yet");
        }
    }
}
```

In the constructor, we expect to receive the base URL of the World Bank API. We didn't hardcode it to allow defining a different URL as needed (for example a different one per environment). This can be useful, especially for testing purposes. After some basic validations, we store the base URL of the main API.

Now, let's start implementing the different methods together.

Implementing the getAllCountries method

This method will use the countries API to retrieve the full list of countries.

We will use the Fetch API to retrieve the data, as well as our `io-ts` validators to make sure that the data matches our expectations at runtime.

Finally, we'll use `async` and `await` to write synchronous-looking code, even if everything is actually asynchronous.

First, add the following utility methods to the class.

There is one to check the status of the response:

```
async checkResponseStatus(response: Response): Promise<Response> {
    if(!response) {
        throw new Error("A response must be provided!");
    }

    if (response.status >= 200 && response.status < 300) {
        return Promise.resolve(response);
    } else {
        return Promise.reject(new Error(response.statusText));
    }
}
```

A second one is to get the JSON content out of the response:

```
async getJsonContent(response: Response): Promise<unknown> {
    if(!response) {
```

```
        throw new Error("A response must be provided!");
    }

    let jsonContent: unknown = undefined;
    try {
        jsonContent = await response.json();
    } catch (error) {
        console.error("Failed to parse the response as JSON: ",
          error);
        throw new Error(`Could not parse the response body as JSON.
          Error: ${error.message}`);
    }
    return jsonContent;
}
```

We'll use the `checkResponseStatus` method to check that API responses are successful (that is, that they at least return a 2xx HTTP status code).

The `getJsonContent` method uses `await` to wait until the conversion of the response body to JSON is completed. Since this operation might fail, we've done this within a `try-catch` block in order to be able to return a meaningful response back to the calling code.

In the catch block, we've used `Promise.reject(...)` to return a custom error message back, but we could also have simply used `throw new Error(...)` to achieve the same result.

Now, implement the `getAllCountries` method as follows:

```
async getAllCountries(): Promise<Country[]> { // <1>

    const response: Response = await fetch(${this.
     countriesApiBaseUrl}?${WorldBankApiV2Params.FORMAT}=
     ${WorldBankApiV2Formats.JSON}&
     ${WorldBankApiV2Params.PER_PAGE}=320); // <2>

    const checkedResponse: Response = await
     this.checkResponseStatus(response); // <3>
    let jsonContent: unknown = await
     this.getJsonContent(checkedResponse);
    const validationResult = worldBankApiV2CountryResponseValidator.
     decode(jsonContent); // <4>
    // throw an error if validation fails
    ThrowReporter.report(validationResult); // <5>
    console.log("Response received and validated");
    // from here on, we know that the validation has passed
    const countries = (validationResult.value as
```

```
            WorldBankApiV2CountryResponse)[1]; // <6>
        console.log(`Found ${countries.length} countries`);

        let retVal: Country[] = countries.map(country => // <7>
            new Country(
                country.name,
                country.id,
                country.iso2Code,
                country.capitalCity,
                country.longitude,
                country.latitude
            )
        );
        return retVal; // <8>
    }
```

Let's go through the code together:

1. We've marked the function as `async`. This is what allows us to use `await` and write synchronous-looking code.
2. We've used `await` to wait until `fetch` returns with the response of our API call.
3. We've used `await` again to wait until the response has been checked by our utility function.
4. We've used our `io-ts` validator (that is, `worldBankApiV2CountryResponseValidator`) to check the validity of the response.
5. We've called `ThrowReporter.report(...)` to make sure that we throw an error if validation fails. We could also have checked the validity ourselves using `if (validationResult.isLeft) { ... }`, but `ThrowReporter` is clearer.
6. We've cast the validation result as `WorldBankApiV2CountryResponse`, which is safe at this point (we've gone through the validation successfully!). Note that since the World Bank APIs always return data in the form `[{pagination_data}, {data}]`, we've used `[1]` to simply get the data.
7. We've then mapped our array to a new array of `Country` class instances.
8. Finally, we've returned the resulting array directly.

Notice that we simply return our array. In this case, we don't need to use `Promise.resolve`. Since the function is marked as `async`, the returned value will be wrapped in `Promise` in any case.

The map function on the array type is very useful, as demonstrated earlier. It allows us to write more functional code. Instead of manually looping through the array to construct a new one, we simply **map** each element to the new type and keep a reference to the resulting array. You can learn more about Array.map here: https://developer.mozilla.org/en-US/docs/Web/JavaScript/Reference/Global_Objects/Array/map.

Doesn't this code look and feel like synchronous code?

Implementing the getCountry method

Now we will take care of the getCountry method.

The getCountry method is very similar:

```
async getCountry(countryCode: string): Promise<Country> {
    if(!countryCode || '' === countryCode.trim()) {
        throw new Error("The country code must be provided!");
    }

    const response: Response = await fetch(`${this.
     countriesApiBaseUrl}/${countryCode}?
     ${WorldBankApiV2Params.FORMAT}=
     ${WorldBankApiV2Formats.JSON}`);

    const checkedResponse: Response = await
     this.checkResponseStatus(response);
    let jsonContent: unknown = await
     this.getJsonContent(checkedResponse);

    const validationResult = worldBankApiV2Country
     ResponseValidator.decode(jsonContent);
    ThrowReporter.report(validationResult);

    // add the second part here
}
```

In this first part, we perform some validation, then invoke the API. Once we have the response, we simply ensure that there is, at most, one country returned.

Next, add the second part of the method:

```
// from here on, we know that the validation has passed
const countries = (validationResult.value as
 WorldBankApiV2CountryResponse)[1];

if (countries.length > 1) {
    return Promise.reject("More than one country
    was returned. This should not happen");
}

const country = countries[0];

return new Country(
    country.name,
    country.id,
    country.iso2Code,
    country.capitalCity,
    country.longitude,
    country.latitude
);
```

In this second part, we extract the list of countries from the validation result. The typecast is safe to perform since we have validated that the object matches our expectations.

We then make sure that there is only one element; if it isn't the case, then we reject the `Promise`.

Finally, we return a new `Country` object created using the different properties of the object that we've extracted from the response.

Implementing the getTotalPopulation method

For this next method, we'll start using the Indicators API. Our function accepts two input parameters: a `Country` object and a date range string. For a production application, the date range would probably require a few safety checks since it must correspond to the World Bank API rules, but we'll be optimistic for now.

First of all, add the following import at the top of the file:

```
import {WorldBankApiV2Indicators} from "./world-bank-api";
```

Then, add the following utility function:

```
getBaseIndicatorApiUrlFor(indicator: WorldBankApiV2Indicators,
country?: Country) {
    let countryCode = "all";
    if(country) {
        countryCode = country.id;
    }
    return `${this.countriesApiBaseUrl}/${countryCode}
      ${WorldBankApiV2.INDICATORS_API_PREFIX}/${indicator}`;

}
```

This function constructs the base URL for the requested indicator (for example, total population) and the given country. If no country is provided, then `all` is used by default.

The implementation of `getTotalPopulation` follows the same idea as the previous methods:

```
async getTotalPopulation(country: Country, dateRange: string):
Promise<DataPoint[]> {
    const response: Response = await fetch(`${this.
    getBaseIndicatorApiUrlFor
    (WorldBankApiV2Indicators.TOTAL_POPULATION, country)}?
    ${WorldBankApiV2Params.FORMAT}=
    ${WorldBankApiV2Formats.JSON}&${WorldBankApiV2Params.
    PER_PAGE}=1000&${WorldBankApiV2Params.DATE}=
    ${dateRange}`);
    const checkedResponse: Response = await
    this.checkResponseStatus(response);
    let jsonContent: unknown = await
     this.getJsonContent(checkedResponse);
    const validationResult = worldBankApiV2Indicator
    ResponseValidator.decode(jsonContent);
    ThrowReporter.report(validationResult);
    // from here on, we know that the validation has passed
    const dataPoints = (validationResult.value as
    WorldBankApiV2IndicatorResponse)[1];

    let retVal: DataPoint[] = [];
    if (dataPoints) { // we might not get anything back
        retVal = dataPoints
            .filter(dataPoint => dataPoint.value !== null)
            // we only include data points for which we have
            // a value
            .map(dataPoint => new DataPoint(
                dataPoint.date,
```

```
                    dataPoint.value as number
          ));
     }
     return retVal;
  }
```

This time around, we check whether the data points could be retrieved or not. This is necessary because sometimes there might be no data available for the given search criteria. If there are data points, then we convert those to our own data model.

 In the preceding code, we skipped data points for which no value is available using the `filter` array method. Again, this makes for a nice functional composition, since the filtered array returned by the `filter` function is then mapped to return the final array.

We've now looked at the most important parts of the population service.

Implementing the other methods

You can, in fact, very easily implement the rest of the methods for the indicator API calls.

Here's a utility function that will heavily simplify the implementation of our contract:

```
async getIndicatorData(indicator: WorldBankApiV2Indicators, country:
Country, dateRange: string, perPage: number): Promise<DataPoint[]> {
   const response: Response = await
fetch(`${this.getBaseIndicatorApiUrlFor(indicator,
country)}?${WorldBankApiV2Params.FORMAT}=${WorldBankApiV2Formats.JSON}
&${WorldBankApiV2Params.PER_PAGE}=${perPage}&${WorldBankApiV2Params.DA
TE}=${dateRange}`);
   const checkedResponse: Response = await
    this.checkResponseStatus(response);
   let jsonContent: unknown = await
    this.getJsonContent(checkedResponse);
   const validationResult = worldBankApiV2IndicatorResponse
      Validator.decode(jsonContent);
   ThrowReporter.report(validationResult);

   // from here on, we know that the validation has passed
   const dataPoints = (validationResult.value as
    WorldBankApiV2IndicatorResponse)[1];

   let retVal: DataPoint[] = [];
   if (dataPoints) { // we might not get anything back
```

```
            retVal = dataPoints
                .filter(dataPoint => dataPoint.value !== null)
                // we only include data points for
                // which we have a value
                .map(dataPoint => new DataPoint(
                    dataPoint.date,
                    dataPoint.value as number
                ));
    }
    return retVal;
}
```

This method accepts an indicator name as input as well as some additional parameters. Then, it takes care of fetching, validating, and returning the corresponding data.

Thanks to this method, we can simply implement the other methods of our service as follows:

```
async getFemalePopulation(country: Country, dateRange: string):
 Promise<DataPoint[]> {
    return this.getIndicatorData(WorldBankApiV2Indicators
    .TOTAL_FEMALE_POPULATION, country, dateRange, 1000);
}

async getMalePopulation(country: Country, dateRange: string):
 Promise<DataPoint[]> {
    return this.getIndicatorData(WorldBankApiV2Indicators.
    TOTAL_MALE_POPULATION, country, dateRange, 1000);
}

async getAdultFemaleLiteracy(country: Country, dateRange: string):
 Promise<DataPoint[]> {
    return this.getIndicatorData(WorldBankApiV2Indicators.
    ADULT_FEMALE_LITERACY, country, dateRange, 1000);
}

async getAdultMaleLiteracy(country: Country, dateRange: string):
 Promise<DataPoint[]> {
    return this.getIndicatorData(WorldBankApiV2Indicators.
    ADULT_MALE_LITERACY, country, dateRange, 1000);
}

async getFemaleSurvivalToAge65(country: Country, dateRange: string):
 Promise<DataPoint[]> {
    return this.getIndicatorData(WorldBankApiV2Indicators.
    ADULT_FEMALE_SURVIVAL_TO_65, country, dateRange, 1000);
}
```

```
async getLifeExpectancy(country: Country, dateRange: string):
 Promise<DataPoint[]> {
    return this.getIndicatorData(WorldBankApiV2Indicators.
    LIFE_EXPECTANCY, country, dateRange, 1000);
}

async getMaleSurvivalToAge65(country: Country, dateRange: string):
 Promise<DataPoint[]> {
    return this.getIndicatorData(WorldBankApiV2Indicators.
    ADULT_MALE_SURVIVAL_TO_65, country, dateRange, 1000);
}
```

This looks much cleaner already, don't you think?

At this point, we could actually refine the service interface and make it more generic, but we'll leave that as an exercise for you.

Creating the service layer barrel

To finish up, create a barrel for the service layer. To do so, create an `index.ts` file and export the following elements in it:

```
export * from "./population-service.intf";
export * from "./population-service";
export * from "./world-bank-api";
```

This barrel will allow us to easily import elements of the service layer from anywhere in the application. As we saw earlier, this simplifies imports, which is valuable.

High-level design

Let's again look at our application from a higher point of view and see how we can design the modules and their relationships:

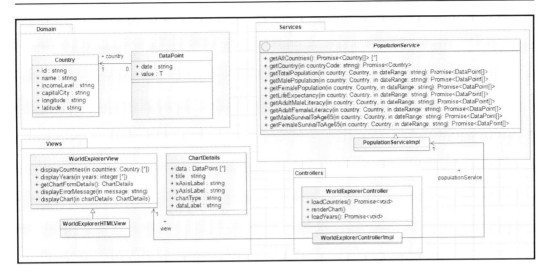

Packages make things even clearer, don't you think? Once we introduce modules/packages, our code immediately gains in terms of organization and navigability:

Let's go over our design package by package.

The controller package

Our controller interface is really straightforward. It exposes a set of methods that can be used in the HTML template to trigger operations:

1. `loadCountries` will be invoked when the application starts. This method will retrieve the list of countries from the World Bank API using the population service. That list will then be displayed onscreen by the view layer.

2. `loadYears` will also be called when the application starts. It will generate a list of years that the user can choose via select boxes. These will be used to define the range of data to fetch in order to create the charts (for example, 2000-2010).

3. `renderChart` will gather the information needed to create a new chart and will then ask the view to render it onscreen.

 `loadYears` and `loadCountries` are both asynchronous. For the list of countries, it is obviously because we need to make an API call. In the case of `loadYears`, we'll see later why that is the case.

Our controller implementation will have a view at its disposal, as well as an instance of the population service to fetch the data.

The view package

Our view interface (that is, `WorldExplorerView`) exposes only a few methods:

1. `displayCountries`: Accepts an array of `Country` objects and displays them onscreen (in our case, simply within an HTML select element).

2. `displayYears`: Displays a list of years in two HTML `select` elements: `from` and `to`.

3. `displayChart`: Renders a chart onscreen, based on the chart description given as a `ChartDetails` object.

4. `displayErrorMessage`: Just like in the previous chapter, this method allows you to display an error message to the user.

5. `getChartFormDetails`: This method can be called by the controller to retrieve the contents of the form. That form will be used to configure the chart to generate.

The chart form will let the user select the following:

1. The country to fetch data for
2. The indicator (for example, total population, life expectancy, and so on)
3. The start year
4. The end year
5. The type of chart to create (for example, line, bar, and so on)

When the user wants to render a new chart, a `ChartDetails` object will be created, containing everything required to render it:

1. `data`: The data points
2. `dataLabel`: The label for the data (this could be useful if we decide to display multiple datasets at once)
3. `title`: The title of the chart
4. `xAxisLabel`: The label for the *x* axis
5. `yAxisLabel`: The label for the *y* axis
6. `chartType`: The type of chart to render

Implementing the view layer

Now that we have our design, let's move on by implementing the view layer:

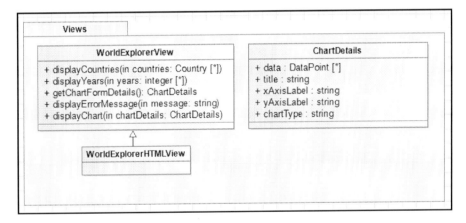

Let's start with the view template.

HTML template

First of all, adapt the `src/index.html` file as follows:

```
<!DOCTYPE html>
<html lang="en">
<head>
    <meta charset="UTF-8">
    <title>WorldExplorer</title>
```

```
        <link rel="stylesheet" type="text/css" href="world-explorer.css">
    </head>

    <body id="worldExplorer">
    <h1>WorldExplorer</h1>

    <form id="chartConfigurationForm" target="#">
        ...
    </form>
    <br />
    <div id="worldExplorerChartContainer">
        <canvas id="worldExplorerChart"></canvas>
    </div>

    <script src="world-explorer.ts"></script>
    </body>
    </html>
```

This defines the base structure of the page. Again, note that the world-explorer.ts file is loaded directly in the template. The Parcel bundler will take care of invoking the TypeScript compiler for us to convert it to JavaScript.

Now, we'll add the contents of the chartConfigurationForm form:

```
        <select id="countrySelect" required>
            <option value="">Loading...</option>
        </select>

        <select id="indicatorSelect" required>
            <option value="TOTAL_POPULATION">Total population</option>
            <option value="TOTAL_MALE_POPULATION">Male population</option>
            <option value="TOTAL_FEMALE_POPULATION">Female
             population</option>
            <option value="ADULT_MALE_LITERACY">Adult male
             literacy</option>
            <option value="ADULT_FEMALE_LITERACY">Adult female
             literacy</option>
            <option value="LIFE_EXPECTANCY">Life expectancy</option>
            <option value="ADULT_MALE_SURVIVAL_TO_65">Adult male survival
             to age 65</option>
            <option value="ADULT_FEMALE_SURVIVAL_TO_65">Adult female
             survival to age 65</option>
        </select>

        <select id="fromYearSelect" required>
            <option value="">Loading...</option>
        </select>
```

```
<select id="toYearSelect" required>
    <option value="">Loading...</option>
</select>

<select id="chartTypeSelect" required>
    <option value="line">Line</option>
    <option value="bar">Bar</option>
    <option value="horizontalBar">Horizontal Bar</option>
    <option value="polarArea">Polar Area</option>
    <option value="radar">Radar</option>
</select>
<input type="button" value="Show"
 onclick="worldExplorerController.renderChart();" />
```

Elements to notice:

1. `chartConfigurationForm`: This is the form that will contain all the elements defining the chart to generate, shown as follows:
    - `countrySelect`: This is the element that will be used to select a country to gather statistics for. Note that the list is not there at this point; it will be filled in when the application starts.
    - `indicatorSelect`: This is the element that will be used to select the statistic of interest. This list is hardcoded, but it could also be made dynamic. The options values match the keys in the corresponding World Bank Indicator API enum (that is, `WorldBankApiV2Indicators`).
    - `fromYearSelect`: This defines the start of the date range. This will also be filled in when the application starts.
    - `toYearSelect`: This defines the end of the date range.
    - `chartTypeSelect`: This allows the user to select the type of chart that they want to generate. The options values match existing Chart.js chart types (`https://www.chartjs.org/docs/latest/charts`).

2. The **Show** button calls `renderChart` on the controller through its click event handler.

The last important piece is the `worldExplorerChart` element. This element is an HTML `canvas` element. We can use this element to draw things using JavaScript. Using `canvas`, we can render images, animations, 3D scenes, games, or charts and graphs!

In our case, we won't manipulate the canvas ourselves. Instead, we'll use Chart.js, which will render charts for us within the targeted `canvas` element.

You can discover the canvas element and the corresponding JavaScript API here: `https://developer.mozilla.org/en-US/docs/Web/API/Canvas_API/Tutorial`.

Here's what our view should look like once completed:

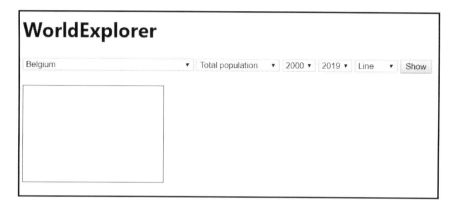

Let's now take care of the code that runs under the hood.

Creating the view package

Go ahead and create the package for our view layer. Create the `src/views` folder.

All the code elements corresponding to the view implementation will be stored there.

Implementing the view model using a Data Transfer Object (DTO)

We first need to create our `ChartDetails` model class. Create a file called `chart-details.intf.ts` inside `src/views`.

Here's the implementation:

```
import {DataPoint} from "../domain";

export interface ChartDetails {
    chartType: string;
```

```
data: DataPoint[];
dataLabel: string;
title: string;
xAxisLabel: string;
yAxisLabel: string;
}
```

 Again, we are using the `.intf.ts` filename suffix to indicate that this file contains an interface.

We have used an interface here and not a class because this model element is a simple **Value Object (VO)**, also called a **Data Transfer Object (DTO)**. It will only be created and used to transfer information from the controller back to our view and we don't need any logic in it.

Defining the view contract

Let's define our contract.

Do the following inside `src/views` and create a file called `world-explorer-view.intf.ts`.

Here's the interface definition that we'll use:

```
import {Country} from "../domain";

import {ChartDetails} from "./chart-details.intf";


export interface WorldExplorerView {
    displayErrorMessage(message: string): void;
    displayCountries(countries: Country[]): void;
    displayYears(years: number[]): void;
    getChartFormDetails(): { error?: string, countryId?: string,
     indicator?: string, fromYear?: number,
     toYear?: number, chartType?: string};
    displayChart(chartDetails: ChartDetails): void;
}
```

For the return type of the `getChartFormDetails` method, we are using the same trick as in the last chapter, allowing us to have clearer and cleaner error handling.

Installing Chart.js

As we mentioned at the beginning of this chapter, we are going to use the Chart.js (`https://www.chartjs.org`) library to generate and render our charts.

Chart.js is a simple to use but very powerful library that can render many different types of interactive charts (for example, line, bar, radar, doughnut, scatter, and many others) and can animate them. It is even possible to create *mixed charts*, combining different types in one.

In this chapter, we'll discover only the basics of using Chart.js. You can check out the official samples to get an idea of what is actually possible with this library: `https://www.chartjs.org/samples/latest`

Follow these steps to install the library and its types:

1. Install the `npm` package using `npm install chart.js --save`.
2. Install the TypeScript typings for Chart.js using `npm install @types/chart.js --save`.

We'll see later how to use it.

Creating the view implementation skeleton

Still inside the `src/views` directory, do the following:

1. Create a file called `world-explorer-view.ts`. Here's the base skeleton to use:

```
import {Country} from "../domain";
import {WorldExplorerView} from "./world-explorer-view.intf";
import {ChartDetails} from "./chart-details.intf";

export class WorldExplorerHTMLView implements
WorldExplorerView {
    private readonly _countrySelect: HTMLSelectElement;
    private readonly _indicatorSelect: HTMLSelectElement;
    private readonly _fromYearSelect: HTMLSelectElement;
    private readonly _toYearSelect: HTMLSelectElement;
    private readonly _chartTypeSelect: HTMLSelectElement;
    private readonly _chartConfigurationForm: HTMLFormElement;

    constructor() {
        // add constructor contents
```

```
        }

        // add method skeletons here
    }
```

2. Next, implement the constructor validation checks and element retrieval:

```
    this._countrySelect = document.getElementById('countrySelect')
    as HTMLSelectElement;
    if (!this._countrySelect) {
        throw new Error("Could not initialize the view. The
          'countrySelect' element id was not found. Was the
    template
          changed?");
    }

    this._indicatorSelect =
    document.getElementById('indicatorSelect') as
    HTMLSelectElement;
    if (!this._indicatorSelect) {
        throw new Error("Could not initialize the view. The
          'indicatorSelect' element id was not found. Was the
    template
          changed?");
    }

    this._fromYearSelect =
    document.getElementById('fromYearSelect') as
    HTMLSelectElement;
    if (!this._fromYearSelect) {
        throw new Error("Could not initialize the view. The
          'fromYearSelect' element id was not found.
          Was the template changed?");
    }

    this._toYearSelect = document.getElementById('toYearSelect')
    as HTMLSelectElement;
    if (!this._toYearSelect) {
        throw new Error("Could not initialize the view. The
    'toYearSelect'
          element id was not found. Was the template changed?");
    }

    this._chartTypeSelect =
    document.getElementById('chartTypeSelect') as
    HTMLSelectElement;
    if (!this._chartTypeSelect) {
        throw new Error("Could not initialize the view. The
```

```
    'chartTypeSelect' element id was not found. Was the
    template changed?");
}

this._chartConfigurationForm =
document.getElementById('chartConfigurationForm') as
HTMLFormElement;
if (!this._chartConfigurationForm) {
    throw new Error("Could not initialize the view. The
    'chartConfigurationForm' element
    id was not found. Was the template changed?");
}
```

Notice that we again retrieve the DOM elements that we need in the constructor function.

3. Finally, add the following skeletons for the methods:

```
displayErrorMessage(errorMessage: string): void {
        if (!errorMessage) {
            throw new Error("An error message must be
            provided!");
        }
        alert(errorMessage); // bad user experience but ignore
                             // this for now
}

displayCountries(countries: Country[]): void {
    // FIX ME implement
}

displayYears(years: number[]): void {
    // FIX ME implement
}

getChartFormDetails(): { error?: string; countryId?:
 string; indicator?: string; fromYear?: number;
 toYear?: number, chartType?: string } {
    // FIX ME implement
}

displayChart(chartDetails: ChartDetails): void {
    // FIX ME implement
}
```

Next up, we'll, of course, replace those empty methods with the actual implementations.

Implementing the displayCountries method

The `displayCountries` method receives an array of `Country` objects and renders those as `<option>` HTML elements as follows:

```
displayCountries(countries: Country[]): void {
    if (!countries) {
        throw new Error("The list of countries to display must be
        provided!");
    } else if (countries.length === 0) {
        throw new Error("The list of countries cannot be empty!");
    }

    console.log("Displaying the countries");
    let countriesOptions = "";
    countries.forEach(country => {
        countriesOptions += `<option
        value="${country.id}">${country.name}</option>`;
    });
    this._countrySelect.innerHTML = countriesOptions;
}
```

Nothing special to mention here; this is a technique that we've already used before.

 If you want to improve the code, you can replace `forEach` with a `map` call instead, using `join()` in the final array.

The next method to implement is `displayYears`.

Implementing the displayYears method

This method is very similar:

```
displayYears(years: number[]): void {
    if (!years) {
        throw new Error("The list of years must be provided!");
    } else if (years.length === 0) {
        throw new Error("The list of years cannot be empty!");
    }
```

```
console.log("Displaying the years");
let fromYearOptions = "";
years.forEach(year => {
    fromYearOptions += `<option value="${year}">${year}</option>`;
});

// reverse order
let toYearOptions = "";
years.reverse().forEach(year => {
    toYearOptions += `<option value="${year}">${year}</option>`;
});
this._fromYearSelect.innerHTML = fromYearOptions;
this._toYearSelect.innerHTML = toYearOptions;
}
```

The only thing to notice here is that, in order to build `toYearOptions`, we iterate through the provided array in reverse order using the `reverse()` method of `Array`. We did this to simplify selecting a date range ending with the last year by default.

Implementing getChartFormDetails and using the property shorthand notation

This method will be used by the controller to retrieve the form selections.

Add the definition of the method as follows:

```
getChartFormDetails(): { error?: string; countryId?: string;
indicator?: string; fromYear?: number; toYear?: number, chartType?:
string } {
    // Continue here
}
```

As stated before, notice the return type again. We reuse the same trick as in the previous chapter, by defining a custom type including an optional error. Then, we check the different form fields and report back to the user when something is invalid.

Note that you could easily abstract the custom response type using a generic type such as `type Result<DataType, ErrorType> = { error?: ErrorType; data?: DataType; };`

Inside that method, we need to add some validation logic:

```
if (this._chartConfigurationForm.checkValidity() === false) {
    this._chartConfigurationForm.reportValidity();
    return {
        error: "The chart configuration form is invalid!"
    }
}

// we check the validity of specific form fields
if (this._countrySelect.checkValidity() === false) {
    this._countrySelect.reportValidity();
    return {
        error: "A country must be selected!"
    }
}

if (this._indicatorSelect.checkValidity() === false) {
    this._indicatorSelect.reportValidity();
    return {
        error: "An indicator must be selected!"
    }
}

if (this._fromYearSelect.checkValidity() === false) {
    this._fromYearSelect.reportValidity();
    return {
        error: "A start year must be selected!"
    }
}

if (this._toYearSelect.checkValidity() === false) {
    this._toYearSelect.reportValidity();
    return {
        error: "An end year must be selected!"
    }
}

if (this._chartTypeSelect.checkValidity() === false) {
    this._chartTypeSelect.reportValidity();
    return {
        error: "A chart type must be selected!"
    }
}
```

Finally, we can create the `return` value if all validation tests have passed successfully:

```
const countryId: string = this._countrySelect.value;
    const indicator: string = this._indicatorSelect.value;
    const fromYear = Number.parseInt(this._fromYearSelect.value);
    const toYear = Number.parseInt(this._toYearSelect.value);
    const chartType: string = this._chartTypeSelect.value;

    return {
        countryId,
        indicator,
        fromYear,
        toYear,
        chartType
    };
```

When the form is fully validated, we return our custom object. For the definition of that object, we have used the **property shorthand notation** introduced by ES2015. It allows us to write `countryId`, for example, instead of `countryId: countryId`. You can learn more about that feature here:

`http://es6-features.org/#PropertyShorthand`.

Implementing the displayChart method

Last but not least, we can now implement the method that will render the chart. The `displayChart` function accepts a `ChartDetails` object, containing everything we need to know in order to render.

Before we implement this method, we first need to import Chart.js and retrieve the `canvas` element from the DOM:

1. Add the following import at the top of the `world-explorer-view.ts` file: `import Chart = require("chart.js");`. That is all we need to do in order to load Chart.js!
2. Add a private and read-only class field for the canvas: `private readonly _canvas: HTMLCanvasElement;`. It can be marked as `readonly` because we won't need to reassign it later.

Now, add the following code to the constructor:

```
this._canvas = document.getElementById("worldExplorerChart") as
HTMLCanvasElement;
if (!this._canvas) {
    throw new Error("Could not initialize the view. The
    'worldExplorerChart' element id was not found. Was the
    template changed?");
}
```

Then, we'll declare an additional private class field for the chart; we'll use that single reference to render our chart: Add the following declaration at the class level: `private _chart?: Chart;`.

Now, implement the `displayChart` method as follows.

First of all, as usual, add a defensive check:

```
if (!chartDetails) {
    throw new Error("The chart details must be provided!");
}
```

Next, we need to create two arrays:

1. One with the labels of our data: In our case, the `date` property of each `DataPoint` instance
2. One with the values: In our case, the `value` property of each `DataPoint` instance

Here's the code:

```
const dataLabels: string[] = [];
const dataValues: number[] = [];

chartDetails.data.forEach(dataPoint => {
    dataLabels.push(dataPoint.date);
    dataValues.push(dataPoint.value);
});
```

Now, we need to make sure that, whenever we try to render a new chart, the previous one (if there was one) gets removed:

```
if(this._chart) {
    this._chart.clear();
    this._chart.destroy();
}
```

Finally, here's the code that generates the chart:

```
this._chart = new Chart(this._canvas, { // <1>
    type: chartDetails.chartType, // <2>
    data: { // <3>
        labels: dataLabels, // <4>
        datasets: [ // <5>
            {
                data: dataValues // <6>
                label: chartDetails.dataLabel, // <7>

                // <8>
                fill: false,
                lineTension: 0.1,
                backgroundColor: "rgba(75,192,192,0.4)",
                borderColor: "rgba(75,192,192,1)",
                borderCapStyle: "butt",
                borderDash: [],
                borderDashOffset: 0.0,
                borderJoinStyle: "miter",
                pointBorderColor: "rgba(75,192,192,1)",
                pointBorderWidth: 1,
                pointHoverRadius: 5,
                pointHoverBackgroundColor: "rgba(75,192,192,1)",
                pointHoverBorderColor: "rgba(220,220,220,1)",
                pointHoverBorderWidth: 2,
                pointRadius: 1,
                pointHitRadius: 10,
            }
        ]
    },
    options: { // <9>
        animation: { // <10>
            animateRotate: true,
            easing: "easeOutQuart"
        },
        responsive: true, // <11>
        scales: {
            xAxes: [{ // <12>
                display: true,
                scaleLabel: {
                    display: true,
                    labelString: chartDetails.yAxisLabel
                }
            }],
            yAxes: [{ // <13>
                display: true,
                scaleLabel: {
```

```
                    display: true,
                    labelString: chartDetails.yAxisLabel
                }
            }]
        },
        title: { // <14>
            display: true,
            text: chartDetails.title
        }
    }
});
```

As you can see, creating a chart using Chart.js is really simple. The **difficulty** arises simply because of the various possibilities of the library.

Here are more details about the preceding code:

1. To create the chart, we create a new instance of the `Chart` class provided by Chart.js:
   1. The first thing that we pass to its constructor is the `canvas` element.
   2. The second thing is the configuration object, which contains the data, the labels, the options, and so on.
2. The `type` property is used to define the type of chart to render. The list of supported types can be found here:
   `https://www.chartjs.org/docs/latest/charts`.
3. The `data` property is used to provide the data of the chart.
4. The data is composed of `labels`, representing the label associated with each data point and `datasets`, accepting an array of data sets.
5. The actual data is passed through the `data` property.
6. Each dataset, of course, contains values and has a specific `label`.
7. It is also possible to define many settings for each dataset, including colors, borders, background, points, and many others.
8. Through the `options` object, we can further configure the chart to generate.
9. With the `animation` options, we can control the animation when the data is rendered.
10. When the `responsive` option is enabled, it adapts the size of the canvas depending on the available screen real estate.

11. With the `scales` option, we can configure the different axes, their labels, and so on.

12. Finally, with the `title` options, we can define and configure the title of the chart.

That's it for the chart generation. Make sure to check the awesome documentation of Chart.js, as there is a whole lot more to discover:
`https://www.chartjs.org/docs/latest`.

Creating the view layer barrel

Now, create a barrel for the view layer. To do so, create an `index.ts` file in `src/views` and export the following elements in it:

```
export * from "./world-explorer-view.intf";
export * from "./world-explorer-view";
export * from "./chart-details.intf";
```

Great—our view layer is now ready!

Implementing the controller layer

It's now time to introduce the brain of our application:

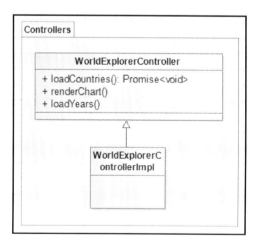

The upcoming sections discuss this topic in detail. Let's go through them!

Creating the controllers package

Go ahead and create the package for our controller layer. Create the `src/controllers` folder.

All the code elements corresponding to the controller implementation will be stored there.

Defining the controller contract

Create a file called `world-explorer-controller.intf.ts` under `src/controllers`.

Here's the interface definition:

```
export interface WorldExplorerController {
    loadCountries(): Promise<void>;
    loadYears(): void;
    renderChart(): void;
}
```

This interface is fairly basic but will take care of everything we need.

Creating the controller implementation skeleton

Let's now implement the skeleton of the controller implementation:

```
import {WorldExplorerController} from "./world-explorer-
controller.intf";
import {PopulationService} from "../services";
import {WorldExplorerView} from "../views";

export class WorldExplorerControllerImpl implements
WorldExplorerController {
    private readonly _view: WorldExplorerView;
    private readonly _populationService: PopulationService;

    constructor(populationService: PopulationService, view:
     WorldExplorerView) {
        if (!populationService) {
            throw new Error("The population service is mandatory!");
        }
```

```
        if (!view) {
            throw new Error("The view is mandatory!");
        }
        this._populationService = populationService;
        this._view = view;
        // TODO complete
    }

    async loadCountries(): Promise<void> {
        // FIX ME implement
    }

    loadYears(): void {
        // FIX ME implement
    }

    async renderChart(): Promise<void> {
        // FIX ME implement
    }
}
```

Our controller implementation requires the following to be provided through the constructor:

- A view
- A population service

As usual, we first make sure that those were indeed provided; then we keep a reference in a private field.

Over the course of the next sections, we will fill in this class skeleton with the actual methods.

Implementing the loadCountries method

The loadCountries method will be invoked when the controller is initialized (that is, through the constructor).

It will do the following:

1. Ask the population service to retrieve information about the countries.
2. Wait for the API call response.
3. Cache the results.
4. Ask the view to display the countries found.

For the Country cache, we will use Map:

1. Add the following import at the top of the file: import {Country} from "../domain";.

2. Add the following private field on the class: private readonly _countriesMap: Map<string, Country> = new Map<string, Country>();.

Now, implement loadCountries as follows:

```
async loadCountries(): Promise<void> {
    console.log("Loading the countries");
    try {
        const countries = await
          this._populationService.getAllCountries();
        countries.forEach(country => {
            this._countriesMap.set(country.id, country);
        });
        this._view.displayCountries(countries);
    } catch(error) {
        console.error("Could not load the list of
          countries! Error: ", error);
        this._view.displayErrorMessage("Could not load the list of
          countries! Are you connected to the Internet?");
    }
}
```

Once more, please take note of the async/await pattern and see how it allows us to simply use a try-catch block, just like we would do for synchronous code. This is pure syntactic sugar bliss!

Now, add the following code to the constructor, to make sure that loadCountries is called when the controller is initialized:

```
this.loadCountries()
    .then(() => console.log("WorldExplorer – Loaded", this))
    .catch(error => {
        console.error("WorldExplorer – Controller failed to load.
          Error: ", error);
        this._view.displayErrorMessage("WorldExplorer failed to load.
          Please contact IT support! ;-)");
    });
```

Great! Now we'll have our countries when the application starts.

Implementing the loadYears method with generators

Now let's look at the `loadYears` method.

The goal of this method is to generate a list of years, which will then be passed to the view for rendering. Those years could be selected as **start year** and **end year** in the user interface. They'll make it possible for the user to select the date range of data.

 We will implement a horrendously complicated solution for this very basic need, but it'll prove useful to demonstrate and explain a concept that was introduced by ES2015 called **generator functions**. We actually mentioned this earlier in the chapter, when covering `async` and `await`.

Here's the code of the method:

```
loadYears(): void {
    console.log("Loading the years");
    const retVal: number[] = [];
    const yearGenerator = this.generateYears(2000, 20);

    let done: boolean = false;
    while (!done) {
        const res = yearGenerator.next();
        done = res.done;
        if (done) {
            break;
        } else {
            retVal.push(res.value);
        }
    }
    this._view.displayYears(retVal);
}
```

Next, we also need to adapt the constructor to invoke this function. Add the following to the constructor: `this.loadYears();`.

For now, you're missing the mysterious `generateYears` function for the code to compile. You can only see that we assign the value returned by the function to a `yearGenerator` constant. After that, we have a loop in which we keep calling `next()` on our `yearGenerator` until it tells us that it is done. While that loop keeps going, it **accumulates** the values in an array.

Okay, so obviously, the `generateYears` function generates values for us and we can iterate over these quite easily. For all we know, the object that we got back from the function call is an iterable (`https://developer.mozilla.org/en-US/docs/Web/JavaScript/Reference/Iteration_protocols`) object.

Here's the implementation of this function. Make sure to add it to your `WorldExplorerControllerImpl` class:

```
private *generateYears(startingYear: number, numberOfYears: number):
IterableIterator<number> {
    let currentYear = startingYear;
    while (currentYear < startingYear + numberOfYears) {
        yield currentYear;
        currentYear++;
    }
}
```

There are three things to notice in this code:

- The `*` character right before the method name. This indicates that this is a **generator function**.
- The return type: `IterableIterator<number>`, which clearly seems to indicate that we are returning an iterable **element**:
    - This type has a `next()` method, which returns an object (that is, an `IteratorResult` instance) containing two basic properties: `value`, which represents the next value in the sequence and `done`, a Boolean indicating whether the sequence has been consumed completely.
- The `yield` keyword.

So, indeed, `generateYears` is a generator function. These were introduced with ES2015 and are supported by TypeScript since version 2.3.

 Sit down on your chair, because the following paragraph might be destabilizing.

Normal functions execute from start to finish, before returning control to the calling code. Generator functions don't work that way! They are quite special since they can actually be **paused** and later **resumed**. We could also say that they can be exited and re-entered. Each time this happens, the execution context (that is, the state) is restored. Isn't that magical?

When a generator function is called, none of its code is immediately executed. Instead, it directly returns the generator to the caller (that is, in our case, we store it in the `yearsGenerator` constant).

 Each time that the generator function is called, it will return a new iterator instance. Each iterator instance can only be consumed once.

When a value is consumed through the generator (that is, when calling `next()` on it), then the generator function is executed right up to the point where it finds the `yield` keyword. When `yield` is used, it defines the value to return for this iteration of the generator.

If we go back to our example, then we can see that, when we yield a year, then we re-enter the generator function, increment the `currentYear` variable, return to the `while` loop condition, and so on. At some point, our generator will be called and the while condition will evaluate to `false`, ending the loop and letting the function actually return. At that point, `done` will be `true` in the returned object.

 The `yield*` expression can also be used to delegate to another generator or iterable object.

Generators are now easy to grasp but they're really powerful.

 Generator functions are **cooperative**, in the sense that when their execution pauses, they hand back control to the calling function, which has to send a signal (that is, call `next()`) to resume the execution of the generator. Here's the signature of the next function: `next(value?: any): IteratorResult<T>`. As a matter of fact, when the code calls the `next` function of a generator, it can pass a value back (that is, cooperate!). When the generator is resumed, the value passed through the `next` function will take the place of the `yield` expression, which can prove very useful.

Generator functions are actually the basic building blocks that are used to make `async` **and** `await` **possible**.

Implementing the renderChart method

Finally, let's now implement the most important piece of our puzzle, the `renderChart` method. We will code it together piece by piece as follows:

1. First of all, we need to retrieve the selections made by the user in the chart form. We can do so using the view's `getChartFormDetails` method:

```
console.log("Rendering the chart");
const chartFormDetails = this._view.getChartFormDetails();
```

Of course, we need to make sure that there are no errors:

```
if (chartFormDetails.error) {
    console.error("Failed to retrieve the chart details",
     chartFormDetails.error);
    return;
}
```

2. Furthermore, we can also verify that all the properties that we expected are defined and available:

```
if (!chartFormDetails.countryId || !chartFormDetails.indicator
|| !chartFormDetails.fromYear || !chartFormDetails.toYear ||
!chartFormDetails.chartType) {
    throw new Error("The chart details couldn't be retrieved
from
    the view!");
}
```

3. For the country, we should normally be able to retrieve it from our cache (that is, the `countriesMap` map); if not, then there is probably an error in the view layer, so we display an error message:

```
let country: Country;
if (this._countriesMap.has(chartFormDetails.countryId)) {
    country =
this._countriesMap.get(chartFormDetails.countryId) as
    Country;
} else {
    console.error("Tried to render a chart for an unknown
    country. Identifier: ", chartFormDetails.countryId);
```

```
this._view.displayErrorMessage("Failed to render the
chart!");
return;
}
```

 We can safely cast the map entry to `Country` because we know that the map contains it and that it actually is a `Country` object. This isn't 100% safe because, of course, at runtime, someone could manipulate our map, but it doesn't matter too much here.

4. For the indicator, we use the same trick as in the previous chapter to find the enum entry. If it fails, then we again simply display an error message:

```
const indicator: WorldBankApiV2Indicators =
WorldBankApiV2Indicators[chartFormDetails.indicator as keyof
typeof WorldBankApiV2Indicators];

if (!indicator) {
    console.error("Tried to render a chart for an unknown
    indicator. Identifier: ", chartFormDetails.indicator);
    this._view.displayErrorMessage("Failed to render the
    chart!");
    return;
}
```

5. Next, we need to validate that the date range is valid:

```
if (chartFormDetails.fromYear > chartFormDetails.toYear) {
    console.error(`Tried to render a chart for an invalid date
    range: from [${chartFormDetails.fromYear}]
    to [${chartFormDetails.toYear}]`);
    this._view.displayErrorMessage("The start year cannot be
    after the end year");
    return;
}
```

6. If it is valid, then we create the string in the format required by the World Bank API:

```
let dateRange: string = `${chartFormDetails.fromYear}`;
if (chartFormDetails.fromYear !== chartFormDetails.toYear) {
    dateRange =
        `${chartFormDetails.fromYear}:${chartFormDetails.toYear}`
}
```

Notice that we continue to leverage template strings whenever we can.

 Here, there is actually an opportunity to improve the code. Instead of requiring a string for the `dateRange` parameter of the population service API calls, we could have introduced a specific data type and moved the logic there instead of polluting our controller layer. You can try to improve this part as an exercise.

For the chart type, we simply take the value as is:

```
let chartType: string = chartFormDetails.chartType;
```

For added safety, we could probably validate that the `chartType` string actually exists in the typings of Chart.js.

Finally, based on the chosen indicator, we can do the following:

1. Fetch the data that we need using the population service.
2. Define the chart's title.
3. Create a `ChartDetails` object.
4. Order the view to render the chart.

Here is the code:

```
try {
    let title = "";
    let xAxisLabel = "";
    let yAxisLabel = "";
    let data: DataPoint[] = [];
    switch (indicator) {
        case WorldBankApiV2Indicators.TOTAL_POPULATION:
            data = await
            this._populationService.getTotalPopulation(country,
             dateRange);
            title = "Total population";
            break;
        case WorldBankApiV2Indicators.TOTAL_MALE_POPULATION:
```

```
            data = await
             this._populationService.getMalePopulation(country,
             dateRange);
            title = "Total male population";
            break;
        case WorldBankApiV2Indicators.TOTAL_FEMALE_POPULATION:
            data = await
             this._populationService.getFemalePopulation(country,
             dateRange);
            title = "Total female population";
            break;
        case WorldBankApiV2Indicators.ADULT_MALE_LITERACY:
            data = await
            this._populationService.getAdultMaleLiteracy(country,
            dateRange);
            title = "Adult male literacy";
            break;
        case WorldBankApiV2Indicators.ADULT_FEMALE_LITERACY:
            data = await
            this._populationService.getAdultFemaleLiteracy(country,
             dateRange);
            title = "Adult female literacy";
            break;
        case WorldBankApiV2Indicators.LIFE_EXPECTANCY:
            data = await
            this._populationService.getLifeExpectancy(country,
             dateRange);
            title = "Life expectancy";
            break;
        case WorldBankApiV2Indicators.ADULT_MALE_SURVIVAL_TO_65:
            data = await
            this._populationService.getMaleSurvivalToAge65(country,
             dateRange);
            title = "Adult male survival to age 65";
            break;
        case WorldBankApiV2Indicators.ADULT_FEMALE_SURVIVAL_TO_65:
            data = await
             this._populationService.getFemaleSurvivalToAge65(country,
             dateRange);
            title = "Adult female survival to age 65";
            break;
        default:
            throw new UnreachableCaseError(indicator); // will
 // fail to compile if we forget a switch case
    }

    const dataLabel = `${title} in ${country.name} for the
     ${chartFormDetails.fromYear}-
```

```
        ${chartFormDetails.toYear} time period`;

    const chartDetails: ChartDetails = {
        chartType,
        data: data.reverse(), // put the oldest data first
        dataLabel,
        title,
        xAxisLabel,
        yAxisLabel
    };

    this._view.displayChart(chartDetails);
} catch(error) {
    console.error("Failed to render the chart. Error: ", error);
    this._view.displayErrorMessage("Failed to render the chart!");
    return;
}
```

In the `default` clause, notice that we have used the trick with `never` that we discussed in the previous chapter. Our code will not compile if we forget a switch case.

As a matter of fact, for our code to compile, we need to implement the `UnreachableCaseError` class. We'll do that next.

Don't forget to add the necessary imports:

```
import {DataPoint} from "../domain";

import {PopulationService, WorldBankApiV2Indicators} from
"../services";

import {ChartDetails, WorldExplorerView} from "../views";
```

Implementing the UnreachableCaseError class

We'll create a `common` package for this class. This will represent a layer of code that is shared between different parts of our code base:

1. Create an `src/common` folder.
2. Create an `errors` folder under `src/common`.

Inside the `src/common/errors` folder, do the following: Create a file called `unreachable-case-error.ts`. Here's the code:

```
export class UnreachableCaseError extends Error {
    constructor(val: never) {
        super(`Unreachable case: ${val}`);
    }
}
```

Next, do the following:

1. Create a barrel for the `errors` package and export the `UnreachableCaseError` class.
2. Create a barrel for the `common` package and re-export everything from the `errors` package using `export * from ./errors`.

With this done, we'll be able to cleanly import things from `common` instead of having to know the exact folder and filenames.

Finally, add the missing import in `src/controllers/world-explorer-controller.ts`: `import {UnreachableCaseError} from "../common";`.

Creating the controller layer barrel

To finish up our controller layer, we should also create a barrel for it. By now, you should be used to this:

1. Create an `index.ts` file in `src/controllers`
2. In it, export the following elements:

```
export * from "./world-explorer-controller.intf";
export * from "./world-explorer-controller";
```

With that done, it'll be easier to later import our controller interface and implementation.

Initializing our application

We are almost done. Now that all our layers are implemented, we only need to Bootstrap our application.

The entry point defined within `index.html` is `src/world-explorer.ts`. You should already have this file. Go ahead and open it now.

Here's the code for this file:

```
import {PopulationService, PopulationServiceImpl} from "services";
import {WorldExplorerHTMLView, WorldExplorerView} from "./views";
import {WorldExplorerControllerImpl, WorldExplorerController} from
"./controllers";

console.log("WorldExplorer - Loading...");
const populationService: PopulationService = new
PopulationServiceImpl('https://api.worldbank.org');

const view: WorldExplorerView = new WorldExplorerHTMLView();

const controller: WorldExplorerController = new
WorldExplorerControllerImpl(populationService, view);

interface CustomWindow extends Window {
    worldExplorerController?: WorldExplorerController
}

const customWindow: CustomWindow = window;
customWindow.worldExplorerController = controller;
```

We simply import the interfaces and classes for our service, our view, and our controller. Then, we instantiate each of those in order, providing the view and service to the controller.

Finally, we customize the global object, just like we did in the previous chapter, allowing us to put our controller on the global scope again.

There we are! `WorldExplorer` is now ready and is fully functioning.

Start the application now using `npm run serve` and you should be able to explore the different indicators that we have added support for.

Here's what the user interface should look like when a chart is loaded:

Go ahead and explore the indicators for a few countries. You'll be surprised!

Leveraging TypeScript path mappings

Our imports already look much better because we have created barrels, which remove the need for knowing the exact filenames. However, our imports still need to indicate the relative paths to the packages that we want to import symbols from.

This is far from ideal because as your applications grow in complexity, your paths will be longer and longer and you might end up with imports like this: `import { foo } from '../../../../../services';`.

A good IDE will go a long way to diminish the annoyance, but it will still have an impact on readability and refactoring. Fortunately, we can improve the situation by adapting the compiler's configuration.

In `tsconfig.json`, we can configure the `paths` option in order to define mappings. Those mappings will let us use non-relative imports (for example, services).

The `paths` mapping values are relative to the `baseUrl` property.

Here's an example:

```
"paths": {
    "services": ["services"]
}
```

With this defined in `tsconfig.json`, we could adapt our imports for the service layer elements like this:

```
import {PopulationService} from "services";
```

However, if you try this out right away, you'll get errors from Parcel (the bundler that we used to build `WorldExplorer`). The thing is that Parcel includes its own module resolution mechanism (`https://parceljs.org/module_resolution.html`), which we need to configure for it to be able to find our modules.

To configure Parcel's module resolution scheme, you need to add an `alias` property to the `package.json` file. For example, here's what you could add for the `services` package:

```
"alias": {
    "services": "./src/services"
}
```

With this defined, both the TypeScript compiler and Parcel will happily resolve your modules using friendlier names.

Why don't you go ahead and adapt all the imports in `WorldExplorer`?

One caveat of the IDEs is that when you use them to add your imports, you might still end up with relative imports, depending on their level of support for TypeScript. In IntelliJ, for example, `paths` will be taken into account, which is nice, but not all IDEs do that.

Summary

In this chapter, we have learned about a *ton* of new things.

First and most importantly, we considered modules, which are crucial in today's JavaScript/TypeScript ecosystem. Using modules, we were able to dramatically improve the organization of our code. Thanks to them, each and every piece of our application is now cleanly isolated and can clearly define what it needs to import (that is, its dependencies) and what it exposes to the outside world using exports (that is, its public API).

We first saw where modules come from, and how they've evolved over time to finally become part of the ECMAScript specification. This led us to discuss the Revealing Module pattern, AMD, CommonJS, System, and UMD. After that, we discovered how to use them with TypeScript, including the following:

1. How to import modules and use destructuring
2. How to export modules
3. How to define barrels using re-exports
4. How module resolution works

Along with that, we also learned about module loaders and bundlers.

Then, we turned our attention to the Fetch API, which is part of modern web browsers and is also usable in other runtime environments, thanks to polyfills. While we were covering that, we also looked at what REST APIs are meant to be.

We briefly mentioned the promise chaining pattern, but only to place emphasis on the fact that there are now better alternatives in terms of code readability. We demonstrated this by introducing `async` and `await`, which enable us to write synchronous-looking asynchronous code, without losing the capability to properly handle errors.

We also introduced the `io-ts` library, which we used to add runtime type checks. This drastically improved the safety of our code.

While coding `WorldExplorer`, we leveraged various techniques, tips, and tricks that we acquired throughout the previous chapters.

During the implementation, we also had the opportunity to learn about some other TypeScript concepts, such as generators and `yield`, the property shorthand notation, path aliases, and others.

Finally, we played with Chart.js to easily render great-looking dynamic charts.

In the next chapter, we are going to take the time to discuss code quality in general and testing in particular.

Further reading

Here are some useful resources related to the subjects covered in this chapter.

Modules

Check out the following links if you want to learn more about ESM and other module types:

- `https://hacks.mozilla.org/2018/03/es-modules-a-cartoon-deep-dive`
- `http://exploringjs.com/es6/ch_modules.html`
- `https://developers.google.com/web/fundamentals/primers/modules`
- `https://developer.mozilla.org/en-US/docs/Web/JavaScript/Reference/Statements/import`
- `https://developer.mozilla.org/en-US/docs/Web/JavaScript/Reference/Statements/export`
- `https://eloquentjavascript.net/10_modules.html`

Namespaces

You can learn more about namespaces here:

- `https://www.typescriptlang.org/docs/handbook/namespaces.html`
- `https://www.typescriptlang.org/docs/handbook/namespaces-and-modules.html`

RESTful APIs

You can find a pretty thorough RESTful API guide here, if you want to learn more: `https://github.com/NationalBankBelgium/REST-API-Design-Guide/wiki`

The Fetch API

You can learn more about the Fetch API here:

- `https://developers.google.com/web/updates/2015/03/introduction-to-fetch`
- `https://davidwalsh.name/fetch`

Async and await

Here are some interesting links, if you want to dive deeper into this subject:

- `https://javascript.info/async-await`
- `https://basarat.gitbooks.io/typescript/docs/async-await.html`
- `https://blog.logrocket.com/promise-chaining-is-dead-long-live-async-await-445897870abc`
- `https://blog.bitsrc.io/keep-your-promises-in-typescript-using-async-await-7bdc57041308`

io-ts and fp-ts

You can learn a lot more about `io-ts` and `fp-ts` here:

- `https://github.com/gcanti/io-ts`
- `https://www.npmjs.com/package/io-ts`
- `https://lorefnon.tech/2018/03/25/typescript-and-validations-at-runtime-boundaries`
- `https://medium.com/@ottoki/runtime-type-checking-with-io-ts-in-typescript-14465169fb02`
- `https://www.olioapps.com/blog/type-driven-development-with-typescript`
- `https://www.olioapps.com/blog/checking-types-real-world-typescript`

Generators

You can learn more about iterators and generators here:

- `https://developer.mozilla.org/en-US/docs/Web/JavaScript/Guide/Iterators_and_Generators`
- `https://developer.mozilla.org/en-US/docs/Web/JavaScript/Reference/Statements/function*`
- `https://developer.mozilla.org/en-US/docs/Web/JavaScript/Reference/Global_Objects/GeneratorFunction`
- `https://developer.mozilla.org/en-US/docs/Web/JavaScript/Reference/Global_Objects/Generator`
- `https://davidwalsh.name/es6-generators`
- `https://www.typescriptlang.org/docs/handbook/release-notes/typescript-2-3.html`

Introduction to Testing

6

In this chapter, we'll explore some ideas about software testing. Then, we'll see how we can write tests for our `WorldExplorer` project using the TypeScript and JavaScript testing libraries. For any real-world application, we should really start thinking about the quality and reliability of our code as early as possible in the development life cycle.

So far in the book, we've tried to raise your awareness about defensive programming techniques, and we have even added runtime type checks to go further, but it is still far from enough!

If you develop applications as we have done so far in the book, then before long you'll most probably end up with unmaintainable and very brittle code. We have approached the different subjects covered so far from an implementation point of view in order to focus on the TypeScript language and its usage, but in a real application, automated tests should be written, ideally, even before the actual code.

We want to take some time to discuss some important ideas around software testing before we move on with our exploration of modern web development.

Let's get started.

Introducing testing

Testing is a very broad subject, and it deserves a lot more space than we can devote to it in this book. Here, we will merely be able to scratch the surface.

Code quality and testing

The population service of `WorldExplorer` might be coded defensively, but we **should** have proof that it will fail gracefully when issues arise.

Here are some examples of things that could go wrong:

- The network could be down when we make a request or before we receive a result.
- The server might be unavailable.
- The server might return unexpected data (for example, missing data, incorrect types, HTTP errors, and many others).
- The code making use of the service could provide invalid input (for example, for the `dateRange` property, for the `country` property, and many others).
- We might have forgotten to handle some error types.
- We might have forgotten to perform some validations.
- Maybe our code will break if too many results are returned at once.
- Maybe our code has security flaws that might get exploited.
- Maybe our code will break if we switch to a newer version of TypeScript or some library.

These only scratch the surface of the myriad of potential errors that could affect our code and thus the users of our application. The only way for us to increase our confidence in the code is to test it.

The objective of testing is to detect as many potential issues as early as possible in the development cycle to reduce their likelihood, their severity, their impact, and so on. The sooner issues can be discovered, the less it should cost to fix them.

 Do not think that software testing is only a job for software testers. Each and every software developer should develop their testing skills and write tests for their code. Testing is an essential skill to master for **any** software craftsperson.

Test types

Issues and bugs can affect our applications at all levels, from the lowest (for example, the wrong variable type) to the highest (for example, bugs in the interface). They can also be **non-functional**, for example, related to security (confidentiality, integrity, and availability), usability, and so on. There are many different types of tests that we can consider here to test both functional and non-functional vulnerabilities, weaknesses, and bugs.

Functional tests

These are tests that validate the correctness of the code, from a features point of view (that is, does the software do what it should?). Functional tests need to validate that everything works as expected:

- **Unit tests**: Unit tests are the lowest level tests that we can write. These tests focus on the smallest units of code (for example, functions and classes). For example, we could write a unit test that checks a specific function or class. Unit tests assume that the system is a white box; this means that we know the inner workings of the system when writing the tests. These tests should work in complete isolation. This means that if the unit of code **under test** relies on other parts of the system, then these should be abstracted away in order to avoid side effects. This can be done using **mocks** and **stubs**. Unit tests are usually the cheapest to develop and maintain and the fastest to execute, compared to other types of tests.

- **Integration tests**: Integration tests are higher-level tests that we can write to verify that different parts of our system integrate as they should with other parts and that, as a whole, they deliver the expected functionality. These tests only require **some** level of isolation; this means that we will focus on specific interactions and that we'll abstract away other ones depending on what we aim to test. Integration tests are often relevant for distributed systems. They're usually slower to execute than unit tests, simply because they need to do more setup work before executing.

- **End-to-end tests**: End-to-end (**E2E**) tests are higher-level tests that can be created in order to validate complex scenarios. Sometimes, **user interface (UI)** tests are performed by E2E tests, but it certainly isn't the only solution. Actually, UI tests can also be performed through unit tests. E2E tests are way above unit tests because they rely on the collaboration of all system parts, from the lowest-level units of code up to the UI layer. The user interface is usually harder to test because it tends to be much less stable than other parts: each modification to the interface will directly affect the tests, and so these are brittle. Generally speaking, E2E tests cost a lot more to create and maintain over time. Importantly, they're also usually much slower to execute.

- **System tests**: System tests are tests that consider the whole application as a black box and validate its behavior according to the requirements.

- **Sanity tests**: Sanity tests are tests that aim to provide some confidence about the overall system. They only aim to check the major features of the system to validate that they work as intended. Sanity tests are usually performed when there is not enough time to go deeper.

- **Smoke tests**: Smoke tests are similar to sanity tests because they also try to touch the main features of the system. The difference is that tests that are marked as smoke tests are the first ones to be executed for any new build. If any of those fail, then there's no need to go further; otherwise, the rest of the tests can be executed. Smoke tests are useful for avoiding useless quality assurance checks. In one sense, we can consider smoke tests as the bare minimum tests that should pass before the rest are even looked at.

- **Regression tests**: As their name indicates, regression tests are tests that we can write to ensure that some previously fixed issue does not resurface. Whenever we fix some important bugs, then we should consider writing a test case to validate that the software continues to work as intended. Whenever those tests get executed, they'll check whether there is any regression in the new code.

- **Acceptance tests**: Acceptance tests are used to decide whether a new version of an application is good enough to make it to production. Acceptance tests are detailed scenarios that represent concrete examples of interactions with the system to achieve business goals. Acceptance tests should ensure that of all the major parts of the system work as intended. In an ideal world, acceptance tests should also be automated and thus be part of the executable specifications. Such scenarios are not easy to write, but there are techniques that can help, such as feature mapping: `https://johnfergusonsmart.com/feature-mapping-a-simpler-path-from-stories-to-executable-acceptance-criteria`.

Non-functional tests

Non-functional tests are complementary to the preceding test types since they focus on other important aspects of the system:

- **Performance tests**: Performance tests ensure that the system works with the intended performance. Performance is sometimes a critical requirement (for example, for games, trading systems, and so on). Performance tests measure the speed at which the system performs some operations.

- **Load/stress tests**: Load tests, also called **stress tests**, are related to performance tests; they verify that the system can withstand the pressure when the load or **stress** on the system increases. For example, an application might work perfectly with a single user but become horrendously slow as the number of concurrent users increases. Again, this might be okay for some systems but problematic for other ones. Load tests perform many operations within a limited time frame and check specific aspects such as CPU usage, memory consumption, and so on.
- **Security/vulnerability tests**: Security tests verify that your application is not susceptible to specific vulnerabilities. Usually, you'll develop such tests when you fix a vulnerability in your system in order to ensure that it does not resurface. In that sense, security tests are also regression tests.
- **Penetration tests**: Penetration tests are closely related to security tests. They are performed by security specialists that try to find all the vulnerabilities that they can in your system. Penetration testers are **white hat hackers**, meaning that they have good intentions; they're trying to help you improve the security of your application and not to take advantage of the vulnerabilities. When vulnerabilities are discovered during penetration tests, they should be fixed and security/regression tests should be added to the application's test suite.
- **Compatibility tests**: Compatibility tests are needed to ensure that your application is compatible with whatever it is supposed to be, whether that is a specific runtime environment, operating system, and so on. Those tests are executed under different conditions and should verify compliance.
- **Usability tests**: Usability tests are checks performed by user interface specialists that aim to ensure that your application is usable, user-friendly, and efficient. This is a very specific category of tests that is much harder to automate as there is a lot of room for interpretation.

Again, there are many books covering this subject alone. In this book, given our space constraints, we'll focus only on unit tests and end-to-end tests.

Testing approach and mindset

When you design and implement tests, you need to start thinking like a malicious hacker. You need to start getting suspicious about everything and to verify everything. You need to think about positive cases, edge cases, and also abnormal scenarios.

A positive case or scenario represents the base case, that is, the ideal world scenario where everything goes according to plan. Of course, that is the first thing to validate. This simply means validating that the code actually works with valid input. Ideally, you should check the full range of valid inputs (when possible).

But you shouldn't stop there. You should then look at more exceptional cases and test the edge cases (that is, the boundaries). For example, if a function works with numbers, then what are the smallest/largest ones allowed? Does the code work with those boundaries?

After that, you can check what happens if you provide invalid or empty input (for example, a value out of the allowed range). Does the code validate data before processing it? Does it throw the expected errors or does it fail in unpredictable ways?

Finally, depending on the type of test, you need to look at non-functional aspects. For example, how much time does the code take to process one item? Then, consider 10 items, then 1,000, and so on.

Mocks and stubs

While writing tests, sometimes we need to abstract away or mock some parts of our system in order to make testing possible and the results reproducible. Mocks are mainly used for unit testing. As we've mentioned, unit tests must work in complete isolation, which means that when we test a specific unit of code (for example, a function), then all of its dependencies should be controlled and should not cause side effects.

Mocks are **imitations** or **fake** units (that is, objects, variables, functions, and so on) that **simulate** the behavior of real units. We can use mocks in order to control the dependencies used by the code that we want to test. For example, if we want to write unit tests for the population service of `WorldExplorer`, then we need to create a mock for the Fetch API. Otherwise, we will remain dependent on its implementation and on the World Bank API, which is not what we need for unit tests. What we want is full isolation.

Mocks are useful because they can be controlled and inspected; for example, you can check whether a mock has been called or not, what the parameters were, and so on. You can also control what mocks will return when called.

Mocks eliminate side effects since they are units that we fully control ourselves during the execution of the test. This means that we decide how they react to specific operations. For example, we can instruct a mock to throw an error or return a specific object when we want to. Thanks to mocks, we can test all the possible scenarios by **faking** the conditions under which our code executes.

Stubs are similar to mocks, but they are usually **simpler**: they implement only the bare minimum to let the code under test work. Libraries that support mocking usually allow us to create mocks and to define and verify our **expectations** (that is, what should be called, how many times, and so on).

The test pyramid

An important metaphor to keep in mind when thinking about software testing is the **test pyramid**. The idea behind it is that we can regroup the different types of tests based on their cost and their execution speed. Based on that segmentation or order, we should write enough cheap tests to cover most of the functionality and cover the rest with other types of tests.

At the base of the pyramid are the unit tests, which are very cheap to create and maintain and are also the fastest to execute. At the top of the pyramid are the end-to-end tests and manual tests, which are more complex to create, much more costly to maintain, and are also slower to execute:

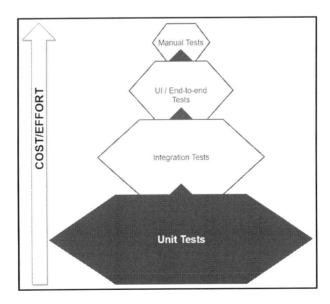

You should always have at least a set of unit tests. Then, depending on the scenarios, you might also need to write integration tests and end-to-end tests to properly cover the different flows.

Test automation and the Definition of Done (DoD)

Test automation is of critical importance. Tests are only valuable if you can automate their execution. Having to manually execute tests costs way too much time and effort. This is why you should write automated test suites during the development of your systems and not afterward. An automated test suite is a set of tests that you can execute automatically as often as you want (for example, with every build of the application).

To make this possible, your development time estimates should always take testing into account. Having a clear **Definition of Done (DoD)** is important as it will list everything that should be accounted for when estimating the time required to implement some feature requests (for example, the time to develop, write tests, document, review, and so on) and will help you convince stakeholders.

To automate tests, you need to write them using tools and libraries that support automation. We'll soon explore some options for test automation in the JavaScript/TypeScript ecosystem.

Test Driven Development

A very popular approach, called **Test Driven Development** (TDD), recommends first focusing on the tests before the implementation. With TDD, you start by writing tests, which effectively become the system's specifications. Only then can you start developing the code that implements those specifications.

The idea is that your tests will fail until you properly implement the necessary code to make them pass. Writing the tests first is beneficial because it forces you to think early enough and more precisely about the functional requirements and the APIs.

By applying the TDD approach and assuming that your specifications are correct, you can improve the quality and reliability of your applications.

You have to think about your test suite as a critical part of the build process. If some tests fail, then your build will fail, and thus you cannot release or deploy your application until you fix the issues. By developing this way, you'll ensure at build time that everything is working according to plan, which is much safer than checking only at runtime.

Behavior Driven Development

Behavior Driven Development (**BDD**) combines ideas and techniques from TDD with those of the domain-driven design approach. As such, it can be considered as an evolution of TDD.

The main focus of the BDD methodology is to improve the collaboration and communication between software developers, quality assurance teams, and analysts and business users. To do so, BDD pushes the idea of describing **stories** composed of **scenarios**, understood by all stakeholders.

Those stories and scenarios become the specifications of the system and can be written along with the tests and validated by them, as part of your code base. When you do so, then those scenarios and stories become **executable specifications**. By executing BDD tests, you effectively validate that your system complies with its specifications.

By applying the BDD approach and writing BDD test specifications, you actually create a close relationship between the specifications and implementation. This is very beneficial as the specifications then become an integral part of the application's code base, versioned with the rest of the code. This is much more powerful and maintainable than having long Word documents, stored **somewhere**, that your code is supposed to comply and stay in sync with. By having the specifications within the code base, both live side by side and evolve together instead of separately.

BDD tests help to focus on the system's behavior and expected outcomes rather than on implementation details.

BDD scenarios usually have the following structure:

- Given: Initial state
- When: Some event occurs
- Then: Expected outcome

Here's an example:

```
Story: Grant access to the system to a new user
As a system administrator
In order to grant access to the system to a new user
I want to create a new user account

Scenario 1: The username is not used yet

Given that the chosen username that is not taken already
And that the username is not too long
When the account has been created
Then I should be able to find it back in the list of users

Scenario 2: The username is already taken
Given that the chosen username is already in use
When the account is being created
Then I should get an error telling me that the username is already in
use
```

BDD scenarios aim to be readable by everyone (not only software developers). To reach that goal, BDD tests use a domain-specific language (that is, the language and terms of the domain experts). This is a concept taken from **Domain-Driven Design (DDD)** (that is, the ubiquitous language idea). The goal is to limit the vocabulary in order to limit communication issues and to use that vocabulary at all levels, from specifications to code.

The domain-specific language is defined project per project and tools can be used to detect the usage of specific words or sentences in the BDD stories and scenarios. For example, Gherkin (`https://docs.cucumber.io/gherkin/reference`) is a specification that is used by the Cucumber library (`https://cucumber.io`) and that defines a set of keywords (for example, `Feature`, `Example`, `Given`, `When`, `Then`, `And`, and so on) that can be extended by project-specific keywords.

JavaScript testing libraries and tools

In the JavaScript ecosystem, there are many testing libraries and tools.

Our goal here is not to express preferences or be exhaustive but simply to list a few options that are currently heavily used in the JavaScript community. It is up to you to evaluate them and decide which ones you prefer or want to use. Also, in this book, we will only use a subset of them.

Let's discover some of them together.

Unit testing

As with many things in the JavaScript/TypeScript ecosystem, there are many different solutions for unit testing. Here are some of the most popular unit testing libraries and tools:

- **Jest** (`https://jestjs.io/`) is a popular unit testing library. It is fast and easy to install, configure, and use. Jest includes support for mocking, asynchronous tests, DOM manipulation code testing, snapshot testing, code-coverage reports, TypeScript, and much more (`https://jestjs.io/docs/en/getting-started`). It also provides basic BDD-like testing support through its `describe` and `it` functions. This can be further improved by using the following utility library: the `jest-cucumber` library (`https://www.npmjs.com/package/jest-cucumber`). Jest was initiated at Facebook and is most notably used to test the React framework.

- **Mocha** (`https://mochajs.org`) is yet another unit testing library. Mocha can be combined with Chai (`https://www.chaijs.com`) to have BDD-style **assertions**.

- **Jasmine** (`https://jasmine.github.io`) is an easy to use unit testing library. It is similar to Jest but provides less features out of the box. It also features basic BDD support through a few utility functions called `given`, `when`, and `then`.

- **Cucumber.js** (`https://github.com/cucumber/cucumber-js`) is the JavaScript version of Cucumber (`https://cucumber.io`), a BDD testing solution. Using Cucumber, you can define BDD stories and scenarios in `.feature` text files, using the Gherkin syntax (`https://docs.cucumber.io/gherkin`) and a domain-specific language. Cucumber stories and scenarios can be written by non-developers, while actual tests validating those specifications are written by developers.

- **Karma** (`https://karma-runner.github.io`) is a test runner for JavaScript. It takes care of executing unit tests against different environments (for example, under Google Chrome, under Mozilla Firefox, and many others). Karma is testing framework agnostic, meaning that it can execute tests written using Jasmine, Mocha, and so on.

Many testing libraries, including some mentioned previously, provide some level of support for BDD-style testing. Most of them do so by providing an API that uses the `Given When Then` structure of BDD, or at least they try to make the tests more readable. Although, in most cases, tests using such libraries cannot be written by non-developers. For reference, check out `https://martinfowler.com/bliki/GivenWhenThen.html`.

Let's now look at tooling for E2E testing.

E2E testing and other tools

As with unit testing, there are also many popular options for writing end-to-end tests:

- **Protractor** (`https://www.protractortest.org`) is an end-to-end test framework created for Angular applications. Protractor tests are executed in a real web browser, interacting with it just like a user would (that is, clicking on buttons, waiting for elements to appear, and so on). Protractor (like many other E2E testing solutions) uses Selenium WebDriver (`https://www.seleniumhq.org/projects/webdriver`) to interact with the browser.
- **Cypress** (`https://www.cypress.io`) is another popular open source E2E testing solution.
- **Istanbul** (`https://istanbul.js.org`) is a tool that you can use to generate test coverage reports, allowing you to verify that you test your code base properly.
- **Puppeteer**: (`https://github.com/GoogleChrome/puppeteer`) is a tool that allows you to easily interact with the Google Chrome (or Chromium) web browser through a high-level API. It runs in headless mode by default (that is, it does not open a browser window). Puppeteer can be used in the context of E2E tests (for example, to make screenshots during tests, export pages as PDFs, and so on).

Testing libraries use **matchers** to define assertions in tests. Here's a basic example using Jest:

```
test('the sum of 1 and 2 is 3', () => {
  expect(1 + 2).toBe(3);
});
```

In the preceding test, we've used the `expect` function to define our expectation and the `toBe` matcher to define the expected result. Different libraries provide different matchers, but the ideas are similar. Here are some of the matchers provided by Jest:

- `toBeNull`
- `toBeDefined`
- `toBeTruthy`
- `not`
- `toBeLessThan`
- `toMatch`

Usually, matchers can be combined. Here's an example: `expect(value).not.toMatch(/foo/)`. You can find the full list of matchers included with Jest at `https://jestjs.io/docs/en/expect`.

And there are even more available, thanks to the Jest community effort: `https://github.com/jest-community/jest-extended`.

Testing the population service of WorldExplorer

Let's make those testing concepts more concrete by implementing some tests for the population service of `WorldExplorer`. To do so, we will use the Jest testing library.

Installing and configuring Jest

First of all, we need to install Jest and the necessary additions:

1. Install Jest using `npm install jest --save-dev`.
2. Install the typings for Jest using `npm install @types/jest --save-dev`.
3. Install the TypeScript preset for Jest using `npm install ts-jest --save-dev`.

   We've used `--save-dev` because Jest will only be used during development.

We've installed `ts-jest` (https://kulshekhar.github.io/ts-jest), a preprocessor plugin for Jest that adds support for TypeScript and source maps.

4. Now, create a file called `jest.config.js` at the root of the project (that is, next to the `package.json` file), with the following contents:

```
module.exports = {
    roots: [
        "<rootDir>/src"
    ],

    preset: 'ts-jest',
    testEnvironment: 'node',
    verbose: false,
    collectCoverage: false,
    globals: {
        'ts-jest': {
            // reference: https://kulshekhar.github.io/ts-
            jest/user/config
        }
    }
};
```

This configuration tells Jest to use its TypeScript preset and also tells it that our source code can be found under `src`. Finally, it also sets the test environment to `node`, which is where we will execute Jest.

You can also define the configuration of Jest directly as part of the `package.json` file. To do so, you just need to add a `jest` key to the file, as described here: https://jestjs.io/docs/en/configuration.html.

If you want to know more about how to configure Jest, check out the official documentation here: https://jestjs.io/docs/en/configuration.html.

There is a great list of resources related to Jest here: https://github.com/jest-community/awesome-jest.

5. Finally, modify the `package.json` file and add the following `"test"` script:

```
"test": "jest"
```

Your `"scripts"` section should then look as follows:

```
"scripts": {
  "tsc": "tsc",
  "build": "cross-env NODE_ENV=production parcel build
   src/index.html --public-url dist",
  "watch": "parcel watch src/index.html",
  "serve": "npm start",
  "start": "parcel serve --open --port 3000 src/index.html",
  "test": "jest"
},
```

6. Once that is done, you should be able to execute Jest using npm test. At this point, Jest should fail since we haven't created any tests so far:

```
$ npm run test

> worldexplorer@1.0.0 test ...
> jest

No tests found
In ...
  10 files checked.
  testMatch: **/__tests__/**/*.js?(x),**/?(*.)+(spec|test).js?
  (x),**/__tests__/**/*.ts?(x),**/?(*.)+(spec|test).ts?(x) -
  0 matches
  testPathIgnorePatterns: \\node_modules\\ - 10 matches
Pattern:  - 0 matches
```

If you notice, Jest has tried to find test files at different locations and different names, but couldn't find any. Let's now create a simple sanity test to ensure that our configuration works.

7. Create a file called `sanity.test.ts` at the root of the `src` folder, with the following contents:

```
test('adding 3 to 2 equals to 5', () => {
    expect(2 + 3).toBe(5);
});
```

In the preceding example, notice that we didn't need to import the Jest functions (that is, `test` and `expect`), thanks to the ambient type definitions.

8. If you now execute the `npm test` command again, the results should look better:

```
$ npm run test

> worldexplorer@1.0.0 test ...
> jest

PASS  src/sanity.test.ts

Test Suites: 1 passed, 1 total
Tests:       1 passed, 1 total
Snapshots:   0 total
Time:        2.593s
Ran all test suites.
```

As the output shows, our test has been found and successfully executed.

Using npm script hooks

At this point, we could add a `pre` script to our existing `build` script in `package.json`, in order to execute our test suite before building the application using Parcel. With that in place, we'll not only be sure that our code compiles, but our confidence will be increased because our application will only be built if the whole test suite passes. Here's an example script that we could use: `"prebuild": "npm run test"`.

This works because `npm` supports **script hooks**.

When `npm` finds a script with the same name as another, but with the **pre** prefix, then it executes that script before the other one. It is also possible to define a script that will be automatically executed after another one using the **post** prefix. You can learn more about hooks here: `https://medium.com/yld-engineering-blog/using-npm-pre-and-post-hooks-d89dcf2d86cf`.

Writing basic tests

Now that everything is configured, let's start writing our tests:

1. Go to the `services` folder.
2. Create a file called `population-service.spec.ts`.

 We recommend putting tests next to the code that they're testing and using the `.spec.ts` filename suffix. This is a common practice that makes it very straightforward to find the tests. Alternatively, you can use the `.test.ts` filename suffix.

3. Add the following code as a starting point:

```
import {PopulationServiceImpl} from "./population-service";

describe('population service', () => {
    let sut: PopulationServiceImpl;

    beforeEach(() => {
        sut = new PopulationServiceImpl('https/foo'); // valid
URL
    });

    // add tests here
});
```

With the preceding code, we've defined a dedicated **scope** for our tests using the `describe` function. You can find its documentation here: `https://jestjs.io/docs/en/api#describename-fn`.
Basically, `describe` creates a group for a set of tests that we could also call a **test suite**, but we'll keep using that term to refer to the whole set of tests of the application.

 Blocks using `describe` can be nested!

Within the `describe` block, we've created a variable corresponding to the unit that we want to focus on: `PopulationService`.

We've called the variable `sut`, which stands for **system under test**. This is a common naming convention used to refer to the unit that we're testing.

4. Finally, with the `beforeEach` function, we've made sure that a new (that is, clean) instance of our `PopulationServiceImpl` class will be created before each test is executed. Basically, `beforeEach` is a part of the setup and teardown functions provided by Jest. There are other setup and teardown methods that can be used, for example, `beforeAll`, `afterAll`, `afterEach`, and so on. You can find the complete list here: `https://jestjs.io/docs/en/setup-teardown`.

Now, let's add some tests inside the `describe` function together. First, we'll focus on the constructor function. Since it accepts a parameter, we need to verify whether it validates the input properly, as follows:

1. Let's start with a positive test (that is, providing a valid input):

```
it('should succeed if the URL is provided and valid', () => {
    expect(new PopulationServiceImpl('https://foo')).
    toBeInstanceOf(PopulationServiceImpl);
    expect(new PopulationServiceImpl('https://foo/')).
    toBeInstanceOf(PopulationServiceImpl);
    expect(new PopulationServiceImpl('http://foo')).
    toBeInstanceOf(PopulationServiceImpl);
    expect(new PopulationServiceImpl('http://foo/')).
    toBeInstanceOf(PopulationServiceImpl);
    expect(new PopulationServiceImpl('HTTP://foo/')).
    toBeInstanceOf(PopulationServiceImpl);
    expect(new PopulationServiceImpl('HTTPS://foo/')).
    toBeInstanceOf(PopulationServiceImpl);
});
```

In this test, we simply create new instances of the class by passing valid inputs each time, and we verify that we do end up with an instance of the class using `toBeInstanceOf`.

We've used the `it` function and have started our description using `should`. This way, the test description becomes easily readable.

2. We can then look at some negative cases:

```
test('should not accept empty input', () => {
    expect(() => new PopulationServiceImpl('')).toThrow();
    expect(() => new PopulationServiceImpl('')).toThrow();
});
```

This time, we've passed some invalid values to the constructor, and we expect it to throw an error. We needed to wrap the instantiation in a dummy function.

Here, we've used `test` instead of `it`; this is just an alias for the same function.

Here's another one that checks whether our constructor correctly checks invalid prefixes:

```
test('should not accept wrong prefix', () => {
    expect(() => new
     PopulationServiceImpl('foo://')).toThrow();
    expect(() => new PopulationServiceImpl('bar')).toThrow();
});
```

The preceding test tries to create instances of the service with invalid prefixes and ensures that the constructor throws an error as expected.

If you want to focus on a single test, you can replace `test` or `it` with `test.only` or `it.only`. When you do so, Jest will execute only that test. This is useful when troubleshooting issues with specific test cases. You can also use `describe.only` to limit the execution to a given test group.

3. Finally, we also need to try passing `null` or `undefined`:

```
test('should not accept null input', () => {
    expect(() => new PopulationServiceImpl(null as unknown as
    string)).toThrow();
    expect(() => new PopulationServiceImpl(undefined as
    unknown as string)).toThrow();
});
```

Great! This way, we know that our service does not accept any input.

Here, we've leveraged the `unknown` TypeScript 3 type with a type cast to bypass the compiler checks. Without this, the code wouldn't compile because we're not supposed to be able to pass `null` or `undefined` to the constructor function. You can use this trick to pass anything you want to a function. Don't forget to validate this, especially for library code, since you never know how your code will actually be used at runtime, when types mostly disappear.

Now that we've covered the basics of using Jest, we can tackle more complex scenarios.

You can also use the `fail('message')` Jest function to force a test to fail in some situations. This can sometimes be useful, for example, if you don't expect your code to fall into some branch during a specific test.

Let's look at how to test asynchronous code.

Testing asynchronous code

The rest of the methods provided by our service are asynchronous and use the Fetch API. To test those methods, we need to discover how to test asynchronous code with Jest and how to use mocks (for example, to avoid side effects when the Fetch API is called).

First of all, the good news is that Jest fully supports testing asynchronous code in general, whether that code works with callbacks, `Promises`, or `async`/`await`. You can find the related official documentation here: `https://jestjs.io/docs/en/asynchronous`. Since we're using `async` and `await`, we'll focus on them.

We can simply create an asynchronous test case by adding the `async` keyword in front of the test function definition:

```
it('should fail if the response does not have a 2xx status code',
async () ⇒ {
    await doSomethingAsync();
    ...
});
```

What we also need now is a polyfill for the Fetch API, since our tests will run in a Node environment, where Fetch is not available. We'll use `cross-fetch` (`https://www.npmjs.com/package/cross-fetch`) for this. Install `cross-fetch` using `npm install --save-dev cross-fetch`.

 Notice that, this time, we've used `--save-dev` since this dependency is only needed for tests.

In addition, we'll need a mock for the Fetch API. For this specific mocking need, we'll use the `jest-fetch-mock` utility library (`https://www.npmjs.com/package/jest-fetch-mock`):

1. Install it using `npm install jest-fetch-mock --save-dev`.
2. Create a file called `jest.setup.ts` at the root of the project (that is, next to `jest.config.js`) and add this to it:

   ```
   import {GlobalWithFetchMock} from "jest-fetch-mock";

   const customGlobal: GlobalWithFetchMock = global as
   GlobalWithFetchMock;

   // load the mock for the Fetch API:
   https://www.npmjs.com/package/jest-fetch-mock
   // and set it on the global scope
   customGlobal.fetch = require('jest-fetch-mock');
   customGlobal.fetchMock = customGlobal.fetch;
   ```

   In this file, we override the global `fetch` variable and we also assign a global `fetchMock` variable. This will make our tests clutter-free.

3. Now, edit the `jest.config.js` file to make sure that our `setup` script is loaded when Jest starts. Add the following property to it:

   ```
   setupFiles: [
       './jest.setup.ts'
   ]
   ```

By doing this, we've instructed Jest to execute the `jest.setup.ts` file when it initializes, right before running our tests. In that file, we've loaded the Fetch API mock and declared it in the global scope, which is not problematic in this specific case. Thanks to this, we'll now be able to control what the Fetch API calls return, using the API documented

here: `https://www.npmjs.com/package/jest-fetch-mock#api`.

Let's start off with a simple test and test our `checkResponseStatus` function as follows:

1. Create a dedicated group of tests for it within `population-service.test.ts`:

   ```
   describe('checkResponseStatus', () => {
       ...
   });
   ```

2. Now add a first test inside the `describe` block:

   ```
   it('should fail if no response object is passed', async () =>
   {
       await expect(sut.checkResponseStatus(null as unknown as
       Response)).rejects.toThrow();
   });
   ```

   Here, we make use of the `async` testing support of Jest to call `checkResponseStatus`. Notice that our test expects the promise to reject/throw using `rejects.toThrow()`.

3. Now, add additional tests for the edge cases of the method:

   ```
   it('should fail if the status is below 200', async () => {
       await expect(sut.checkResponseStatus(new Response(null, {
           status: 199
       }))).rejects.toThrow();
   });

   it('should fail if the status is above 299', async () => {
       await expect(sut.checkResponseStatus(new Response(null, {
           status: 300
       }))).rejects.toThrow();
   });
   ```

You can execute (and debug!) Jest tests using most IDEs. For example, IntelliJ Ultimate has built-in support for Jest: `https://www.jetbrains.com/help/idea/running-unit-tests-on-jest.html`. For Visual Studio Code, you can install this extension: `https://marketplace.visualstudio.com/items?itemName=Orta.vscode-jest`.

4. Finally, let's not forget to test the positive case:

```
it('should succeed if the response has a 2xx status code',
async () => {
    let fakeResponse: Response = new Response(null, {
        status: 200
    });

    await expect(sut.checkResponseStatus(fakeResponse))
    .resolves.toBe(fakeResponse);
    fakeResponse = new Response(null, {
        status: 204
    });

    await expect(sut.checkResponseStatus(
        fakeResponse)).resolves.toBe(fakeResponse);

    fakeResponse = new Response(null, {
        status: 299
    });

    await expect(sut.checkResponseStatus(
        fakeResponse)).resolves.toBe(fakeResponse);
});
```

This time, since we provide valid input to the function, we, of course, verify that the promise resolves to the expected value.

An alternative style to this is to add a `done` argument to the test function and to invoke it when the test is done or to invoke `done.fail` when an error is detected within the test.

Here's a nice article about asynchronous testing with Jest: `https://medium.com/@liran.tal/demystifying-jest-async-testing-patterns-b730d4cca4ec`.

Let's apply this knowledge to test the `getAllCountries` method.

Implementing positive and negative tests for getAllCountries

Now that we've seen how to test asynchronous code, let's see how we can test the getAllCountries method, which uses the Fetch API. For this one, we'll use our Fetch mock:

1. Create a new describe block as follows:

```
describe('getAllCountries', () => {
    beforeEach(() => {
        fetchMock.resetMocks();
    });

    // TODO add tests here
});
```

In the beforeEach function, we use jest-fetch-mock to reset the Fetch API mock. This is useful to avoid side effects between our test cases.

2. In the following beforeEach function, add the following variable:

```
const dummyValidData: WorldBankApiV2CountryResponse =
[{"page": 1, "pages": 7, "per_page": "50", "total": 304}, [{
    "id": "ABW",
    "iso2Code": "AW",
    "name": "Aruba",
    "capitalCity": "Oranjestad",
    "longitude": "-70.0167",
    "latitude": "12.5167"
}, {
    "id": "AFG",
    "iso2Code": "AF",
    "name": "Afghanistan",
    "capitalCity": "Kabul",
    "longitude": "69.1761",
    "latitude": "34.5228"
}]];
```

The variable represents a valid response for the Fetch call. Once added, you can now easily implement a positive test for getAllCountries as follows:

```
it('should succeed and return countries when the request
succeeds and a valid response is received', async () => {
    fetchMock.mockResponse(
        JSON.stringify(dummyValidData),
```

```
                {status: 200}
        );

    await expect(sut.getAllCountries()).resolves.toBeTruthy();

    await sut.getAllCountries()
        .then(countries => {
            expect(countries.length).toBe(2);

            const dummyValidCountries = (dummyValidData[1]);
            expect(countries[0].capitalCity).
            toBe(dummyValidCountries[0].capitalCity);
            expect(countries[0].name).
            toBe(dummyValidCountries[0].name);
            expect(countries[1].capitalCity)
            .toBe(dummyValidCountries[1].capitalCity);
            expect(countries[1].name).
            toBe(dummyValidCountries[1].name);
        })
        .catch(() => fail("Should not throw"));
})
```

The first notable thing that we do in this test case is to instruct `jest-fetch-mock` to always return our dummy data along with an HTTP status code of 200. This is what the `mockResponse` function call does. With that done, any request made by our code using `fetch` will receive our configured response in return. That is, until we call `mockResponse` again or until we call `fetchMock.resetMocks()`.

In the rest of the test, we simply use `await` and call our method under test. Then, using `resolves.toBeTruthy()`, we make sure that the function succeeds as expected. Finally, we repeat the operation and add a few checks to ensure that we do receive the same country data as we've provided through the Fetch API mock in return.

Our `dummyValidCountries` input is useful, but static. Sometimes, it is much more powerful to be able to quickly generate many different objects in order to test various scenarios more easily. Tools such as `cooky-cutter` (`https://www.npmjs.com/package/cooky-cutter`) can help you with that. You can learn more about that tool here: `https://medium.com/@skovy/object-factories-for-testing-in-typescript-501c8f42768e`.

3. Now, add a few negative test cases:

```
it('should fail and throw if the response does not match the
expected format', async () => {
    fetchMock.mockResponse(
        JSON.stringify({foo: "bar"}),
        {status: 200}
    );
    await expect(sut.getAllCountries()).rejects.toBeTruthy();
});
```

The call should fail this time since we're providing an unexpected response back to the function, even though the HTTP status code was 200.

4. Let's now check that the status code is indeed verified:

```
it('should check the response status and fail if
  outside of the allowed range (2xx)', async () => {
    fetchMock.mockResponse(
        JSON.stringify(dummyValidData),
        {status: 199}
    );
    await expect(sut.getAllCountries()).rejects.toBeTruthy();

    fetchMock.mockResponse(
        JSON.stringify(dummyValidData),
        {status: 300}
    );
    await expect(sut.getAllCountries()).rejects.toBeTruthy();
});
```

If you pay attention, you'll notice that by doing this, we're actually checking whether `checkResponseStatus` is called and whether the result of that call influences the result of the `getAllCountries` call. This test is relevant and useful because it makes sure `getAllCountries` does the necessary checks, and here, we don't care how it does so.

Spying on methods with Jest

Now, without implying that it is actually a good idea, let's see how we can spy on method calls using Jest. We'll verify that the `checkResponseStatus` method gets called as expected:

```
it('should call checkResponseStatus', async () => {
    fetchMock.mockResponse(
```

```
        JSON.stringify(dummyValidData),
        {status: 200}
    );

    const checkResponseStatusSpy = jest.spyOn(sut,
    "checkResponseStatus");

    await sut.getAllCountries().catch(() => {
        fail("Should not fail");
    });

    expect(checkResponseStatusSpy).toHaveBeenCalledTimes(1);
});
```

Using the `jest.spyOn` function, we tell Jest that we want to spy on the `checkResponseStatus` method. Then, after having called our `getAllCountries` method, we can verify whether the object that we're spying on has been called or not. In this case, the method is supposed to be called once.

 You can learn more about Jest `spy` objects here: `https://remarkablemark.org/blog/2018/04/10/jest-spyon-function`

We'll stop our small incursion into the world of testing for now. As you can imagine though, there is a lot more ground to cover. Why don't you continue testing the other methods of the class to get more familiar with the subject?

Take some time now to go through the documentation of Jest in order to learn about the Jest object, how to mock functions, modules, and so on. It's a very useful resource. Finally, make sure to read the following article: `https://medium.com/@rickhanlonii/understanding-jest-mocks-f0046c68e53c`. It will teach you everything about Jest's support for mocking.

Summary

In this short but important chapter, we learned about software testing.

We took the opportunity to remind you of the importance of software/code quality in general and of testing in particular. We briefly covered what testing is, as well as different types of tests that can be created to increase the confidence in what we build, mocks and stubs, and many other elements.

We also reviewed some testing approaches, such as TDD and BDD, as well as concepts such as the test pyramid, test automation, and many others.

While covering this subject, we also introduced different testing tools and libraries that are currently heavily used in the JavaScript/TypeScript ecosystem. We then presented the Jest testing library (`https://jestjs.io`).

After adding and configuring Jest, we wrote a few unit tests together and used `jest-fetch-mock` (`https://github.com/jefflau/jest-fetch-mock`), which made it possible to easily test our asynchronous code. Finally, we saw how to use Jest spy objects to verify our expectations.

Don't hesitate to explore some of the resources mentioned in the next section to dive deeper into testing. It will certainly not be a waste of your time and will make you a better developer.

In the next chapter, we're going to learn about modern web frameworks, and we will see how we can leverage TypeScript with them. We will start our exploration with Angular, one of the most popular solutions for creating modern web applications.

We hope that you've enjoyed the journey so far and that you are ready for the next half. We still have a ton of cool things to discover together!

7
Discovering Angular, Angular Material, and RxJS

In the first half of this book, we covered the crucial aspects of TypeScript, from its powerful type system to its support for modules. Even if you haven't realized it yet, you've actually learned the most important parts of TypeScript already! With that done, we can finally step up our game and start having fun with the language.

We still have a ton to learn together, though, but isn't that where all the fun is?

In the previous chapters, we didn't put a lot of effort into our user interfaces (to say the least). Of course, it wasn't our main focus, but we have to face the truth—it would be hard to reach an acceptable level of quality without having enough CSS experience. Notably, we didn't have any reusable user interface components at our disposal, nor the time to create our own.

The fact is that you'll rarely have the opportunity to dedicate a lot of time to the creation of basic user interface components for real-world projects. To make matters worse, given that we live in a mobile world, our applications are supposed to function/render nicely on a wide variety of devices and displays. Supporting this growingly complex ecosystem is insanely difficult.

Moreover, we have seen how tedious it was for us to get data in and out of the **Document Object Model (DOM)** by hand. Even if TypeScript offers an easy-to-use API to query it and make changes, we ended up writing a lot of code just to add or remove elements. If you multiply this hindrance tenfold, then you can imagine how cumbersome and error-prone it quickly becomes.

Finally, structuring our application has also proved to be challenging. Modules have helped us to improve code organization, but it remains for us to stay consistent in maintaining a well-structured code base.

The conclusion is obvious—we need help to make things easier, better structured, better-looking, and more efficient!

The good news is that we are not alone. Tens of thousands of organizations and developers worldwide face the same challenges. Luckily for us, we can stand on the shoulders of giants who have spent many man-years developing world-class solutions that are available for free under open source licenses.

The net result is that, in today's ecosystem, there are literally thousands of libraries and frameworks that we can pick and choose from to develop modern web applications.

In this book, we have chosen to present three different solutions: Angular (https://angular.io), React (https://reactjs.org), and Vue.js (https://vuejs.org), which are all tremendously popular nowadays. This is an arbitrary selection, of course, simply based on our own experience and the current trends in our industry.

 Sadly, we won't be able to do much more than scratch the surface here. Entire books have been written on each of those powerful solutions and we simply don't have enough space to go into them in depth. Still, we intend to present enough for you to gain a clear idea about what they are and how they work so that you can make up your mind about which one you like the most.

In this chapter, we will first take a look at what modern web applications actually are. Then, we'll begin our overview with the Angular framework (https://angular.io) and the Angular Material (https://material.angular.io) user interface component library, which implements the Material Design specification (https://material.io/design).

We will explore how they can be combined with TypeScript, and we'll continue to introduce you to additional TypeScript features.

We will also discover **Reactive Programming (RP)** and **RxJS** (https://rxjs-dev.firebaseapp.com), which are heavily used with Angular but can be applied in many situations, frameworks, and even technology stacks (for example, Java, .NET, and more).

To sum it up, we will cover the following topics in this chapter:

- Modern web applications
- TypeScript decorators
- Angular
- Angular application architecture
- Core concepts of Angular
- RP and RxJS
- Angular forms
- Material Design and Angular Material

Learning about modern web applications

Thanks to TypeScript and tools such as npm and Parcel, we've seen how great the developer experience can be nowadays, with the tooling doing the heavy lifting behind the scenes, letting us focus on adding valuable features.

Still, so far in this book, we have only created **old-school** web applications. If we take a hard look at the user interfaces of the applications that we have created, there's nothing really impressive to brag about.

Don't despair yet, though. Using TypeScript, together with frameworks such as Angular, we can create modern web applications. But what actually are they?

Server-side rendering

Since its inception in the 1990s, the **World Wide Web (WWW)** has never ceased to evolve and amaze us all.

At the beginning, websites were completely *static*. You would insert content into your web pages and these would be served as-is, without any modifications. Then, over the years, the web has become more and more dynamic.

For a long period of time, **server-side rendering (SSR)** was all the rage. Many languages and frameworks allowed developers to inject data into pages before returning the generated HTML to clients.

Frameworks such as Apache Struts (Java), JavaServer Faces (Java), ASP.NET (.NET), Zend (PHP), Django (Python), Flask (Python), Ruby on Rails (Ruby), and many more fall into this category.

At that time, web browsers were considered as dumb Terminals, merely capable of rendering HTML pages. There were multiple reasons for this state of affairs:

- Desktop usage was still predominant.
- Desktop computers were many times slower than our current smartphones.
- The JavaScript engines inside web browsers were much slower than those we have today.
- The web as a platform was far less capable than it is nowadays.

But SSR was not perfect. For instance, it wasn't network- or mobile-friendly. Server responses mixed data and presentation (HTML/CSS/images), which resulted in an enormous waste of bandwidth.

Applications relying on SSR usually maintained user sessions on the backend, which required more resources and more complex setups for high availability. For example, the **JavaServer Faces (JSF)** framework maintained the state of the user interface in memory for all connected users.

From a user's perspective, the main drawback of SSR was that most actions and page transitions required full round-trips to the backend and full page refreshes. This was wasteful and far from ideal for good user experiences.

However, as we'll see, SSR has its merits and is still relevant today. But, it has evolved to complement the experience provided by SPA, which we'll introduce next.

SPAs

When jQuery (`https://jquery.com`) came out and gained popularity, it initiated an important transition on the web. jQuery and similar libraries made it possible to dynamically adapt the content of web pages very easily. Moreover, combined with `XMLHttpRequest` (`https://developer.mozilla.org/en-US/docs/Web/API/XMLHttpRequest`), often called AJAX or XHR, it alleviated the need for full page refreshes. This was a great step forward for user experiences on the web.

The web 2.0 era had begun. This trend kept gaining strength and, combined with the rise of mobile devices, it forced developers to expose more and more services/data through web services (for example, RESTful APIs), so that they could be consumed easily.

Over time, most SSR frameworks have ended up integrating support for so-called partial page refreshes initiated by code executing on the client side. Usually, those frameworks embedded jQuery or similar JavaScript toolkits and provided higher-level APIs to update parts of the page using XHR requests and DOM manipulation.

With the accelerating shift toward mobile devices, the incredible popularity of JavaScript, and the rise in power of client devices, more and more code got written on the client side, which is logical since it made it possible to create superior user experiences while decreasing waste.

This shift was also linked to the evolution of web standards. HTML 5 and the WHATWG standard (`https://spec.whatwg.org`) heavily empowered web developers around the world and made the web platform far more appealing than ever before. Many APIs were introduced back then and were implemented in modern web browsers. The following are some examples:

- **Server-Sent Events (SSE)**:
  `https://developer.mozilla.org/en-US/docs/Web/API/Server-sent_events`
- **LocalStorage**: `https://developer.mozilla.org/en-US/docs/Web/API/Web_Storage_API/Local_storage`
- **SessionStorage**: `https://developer.mozilla.org/en-US/docs/Web/API/Window/sessionStorage`
- **The Notifications API**:
  `https://developer.mozilla.org/en-US/docs/Web/API/Notifications_API`
- **Service Worker API**:
  `https://developer.mozilla.org/en-US/docs/Web/API/Service_Worker_API`
- **The WebSocket API**:
  `https://developer.mozilla.org/en-US/docs/Web/API/Websockets_API`

These APIs are just the tip of the iceberg. The great news is that the trend continues. Each year, new APIs are standardized and added to web browsers. You can find out more at `https://developer.mozilla.org/en-US/docs/Web/API`.

Thanks to all of this, web developers have actually started creating full-blown applications running in the web browser. These applications are usually called **client-side apps** or **Single Page Applications (SPAs)**. They embed a lot of logic and can be stateful. For example, they can manage the state of the user interface, handle navigation from page to page, and much more—all without systematically depending on a remote backend system.

Most importantly, SPAs are very reactive and behave more like desktop applications. To achieve this, they heavily manipulate the DOM and make requests to the backend in order to fetch or push data only when needed.

Over time, it slowly became evident that DOM manipulation through jQuery and the like had its limitations. The lack of structure made it difficult to develop and maintain large applications using that approach. Moreover, dependency management and callback handling were a real nightmare for developers and caused more headaches than you could count.

We'll take a look shortly at how those issues can be solved using modern web frameworks.

Mobile-first and responsive web design (RWD)

As the world became more and more **mobile**, web developers and web designers began pushing heavily toward a reversal of priorities. Where people initially created web applications with desktops in minds, they were now thinking in a mobile-first way.

This is rather logical; if the majority of potential users were using mobile devices, why would we want to treat mobile as an afterthought during development?

Web developers started using **CSS media queries** (https://developer.mozilla.org/en-US/docs/Web/CSS/Media_Queries/Using_media_queries) to define **breakpoints**: points at which the different CSS rules start getting applied. Media queries make it possible to define specific rules that apply depending on the device's size, orientation, pixel density, and much more.

 This is beyond the scope of this book, but you can find a number of great examples at https://css-tricks.com/snippets/css/media-queries-for-standard-devices.

These are usually referred to as RWD techniques.

PWAs

In recent years, novel means of improving user experience have emerged. One very powerful approach is to create web applications that act more like desktop applications. We usually call these **Progressive Web Applications (PWAs)**.

For instance, PWAs can do the following:

- Function even if the user is disconnected from the network
- Make use of **push notifications** (that is, desktop-like notifications even if the application is closed)
- Access native features usually reserved for native applications (for example, GPS positions, device orientation, and more)

The core idea of PWAs is to provide **progressive enhancement** to end users. Here are some examples of what this means in practice:

- If users are online, the save functionality of a PWA will be available to them. If they are not, then the application can persist modifications locally and wait until the network is reachable again, at which point the data will be synchronized automatically.
- Users automatically get an up-to-date version of the application when they go online.
- Users can **install** the application on their desktop or mobile devices just as if it was a native one.

Modern web APIs, such as those that we have previously mentioned, make these scenarios possible (for example, web application manifests, service workers, web workers, IndexedDB, LocalStorage, SessionStorage, and more).

PWAs shouldn't be negatively impacted by disconnections. As we've mentioned, they're supposed to work offline (among other things). A good idea is to consider PWAs as **offline-first** web applications—think about how the different features of your applications should behave when the network is not reachable and what to do when it is.

Of course, creating a PWA requires more upfront effort, but the benefits for end users are important. Also, as we'll see shortly, modern web frameworks can also help and make this easier. Angular, which is the main subject of this chapter, has great support for PWAs: https://angular.io/guide/service-worker-intro.

An interesting tool to mention here is **Lighthouse**, developed by Google. Lighthouse allows you to automate a series of quality audits for modern web applications, including multiple ones for PWAs:

- `https://developers.google.com/web/tools/lighthouse`
- `https://developers.google.com/web/ilt/pwa/lighthouse-pwa-analysis-tool`

Modern web frameworks

Fortunately for us all, a new generation of web frameworks has emerged to alleviate the recurring pains that arise when developing web applications. Angular and React are among the top contenders, but there are dozens of others such as Aurelia (`https://aurelia.io`), Ember (`https://www.emberjs.com`), Dojo (`https://dojo.io`), Meteor (`https://www.meteor.com`), and more.

> **Most, if not all, of these have one thing in common: they make it very easy to perform DOM transformations without necessarily having to manipulate DOM nodes directly or manually**, as we did in previous chapters. That alone is a huge time-saver.

Before we go any further, keep in mind that nobody has to use a framework, but there are very compelling arguments for doing so nowadays. Frameworks provide reference architectures, high-level designs, naming conventions, formatting rules, skeletons for new applications, tooling to easily scaffold new projects, components, and so much more.

Of course, there are also arguments against using frameworks, but as soon as you're part of a team, then the value they bring to the table is quickly visible. You can read an interesting argument on this subject at `https://www.sitepen.com/blog/2017/11/10/web-frameworks-conclusions`.

Each framework has its own peculiarities and provides more or less built-in support for certain features; for example, dependency management, **dependency injection (DI)**, internationalization, HTTP call handling, routing/navigation, animation, and much more. Some also have varying degrees of support for PWAs, SSR, and many others.

Many of them provide ways to create and reuse user interface components and thus avoid code duplication, which increases safety and reduces maintenance costs. Many of them also support **web components** (https://www.webcomponents.org), which are very promising for the future of web development.

Modern web frameworks take advantage of powerful tools such as the module loaders and bundlers we discussed earlier. It slowly becomes trivial to automate the build of large/complex web applications and to create production-grade deliverables that are fully optimized. For instance, the Angular tooling (currently) uses webpack to create minified/uglified bundles and supports lazy loading and code splitting to load only parts of the application when they're accessed.

Most of these frameworks also make it much easier to test your frontend applications. For example, Angular applications can easily be unit-tested using any of the tools we've covered earlier. End-to-end tests can also be created easily using tools such as Protractor (https://www.protractortest.org).

As we've stated earlier, SSR still has value nowadays. For example, it can be very helpful for **search engine optimization (SEO)**, **graceful degradation** (for example, this functions even if JavaScript is not available), and pre-rendering to improve perceived performance. SSR is supported by multiple modern web frameworks. Angular is among them thanks to the Angular Universal project: https://angular.io/guide/universal.

There is also a lot of variety around what is included out of the box or supported through extensions/modules. For example, Angular is a framework that tries to come with the batteries included; it provides a lot of functionality as part of its core. React, on the other hand, is closer to a library and tries to be more minimalist.

Once again, there is value at both ends of the spectrum. Frameworks are more opinionated, which can help teams avoid wasting time making choices for many low-level details. Libraries, on the other hand, tend to be less opinionated, provide more freedom, and try to stay out of the way as much as possible. There are many shades of gray and there is no **better** or **worse** choice.

To a large extent, choosing between both depends on many factors, including personal taste, team maturity, background, skills, project budget, and timing.

Last but not least, more and more modern web frameworks support TypeScript to some extent, which, of course, brings many more benefits to the table.

Before we start our excursion into the Angular universe, we need to take a brief detour to discover TypeScript decorators. We have already mentioned and used them in Chapter 4, *Leveraging Generics and Enums to Build a Media Management Web Application*, but we haven't yet taken the time to understand what they actually are.

Understanding TypeScript decorators

It makes sense to discuss **decorators** now because they are heavily used by Angular.

We will only scratch the surface here, as decorators are fairly advanced and, most of the time, you'll be using them rather than writing your own.

What are decorators?

Decorators provide a way to do *metaprogramming* and attach *metadata* to classes and class members (that is, methods, accessors, fields, and parameters). They're sometimes referred to as *annotations*, but they are more than that (in TypeScript at least).

Annotations provide a way to attach metadata to annotated elements. While decorators can do the same, they can also expand and/or modify the behavior of the elements they're applied to.

 A **decorator** is actually a well-known design pattern that is generally used to wrap existing constructs and provide additional behavior/data to the decorated element.

In TypeScript, decorators are declared using functions with specific arguments and can be attached to classes and class members using the following notation: `@prefix`.

For example, a decorator called `Secured` would be applied to a class as follows:

```
@Secured
class Something
```

In fact, what follows the @ sign must be an expression that evaluates to a decorator function.

The following code is actually valid (but not very useful or readable):

```
@((target: any, propertyKey: string, descriptor: PropertyDescriptor)
=> {})
```

This works because what follows the @ sign is an expression that evaluates to a decorator function. Decorator functions receive the following:

- A target
- The name of the property that they decorate
- The descriptor of that property

We don't need to know much more for our purposes but do check out the official documentation for more details: `https://www.typescriptlang.org/docs/handbook/decorators.html`.

Decorators are not TypeScript-specific. They're actually on the ECMAScript standards track, meaning that they'll probably end up becoming part of the language. At the time of writing, decorators are in stage 2, thus they aren't ready for prime time, but they're getting closer.

You can find the state of all proposals that are being reviewed/prepared by the TC39 committee at: `https://github.com/tc39/proposals`.

Given that the official specifications aren't finalized yet, decorators remain **experimental** in TypeScript. Don't sweat it, though; they've been battle-tested as they are already used in production by thousands of applications. The only thing to keep in mind is that their syntax/semantics *could* change once they officially become part of ECMAScript.

To enable support for decorators in TypeScript, you need to enable the `experimentalDecorators` option in `tsconfig.json`.

Now, let's cover some use cases for TypeScript decorators.

When are decorators useful?

Decorators can be used to deal with **cross-cutting concerns** in your application—that is, concerns that are not directly related to application features but are instead present everywhere in the system and can't be isolated from the rest of the application.

Examples of cross-cutting concerns include logging, authorization, exception handling, transaction management, validation, caching, and more. All of these are **secondary**, but can't be taken out or isolated without loss.

Decorators help us to tackle such concerns cleanly. By annotating classes and their fields with decorators, and therefore adding metadata/behavior, you can add specific information/logic where needed, without necessarily cluttering your code.

Let's look at an example that demonstrates how badly cross-cutting concerns can **pollute** your code:

```
class BankService {
    constructor() { }

    public depositMoney(amount: number): void {
        log(`Persisting account change - start: ${new Date()}`);
        if(!isAuthenticated) {
            log('Refused to deposit money');
            throw new Error('Only authenticated users can deposit
            money');
        }

        if(!amount || amount <= 0) {
            throw new Error('The amount is not valid');
        }

        try {
            doInTransaction(() => {
              // try to do something interesting
              commitTransaction();
            });
        } catch(error) {
            log(`Operation failed: ${error}`);
            rollbackTransaction();
        }
        log(`Persisting account change - end: ${new Date()}`);
    }
}
```

In the preceding example, the actual business logic only represents a fraction of the code. The rest is exclusively dealing with cross-cutting concerns.

The following is how the same code could be rewritten with the help of decorators:

```
import {Authenticated, Traced, Transactional, ValidNumber} from "./02-
cross-cutting-utils";

class NewBankService {
  constructor() {
  }

  @Traced
  @Authenticated
  @Transactional
  public depositMoney(@ValidNumber({min: 0}) amount: number):
  void {
    // try to do something interesting
  }
}

new NewBankService().depositMoney(500);
```

Decorators are now responsible for handling secondary concerns while the method itself fully focuses on business logic. This is much better for readability, reusability, and maintainability.

Aspect-Oriented Programming

Thanks to decorators, you can actually develop applications using **Aspect-Oriented Programming (AOP)**. AOP is a programming paradigm that we haven't had the chance to discuss yet. It is a technique that is meant to deal with cross-cutting concerns.

The idea of AOP is to implement the logic for cross-cutting concerns once and reuse it declaratively and, as we've just seen, this is exactly what decorators enable us to do!

By adding decorators to elements, you can instrument those. For example, you could create and use a decorator for all your service methods, ensuring that logging is performed before/after each method call.

Exploring Angular

Angular (`https://angular.io`) is the first modern web framework that we'll explore together. Being a framework, you'll see that there is a lot of ground to cover. Consider these sections as introductory material, but don't try to memorize everything right away. Instead, focus on understanding the concepts and come back to the theory when you feel the need to.

What is Angular?

Angular was created at Google and published under an open source license around 2009. It quickly gained popularity due to its ease of use and performance capabilities. The official logo of Angular is as follows:

Angular is tremendously popular and is surrounded by a very large community, which is probably its greatest asset. There is a lot of innovation around it and a ton of community-driven materials that are available online (for example, libraries, modules, tools, articles, courses, conference talks, and more). In addition to this, Angular has been adopted by many organizations all around the World, from startups to Fortune 500 companies. Google itself uses Angular extensively for many of its flagship products.

The first versions of Angular were called AngularJS and were written in pure JavaScript. The framework has evolved a lot over time and was even rebuilt from the ground up in 2016 using TypeScript. With effect from then, the framework is simply called Angular.

While preparing the rewrite of AngularJS, Google had initially started working on a new programming language called AtScript. Then, they realized that joining forces with Microsoft and using TypeScript would be more beneficial for everyone.

The fact that Angular was rewritten using TypeScript is one of many factors that have contributed to the rise in popularity of TypeScript and its mainstream use. Many developers have discovered TypeScript while learning about new versions of Angular.

You can learn more about this story at the following address: `https://blogs.msdn.microsoft.com/typescript/2015/03/05/angular-2-built-on-typescript`.

Angular's feature set is quite extensive: components, templating, data binding, modules, DI, services, directives, routing, pipes, form validation, internationalization, accessibility, testing, HTTP requests handling, SSR, PWAs, code splitting, lazy loading, and so much more!

Angular also has a great (and very opinionated) style guide that you can find here: `https://angular.io/guide/styleguide`.

To be fair, Angular should be considered as a whole *platform* rather than *just* as a frontend web framework. For this reason, the learning curve can feel quite steep, but the rewards far outweigh the learning effort. Angular is hugely popular and there is a lot of demand in the job market for Angular developers.

Angular has a great introductory tutorial that you should absolutely follow in order to get started quickly: `https://angular.io/tutorial`.

Over the course of the next sections, we'll explore the core concepts of the framework. We will put that knowledge to good use while creating our application in the next chapter.

Model View Whatever (MV*)

Angular is commonly referred to as a Model View* framework. The asterisk is used to highlight the fact that Angular does support more than **just** MVC. For example, you can apply the Model View Model approach if you like **Model View Presenter** (**MVP**) or any other pattern you fancy.

Angular defines a set of concepts that help you to keep a good separation of concerns, but it's up to you to make use of those primitives to architect your own applications as you see fit.

Angular CLI

Let's learn some things about the official **Angular command-line interface (Angular CLI)**.

The Angular CLI is a command-line interface and is available as an npm package that you can use to quickly generate new Angular applications and do many other things (for example, create modules, components, services, and more). This tool is great for getting started, but it is also very useful on a daily basis when developing Angular applications. It is a powerful productivity tool that is customizable in many ways.

Let's look at how we can install it on our machine: run npm install -g @angular/cli to install the package globally.

Once installed, you should have the ng executable at your disposal.

 Alternatively, don't forget that you can also use the npx command to avoid installing packages globally: npx @angular/cli.

Here are some useful commands that you should know about:

- ng help: For general help
- ng <command> help: For help related to a specific command
- ng new <project name>: For creating a new project
- ng doc <keyword>: For searching for something in the official Angular documentation
- ng version: For displaying the version of the CLI

Once a project has been created using the ng command, you can use other Angular CLI commands to perform many useful operations:

- ng build: For building the current project and generating output in a dist folder.

- `ng generate <schematic>`: For generating elements or file changes based on **schematics** (for example, components, directives, enums, guards, interfaces, and more).
- `ng serve`: For running and serving your application, and then automatically rebuilding when file changes are detected.
- `ng test`: For executing unit tests for your application (by default, using Karma or Jasmine).
- `ng e2e`: For executing end-to-end tests for your application (by default, using Protractor).
- `ng lint`: For checking the quality of your code with respect to the default coding conventions. Behind the scenes, this command makes use of the TSLint tool: `https://palantir.github.io/tslint`.
- `ng update`: For updating your application and its dependencies.

There are many commands that you can use within an Angular project when it has been set up to use the Angular CLI. This might not be well known, but there is actually an incredible amount of complexity hidden behind those commands. By simply generating a new project using the CLI, you get (among other things) the following for free:

- A fully configured and ready-to-be-used Angular application
- A great starting structure for your application's code
- A complete build hidden behind Angular CLI commands:
    - Including a local web server with auto-reloading, a way to generate a minified production version, and more
    - All while keeping control over the build through the `angular.json` file (covered later in this chapter)
- A set of dependencies that are useful for any Angular application: Angular and its different modules, `core-js` (polyfills), `tslib`, and `zone.js`
- A preconfigured testing environment based on Jasmine and Karma for unit testing and on Protractor for end-to-end testing:
    - Including code coverage reports as well as the option to execute tests in different web browsers
- Quality and code convention checking automation through TSLint and Codelyzer:
    - Including sensible defaults (through the `tslint.json` file)
- A default `.gitignore` file
- The `.editorconfig` file (see the following tip)

- A default TypeScript compiler configuration (that is, the `tsconfig.json` file)
- Support for CSS, SASS, LESS, or Stylus (depending on your preference)
- With the Angular router configured (depending on your choice)

Isn't that list impressive? We didn't lift a finger and now we get all this! There's actually a whole lot more hidden under the hood! Thanks to its **batteries-included** approach, the Angular CLI can help you avoid a lot of bikeshedding and lets you concentrate simply on delivering added business value instead of having to worry about how to integrate all the tools and libraries together.

If you have ever gone through the complexity of setting all of this up for a project, you'll realize how helpful this really is.

The `ng generate` command is extremely useful because it can help you to be more productive by generating different types of elements (or transforming files) based on **schematics**.

 The `.editorconfig` file is a sort of de-facto standard for describing how files in a project should be treated by text editors; this helps keep some consistency across editors and IDEs. Through this file, you can, for example, configure (for each file extension) whether the files should use tabs or spaces, whether there should be a final blank line, whether white space should be trimmed, and more. Many editors either have a native support—editorconfig—or have plugins that do. You can learn more about this here: `https://editorconfig.org/`.

Another very useful command provided by the CLI is `ng update`. It allows you to easily update your project to use newer versions of Angular without hassle, but also to update your other dependencies. You can learn more about it here: `https://update.angular.io`.

Bonus: Schematics

The schematics mentioned previously are sort of **blueprints** for transformations. This might sound vague, but it is simply because you can do many things with them. Schematics provide the logic for modifying your project; they **explain** to the CLI how to perform specific modifications.

For example, a schematic could add and configure an additional library into your project, fix a known bug, or update libraries. The CLI comes with a large set of schematics out of the box, but it is also possible to create your own. You can use these through the `ng generate` command. You can find a detailed introduction to schematics on the official Angular blog:

`https://blog.angular.io/schematics-an-introduction-dc1dfbc2a2b2`.

Many tools and libraries in the Angular ecosystem provide their own schematics. For instance, the NgRx library, which we'll touch on later in the chapter, provides schematics to easily generate code.

Let's play with the CLI right away!

Bonus: Hello world with the Angular CLI

Why don't we go ahead and create an example project using the CLI?

Follow these steps to create a project:

1. Open your favorite Terminal.
2. Create a project using `ng new cli1` or `npx @angular/cli new cli1`.

Congratulations! You now have your own Angular playground application.

The creation of the project could take a bit of time, given that the CLI will trigger the installation of the project's dependencies.

Once everything is installed, you'll be able to start the application by following these instructions:

1. Go into the "`cli1`" folder: `cd cli1`.
2. Run the following command: `ng serve --open`.

The `ng serve` command will start a local web server to serve your application, by default, on port `4200`. You can learn more about this command here: `https://angular.io/cli/serve`.

You should see a output resembling the following in the Terminal:

```
$ ng serve --open
** Angular Live Development Server is listening on localhost:4200,
open your browser on http://localhost:4200/ **
```

```
Date: 2018-12-14T10:33:56.490Z
Hash: ada5c275f4df6e78fb66
Time: 19542ms
chunk {main} main.js, main.js.map (main) 9.82 kB [initial]
[rendered]
chunk {polyfills} polyfills.js, polyfills.js.map (polyfills) 223 kB
[initial] [rendered]
chunk {runtime} runtime.js, runtime.js.map (runtime) 6.08 kB
[entry] [rendered]
chunk {styles} styles.js, styles.js.map (styles) 16.7 kB [initial]
[rendered]
chunk {vendor} vendor.js, vendor.js.map (vendor) 3.43 MB [initial]
[rendered]
i [wdm]: Compiled successfully.
```

Notice that the Angular CLI has defined a set of module **bundles** for us:

- `main`: Our application code
- `polyfills`: All the polyfills necessary for the application to function
- `runtime`: Specific libraries that we need at runtime
- `styles`: Application styles
- `vendor`: All third-party libraries that we need (for example, Angular, RxJS, Zone.js, and more)

Thanks to the `--open` flag, a web browser page should have opened automatically.

You should now see the following default content:

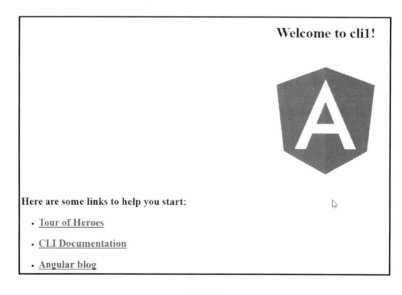

Note that, by the time you read this, the default content will most probably have changed with newer Angular CLI releases.

Keep the browser window open and do the following:

1. Open `src/app/app.component.html`.
2. Make some random changes.
3. Save the file.

If you keep an eye on the web browser tab, you'll see that the page is automatically adapted thanks to the live reloading feature of the development server started through `ng serve`. Neat!

If you take a look at the Terminal, you'll see that the Angular CLI has rebuilt our application and has only recompiled the parts that were changed (`main.js`, in this case):

```
Date: 2018-12-14T10:41:10.037Z - Hash: a7f2f75c5ab34e56eda5 - Time:
2186ms
4 unchanged chunks
chunk {main} main.js, main.js.map (main) 8.83 kB [initial]
[rendered]
i [wdm]: Compiled successfully.
i [wdm]: Compiling...
```

Now, let's adapt the class behind our component:

1. Open `src/app/app.component.ts`.
2. Change the value of the `title` field.

Again, the change should be picked up immediately, the code recompiled, and the page automatically updated!

 If you've ever wondered how the value of the title field ends up being displayed in your web browser, then locate the following expression in the `app.component.html` template: `{{ title }}`. We will learn more about these expressions soon.

Now, let's add a new component: execute `ng generate component foo`.

You should see the following in the Terminal:

```
$ ng generate component foo
CREATE src/app/foo/foo.component.html (32 bytes)
CREATE src/app/foo/foo.component.spec.ts (671 bytes)
```

```
CREATE src/app/foo/foo.component.ts (297 bytes)
CREATE src/app/foo/foo.component.scss (0 bytes)
UPDATE src/app/app.module.ts (422 bytes)
```

As you can see, our new component was generated under `src/app/foo`. If you now open `src/app/app.module.ts` (that is, the default **module**), you'll see that our `FooComponent` component has been added to the `declarations` array within the `@NgModule` decorator (more on this later!).

Let's use this new component:

1. Open `src/app/app.component.html`.
2. Add this line somewhere in the template: `<app-foo></app-foo>`.

If you look at the page now, you should see the following message appear, indicating that the component was indeed loaded:

```
Foo works!
```

Isn't that cool?

Now, take some time to play around with your Angular application. Also, why don't you try some of the other CLI commands and options?

Don't worry about the details—we'll explore those in the rest of this chapter, one step at a time.

Learning the Angular application architecture

This section contains an extremely condensed explanation of the architecture of Angular applications. In the sections that follow, we will review most of the concepts in more detail.

At the highest level, Angular applications are composed of **modules** called **NgModules**. Each of these modules represents a separate **compilation context** for application components. Usually, Angular applications have one module per feature or per group of features; the decomposition is left to the discretion of the developers.

Modules are very useful for ensuring the clean structure of your applications and also to support lazy loading for certain features (among other benefits). By leveraging Angular's lazy loading support, you can avoid wasting the bandwidth of your users by loading specific modules only when they are actually going to be used.

 You can learn more about Angular's support for lazy loading at `https://angular.io/guide/lazy-loading-ngmodules`.

Each module may be composed of different primitives that we will soon discover, such as components, directives, services, pipes (and more) as shown here:

Module A	Module B
Component	Service
{ }	{ }
Module C	**Module D**
Directive	Fn value
{ }	λ 3.1415

In each and every Angular application, there is always at least a **root module**, usually called `AppModule`. The root module enables bootstrapping the application (that is, it serves as an entry point).

Components define and control parts of the user interface (that is, **view fragments**). Those parts can be as small or as large as you want. Of course, components can (and should!) reuse other components.

They make use of **services**, for example, to exchange data with remote sources. Services can do anything you fancy. For example, we'll see later on that the services we have created in our previous applications could easily be converted to Angular ones!

Angular components and services can be declared using simple classes (usually written in TypeScript) and annotated with Angular decorators, which are, in fact, TypeScript decorators! Those decorators define their type as well as *metadata*. For example, in Angular component classes, the `@Component` decorator is the one that makes the link between the class and the **template**, which defines the associated view.

Component templates make use of what we could call **enhanced HTML**. That is, standard HTML tags, custom ones, but also Angular-specific **directives**, **bindings**, and **expressions**. Through bindings and expressions, you can handle inputs and outputs, react to events, and render data provided by the component's controller.

Angular has built-in support for DI. When an application element requires access to some service, then Angular provides it automatically by means of an **injector**. Angular actually takes care of creating and managing instances of application components, services, and much more. Angular's DI system also relies on metadata defined through other Angular decorators.

DI, also called **Inversion of Control (IoC)**, is a hugely popular design pattern used to decouple code by injecting dependencies where they are needed instead of instantiating them manually. **DI systems are responsible for identifying the required dependencies and implementations, as well as instantiating and injecting them where needed**. In addition to this, they also take care of the life cycle of those dependencies. Thanks to this pattern, the application code becomes more easily testable. We'll explore DI and IoC more in detail in the rest of this book. If you're impatient, then you can learn more about DI at `https://martinfowler.com/articles/injection.html` **and** at `https://stackify.com/dependency-injection`.

Here's a small diagram, taken from the official Angular documentation, that illustrates all of this:

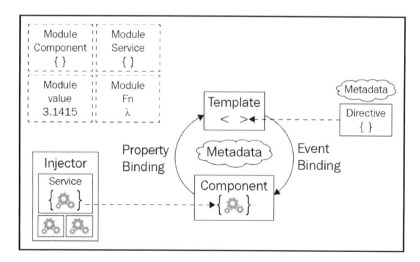

In the preceding diagram, you can see the following:

- A template and its component class can communicate through **property bindings** and **event bindings**.
- An **injector** handles the injection of dependencies into the component.
- Modules contain different elements (values, functions, services, components, and more).

Finally, since Angular supports the creation of SPAs, it also provides a **router** that can be used to navigate between different routes. When a route is accessed, the router adapts the view and renders the corresponding components. To use the router, you need to import `Router NgModule`.

There you go—this is Angular in a nutshell.

You can find the official architecture overview here: `https://angular.io/guide/architecture`.

Exploring core Angular concepts

Let's now take some time to introduce the core Angular concepts mentioned in the previous section in a bit more detail.

Modules

As we briefly explained in the *Learning the Angular application architecture* section, modules and `NgModule` decorators are great for reusability and encapsulation. They provide a way to decompose applications in sets of features and to encapsulate/isolate the different pieces. You can more or less compare them to packages in Java or namespaces in .NET.

 ES2015/TypeScript modules are not the same as `NgModule` decorators! Those concepts are different, even if there are some similarities. You can view all the differences at `https://angular.io/guide/ngmodule-vs-jsmodule`.

Usually, within your applications, you'll be creating so-called **feature modules**: `https://angular.io/guide/feature-modules`.

Each Angular module is declared by creating a TypeScript class and by decorating it with the `@NgModule` decorator. Here's an example of `NgModule` from the `src/app/app.module.ts` file of the application that we created earlier using the Angular CLI:

```typescript
import { BrowserModule } from '@angular/platform-browser';
import { NgModule } from '@angular/core';

import { AppComponent } from './app.component';
import { FooComponent } from './foo/foo.component';

@NgModule({
  declarations: [
    AppComponent,
    FooComponent
  ],
  imports: [
    BrowserModule
  ],
  providers: [],
  bootstrap: [AppComponent]
})
export class AppModule { }
```

This `NgModule` decorator is a function that takes a single metadata object as a parameter. Through this object, you can define the following:

- `declarations`: Elements (that is, components, directives, and pipes) that belong to this module (that is, that are local). **All elements should be declared in exactly one module of the application!**
- `exports`: The subset of the elements of this module that should be accessible/usable in other modules.
- `imports`: Other modules that export elements needed by this module.
- `providers`: Service factories that this module contains. Once declared, providers can be used by Angular to instantiate and inject dependencies in the rest of the application (that is, not only in the current module!).
- `bootstrap`: The component that holds the view to be inserted into the `index.html` page. This should only be set in the root module of the application.

Note that some elements can appear in multiple properties, but each serves a different purpose!

The Angular team has also published a very interesting FAQ about NgModule decorators here: https://angular.io/guide/ngmodule-faq.

If you take a close look at the preceding example, you'll notice the following import:

```
import { BrowserModule } from '@angular/platform-browser';
```

This is later added to the imports parameter of the NgModule metadata object:

```
imports: [
    BrowserModule
]
```

The BrowserModule (https://angular.io/api/platform-browser/BrowserModule) of Angular is NgModule, which provides everything required to create web applications using Angular. This module re-exports everything from ApplicationModule (https://angular.io/api/core/ApplicationModule) as well as everything from CommonModule (https://angular.io/api/common/CommonModule). The CommonModule of Angular is the one that provides the most used elements of Angular, such as NgIf, NgForOf, and NgStyle. We will learn more about them later.

You can find a list of commonly used NgModule decorators at https://angular.io/guide/frequent-ngmodules, and the full list at https://angular.io/api?type=ngmodule.

That's enough about modules—let's delve into the coolest part of Angular: components!

Components

Components are at the very core of Angular applications. An Angular application is materialized by a **component tree** that, as a whole, defines the user interface and behavior of your application.

At the top of this tree is the **App** component, which is the one that you will define first. In this component, you will be able to compose/assemble other components, which will, in turn, also be able to use other ones in different ways.

Here's what this tree could look like:

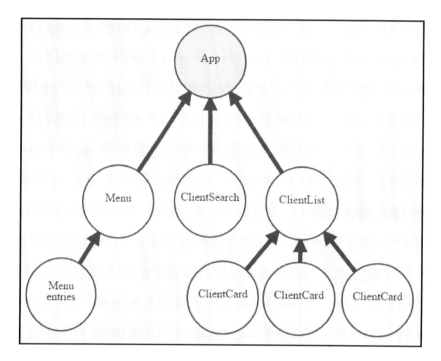

The **App** component at the top is the one that will be loaded first when the Angular application starts (we'll quickly explore the bootstrap process later in this chapter). In this example, the app component includes a menu component, which, in turn, includes menu entries. Let's say that this component renders the menu of the application, allowing its users to move around from page to page.

Below the app component, there is also a **ClientSearch** component, which will render a search box on the screen. Finally, the last child of the app component is a **ClientList**, which must render a list of clients. As you can see, the **ClientList** component has children of its own: a set of **ClientCard** components, each probably rendering information about a specific client on the screen.

As highlighted through this example, having a component tree makes it easier to navigate and understand the composition of the application. Additionally, it makes it possible and more natural to reuse code and parts of the user interface.

But what are components really? Well, the simplest way to think about them is in terms of what they're composed of:

1. An HTML template made of the following:
   - Standard, as well as custom, HTML tags
   - Angular directives, expressions, bindings, pipes, and more
2. A component class with the following:
   - Metadata
   - Logic
   - Data
   - Inputs and outputs

That's it! Based on this explanation, we can state that **creating a component is a way to encapsulate and reuse the logic and HTML needed to render a part of the user interface**.

A component can be as simple as a text field or as large as the whole page, and can be composed of images, forms, fields, tables, and much more. Actually, as we've just mentioned, it can even represent the complete user interface, such as the root **app** component.

 Even if it is actually possible to define the whole application as part of the app component, it is much better to decompose it into many, smaller (and thus more reusable), components.

Component templates are where most of the magic of Angular happens. We'll learn more about templates and how to write them in a moment.

Component templates and data bindings

Here's a quick introduction to templating with Angular.

To write templates, you can use most standard HTML tags as well as many additional features that Angular provides. Using those, you can render data held by your controller, perform transformations, loop over arrays, define events and event handlers, and much more.

The following is an example template that is taken directly from the official documentation:

```
<h2>Hero List</h2>

<p><i>Pick a hero from the list</i></p>
<ul>
  <li *ngFor="let hero of heroes" (click)="selectHero(hero)">
    {{ hero.name }}
  </li>
</ul>

<app-hero-detail *ngIf="selectedHero" [hero]="selectedHero"></app-
hero-detail>
```

In this example, you will notice the following:

- Standard HTML tags are used (for example, h2, p, ul, and li).
- {{ hero.name }} is an **interpolation**. It can be used to render a value held by the controller or display the results returned by a function. The same double-curly-brace syntax can also be used to evaluate more complex **expressions**. Here is an example: {{ 1 + 1 + getTotal() }}.
- The *ngFor directive is used to loop over the heroes list of the controller. For each item in the array, a hero variable is defined, which is then used within the <li> tag to display the name of the hero.
- An event handler is associated with the click event using the (eventName) = syntax. In this case, the event is associated with the selectHero method on the controller of the component.
- A custom HTML tag, <app-hero-detail>, is used. This tag actually corresponds to an Angular component. This element will only appear if the condition defined using the *ngIf directive is evaluated to true. In this case, the element will only be present in the DOM if the selectedHero property of the controller is **truthy**.
- Finally, we pass an input to the <app-hero-detail> component using the [inputName] = syntax.

As demonstrated here, using the template syntax and data binding capabilities of Angular, we can easily create links between component templates and their controllers. We can also define event handlers and pass data around between components.

There are a few limitations to templates. For one, you cannot use `script` tags for security reasons (to limit the possibility of injection attacks). Other tags simply don't make sense in component templates (for example, `html` and `body`).

Angular's template syntax is very powerful and there is a lot more to learn. You can find the complete template syntax reference here: `https://angular.io/guide/template-syntax.`

 The Angular team has some interesting guidelines for template expressions. Notably, these shouldn't have any visible side-effects (that is, they should not break the **unidirectional data flow** policy of Angular). Also, they should be cheap to execute, because they'll be evaluated each time Angular performs a **change detection cycle**. Expressions should also be kept simple; complex expressions indicate that too much logic is placed within the template instead of in the controller. Finally, expressions should ideally be *idempotent*, in order to avoid side-effects.

Just like `NgModules`, components are declared using a specific decorator set on a class—in this case, the `Component` (`https://angular.io/api/core/Component`) decorator. Through it, you can define how your components should be instantiated and used.

Here's an example:

```
import { Component } from '@angular/core';

@Component({
  selector: 'app-root',
  templateUrl: './app.component.html',
  styleUrls: ['./app.component.scss']
})
export class AppComponent {
  title = 'Foo';
}
```

The `Component` decorator has many options, but the following are the ones that you'll use most of the time:

- `selector`: This is the selector for the component. It is used as a CSS selector, but also as a custom HTML tag name, usable in the templates, for example, `client-card`.

- `template`: An inline template (useful for simple components or demonstrations), for example, `<span>Hello {{ username }}</span>`.
- `templateUrl`: An external template file (this is usually preferable for separation of concerns).
- `styles`: Inline styles for the component (again, this is better suited for demonstrations and simple cases), for example, `['span { background-color: red; }']`.
- `styleUrls`: Files containing the CSS style sheets for this component.
- `providers`: Related to DI; configures the *injector* of this component.
- `changeDetection`: The strategy that Angular should use to detect changes in this component.

 Components are actually specialized directives (`https://angular.io/api/core/Directive`), which we will discuss later.

As we have briefly shown in the template example, Angular components can actually interact with one another. That is what makes them so powerful.

Component bindings, HTML attributes, and DOM properties

Each component can have **inputs** and **outputs**. By creating **bindings**, it is possible to feed data into other components. Additionally, through their outputs, components can provide information to the outside world. Components that make use of other components can bind to their outputs in order to be able to react to the events emitted by them.

Here's a useful diagram from the official documentation that gives a summary of the binding possibilities and the associated syntax:

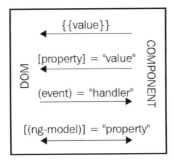

As you can see, we can define the following:

- **One-way bindings** use the following:
    - Interpolation/expressions: `{{ expression }}`
    - Property bindings: `[property]="..."`
    - Event bindings: `(event)="..."`, associated with **template statements**
- **Two-way bindings** use the so-called **banana-in-a-box** syntax: `[(ng-model)]="..."`.

These bindings can be grouped into multiple categories depending on the direction of the data flow, as proposed in the official Angular documentation:

- From data source to view (that is, from components to elements) using expressions and property bindings
- From view to data source (that is, from elements to components) using event bindings
- From view to data source to view, using two-way bindings

Using **property bindings**, you can set properties of view elements, directives, and components. Note that interpolation is usually a **nicer** alternative, syntax-and readability-wise, to property bindings.

 Don't forget the brackets (that is, `[]`) for property bindings, otherwise Angular will not try to evaluate associated expressions.

In practice, when you're defining data bindings, they only refer to properties and events of the target objects; HTML attributes don't remain. Stated differently, the target of a data binding is *something* in the DOM.

It is important to understand the difference between **HTML attributes and DOM properties** in order to grasp how Angular bindings work. **Attributes are defined through HTML, but properties are defined at the DOM level**.

 Some HTML attributes have a one-to-one mapping to properties, but some do not have corresponding properties. The opposite is also true: some DOM properties do not have matching attributes.

Finally, **attributes initialize DOM properties**. While property values can change after initialization, attribute values cannot. With Angular, attributes only initialize the element/directive state. You can refer to the following section in the Angular documentation to learn more:

`https://angular.io/guide/template-syntax#html-attribute-vs-dom-property.`

When you define event bindings, you associate specific events with **template statements** that are executed as a reaction to those events. Of course, events have side-effects. For example, you can update the state of your application and perform subsequent actions if needed. We'll make use of event bindings and learn a bit more about them later on in this chapter.

 Template statements should be simple, just like template expressions. They also have a specific syntax with some limitations, as explained here:
`https://angular.io/guide/template-syntax#template-statement s.`

Let's delve more deeply into components.

Defining component inputs and outputs

Now, the question that remains is: How do we define the inputs and outputs of a component?

To define an **input property** on a component, you can use an `@Input` (`https://angular.io/api/core/Input`) decorator on a *settable* property in the controller class (for example, a writable field or a setter method). When a property binding (`https://angular.io/guide/template-syntax#property-binding`) is defined, the values will be passed to the class instance by Angular.

For outputs, you use the `@Output` (https://angular.io/api/core/Output) decorator on `EventEmitter` (https://angular.io/api/core/EventEmitter). **Outputs are represented by events**, which can be listened to and reacted upon.

By default, the name of the property for the event corresponds to the output field's name. For instance, if the field name is `deleteRequested`, then the property on the component will be called `delete-requested`. Users of that component will be able to react to those events using the following syntax: `(deleteRequested)="..."`.

The name of the property can be customized via the `bindingPropertyName` property of the `@Output` decorator.

Let's take an example from our graph earlier from *Components* section. We'll illustrate how a hypothetical `ClientList` component can react to events raised by a `ClientCard` child component.

In this example, the following will happen:

1. The `ClientCard` component will require a `Client` object instance as input (that is, the client object to be rendered).
2. The `ClientCard` component will display a **Delete** button and will emit an event whenever that button is clicked on.

Here's what the template of the `ClientCard` component looks like:

```
import { Component, EventEmitter, Input, OnInit, Output } from
'@angular/core';
import { Client } from '../domain/client';

@Component({
  selector: 'app-client-card',
  template: `
    <h3>{{ client.name }}</h3>
    <ul>
      <li>Address: {{ client.address }}</li>
      <li>
        <button (click)="delete()">Delete!</button>
      </li>
    </ul>
  `,
  styleUrls: ['./client-card.component.css']
})
export class ClientCardComponent implements OnInit {
```

```
@Input()
client: Client;

@Output()
deleteRequested = new EventEmitter<void>();

constructor() {
}

delete() {
  this.deleteRequested.emit(); // here we simply emit an empty
  event, but we could also pass data in the event
}

ngOnInit() {
}
}
```

As you can see, this is pretty straightforward. Our component accepts a `Client` object as input and will emit events using the `deleteRequested` event emitter in the `delete` method.

> Did you notice the `ngOnInit` method? This is a **life cycle hook**. We'll learn more about these later in this chapter.

Now, let's look at the `ClientList` component:

```
import { Component, OnInit } from '@angular/core';
import { Client } from '../domain/client';

@Component({
  selector: 'app-client-list',
  template: `
    <h2>Client list</h2>

    <app-client-card *ngFor="let client of clients"
                     [client]="client"
                     (deleteRequested)="onDeleteRequested()">
    </app-client-card>
  `,
  styleUrls: ['./client-list.component.css']
})
export class ClientListComponent implements OnInit {

  public clients = [
```

```
  new Client('1', 'foo', 'fooAddress'),
  new Client('2', 'bar', 'barAddress')
];

constructor() {
}

onDeleteRequested() {
  alert('A delete has been requested!');
}

ngOnInit() {
}

}
```

In this example, when a `deleteRequested` event is raised by a `ClientCard` component instance, the `ClientList` component simply calls its controller's `onDeleteRequested` method.

 You can find the source code for this example in the book's sample code under `Chapter07/clientlist`.

Here we haven't done so, but while creating the new version of MediaMan in the next chapter, we'll see in practice how we can pass/retrieve data along with our events, using the `$event` object.

One final interesting thing to learn (for now) about components is how we can create **template reference variables**. In the previous chapters, we often had to use `document.getElementById` in our controllers to get a reference to specific DOM nodes that we needed to manipulate. Angular actually provides multiple alternatives for doing just that.

One of them is to declare template reference variables. These are basically variables that you define in your templates and that you can then refer to anywhere else in the template. These variables point to specific DOM elements.

Here's an example:

```
<input type="text" #firstName placeholder="First name">
...
<button (click)="sayHiTo(firstName.value)">Say hi!</button>
```

As you can see from the preceding code, thanks to the `#firstName` template reference variable, we are able to directly pass the value of the HTML input to the `sayHiTo` method when the button gets clicked on. Isn't that awesome?

> If you've ever wondered about how to name things within your Angular applications, then you should go ahead and read the official naming conventions for Angular:
> `https://github.com/angular/angular/blob/master/docs/NAMING.md`.

That's it for our brief introduction to Angular components. Of course, we've had to take a few shortcuts here and there, but we simply wanted to give you the gist.

Smart versus dumb components

The `ClientCard` component in our previous example is what we usually call a **dumb component**. Such components are also known as **presentational components** or **pure components**.

The difference between **smart components** and dumb, presentational, or pure ones is that the latter don't fetch data themselves and, generally, don't include too much logic. For example, in our case, the `ClientCard` component receives a list of clients to display; it doesn't know where the data came from. Also, when a deletion is requested, this component only emits an event (that is, a signal). It doesn't have to decide what to do next.

Of course, you'll need some smarter components to make the link between your view layer and the rest of your application. That being said, generally speaking, you should try to have as many dumb components as you can in order to maximize reusability.

> Speaking of reusability, you could also create Angular libraries for your shared components. This is explained here:
> `https://angular.io/guide/creating-libraries`. You can also take advantage of solutions such as `nrwl nx`
> (`https://github.com/nrwl/nx`), which we'll discuss in the *What's Next?* chapter.

The following article further discusses the dichotomy between smart and dumb components:
`https://blog.angular-university.io/angular-2-smart-components-vs-presentation-components-whats-the-difference-when-to-use-each-and-why`.

Component life cycle hooks

In the section about components, we briefly mentioned **life cycle hooks**. Angular really makes it easy to plug in logic at different points in the life cycle of your applications/components (for example, when a component is created, rendered, or when it renders its children).

Using life cycle hooks is a breeze. All you need to do is implement the interface of the hook that you want to attach logic to.

Here's an example:

```
export class SomeComponent implements OnInit {
  constructor() { }

  // implement OnInit's method
  ngOnInit() {
    console.log('SomeComponent was just initialized');
  }
}
```

Here, we have used the `OnInit` life cycle hook, which requires us to implement the `ngOnInit` method. That method will be called each time this component gets initialized.

Here is a list of the most commonly used hooks:

- `ngOnChanges`: This allows you to react when input properties change.
- `ngOnInit`: This is called when Angular has initialized a component and has set its input properties.
- `ngAfterContentInit`: This allows you to react when external content has been projected into the component.
- `ngAfterViewInit`: This allows you to react once Angular has initialized the component's view.
- `ngOnDestroy`: This is called before Angular destroys the component/directive. This hook is very useful for performing cleanups (for example, unsubscribing from observables, which we'll soon learn about).

Routing

One thing that you might ask yourself now is: *How do I go from page to page in an Angular application?* Well, actually this is a great question!

In most SPA frameworks, there is something called a **router**, which maintains a set of *routes* with their associated **views**. The router renders the correct view(s) depending on the active route(s).

Angular, being a framework, has its own router built in (https://angular.io/guide/router).

With the Angular router, each route points toward an Angular component.

 Note that there are third-party routers as well, such as ui-router (https://github.com/ui-router/angular).

Given our space constraints, we won't have the opportunity to delve into how routing works, but it is certainly worth exploring on your own, as any decently-sized application will require you to use routing!

Directives

Earlier, we said that components are actually specialized directives that have a template. But what are directives then?

Directives are Angular elements that you can use to dynamically modify the DOM.

They are implemented using simple classes and can have inputs and outputs. To declare a directive, you simply have to annotate it with the @Directive (https://angular.io/api/core/Directive) decorator.

Just like components, directives have a selector that makes it possible to refer to them from inside templates.

There are three types of directive:

1. Components: As we've seen before!
2. Structural directives: These modify the structure of the DOM, for example, by adding, removing, or replacing elements in the tree. Angular provides a number of structural directives, such as *ngFor and *ngIf, which we learned about earlier.
3. Attribute directives: These alter or transform existing elements. Angular also provides a set of attribute directives, such as ngModel, ngStyle, ngClass, and ngSwitch.

You can find a full list of directives that Angular includes out of the box here: `https://angular.io/api?type=directive`.

> You might be wondering why there's an asterisk before directives such as `*ngFor` and `*ngIf`. You can find an explanation here: `https://angular.io/guide/structural-directives#asterisk`.

Here's a bit of information about some attribute directives:

- `ngClass`: This allows you to dynamically add or remove CSS classes easily.
- `ngStyle`: This allows you to define inline CSS styles dynamically. Here's an example: `<div [style.background-color]="isEnabled ? 'green' : 'red'">`.
- `ngSwitch`: Just like a JavaScript/TypeScript `switch` statement, this directive allows you to switch to a condition and display something based on the value.

> Angular supports keyboard events as well as *key event filtering*. This feature makes it really easy to implement listeners for complex keyboard combinations. For instance, implementing a listener that reacts when the *Enter* key is pressed can be done using `(keyup.enter)='enterWasPressed()`. Here's another for *Ctrl* + *Z*: `(keydown.control.z)='undo()'`. With this trick, you can easily improve the accessibility of your applications by using keyboard shortcuts. Learn more about this here: `https://angular.io/guide/user-input#key-event-filtering-with-keyenter`.

Directives are great. Actually, they're the basis of more advanced concepts, such as pipes, which we will cover next.

Pipes

With Angular **pipes**, an perform display-time transformation. Pipes are invoked through the **pipe operator**, `|`, which should look familiar if you are used to Unix or Windows shells.

Pipes are useful for simple transformations such as date formatting, translations, filtering, and case changes.

Using them is rather intuitive:

```
{{ 'hello' | uppercase }}
<br>
{{ 'HELLO' | lowercase }}
<br>
{{ 1234.56 | currency:"EUR" }}
<br>
{{ '2018-08-13' | date:'E yy-MM-d' }}
<br>
{{ 1337000000.420545 | number: '1.1-2' }}
<br>
{{ 0.421 | percent }}
<br>
{{ [9,8,7,6,5,4] | slice:0:3 }}
```

Here is the corresponding output:

```
HELLO
hello
€1,234.56
Mon 18-08-13
1,337,000,000.42
42%
9,8,7
```

These are just some of the built-in pipes that Angular provides. You can find the full list here: https://angular.io/api?type=pipe.

Here's one more example:

```
{{ someMessageKey | translate }}
```

Here, we ask Angular to render the someMessageKey property and apply the translate pipe on it before displaying the result. In this example, we can imagine that someMessageKey is a key, such as user.name, that corresponds to a specific message in the application. The translate pipe takes that value as input and knows how to fetch the corresponding translation depending on the current language (for example, Nom de l'utilisateur in French).

The translate pipe is not a part of Angular's core concepts but is provided by the ngx-translate library (http://www.ngx-translate.com).

Pipes are declared using the @Pipe (https://angular.io/api/core/Pipe) decorator.

Change detection

Angular can feel pretty **magical** when you start using it.

For instance, how does it know when inputs change? How does it re-render elements? We won't be able to delve very deeply into how things work under the hood, but we can at least give you a rough idea.

When Angular is loaded, it patches many browser APIs in order to know when some things happen. Most of these patches are handled by the `zone.js` (`https://github.com/angular/zone.js`) library that Angular uses (and which might also get standardized at some point in the future). Thanks to those patches, Angular knows when buttons are clicked on, when event listeners are triggered, when (most) asynchronous operations are completed, and more.

When Angular notices that something relevant has happened, it triggers a **change detection cycle**. The goal of that process is indeed to detect changes in order to re-render only necessary elements.

Each Angular component has an implicit *change detector* that will verify whether anything has changed in that component. This means that there is a parallel **change detector tree** right next to the component tree of your application.

By querying that change detector tree, Angular can precisely determine what has changed (if anything) in your application and can then re-render only the changed parts. The change detection cycle goes from the top of the component tree (that is, your root/app component) to the bottom and can fully check your application in one pass.

By default, Angular checks whether any values of template expressions differ from their previous state. This method is usually called **dirty-checking** and the verification is performed for all components.

Angular is really fast and can perform thousands of checks in a few milliseconds. Of course, as applications grow larger, things take longer. It is possible to optimize the process, for example, by using immutable data structures. **Immutable objects provide the stability guarantee that values won't change unless the corresponding variable is reassigned.** While using immutable data structures, we can simply tell Angular to skip some checks by setting the `changeDetection` property of specific components to `ChangeDetectionStrategy.OnPush`. You can learn more about that as follows:
`https://netbasal.com/a-comprehensive-guide-to-angular-onpush-change-detection-strategy-5bac493074a4`.

Let's introduce Angular services.

Services

A **service** in Angular is usually a class (by convention, with the `Service` suffix) that provides some reusable behavior, just like `MediaService` in our MediaMan application.

Services are marked as injectable using the `@Injectable` decorator. Angular can automatically instantiate services and inject them when and where needed; we'll discuss that in the next section.

Here's an example service:

```
import { Injectable } from '@angular/core';

@Injectable(
  providedIn: 'root'
)
export class BookServiceImpl implements BookService {
  ...
}
```

Since components are user-facing, they are not supposed to worry too about much business logic and interaction with other parts of the application or other systems. Instead, components should focus on user experience and delegate processing to services.

We have already covered the benefits of services in previous chapters, so we won't repeat the discussion. The good news is that services are first-class citizens in Angular. In our application, we'll, of course, take advantage of services.

The **facade** design pattern is a great one to leverage when designing and using application services. When complexity rises, you might have multiple services that need to collaborate. To limit coupling, you can create **facades**, which are **simple interfaces on top of more complex subsystems**. By using the facade pattern, you can hide away a lot of complexity, inherently reducing the amount of knowledge needed to use the subsystems hidden behind the facades. Check out the following article to learn more about this design pattern: `https://www.baeldung.com/java-facade-pattern`. This example uses Java, but the pattern itself is easily applicable to TypeScript and Angular applications.

Let's discuss DI next.

DI

When a component (in the broad sense) in your application depends on others, those dependencies must be made available at runtime in one way or another. The manner in which dependencies are located, instantiated, and provided actually matters a lot. If you're not careful, you'll quickly create strong ties (that is, strong coupling) between different pieces of your application.

Down the line, **unnecessary coupling leads to code that is harder to maintain, test, and debug**.

DI, also known as **Inversion of Control (IoC)**, is a design pattern that can help us to limit coupling and thus avoid those pitfalls. With that pattern, we can use a declarative approach rather than an imperative one to define our dependencies. Using DI/IoC, each component in our application can declare its dependencies and, at runtime, the injection system will provide those dependencies for us. That way, our code will not have to care about where the dependency comes from, what precise implementation it is, and, more importantly, how it was instantiated.

Be wary of using the `new` keyword in your code for dependencies. Each time you `new-up` a dependency yourself, you're creating a coupling that you might avoid using DI/IoC or factories (another related design pattern).

By combining DI and programming against interfaces, we can limit the touchpoints between application elements to the bare minimum: a contract.

We've used this approach with MediaMan earlier. Do you remember when our `MediaManController` class required an instance of `MediaManView` and `MediaService`? The `MediaManController` class didn't get its dependencies itself—it simply required those to be passed to its constructor. That way, we could limit the coupling.

With MediaMan, the entry point of the application took care of instantiating the implementation of the orchestration. By doing that, we actually applied the IoC pattern (manually, though). The IoC pattern's name comes from the fact that we invert the responsibilities. Instead of letting the dependent **components** take care of instantiating their dependencies on their own, we pass over that responsibility to the "thing" that instantiates them.

DI systems can actually instantiate/configure whole graphs of objects for us and inject specific elements only where and when needed. DI/IoC is supported by many frameworks in various programming languages; for example, Spring for Java and Unity for .NET. Of course, we have introduced DI here because Angular also supports this pattern!

Creating so-called **injectable** elements in Angular is really easy. Most of the time, you'll be injecting **services**, which should be marked as injectable so that Angular's DI framework can instantiate and inject them.

If you're curious, you can find a concrete example here with a service implementation:
`https://github.com/NationalBankBelgium/stark/blob/master/packages/stark-core/src/modules/session/services/session.service.ts`. You can also find a service interface here:
`https://github.com/NationalBankBelgium/stark/blob/master/packages/stark-core/src/modules/session/services/session.service.intf.ts`.

Annotating a class with the `@Injectable` (`https://angular.io/api/core/Injectable`) decorator tells Angular that this element can be injected elsewhere. However, that isn't enough for Angular to be able to actually instantiate and inject that element.

In Angular terms, we say that an injectable service **provides** a service. For Angular to be able to inject an actual instance of an injectable service somewhere, it needs to use **injectors** (https://angular.io/guide/glossary#injector).

Learning about injectors and the singleton design pattern

Injectors are elements that Angular uses to actually instantiate, retrieve, and inject dependencies where they are needed. Injectors instantiate dependencies once and store the created instances in a **DI container**. Each time a dependency is needed, the injector first checks whether it already has an instance of it in its container. If it does, then it returns that instance instead of creating a new one.

 By creating a single instance of each injectable element, injectors apply the **singleton design pattern**. Singleton is a pattern that you should definitely be aware of.

If we simplify this, we can consider these containers as simple maps storing token-instance pairs. Each pair is composed of some **token** (for example, a unique **name** for a dependency) and an instance of the corresponding dependency. With the help of these containers, injectors improve application performance.

To complete the picture, **providers** are objects that describe how to get or create a given dependency. When you define injectable elements in your application, you also need to register a provider with an injector so that this injector can use it to instantiate the corresponding dependency. Most of the time for services, the provider is the service class itself, with the constructor acting as a factory (which it is, after all).

Thanks to all of the preceding, when Angular instantiates a component for us, it can identify its dependencies (by analyzing the constructor parameters) and ask an injector for an instance of each of those dependencies. If the injector does not already have an instance for a given dependency in its container, it will use the registered provider to create one and cache it, before returning it to Angular. Finally, once Angular has all the required dependencies, it can instantiate the component.

Injectors also maintain a map containing token-provider pairs, making a link between an injection token (`https://angular.io/guide/glossary#di-token`) and a provider.

Let's continue.

A brief note about the root application injector

When Angular bootstraps, it creates a default application-wide injector called the **root application injector**, which is linked to `AppModule` (that is, the root application module). By default, service providers are registered in it.

To register a service globally (that is, to make it injectable anywhere in your application), you can use the `providedIn: 'root'` property of the `@Injectable` decorator, as we did in the previous section. This will register the service in the `root` application injector.

To be thorough, you should know that Angular's DI framework defines a **tree of injectors**, which is somewhat akin to the change detection tree. Similarly, the injector tree reflects and lies next to the component tree.

When the injector of a component cannot find a required dependency, then the parent injector is queried, and so on, until the root application injector is reached. This process is called **injector bubbling** (to make the parallel with DOM event bubbling) and is explained in detail here:
`https://angular.io/guide/hierarchical-dependency-injection#injector-bubbling`.

As you can guess, the **root application injector** sits at the top of that tree. This root injector is used for most services. This is intuitive because most services should be stateless, hence it is better to maximize the reuse of existing instances instead of having to create new instances depending on where things need to be injected. Sometimes, though (usually for performance reasons), it actually makes sense to register some providers locally within specific modules that can be loaded lazily or even tree-shaken (that is, removed) if not needed, resulting in lighter application bundles.

You can register a service locally in a specific module either by using `providedIn: SomeModule` or by adding the provider to the `providers` property of the `@NgModule()` decorator. You can learn more about that here: `https://medium.com/@tomastrajan/total-guide-to-angular-6-dependency-inject ion-providedin-vs-providers-85b7a347b59f`.

 If you want a new instance of a given dependency each time a component is instantiated, then you can register the provider through the `providers` array property of the `@Component` decorator at `https://angular.io/api/core/Component`.

Obviously, the reality is more complicated than this and there are quite a few subtleties; however, we'll stop here since this should already have given you a pretty solid understanding of what DI is and how it works in Angular.

Angular's bootstrap process

At this point, you should already have a good idea about the main pieces of the Angular puzzle. This might still be fuzzy, but it'll all become much clearer once we put things together (that is, pretty soon!).

As promised earlier, let's now examine how the Angular bootstrap process works.

If you take a look at an application generated by the Angular CLI, you should find the following tag in the `src/index.html` file: `<app-root></app-root>`. This is where the root component of your application (that is, the app component) gets added. However, before Angular can kick in and effectively replace that element with the DOM of the actual app component, it needs to be loaded and initialized.

By default, even if you don't see it, the Angular CLI (currently) uses `webpack` behind the scenes to build and serve your application. If we try to oversimplify, then when you execute the `ng serve` command, your `webpack` kicks in, generates JavaScript bundles out of your application, and the `webpack` development server ends up being started, serving your application and loading its bundles in the page.

Without going into too many details, you should also know that the `webpack` configuration has an **entry point**, which is the code that `webpack` considers to be the starting point of the application. By default, with the Angular CLI, that starting point is the `src/main.ts` file.

Here's what `main.ts` looks like:

```
import { enableProdMode } from '@angular/core';
import { platformBrowserDynamic } from '@angular/platform-browser-
dynamic';

import { AppModule } from './app/app.module';
import { environment } from './environments/environment';

if (environment.production) {
  enableProdMode();
}

platformBrowserDynamic().bootstrapModule(AppModule)
  .catch(err => console.error(err));
```

Here, the most important part is the
`platformBrowserDynamic().bootstrapModule(AppModule)` call. This is how
we tell Angular which module to load to kick-start the application. From there, the
`AppModule` gets loaded, and at this point, Angular knows about the `App` component.

 Did you notice the `.catch` call at the end? This hints at the fact that
the `bootstrapModule` method returns `Promise`.

Now, take a look at the `src/app/app.module.ts` file:

```
import { BrowserModule } from '@angular/platform-browser';
import { NgModule } from '@angular/core';

import { AppComponent } from './app.component';
import { FooComponent } from './foo/foo.component';

@NgModule({
  declarations: [
    AppComponent,
    FooComponent,
  ],
  imports: [
    BrowserModule
  ],
  providers: [],
  bootstrap: [AppComponent]
})
export class AppModule { }
```

Notice the `bootstrap: [AppComponent]` line. This tells Angular which component to add to the `index.html` page.

The `declarations` array is used to list all components, pipes, and directives that are part of the module. As new components are created in the module, they need to be added to this array.

 All Angular components must be declared in (exactly) one module (in the `declarations` array). If you forget to declare a component before you use it, Angular will complain. This also applies to pipes and directives in general.

Once declared, you can use those elements within the module. To use them outside the module, you'll need to import the module in which they are declared using the `imports` array of the `NgModule` decorator. In addition, you'll also have to include them in the `exports` array of the `NgModule` decorator so that other modules can use them.

Angular workspaces and the angular.json file

When you generate an Angular application using the Angular CLI (that is, `ng new` . . .), it creates a **workspace** for you. An Angular workspace is simply a directory that contains one or more Angular projects, which are themselves either **applications** or **libraries**.

 Angular libraries aren't full-blown applications, but they contain reusable elements. They become useful when you work on multiple applications in parallel that share some elements like components, directives, services.

At the root of every Angular workspace, you should find an `angular.json` file. This is the configuration file of the workspace. Inside it, all projects that are part of the workspace are listed, along with their configurations. Additionally, you can fine-tune the build system and tools (either for the whole workspace or project-by-project).

Here are a few simple examples of things that you can configure for a project:

- `outputPath`: The folder where the build output will be saved
- `index`: The HTML file to use as an entry point (this defaults to `src/index.html`)
- `main`: The file to use as an entry point (this defaults to `src/main.ts`)

- assets: An array of assets to include in the output of the build
- configurations: Environment-specific configurations or customizations
- budgets: A way to keep an eye on build sizes by setting soft and hard limits

> You can learn more about Angular budgets here: https://medium.com/dailyjs/how-did-angular-cli-budgets-save-my-day-and-how-they-can-save-yours-300d534aae7a.

The angular.json file provides extensive control over the build process. Once you get more familiar with the framework, you'll come to appreciate this flexibility.

Angular testing support and coverage reports

Angular's testing support covers unit-as well as end-to-end testing.

By default, the Angular CLI configures Jasmine (https://jasmine.github.io) for unit tests, along with Karma (https://karma-runner.github.io) as the test runner. For end-to-end testing, Protractor (https://www.protractortest.org) is the default.

The CLI also makes it easy to generate code coverage reports using Istanbul (https://istanbul.js.org). **Coverage reports help to shed some light on the parts of the code base that need additional testing efforts** (for example, classes, functions, or code branches that have not been tested).

Executing unit tests and generating coverage reports is as simple as running ng test --no-watch --code-coverage.

Once the command completes, you should find a coverage folder in your project, containing the reports in different formats (including HTML).

The fact that the CLI manages configuration for us is great because it really spares us a huge amount of time and effort researching and configuring the different tools and their integrations. In the past, all the wiring had to be done manually and it was really far from trivial. It was also especially challenging to maintain build configurations over time, given how fast the JavaScript ecosystem evolves.

Angular testing utilities

Angular also includes a number of utilities to help you write unit and integration tests. TestBed (https://angular.io/api/core/testing/TestBed) is a notable example. With it, you can dynamically create a fake Angular module (that is, NgModule) in your test code. This enables you to test the actual behavior of components and to use Angular's DI capabilities in the tests. Another example is HttpClientTestingModule (https://angular.io/api/common/http/testing/HttpClientTestingModule), which enables testing services that rely on Angular's HttpClient module.

Another important aspect to consider when testing Angular applications is ensuring that components do what they should. This means verifying not only the behavior of the component's class, but also its interactions with the associated template. This is important because both work hand-in-hand at runtime. For this reason, you should verify that they collaborate as intended.

Once again, Angular's TestBed interface can help. It provides many utility methods to ease testing, such as configureTestingModule.

Another method it provides is createComponent, which returns ComponentFixture (https://angular.io/api/core/testing/ComponentFixture) through which you can interact with the components being tested, inspect them, and detect changes.

> Unit tests are named after the class they test and have the following suffix: .spec.ts. For example, if you write unit tests for footer.component.ts, then the tests will be located in footer.component.spec.ts, right next to the class it corresponds to. This makes the file structure very intuitive to browse.

We need to move forward now—but make sure you stop by the official user guide to discover much more: https://angular.io/guide/testing.

If you do so, you'll begin to realize the huge amount of support that Angular provides for testing various scenarios.

> **One recommendation of the Angular team is to test the interactions of your components with the DOM using unit tests whenever possible.** They recommend this because unit tests are usually faster, easier to write, and easier to maintain.

We'll now take a look at Angular Console.

Bonus: Angular Console

Angular Console (`https://angularconsole.com`) is a very useful companion application for Angular developers. It can be installed on Linux, macOS, and Windows, but also directly within VS Code:

`https://marketplace.visualstudio.com/items?itemName=nrwl.angular-console.`

It is a graphical tool built on top of the Angular CLI. With it, you can easily create new Angular projects and manage existing ones:

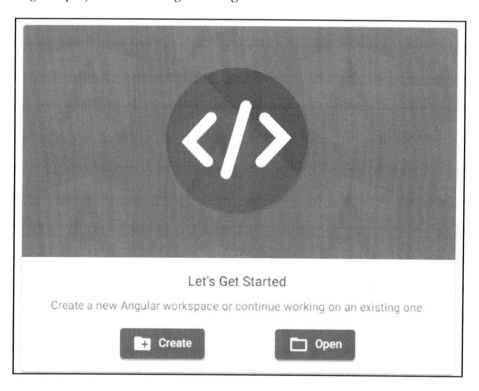

When you create a project with Angular Console, you just have to follow the wizard and customize the options as you see fit:

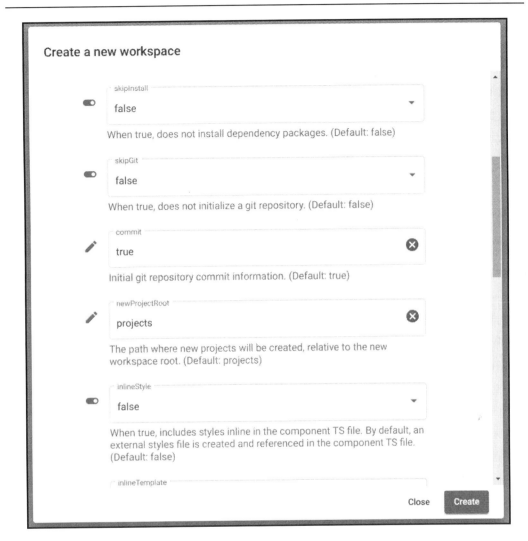

The tool will create a new workspace and project for you automatically, using the Angular CLI:

```
Create a new workspace

new-workspace test --directory=test --collection=@schematics/angular --no-experiment
alIvy --no-skipInstall --no-skipGit --no-inlineStyle --no-inlineTemplate --no-routin
g --no-skipTests --createApplication --no-minimal --no-interactive
```

We strongly believe that mastering the command line is key to greater productivity levels, which is why we have discussed shell and Git Bash early on in this book. That said, graphical tools also have their advantages too. For instance, by using Angular Console, you can actually discover some otherwise **hidden** gems in the CLI. The thing is that tools such as the Angular CLI have so many options and evolve so fast that they're hard to master.

Once you have created or opened a project with Angular Console, you can perform operations on it through the user interface; for example, you can execute the build, serve the application, execute tests, and more. To summarize, you can do anything the CLI can do but with visual assistance:

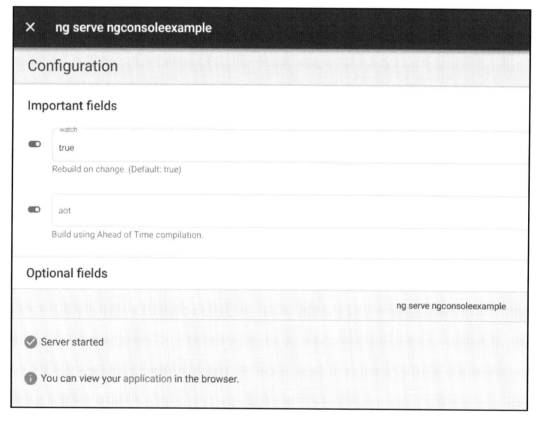

Have you heard about Augury yet? No? Okay, let's introduce it next.

Bonus: Augury

Augury (`https://augury.rangle.io`) is a very useful debugging tool for Angular that can be installed as an extension for both Google Chrome and Mozilla Firefox. It extends the built-in developer tools with Angular-specific utilities:

With the help of Augury, you can visualize your Angular application's component tree, inspect the state of its components, and analyze what is going on behind the scenes:

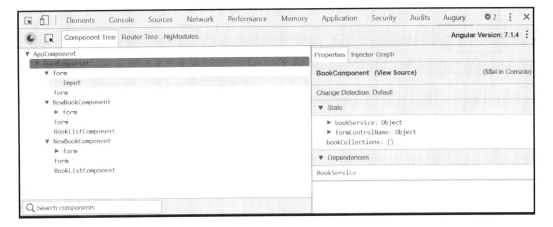

In the preceding example, the **Component Tree** view clearly shows the structure of the page. Whenever an element is selected on the left, its properties are shown on the right.

Introducing RP and RxJS

One programming paradigm that we haven't talked about so far but that Angular heavily relies on/encourages is called **Reactive Programming** (**RP**) or, more specifically, **Functional Reactive Programming** (**FRP**).

RP is not new at all; its principles have been described and studied since the early 1970s. RP and FRP have gained a lot of traction in recent years thanks to the rise of microservice-based architectures and the decline of Moore's law (https://www.scientificamerican.com/article/end-of-moores-law-its-not-just -about-physics). With the now much slower yearly increase in raw CPU power, the alternative is to develop systems that can take advantage of more CPUs or CPU cores through *parallelism* and workload distribution.

The RP paradigm is based on the idea that, most of the time, we can treat/manipulate inputs and outputs as **streams** of events/data. Simply put, we can treat most inputs and outputs as **asynchronous data streams** and perform stream processing in a non-blocking fashion.

A famous design pattern that RP is related to is called the **observer pattern**. That design pattern is useful when the state of a **subject** is of interest to outside parties called **observers**. The observers can **subscribe** to a subject and be **notified** whenever an event occurs. There are **observable** elements (that is, subjects) and **observers**.

 One useful analogy for data streams is water system pipes. If the pipes were transparent, then you could observe the flow of water going through them. If you wanted to filter out residues, then you could add filters to the system. If you wanted the water to be hotter, then you could add a heater next to the pipes to change the temperature. You could also tie two different pipe systems together and redirect the flow from one direction to another, and much more—you get the idea!

With RP, we subscribe to streams and use a *declarative approach* to define what to do when new data arrives or when events occur. This approach is powerful because it means that, at runtime, the processing itself can be performed in a non-blocking way, potentially on different threads or CPU cores.

RP, therefore, embraces an **event-driven approach** through which we can **react** to events pushed into a stream that we are **observing**. Using RP, we can, of course, also define and publish our own streams and events and use those to create virtual pipes between different parts of our applications.

Event-driven architectures put a lot of emphasis on observing or reacting to changes in **streams of events**. For instance, if you write an application for the stock market, you might be interested in **observing** the stream of values corresponding to all changes in valuation for specific stocks. Using RP, you can then describe what should be done when events are received. For example, you could instruct your program to sell when prices go below a certain threshold in order to cut losses, and much more.

If you think about it, events are omnipresent in web browsers—literally, thousands of events are generated each second when the following happen:

- You move your mouse.
- You click on elements on the page.
- You touch the screen.
- The browser receives a response to an HTTP call.
- The DOM is modified.
- The browser window is resized.
- You zoom in or out.
- You type something.
- You go online or offline.

The examples are countless! In addition, most of these *events are asynchronous in nature*. If you are interested in specific events, then you declare callback functions that will be invoked when those events occur.

But what if we could *subscribe* to a stream of mouse click events? Or to a stream of DOM modification events? Or even to a stream of application-specific events (for example, when a new comment has just been added on a screen)?

Well, thanks to RP libraries, we can do exactly that and much more!

RP libraries

RP is found everywhere nowadays; for example, in C# with ReactiveX (http://reactivex.io), in Java with the RxJava (https://github.com/ReactiveX/RxJava) and Reactor (https://projectreactor.io) projects, and in many other languages such as Scala (https://github.com/politrons/reactiveScala) or Haskell (https://wiki.haskell.org/Functional_Reactive_Programming). A *Reactive Streams* manifesto (http://www.reactive-streams.org) has also helped push the *standardization* of APIs forward.

The JavaScript/TypeScript ecosystem also has its own flagship implementation called RxJS (`https://rxjs-dev.firebaseapp.com`), which Angular uses and recommends.

RxJS is usually referred to as an FRP library. It provides an API for handling and composing streams of arbitrary data that combines the following:

- The **observer pattern**
- The **iterator pattern**
- Many functional programming-inspired operators

RxJS basics – observables

The main concept of the RxJS library is `Observable`, which is an abstraction for an *array of items over time* (that is, a stream of values).

Observables can do the following:

- Be subscribed to (that is, observed)
- Emit values when they become available
- Automatically push the values they emit to their subscribers (depending on the type of observable!)

Creating observables is easy, and RxJS provides **operators** which can create `Observable` instances from different sources.

Here are a few examples.

The `of` (`https://www.learnrxjs.io/operators/creation/of.html`) operator lets you create observables from a set of values:

```
import { of } from 'rxjs';
const myObservable = of(1,3,3,7);
//...
```

The `from` (`https://www.learnrxjs.io/operators/creation/from.html`) operator lets you create observables from arrays, iterables, and promises! This might seem like a detail, but this is actually a very important statement. Once you fully realize how powerful RxJS really is, you'll see that promises aren't so great in comparison.

Here is an example of how `from` can be used:

```
import { from } from 'rxjs';
const myObservable1 = from([1,2,3]);
const myObservable2 = from(new Promise(resolveFn =>
resolveFn('Foo')));
```

In the second example, an observable is created from `Promise`.

It is also possible to convert an `Observable` instance into a `Promise` instance using the `toPromise` (`https://www.learnrxjs.io/operators/utility/topromise.html`) operator. This is very useful when you need to return or use promises in some parts of your code base (for example, in order to interact with a third-party API that only supports promises.)

Creating `Observable` instances from events, as discussed earlier, is really simple using the `fromEvent` (`https://www.learnrxjs.io/operators/creation/fromevent.html`) operator:

```
import { fromEvent } from 'rxjs';
const myClicksObservable = fromEvent(document, 'click');
```

There are also other creation operators that you can explore at `https://www.learnrxjs.io/operators/creation`.

RxJS basics – observers

Creating observables is only half the battle. Having a data source is one thing, but if nobody *observes*, listens, or watches, then it is pretty much useless. As a matter of fact, **an observable will only be executed if there is at least one observer**.

With RxJS, each subscriber is called `Observer`. These are listeners for the values emitted/produced by `Observable`.

Here's a basic example:

```
const observer = {
    next: (x:any) => console.log(`Observer got a next value: ${x}`),
    error: (err:any) => console.error(`Observer got an error:
${err}`),
    complete: () => console.log('Observer got a completion
notification')
};
```

Here, the `observer` object is a valid observer. As illustrated in the preceding code block, it should have three basic functions called `next`, `error`, and `complete`, which are part of the **Observable API contract**.

This contract is quite simple:

- `next`: Can be called 0-n times (that is, each time a new value is available)
- `error`: Can be called only once, then nothing else can be emitted through the observable (that is, called if an error occurs)
- `complete`: Can be called only once, then nothing else can be emitted through the observable (that is, called if no more values will ever be emitted)

Let's explore what this contract means in practice. Consider the following example:

```
observer.next(1);
observer.next(2);
observer.next(3);
observer.complete();
observer.next(4); // 4 will not be delivered!
```

In this example, the `next` method of the observer is called multiple times. After that, the `complete` function is called once. After that, calling `next` again won't have any effect because the stream has been terminated.

RxJS basics – subscriptions

To register an observer with `Observable`, you have to call its `.subscribe(...)` method and pass your observer as an argument. In return, you'll get a `Subscription` object, which you can use to *cancel* the subscription once you are not interested anymore:

```
import { of } from 'rxjs';

const myObservable = of(1,3,3,7);
const mySubscription = myObservable.subscribe(x => console.log(x));
...
mySubscription.unsubscribe();
```

 As you might have noticed in this example, you are not forced to define all the contract methods (that is, `next`, `error`, and `complete`). However, just like the promises, it is best to handle at least the `error` case!

When you subscribe to `Observable`, you actually create an *execution* of it. This is an important thing to keep in mind: simply creating `Observable` will do nothing. Actual work will only start as soon as there is at least one observer.

 Properly handling subscriptions is very important, as you could easily introduce memory leaks by not cleaning things up. You can refer to this article to understand how to handle this: `https://blog.angularindepth.com/the-best-way-to-unsubscribe-rxjs-observable-in-the-angular-applications-d8f9aa42f6a0`.

Let's now look at subjects.

RxJS basics – subjects

`Subject` (`https://rxjs-dev.firebaseapp.com/guide/subject`) is both `Observable` and `Observer`. As `Observer`, it watches over a data source (for example, a type of event or an external data source) and as `Observable`, it can be subscribed to, and therefore emit events or values to its subscribers (that is, observers).

Here is an example:

```
import { Subject } from 'rxjs';

const observer1 = {
    next: (value: string) => console.log(`Observer 1: ${value}`)
};

const observer2 = {
    next: (value: string) => console.log(`Observer 1: ${value}`)
};

const mySubject = new Subject<string>();

mySubject.subscribe(observer1);
mySubject.subscribe(observer2);

mySubject.next("Hello");
mySubject.next("World");

// Output:
// Observer 1: Hello
// Observer 2: Hello
// Observer 1: World
// Observer 2: World
```

Previously, the `observer1` and `observer2` observers get called for each of the next calls on the observed subject.

 There are multiple `Subject` implementations in RxJS: `BehaviorSubject`, `ReplaySubject`, `AsyncSubject`, and many more.

Great—let's keep going!

RxJS basics – hot and cold observables

Observables can be **hot** or **cold**.

Cold observables start executing upon subscription (that is, they only start producing values when `subscribe` is called). **You can compare cold observables to online video streaming solutions: that is, they only stream data when a client is connected and requests it**.

Hot observables are different—they produce values whether there are subscribers or not. **You can compare hot observables to a radio: it keeps streaming, hoping that there are listeners out there**.

RxJS basics – operators and marble diagrams

Operators are one of the greatest strengths of RxJS, but what are they?

Operators are functions that can be applied to streams in order to **transform** them in various ways. Most operators are also *fluent*: you can chain them because **applying an operation to a stream usually returns a new stream**. Thanks to this feature, you can declare a set of operations to be performed whenever a value arrives, therefore defining complex stream processing rules in a declarative manner.

The composability of operators represents a key advantage of RxJS, but it should not be abused. You need to be careful because it is easy to make your code complex to read and understand if you go overboard.

RxJS provides dozens of operators out of the box (`https://rxjs-dev.firebaseapp.com/api?type=function`). Here are some examples of functional ones: `map`, `flatMap`, `concat`, and `reduce`. If you are already familiar with functional programming, then you'll surely recognize these terms.

There are many operators that you'll combine depending on your requirements. Some of them are not straightforward to use, but there is a nice concept that can help you understand how they work: **marble diagrams**.

Marble diagrams help visualize how operators work. They represent input streams and output streams after operators are applied. On these diagrams, time flows from left to right.

Here is an example for the `map` operator:

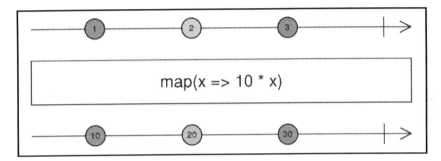

In this example, you can see that the `map` operator applies a provided function to the values that are emitted by `Observable`; in this case, it is multiplied by 10. The **map** function is applied to each element of the input stream as they are *emitted*. After the operator has been applied to a value, the mapped value is emitted on the output stream.

Marble diagrams offer a great mental model for what happens with streams and values. If you apply multiple operations to a stream, then you have to imagine that values coming into the original stream **fall down** into the operator, get modified, and are then pushed into a new stream down below.

 Subscribers to the original stream will get the untouched emitted values, while subscribers to derived streams will get the values resulting from the application of all the intermediary operators.

We won't explore RxJS in any more detail, but rest assured that this is a library that you should definitely understand, if not master. The `Observable` API is a candidate for being integrated into future versions of ECMAScript, as a companion to the existing `Promise` API that we learned about previously.

While using RxJS and observables, you'll quickly realize that observables are much more interesting and powerful than promises. With them, you can do a lot more with much less code. Moreover, observables can have many subscribers and can emit many values over time, while promises can only result in one value being returned.

Let's now take a look at Angular forms and examine how RP can be leveraged to make them really powerful.

Exploring Angular forms

Now that you know about RP, we can also mention Angular forms. Angular supports two different ways of managing/handling them:

- Template-based: This is useful for simple and basic use cases.
- Reactive: This is far more powerful and easily testable.

Both of those approaches rely on the same API foundations, but template-based forms are more abstract and require less knowledge of Angular.

Template-based forms

Template-based forms are defined in templates, while the logic behind them is implemented in component classes. To be able to use them, you'll need to import the `FormsModule` module in your `@NgModule` decorator.

Here is an example taken from the official Angular documentation:

```html
<div>
  <label for="name">Name</label>
  <input type="text" id="name" required
    [(ngModel)]="model.name" name="name">
</div>

<div>
  <label for="alterEgo">Alter Ego</label>
  <input type="text" id="alterEgo" [(ngModel)]="model.alterEgo"
name="alterEgo">
</div>

<div>
```

```
    <label for="power">Hero Power</label>
    <select id="power" required [(ngModel)]="model.power" name="power">
      <option *ngFor="let pow of powers" [value]="pow">{{ pow
}}</option>
    </select>
</div>
```

Template-based forms are actually very similar to the forms that we created earlier in the book; they rely on HTML5 attributes, labels, and much more.

 The `form` tag doesn't require a target; this is taken care of by `FormsModule`, which automatically adds the `NgForm` (`https://angular.io/api/forms/NgForm`) directive to your forms.

The advantage of template-based forms is that they are simple to grasp and use. Since you are writing the template, you can use all the directives that you want, such as `*ngFor` to iterate over collections and `ngModel` to have two-way bindings between your form and your component class.

As a matter of fact, template-based forms are exactly the same as in AngularJS. As such, they're very useful for migration scenarios, as a way to ease the transition of an existing AngularJS application to Angular.

 If you use `ngModel` to bind form controls, Angular will automatically track their state. Based on what it detects (for example, whether the element is valid, invalid, or modified or not) it will add or remove CSS classes such as `ng-touched`, `ng-untouched`, `ng-dirty`, and `ng-pristine`. This is great because it lets you easily adapt the styling of your form's elements based on their state. Without Angular, this would require quite some code to achieve.

With template-based forms, form changes flow asynchronously from the view to the model (that is, the component class members that are bound to your form elements). Behind the scenes, what happens is that those form elements declared in the templates are associated with a form model by Angular. That form model keeps track of data changes and differences between the HTML inputs and Angular's representation.

When changes are detected (for example, after you type something in a form field), events are triggered, which then causes the corresponding component class member properties to be updated.

Reactive forms

Reactive forms are *synchronous* and more explicit. With them, you define the form model programmatically in the component class, including the form controls, control groups, and so on. When changes occur on either side (that is, user inputs or form model controller), the other side is updated synchronously. This means that *reactive forms are more predictable.*

Here is an example from the official documentation of Angular:

```
import { Component } from '@angular/core';
import { FormGroup, FormControl } from '@angular/forms';

@Component({
  selector: 'app-profile-editor',
  templateUrl: './profile-editor.component.html',
  styleUrls: ['./profile-editor.component.css']
})
export class ProfileEditorComponent {
  profileForm = new FormGroup({
    firstName: new FormControl(''),
    lastName: new FormControl(''),
  });
}
```

In the preceding code sample, `ProfileEditorComponent` declares a form by instantiating the `FormGroup` class and defining a set of `FormControl` elements.

The corresponding template simply binds the form elements to the backing model:

```
<form [formGroup]="profileForm">

  <label>
    First Name:
    <input type="text" formControlName="firstName">
  </label>

  <label>
    Last Name:
    <input type="text" formControlName="lastName">
  </label>

</form>
```

There is no indirection with this approach. Since the template's form is bound to `FormGroup` declared in the component, changes are directly reflected.

`FormControl` instances expose a `valueChanges` observable—any observer will be immediately notified whenever the value of that control changes.

We'll use reactive forms in our application. For now, just keep in mind that **reactive forms might be a bit more complex, but offer much more flexibility, control, reusability, predictability, and performance in return**.

Introducing Material Design and Angular Material

Creating a great user interface design system is insanely hard and most of us don't have the skills, experience, or simply time to go about creating a decent one. Luckily for us, Google's world-class designers have created Material Design (`https://material.io`).

Material Design is an open design specification created by Google and publicly announced in 2014. Nowadays, most Google products (including Android mobile applications) are based on it.

Material Design was built with mobile-first and *adaptive* user interfaces in mind. It provides a great starting point for anyone looking to create modern user experiences that work seamlessly on desktop and mobile.

If you take a look at the official website, you'll see that it covers many topics, such as how to handle layout, navigation, colors, typography, iconography, shapes, motion, interaction, and much more.

In addition, the specification also provides many guidelines to help you create great user experiences (for example, from a usability point of view). Finally, it also describes many user interface components in great detail (for example, buttons, cards, data tables, dialogs, and lists).

Many big brands also have their own design system, such as Microsoft's Fluent (`https://www.microsoft.com/design/fluent`), but not all of them are open and free to use.

Having a design system specification is a huge win for everyone, but also having an actual implementation is even nicer. Again, luckily for us, the Angular team at Google has created Angular Material (`https://material.angular.io`), an open source Angular-based library that implements Material Design.

Angular Material includes a ton of reusable Angular components (`https://material.angular.io/components/categories`) that respect Material Design's guidelines. Angular Material has great support for theming and accessibility (for example, ARIA, keyboard control, and more). Finally, it provides many APIs to programmatically control the interface, a set of Angular CLI schematics, and much more.

 Note that there is also an official implementation of Material Design written in pure CSS. You can find information about it at `https://github.com/material-components/material-components-web` and at `https://material.io/develop/web`. Over time, Angular Material might make use of these components, but for the time being you can mix and match both in your projects if you feel the need to. Just be aware of what it means for the long term: `https://stackoverflow.com/questions/41180498/material-components-for-the-web-vs-angular-material-2`.

In the next chapter, we'll leverage Angular Material to improve our application's user interface.

Summary

This chapter was once again packed with content. Congratulations on making it this far!

We started by learning about what modern web applications are all about and how they differ from old-school ones. We learned about the differences between SSR and SPA. We also briefly talked about mobile-first, RWD, and PWA.

These ideas are all at the core of the modern web and any developer who is serious about building web applications should learn as much as possible about these concepts.

Following that, we defined what modern web frameworks can do for us. This, of course, led us into the main topic of this chapter: Angular!

Before diving into it, we finally discovered a bit more about TypeScript decorators, which are extensively used by Angular.

Given that Angular is a large framework, we had to introduce many concepts and ideas, such as modules, components, templates, bindings, life cycle hooks, directives, pipes, forms, DI, and more.

Of course, being faced with so much information all at once can be overwhelming, but the goal, above all, was to at least make you aware of the depth of Angular.

Its learning curve is certainly steep, but you don't need to learn everything at once. Learning a framework is always a journey. You'll never know everything about it, but if you use it for a while, you'll start recognizing patterns, and then gain confidence and increase your productivity.

Knowing that Angular has so much to offer is important when assessing which frontend framework or library to use. Of course, it is huge and you might only need a fraction of it for now; however, if you need to use it later, you know that it'll probably be there, waiting for you.

In this chapter, we've also learned about a few more design patterns such as the observer pattern, as well as programming paradigms such as AOP, RP, and FRP.

Finally, we also explored RxJS and the `Observable` contract. We could only go so far on those topics, but don't hesitate to go further on your own—you won't regret it!

In the next chapter, we will use our newly acquired skills to rewrite the MediaMan application using Angular.

Further reading

Here are some useful resources related to the subjects covered in this chapter.

PWAs

Here are some interesting links if you want to learn more about PWA:

- `https://developers.google.com/web/progressive-web-apps`
- `https://developers.google.com/web/progressive-web-apps/checklist`

TypeScript decorators

Here are some useful resources if you want to learn more about decorators:

- https://www.typescriptlang.org/docs/handbook/decorators.html
- http://blog.wolksoftware.com/decorators-reflection-javascript-typescript

RP and RxJS

Here are some useful resources about RxJS and observables:

- **Official website:** https://rxjs-dev.firebaseapp.com
- **Marble diagrams:** http://rxmarbles.com
- **Operators documentation:** https://www.learnrxjs.io/operators
- **Marble testing library:** https://cartant.github.io/rxjs-marbles

If you want to read more about RP, refer to the following:

- **A great article by Andre Staltz:**
  https://gist.github.com/staltz/868e7e9bc2a7b8c1f754
- **A great article about cold versus hot observables:**
  http://blog.thoughtram.io/angular/2016/06/16/cold-vs-hot-observables.html
- https://blog.angular-university.io/functional-reactive-programming-for-angular-2-developers-rxjs-and-observables
- https://blog.angularindepth.com/learn-to-combine-rxjs-sequences-with-super-intuitive-interactive-diagrams-20fce8e6511
- http://paulstovell.com/blog/reactive-programming
- https://medium.freecodecamp.org/functional-reactive-programming-frp-imperative-vs-declarative-vs-reactive-style-84878272c77f
- https://infoscience.epfl.ch/record/148043/files/DeprecatingObserversTR2010.pdf?version=1
- https://angular.io/guide/rx-library
- https://medium.com/@jshvarts/read-marble-diagrams-like-a-pro-3d72934d3ef5

Angular

Here are some useful general resources around Angular:

- The official documentation: `https://angular.io/docs`
- A useful cheatsheet: `https://angular.io/guide/cheatsheet`
- The official style guide: `https://angular.io/guide/styleguide`
- Angular sources: `https://github.com/angular`
- Angular Playground (`http://www.angularplayground.it`): a nice project to learn about Angular and try things out
- Angular's CLI documentation: `https://cli.angular.io`
- The Angular API documentation: `https://angular.io/api`
- In-depth tutorials about Angular: `https://blog.angularindepth.com`
- Augury (`https://augury.rangle.io`): a browser extension for debugging Angular applications
- Many more resources that can be found on the official website: `https://angular.io/resources`
- A great article by Vasco from Angular University: `https://blog.angular-university.io/why-angular-angular-vs-jquery-a-beginner-friendly-explanation-on-the-advantages-of-angular-and-mvc`

CLI

Here is the official documentation of the Angular CLI: `https://angular.io/cli`.

Router

You can learn more about the Angular router here:

- `https://angular.io/guide/router`
- `https://www.smashingmagazine.com/2018/11/a-complete-guide-to-routing-in-angular`

Modules

Here are some links about Angular modules:

- `https://angular.io/guide/architecture-modules`
- `https://angular.io/guide/ngmodules`
- `https://angular.io/guide/module-types`
- `https://angular.io/guide/ngmodule-api`
- `https://juristr.com/blog/2017/03/angular-modules-vs-es6-modules`

Life cycle hooks

You can learn more about life cycle hooks and find a full list of hooks, along with examples, here: `https://angular.io/guide/lifecycle-hooks`.

Directives

If you want to learn more about directives, check out the following from the official documentation:

- `https://angular.io/guide/architecture-components#directives`
- `https://angular.io/guide/structural-directives`
- `https://angular.io/guide/attribute-directives`
- `https://netbasal.com/understanding-angular-structural-directives-659acd0f67e`
- `https://netbasal.com/the-power-of-structural-directives-in-angular-bfe4d8c44fb1`

Components

You can learn a lot more about Angular components and how they can interact with one another here:

- `https://angular.io/api/core/Component`
- `https://angular.io/guide/component-interaction`
- `https://angular.io/guide/architecture-components`
- `https://angular.io/guide/template-syntax`

Pipes

You can learn more about pipes here:

- `https://angular.io/guide/architecture-components#pipes`
- `https://codecraft.tv/courses/angular/pipes/built-in-pipes`

Services

You can learn more about services here:

- `https://angular.io/guide/architecture-services`
- `https://medium.com/@balramchavan/best-practices-building-angular-services-using-facade-design-pattern-for-complex-systems-d8c516cb95eb`

DI

Here are some links about DI support and its providers:

- **DI entry point:** `https://angular.io/guide/dependency-injection`
- **Providers:** `https://angular.io/guide/providers`
- **DI providers:** `https://angular.io/guide/dependency-injection-providers`
- **Injector tree/inheritance:** `https://angular.io/guide/hierarchical-dependency-injection`
- **Injectors:** `https://angular.io/guide/glossary#injector`
- **DI tokens:** `https://angular.io/guide/glossary#di-token`
- **DI in action:** `https://angular.io/guide/dependency-injection-in-action`
- **In-depth article:** `https://blog.angularindepth.com/angular-dependency-injection-and-tree-shakeable-tokens-4588a8f70d5d`

Change detection

If you want to understand more details about change detection, then take a look at the following:

- `https://blog.thoughtram.io/angular/2016/02/22/angular-2-change-detection-explained.html`
- `https://angular.io/api/core/Component#changeDetection`
- `https://blog.angular-university.io/how-does-angular-2-change-detection-really-work`
- `https://www.sitepoint.com/change-detection-angular`
- `https://github.com/angular/zone.js`

Forms

The best place to start if you want to learn more about Angular forms is the official documentation, which also covers how to test and validate forms:

- `https://angular.io/guide/forms-overview`
- `https://angular.io/guide/reactive-forms`

Miscellaneous

Finally, here are some additional resources:

- The bootstrap process of Angular:
  `https://angular.io/guide/bootstrapping`
- The file and folder structure of Angular applications:
  `https://angular.io/guide/file-structure`
- Workspace configuration with `angular.json`:
  - `https://angular.io/guide/workspace-config`
  - `https://nitayneeman.com/posts/understanding-the-angular-cli-workspace-file`

8
Rewriting MediaMan Using Angular and Angular Material

Now that you have a rough idea about what Angular really is, what it is composed of, and how to write components, we're going to apply this new knowledge of yours to revisit the MediaMan application.

Going through this exercise will give you the opportunity to witness the impact of such a migration on the existing code and quality of the overall application. It will also give you a more concrete understanding of the framework and should clarify why Angular can be used to rapidly build large enterprise applications with ease.

In this chapter, we will cover the following topics:

- Creating the project (using the Angular CLI)
- Integrating the shared logic
- Implementing the book module
- Revisiting the user interface with Angular Material

What will you build?

Instead of rewriting MediaMan from scratch, we are going to port the existing code step by step. This will let us focus on the Angular way of doing things.

We will start by creating a new application using the Angular CLI. Then, we will integrate our existing data model, services, and visual elements, making sure that we leverage the Angular concepts that we learned about in the previous chapter.

We will go through two stages. During the first iteration, we will create MediaMan v2, which will keep the same user interface as before. After that, we will add Angular Material to the project and then we'll recreate the user interface using Angular Material components.

From a functional point of view, our application will remain exactly the same as before, but it'll have a better code structure and a nicer user interface. As an added benefit, any other Angular developer should be able to quickly join the project and get up to speed.

Going through the migration process will give you a clear understanding of how Angular and Angular Material work.

Let's get started!

Creating the project

Let's prepare our project. This time around, we did not prepare the project beforehand. Instead, we'll let you do everything on your own. Don't worry though, the Angular CLI will be a great companion and we'll stick around to guide you.

Creating the project using the CLI

Go ahead and create a new folder for the project using the CLI, and run the following command:

```
ng new mediaman-v2
```

The CLI will ask you a couple of questions. Here are the answers that you should provide:

1. **Would you like to add Angular routing? (Y/N):** N
2. **Which stylesheet format would you like to use?:** SCSS (.scss) (http://sass-lang.com)

The Angular CLI will then generate the project files and trigger the installation of all of the required dependencies.

Reviewing the application structure

If you take a look at the list of files that the CLI has generated for you, then some filenames should already look familiar, but others probably less so.

Let's have a look at them:

- `tslint.json`: This is the TSLint configuration.
- `src/favicon.ico`: This is a default favorite icon for our application.
- `src/polyfills.ts`: This is the file used to import all required polyfills.
- `src/styles.scss`: This is the main stylesheet for the application. Notice the file extension: it corresponds to SASS (`https://sass-lang.com`), which we have chosen to use here.
- `src/browserslist`: This is a configuration file used to determine browser support rules.
- `src/assets/.gitkeep`: This is an empty file that simply tells Git to track the currently empty `assets` folder. The `assets` folder is where you can place your images, fonts, and much more.
- `src/environments/environment.ts`: These are the environment definitions for development time.
- `src/environments/environment.prod.ts`: The contents of this file are taken instead of those in `environment.ts` for production (that is, when the application is built with the `--production` flag).
- `e2e/protractor.conf.js`: This is the configuration of Protractor, the default E2E testing library of Angular.
- `e2e/tsconfig.e2e.json`: This is a TypeScript configuration file dedicated to E2E testing.
- `e2e/src/app.e2e-spec.ts`: This is an example E2E test.
- `e2e/src/app.po.ts`: This is an example **page object**. Page objects are related to the page object design pattern for improving the maintainability of your tests. You can learn more about that pattern here: `https://www.automatetheplanet.com/page-object-pattern`.

Keep in mind that this structure evolves over time. For instance, thanks to one of our technical reviewers, we have realized that the `browserslist` file is now located at the root of the project, while it was under `src` when we initially wrote this chapter! Don't attach too much importance to the filenames and their location; it's much more important to understand the role that they play, as that doesn't change that often.

Extending another TypeScript configuration

If you take a look at the `e2e/tsconfig.e2e.json` file, you'll see that it starts with the following line: `"extends": "../tsconfig.json"`.

 The file might be called `tsconfig.json` if you're using a more recent version of the Angular CLI!

Using this directive, you can inherit from another TypeScript configuration (and even chain multiple ones). This is very useful for larger projects where only specific settings differ in some parts of the system.

You can read more about this here:
`https://www.typescriptlang.org/docs/handbook/tsconfig-json.html#configuration-inheritance-with-extends`.

Folder structure and the LIFT principle

The base folder structure of the project is simple, easy to understand, and great for smaller applications:

```
. e2e/
. src/
.. app/
.. assets/
.. environments
```

As you can guess, the bulk of the application code will go into the `app` folder. Within this folder, we will create modules for the different functional parts and features of our application. Within each of those modules, we'll organize elements by type (for example, components, entities, services, and more). This will help us to better structure our code.

The Angular structure is based on the **LIFT principle** described in the official style guide: `https://angular.io/guide/styleguide#lift`.

LIFT stands for the following:

- Locate code easily
- Identify code at a glance

- Flattened structure as long as possible
- Try to stay DRY

 Keep in mind that the main goal of the file and folder structure in any software project is to make it easy to find your way around it and to make navigation easy. So, don't make it too complex unless you really need to.

The good news is that Angular is rather flexible and doesn't enforce its own structure for all applications. Larger ones will go further and create different libraries and projects, but this will do for MediaMan.

Adding required dependencies

As you know, the previous version of MediaMan used the following libraries:

- `localforage`: To persist/load media collections
- `class-transformer`: To serialize/deserialize classes

Go ahead and do the following:

1. Add these dependencies to the `package.json` file.
2. Run `npm install` to retrieve them.

Alternatively, you can do it all at once using `npm install localforage class-transformer --save`.

Starting the development server

Now that the project is created and that all of the necessary dependencies are available, go ahead and start the development server:

```
ng serve --open
```

Once this is done, you should be able to access the application at the following location: `http://localhost:4200`.

 Most of the time, the changes that you will make should be picked up automatically. Sometimes, though, you might need to restart the server (for example, after renaming/moving files around).

You can leave the server running during development.

Defining the application title

We'll start small and modify the application's entry point to display the application name.

As we saw earlier, the bootstrapped element of Angular applications is the App component, composed of `app.component.html` and `app.component.ts`. These files have been generated automatically by the CLI.

Go ahead and replace the contents of `src/app/app.component.html` with the following:

```
<h1>{{ title }}</h1>
```

Now, let's adapt the `app.component.ts` file by changing the title from `mediaman-v2` to `Mediaman`:

```
title = 'Mediaman'
```

If you look at the application in your browser, you should see that it was updated automatically.

Integrating the shared logic

Without a doubt, we want to reuse as much code as possible in our new and awesome Angular application! The good news is that we can, and, as you'll see, it is really straightforward. It wouldn't be the case for just any project, but the fact is that our code is already written in TypeScript, uses modules, and is pretty well-structured.

We will now create an Angular module called `shared`. We will use it to store elements that can be reused across the application. In this `shared` module, we will store our generic domain model classes, services, and more. Obviously, this module will contain everything about `Media`.

Open up a Terminal and go to the application's `src/app` folder. Then, create the new module using the following command:

```
ng generate module shared
```

Let's start by migrating the `Genre` enum from MediaMan v1, as we will require it soon. We will put it inside our newly created `shared` module.

At this point, the `shared` module's folder only contains the module definition (that is, the `shared.module.ts` file).

Before you continue, make sure to use the `cd` command to get into the `shared` folder.

 This step is important because the **Angular CLI commands are contextual**. If a command is executed in a module's folder, then the elements will be created and declared in that same module.

To gain some time, let's use the CLI to generate the enum for us:

```
ng generate enum enums/genre
```

Here is the expected output:

```
CREATE src/app/shared/enums/genre.enum.ts (22 bytes)
```

Next, let's edit this file and copy the content of the previous implementation we had for our enum, `Genre`:

```
export enum Genre {
  Horror = 'Horror',
  Fantastic = 'Fantastic',
  Thriller = 'Thriller',
  Romance = 'Romance',
  Fiction = 'Fiction'
}
```

A pattern that we've also applied here and that we'll try to use consistently across the application is to limit each file to one **concept**. We won't be putting anything other than the `Genre` enum in this file. This is related to the LIFT pattern that we mentioned before: the filename clearly indicates what it contains.

 We are structuring our `shared` module per element type. This is useful for utility modules such as this one.

Before creating our next class, we need to import the `reflect` polyfill. This polyfill is required by `class-transformer`.

We need to open the `src/polyfills.ts` file and add the following import:

```
import 'core-js/es/reflect';
```

Let's continue the migration with our abstract `Media` class.

First, still from the `src/app/shared` folder, create the skeleton using the following:

ng generate class entities/abstract-media --type="entity"

Did you notice the `--type=` option? This is recommended as it lets the Angular CLI worry about the filename suffix for us.

Then, copy the content of the following file from this book's sample code: `Chapter08/mediaman-v2/src/app/shared/entities/abstract-media.entity.ts`. This is a copy of the previous implementation.

Now, we can migrate to our `MediaCollection` class. Again, create the file with the CLI:

ng g class entities/media-collection --type="entity"

We've used the `g` shorthand for `generate`.

Now, replace the generated code with the contents of this file: `Chapter08/mediaman-v2/src/app/shared/entities/media-collection.entity.ts`.

Next up is the `MediaService` class. Generate the TypeScript file using the CLI:

ng g class services/abstract-media.service

Notice that we haven't used the `--type=` option. The end result is the same, but it is actually preferable to use `--type` for simplicity's sake.

Once again, replace the generated code with the previous implementation, located here in the code sample: `Chapter08/mediaman-v2/src/app/shared/services/abstract-media.service.ts`.

So far, we haven't modified anything from our previous code, apart from splitting the content up in multiple files.

Great, our `shared` module is ready!

Implementing the book module

Now that we've laid out the base structure and integrated our `shared` module, we can turn our attention to the books.

Creating the module

Go back to the application's app module folder (that is, `src/app`) and create a new `book` module to encapsulate the code specific to books:

- `cd <path to mediaman-v2>/src/app`
- `ng g module book`
- `cd book`

Then, create the `book` entity:

`ng g class entities/book --type="entity"`

Then, copy over the code from the previous implementation, which you can find here: `Chapter08/mediaman-v2/src/app/book/entities/book.entity.ts`.

The next element on our list is the book service. Create it using the following:

`ng g service services/book`

In the previous version of MediaMan, we had `MediaController`, which was responsible for managing the collection of books. Also, we didn't have a service dedicated to books. With our Angular version, we can actually create such a service, make it stateful, and integrate the methods from `MediaController`.

Let's modify `BookService` a bit, in order to extend the abstract `MediaService`.

Replace the generated code with the following:

```
import { Injectable } from '@angular/core';
import { MediaService } from '../../shared/services/abstract-
media.service';
```

```
import { Book } from '../entities/book.entity';
import { MediaCollection } from '../../shared/entities/media-
collection.entity';

@Injectable({
  providedIn: 'root'
})
export class BookService extends MediaService<Book> {
  private _bookCollections: Map<string, MediaCollection<Book>> = new
  Map<string, MediaCollection<Book>>();

  constructor() {
    super(Book);
  }

  get bookCollections(): Map<string, MediaCollection<Book>> {
    return this._bookCollections;
  }
}
```

Our service uses the @Injectable decorator to declare the service with Angular's DI system.

Our service also has a private state, our book collections map. Since this service will only be instantiated once by Angular, this will be fine.

Implementing the bookCollection methods

The first method that we can add from the previous version of MediaManControllerImpl is reloadBookCollections(): void.

Here's the code that you can add for it:

```
reloadBookCollections(): void {
    this.getMediaCollectionIdentifiersList().then(keys => {
      this._bookCollections.clear(); // clear the current state
      keys.forEach(key => {
        this.loadMediaCollection(key).then(collection => {
          this._bookCollections.set(key, collection);
        });
      });
    });
}
```

Notice that now we are extending from `MediaService`, we have removed
the `this._bookService.` prefix and replaced it with `this.` in order to call the
method from the parent `MediaService` class.

Also, since we manage the view with an Angular template, we don't need to call any
method from `MediaManView` anymore. We can simply remove the two mentions
to `this._view` in our method.

Now, copy the `createBookCollection` method. For this one, we have to change the
signature to add a `name` parameter: `createBookCollection(name: string):
void`.

Here's the adapted code:

```
createBookCollection(name: string): void {
  console.log('Creating a new book collection: ', name);

  const newBookCollection: MediaCollection<Book> = new
  MediaCollection<Book>(Book, name);
  this._bookCollections.set(newBookCollection.identifier,
  newBookCollection);

  this.saveMediaCollection(newBookCollection).then(() => {
    console.log(`New book collection called
    "${newBookCollection.name}"
    saved successfully. Identifier: `, newBookCollection.identifier);
    }).catch(_ => {
    this.displayErrorMessage(`Failed to save the new book collection
    called ${name}`);
  });
}
```

Again, we have removed mentions to `this._view`, except for the one in `catch()` of
our promise. For that one, we have
replaced `this._view.displayErrorMessage` with `this.displayErrorMessage`
order to call the parent method.

 In the preceding code, we have completely ignored the error
received in the `catch` block. Keep in mind that we did this only to
simplify the examples. In a real application, you should instead log
the errors appropriately so that you can later troubleshoot issues.
Production-grade systems should actually collect errors centrally to
proactively resolve issues rather than waiting for end users to call
for help!

The next method in our list is `removeBookCollection`:

```
removeBookCollection(identifier: string): void {
  if (!identifier) {
    throw new Error('An identifier must be provided');
  }

  this._bookCollections.delete(identifier);
  this.removeMediaCollection(identifier).then(() => {
    console.log('Removed the collection with identifier: ',
    identifier);
  }).catch(_ => {
    this.displayErrorMessage('Failed to remove the collection!');
  });
}
```

So far, so good; let's continue.

Implementing the book method

Next, let's copy and adapt the `createBook` method.

For this one, we need to add a `book: Book` parameter. That way, users of the service will be able to pass in the book to add to the collection.

Here is the new code for this method:

```
createBook(collectionIdentifier: string, book: Book): void {
  if (!collectionIdentifier) {
    throw new Error('The collection identifier is required to create a
    new book!');
  }

  if (!this._bookCollections.has(collectionIdentifier) ||
    !this._bookCollections.get(collectionIdentifier)) {
    console.error('Tried to add a book to an unknown collection.
    Identifier: ', collectionIdentifier);
    this.displayErrorMessage('Failed to create the new book!');
    return;
  }

  const existingCollection =
    this._bookCollections.get(collectionIdentifier);
  if (!existingCollection || !book) {
    throw new Error(`The collection couldn't be retrieved or we
    could not get the book details from the view!`);
```

```
    }

    existingCollection.addMedia(book);

    this.saveMediaCollection(existingCollection)
      .then(() => {
        console.log(`Book collection called "${existingCollection.name}"
        updated successfully.`);
      })
      .catch(error => {
        console.error('Error while updating an existing book collection:
        ', error);
        this.displayErrorMessage(`Failed to update the existing book
        collection called ${existingCollection.name}`);
      });
  }
```

If you compare it with the previous implementation, you will notice that we have also removed the code that was previously used to retrieve the book. We don't need to retrieve it anymore since we now receive it through a method parameter.

The last method we have to migrate is removeBook. For this one, we only have to remove bookService and replace it with this to use the parent method.

We can now apply the same changes as before (about _view):

```
    removeBook(collectionIdentifier: string, bookIdentifier: string) {
      if (!collectionIdentifier) {
        throw new Error('The collection identifier must be provided!');
      }

      if (!bookIdentifier) {
        throw new Error('The book identifier must be provided!');
      }

      console.log(`Removing book ${bookIdentifier} which should be part
      of collection ${collectionIdentifier}`);

      const existingCollection = this._bookCollections.
      get(collectionIdentifier);
      if (!existingCollection) {
        throw new Error('The collection couldn't be retrieved or we
          could not get the book details from the view!');
      }

      existingCollection.removeMedia(bookIdentifier);
      this.saveMediaCollection(existingCollection)
        .then(() => {
```

```
        console.log(`Book collection called
        "${existingCollection.name}" updated successfully.`);
      })
      .catch(error => {
        console.error('Error while updating an existing book
        collection: ', error);
        this.displayErrorMessage(`Failed to save the modifications`);
      });
    }
```

That's it—our service is now ready to use. Wasn't that easy?

Apart from the @Injectable decorator added on top and a few minor changes, the implementation remains globally the same as before.

The main difference is that we can now leverage Angular's DI capabilities to inject our service anywhere we need.

Of course, having a service and some entities is not enough. At this point, we still have no visual elements. Fortunately, with Angular, this will be easy to implement.

Creating the book page component

Let's create a **page** for managing book collections.

This page will display all book collections and will allow us to manage them. Moreover, the controller of the page will be aware of the fact that the BookService exists and will use it when modifications need to be made to books/collections. Because of that added responsibility, it should be considered a **smart component**.

From here on, you'll start noticing more important changes in how we are going to construct the view. Rather than putting all of the elements and logic in the same place, we will instead decompose our view in multiple Angular components, with each responsible for a smaller part.

Still from the book module's folder, let's go ahead and create the page using the CLI:

```
ng g component pages/book-page
```

The output should look as follows:

```
CREATE src/app/book/pages/book-page/book-page.component.html (28
bytes)
CREATE src/app/book/pages/book-page/book-page.component.spec.ts (643
```

```
bytes)
CREATE src/app/book/pages/book-page/book-page.component.ts (281 bytes)
CREATE src/app/book/pages/book-page/book-page.component.scss (0 bytes)
UPDATE src/app/book/book.module.ts (280 bytes)
```

As you can see, the CLI has generated the HTML template, the controller, an SASS (with the `.scss` extension) file for the styles and a file for the unit tests. The CLI has also already registered the page in `declarations` of the `module` file.

Now, let's adapt the generated controller (that is, `book-page.component.ts`) in order to inject `BookService`:

1. Add the following import at the top:
   ```
   import {BookService} from '../../services/book.service';
   ```
2. Add the following parameter to the constructor: `private bookService: BookService`.

Angular will take care of resolving and injecting this dependency for us.

 When a variable is used only within the controller, it's a best practice to declare it as private in order to be sure it cannot be modified from the outside.

Next, we need to declare the `bookCollections` map that we'll use in the template: `public bookCollections: Map<string, MediaCollection<Book>>;`.

Of course, you'll also need to add the corresponding imports:

- `import {MediaCollection} from '../../../shared/entities/media-collection.entity';`
- `import {Book} from '../../entities/book.entity';`

 This time, we have declared our variable as public because we'll need to access it from the template of our component.

Another thing that we need to add and instantiate ourselves is `FormControl`. We will use it in our template to back the form input field used for the creation of a book collection.

In order to add it, we need to do the following:

1. Add the following import: `import { FormControl } from '@angular/forms';`
2. Declare the following class field: `public formControl: FormControl;`

By using `FormControl` (which is a part of reactive forms), we'll be able to fully configure the field and its validation rules programmatically. This approach should be preferred in general, as it is more powerful than defining the validation rules through the templates. Also, as we saw in the previous chapter, reactive forms work synchronously, which is far more predictable.

We need to configure our form control during the initialization life cycle phase of Angular. To do so, let's implement the `OnInit` interface:

1. Import the interface: `import { OnInit } from '@angular/core';`
2. Implement it: `... BookPageComponent implements OnInit`

Now, implement the `ngOnInit` method as follows:

```
ngOnInit() {
    this.formControl = new FormControl('', Validators.required);
    this.bookService.reloadBookCollections();
    this.bookCollections = this.bookService.bookCollections;
}
```

You'll also need to import the `Validators` class from the `@angular/forms` module.

Take a closer look at how we create and configure `FormControl`. As you can see, we define the default value as `''` and we use `Validators.required` to mark the input as required.

Next, we are going to create a method that will be called when a new book collection needs to be created. We will bind this method to the `submit` action of the book collection creation form:

```
createBookCollection(): void {
    if (this.formControl.valid) {
        this.bookService.createBookCollection(this.formControl.value);
        this.formControl.reset();
    }
}
```

In this method, the first thing that we do is check the validity of our form control. If it is valid, then we call the `createBookCollection` method of our book service with the current value of `formControl` as a parameter. Finally, we reset our `formControl` instance to have a blank input again.

Next, we'll add some additional methods using the **delegate design pattern**. For these, we don't need to add specific checks:

```
removeBookCollection(identifier: string): void {
  this.bookService.removeBookCollection(identifier);
}

createBook(book: Book, collectionIdentifier: string): void {
  this.bookService.createBook(collectionIdentifier, book);
}

removeBook(collectionIdentifier: string, bookIdentifier: string) {
  this.bookService.removeBook(collectionIdentifier, bookIdentifier);
}

reloadBookCollections(): void {
  this.bookService.reloadBookCollections();
}
```

Now that our controller is ready, it is time to implement the template of our page. We'll simply reuse the code from our first implementation of MediaMan and adapt it to take advantage of Angular's templating features.

Open `index.html`, located in the following folder of the code samples: `Chapter04/mediaman-v1`. Then, copy the HTML code from line **12** (that is, this line: `<h2>Book collections</h2>`) to line **33** (included) into the `book-page.component.html` template, replacing what is already there.

Because we will manage and display book collections differently, you can safely remove the following code from the template:

```
<div id="bookCollections" class="containerGroup">
</div>
```

The next step that we need to take is to adapt the template to bind its elements to our controller.

First of all, add the following binding to the input field of the `newBookCollection` form: `[formControl]="formControl"`. This will tie the input to `FormControl`.

Now, we want to display warnings when required (for example, when the input has been **touched** and if no value has been defined).

To do this, let's add the following code right underneath the `Name` input of the `newBookCollection` form:

```
<div *ngIf="formControl.invalid && (formControl.dirty ||
formControl.touched)" class="alert alert-danger">
  <span *ngIf="formControl.hasError('required')">
    Name is required.
  </span>
</div>
```

Notice that we can easily adapt our view based on the form control state.

We need to make a few last changes to this first form:

1. Change the `onclick` DOM event binding to an Angular `click` binding: `(click)`.
2. Associate that binding with the `createBookCollection()` method of our controller (no need for `mediaManController` this time).
3. Change the button's type to `submit`. This will allow us to send the form using the *Enter* key easily.

In the second form (that is, the one used to reload the book collections), we need to make the following modifications:

1. Adapt the input's click event binding to an Angular binding (the same as earlier).
2. Also, change the button's type to `submit`.

You can find the completed file at the following location in this book's assets: `Chapter08/mediaman-v2/src/app/book/book-page.component.html`.

Adapting the book module

The page is almost ready to be displayed. So far, we haven't imported the `FormModule` and `ReactiveFormsModule` Angular modules. We need to do that now in the `book` module (that is, `src/app/book/book.module.ts`).

Last but not least, we also need to add `BookPageComponent` to the `exports` property of the module. If we don't, then we won't be able to use it from the outside later on!

Here's what your `book.module.ts` file should look like after these modifications:

```
...
import { FormsModule, ReactiveFormsModule } from '@angular/forms';

@NgModule({
  declarations: [BookPageComponent],
  imports: [
    CommonModule,
    FormsModule,          // <-- Add this line
    ReactiveFormsModule, // <-- Add this line
  ],
  exports: [BookPageComponent], // <-- Add this line
})
export class BookModule { }
```

Notice that we have added the necessary imports for `FormsModule` and `ReactiveFormsModule`.

Now that the required modules have been imported, we will be able to leverage reactive forms in our book module.

Importing the book module

The next step is to import the `NgModule` book in the app module so that we can use its components:

```
import { BookModule } from './book/book.module';
...
@NgModule({
  declarations: [
    AppComponent
  ],
  imports: [
    BrowserModule,
    BookModule,      // <-- Add this line
  ],
  providers: [],
  bootstrap: [AppComponent],
})
export class AppModule {
}
```

Great! With that done, we can now display our component page in the application. Let's update the app component's template.

To do so, edit the `app.component.html` file and add `book-page` under the title, as follows:

```
<h1>{{ title }}</h1>

<app-book-page></app-book-page>
```

At this point, our book page should be displayed. Let's now move on to the styling.

Migrating the styles

The user interface doesn't really look as we would like it to. This is because we haven't imported the styles of the previous version.

Go ahead and copy the previous styles over to `src/styles.scss`. You can find a copy of the old stylesheet in the assets of this book, under `Chapter08/mediaman-v2/src/styles.scss`. The user interface should now look better!

Also, if you look at the console, you'll see that the book collection creation already works. We're just lacking a way to add books and display the collections. Let's do that next!

Implementing book creation

We will now create a component that will add support for creating new books.

That component will ensure that the required information is provided by end users. Its responsibility will only be to gather the information though. It won't take care of persisting the book. We will keep this component ignorant of what happens with the data. As such, it'll be a dumb component.

Our component will have an output through which it will emit events containing the `Book` objects to persist. That output stream will be watched by a smarter component (in other words, our page component) that will decide what to do (for example, make use of `BookService`). To emit those events, we will make use of the `EventEmitter` class provided by Angular (based on RxJS Observables).

Let's create the component. In your console, go back to `src/app/book` and run the following:

```
ng g c components/book-new
```

We've used the `c` shorthand for `component`.

Here is the code for the controller:

```
import { Component, EventEmitter, OnInit, Output } from
'@angular/core';
import { FormControl, FormGroup, Validators } from '@angular/forms';
import { Genre } from '../../../shared/enums/genre.enum';
import { Book } from '../../entities/book.entity';

@Component({
  selector: 'app-book-new',
  templateUrl: './book-new.component.html',
  styleUrls: ['./book-new.component.scss']
})
export class BookNewComponent implements OnInit {
  @Output()
  created: EventEmitter<Book> = new EventEmitter<Book>();

  formGroup: FormGroup;
  genres: string[] = [];

  constructor() {
  }

  // insert the rest of the code here
}
```

Note that we've already defined `EventEmitter`, `FormGroup`, and an empty array for book genres; we'll fill it during the initialization of the component.

Add the `ngOnInit` life cycle method as follows:

```
ngOnInit() {
    // fill-in the array of genres
    for (const genreKey of Object.keys(Genre)) {
      this.genres.push(genreKey);
    }

    this.formGroup = new FormGroup({
      name: new FormControl('', [Validators.required]),
      author: new FormControl('', [Validators.required]),
      genre: new FormControl('', [Validators.required]),
      numberOfPages: new FormControl('', [Validators.required,
```

```
        Validators.pattern(/^[0-9]+$/)]),
      pictureLocation: new FormControl(''),
      description: new FormControl('')
    });
  }
```

In this method, we have defined different `FormControl` elements in `FormGroup`, along with their validation rules. We will soon attach those controls to the elements of our template.

 In the previous code sample, we decided to explore the list of `Genre` types into a simple array of strings that can be used within the template. In this case, we have done this through the `ngOnInit` life cycle method to give you an example. In practice though, you can avoid that and directly use the `Genre` type as follows: `genres: Genre[] = Object.values(Genre);`.

Next, add the `createBook` method:

```
createBook(): void {
    if (this.formGroup.valid) {
      const rawValue: any = this.formGroup.getRawValue();

      for (const key of Object.keys(rawValue)) {
        rawValue[key] = rawValue[key] === null ? undefined :
        rawValue[key];
      }

      const bookToCreate: Book = new Book(rawValue.name,
      rawValue.description === null ? undefined : rawValue.
      description,
        rawValue.pictureLocation === null ? undefined :
        rawValue.pictureLocation,
        Genre[rawValue.genre as keyof typeof Genre], rawValue.author,
        rawValue.numberOfPages);

      this.created.emit(bookToCreate);
      this.formGroup.reset();
    }
  }
```

The `createBook` method first checks whether `formGroup` is valid; if it is, then it initializes a `Book` object corresponding to the filled-in form information, including the name, the description, the picture, and the genre.

Notice that we get the `formGroup` raw value and that we extract the different user inputs out of it. We chose to explicitly type the `this` constant to `any` to make it obvious that the type is not safe to use (that is, we don't have strong typing here); this is not strictly mandatory but makes this fact visible. In the future, Angular might provide us with stronger type safety.

Finally, it emits a `created` event with the new book as payload in order to signal that a book should be created.

Thanks to the fact that we are using reactive forms, we could configure validation rules programmatically: `numberOfPages: new FormControl('', [Validators.required, Validators.pattern(/^[0-9]+$/)]),`. We can configure as many validators as we want. For more information about them, check out the official documentation: `https://angular.io/api/forms/Validators`.

Now go ahead and implement the template for this component:

```html
<h3>New book</h3>

<form [formGroup]="formGroup" novalidate>
  <ul>
    <li>
      <input formControlName="name" type="text" placeholder="Name"
      required/>
      <input formControlName="author" type="text" placeholder="Author"
      required/>
    </li>
    <li>
      <select formControlName="genre" required>
        <option *ngFor="let genre of genres" [value]="genre">{{ genre
        }}</option>
      </select>
      <input formControlName="numberOfPages" type="number"
      placeholder="Pages" required>
    </li>
    <li>
      <input formControlName="pictureLocation" type="url"
        title="Picture" placeholder="Picture URL">
    </li>
    <li>
      <textarea formControlName="description"
        placeholder="Description"></textarea>
    </li>
```

```
    </ul>

    <button type="button" (click)="createBook()">Create</button>
</form>
```

Notice how we render the list of genres, simply by iterating on the array using the *ngFor directive.

Displaying book collections

We will now create the component that will receive and render a book collection. Again, this component can remain dumb:

1. It will accept a list of books as input (that is, the collection to display).
2. It will emit events when actions are performed on the elements in the list (for example, request to delete book from the collection).

Start by creating the component using the CLI:

```
ng g c components/book-list
```

Then, adapt the controller as follows:

```
import { Component, EventEmitter, Input, OnInit, Output } from
'@angular/core';
import { Book } from '../../entities/book.entity';

@Component({
  selector: 'app-book-list',
  templateUrl: './book-list.component.html',
  styleUrls: ['./book-list.component.scss']
})
export class BookListComponent implements OnInit {
  @Input()
  books: Book[];

  @Output()
  removedBook: EventEmitter<string> = new EventEmitter<string>();

  constructor() {
  }

  ngOnInit() {
  }

  removeBook(bookId: string): void {
```

```
      this.removedBook.emit(bookId);
  }

  trackById(book: Book): string {
    return book.identifier;
  }
}
```

And continue with the template:

```
<table class="collectionTable">
  <thead>
  <tr>
    <td>Picture</td>
    <td>Name</td>
    <td>Genre</td>
    <td>Description</td>
    <td>Author</td>
    <td>Pages</td>
    <td>Remove</td>
  </tr>
  </thead>
  <tbody>
  <tr *ngFor="let book of books; trackBy: trackById">
    <td>
      <img [src]="book.pictureLocation" class="mediaImage">
    </td>
    <td>
      {{ book.name }}
    </td>
    <td>
      {{ book.genre }}
    </td>
    <td>
      {{ book.description }}
    </td>
    <td>
      {{ book.author }}
    </td>
    <td>
      {{ book.numberOfPages }}
    </td>
    <td>
      <button (click)="removeBook(book.identifier)">X</button>
    </td>
  </tr>
  </tbody>
</table>
```

Notice the `[src]` binding for the book's picture location.

In the template, we used the `trackBy` attribute within our `*ngFor` loop and we've associated it with the `trackById` method in our controller. If you're curious about this, then you should definitely check this article: `https://netbasal.com/angular-2-improve-performance-with-trackby-cc147b5104e5`.

Let's quickly take a look at `BookModule` to see how magic the Angular CLI is:

```
import { NgModule } from '@angular/core';
import { CommonModule } from '@angular/common';
import { BookNewComponent } from './components/book-new/book-
new.component';
import { BookPageComponent } from './pages/book-page/book-
page.component';
import { BookListComponent } from './components/book-list/book-
list.component';
import { FormsModule, ReactiveFormsModule } from '@angular/forms';

@NgModule({
  declarations: [BookPageComponent, BookNewComponent,
  BookListComponent],
  imports: [
    CommonModule,
    FormsModule,
    ReactiveFormsModule,
  ],
  exports: [BookPageComponent]
})
export class BookModule {
}
```

As you can see, the two newly created components have automatically been added to the `declarations` array. Thanks to that, we can directly use these components inside of `BookModule`.

There's no need to export anything this time because we'll only use these components inside of the module.

We have now reached the very last steps of our migration to Angular!

Adding the components to the page

Let's adapt the `book-page.component.html` template to start using our
components:

```html
<h2>Book collections</h2>

<div class="collectionContainerGroup">
  <div class="containerGroup">
    <div class="container">
      <h3>New collection</h3>
      <form id="newBookCollection" action="#">
        <div>
          <input type="text" [formControl]="formControl" title="Name"
            placeholder="Name" required />
          <div *ngIf="formControl.invalid && (formControl.dirty ||
            formControl.touched)"
              class="alert alert-danger">
            <span *ngIf="formControl.hasError('required')">The name is
            required.</span>
          </div>
        </div>
        <input type="submit" value="Create"
        (click)="createBookCollection()" />
      </form>
    </div>
    <div class="container">
      <h3>Tools</h3>
      <form action="#">
        <input type="button" value="Reload collections"
          (click)="reloadBookCollections()"/>
      </form>
    </div>
  </div>

  <div class="containerGroup" *ngFor="let bookCollection of
    bookCollections | keyvalue; trackBy:trackById">
    <div class="collection">
      <h3 class="collectionName">{{ bookCollection.value.name }}</h3>
      <div class="containerGroup">
        <app-book-new class="container"
                    (created)="createBook($event,
                    bookCollection.key)"></app-book-new>
        <div class="collectionToolsContainer">
          <h3>Tools</h3>
          <form action="#">
            <button (click)="removeBookCollection
            (bookCollection.key)">Remove collection</button>
```

```
          </form>
        </div>
      </div>
      <div class="containerGroup">
        <app-book-list class="container" (removedBook)="
          removeBook(bookCollection.key, $event)"
          [books]="bookCollection.value.collection"></app-book-list>
      </div>
    </div>
  </div>
</div>
```

With this done, we are now using our Angular components. Great!

Revisiting the user interface with Angular Material

At this point, we have migrated our application to Angular, but our user interface is still exactly the same. At this point, you might be thinking: we could certainly create a more beautiful UI now.

In the previous chapter, we talked a bit about Material Design and Angular Material. We'll now refactor the user interface to use Angular Material.

 If you want to make sure to that you have the same starting point as we do to follow along, then you can copy the `Chapter08/mediaman-v2` folder from this book's sample code. This version of the application includes all of the changes that we have discussed so far in this chapter.

Let's start by installing Angular Material into our project.

Installing Angular Material

In order to install Angular Material in the project, all you have to do is use the CLI!

Open your console, go into the project folder, and execute the following command:

```
ng add @angular/material
```

You'll have the choice between different themes. Pick the one that you want. We'll take the `Indigo/Pink` theme for this example:

```
$ ng add @angular/material
Installing packages for tooling via npm.
npm WARN ajv-keywords@3.4.0 requires a peer of ajv@^6.9.1 but none is
installed. You must install peer dependencies yourself.
npm WARN @angular/material@7.3.3 requires a peer of @angular/cdk@7.3.3
but none is installed. You must install peer dependencies yourself.
npm WARN optional SKIPPING OPTIONAL DEPENDENCY: fsevents@1.2.7
(node_modules\fsevents):
npm WARN notsup SKIPPING OPTIONAL DEPENDENCY: Unsupported platform for
fsevents@1.2.7: wanted {"os":"darwin","arch":"any"} (current:
{"os":"win32","arch":"x64"})

+ @angular/material@7.3.3
added 1 package and audited 40191 packages in 15.693s
found 3 vulnerabilities (2 low, 1 high)
  run `npm audit fix` to fix them, or `npm audit` for details
Installed packages for tooling via npm.
? Choose a prebuilt theme name, or "custom" for a custom theme:
> Indigo/Pink        [ Preview:
https://material.angular.io?theme=indigo-pink ]
  Deep Purple/Amber  [ Preview:
https://material.angular.io?theme=deeppurple-amber ]
  Pink/Blue Grey     [ Preview:
https://material.angular.io?theme=pink-bluegrey ]
  Purple/Green       [ Preview:
https://material.angular.io?theme=purple-green ]
  Custom
```

Next, you can enable HammerJS and set up the browser animations :

```
? Choose a prebuilt theme name, or "custom" for a custom theme:
Pink/Blue Grey     [ Preview:
https://material.angular.io?theme=pink-bluegrey ]
? Set up HammerJS for gesture recognition? (Y/n) y
? Set up browser animations for Angular Material? (Y/n) y
```

The installation will make modifications to some files automatically:

```
UPDATE src/main.ts (391 bytes)
UPDATE src/app/app.module.ts (512 bytes)
UPDATE angular.json (4072 bytes)
UPDATE src/index.html (478 bytes)
UPDATE src/styles.scss (2515 bytes)
```

Angular Material has installed the application. Let's start using some Angular Material components to see how it works!

 You can find the full list of components included in Angular Material on its official website:
https://material.angular.io/components/categories.

Let's add some components now that Angular Material is available.

Adding a toolbar

Let's start our user interface refresh by adding a toolbar. You can find examples here: https://material.angular.io/components/toolbar/overview.

To use Angular Material components, you need to import their corresponding modules separately. You can do so at the application level (that is, in the App module) or, rather, in specific modules if you only plan to use these in particular parts of your application.

The Angular Material documentation actually proposes two different approaches. Either you import the modules for the components you need in each module, or you create a shared module in which you import those and reexport them.

Since we already have a shared module in place, we'll use the latter approach.

Adapt the src/app/shared/shared.module.ts file of your project to reexport MatToolbarModule:

```
import { MatToolbarModule } from '@angular/material';

@NgModule({
  ...
  exports: [
    ...
    MatToolbarModule,   // <-- Add this one
  ]
  ...
})
export class SharedModule {
}
```

By reexporting `MatToolbarModule`, we're allowing any module that imports our `shared` module to directly have access to it. This is very similar to the TypeScript barrels that we've discussed earlier in this book. Neat!

 Of course, you can also add `MatToolbarModule` to make it available within the `shared` module. This can be useful if you integrate visual components in your `shared` module.

Now, you have to import `SharedModule` in `AppModule` (that is, `src/app/app.module.ts`):

```
import { SharedModule } from './shared/shared.module';

@NgModule({
  imports: [
    ...
    SharedModule, // <-- Add this line
  ]
})
export class AppModule {}
```

Now, you can modify the app component's template, located in `src/app/app.component.html`, like this:

```
<mat-toolbar color="primary">{{ title }}</mat-toolbar>
```

If you get errors about `mat-toolbar` not being found, just restart the server.

Here's how the application should look now:

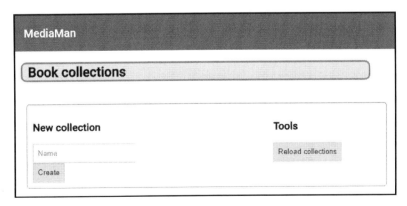

This already looks better, doesn't it?

With Angular Material, you can use colors from different palettes in your application, such as `primary`, `accent`, and `warn`. Each palette has different colors and shades, varying depending on the theme. Check out the official theming guide: `https://material.angular.io/guide/theming`.

Let's improve things further.

Making the application responsive

To make our application perfectly responsive, we will use `@angular/flex-layout`, a library that provides a layout API based on Flexbox and media queries. More importantly, it also provides a responsive API allowing you to easily specify layouts, sizes, and visibility depending on the display device types/viewport sizes. You can find all of the details about it here: `https://github.com/angular/flex-layout`.

Use the following command to install this module:

```
npm install --save @angular/flex-layout
```

Then, add `FlexLayoutModule` to the `exports` array of the `shared` module (that is, `src/app/shared/shared.module.ts`):

```
...
import { FlexLayoutModule } from '@angular/flex-layout';
...

@NgModule({
  ...
  exports: [
    ...
    FlexLayoutModule, // <-- add this line
  ]
})
export class SharedModule {
}
```

With this done, we'll be able to use the APIs provided by the `flex-layout` library in MediaMan.

Revisiting the book page

Let's import some additional Angular Material modules to improve our book page.

Edit the `shared` module again to import a few more Angular Material components:

```
import { NgModule } from '@angular/core';
import { CommonModule } from '@angular/common';
import { FlexLayoutModule } from '@angular/flex-layout';
import {
  MatButtonModule,
  MatCardModule,
  MatDividerModule,
  MatFormFieldModule,
  MatIconModule,
  MatInputModule,
  MatOptionModule,
  MatSelectModule,
  MatTableModule,
  MatToolbarModule,
} from '@angular/material';
...
```

Then, update the module's `exports` array accordingly:

```
@NgModule({
  declarations: [],
  imports: [
    CommonModule,
  ],
  exports: [
    FlexLayoutModule,
    MatButtonModule,
    MatCardModule,
    MatDividerModule,
    MatFormFieldModule,
    MatIconModule,
    MatInputModule,
    MatOptionModule,
    MatSelectModule,
    MatTableModule,
    MatToolbarModule,
  ]
})
export class SharedModule {
}
```

Next, in order to be able to use those reexported modules in the `Book` module, don't forget to import `SharedModule` in it:

```
import { SharedModule } from '../shared/shared.module';

@NgModule({
  imports: [
    ...
    SharedModule, // <-- add this line
  ]
})
export class BookModule {}
```

Now, let's rewrite the template of the `BookPage` component to use the Angular Material modules that we have just imported. Through this process, we'll also stop using many of the styles that had to be defined in the first version of MediaMan.

First of all, add a toolbar with the title of the page:

```
<mat-toolbar color="warn">Book collections</mat-toolbar>
```

Then, add a first Material Card (another Material component) right after the toolbar:

```
<mat-card fxLayoutGap="20px">
    ...
</mat-card>
```

Cards are containers for text, photos, and actions. They are very versatile. Inside of this first card, we will add different sections.

 We have used the `fxLayoutGap` directive from the flex layout to insert some space between the elements in our card.

Now, within the card, add the first section for creating new books:

```
<section fxFlex>
  <h2>New collection</h2>
  <form action="#" fxLayoutGap="10px">
    <mat-form-field>
      <input matInput type="text" [formControl]="formControl"
       title="Name" placeholder="Name" required/>
      <mat-error *ngIf="formControl.invalid && (formControl.dirty ||
       formControl.touched)"
                 class="alert alert-danger">
        <span *ngIf="formControl.hasError('required')">
```

```
        Name is required.
      </span>
    </mat-error>
  </mat-form-field>
  <button mat-button mat-raised-button color="accent" type="submit"
  (click)="createBookCollection()">Create</button>
  </form>
</section>
```

There are interesting things to notice here:

- The `mat-form-field` directive is used to wrap compatible Angular Material components (for example, `input`, `textarea`, `select`, `mat-select`, and `mat-chip-list`) and to apply text field styles to these.
- The `matInput` directive makes the text input field compatible with `mat-form-field`.
- The `mat-error` directive is used to display errors when the corresponding field is invalid.
- The button now has a `submit` type.
- The `mat-button` and `mat-raised-button` directives have been added to the button to style it. In addition, the `accent` color has been used on it.

Now, add a second section for `Tools`:

```
<section fxFlex>
    <h2>Tools</h2>
    <button mat-raised-button color="primary" type="button"
(click)="reloadBookCollections()">Reload collections</button>
</section>
```

This time, the button uses the `primary` color of the theme.

 Material Design uses specific colors and effects to denote `primary` and `secondary` actions.

Finally, add `mat-card` to the template for the book collections:

```
<mat-card *ngFor="let bookCollection of bookCollections | keyvalue;
trackBy:trackById">
  <h3 mat-card-title>{{ bookCollection.value.name }}</h3>
  <mat-card fxLayout="row" fxLayoutGap="20px">
    <app-book-new fxFlex (created)="createBook($event,
    bookCollection.key)"></app-book-new>
```

```
    <div fxFlex>
      <h3>Tools</h3>
      <button mat-raised-button (click)="removeBookCollection
        (bookCollection.key)">Remove collection</button>
    </div>
  </mat-card>
  <mat-card fxLayout="row">
    <app-book-list fxFlex
(removedBook)="removeBook(bookCollection.key,
    $event)"
      [books]="bookCollection.value.collection"></app-book-list>
  </mat-card>
</mat-card>
```

The following are some things to notice here:

- We have replaced some `div` elements with Angular Material components.
- `mat-card` uses the `row` flex layout. This is set by `fxLayout="row"`.
- The `fxFlex` directive enables automatic sizing of the corresponding element, using Flexbox.

 Did you notice `|` `keyvalue` in `*ngFor`? The `keyvalue` pipe is used to transform objects and maps into arrays of `key-value` pairs. This is useful to avoid adding logic in the controller for doing the conversion. Check out this article to learn more: `https://grokonez.com/frontend/angular/angular-6/angular-6-keyvalue-pipe-ngfor-loop-through-object-map-example`.

You can find the completed template at the following location in this book's repository: `Chapter08/mediaman-v3/src/app/book/pages/book-page/book-page.component.html`.

To be honest, this probably doesn't look great so far. We still have other components to adapt.

Angular Material makes it very easy to compose advanced UI components together to create full fledged applications, while drastically reducing the amount of custom styling required. As you'll see, we'll be able to do quite a bit of cleanup in our global stylesheet (that is, `src/styles.scss`). Actually, we can already remove the styles for `h2` to get a better look and feel:

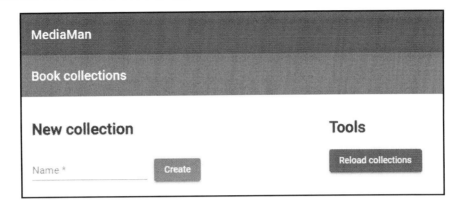

Let's continue.

Improving the book creation component

Let's improve the book creation component (that is,
`src/app/book/components/book-new`).

To do so, we will not only leverage the `matInput` directive and `mat-form-field`,
but also `mat-select` and `mat-option`.

Before we move on, let's do a small change to the controller. Adapt its constructor as
follows:

```
constructor(private formBuilder: FormBuilder) { }
```

For this code to compile, you'll of course also need to add the corresponding `import`
statements:

```
import { FormBuilder } from '@angular/forms';
```

Next, adapt the `ngOnInit` function, like this:

```
ngOnInit() {
    ...

    this.formGroup = this.formBuilder.group({
      name: ['', Validators.required],
      author: ['', Validators.required],
      genre: ['', Validators.required],
      numberOfPages: ['', [Validators.required,
        Validators.pattern(/^[0-9]+$/)]],
      pictureLocation: '',
```

```
      description: ''
  });

  ...
```

`FormBuilder` that we have used here is part of `@angular/forms`. It makes it a breeze to create `FormGroup` elements. Rather than using `new FormControl(...)` many times, we simply declare all controls at once with a nicer syntax.

If we compare this to what we had before, we can easily see the benefits of using `FormBuilder`:

```
this.formGroup = new FormGroup({
  name: new FormControl('', Validators.required),
  author: new FormControl('', Validators.required)
})
```

Obviously, the new syntax is more concise and readable. You can learn more about the `FormBuilder` utility here: `https://angular.io/api/forms/FormBuilder`.

Now, adapt the template as follows.

First, add the base structure:

```
<h3>New book</h3>

<form [formGroup]="formGroup" novalidate>
  <!-- Add the form elements here -->
</form>
```

Next, add the name and author fields:

```
<section fxLayoutGap="10px">
  <mat-form-field fxFlex>
    <input matInput formControlName="name" type="text"
      placeholder="Name" required />
  </mat-form-field>
  <mat-form-field fxFlex>
    <input matInput formControlName="author" type="text"
      placeholder="Author" required />
  </mat-form-field>
</section>
```

Notice how we have isolated the fields in a section and defined a gap of 10 pixels using the `fxLayoutGap` directive.

Next, add a select for the book genres using the `mat-select` Angular Material component, as well as an input for the number of pages:

```
<section fxLayoutGap="10px">
  <mat-form-field fxFlex>
    <mat-select placeholder="Genre" formControlName
      ="genre" required>
      <mat-option *ngFor="let genre of genres" [value]="genre">{{
        genre }}</mat-option>
    </mat-select>
  </mat-form-field>
  <mat-form-field fxFlex>
    <input matInput formControlName="numberOfPages" type="number"
      placeholder="Pages" required />
  </mat-form-field>
</section>
```

Next, insert additional sections for the picture and the description:

```
<section fxLayoutGap="10px">
  <mat-form-field fxFlex>
    <input matInput formControlName="pictureLocation" type="url"
      title="Picture" placeholder="Picture URL" />
  </mat-form-field>
</section>
<section>
  <mat-form-field fxFlex>
    <textarea matInput formControlName="description"
      placeholder="Description"></textarea>
  </mat-form-field>
</section>
```

Finally, add a button to invoke the book creation method:

```
<button mat-raised-button color="primary" type="button"
  (click)="createBook()">Create</button>
```

The `required` attribute is still present in your template because Angular Material needs it to style the input correctly, even if it is already required in the `formGroup` declaration.

> The `mat-form-field` component is needed around `matInput` to style it and add visual effects to it.

Next up is the book list component.

Improving the book list component

To finish our upgrade to Angular Material, we'll work on the `book-list` component.

In this case, we will use the following Angular Material components: `mat-button`, `mat-table`, and `mat-icon`.

Open the controller (that is, `src/app/book/components/book-list/book-list.component.ts`) and add the following `public` field to the class:

```
public displayedColumns: string[] = [
    'pictureLocation', 'name', 'genre', 'description', 'author',
    'numberOfPages', 'identifier'
];
```

This field will be used by the `mat-table` component to identify the columns that should be displayed or hidden.

Now, adapt the template of the component, as follows:

```
<table mat-table [dataSource]="books" fxFlex>
  <ng-container matColumnDef="pictureLocation">
    <th mat-header-cell *matHeaderCellDef>Picture</th>
    <td mat-cell *matCellDef="let book"><img alt="picture"
    [src]="book.pictureLocation" class="mediaImage"></td>
  </ng-container>

  <ng-container matColumnDef="name">
    <th mat-header-cell *matHeaderCellDef>Name</th>
    <td mat-cell *matCellDef="let book"> {{ book.name }} </td>
  </ng-container>

  <ng-container matColumnDef="genre">
    <th mat-header-cell *matHeaderCellDef>Genre</th>
    <td mat-cell *matCellDef="let book"> {{ book.genre }} </td>
  </ng-container>

  <ng-container matColumnDef="description">
    <th mat-header-cell *matHeaderCellDef>Description</th>
    <td mat-cell *matCellDef="let book"> {{ book.description }} </td>
  </ng-container>

  <ng-container matColumnDef="author">
    <th mat-header-cell *matHeaderCellDef>Author</th>
    <td mat-cell *matCellDef="let book"> {{ book.author }} </td>
  </ng-container>
```

```
  <ng-container matColumnDef="numberOfPages">
    <th mat-header-cell *matHeaderCellDef>Pages</th>
    <td mat-cell *matCellDef="let book"> {{ book.numberOfPages }}
</td>
  </ng-container>

  <ng-container matColumnDef="identifier">
    <th mat-header-cell *matHeaderCellDef>Remove</th>
    <td mat-cell *matCellDef="let book">
      <button mat-icon-button color="warn"
        (click)="removeBook(book.identifier)">
        <mat-icon>cancel</mat-icon>
      </button>
    </td>
  </ng-container>

  <tr mat-header-row *matHeaderRowDef="displayedColumns"></tr>
  <tr mat-row *matRowDef="let row; columns: displayedColumns;"></tr>
</table>
```

As you can see, creating a Material table is easy:

1. First, we defined a simple HTML table.
2. Then, we added the `mat-table` directive to it.
3. After that, we added a binding defining the data source for the table with `[dataSource]="books"`.
4. Then, for each column in our table, we defined an `ng-container` element, wrapping `th` and `td` elements and using other Angular Material directives.

Cleaning things up

The last thing that we need to take care of is to clean up the stylesheet of the application by removing all of the style definitions that have now become obsolete and adding a small rule to improve our table.

Adapt the `src/styles.scss` file as follows:

```scss
@import url('https://fonts.googleapis.com/css?family=Roboto');

html, body { height: 100%; }
body { margin: 0; font-family: Roboto, "Helvetica Neue", sans-serif; }

.mediaImage { max-height: 120px; }

table td.mat-cell, table th.mat-cell { padding-right:20px; }
```

Now we can see the new styled implementation of `mediaman-v3`:

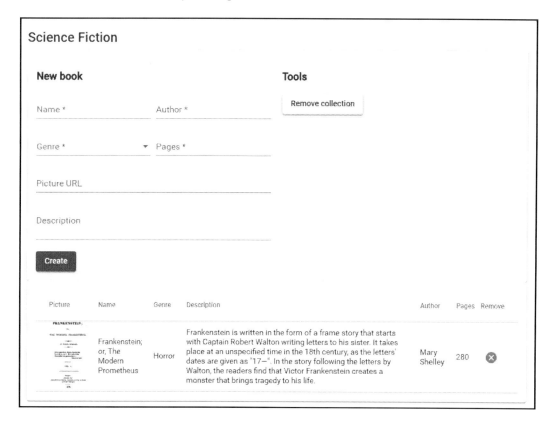

Hopefully, you can appreciate the improvements that we've made together!

Summary

In this chapter, we have put all of the knowledge acquired so far to good use by migrating our MediaMan application to Angular.

Then, with MediaMan v3, we improved the user interface by introducing and using Material Design with Angular Material.

While doing all of this, we have hopefully demonstrated that Angular and Angular Material are really easy to integrate in a clean application. Also, we have seen how marvelous TypeScript support is with Angular.

Angular and Angular Material deserve a lot more than two chapters, but this little introduction should have convinced you that it isn't that hard to get started. Once you dive into the code, you can quickly get productive.

Frustratingly, due to space constraints, there are many aspects that we had to leave out, such as routing, state management, internationalization, error handling, PWAs, and many more. If you are serious about building modern web applications, then you should definitely invest time in learning these subjects.

In the next chapter, we will continue our exploration of modern web frameworks with Vue.js. As we will see together, Vue is much lighter than Angular, which is both a strength and a weakness, depending on how you look at it!

Introducing Vue.js

9

Now that you've become one of the cool kids that uses Angular, why don't we step it up a notch and learn about one more trendy modern web framework? In this chapter, we will discover Vue.js (`https://vuejs.org`), as well as its CLI (`https://cli.vuejs.org`) and the Element (`https://element.eleme.io`) UI library. We will, of course, take some time to cover the most important aspects of the framework, as well as the surrounding tools and the library ecosystem.

Learning about one more JavaScript web framework will help you get a feel for another way in which you can develop modern web applications that may be more appropriate for certain situations and requirements. You'll also see that Vue.js is similar to Angular in certain aspects, which means that you'll understand most Vue concepts in no time.

In this chapter, we will cover the following topics:

- Vue.js
- Hello Vue!
- Understanding Vue concepts
- Vue developer tools
- The Vue CLI
- TypeScript support
- Dependency injection
- User interface component libraries
- Routing
- State management for modern web applications

Let's get started!

Vue.js

Vue.js (`https://vuejs.org`), also known as Vue, is a modern web framework that can be used to easily create SPAs:

Vue is open source and was created in 2014 by Evan You (`https://evanyou.me`), who was working on AngularJS projects at Google at the time. While creating Vue.js, Evan's goal was to take the good parts of AngularJS and create a **simpler** and **lighter** alternative.

One of the key advantages of Vue.js is that it is really lightweight (~30 KB when gzipped!), highly performant, approachable, and easy to learn. As we'll see shortly, compared to Angular, there are **fewer concepts to learn about before you can get started with Vue**.

Vue.js is also easy to integrate into existing applications, including legacy ones that are rendered on the server side. This fact alone is a good reason to choose Vue instead of Angular or React, depending on your project.

Just like Angular, Vue.js embraces the standards of the web (any valid HTML code is also a valid Vue template) and reactive programming and has a component-based architecture. It also features a set of official services and APIs around the core of the framework; for example, there is an official routing mechanism, and an official state management library.

As an added benefit, learning Vue.js is actually fun. You can start with the core, which is focused on the view layer, and then learn some more if you want to and start using some of the officially supported extensions/libraries.

Although Vue.js is *small-ish*/minimalist in comparison to Angular, **it doesn't try to give you everything and the kitchen sink**, like Angular does with its numerous built-in modules. As a result, community-driven packages that support specific requirements need to be added to Vue projects. This means that creating a large/complex application that requires many features may be more complex, given that you would need to choose different solutions yourself and figure out how to integrate everything properly.

Like most modern web frameworks, Vue has a very efficient rendering pipeline, but it wouldn't be useful to try and compare the performance of each framework since performance is a moving target: it evolves all the time. One point to mention, though, is that Vue (like React) uses a **virtual DOM**, a technique that was initially made popular by React.

The virtual DOM, as its name implies, is an abstraction of the actual DOM that the browser is aware of. Whenever a component needs to be rerendered, a new virtual DOM is generated in memory, which is then compared to the previous one. The differences are identified and a set of transformations are derived and applied to the actual DOM of the page, making the changes effective in your application.

 Don't waste too much time digging into virtual DOM, incremental DOM, or similar techniques at this point unless you plan on contributing to the frameworks themselves. Each major framework tends to evolve very rapidly, and what is true today will probably not be true forever. For example, at the time of writing, Angular is preparing to move toward using an incremental DOM technique with Ivy, its new rendering engine: `https://blog.nrwl.io/understanding-angular-ivy-incremental-dom-and-virtual-dom-243be844bf36`.

Another interesting thing to mention is that, in comparison to Angular, Vue is not backed by a large company. Instead, it is led by an independent core team that accepts donations and is surrounded by a large developer community.

Hello Vue!

Let's complete a quick practical exercise with Vue. This will give you an idea of how easy it is to get started:

1. Create a new folder called `01-hello-vue`. Inside this folder, create an `index.html` file with the following content:

```
<!DOCTYPE html>
<html lang="en">
<head>
    <meta charset="UTF-8">
    <title>Hello Vue!</title>

    <!-- development version of Vue.js -->
    <script src="https://cdn.jsdelivr.net/
     npm/vue/dist/vue.js"></script>
</head>
<body>

<div id="app">
    {{ message }}
</div>

<script type="text/javascript">
    var app = new Vue({
        el: '#app',
        data: {
            message: 'Hello world!'
        }
    });
</script>

</body>
</html>
```

You have just written your first Vue application! Yes, it really is that simple.

2. Now, open the page in your web browser to see the result. You should see the following interpolated message:

```
Hello world!
```

3. Now, open up the Developer Tools (*F12*), go to the **Console** tab, and type in the following:

```
app.message = "Cool!";
```

The message on the page should have changed. Isn't that nice?

Thanks to this little experiment, we already know that Vue apps are dynamic and **reactive**.

Just for fun, you can also try defining two different Vue applications in a single page; there's nothing wrong with that:

```html
<!DOCTYPE html>
<html lang="en">
<head>
    <meta charset="UTF-8">
    <title>A story of two Vue apps!</title>

    <!-- development version of Vue.js -->
    <script
src="https://cdn.jsdelivr.net/npm/vue/dist/vue.js"></script>
</head>
<body>

<div id="app">
    {{ message }}
</div>

<div id="otherApp">
    {{ otherMessage }}
</div>

<script type="text/javascript">
    const app = new Vue({
        el: '#app',
        data: {
            message: 'Hello world!'
        }
    });

    const otherApp = new Vue({
        el: '#otherApp',
        data: {
            otherMessage: 'Foobar'
        }
    })
</script>

</body>
</html>
```

In the preceding code, app and otherApp are defined as two separate Vue applications that take care of different parts of the actual DOM tree.

 If you're using VS Code, then take a look at the Vetur (https://marketplace.visualstudio.com/items?itemName=octref .vetur) plugin. It provides syntax highlighting, code snippets, linting, auto completion, debugging support, and more.

Now, let's learn about the core concepts of Vue.

Understanding Vue concepts

Now that we've learned how to run a small Vue application, let's go a step further and discover the main concepts of Vue.

Directives

Vue uses the concept of **directives**; these are similar to Angular directives. Just like Angular, Vue provides a set of built-in directives.

The following is an example of how to bind a value to an element attribute using the built-in v-bind directive:

```
<!DOCTYPE html>
<html lang="en">
<head>
    <meta charset="UTF-8">
    <title>Bind me!</title>

    <!-- development version of Vue.js -->
    <script
src="https://cdn.jsdelivr.net/npm/vue/dist/vue.js"></script>
</head>
<body>

<div id="app">
    <input type="text" v-bind:placeholder="defaultMessage">
</div>

<script type="text/javascript">
    let app = new Vue({
        el: '#app',
        data: {
```

```
            defaultMessage: 'Username'
        }
    });
</script>

</body>
</html>
```

Another built-in directive, called `v-if`, allows us to conditionally render elements, as shown in the following code:

```
<!DOCTYPE html>
<html lang="en">
<head>
    <meta charset="UTF-8">
    <title>If only...</title>

    <!-- development version of Vue.js -->
    <script
src="https://cdn.jsdelivr.net/npm/vue/dist/vue.js"></script>
</head>
<body>

<div id="app">
    <div id="invisible" v-if="shouldBeRendered">You can't see
me!</div>
</div>

<script type="text/javascript">
    let app = new Vue({
        el: '#app',
        data: {
            shouldBeRendered: false
        }
    });
</script>

</body>
</html>
```

In the preceding example, the `invisible` div element will not be **rendered** unless `shouldBeRendered` becomes `true`. Go ahead and type this into the console to make it appear as follows:

```
app.shouldBeRendered = true;
```

v-if defines whether the element is to be added to the DOM. It is the same as Angular's ngIf.

> If you only want to show/hide an element (that is, play with the CSS display property), then you can use v-show instead of v-if.

Vue includes many directives (https://vuejs.org/v2/api/#Directives) out of the box and you can, of course, create your own.

Here are a few other built-in directives:

- v-for: Loops over a data source to render multiple elements.
- v-if, v-else, and v-else-if: Can be combined together.
- v-text: Updates the text content of an element.
- v-html: Updates the innerHTML of an element.
- v-on: Attaches an event handler to an element.
- v-model: Defines a two-way binding on a form element or component. This is very similar to the **banana-in-a-box** syntax that's used by Angular: [(ngModel)].

Let's now look at how v-for works:

```
<!DOCTYPE html>
<html lang="en">
<head>
    <meta charset="UTF-8">
    <title>For...</title>

    <!-- development version of Vue.js -->
    <script
src="https://cdn.jsdelivr.net/npm/vue/dist/vue.js"></script>
</head>
<body>

<div id="app">
    <ul>
        <li v-for="movie of movies">{{movie.name}}</li>
    </ul>
</div>

<script type="text/javascript">
    let app = new Vue({
```

```
        el: '#app',
        data: {
            movies: [
                {name: "The Shawshank Redemption (1994)"},
                {name: "The Dark Knight (2008)"},
                {name: "The Lord of the Rings: The Fellowship of the
                Ring (2001)"},
                {name: "Forrest Gump (1994)"}
            ]
        }
    });
</script>

</body>
</html>
```

In this example, we've looped over the `movies` collection, just like we would have done using `*ngFor` with Angular.

 `v-for` can also iterate over object properties and iterable (`https://developer.mozilla.org/en-US/docs/Web/JavaScript/Reference/Iteration_protocols#The_iterable_protocol`) values in general.

Let's look at one final example. The following code demonstrates how event bindings work when we use the `v-on` directive:

```
<!DOCTYPE html>
<html lang="en">
<head>
    <meta charset="UTF-8">
    <title>Click on it!</title>

    <!-- development version of Vue.js -->
    <script
src="https://cdn.jsdelivr.net/npm/vue/dist/vue.js"></script>
</head>
<body>

<div id="app">
    <button v-on:click="sayHi">Click to say hi!</button>
</div>

<script type="text/javascript">
    let app = new Vue({
        el: '#app',
        data: {
```

```
        sayHi: () => {
            alert('Hi there!')
        }
    }
  });
</script>

</body>
</html>
```

By using `v-on:click="sayHi()"`, we've bound the `click` event of the button to our `sayHi` function. Pretty straightforward, right?

There's a lot more to say about Vue directives, but this should be enough to get you started!

Do you remember the `isEnter` function that we had to write in Chapter 2, *Building TodoIt - Your Own todo Management Web Application with TypeScript*? Handling keyboard events and key modifiers is easy with Vue. You can simply do this: `v-on:keyup.enter="someFunction"`. We'll use this trick for our application. You can learn more about this at https://vuejs.org/v2/guide/events.html#Key-Modifiers.

Vue also provides support for event modifiers so that it can handle things such as stopping or preventing the propagation of DOM events (a frequent requirement of web applications). You can read more about this at https://vuejs.org/v2/guide/events.html#Event-Modifiers. Here are a few examples that have been taken from Vue's official documentation:

```
<!-- the click event's propagation will be stopped -->
<a v-on:click.stop="doThis"></a>

<!-- the submit event will no longer reload the page -->
<form v-on:submit.prevent="onSubmit"></form>

<!-- modifiers can be chained -->
<a v-on:click.stop.prevent="doThat"></a>

<!-- just the modifier -->
<form v-on:submit.prevent></form>

<!-- use capture mode when adding the event listener -->
<!-- i.e. an event targeting an inner element is handled here before
being handled by that element -->
<div v-on:click.capture="doThis">...</div>
```

```
<!-- only trigger handler if event.target is the element itself -->
<!-- i.e. not from a child element -->
<div v-on:click.self="doThat">...</div>
```

Finally, as we mentioned earlier, you can also implement your own directives (https://vuejs.org/v2/guide/custom-directive.html).

Components and props

Vue has also embraced a **component architecture**, and for good reason! As we discussed in the previous chapter, components make it easy for us to compose/reuse simple concepts and build large and complex applications in a tractable way.

Conceptually, all the user interfaces can be decomposed into a component tree:

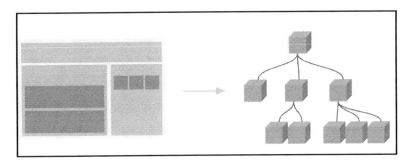

Here's how you can declare a **component** with Vue:

```
Vue.component('todo-task', {
    props: ['description'],
    template: '<li>{{description}}</li>'
});
```

The component declaration is quite easy to understand. The component name is the first argument of the function, while the second argument is an object that contains different options:

- props: This is used to declare the component properties. In this case, we can pass description when defining a todo-task element. (Reference: https://vuejs.org/v2/guide/components-props.html.)
- template: This is used to define the template of the component.

The naming convention for Vue components varies, depending on how the components will be used. If the component is to be used in the DOM, then the name should be in **kebab-case** (that is, lowercase and delimited using hyphens) and should contain at least one hyphen.

Once declared, this component can be used globally in any Vue instance very easily:

```
<todo-task description="Finish writing the book"></todo-task>
```

Here, we have hardcoded the `description` property of `todo-task`. However, we could use directives to bind a value dynamically or even loop over collections with `v-for` and render many components at once. As you can see, this is all very similar to what we did using Angular.

You can find this example, along with a few additional ones, in the code samples for this chapter: `https://github.com/PacktPublishing/-Typescript-3.0-Projects---Learn-Typescript-by-Building-Web-Applications/tree/master/9`.

Property names should be defined using camelCase in JavaScript and kebab-case in HTML. Again, this is the same as with Angular.

When components need to handle more complex inputs, it can become tedious to go and create a separate prop for each input. In such cases, it is easier to pass the complex object directly. Here's an example of doing this:

```html
<!DOCTYPE html>
<html lang="en">
  <head>
    <meta charset="UTF-8" />
    <title>Todo task complex input</title>

    <!-- development version of Vue.js -->
    <script
src="https://cdn.jsdelivr.net/npm/vue/dist/vue.js"></script>
  </head>
  <body>
    <div id="app">
      <ul>
        <todo-task v-for="todo of todos" :key="todo.id" v-
        bind:todo="todo"></todo-task>
      </ul>
    </div>
```

```
<script type="text/javascript">
  Vue.component("todo-task", {
    props: ["todo"],
    template: '<li class="todoTask">{{todo.description}}</li>'
  });

  let app = new Vue({
    el: "#app",
    data: {
      todos: [
        { id: 1, description: "Learn about React" },
        { id: 2, description: "Follow @dSebastien on Twitter" },
        { id: 3, description: "Conquer the world" }
      ]
    }
  });
</script>
</body>
</html>
```

Here, we have simply bound a todo task object. Then, in the template, we were able to easily access its properties.

Did you notice the :key attribute on the todo-task element, right next to v-for? This tells Vue that it can render the elements more efficiently. Thanks to that unique identifier (uniqueness is important!), Vue is able to track the elements and reuse them while rerendering. For instance, if you have changed the order of the elements in the list, then Vue will be able to simply reorder the DOM elements without recreating them from scratch. This is explained here: https://vuejs.org/v2/guide/list.html#key. Note that this is similar to Angular's trackBy feature.

There are more tricks you can learn about in terms of rendering lists with Vue, but we cannot cover all of these here. Please check out https://vuejs.org/v2/guide/list.html for more information.

Component prop types and validation rules

In addition to their name, `props` **can have types, as well as validation rules**:

```
props: {
  title: String,
  link: String,
  visitors: Number,
  isVisible: Boolean,
  messages: Array,
  owner: Object,
  children: [Object, String] // multiple accepted types
}
```

If a type is defined for a property, Vue will ensure that you pass the expected types before creating the component.

 It is possible to use custom constructor functions as types; in that case, Vue will use an `instanceof` check. Unfortunately, this is much less interesting than what Angular can do with its native (compile-time) TypeScript support. However, as we'll see later, we can also use TypeScript with Vue.

Here's a more advanced example, with a required `Object` property that has a default value and a custom validation function:

```
props: {
  task: {
    type: Object,
    required: true,
    default: function() {
        return {
            id: -1,
            description: "Default",
        };
    },
    validator: function(value) {
        return typeof value.id === 'number' && typeof
         value.description
        === 'string';
    }
  }
}
```

In the preceding code, the validator ensures that the value has an `id` property of the `number` type and a `string` description. Note that those are pure JavaScript runtime type checks.

The internal state of a component

Components can also have their own internal state/data:

```
props: ['someInput'],
data: function() {
    return {
        foo: this.someInput,
    };
}
```

In the preceding example, `someInput` is passed in and used for the internal state of the component in a `foo` property. The function needs to be defined so that the state remains internal (remember our previous discussions about encapsulation!).

 Components shouldn't try to mutate their properties. Such mutations will be lost whenever Vue refreshes the bindings (for example, when the parent component is updated). If you need to mutate a property, then add it to the data of the component, like we did previously, or to the `computed` object, which is there to hold derived properties (which we will cover in the next section).

Now, let's learn how to listen to events.

Listening to events that have been triggered by child components

Listening to events that have been emitted by children components is done using the `v-on` directive and, just like with Angular, you can also pass data along. Here's an example:

```
<!DOCTYPE html>
<html lang="en">
<head>
    <meta charset="UTF-8">
    <title>Todo task list listen</title>

    <!-- development version of Vue.js -->
```

```
    <script src="https://cdn.jsdelivr.net/npm/vue/dist/vue.js">
</script>

    <style>
        .todoTask {
            cursor: pointer;
        }
        .todoTask:hover {
            background-color: #1e9;
        }
    </style>
</head>
```

In the `head` tag, we define some styles for our example and, as usual, we define the logic for our example in the `body` tag:

```
<body>

<div id="app">
    <todo-list v-bind:items="todos"></todo-list>
</div>

<script type="text/javascript">
    Vue.component('todo-task', {
        props: ['todo'],
        template: `<li class="todoTask" v-on:click="$emit('delete',
        todo.id)">{{todo.description}}</li>`
    });

    Vue.component('todo-list', {
        props: ['items'],
        template: `
            <ul>
                <todo-task v-for="todo of todos" :key="todo.id" v-
                bind:todo="todo" v-on:delete="
                onDelete($event)"></todo-
                 task>
            </ul>
        `,
        data: function() {
            return {
                todos: this.items
            };
        },
        methods: {
            onDelete(id) {
                console.log("Deleting id: ", id);
                this.todos = this.todos.filter((value) => value.id !==
```

```
                                id);
                    }
                }
            });

    let app = new Vue({
        el: '#app',
        data: {
            todos: [
                {id: 1, description: "Learn about React"},
                {id: 2, description: "Follow @dSebastien on Twitter"},
                {id: 3, description: "Conquer the world"}
            ]
        }
    });
</script>

</body>
</html>
```

In this example, we have introduced a `todo-list` component that accepts a list of todo tasks as input and renders a list of `todo-task` elements.

When the user clicks on one of these tasks, an event is emitted by the corresponding `todo-task` using the following code:

```
v-on:click="$emit('delete', todo.id)"
```

As you can see, emitting an event is done using the `$emit` built-in function; its first parameter is the event name, while the second one is the data structure to pass along with the event. In this case, we include the unique identifier of the element to remove.

Emitting the event is only half of the story. For it to do anything, something must react to it. In our example, the parent `todo-list` component listens to the event using `v-on:delete="onDelete($event)"`. Each time a `delete` event is emitted, the `onDelete` function gets called and receives the event data thanks to `$event`.

> Instead of using `v-on:delete=...`, we could've used the shorthand notation, that is, `@delete=...`. This is a matter of taste, so it's up to you!

As we discussed in the previous chapter, this approach is recommended as it helps in creating **dumb** components. In this case, the `todo-item` component doesn't need to know or care about what happens with the event.

It just fires a signal and forgets about it. Then, something else is responsible for reacting to and making decisions. This improves reusability and respects the valuable **single responsibility principle (SRP)** that we learned about earlier in this book.

Single File Components (SFCs)

In larger applications, declaring components globally, as we've seen up until now (that is, using `Vue.component(...)`), can quickly become problematic. Fortunately, it is also possible to define components locally or in dedicated files using the `.vue` file extension.

These are called SFCs. We will leverage SFCs in this chapter. If you're impatient, you can take a look at the documentation for it here:
`https://vuejs.org/v2/guide/single-file-components.html`.

Similarities with Angular

So, what do you think so far? If we put the application's bootstrap process aside, which is a bit more involved with Angular, don't you feel like Vue is very close in philosophy to Angular? Given the background of the creator, this should be no surprise.

As usual, there's so much more to say! We could discuss web components, component slots, dynamic and asynchronous components, recursive ones, and so many other things, but we need to move forward!

 Vue.js has quite a lot of tricks up its sleeve. For example, take a look at **instance properties**: `https://vuejs.org/v2/cookbook/adding-instance-properties.html`. We won't cover these in this book, but they're definitely worth learning about.

Computed properties

Vue.js, like Angular, advises against putting too much logic inside component templates. The reasons for this are obvious: bugs can quickly creep in, template logic is hard to test, the logic inside templates is not reusable, and, last but not least, templates become harder to understand, which is bad for maintainability.

By using **computed properties**, you can move logic to where it belongs: inside the controller.

Here's an example we've taken from Vue's official documentation.

The following is an example of a component template without a computed property:

```
<div id="example">
  {{ message.split('').reverse().join('') }}
</div>
```

The following is the same example, but with the logic inside a computed property:

```
<div id="example">
  "{{ reversedMessage }}"
</div>

...

var vm = new Vue({
  el: '#example',
  data: {
    message: 'Hello'
  },
  computed: {
    // a computed getter
    reversedMessage: function () {
      // `this` points to the vm instance
      return this.message.split('').reverse().join('')
    }
  }
})
```

As you can see, computed properties are simply added to a `computed` object, and each computed property is defined as a function that returns the derived value.

Inside the template, we can simply use `reversedMessage` as if it were any other property. Inside the controller, though, it is clear that this property is derived/computed. If the value of the backing `message` property changes, then the computed property will change as well.

As stated in the documentation, the same result can be achieved by defining a method and invoking it in the template, but the difference lies in how the values are resolved. With computed properties, the value is resolved once, cached, and then reused until the properties that they depend on change. This, of course, makes computed properties much more efficient than systematically calling a function.

Using computed properties with dependencies that are not reactive (that is, not **tracked** by Vue.js) can cause surprises, so be cautious.

Here's an example from the official documentation demonstrating such an issue:

```
computed: {
  now: function () {
    return Date.now()
  }
}
```

The issue with the preceding code is that the result of calling `Date.now()` will be *cached*. The same value will always be returned, even if you may want/expect the value to be kept up to date whenever the element is rerendered.

Watchers

Vue.js provides us with a way to programmatically react to value changes in other properties. These are known as **watcher functions**, and they are defined through the `watch` option.

Each watcher is defined as a **property name – function** mapping, where the property name is the name of the property to watch and the function is called whenever the property value changes.

Here's an example:

```
var watcherExample = new Vue({
  el: '#watcher-example',
  data: {
    something: '',
    lastUpdated: '',
  },
  watch: {
    // whenever 'something' changes the function below will get
      invoked something: function (newValue, oldValue) {
      console.log(`Old value: ${oldValue}`);
      console.log(`New value: ${newValue}`);
      this.lastUpdated = Date.now();
    }
  },
})
```

In this example, whenever the value of the `something` property changes, the associated watch function will be called.

Generally speaking, **you should prefer computed properties to watchers as they're less verbose and less repetitive**. Watchers are mostly useful for cases where you need to perform operations that take longer or are more costly.

We'll look at filters next.

Filters

Formatting text is something that we need to do often while developing applications, whether that is to render monetary amounts, dates, or to transform/translate text.

Vue **filters** allow us to do this easily in a reusable manner. We can use Vue filters by using the pipe symbol: |. This is indeed inspired by Angular (this is getting old already), which itself has taken inspiration from classic Unix shells for its pipes.

Here's an example:

```
<!DOCTYPE html>
<html lang="en">
<head>
    <meta charset="UTF-8">
    <title>Vue filter</title>

    <!-- development version of Vue.js -->
    <script
src="https://cdn.jsdelivr.net/npm/vue/dist/vue.js"></script>
</head>
<body>

<div id="app">
    {{ message | reverse }}
</div>

<script type="text/javascript">
    let app = new Vue({
        el: '#app',
        data: {
            message: "Hello world!"
        },
        filters: {
            reverse: (value) =>
                value.split('').reduce((reversedString, char)
                => char +
                reversedString, '')
```

```
        }
    });
</script>

</body>
</html>
```

There's not much more to say here; if you understand Angular pipes, then Vue filters are quite intuitive.

Next up are lifecycle hooks.

Lifecycle hooks

Vue instances and Vue components, in general, have an associated lifecycle. You can use **lifecycle hooks** to add your own logic at certain points of this lifecycle.

The following example has been taken from the official documentation; it demonstrates how we can write a lifecycle hook that will be invoked when an instance has just been created:

```
new Vue({
  data: {
    a: 1
  },
  created: function () {
    console.log(`a is: ${this.a}`); // "a is: 1"
  }
})
```

In the preceding code, the `this` keyword points to the current Vue (component) context, also called the **VM**. Check out the following documentation to find out more: `https://vuejs.org/v2/guide/instance.html`.

There are quite a few different hooks, as shown in the following diagram:

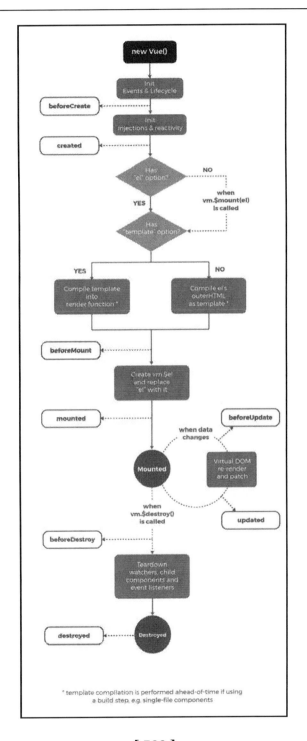

Don't worry, though – there's no need to memorize all of this. Just keep this idea in mind in case you ever need to attach some code to one of these phases.

 The official documentation on lifecycle hooks can be found at `https://vuejs.org/v2/guide/instance.html#Instance-Lifecyc le-Hooks`.

Mixins and pure functions

Sometimes, you'll face situations where an existing component almost fits your new requirements but not quite. Some other times, you'll notice that different components actually have quite a lot in common, but also diverge too much in some respects.

Application design choices are often very situational, and there aren't many solutions that you can blindly apply, no matter what. For example, splitting components means introducing some level of duplication and breaking the DRY principle, while extending or combining existing components can lead to bloat (for example, too many properties on a single component) or introduce leaky abstractions and more trouble down the line.

Vue.js `mixins` (not to be confused with TypeScript `mixins`!) provide a way for us to share/reuse functionality between Vue components. Mixins are inherently *functional*; they make it possible for us to encapsulate a single feature/functionality and reuse it across different components in the application.

 Ideal `mixins` should be **pure functions**: they should not have side effects and they shouldn't have dependencies that could influence their results. Given the same inputs, a pure function or `mixin` should always return the same outputs. Pure functions are part of the functional programming paradigm and are very valuable since they are predictable and easily testable. You can learn more about them here: `https://medium.com/javascript-scene/master-the-javascript-i nterview-what-is-a-pure-function-d1c076bec976`.

With Vue.js, `mixin` objects may contain any Vue component option. When a `mixin` is used in a component, all of the options that are defined by the `mixin` are merged with the **host** component's options.

Let's go through a few examples to make this more tractable.

Here is a very simple `mixin` that will log a message whenever a component that uses it is created:

```
const loggingMixin = {
    created() {
        console.log("I'm the logging mixin");
    }
};
```

As we mentioned previously, `mixin` is a simple object that includes Vue component options. In this example, we've used the `created` lifecycle hook.

Using this `mixin` in a component is as simple as adding it to the `mixins` option's array:

```
Vue.component('foo', {
    template: '<div>bar</div>',
    mixins: [
        loggingMixin,
    ],
});
```

Any code that's declared in mixins has priority over the code of the host component. This means that methods such as the `created` lifecycle method will execute first.

In the case of conflicting data or conflicting object properties (for example, `prop` with the same name declared on both), then the component wins over the `mixins`. The option merging rules are described here:
https://vuejs.org/v2/guide/mixins.html#Option-Merging.

 Mixins can also be declared globally using `Vue.mixin(...)`. Be careful, however: declaring a global `mixin` has an impact on all the components, including third-party ones. This can cause surprises if you're not careful, so it is clearly not a recommended practice.

One limitation of Vue.js `mixins` to be aware of is the fact that they can't rely on or use the state that's held by another `mixin`/component, or share its state with them. This is actually a good characteristic since it prevents us from mixing concerns and needlessly introducing strong coupling.

An important downside of using `mixins` is that they introduce *magic* and, thus, indirection. Once `mixins` have been introduced to a project, it becomes less obvious where data/logic is held/coming from.

In Chapter 11, *Diving into React, NestJS, GraphQL, and Apollo,* we'll talk about **hooks**, which provide a more powerful alternative to mixins. At the time of writing, hooks aren't yet supported by Vue.js, but they probably will be in the future. For now, there's just an experimental library: https://github.com/yyx990803/vue-hooks. Don't try to use it in production, though!

You can find a few more example mixins in this book's sample code, under Chapter09/mixins/index-01-mixin-basic.html.

Render functions

Most of the time, you should be able to construct the user interfaces of your applications using simple components and templates. However, there are certain cases where it won't be practical to do so.

One example is when you want to benefit from the flexibility of JavaScript so that you can adapt the DOM and it can be rendered. You can find a detailed example at https://vuejs.org/v2/guide/render-function.html.

Render functions were introduced precisely for such cases. By using such functions, you can programmatically define what the component will be rendered into.

A render function is defined just like any other Vue component option:

```
<!DOCTYPE html>
<html lang="en">
<head>
    <meta charset="UTF-8">
    <title>Render function</title>

    <!-- development version of Vue.js -->
    <script
src="https://cdn.jsdelivr.net/npm/vue/dist/vue.js"></script>
</head>
<body>

<div id="app">
    <custom-heading v-bind:level="3">{{message}}</custom-heading>
</div>

<script type="text/javascript">
    "use strict";
```

```
Vue.component('custom-heading', {
    render: function (createElement) {
        return createElement(
            'h' + this.level,      // the first parameter
                // is the name of the tag to create
            this.$slots.default, // the children
        )
    },
    props: {
        level: {
            type: Number,
            required: true,
        }
    }
});

let app = new Vue({
    el: '#app',
    data() {
        return {
            message: "I'm the component"
        };
    },
});
</script>

</body>
</html>
```

In the preceding example, you can see that our function returns the result that was generated by the createElement function call. The createElement function simply creates a new (virtual) DOM element/node (also called VNode) for us. The first parameter that we pass to it is the name of the element to create (in this case, a heading tag). The second (optional) argument is an object representing the element's attributes. The last argument is the array of element's children or a string representing text nodes.

 If you're curious about the this.$slots.default value that we've passed to the createElement function, then take a look at https://vuejs.org/v2/guide/render-function.html#Slots. While you're at it, you can also read the API documentation for instance properties: https://vuejs.org/v2/api/#Instance-Properties.

We won't dive into render functions in any more depth for Vue, but don't hesitate to explore them on your own. Later in this book, we will see that render functions are central to React applications. The same is true for JSX and TSX, which we'll also look at later in this book, while discovering React:
`https://vuejs.org/v2/guide/render-function.html#JSX`.

 You can find code examples in this book's assets folder under `Chapter09/render-functions`.

Testing support

Vue offers excellent support for unit testing components, notably through its `@vue/test-utils` entry point. Using these testing utilities, you can easily *mount* a component and validate that it behaves as expected.

The Vue CLI (which we'll discuss soon) also includes built-in support for unit testing with Jest or Mocha.

We won't cover this here, unfortunately, but don't hesitate to explore this subject on your own.

Vue developer tools

Similar to the Augury (`https://chrome.google.com/webstore/detail/augury/elgalmkoelokbchhkhacckoklkejnhcd`) utility that we presented in the previous chapter, Vue also has its own developer tools (`https://github.com/vuejs/vue-devtools`).

To install them, you can go to the official website or directly download any of the following:

- The Google Chrome extension:
  `https://chrome.google.com/webstore/detail/vuejs-devtools/nhdogjmejiglipccpnnnanhbledajbpd`
- The Firefox extension:
  `https://addons.mozilla.org/en-US/firefox/addon/vue-js-devtools`

- The portable and browser-independent version:
  `https://github.com/vuejs/vue-devtools/blob/master/shells/electron/README.md`

We'll use the Google Chrome extension as an example here.

Once installed, if you open up a page running a Vue application and then press *F12* to show the Developer Tools, you should see a **Vue** tab:

If you click on the **Vue** tab, you will be presented with the component tree of your application in the **Components** view:

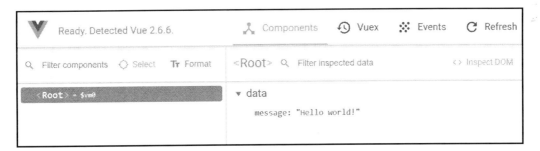

The **Components** view allows you to inspect and manipulate the state of the components in your application, including their internal data.

The **Vuex** tab is dedicated to Vuex, the official state management solution for Vue. We will cover Vuex later in this chapter.

Finally, in the **Events** tab, you can gain some insight into the various events that are triggered by your application:

The Vue dev tools are very useful during development. They're also great (just like the Angular CLI) at helping juniors do more on their own.

 If you're looking for a prototyping solution, then take a look at **PreVue** (`https://prevue.io`), a nice utility that you can use to quickly create prototypes.

Now, let's take a look at the official Vue CLI.

The Vue CLI

The Vue CLI (`https://cli.vuejs.org/`) is the perfect companion for creating Vue.js applications, similar to what the Angular CLI is to Angular.

Installing this tool is very simple; you just need to execute the `npm install -g @vue/cli` command (or `yarn global add @vue/cli` if you prefer using Yarn).

 If you remember our advice from the first few chapters of this book about avoiding installing `npm` packages globally, then congratulations! You can execute the Vue CLI through `npx vue`. Unfortunately, you will need to install (as far as we know) the `@vue/cli-service-global` package globally.

Using the Vue CLI, you can easily scaffold new applications. While doing so, you can pick and choose from the different tools that you're interested in using (for example, Babel, TypeScript, PostCSS, Jest, and many others). This means that you can easily set up new applications that correspond to your needs/preferences. Many libraries and tools are supported out of the box.

The Vue CLI also includes an easy-to-use development web server with **hot reloading** support (that is, a build feature that detects changes in the code and automatically reloads the page to include those).

It does not, however, allow you to generate code like the Angular CLI is able to.

Finally, just like the Angular Console, which we mentioned in the previous chapter, the Vue CLI also includes a web user interface that you can use to create and manage Vue projects:

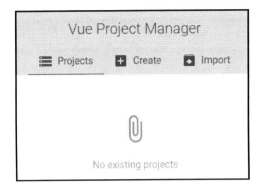

You can start the Vue UI by executing the following command:

```
vue ui
```

Once you have created or imported a project using the Vue UI, you'll have access to many more features, which makes this a great companion app to use while developing with Vue. Here are a few examples.

The project configuration can be adapted from the following screen:

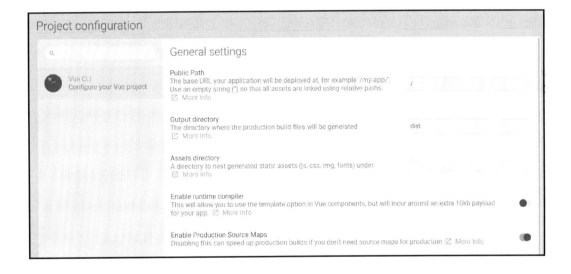

Project dependencies can be managed from the following screen:

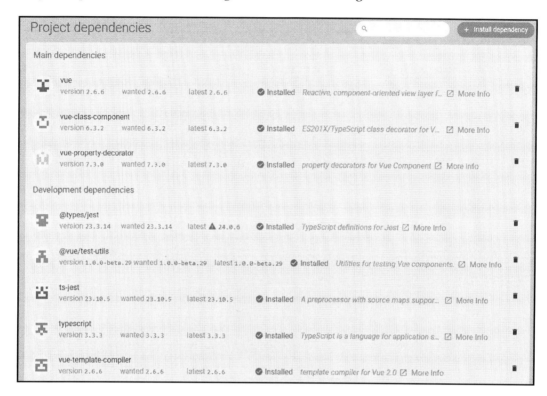

The same goes for project plugins, which can also be adjusted:

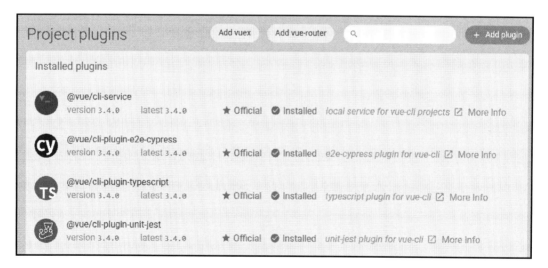

The ability to manage the application's configuration through a GUI is great for discoverability as it helps us find out more about the CLI's features.

One area where the Vue CLI particularly shines is its **Tasks** panel, which allows us to execute different project scripts.

For example, through the serve task, you can run the build of your application and get a visual analysis of your assets, modules, and dependencies, as well as how long each one should take to load, depending on the network's conditions:

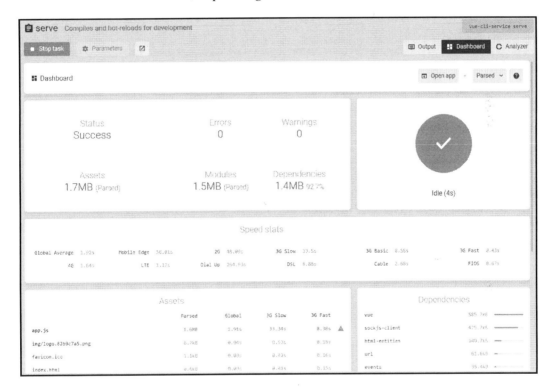

This is a great place to go to when you want to identify bottlenecks and improve performance.

Behind the scenes, the Vue CLI relies heavily on Webpack for the build part. This is great as it means that there is inherent support for many advanced features, such as code splitting, tree shaking, caching, hot module replacement, and resource prefetching. As a matter of fact, Vue is transparent about that and allows us to inspect and customize the build process if we ever need to (https://cli.vuejs.org/guide/webpack.html#simple-configuration).

You can use `vue inspect` to take a look at Webpack's configuration.

Now, let's use the CLI.

Bonus – creating a new project using the Vue CLI

We've used the Vue CLI to create an example application with TypeScript support enabled. You can find it in the code samples for this book, under `Chapter09/04-vue-cli/01-empty`.

When you use the Vue CLI to create an application, it asks a series of questions that let you customize the project creation process.

Here's how we created our example application and the options that we used:

- Command: `vue create 01-empty`
- Manually select features
- Package manager? Yarn
- Features:
  - TypeScript
  - Linter/Format
  - Unit testing
  - E2E testing

At the second stage, the CLI has asked us the following questions:

- *Use class-style component syntax?* Yes
- *Which linter to use?* TSLint
- *When to lint?* Lint on save
- *Which library for unit tests?* Jest
- *Which library to use for E2E tests?* Cypress
- *Where to store configurations?* In dedicated config files

Like the Angular CLI, the tools surrounding Vue always evolve, so don't worry if you don't see the exact same list of questions when you go through this! The frontend ecosystem moves blazingly fast!

Once we have provided our answers, the CLI generates the following files for us:

```
-rw-rw-rw- 1 Sebastien Sebastien    33 Feb 18 07:13 .browserslistrc
-rw-rw-rw- 1 Sebastien Sebastien    50 Feb 18 07:13 cypress.json
-rw-rw-rw- 1 Sebastien Sebastien   258 Feb 18 07:13 .gitignore
-rw-rw-rw- 1 Sebastien Sebastien   530 Feb 18 07:13 jest.config.js
drwxrwxrwx 1 Sebastien Sebastien   512 Feb 18 07:14 node_modules
-rw-rw-rw- 1 Sebastien Sebastien   768 Feb 18 07:13 package.json
-rw-rw-rw- 1 Sebastien Sebastien    59 Feb 18 07:13 postcss.config.js
drwxrwxrwx 1 Sebastien Sebastien   512 Feb 18 07:13 public
-rw-rw-rw- 1 Sebastien Sebastien   475 Feb 18 07:14 README.md
drwxrwxrwx 1 Sebastien Sebastien   512 Feb 18 07:13 src
drwxrwxrwx 1 Sebastien Sebastien   512 Feb 18 07:13 tests
-rw-rw-rw- 1 Sebastien Sebastien   694 Feb 18 07:13 tsconfig.json
-rw-rw-rw- 1 Sebastien Sebastien   379 Feb 18 07:13 tslint.json
-rw-rw-rw- 1 Sebastien Sebastien  347K Feb 18 07:14 yarn.lock
```

As you can see, the TypeScript configuration files are here, a Jest configuration file has been generated for us, and some others have been generated for Cypress (E2E tests), PostCSS, and TSLint. This may not seem like much, but this actually saves us a lot of effort.

 While we're busy discussing Vue's supporting tools, note that VS Code has great support for Vue, notably through the Vetur (`https://github.com/vuejs/vetur`) plugin. There is also a page on the official website that explains how to debug Vue applications in VS Code:
`https://vuejs.org/v2/cookbook/debugging-in-vscode.html`.

The folder structure that's put in place for us by the CLI is quite simple:

- The `src` folder contains our project files.
- The `tests` folder contains E2E tests (and unit tests if you wish to isolate those as well).
- The `public` folder contains static assets, including the `index.html` file.

The source folder is organized as follows:

```
-rw-rw-rw- 1 Sebastien Sebastien 616 Feb 18 07:13 App.vue
drwxrwxrwx 1 Sebastien Sebastien 512 Feb 18 07:13 assets
drwxrwxrwx 1 Sebastien Sebastien 512 Feb 18 07:13 components
-rw-rw-rw- 1 Sebastien Sebastien 142 Feb 18 07:14 main.ts
-rw-rw-rw- 1 Sebastien Sebastien 306 Feb 18 07:14 shims-tsx.d.ts
-rw-rw-rw- 1 Sebastien Sebastien  74 Feb 18 07:14 shims-vue.d.ts
```

The bootstrap process is very straightforward:

- `App.vue` is the **root** application component (similar to the `App` component with Angular).
- `main.ts` creates the `Vue` instance for us and attaches (or **mounts**) the `App` component to the `#app` div.

> The curious among you may have noticed the `shims-vue.d.ts` file. This file declares a TypeScript module named `*.vue`; this is what allows `main.ts` to import the `App.vue` file using `import App from './App.vue';`. Under the hood, the Vue build process uses the officially supported `vue-loader` (`https://github.com/vuejs/vue-loader`) library, which is a Webpack loader for SFCs.

This example leads us directly to TypeScript support!

TypeScript support

Vue.js provides official support for TypeScript, and that support keeps getting better and better. The documentation for Vue.js's TypeScript support is located at `https://vuejs.org/v2/guide/typescript.html`.

The main `npm` package of Vue includes TypeScript type definitions (`https://github.com/vuejs/vue/tree/dev/types`), which is nice because those should stay well aligned with the project as it evolves.

At the time of writing, the latest release of Vue is 2.6, also known as **Macross**.

Vue 3.0, which should be released in 2019 (or early 2020), will feature full TypeScript support. Moreover, Vue.js itself will be written in TypeScript.

Compiler configuration

In the official documentation, the Vue team recommends that we configure the TypeScript compiler as follows:

```
{
  "compilerOptions": {
    // this aligns with Vue's browser support
    // feel free to go higher if you don't need to support older
    // environments
    "target": "es5",
    // we've seen how stricter inference is beneficial
    "strict": true,
    // to leverage tree shaking with Webpack, rollup and
    // other bundlers
    "module": "es2015",
    "moduleResolution": "node"
  }
}
```

The `strict` mode and, in particular, the implied `noImplicitThis: true` option, allow us to benefit from type checking `this` when writing Vue components.

 Of course, you can target a higher version than ES5 if you don't need to support older web browsers such as IE11.

The Vue CLI that we introduced previously also includes support for TypeScript, so you can use it to create projects that have everything you need in order to write TypeScript-based Vue applications.

SFC with vue-class-component

Using the officially supported `vue-class-component` (`https://github.com/vuejs/vue-class-component`) library, we can actually write Vue components using TypeScript classes, which will be more familiar to you now that we've played with Angular.

The `vue-class-component` library provides an `@Component` decorator that you can add to your classes to transform them into Vue components. For this to work, you need to set the `experimentalDecorators` option to `true` in your `tsconfig.json` file.

Vue components that have been written using TypeScript can be stored in files with the `.vue` extension. In the next section, we'll also see how we can isolate this TypeScript code by splitting Vue components into multiple files.

Here is an example of what an SFC looks like when written using TypeScript:

```
<template>
    <div class="hello">
        <h1>{{ message }}</h1>
        <p>
            <span>Count:</span> {{ count }}
        </p>
        <p>
            <span>Computed property:</span> {{ someComputedProperty }}
        </p>
        <p>
            <span>Event listener:</span> <input type="button"
            @click="onClickHandler($event)" value="Click me!" />
        </p>
        <p>
            <span>Increment counter and emit an event:</span> <input
            type="button" @click="incrementCount()" value="Click me!"
            />
        </p>
    </div>
</template>

<script lang="ts">
    import {Component, Emit, Prop, Vue} from 'vue-property-decorator';

    @Component({})
    export default class ExampleSFC extends Vue {
        // Property
        @Prop({
            default: 'default message',
            required: false,
        })
        private message!: string;

        // Data property
        private count: number = 0;

        // Lifecycle hook
        public mounted() {
            // alert('The ExampleSFC component has just
            // been mounted');
```

```
        }

        // Computed property
        public get someComputedProperty() {
            return 123;
        }

        // Event handler
        public onClickHandler(event: MouseEvent) {
            alert(`The button was clicked. Event: ${event}`);
        }

        // Event emitter
        @Emit('count-increased') // if not specified, then the method
        name is used and changed to kebab case
        public incrementCount() {
            this.count += 1;
            return this.count; // this value will be emitted
        }
    }
</script>

<!-- "scoped" below means that the styles of this component won't leak
out and will only apply to this component -->
<style scoped>
    h1 {
        margin: 40px 0 0;
    }
</style>
```

Here is how this example component can be used in the example application
(the `src/App.vue` file):

```
<template>
    <div id="app">
        <ExampleSFC message="Custom message" v-on:count-
        increased="onCountIncreased($event)" />
    </div>
</template>

<script lang="ts">
    import {Component, Vue} from 'vue-property-decorator';
    import ExampleSFC from './components/ExampleSFC.vue';

    @Component({
        components: {
            ExampleSFC,
        },
```

```
        })
        export default class App extends Vue {
            public onCountIncreased(event: any) {
                alert(`New count: ${event}`);
            }
        }
</script>

<style>
</style>
```

The following are some things to take note of from the preceding example:

- The TypeScript code is placed within a `script` block starting with `<script lang="ts">`.
- The component is declared with an `@Component` decorator, which is provided by the `vue-property-decorator` library (the CLI has added this for us).
- The properties are declared by adding the `@Prop` decorator to class fields.
- The `@Prop` decorator is also provided by `vue-property-decorator`.
- Properties that are not decorated with `@Prop` are part of the component's **data**.
- Component methods are declared as class members: `incrementCount()` `{ ... }`.
- Computed properties are declared using property accessors: `get computedMsg(...)`.
- Lifecycle hooks are declared as class members: `mounted() { ... }`.
- Event handlers are simple class member functions that accept the event as a parameter: `onClickHandler(...) { ... }`.
- Methods that emit events can be annotated with `@Emit`, which takes the return value of the function and emits it using `$emit`.
- The event name can be specified in `@Emit`. If no name is specified through the decorator, then the method's name will be used instead (in kebab-case).
- Component dependencies are declared within the `@Component` declaration (you can see this in the `App.vue` file).

Did you notice how we've used the `default` keyword while exporting the `ExampleSFC` component's class? This demonstrates how we can define a default export in a module. Also, pay attention to how the class is then imported into the `App` module. We don't recommend using default exports, but we wanted to show you at least one in this book!

You can find the complete source code for this example in this book's samples, under `Chapter09/05-vue-ts`.

The `vue-class-component` library also supports `mixins`: https://github.com/vuejs/vue-class-component#using-mixins.

This is quite nice already, but we can do better.

Splitting components into multiple files

So far, we have always kept our controllers separate from templates/views and styles. You may not be pleased with SFC as there are mixing concerns. To some extent, this is a matter of taste, but as components grow, it makes less and less sense to keep everything in a single file.

Actually, we can also separate the different parts of a component with Vue.js and TypeScript. We'll see how in this section.

This approach has been described by George Hanson in the following article: https://dev.to/georgehanson/building-vuejs-applications-with-typescript-1j2n. This section is directly inspired by that blog post, with George's permission.

We'll use the previous code sample as a starting point. Make a copy of the `Chapter09/05-vue-ts` folder from this book's assets if you want to follow along.

We then need to add the following dependencies:

```
npm install vue-template-loader webpack-stream --save-dev
```

Now, we will recreate the `ExampleSFC` component using multiple files. We don't need that file anymore, so you can safely delete it: `src/components/ExampleSFC.vue`.

Create an `example.ts` file under `src/components` with the following content:

```
import {Component, Prop, Vue} from 'vue-property-decorator';

@Component
export default class Example extends Vue {
    @Prop({
        default: 'default message',
        required: false,
    })
    private message!: string;
}
```

For brevity, we've only kept the `message` property.

Now, create `example.html` next to the TS file. For now, we'll simply render the `message` property:

```
<span>The message is: {{message}}</span>
```

To establish a link between the component class and our HTML template, we'll leverage the `vue-template-loader` (`https://github.com/ktsn/vue-template-loader`) library that we added earlier. This library is a `webpack` loader: `https://webpack.js.org/loaders`.

 Loaders are at the very core of Webpack and allow us to easily load all sorts of assets.

To load our HTML template, we need to create a **shim**.

Go ahead and create a `shims-html.d.ts` file in the `src` folder with the following content:

```
// reference: https://dev.to/georgehanson/building-vuejs-
// applications-with-typescript-1j2n

declare module '*.html' {
    import Vue, {ComponentOptions, FunctionalComponentOptions} from
    'vue';
```

```
interface WithRender {
    <V extends Vue, U extends ComponentOptions<V> |
    FunctionalComponentOptions>(options: U): U;
    <V extends typeof Vue>(component: V): V;
}

const withRender: WithRender;
export default withRender;
}
```

Don't worry too much if you don't understand this code; it is quite involved. All you need to care about is the fact that this *shim* simply helps TypeScript understand what is returned when HTML files are imported. Without this, TypeScript wouldn't be able to compile the next bit.

Now that we have the template and HTML shim in place, let's go ahead and load our template.

Replace the code in the `src/components/example.ts` file with the following code:

```
import { Component, Prop, Vue } from 'vue-property-decorator';

import WithRender from './example.html';

@WithRender
@Component
export class Example extends Vue {
    @Prop({
        default: 'default message',
        required: false,
    })
    private message!: string;
}
```

Here, we are importing our template file and using the `WithRender` token as a decorator for our class.

There are a few more steps we need to take before we've completed our task.

Obviously, we need to adapt the `src/App.vue` component so that it loads the new component:

```
<template>
    <div id="app">
        <Example message="Custom message" />
    </div>
</template>
```

```
<script lang="ts">
    import {Component, Vue} from 'vue-property-decorator';
    import {Example} from './components/example';

    @Component({
        components: {
            Example,
        },
    })
    export default class App extends Vue {
    }
</script>

<style>
</style>
```

Finally, we need to customize the build of Vue in order to configure the HTML template loader.

If you try to launch the application at this point, you'll probably get the following error:

```
Failed to compile.

./src/components/example.html 1:4
Module parse failed: Unexpected token (1:4)
You may need an appropriate loader to handle this file type.
> The message is: {{message}}
```

As the error indicates, no loader can currently handle the HTML files.

Just like the Angular CLI, Vue.js sports a **batteries included** Webpack build. Moreover, similar to Angular, Vue.js also allows us to tweak the build process as required. The official documentation covers this in detail:
https://cli.vuejs.org/guide/webpack.html.

 To learn more about configuring Vue, check out https://vuejs.org/v2/api/#Global-Config and https://cli.vuejs.org/config.

Create a vue.config.js file at the root of the project with the following content:

```
module.exports = {
    configureWebpack: {
        module: {
            rules: [
```

```
                {
                    test: /.html$/,
                    loader: "vue-template-loader",
                    exclude: /index.html/
                }
            ]
        }
    }
};
```

In this file, we have declared a Webpack *rule* that links `.html` files (except `index.html`) with `vue-template-loader`.

 This configuration will be merged with the rest of the Webpack configuration of Vue.js; this is how Vue supports the ability to customize the build process.

That's it! If you run the application, you should see the output that was shown in this example.

This was a bit tedious, but the good news is that these are manipulations that you only need to do *once*.

There are pros and cons to SFCs, and we won't argue about which approach is best. It'll be up to you and your team to decide.

Dependency injection

As we've already seen, **dependency injection (DI)** is a great pattern with huge benefits that helps us create loosely coupled elements. Let's look at how we can apply DI to Vue projects. This is something that's useful for us to understand and master.

Built-in support

Unfortunately, out of the box, Vue doesn't provide much support for dependency injection in its current version.

However, Vue does include two options: `provide` and `inject`. They are described in the official documentation (`https://vuejs.org/v2/api/#provide-inject`). These two options are normally intended for plugin development, but can actually be used in any Vue application. We'll see that we can leverage them in our applications to define/provide dependencies and inject them where needed.

Through the `provide` option, components can define elements that can be injected into any of their descendants using `inject`.

 This feature is quite similar to the `providers` array in Angular. As a matter of fact, it is also close to React's **context** feature, which we'll talk about later in this book.

We can also use `inject` to get access to *injectable* elements.

Here's a basic example of using the more classic Vue syntax:

```
// a parent component provides 'foo'
var Provider = {
  provide: {
    foo: 'bar'
  },
  // ...
}

// a child component injects 'foo'
var Child = {
  inject: ['foo'],
  created () {
    console.log(this.foo) // => "bar"
  }
  // ...
}
```

As you can see, it isn't too complicated.

TypeScript support

Now, let's take a look at an example of leveraging TypeScript support.

Let's assume that we have the following component tree:

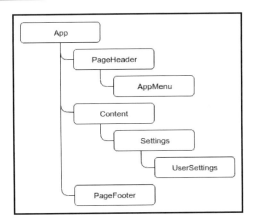

If we want to define a dependency that can be injected into the **UserSettings** component, then we can introduce a **provider** for it in any of its ancestors: **Settings**, **Content**, or **App**. Providers that are defined at the **App** level can be used anywhere in the component tree.

Once again, we can draw a parallel with Angular features since this **provider hierarchy is somewhat similar to Angular's injector tree**.

In the following example, we'll simply make a `username` string available for injection, but we could do the same with any other object type:

```ts
<template>
    <div id="app">
        <PageHeader />
        <Content />
        <PageFooter />
    </div>
</template>

<script lang="ts">
    import {Component, Vue} from 'vue-property-decorator';
    import PageHeader from '@/components/PageHeader.vue';
    import PageFooter from '@/components/PageFooter.vue';
    import Content from '@/components/Content.vue';

    @Component({
        components: {
            PageHeader,
            Content,
            PageFooter,
```

```
        },
        provide: {
            'username': 'dSebastien',
        },
    })
    export default class App extends Vue {
    }
</script>

<style>
</style>
```

We have simply used the `provide` property to define the value.

Take note of how the `App` component registers the `PageHeader`, `Content`, and `PageFooter` components. These are registered locally, as opposed to the global registration approach that we used earlier using `Vue.component(...)`. The advantage of declaring component dependencies locally is that it enables additional build optimizations, such as **tree shaking** and better **code splitting**: `https://vuejs.org/v2/guide/components-registration.html#Local-Reg istration`.

If you pay attention to the TypeScript imports, you'll see that there is a weird leading @ symbol before the path to the file to import. This is actually a TypeScript **path mapping** that's defined for us in the TypeScript compiler configuration (that is, in `tsconfig.json`) by the Vue CLI. We covered this concept in Chapter 5, *Coding WorldExplorer to Explore the Population of the World*.

Here is how we can inject the value into the `UserSettings` component:

```
<template>
    <div class="header">
        <h3>User settings</h3>
        <span>Username: {{username}}</span>
        <div>
            <label> Likes chocolate?
                <input type="checkbox" value="Like chocolate" v-
                model="likeChocolate" />
            </label>
        </div>
    </div>
</template>

<script lang="ts">
    import {Component, Inject, Vue} from 'vue-property-decorator';
```

```
@Component({})
export default class UserSettings extends Vue {
    @Inject('username')
    username!: string; // definite assignment assertion

    likeChocolate: boolean = true;
}
</script>

<style scoped>

</style>
```

As you can see, we've leveraged the `vue-property-decorator` library again to achieve more idiomatic TypeScript code. Injecting using a decorator feels natural if you've used Angular or the Spring framework in Java before.

In fact, `vue-property-decorator` also includes a decorator called `@Provide`. Here's how we can use it to declare a similar provider in a more TypeScript-friendly way:

```
export default class PageHeader extends Vue {
    @Provide("menu-title")
    menuContents: { title: string } = { title: "Foo" };
}
```

These examples are contrived, but convey how things work out of the box with Vue and TypeScript.

 You can find these code samples under `Chapter09/06-vue-injection-basic`.

By taking advantage of this basic dependency injection support, you can improve the maintainability of your code.

Limitations

Vue's dependency injection constructs help decouple your components, but there are some drawbacks that you should be aware of. Some of them can be mitigated, but others cannot.

For starters, Vue's injection feature works by matching the provider **key** with the one that was requested when injecting. This means that if you use the same injection **key** for multiple providers in the ancestor's chain of a component, then you'll shadow providers who are higher in the hierarchy. In practice, the last writer wins (that is, the provider closest to the injection point will be used). This is a drawback because it could cause surprises. We will address this issue in the next section.

Another limitation to consider is that the `provide` and `inject` bindings are (intentionally) not reactive, which means that changes won't be tracked by Vue, apart from if you inject objects that have already been observed by Vue's change tracking system: `https://vuejs.org/v2/guide/reactivity.html`.

One more drawback of Vue's DI support is that it cannot perform constructor injection. This is problematic with TypeScript because it means that our component class properties won't be fully initialized by the constructor, but set afterward. We'll see how we can work our way around this issue by leveraging TypeScript's **definite assignment assertions**, later in this book.

Moreover, Vue's DI support, since it's quite rudimentary, can only perform simple bindings between a provider and an injection point. If you have multiple implementations of a given interface, then the only way to distinguish those with regard to Vue's DI system is to create separate providers and have the **client** code be aware of those.

Finally, it is only possible to leverage this DI support from within Vue components, which means that you cannot wire other elements, such as services.

These limitations truly mean that we can't do **pure** dependency injection with Vue; we can only do basic things. Not all hope is lost, though, as future versions of Vue may improve this situation. Meanwhile, we can counter some of these limitations. Let's see how!

Improving our code with ES2015 symbols

The **key** issue (pun intended) that we mentioned previously can actually easily be avoided by leveraging ECMAScript **symbols**, a new primitive type that was introduced with ES2015 and is now well supported in all modern web browsers.

Symbols are interesting because every single one of them is *unique*; you cannot create the same Symbol twice:

```
const foo: Symbol = Symbol();
const bar: Symbol = Symbol();
console.log(foo === bar); // false
```

In the preceding example, foo and bar are *not* the same! A symbol is a primitive type that can't be recreated, unlike strings and numbers, for example. However, it shares the immutability property of the other primitives: once a symbol has been created, it cannot be modified.

When creating a Symbol, you can pass in a description using a string or number. This description is optional and only useful for debugging. Setting a symbol description doesn't have any impact on its uniqueness:

```
const theAnswer = Symbol(42);
const anotherAnswer = Symbol(42);

// The following would fail to compile in TypeScript but would just
return false in JavaScript
// here's the TypeScript error it triggers: TS2367: This condition
will always return 'false' since the types 'unique symbol' and 'unique
symbol' have no overlap.
//console.log(theAnswer === anotherAnswer); // false

const mySuperSymbol = Symbol('This is a fantastic symbol');
```

Before symbols were introduced in ECMAScript 2015, only strings could be used as object keys, but now symbols can also be used:

```
const mySymbol = Symbol('foo');
const myObject = {
    [mySymbol]: 'baz',
};

console.log(myObject[mySymbol]);
```

Actually, this usage pattern is the *raison d'être* of symbols: it provides us with a way to define unique object keys.related ones. Moreover, we'll become more versatile, given how powerful InversifyJS is compared to Vue's built-in DI support

We have to use [] around the `Symbol` here, otherwise, the object key would be the `mySymbol` string and not our actual symbol.

Now that we know what symbols are, we can leverage them to add more safety to our previous DI code.

Instead of using the same string key on the provider and injection sides, we can define, export, and use `Symbol`. This will ensure that we get precisely the dependency that we care about and not another one.

We'll leave this as an exercise for you, but you'll see this technique being used in practice in the upcoming sections.

You can find the examples that were used in this section in the assets folder of this book, under `Chapter09/symbols`.

Late binding and TypeScript definite assignment assertions

If you take a close look at the code for the previous `UserSettings` example component, you may notice a weird exclamation mark:

```
@Inject("username")
username!: string; // definite assignment assertion
```

Now, what is it and why did we need it?

As the official TypeScript documentation (https://www.typescriptlang.org/docs/handbook/release-notes/typescript-2-7.html#definite-assignment-assertions) states, **definite assignment assertions can be used to tell the compiler that variables will indeed be assigned, even if TypeScript can't determine this on its own.**

The definite assignment assertion is used through the `!` character, and is defined after a property or variable declaration.

If we consider the preceding code, at compile time, the type checker *cannot* possibly know that Vue's dependency injection system is going to provide the field's value after the object's construction.

From the type checker's point of view, once it is told that the value is not defined through an **initializer** or via a constructor, then the value is considered as not being properly initialized at construction time. Because of this, the compiler considers that the property could be `undefined`, which is not compliant with the defined type (at least in strict mode).

One way to fix this issue would be to change the type of the username field to `string | null | undefined`, but this is clearly not the best approach to take. We don't actually want our dependency to be `null` or `undefined`, and we don't want to be able to set it to such a value inadvertently.

Obviously, the better answer here is to use a definite assignment assertion, just like we did, since it allows the value to not be defined immediately at construction time, while still preventing us from intentionally setting the value to `null` or `undefined`, which is nice.

Of course, this workaround still leaves us with *weaker type safety* since any misconfiguration of the dependency injection could lead to errors that cannot be caught at compile time. These can only be caught at runtime.

If Vue had support for constructor injection like Angular does, then we wouldn't have this issue. We could check for the availability of our dependencies right away and we also wouldn't need to use this TypeScript feature.

The SL design pattern and InversifyJS

Now that we have a good understanding of the limitations of Vue's current DI system, we can take a look at alternatives and possible improvements.

One thing that we can do to improve the code is to leverage a third-party dependency injection library. In this section, we'll be using **InversifyJS** (`http://inversify.io`), a lightweight DI library written in TypeScript that acts as an IoC container.

InversifyJS supports setter injection and using symbols, just like Vue does, but it is much more powerful as it also supports the following:

- Controller injection
- Optional dependencies
- Default values
- Injecting factories
- Middleware

- Tagged and named bindings
- Circular dependencies
- Testing

By using InversifyJS, we will be able to configure *all* of our injectable elements, not just the Vue-related ones. Moreover, we'll become more versatile, given how powerful InversifyJS is compared to Vue's built-in DI support.

To integrate InversifyJS with Vue, we'll leverage symbols, `provide` and `inject`, and a design pattern called **Service Locator** (**SL**).

The SL pattern is an alternative way of reducing coupling between application components. With this design pattern, an object can use a *service locator* to create/retrieve the things it needs, without necessarily having to know too much about how those are constructed.

The SL pattern is not as great as pure DI/IoC, as we have seen with Angular, because it requires our code to be aware of the service locator. With pure DI/IoC, our code would receive its dependencies and would not need to have any knowledge about where those are coming from or how they're constructed.

The reason why using this pattern makes sense here is because Vue does not support constructor injection. Because of this, and in order to avoid abusing definite assignment assertions, we'll simply inject the service locator into our components. Once our components get hold of the service locator, they'll be able to use it to get instances of their dependencies, limiting the knowledge they require.

SL using InversifyJS and reflect-metadata

Let's make this more concrete with an example. We will create a simple Vue application with the following component tree:

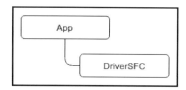

This application will simply render a **DriverSFC** component, which will display a message on the screen. To do so, it'll need to get/use a `Driver` object.

The `Driver` instance will, of course, need to be created, but the `DriverSFC` component will not know how to do so. As a matter of fact, the `Driver` instance will be created by InversifyJS and will be the only one that knows how to construct it.

To spice things up a bit, in order to create a `Driver` instance, InversifyJS will have to create a `Car` object of the correct subtype. It will need to know the following information:

- Instances of the `CalmDriver` type should be provided with an instance of `SilentCar`.
- Instances of the `CrazyDriver` type should be provided with an instance of `LoudCar`.

Here are the steps that we'll go through in this example:

1. Install InversifyJS.
2. Create the domain model and annotate it for dependency injection.
3. Configure the IoC container to wire everything together.
4. Use the `provide` option of Vue.js to make the IoC container instance available to all the components within the application.
5. Use the IoC container in a component to retrieve its dependencies without needing to use `new` (that is, the IoC container will serve as a service locator!).

 If you want to follow along, then the sources for this example are available in the code samples of this book under `Chapter09/07-vue-injection-inversify`.

Let's get started:

1. To install InversifyJS, we need its `npm` package, along with the `reflect-metadata` library. InversifyJS uses this library to add support for metadata on elements, which it does through decorators:

   ```
   npm install inversify reflect-metadata --save
   ```

   Once installed, we will be able to import and use Inversify in our code.

InversifyJS includes its own type definitions, so there's no need for an `@types/` dependency here.

2. Next, we need to make sure that the following compiler options are configured in `tsconfig.json` (at the very least):

   - `"experimentalDecorators": true`
   - `"emitDecoratorMetadata": true`
   - `"types": ["reflect-metadata", "tslib"]`

The `reflect-metadata` library allows us to perform **reflection** at runtime by attaching additional type metadata to the transpiled classes. To work, we need to enable the `emitDecoratorMetadata` option and load the `reflect-metadata` polyfill. This polyfill provides the `Reflect` object.

This may sound vague, but thanks to this, at runtime, libraries such as InversifyJS can find out design-time information such as the original type (`design:type`), the parameters (`design:paramtypes`), and the return type (`design:returntype`) of decorated elements. This allows those libraries to do interesting things at **runtime**, such as creating instances of specific classes dynamically.

Of course, you can do this too! The following example shows how we can retrieve the design-time type of a target element:

```
Reflect.getMetadata("design:type", target, key);
```

 In the previous chapters, we explained how decorators work and mentioned that they're on their way to becoming part of the language. Actually, the draft decorator's specification currently describes a `@metadata` decorator that will allow us to attach arbitrary metadata:

https://github.com/tc39/proposal-decorators#metadata.

The following are the base interfaces that we will use:

- The first one defines a `Car`:

```
export interface Car {
    type: string;
    makeNoise(): void;
}
```

- The second defines a `Driver`:

```
import {Car} from './car';

export interface Driver {
    description: string;
    car: Car;
}
```

Once again, we will program **against** interfaces. Our Vue component will not be aware of the existence of these implementations.

We will also have `CalmDriver` and `CrazyDriver`, as shown in the following code block:

```
import {Driver} from './driver';
import {inject, injectable, tagged} from 'inversify';
import {Car} from './car';
import {TYPES} from '@/ioc-types';
import {TAGS} from '@/ioc-tags';

@injectable()
export class CalmDriver implements Driver {

    public constructor(
        @inject(TYPES.CAR)
        @tagged(TAGS.CRAZY, false)
        private _car: Car,
    ) {
        console.log('Calm driver instance created');
    }

    public get car(): Car {
        return this._car;
    }

    public get description(): string {
        return `I'm a calm guy driving a ${this._car.type}`; }
}
```

As you can see, the implementation is straightforward.

> The `CrazyDriver` class is very similar; only its name and the `@tagged` annotation differ.

There are a few things to notice here:

- The class is marked as `injectable` using a decorator provided by InversifyJS.
- This is similar to Angular's `@Injectable` decorator.
- The `car` field is annotated with two additional InversifyJS decorators.

The `@inject` decorator instructs InversifyJS to inject an instance; in this case, this is identified by `Symbol` (as we'll see shortly).

The `@tagged` decorator tells InversifyJS to identify the exact type that we're interested in. Using this feature of InversifyJS is useful when there are multiple implementations of the same interface. The tag acts as a discriminator.

Here is how we have defined our `TYPES` constant:

```
export const TYPES = {
    CONTAINER: Symbol('CONTAINER'),
    DRIVER: Symbol('DRIVER'),
    CAR: Symbol('CAR'),
};
```

As you can see, we have simply defined a few symbols. We've used symbols here because they act as great **markers**.

The following is the definition of the tag that we have used:

```
export const TAGS = {
    CRAZY: Symbol('CRAZY'),
};
```

Again, the tag itself is simply another `Symbol`. Through the `@tagged` decorator, we have simply associated a value with that tag. In the case of `CrazyDriver`, we've associated it with `true`; and we've associated `false` with `CalmDriver`.

Now, we can take a look at the `ioc-config.ts` file, which is where we configure the IoC container of InversifyJS:

```
import 'reflect-metadata';

import {Container} from 'inversify';
import {Driver} from '@/domain/driver';
import {CalmDriver} from '@/domain/calm-driver';
import {LoudCar} from '@/domain/loud-car';
import {Car} from '@/domain/car';
import {SilentCar} from '@/domain/silent-car';
```

```
import {TYPES} from '@/ioc-types';
import {TAGS} from '@/ioc-tags';

export const container = new Container();

// configuration of our container
container.bind<Driver>(TYPES.DRIVER).to(CalmDriver);
container.bind<Car>(TYPES.CAR).to(LoudCar).whenTargetTagged(TAGS.CRAZY
, true); // crazy drivers drive loud cars
container.bind<Car>(TYPES.CAR).to(SilentCar).whenTargetTagged(TAGS.CRA
ZY, false); // calm drivers drive silent cars
```

We start by creating and exporting a `Container` instance. Then, we use the `bind` method of the container to associate a symbol with a specific class.

The simplest example is using `container.bind<Driver>(TYPES.DRIVER).to(CalmDriver);`, which binds `TYPES.DRIVER` to the `CalmDriver` class. With that binding defined, we can use `@inject(TYPES.DRIVER)` anywhere to ask InversifyJS to instantiate and inject that dependency.

Of course, that alone wouldn't be enough since the `Driver` implementations also have dependencies of their own. The next few lines actually define the additional required bindings.

These bindings use a more advanced form to determine which implementation to use, depending on the tags. This one, for example, binds the `LoudCar` implementation when the `CRAZY` tag is set to `true`:

```
container.bind<Car>(TYPES.CAR).to(LoudCar).whenTargetTagged(TAGS.CRAZY
, true);
```

Great – our model has been defined and the IoC container has been configured. But how can we bootstrap the application and get hold of our dependencies in the components?

Let's take look at the `App` component to see how the IoC container is defined and made available by the rest of the application:

```
<template>
    <div id="app">
        <DriverSFC />
    </div>
</template>

<script lang="ts">
```

```
import {Component, Provide, Vue} from 'vue-property-decorator';
import DriverSFC from '@/components/DriverSFC.vue';
import {container as iocContainer} from '@/ioc-config';
import {TYPES} from '@/ioc-types';
import {Container} from 'inversify';

@Component({
    components: {
        DriverSFC,
    },
})
export default class App extends Vue {
    @Provide(TYPES.CONTAINER)
    private container: Container = iocContainer;
}
</script>

<style>
</style>
```

In our template, we simply use the `DriverSFC` component (which we'll look at next). Then, in the App class, we use the `@Provide` decorator on a `Container` field:

```
@Provide(TYPES.CONTAINER)
private container: Container = iocContainer;
```

This `container` will be our service locator. Given that we have used `Symbol` to put a unique label on it, we will be able to retrieve it easily in `DriverSFC` using the `@Inject` decorator.

Finally, here is how we retrieve and use the `container` instance to fetch our dependencies from the `DriverSFC` component:

```
<template>
    <div class="hello">
        <h1>{{ driver }}</h1>
    </div>
</template>

<script lang="ts">
    import {Component, Inject, Vue} from 'vue-property-decorator';
    import {Container} from 'inversify';
    import {Driver} from '@/domain/driver';
    import {TYPES} from '@/ioc-types';

    @Component({})
    export default class DriverSFC extends Vue {
```

```
@Inject(TYPES.CONTAINER)
private _container!: Container;
private _driver!: Driver;

// Lifecycle hook
public created() {
    console.log('Initializing Driver');
    console.log('IoC container retrieved: ', this._container);
    this._driver = this._container.get<Driver>(TYPES.DRIVER);
    console.log('Retrieved driver: ', this._driver);
    console.log('Driver initialized');
}

public get driver(): string {
    return this._driver.description;
}
    }
}
</script>

<style scoped>

</style>
```

This is the final piece of this little puzzle: our component uses the `@Inject` decorator of `vue-property-decorator` to get the `Container` instance. Then, after its creation, it uses it to retrieve an instance of its `Driver` dependency.

Again, using the SL pattern is simply a workaround due to there being a lack of proper dependency injection support in Vue.js. However, as we have just seen, this provides us with a way to avoid using `new` ourselves, along with a solution to manage dependency graphs outside of Vue. As an added benefit, we also get the more advanced DI configuration capabilities that InversifyJS offers.

You can find the sources for this example in the code samples for this book, under `Chapter09/07-vue-injection-inversify`. If you install and execute this code, you'll see that `DriverSFC` gets its `Driver` instance and that it's properly initialized and configured. It actually gets a `CalmDriver` instance (since we've bound that implementation by default), along with a `SilentCar` instance.

> If you want good support for Vue.js in VS Code, then take a look at Vetur: `https://github.com/vuejs/vetur`.

However, we can do even better!

Better InversifyJS integration

It was interesting to discover the SL pattern, but, as we've seen, it isn't ideal. As a matter of fact, there are better ways for us to integrate InversifyJS.

As we've already discussed, the main issue of integrating InversifyJS and Vue.js is the fact that Vue handles the construction of the class instances, making it impossible for us to use constructor injection, and forcing us to use definite assignment assertions.

Let's discover and use the `inversify-inject-decorators` library (`https://github.com/inversify/inversify-inject-decorators`). This library provides a set of decorators that add support for *lazy injection* of InversifyJS-managed dependencies. With it, we will be able to *declare* our dependencies through decorators instead of having to retrieve them programmatically through a service locator. This library will take care of doing the lookup for us in the IoC container and inject the necessary dependencies.

Let's see how this works:

You can find the source code for this example in the code samples for this book under `Chapter09/08-vue-injection-inversify-improved`. If you wish to follow along, then just make a copy of the previous project (that is, `Chapter09/07-vue-injection-inversify`).

1. The first thing we need to do is add the library to our dependencies:

   ```
   npm install inversify-inject-decorators
   ```

   As usual, you can use either `npm` or `yarn`, depending on what you prefer.

We didn't specify `--save` here because `npm` does this automatically.

2. Next, we can remove everything related to InversifyJS from our `App.vue` file as we won't be using the SL pattern anymore:

   ```
   <template>
       <div id="app">
           <DriverSFC />
       </div>
   </template>
   ```

```
<script lang="ts">
    import {Component, Vue} from 'vue-property-decorator';
    import DriverSFC from '@/components/DriverSFC.vue';

    @Component({
        components: {
            DriverSFC,
        },
    })
    export default class App extends Vue {
    }
</script>

<style>
</style>
```

3. Finally, we can update our `DriverSFC.vue` file, as follows:

```
<template>
    <div class="hello">
        <h1>{{ driver }}</h1>
    </div>
</template>

<script lang="ts">
    import {Component, Vue} from 'vue-property-decorator';
    import {Driver} from '../domain/driver';
    import {TYPES} from '@/ioc-types';
    import {container} from '../ioc-config';
    import getDecorators from 'inversify-inject-decorators';

    const { lazyInject } = getDecorators(container);

    @Component({})
    export default class DriverSFC extends Vue {

        @lazyInject(TYPES.DRIVER)
        private _driver!: Driver;

        // Lifecycle hook
        public created() {
            console.log('Retrieved driver: ', this._driver);
            console.log('Driver initialized');
        }

        public get driver(): string {
            return this._driver.description;
        }
```

```
        }
    </script>

    <style scoped>

    </style>
```

As you can see, the following are the only things that we need to do now:

- Get a configured `lazyInject` decorator by calling the `getDecorators` function and passing it our InversifyJS container as follows: `const { lazyInject } = getDecorators(container);`
- Request the lazy injection of the `Driver` field using `@lazyInject(TYPES.DRIVER)`

Of course, this remains a post-construction injection and, hence, the definite assignment assertions remain necessary, but at least our component doesn't need to interact directly with the IoC container anymore.

This is a very useful improvement over our previous code and it brings us one step closer to a clean dependency injection design.

 You can reuse this approach with React, which also instantiates components and prevents controller injection.

Now, let's talk about the user interface component libraries for Vue.

User interface component libraries

There are many user interface component libraries to choose from when using Vue.js, just like all the popular frontend frameworks. In this section, we'll talk about a few of those libraries.

Vuetify

One of the most popular component toolkits for Vue is called **Vuetify** (`https://vuetifyjs.com/en`). It is based on the Material Design specification and implements almost 100 different components.

Vuetify is very easy to install thanks to its Vue CLI plugin (`https://github.com/vuetifyjs/vue-cli-plugin-vuetify`), which makes it possible for us to install Vuetify in a new project with a single CLI command:

```
vue add vuetify
```

Alternatively, Vuetify can also be installed through Vue UI.

 You can find the getting started guide for Vuetify here: `https://vuetifyjs.com/en/getting-started/quick-start`.

In this chapter, we won't be using Vuetify, simply because we want to explore a design system other than Material Design, but rest assured that Vuetify is a great choice.

Buefy

Another popular option for creating user interfaces with Vue is **Buefy** (`https://buefy.org`). This is a much lighter alternative (<100 KB) and is based on **Bulma** (`https://bulma.io`), a really nice CSS framework that leverages the Flexbox API.

With Buefy, you can easily create custom layouts, themes, and forms and use its user interface components. Buefy only includes a handful of components, but, for simpler applications, this may be enough.

Installing Buefy only requires a few steps, as described here: `https://github.com/buefy/buefy`.

Quasar

Quasar (`https://quasar-framework.org`) lies on the other side of the size/feature set spectrum. It is a large toolkit that helps create hybrid mobile applications with a native look and feel. Quasar can be used to create responsive web applications, PWAs, and desktop-like applications using **Electron**.

The advantage of Quasar is that it allows us to do all of this with a single code base rather than us having to create a separate client application per platform.

Quasar also includes many user interface components based on the Material Design specification, which are written as **web components**.

Finally, it even sports a CLI (`https://quasar.dev/quasar-cli`) to help us easily create new applications and scaffold pages, layouts, components, and many other things besides.

Quasar has a great user guide to get you started: `https://quasar.dev/introduction-to-quasar`.

We will not be using Quasar, but you should definitely give it a try.

Element

Element (`https://element.eleme.io`) is the last library that we'll discuss here and the one that we will be using for our application in the next chapter.

Element includes many user interface components (around 50) and is very simple to use.

 Interestingly, Element is available for Vue, React, and Angular.

As we'll see while developing our application, installing Element is really straightforward.

Here is a curated list of Element-related resources: `https://github.com/ElementUI/awesome-element`.

And many others

There are many other options out there, so feel free to explore them. Some of these are as follows:

- BootstrapVue: `https://bootstrap-vue.js.org`
- Vux: `https://github.com/airyland/vux`
- Vue Material: `https://vuematerial.io/`
- Fish-ui: `https://github.com/myliang/fish-ui`
- Muse-UI: `https://github.com/museui/muse-ui`

- View UI: `https://www.iviewui.com`
- Keen UI: `https://github.com/JosephusPaye/Keen-UI`

Routing

Like Angular and React, Vue.js has its own router. Vue's official router library is called the Vue Router (`https://router.vuejs.org`). Vue Router offers a really easy-to-use solution for managing **routing** on the client side with Vue.js.

While covering Angular in the previous chapters, we couldn't look at its router due to space constraints. In the next chapter, we'll take some time to introduce routing so that we can structure our application and learn how to leverage this important concept of modern web applications.

As we'll see, **the router will allow us to split our application into multiple pages and associate each of those with a specific route (URL). The Vue Router is a URL router**, as opposed to a *state router*, like the Angular router is. If you already know about Angular's router, you'll quickly see the difference between them.

Basically, the idea is that **a state router associates a set of components with a state, and states can be nested if needed**. Most importantly, a state router does not mandate each state to be associated with a different URL, while **a URL router uses URLs as the top-level concept**.

The Vue Router library is very powerful and has a broad feature set. For example, it supports route parameters/queries/wildcards, transition effects, fine-grained navigation control, the HTML 5 history API (which is used to update the browser's history while navigating within the client-side application), and much more.

While developing the LyricsFinder application in the next chapter, we'll only use a small subset of features of Vue Router, but don't hesitate to explore on your own. Installing, configuring, and using it will help you understand what it is and how it works.

State management for modern web applications

One subject that we haven't discussed so far in this book is **state management**.

Since modern web applications manage the state of the user interface on their own, they need to take great care of the consistency of the displayed data.

Components are a good way for us to decompose complex user interfaces into many smaller pieces, each taking care of specific parts of the UI, along with the data that those should render.

As the complexity of an application grows, it becomes more and more challenging to maintain data consistency across components. As soon as multiple components need to display the same data, there is a risk that one of those will not be aware of changes and will display stale/incorrect data to the user, leading to a bad user experience (at best).

Naive approach – propagating state changes using custom events and props

One approach to passing data around the application is to leverage custom events and component inputs (that is, props), as shown in the following schema:

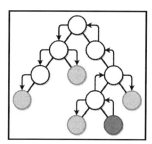

In this example, the component in dark gray has changed a piece of data and emits an event to let the rest of the application know about the modification. Components in light gray depend on this data and need to receive the new **state**.

As the diagram clearly depicts, the issue is obvious: for light gray components to receive the new state, many intermediary components need to receive it through props and emit it through events.

Of course, the more components there are in the tree and the more states to exchange, the worse it gets. This approach is not scalable at all.

Broadcasting state changes

Another solution that was popular a few years ago was to use a **broadcasting** mechanism, through which application code would simply emit custom **global** events, along with arbitrary data. The rest of the application was then able to retrieve the data and react to the changes by listening to those global events.

The advantage of broadcasting is that different and **unconnected** application components can easily communicate without us having to introduce strong coupling and without us needing many unrelated components to participate in the data exchange.

Broadcasting was actually supported in Vue.js 1.x through `$broadcast`, as well as in older AngularJS versions through `$rootScope.$broadcast`. These were never heavily recommended and have been deprecated/removed during the evolution of their respective frameworks.

For instance, the official migration guide from Vue 1.x to 2.0 proposed that we should use the following pattern to let distant components communicate with each other:

```
var eventHub = new Vue();

// Somewhere in the application
eventHub.$emit('add-todo', { text: this.newTodoText });

// Elsewhere in the application
eventHub.$on('add-todo', this.addTodo);
```

The idea simply consists of using a separate instance of Vue and using it as an *event hub*. This is possible because the `Vue` instance can be made *global* and it includes methods that we can use publish and react to events:

- Emit: `https://vuejs.org/v2/api/#vm-emit`
- Listen: `https://vuejs.org/v2/api/#vm-on`

Broadcasting is compelling, but has important drawbacks to be aware of.

If you start broadcasting events, then you're actually introducing the equivalent of global variables to your code base. Any application component can broadcast the same events and wreak havoc in the application.

Also, the more events you broadcast, the harder it'll become to track the application's logical flow.

Finally, broadcasting does not scale and rapidly makes application code hard to reason about (for example, what emitted an event and why?).

For those reasons, broadcasting only makes sense for very small applications.

Simple store pattern

For simple applications, the Vue.js documentation proposes a simple **store pattern**: `https://vuejs.org/v2/guide/state-management.html#Simple-State-Management-from-Scratch`.

The idea behind this simple pattern is to hold the application state in a **store**, acting as a *single source of truth* for the whole application. This store can be as simple as a global object holding the data state, along with methods that allow us to modify it (so as to keep those modifications under control).

Here's how this looks in practice (we've taken the following example from the official Vue guide):

```
const store = {
  debug: true,
  state: {
    message: 'Hello!'
  },
  setMessageAction (newValue) {
    if (this.debug) console.log('setMessageAction triggered with',
    newValue)
    this.state.message = newValue
  },
  clearMessageAction () {
    if (this.debug) console.log('clearMessageAction triggered')
    this.state.message = ''
  }
}
```

Using the data in the store is really simple:

```
const vmA = new Vue({
  data: {
    privateState: {},
    sharedState: store.state
  }
})

const vmB = new Vue({
```

```
  data: {
    privateState: {},
    sharedState: store.state
  }
})
```

Updating the store is as simple as calling the store methods, like so:

```
store.setMessageAction('foo');
```

Again, this pattern is only relevant for small applications.

Now, let's take a look at a more advanced solution that's more suited for medium to large applications.

Redux and the unidirectional data flow

During the last few years, some client-side state management solutions have gained traction and have become hugely popular in the JavaScript community. These include Flux and its **grandchild**, **Redux**, both of which were created by Facebook:

Both were introduced to try and solve the state management issue that impacted Facebook more and more as its user interface grew in size and complexity.

 Redux is related to React, but can actually be used with other frameworks, including Vue.js and Angular. There are also other implementations of Redux, such as NGRX (`https://github.com/ngrx`) for Angular, which makes use of RxJS.

We won't be using Redux in this book, but nevertheless, it is very interesting to understand what it is and how it works.

Redux aims to help you write applications that do the following:

- Behave consistently thanks to the *single source of truth* represented by the Redux **store**
- Run in different environments (for example, client, server, native)
- Remain easy to test

Redux (`https://redux.js.org`) is, in fact, both an *architectural pattern* and a *library*.

The Redux pattern prescribes how data/state changes should flow in the application so as to maximize predictability and consistency. Simply put, the Redux pattern recommends a **unidirectional data flow**. We'll discover what this actually means soon.

On the other hand, the main goal of the library is to provide a *predictable state container* or *store* for JavaScript applications.

Redux also focuses on the developer experience and provides great support for debugging. Notably, it supports **time travel debugging** through web browser extensions. The idea behind time travel debugging is that, through browser extensions, you can explore the content of the store, replay past events, or even go back in time.

With Redux, the **whole** state of the application is stored in an object tree within a store, which acts as the single source of truth for the whole application. Any component within the application can *subscribe* to the store and be *notified* whenever the subset of the stored data it cares about has changed.

Here's an updated version of the schema that we discussed earlier:

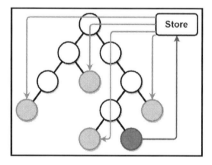

With this approach, when the component in dark gray pushes information into the store, all the light gray components that have subscribed are notified of the change. This is much more efficient than the naive approach of using custom events and props. It is also cleaner than blind broadcasting. This alone makes Redux a much more interesting solution, but it doesn't stop there.

If we zoom in a bit, we can see how the state data flows within the application:

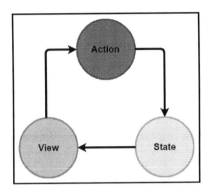

The component in dark gray triggers an **action**, which ends up updating the **state** of the application, which, in turn, causes an update of the **view**. This is the **unidirectional data flow**.

If we zoom in even further, then we can see what a pattern looks like in action:

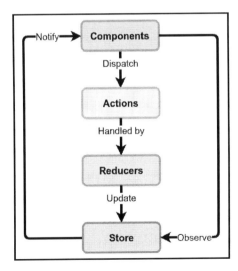

All of the components in the application dispatch **Actions**, which are handled by **Reducers**, which in turn update the store. Also, components can observe the store and the store will notify them whenever the *slice* of the state they care about has changed.

This way, the application's behavior can easily be *observed* and the data flow becomes clear and *predictable*.

With Redux, the store is also **immutable** and **read-only**. The only way to change it is to dispatch an action and let the reducers derive a new state. Deriving a new state means constructing a new state object tree, not mutating the existing one! This immutability constraint is the one that makes it possible to travel back in time. By keeping track of actions and store state changes, it becomes very easy to replay events and put the application back into a previous state (simply by replacing the current state with a previous one).

When an application follows the Redux pattern, it has to implement the following:

- **Actions**: These describe a change to make. Each action has a type (for example, SET_USERNAME) and an optional **payload**. Actions follow the **command design pattern**.
- **Reducers**: These determine whether and how the state changes in response to actions. Reducers update the state tree in the store:
    - The input for a reducer is the current state, as well as an action
    - The output of a reducer is a new state (again, the existing state is not mutated!)
- **Store structure**: The store should be considered as a database that contains a tree of data that will be manipulated by the reducers as a result of their actions:
    - In JavaScript, the store can be a **Plain Old JavaScript Object (POJO)**.

So, what data should be put inside the store?

- The UI and the related state that should be kept when switching between views (for example, data that allows us to restore the state of a search form when navigating back to a previous screen)
- Data that allows us to **rehydrate** the store when the application starts (that is, restore the state of the application when it is accessed anew)

In any case, don't go overboard: only the state that is relevant to one component should remain local to it. **The store is only useful for shared states**.

> The store is actually a *tree* data structure; you can organize its content as you see fit (flat, nested – whatever you want). Usually, the recommendation is to *normalize* the state tree in order to limit the difficulty of updating it. This means we avoid having the same information in multiple places. You can find out more about this here: `https://redux.js.org/recipes/structuring-reducers/normalizing-state-shape`.

As we've already mentioned, Redux can be used with Vue.js, as explained at the following link: `https://snipcart.com/blog/redux-vue`.

A note about pure functions

Redux reducers should be **pure functions**. As we discussed earlier in this chapter, pure functions are related to functional programming and are supposed to be **stable**. Given the same inputs, they should always return the same outputs. To guarantee that, pure functions cannot rely on the external state. Also, pure functions should not have side effects.

Here's a useful reference to understand what pure functions are: `https://medium.com/javascript-scene/master-the-javascript-interview-what-is-a-pure-function-d1c076bec976#.uw1h6nv66`.

With Redux, reducers are organized as a tree; each reducer only takes care of specific action types.

VueX

VueX (`https://vuex.vuejs.org`) is the official state management library that's offered by Vue.js. VueX is mainly useful for medium- and large-sized applications. For small ones, the signal-to-noise ratio is too low to really justify it.

To understand what VueX is about and how it works, start by taking a look at the official schema of VueX:

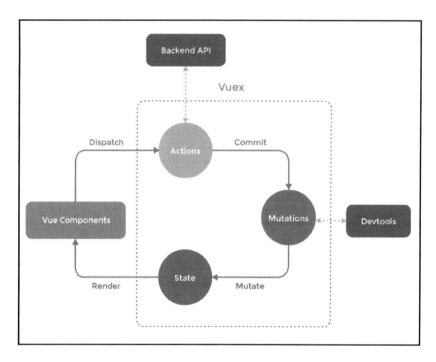

Does it look familiar to you now that we've learned about Redux? Indeed it does! Vuex is actually heavily inspired by Flux and Redux (among others).

The major benefit of VueX, compared to Redux, is the fact that it is made specifically for Vue.js and thus integrates perfectly with it. In addition, VueX is also supported by the Vue dev tools that we covered earlier in this chapter.

 If you need to select a state management solution for your next Vue.js project, then you need to determine whether you care about the *framework independence* of the solution. If you do, then favor Redux, as you'll be able to reuse your code with another frontend framework. If you don't, then go for VueX as it will provide the best integration.

In this section, we'll concentrate on explaining the concepts of VueX.

Just like Redux, at the core of VueX lies the store. As we've already learned, **the store is a single object in which the application state is held and that acts as the single source of truth for the rest of the code**.

Creating a VueX store is straightforward. The following is an example that's been taken from the official VueX documentation:

```
const store = new Vuex.Store({
  state: {
    todos: [
      { id: 1, text: '...', done: true },
      { id: 2, text: '...', done: false }
    ]
  },
  getters: {
    doneTodos: state => {
      return state.todos.filter(todo => todo.done)
    }
  }
})
```

The `state` object holds the current state of the application. In the `getters` object, we can define functions that derive things from the state (what those functions get as their first arguments).

> **You can think of those getter functions as computed properties for the store**. Getters are great if we wish to create multiple representations of the same store data without mutating it. This can eliminate some duplication in your components. Another name for getters in the context of Redux-like libraries such as VueX is **selectors**; their role is to select/extract some piece(s) of information out of the store.

Since VueX is nicely integrated with Vue.js, the store can be passed as an option in the `Vue` object. Doing so will automatically inject the store into all of the Vue components as `this.$store`, making it really easy to access and use.

Here's an example of doing this:

```
const app = new Vue({
  el: '#app',
  // provide the store using the "store" option.
  // this will inject the store instance to all child components.
  store,
  components: { Counter },
  template: `
    <div class="app">
      <counter></counter>
    </div>
  `
})
```

Since components will be injected with the store, they can easily retrieve data out of it. Components should usually use computed properties for this since they will be updated whenever the state changes.

Here is an example of this:

```
const Counter = {
  template: `<div>{{ count }}</div>`,
  computed: {
    count () {
      return this.$store.state.count;
    },
  },
};
```

Getters can be accessed as properties using the following syntax:

```
store.getters.<name>
```

Getters can also be called as functions, which is useful if you need to pass input.

If your component needs to use multiple pieces of the store's state, then it can be tedious to declare all of the computed object functions. To make this easier, VueX provides a helper called `mapState`, which will create those functions on the fly for you. This is explained in the official guide: `https://vuex.vuejs.org/guide/state.html#the-mapstate-helper`. VueX also provides a `mapGetters` helper so that we can map store getters to local computed properties.

Changing the VueX store's state is done by performing **mutations**. Mutations are akin to reducers in Redux. They are functions that receive the current state as its first argument, receive other arguments, and modify the state if needed.

Here's an example of this:

```
const store = new Vuex.Store({
  state: {
    count: 1,
  },
  mutations: {
    increment (state, incrementBy) {
      // mutate state
      state.count += incrementBy;
    },
  },
});
```

Since the VueX store is *reactive,* when a mutation occurs, all the components that watch the corresponding part of the state tree are updated automatically.

Like in Redux, reducers are never called directly. Declaring a mutation just states that *this is what should be done when this mutation needs to occur.* As such, mutation functions implement the logic that we need in order to react to specific *events.* The event that a mutation reacts to is simply defined as its function name. In the previous example, the event name is increment.

To trigger a mutation, store.commit must be called and provided with the mutation/event name, along with any additional arguments that are expected by the mutation function (this is optional).

Here's an example:

```
store.commit('increment', 10);
```

Another way to trigger a mutation is by using syntax that's closer to that of Redux:

```
store.commit({
  type: 'increment',
  incrementBy: 10,
});
```

When using this style, the object that's passed to the `commit` method is passed as a payload to the mutation function:

```
mutations: {
  increment (state, payload) {
    state.count += payload.incrementBy;
  },
},
```

Notice how simple it is to declare the mutation.

> In a mutation function, if you want to add/remove a single property to/from an existing object of the state tree, you can use the ES2015 **object spread syntax**. Here's an example: `state.obj = { ...  state.obj, newProp: 123 }`. This is necessary because of how reactivity is currently implemented in Vue. This will create a (shallow) copy of all the properties of `state.obj` in a new object and will add/set the `newProp` property to/on it. You can learn more about this very useful syntax
> at `https://github.com/tc39/proposal-object-rest-spread`
> and `https://alligator.io/typescript/object-rest-spread`.

Finally, mutations can also be committed easily using the `mapMutations` helper that's provided by VueX. This simply maps component methods to calls toward `$store.commit(...)`.

VueX mutations must be *synchronous*. If you need to perform asynchronous operations, then you should use **actions** instead (`https://vuex.vuejs.org/guide/actions.html#actions`). Actions differ from mutations in that, instead of mutating the state, they actually commit mutations. As such, you can think of them as layers on top of mutations.

Here's a simple example that's been taken from the official guide:

```
const store = new Vuex.Store({
  state: {
    count: 0,
  },
  mutations: {
    increment (state) {
      state.count++;
    },
  },
  actions: {
    increment (context) {
      context.commit('increment');
    },
  },
});
```

As we can see, actions receive a `context` object as an argument. This object has the same methods and properties as the store object, so you can use it to call `context.commit`, `context.getters`, and many others.

As stated in the official guide, you can use ES2015 **argument destructuring** to easily access the commit function (or anything else you fancy, actually). Here is how it works: `increment ({ commit })` `{ ... }`. Notice `{}` around `commit` in the arguments list. The idea here is that we're only taking the `commit` property/function from the argument that was passed to the function. With that, `commit` can be called directly. You can learn more about destructuring here: `https://github.com/lukehoban/es6features#destructuring`.

To trigger an action, you simply need to call `store.dispatch('increment');`. This is very similar to how things work with Redux and NGRX (the Redux inspired state management solution for Angular).

When calling `dispatch`, you can also use the object syntax for mutations.

Here's a more elaborate example:

```
actions: {
  checkout ({ commit, state }, products) {
    // save the items currently in the cart
    const savedCartItems = [...state.cart.added];
    // send out checkout request, and optimistically
    // clear the cart
    commit(types.CHECKOUT_REQUEST);
    // the shop API accepts a success callback and a failure callback
    shop.buyProducts(
      products,
      // handle success
      () => commit(types.CHECKOUT_SUCCESS),
      // handle failure
      () => commit(types.CHECKOUT_FAILURE, savedCartItems),
    );
  },
},
```

The `checkout` action uses argument **destructuring** to get the `commit` and `state` properties out of the first function argument. It also accepts a list of products. Inside the function, the **object spread** syntax is used to get the items (held inside the state tree) and put them into a new array:

```
[...state.card.added]
```

The `commit` function is called and then an asynchronous operation is performed (that is, an external API is called). When the response is received, the results are committed too, triggering the appropriate mutations.

Actions can also be chained/composed using `async` and `await`:

```
actions: {
  async actionA ({ commit }) {
    commit('gotData', await getData());
  },
  async actionB ({ dispatch, commit }) {
    await dispatch('actionA'); // wait for `actionA` to finish
    commit('gotOtherData', await getOtherData());
  },
},
```

Here's a useful summary of the VueX store structure:

```
const store = new Vuex.Store({
  state: {
  },
  getters: {
  },
  mutations: {
  },
  actions: {
  },
});
```

In larger applications, the store can be modularized. For example, you could isolate the state that's used in a specific part of the application and put it in a dedicated store module.

In conclusion, the VueX library is really approachable because there are only a few key concepts to learn about and the syntax isn't hard to grasp. There's more to say about VueX, but we need to stop here. Check out the *Further reading* section at the end of this chapter for more information.

Summary

In this chapter, we have continued our exploration of modern web frameworks with Vue.js. We hope that you're enjoying the trip as much as we are!

We have seen that Vue.js has many similarities with Angular, but is also *much lighter* than its larger cousin. Vue has its own merits, and clearly its learning curve is not as steep as Angular's.

We have actually covered a good portion of the basic features of Vue, which should have given you a decent overview of its capabilities.

We hope you have appreciated how simple it was for us to use TypeScript with Vue.js and its surrounding libraries. Overall, the level of support for TypeScript is quite good already, and the next few iterations of Vue.js will keep on improving the situation. There's no doubt about it: TypeScript is gaining in popularity and is here to stay.

In this chapter, we have also discussed state management. We have covered the main concepts of Redux (for example, the one-way data flow) and seen how VueX works and how close it is to Redux.

We've also learned about symbols, which are very useful if we want to get truly *unique* immutable references. We also looked at how we can leverage them with InversifyJS to integrate better dependency injection support into Vue.js applications! This is very useful to know about since the DI support for Vue is rather primitive at the moment. Using InversifyJS allows us to improve the quality of our code. As an added benefit, the same approach can actually be used with React as well.

In the next chapter, we will write a new application using Vue: LyricsFinder!

Further reading

Here are some useful resources related to the subjects that we covered in this chapter:

Vue

The following references are related to Vue:

General

General references pertaining to Vue:

- Sources related to Vue.js can be found on GitHub: `https://github.com/vuejs/vue`
- API: `https://vuejs.org/v2/api`
- Cookbook: `https://vuejs.org/v2/cookbook`
- Official style guide: `https://vuejs.org/v2/style-guide`
- Official blog: `https://medium.com/the-vue-point`
- Official roadmap: `https://github.com/vuejs/vue/projects`
- Structuring Vue projects: `https://medium.com/glovo-engineering/how-to-structure-your-vue-project-for-the-long-term-657817a2a002`

Components

The following are some useful links pertaining to components if you want to learn more:

- **Component Basics:** https://vuejs.org/v2/guide/components.html
- **Component Props:** https://vuejs.org/v2/guide/components-props.html
- **Component Slots:** https://vuejs.org/v2/guide/components-slots.html
- **Dynamic & Async Components:**
  https://vuejs.org/v2/guide/components-dynamic-async.html

Computed properties

The following references relate to computed properties:

- **Computed Properties and Watchers:**
  https://vuejs.org/v2/guide/computed.html
- **Computed Setter:**
  https://vuejs.org/v2/guide/computed.html#Computed-Setter

Filters

The following references relate to filters:

- **Filters:** https://vuejs.org/v2/guide/filters.html
- **Filter examples:** https://scotch.io/tutorials/how-to-create-filters-in-vue js-with-examples

Mixins

The following references relate to `mixins`:

- **Official documentation:** https://vuejs.org/v2/guide/mixins.html
- **Related article:** https://css-tricks.com/using-mixins-vue-js

Render functions

The following references relate to functions:

- Render functions: https://vuejs.org/v2/guide/render-function.html
- The arguments of the createElement function: https://vuejs.org/v2/guide/render-function.html#createElement-Arguments

Testing support

You can learn more about testing support here:

- Unit testing: https://vuejs.org/v2/guide/unit-testing.html
- Vue testing utilities: https://vue-test-utils.vuejs.org
- Cookbook for unit testing Vue components: https://vuejs.org/v2/cookbook/unit-testing-vue-components.html

Router

The following references relate to the Vue Router:

- Vue Router home page: https://router.vuejs.org
- Vue Router sources: https://github.com/vuejs/vue-router

VueX

The following references relate to VueX:

- Official state management guide: https://vuejs.org/v2/guide/state-management.html
- VueX documentation: https://vuex.vuejs.org
- VueX sources: https://github.com/vuejs/vuex
- vuex-class: https://github.com/ktsn/vuex-class
- Alternative: https://snipcart.com/blog/redux-vue

TypeScript

The following references are related to TypeScript:

Symbols

You can learn more about symbols here:

- MDN – Symbol documentation:
  `https://developer.mozilla.org/en-US/docs/Web/JavaScript/Reference/Global_Objects/Symbol`
- *JavaScript Symbols: But Why?*:
  `https://medium.com/intrinsic/javascript-symbols-but-why-6b02768f4a5c`

10
Creating LyricsFinder with Vue.js

Now that we have discovered the main concepts of Vue, we will build a new application together, which will make things much more concrete and clear.

In this chapter, we have decided to create a tool to find artists, songs, and lyrics using Vue.js. We'll call this application **LyricsFinder**.

While implementing it, we will take advantage of Vue, but also TypeScript, of course!

We cover the following topics in this chapter:

- High-level design and technical stack
- Getting started with the project
- Getting a MusixMatch API key
- Configuring InversifyJS
- Creating the home view
- Implementing the basic layout of the application
- Creating the search component and using Vue slots
- Handling search using `MusicService`
- Creating and using the songs list component
- Creating and using the lyrics view

What will you build?

It is now time for us to develop a new application together!

To fetch information about artists, songs, and lyrics, our application will interact with the MusixMatch (`https://www.musixmatch.com`) API. MusixMatch is an online service that has a catalog of more than 14 million lyrics in more than 50 languages.

The user interface of the application will be quite rudimentary. The home page will provide a single input field. Once a search is executed, LyricsFinder will try to find matching artists and songs based on the search criteria.

When the user selects a song in the list, they will be presented with a view showing the lyrics of that song (if they are available). On that screen, the user will also have a link to go back to the home page.

This is simple, but it will allow us to use many of the concepts that we introduced in the previous chapter.

Let's get started!

High-level design and technical stack

Before we start writing our application, let's have a look at the high-level design and the technical stack we are going to use.

Schema

For this new application, we'll keep the high-level design simple:

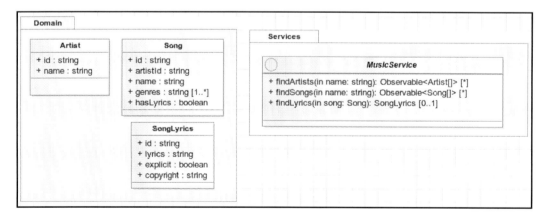

As we can see in the diagram, our domain model will be composed of a few concepts: `Artist`, `Song`, and `SongLyrics`. To get access to instances of those objects, our application will use `MusicService`, which will take care of interacting with the MusixMatch API. The service will also handle the deserialization of the MusixMatch responses into our domain model concepts.

Music service

To make the HTTP requests, our music service will use Axios (`https://github.com/axios/axios`), a popular and easy-to-use `Promise`-based HTTP client library.

Our service will also use the `io-ts` library to validate the payloads and ensure that the responses match our expectations.

Since we prefer `Observable` instances to `Promise` instances for reasons explained in `Chapter 7`, *Discovering Angular, Angular Material, and RxJS*, we will use RxJS (`https://rxjs-dev.firebaseapp.com`) to convert from `Promise` to `Observable` instances.

Instead of Axios, we could've used `rx-http-request` (`https://www.npmjs.com/package/@akanass/rx-http-request`), a TypeScript and RxJS-based rewrite of a popular HTTP client called request (`https://github.com/request/request`). We didn't do it simply to show you how you can **wrap** a `Promise`-based API with RxJS.

Finally, we will use InversifyJS to add dependency injection support, along with the `inversify-inject-decorators` library that we covered in the previous chapter.

User interface

To create the user interface of LyricsFinder, we will install and use the Element components library. We will be creating single-file Vue.js components, which is preferable for simplicity's sake, given the small size of our application.

The user interface will really contain two main views (that is, pages):

- The home view, where we will be able to search for artists and songs
- The lyrics view, which will display song lyrics

To handle the navigation between those views, we will use the Vue Router library, which we introduced in the previous chapter.

TypeScript

Of course, since we're focusing our attention on TypeScript in this book, we'll leverage it as much as we can throughout the application.

Getting started

Let's start by creating the project and analyzing the structure we need.

Creating the project

We've prepared a skeleton for the project, which you can find in the book's assets under `Chapter10/lyricsfinder-initial`.

The skeleton already includes Vue, InversifyJS, RxJS, and Axios.

More importantly, the domain and service layers are already included in the skeleton, along with a number of unit tests. This means that all the wiring has already been done to retrieve information about artists, songs, and lyrics.

We have done this so that we can concentrate on integrating and using Vue in the higher layers of the application.

 Don't hesitate to dive into the service layer code to understand how it works. Since we have used a test-driven development approach, the best place to start your investigation is the test suite of the music service, located in `src/services/music-service.spec.ts`.

Follow these steps:

1. Copy the `Chapter10/lyricsfinder-initial` folder in your workspace.
2. Install the project dependencies using `npm install`.

You can validate that everything is in order by executing `npm test` from the root folder of the project. All tests should be green.

If you're really curious, you might notice that we have customized the TSLint and Jest configuration files. TSLint has been made stricter, while Jest has been configured to also include test files within the `src` folder.

We can now start the application.

Starting the development server

To start the server, simply execute `npm run serve` in the project's root folder. Look at the console to find the port number that the server listens on.

Project structure and conventions

Even if Vue.js is small and lightweight, we need to properly organize our code to make it easier to locate elements. We can, of course, apply the LIFT pattern recommended by Angular.

Here's an overview of the project's `src` folder structure that we will use:

```
├──── api-key.ts        # holds the API key for the MusixMatch
├──── App.vue           # application's root component
├──── main.ts           # entry point
├──── assets/           # images, fonts, ...
├──── components/       # Vue.JS components (i.e., dumb components)
├──── domain/           # domain model
├──── ioc/              # InversifyJS configuration, types and tags
├──── mixins/           # Vue.JS mixins
├──── router/           # router configuration
├──── services/         # application services
├──── store/            # VueX store, actions and mutations
├──── styles/           # project-specific CSS stylesheets
├──── views/            # Vue.JS page components (i.e., smart components)
```

We could decompose things further into modules, but it wouldn't make sense for a small application like ours. If you are interested in how to structure larger applications, then take a look at the following article: `https://medium.com/3yourmind/large-scale-vuex-applic ation-structures-651e44863e2f`.

Next to the code structure, we also need to pay attention to naming and code style conventions.

Luckily for us, Vue.js also has an official style guide that you can find at `https://vuejs.org/v2/style-guide`. We'll try to respect it while developing our application.

We have chosen to use kebab-case for TypeScript files and PascalCase for `.vue` files. Of course, this is just a matter of taste; the most important thing is to stay consistent. For interfaces, we'll continue to use the `intf.ts` suffix.

Getting a MusixMatch API key

The MusixMatch API cannot be used anonymously. For this reason, you'll need to sign up for an account over at `https://developer.musixmatch.com/signup`.

Don't worry; this is free. The MusixMatch API's free tier will allow us to do enough for the purposes of this book. If you skip this, you won't be able to use the live API. Once you have filled in the registration form, you'll get a confirmation email.

Once your account has been confirmed, go to your applications administration page over at `https://developer.musixmatch.com/admin/applications`. There, you should see a default application listed. Click on the **View** button next to it to see its details.

On the details page, you should find your API key. Go ahead and add it to the `src/api-key.ts` file.

Configuring InversifyJS

As we've explained, the service layer is already implemented, but InversifyJS hasn't been fully configured yet. Let's do it now and make sure that we can use dependency injection to get an instance of the `MusicService` service.

First off, add a few symbols to the `src/ioc/types.ts` file:

```
export const TYPES = {
  MUSIC_SERVICE: Symbol('MUSIC_SERVICE'),
  MUSIXMATCH_BASE_URL: Symbol('MUSIXMATCH_BASE_URL'),
  AXIOS_INSTANCE: Symbol('AXIOS-INSTANCE'),
};
```

We'll use `MUSIC_SERVICE` `Symbol` as the unique token for the music service.

Next, adapt the `MusicService` implementation in `src/services/music-service.ts` to introduce the necessary InversifyJS decorators:

1. Add the following imports on top:
   `import {inject, injectable} from 'inversify';`.
2. Add `@injectable()` to the class.
3. Add `@inject(TYPES.MUSIXMATCH_BASE_URL)` above the `baseUrl` constructor argument.
4. Add `@inject(TYPES.AXIOS_INSTANCE)` above the `axios` constructor argument.

Thanks to these decorators, InversifyJS will know that the class is **injectable** and that it needs to inject the constructor arguments.

Next, modify the IoC configuration in the `src/ioc/config.ts` file like this:

```
import {Container} from 'inversify';
import {TYPES} from '@/ioc/types';
import {MusicService, MusicServiceImpl} from '@/services';
import getDecorators from 'inversify-inject-decorators';
import {AxiosInstance} from 'axios';
import axios from 'axios';

export const container = new Container();

// configuration of our container
container.bind<string>(TYPES.MUSIXMATCH_BASE_URL).toConstantValue('htt
ps://cors-anywhere.herokuapp.com/http://api.musixmatch.com/ws/');
container.bind<AxiosInstance>(TYPES.AXIOS_INSTANCE).toConstantValue(ax
ios);
container.bind<MusicService>(TYPES.MUSIC_SERVICE).to(MusicServiceImpl)
;

export const { lazyInject } = getDecorators(container);
```

That's it! Now InversifyJS knows about our service and its dependencies (`axios` and the API base URL). We can now inject it!

 If you take a look at the `src/main.ts` file, you'll see that we have already imported the `reflect-metadata` polyfill there. That way, it is globally available for our application.

Let's now create the home view of the application.

Creating the home view

Now that our `MusicService` is ready for use through injection, let's focus on the Vue application.

Creating the skeleton

Let's create our home view. At first, we'll keep it really basic. We just need to introduce it for now (you'll see why in a minute) but don't worry, as we will come back to it real soon.

Go ahead and create a `src/views/Home.vue` file.

Add the following code to it:

```ts
<template>
  <div class="lf-home-vue">
    <h1>LyricsFinder v1 - Home</h1>
    <span>Coming soon...</span>
  </div>
</template>

<script lang="ts">
  import {Component, Vue} from 'vue-property-decorator';

  @Component({})
  export default class Home extends Vue {
    // Lifecycle hook
    public mounted() {
      console.log('Home component mounted');
    }
  }
</script>

<style scoped>

</style>
```

As you can see, this is a simple SFC.

Let's put it aside for now and see how we can display it.

Installing and configuring Vue Router

Now that we have a first view (even if an overly simplistic one), we can display it. To do so, we will now install and configure Vue Router in our application:

1. Install the library:

   ```
   npm install vue-router
   ```

2. Once installed, modify the src/router/router.ts file as follows:

   ```
   import VueRouter from 'vue-router';
   import Home from '@/views/Home.vue';

   export const router = new VueRouter({
     mode: 'history',
     base: '', // useful for sub-domains
     routes: [
       { path: '/', component: Home },
       { path: '/home', component: Home },
       { path: '*', redirect: '/' },
     ],
   });
   ```

There are a few things to know about this code:

- We first import VueRouter: This is the class that is used to create a router instance and configure it.
- In this file, we create and export an instance of VueRouter.
- We have set the mode option to 'history': This is useful to get nicer looking URLs. This leverages the History API of modern web browsers (that is, history.pushState).
- We have defined an array of routes. Each route is composed of path and component.
- Our / and /home routes are associated with the Home component.
- We have also defined a wildcard route that redirects to /. Thanks to this, even if the user types the wrong URL, they'll get back to the home page.

The default mode for the router is hash, which uses a URL fragment (that is, http://some-url#some-route) instead of the History API. Using the History API and changing the URL requires the web server hosting the application to perform redirects towards the index.html file in case of 404 errors. The webpack development server does it, but for production, it is something that must be considered.

Don't hesitate to check out the documentation of Vue Router if you want to learn more about what is possible: https://router.vuejs.org/guide.

Our router is now configured, but we haven't told Vue to use it. Let's do that right away.

Modify the src/main.ts file as follows:

```
import './polyfills';
import './styles/lyricsfinder.css';

import Vue from 'vue';
import App from './App.vue';
import VueRouter from 'vue-router';
import {router} from '@/router/router';

Vue.config.productionTip = false;

Vue.use(VueRouter);

new Vue({
  render: (h) => h(App),
  router, // shorthand for router: router
}).$mount('#app');
```

The changes are very simple:

- First, we have told Vue to use the router with Vue.use(VueRouter);.
- Second, we have associated the router configuration with our Vue instance using router.

We are almost there! The last thing that we need to do is to display the component associated with the **active route**.

The active route is the one for which there is currently a (URL) match in the router configuration. Given that we have configured a catch-all route, there will always be an active route in our application.

Go ahead and do the following:

1. Open the `src/App.vue` file.
2. Replace the `div` contents with `<router-view></router-view>`.

The `<router-view>` tag is where the component associated with the active route will be rendered by Vue.

That's it! If you now open the application in your web browser, you should see the rendered `Home` view:

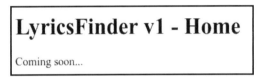

This demonstrates that the `Home` view associated with the default route has been loaded as expected.

If you take a look at the Vue developer tools, you should clearly see that the `Home` component is loaded:

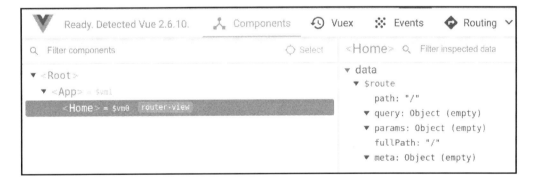

On the right side of the image, notice the `$route` variable within the data of the `Home` component. As we explained earlier, all components have access to the current route information.

While you're in the developer tools, also take a look at the **Routing** tab:

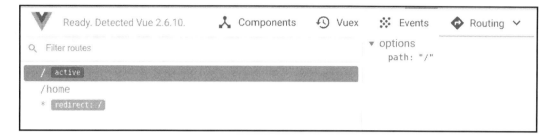

Vue Router is well integrated, and you can easily inspect the routes configuration, see which route is currently active, and many other things.

 If you're using VS Code, then note that you can install the Vetur extension, dedicated to Vue.JS: `https://marketplace.visualstudio.com/items?itemName=octref.vetur`.

Let's continue.

Installing and configuring Element

We are now going to add the Element component library to the project.

As usual, the installation starts with `npm`:

```
npm install element-ui
```

Once installed, we need to load Element and associate it with Vue. There are two approaches:

1. Load all Element components at once.
2. Load only the Element components that we actually need.

 For simplicity, we'll use the first approach, but keep in mind that the alternative is probably better for production code. You can find more details here: `https://element.eleme.io/#/en-US/component/quickstart`.

Open the `src/main.ts` file:

1. Import the Element library reset stylesheet: `import 'element-ui/lib/theme-chalk/reset.css';`.
2. Import the Element library stylesheet: `import 'element-ui/lib/theme-chalk/index.css';`.
3. Import `ElementUI`: `import ElementUI from 'element-ui';`.
4. Import the English locale: `import * as enLocale from 'element-ui/lib/locale/lang/en';`.
5. Register the Element components with Vue: `Vue.use(ElementUI, { locale: enLocale });`.

Element's default language is Chinese, which is why we have loaded a custom locale.

Great, now we can use Element in our application!

Implementing the basic layout of the application

We will now add some chrome to our application. Let's see how quickly we can create a simple layout for LyricsFinder using Element.

Out of the box, Element offers support for defining layouts using a 24-column **grid system** through its `el-row` and `el-column` components.

Those components are easy to use and powerful. You can easily define multiple rows and columns, with different spacing between columns, different alignments, offsets, and many more things.

All Element components are prefixed by `el-`, for example, `el-card`.

Responsive web design is also supported by Element. Multiple **breakpoints** are defined by default: xs, sm, md, lg, and xl. These allow us to create a responsive interface that adapts nicely to the available screen real estate.

 Element also provides classes for hiding elements based on breakpoints: https://element.eleme.io/#/en-US/component/layout.

In addition to its grid system, Element also includes **container** components, which are useful for clearly structuring pages. These include the following:

- el-container: Wrapper for other elements
- el-header: Container for the header
- el-aside: Container for side elements (for example, a side menu)
- el-main: Container for the main content
- el-footer: Container for the footer

Those container components all use the Flexbox API. We will use them in LyricsFinder.

First of all, open the src/App.vue file and replace the template tag with the following code:

```
<template>
  <el-container class="lf-wrapper">
    <el-header height="150px" class="lf-header">
      <el-image :src='require(`@/assets/logo.png`)' class="lf-header-
        logo" fit="contain" lazy/>
    </el-header>
    <el-main class="lf-main">
      <el-row type="flex">
        <el-col :span="4"></el-col>
        <el-col :span="16">
          <router-view></router-view>
        </el-col>
        <el-col :span="4"></el-col>
      </el-row>
    </el-main>
    <el-footer class="lf-footer">
      Powered by TypeScript and Vue.JS!
    </el-footer>
  </el-container>
</template>
```

Here are a few things that you should notice:

- The top-level element in our template is `el-container`, and it has become a wrapper for the whole application. Within it, elements are organized vertically because we have defined a header/footer.
- Inside the container, we have added a header, a main section, and a footer.
- Within the header, we have used the `el-image` tag to display the logo of the application. The `el-image` tag is interesting because it supports lazy loading, load failure messages, and many other things.
- Within the `el-main` element, we have kept our router outlet. We have also used `el-row` and `el-col` to limit the width of this section.

At this point, the application doesn't look very nice, but you can easily improve the situation with a bit of time and effort.

Here's a basic starting point. Go ahead and replace the `style` tag with the following code:

```
<style>
  :root {
    --font-color: #fff;
    --background-color: #0e4868;
  }

  .lf-wrapper {
    border-radius: 3px 3px 20px 20px;
    border: 20px solid var(--background-color);
  }

  .lf-header, .lf-main, .lf-footer {
    background-color: var(--background-color);
    text-align: center;
  }

  .lf-header, .lf-footer {
    vertical-align: middle;
    color: var(--font-color);
  }

  .lf-header-logo {
    height: 100%;
  }

  .lf-footer {
    line-height: 60px;
```

```
  }
</style>
```

With that in place, here's how the application should look:

Here is a list of references:

- Layout
  components: `https://element.eleme.io/#/en-US/component/layout`
- Layout
  containers: `https://element.eleme.io/#/en-US/component/container`
- Image component: `https://element.eleme.io/#/en-US/component/image`

Creating the search component and using Vue slots

In order to let the users of LyricsFinder easily look for artists and songs, we will now create a search component.

Our specifications for this component are quite simple:

- Display a search input field, allowing users to type in the name of an artist or song they want to look for.
- Pressing *Enter* in the input field should automatically trigger an event containing the entered text.
- Include a search button, allowing users to trigger a search manually.

- Clicking on the search button should automatically trigger an event containing the entered text.
- Clearing the input field should automatically trigger an event. This event will later allow us to reset the artists and songs lists.

The search component will be a dumb component: it will emit events but will not know or care about what happens next. Actually, the home view will be responsible for listening and reacting to those events; as such, that view will be a smarter component.

Let's get started! Go ahead and create a `Search.vue` file in `src/components`.

To begin with, use the following skeleton for the component:

```
<template>
  <el-container class="lf-search">
    TODO
  </el-container>
</template>

<script lang="ts">
  import {Component, Vue} from 'vue-property-decorator';

  @Component({})
  export default class Search extends Vue {
  }
</script>

<style scoped>

</style>
```

 Notice that we've used an `el-container` again to wrap our content. Our component also uses a custom `lf-search` CSS class.

Let's work on the template.

Replace the `TODO` line in the `el-container` with the following code:

```
<el-input clearable placeholder="Artist or song to search for" prefix-
  icon="el-icon-search">
  <el-button slot="append" type="primary" icon="el-icon-
  search">Search</el-button>
</el-input>
```

We have now added the input field and the search button.

There are some interesting things in this code:

- The el-input has the clearable directive set on it. It adds a button on the right of the field to easily clear it.
- The el-input has a prefix icon (that is, an icon on the left side).
- The button also has an icon defined.

Another interesting detail is that the button is nested in el-input and has a slot property set to append. You might wonder what this all means.

Slots are a feature of Vue components enabling **content projection**. They're actually one more of those ideas borrowed from Angular. The concept of slots is that components can define **places** where elements can be inserted by its users.

 Check out the references if you want to learn more about slots. If you're curious about the equivalent feature in Angular, then take a look at this article: https://blog.angular-university.io/angular-ng-content.

In this case, we have used the slot named append of the el-input component, which adds content after the input field. This approach is described here in detail: https://element.eleme.io/#/en-US/component/input.

Now, adapt the style tag as follows:

```
<style scoped>
  .lf-search {
    width: 100%;
  }
</style>
```

This will increase the width of the container.

Now let's bind the input to the component's class. To do so, first add the following field to the class:

```
private searchText = '';
```

Then, in order to define the binding, follow these steps:

1. Add `v-model="searchText"` to the `el-input` tag. To finish up, we need to implement the event handling as described in our specifications. Adapt the template again to handle the `keyup`, `clear` and `click` events.

2. Add `@keyup.enter.native="searchHandler()"` to the `el-input` tag.

3. Add `@click="searchHandler()"` to the `el-button` tag.

Thanks to those event handlers, LyricsFinder will now react to the *Enter* key press and to the button click.

 Instead of the `keyup` event, you could also hook your event handler to the `change` event in order to react to more interactions (for example, copy/paste).

Next, import the `Emit` decorator at the top of the component's class:

```
import {Emit} from 'vue-property-decorator';
```

Finally, add the following methods to the same class:

```
public searchHandler(): void {
  if ('' !== this.searchText) {
    this.emitSearchEvent();
  } else {
    this.emitSearchClearedEvent();
  }
}

@Emit('search-triggered')
public emitSearchEvent(): string {
  console.log('Emitting search triggered event');
  return this.searchText;
}

@Emit('search-cleared')
public emitSearchClearedEvent(): void { }
```

Our `searchHandler` method checks the state of the input field in order to decide whether to emit a `search-triggered` or a `search-cleared` event.

You can find the completed code of the search component here in the code samples: `Chapter10/lyricsfinder-v1/src/components/Search.vue`.

Our component is now ready; we can now add it to the `Home` view:

1. Open the `src/views/Home.vue` file and update the template as follows:

```
<template>
  <el-container class="lf-home-view" direction="vertical">
    <Search></Search>
  </el-container>
</template>
```

2. Then, update the `@Component` decorator as well:

```
@Component({
  components: {
    Search,
  },
})
```

Again, you'll need to also add the import.

3. Take a look at the application now:

Great, now we're getting somewhere!

We have used `direction="vertical"` in order for the elements to stack *vertically*.

Next up, we're going to implement the event handling on the `Home` view and see how to fetch artists and songs using `MusicService`.

Here are a list of references:

- Input component: `https://element.eleme.io/#/en-US/component/input`
- Button component: `https://element.eleme.io/#/en-US/component/button`
- Slots: `https://vuejs.org/v2/guide/components-slots.html`

Handling search using the MusicService

Before we can use the `MusicService` in our `Home` view, we need to inject it. Since we have already configured InversifyJS, we can do that really quickly:

1. First of all, open the `src/views/Home.vue` file and add the following imports:

```
import {MusicService} from '@/services';
import {TYPES} from '@/ioc/types';
import {lazyInject} from '@/ioc/config';
```

2. Then, create a new field for the service inside the class and decorate it with `@lazyInject` as follows:

```
@lazyInject(TYPES.MUSIC_SERVICE)
private musicService!: MusicService;
```

3. We can verify that our service correctly gets injected by modifying the `mounted` life cycle hook:

```
public mounted() {
  console.log('Home component mounted');
  console.log('Music service instance: ', this.musicService);
}
```

With this done, we can now easily get the information we need using the service. Actually, we'll only need to interact with it when events are emitted by the search component.

Let's implement the event handlers:

1. Change the `Search` tag in the template to `<Search @search-triggered="search($event)" @search-cleared="searchCleared()"></Search>`.

2. Then, don't forget to implement the two following functions:

```
public search(searchText: string): void {
  console.log('Handling search: ', searchText);
}

public searchCleared(): void {
  console.log('Handling search cleared');
}
```

If you try now, you should see that our event handlers are indeed invoked when we type something in the search input, click the button, or clear the input. Great!

Now it is time to use the service and to display some actual results.

Add these to the class:

- `import { Artist } from '@/domain';`
- `private artists: Artist[] = [];`
- `private artistsLoading = false;`

Notice that, in this case, we have decided not to add a type annotation to the `artistsLoading` field. We have omitted it because the compiler clearly sees that we immediately assign a `boolean` to value it, so adding a type annotation is useless in this case.

Then, adapt the `search` method as follows:

```
public search(searchText: string): void {
  console.log('Handling search: ', searchText);

  this.artistsLoading = true;
  const artistsSearchSubscription =
    this.musicService.findArtists(searchText).subscribe({
      next: (artists: Artist[]) => {
```

```
            console.log(`Artists search result received. Found
              ${artists.length} artists`);
            this.artists = artists;
            this.artistsLoading = false;
        },
      error: (err: any) => {
          console.error('Error: ', err);
          this.artistsLoading = false;
          artistsSearchSubscription.unsubscribe();

        },
      complete: () => {
          this.artistsLoading = false;
          artistsSearchSubscription.unsubscribe();
        },
      });
  }
```

This code leverages the `Observable` instance returned by our service layer.

This reactive programming approach takes some getting used to, but is very elegant:

1. We call the `findArtists` method of our service and `subscribe` to the returned `Observable` (which we get immediately).
2. We keep a reference to the `Subscription` object returned by the `subscribe` method call so that we can later unsubscribe (and avoid introducing a memory leak).
3. We pass an `observer` to the `subscribe` method, with the `next`, `error`, and `complete` methods (that is, the complete `Observable` contract).
4. When either `complete` or `error` is called, we unsubscribe. Alternatively, we could use the `vue-rx` library to transparently handle the subscriptions for us (more about it later)

We have also kept track of the loading state. Thanks to this, and with the help of Element, we can easily display a loading indicator on the page.

To render the artists list and handle the loading state, go ahead and add the following code to the template, right below the `Search` tag:

```
<el-divider></el-divider>
<el-row class="lf-home-view-results">
  <el-col :span="12">
    <el-container class="lf-home-view-results-artists"
        direction="vertical">
```

```
          <h3>Artists</h3>
          <el-container v-loading="artistsLoading">
            <ul>
              <li v-for="artist in artists" :key="artist.id">
                {{artist.name}}</li>
            </ul>
          </el-container>
        </el-container>
      </el-col>
    </el-row>
```

If you test the application now, you should see that it works and that we even get a nice loading icon while the search operation is ongoing, thanks to the v-loading directive set on the container. We can build upon this basic structure to also search for songs using the same input.

Add two more fields to the class:

- private songs: Song[] = [];
- private songsLoading = false;

Of course, don't forget to add the necessary import for the Song class:

```
import {Song} from '@/domain';
```

Then, add the following code to the search method:

```
this.songsLoading = true;
const songsSearchSubscription =
this.musicService.findSongs(searchText).subscribe({
  next: (songs: Song[]) => {
    console.log(`Songs search result received. Found ${songs.length}
     artists`);
    this.songs = songs;
    this.songsLoading = false;
  },
  error: (err: any) => {
    console.error('Error: ', err);
    this.songsLoading = false;
    songsSearchSubscription.unsubscribe();

  },
  complete: () => {
    this.songsLoading = false;
    songsSearchSubscription.unsubscribe();
  },
});
```

Indeed, this code has the exact same structure as before but searches for songs instead of artists.

We have kept both search operations independent; depending on the server and network conditions, one result will arrive before the other. In this case, we do not care about the order but know that RxJS observables can be coordinated/chained if needed. For example, you could decide to wait for all results to arrive before updating the view. There are many operators that you can use to help you, such as `groupBy`: `https://www.learnrxjs.io/operators/transformation/groupby.html`.

To continue, modify the template to display the retrieved songs by adding a new `el-col` (similar to the previous one, but for songs) below the first `el-col` element:

```
<el-col :span="12">
  <el-container class="lf-home-view-results-songs"
    direction="vertical">
    <h3>Songs</h3>
    <el-container v-loading="songsLoading">
      <ul>
        <li v-for="song in songs" :key="song.id">{{song.name}}</li>
      </ul>
    </el-container>
  </el-container>
</el-col>
```

Finally, adapt the `style` tag as follows:

```
<style scoped>
  .lf-artists > h3 {
    color: var(--font-color);
  }

  .lf-artists ul {
    text-align: initial;
  }

  .lf-home-view-results {
    color: var(--font-color);
  }
</style>
```

Let's not worry too much about the styling at this point. If you're motivated, though, feel free to improve the display before moving on.

> The preceding code that handles RxJS observables/subscriptions could be improved and made safer by introducing and using `vue-rx` (`https://github.com/vuejs/vue-rx`), a library that adds support for RxJS in Vue.js. If you have time, then also take a look at `vue-rx-decorators` (`https://github.com/MinuKang/vue-rx-decorators`). We won't cover those libraries here due to space constraints, but they are great if you combine Vue.js and RxJS in your project. Check out this article to learn more: `https://codeburst.io/combining-vue-typescript-and-rxjs-with-vue-rx-a084d60b6eac`.

Here is a list of references:

- Loading indicators: `https://element.eleme.io/#/en-US/component/loading`

Creating and using the songs list component

For now, we have simply displayed the list of songs within the `Home` view, but this isn't great. We should actually create a dedicated component to do that. What we actually want is a component that we can pass the list of songs to, which will render it nicely and let us know when a selection has been made in that list.

Here are the specifications for the `SongsList` component:

- Accept an array of `Song` objects as input.
- Accept a loading state `boolean` as input (which will be used to render the loading indicator when needed).
- Display the provided list of songs; each item should be clickable.
- Emit an event whenever a song in the list has been clicked upon; attach the corresponding `Song` object to the event.

In the `Home` view, we will later implement an event handler for the song selection event.

Create the component file, `src/components/SongsList.vue`, then add the following base structure to it:

```
<template>
</template>

<script lang="ts">
</script>

<style scoped>
</style>
```

Then, replace the `script` tag with the following:

```
<script lang="ts">
  import {Component, Emit, Prop, Vue} from 'vue-property-decorator';
  import {Song} from '@/domain';

  @Component({})
  export default class SongsList extends Vue {
    @Prop({
      required: true,
    })
    private songs!: Song[];

    @Prop({
      required: false,
      type: Boolean,
    })
    private songsLoading = false;

    @Emit('song-selected')
    public emitSongSelectedEvent(selectedSong: Song): Song {
      console.log('Emitting song selected event: ',
      selectedSong.name);
      return selectedSong;
    }
  }
</script>
```

As required, our component has two input properties:

- The songs list: `songs`
- The loading state: `songsLoading`

In addition, notice the `emitSongSelectedEvent` method. This is the one that will emit the event (which should be quite clear given the name of the method). As we saw in the previous chapter, to emit events, we just need to add the `@Emit` decorator on a method and the return value of that method will be added as payload for the event.

In this case, this method will emit a `song-selected` event with the song as the payload.

 Notice that we had to specify the data type for the `songsLoading` property.

Next, change the template to the following:

```
<template>
  <el-card class="box-card lf-songs">
    <div slot="header" class="clearfix">
      <h3>Songs</h3>
    </div>
    <el-container v-loading="songsLoading" direction="vertical">
      <el-row v-for="song in songs" :key="song.id" class="item
        lf-song"
        v-if="song.hasLyrics">
        <el-col :span="22" class="lf-song-name">
          <span>{{song.name}}</span>
        </el-col>
        <el-col :span="2">
          <el-button @click="emitSongSelectedEvent(song)" style=""
            icon="el-icon-video-play"></el-button>
        </el-col>
      </el-row>
    </el-container>
  </el-card>
</template>
```

Here, we're using a new component of the Element library: `el-card`. Cards are actually inspired by Material Design.

Our card has a header corresponding to the `slot="header"` div. In this header, we have simply displayed the title of the section.

Underneath the header, we have added a container for the list of songs. This container has the v-loading directive defined, which will cause the loading indicator to be displayed if the bound property (that is, songsLoading) is set to true.

Notice that the direction property of the el-container element is set to "vertical", indicating that the contained elements should be stacked vertically.

Within the container, we render el-row elements using the v-for directive, which will loop over the collection of songs.

The v-if directive is used to avoid rendering an el-row if the song it is created for does not have lyrics.

This code can, of course, be improved (quite a bit, actually). For instance, the v-if directive can be eliminated by replacing the songs property with a computed property returning an already filtered version of the songs array. We wrote it this way here to avoid introducing more complexity at once.

Within each el-row element, we display the song name and a button to let the user select a song. When the user clicks on that button, we call the emitSongSelectedEvent method, passing the selected song object along. This is handled through the @click event binding.

Finally, notice that we have added some CSS class names to the different elements of the template. This will allow us to improve the user interface through CSS.

Let's try and do a first iteration of the styling.

Modify the styles section of the template as follows:

```
<style scoped>
  .lf-songs {
    background-color: var(--background-color);
  }

  .lf-songs h3 {
    color: var(--font-color);
  }

  .lf-song {
    margin-top: 5px;
  }
```

```css
  .lf-song-name {
    vertical-align: middle;
  }

  .lf-song-name::before {
    content: '';
    display: inline-block;
    height: 100%;
    vertical-align: middle;
    margin-right: -0.25em; /* Adjusts for spacing */
  }

  .lf-song-name > span {
    color: var(--font-color);
    display: block;
    width: 100%;
    text-align: left;
  }
</style>
```

With this done, the list will look much better, as we will see in a minute.

 You can add some styles to improve the look and feel. Take a look at the end result if you need some inspiration: `Chapter10/lyricsfinder-v1/src/components/SongsList.vue`.

Next, go back to `src/views/Home.vue` and replace the second `el-col` tag (that is, the one for songs) with the following code:

```
<SongsList :songs="songs" :songsLoading="songsLoading"></SongsList>
```

This will make use of our freshly created `SongsList` component. As you can see, we simply provide the two required bindings to it.

Don't forget to also update the `@Component` decorator:

```
import SongsList from '@/components/SongsList.vue';
...
@Component({
  components: {
    SongsList, // add this line
    Search,
  },
})
```

Great! Our songs list is already looking better:

Moreover, our code is also much cleaner now. We can take care of the last step for our `Home` view by adding a handler to react to the `song-selected` event.

Modify the `SongsList` tag in the `Home` view template to call the handler:

```
@song-selected="songSelected($event)"
```

Then, add a first iteration of the method implementation:

```
public songSelected(selectedSong: Song): void {
  console.log(`Song selected: [${selectedSong.name}]. Loading its
    lyrics`);

  const lyricsSearchSubscription =
    this.musicService.findLyrics(selectedSong).subscribe({
    next: (lyrics) => {
```

```
      console.log(`Lyrics loaded for [${selectedSong.name}]:
        ${lyrics.lyrics}`);

      // TODO redirect to the lyrics view!
    },
    error: (err: any) => {
      console.error('Error: ', err);
      lyricsSearchSubscription.unsubscribe();
    },
    complete: () => {
      lyricsSearchSubscription.unsubscribe();
    },
  });
}
```

This event handler continues to follow the same pattern as before. Once a song has been selected, we directly try to fetch its lyrics. Go ahead and try it out now.

In the next section, we're going to implement the `Lyrics` view to render the song lyrics. Once done, we will add a new route to the application and will come back to the preceding event handler in order to take care of the redirection to our new view.

Here is a list of references:

- Card component: `https://element.eleme.io/#/en-US/component/card`

Creating and using the lyrics view

We have almost reached our goal. Let's now create the lyrics view:

1. Create a `Lyrics.vue` file under `src/views` with the following template:

```
<template>
  <el-container class="lf-lyrics-view" direction="vertical">
    <span>{{song.name}}</span>
    <el-divider></el-divider>

    <el-container class="lf-lyrics-view-lyrics"
        direction="vertical">
      <span v-for="lyricsLine in songLyricsLines">
        <span>{{lyricsLine}}<br /><br /></span>
      </span>
    </el-container>
    <router-link to="/"><i class="el-icon-back"></i></router-
link>
```

```
      <el-divider></el-divider>
      <span>{{songLyrics.copyright}}</span>
    </el-container>
  </template>
```

Here, we simply display the song lyrics and their copyright.

For the lyrics, we display them one line at a time using the `v-for` directive.

We have added a `router-link` to the page, which allows us to go back to the home page of the application. In this case, the link simply points to the `/` route.

2. To finish the implementation, add the following code:

```ts
<script lang="ts">
import {Component, Prop, Vue} from 'vue-property-decorator';
import {Song, SongLyrics} from '@/domain';

@Component({})
export default class Lyrics extends Vue {
  @Prop({
    required: true,
    type: SongLyrics,
  })
  private songLyrics!: SongLyrics;

  private songLyricsLines: string[] = [];

  @Prop({
    required: true,
    type: Song,
  })
  private song!: Song;

  public mounted() {
    console.log('Lyrics component mounted');

    if (this.songLyrics.lyrics) {
      this.songLyricsLines =
this.songLyrics.lyrics.split('\n');
    }
  }
}
</script>
```

Here, we're again leveraging the `vue-property-decorator` library.

In addition, we have used the `mounted` life cycle hook in order to split the lyrics into an array of lines. We chose to do this because MusixMatch returns a single string value containing newline (that is, `'\n'`) characters. Another approach for adding the lyrics to the page would've been to directly bind the value to the DOM using the `v-html` directive of Vue, but this would have introduced a **cross-site scripting (XSS)** vulnerability into our application.

 Be very careful with directives such as `v-html` (with Vue.js or other frameworks for that matter). **Binding data directly to the DOM is risky and must be done cautiously and only with trusted content. If you bind untrusted data to the DOM, then you can introduce severe security issues in your application**.

3. Then adapt the styles:

```
<style scoped>
  .lf-lyrics-view {
    color: var(--font-color);
  }

  .lf-lyrics-view-lyrics > span {
    width: 100%;
  }

  i {
    font-size: 50px;
  }
</style>
```

Nothing new or fancy here.

Now that our `Lyrics` view is defined, we need to update our router configuration.

Open the `src/router/router.ts` file and adapt it to introduce a new route:

```
import VueRouter from 'vue-router';
import Home from '@/views/Home.vue';
import Lyrics from '@/views/Lyrics.vue';

export const ROUTES = {
  HOME: 'home',
  LYRICS: 'lyrics',
```

```
};

export const router = new VueRouter({
  mode: 'history',
  base: '', // useful for sub-domains
  routes: [
    { path: '/', component: Home },
    { path: `/${ROUTES.HOME}`, component: Home, name: ROUTES.HOME },
      { path: `/${ROUTES.LYRICS}`, component: Lyrics, name:
        ROUTES.LYRICS, props: true },
    { path: '*', redirect: '/' },
  ],
});
```

If you compare this code with the previous implementation, notice the following:

- We have added a name property to our routes.
- We have exported the route names as a constant: ROUTES.
- We have set the props property to true for the lyrics route. This will allow us to pass route parameters as properties for the Lyrics component.

To finish the implementation, go back to the src/views/Home.vue file.

In it, first add the following import:

```
import {ROUTES} from '@/router/router';
```

Then, replace the TODO that we left before with this:

```
this.$router.push({
  name: ROUTES.LYRICS,
  params: {
    song: selectedSong,
    songLyrics: lyrics,
  },
} as any); // opportunity to improve
```

The code uses $route to programmatically route the user to the Lyrics view. Now you can see why we have exported the route names. Thanks to this, we avoid hardcoding the same strings all over the application. We have also passed the song and its lyrics to the route, which will be pushed to the properties of the Lyrics component.

In the last code snippet, we had to cast the object to `any` because of an issue with the Vue router type definitions. Our code is actually valid, but, at the time of writing, the TypeScript typings are not in line with the actual API. Unfortunately, this still happens from time to time with various libraries. This is definitely one of the weaknesses of TypeScript; the experience of using third-party JavaScript libraries largely depends on the quality and correctness of the type definitions. The good news is that typings are open source, so everyone is welcome to improve them! Open source is great, so don't hesitate to jump in and contribute!

There we are! LyricsFinder is now (almost) ready for prime time! Congratulations!

Here is a list of references:

- Router
  navigation: `https://router.vuejs.org/guide/essentials/navigation.html`
- Passing props to
  routes: `https://router.vuejs.org/guide/essentials/passing-props.html`

Summary

Through our small prototype, we have gone from a simple idea to a concrete application in no time. Of course, LyricsFinder lacks all the bells and whistles that end users would expect from a production application, and there is a lot of room for improvement, but the base functionality is there and the code is simple and easy to understand.

We have created a few SFCs and handled inputs with props as well as outputs using properties and event handlers.

We have also installed the Vue Router library, configured it, and defined a few routes together, allowing us to easily implement navigation within our SPA.

The Element component library has also helped us move forward efficiently. We have seen that it is both very approachable and efficient. The choice of Element was quite arbitrary and, in fact, many other libraries would have been just as good (for example, those that we mentioned in the previous chapter: Quasar, Vuetify, Buex, and many others).

Initially, our plan was to integrate VueX into LyricsFinder as part of the chapter, but this would have introduced too much complexity at once, which might have left you with the wrong impression about Vue.js. Ultimately, we have chosen to keep things simple to reflect the true nature of Vue.

Nevertheless, take our advice and dig deeper into VueX (NGRX for Angular or Redux for React), as state management libraries are the key for great frontend applications!

Our next chapter is dedicated to React, the other superstar among modern web frameworks. Get ready for a change, because React is quite different from what we've seen so far!

Further reading

Here are some useful resources:

- MusixMatch API
  documentation: `https://developer.musixmatch.com/documentation`
- MusixMatch OpenAPI
  documentation: `https://playground.musixmatch.com`

11

Diving into React, NestJS, GraphQL, and Apollo

Do you know what is cooler than knowing about two modern web development solutions? Knowing about three (or more)! And do you know what is even greater? Also knowing something about backend development!

In this chapter, we will learn about React (`https://reactjs.org`) and its ecosystem. Programming with React is one of the most demanded skills for web developers on the market today, so learning it is certainly valuable. But this book isn't about money; it is about *passion* and *fun*. And don't worry about fun—we'll have quite some in this chapter!

We won't stop there though! We will go above and beyond and learn about GraphQL (`https://graphql.org`), Apollo GraphQL (`https://www.apollographql.com`), and NestJS (`https://nestjs.com`).

Of course, we will also see how all of those can benefit from TypeScript support.

Let's look at the important topics that we are going to cover in this chapter:

- React
- JSX
- React elements
- Components and `props`
- Rendering lists
- Hooks
- Learning about React developer tools
- Exploring the **Create React App (CRA)**

- Understanding React with TypeScript
- Discovering NestJS in a jiffy
- Introducing GraphQL

This whole chapter will actually prepare you for the last important milestone of the book: using all of those frameworks, libraries, and tools to revisit the LyricsFinder application in the next chapter!

Let's dive right in!

Introducing React

"React is as a declarative, efficient, and flexible JavaScript library for building user interfaces."

- React website

React (`https://reactjs.org`) is the last modern web development solution that we will cover in this book. It is also called React.js or ReactJS. Like Angular and Vue.js, you can use it to create SPAs, but that's not all.

At the time of writing, React has more than 135,000 stars on GitHub and 1,300 contributors, which makes it one of the most popular projects on the platform:

The official React logo

We are currently exploring modern web *frameworks* but in reality, *React is not a framework*, but *just* a library. It does not try to provide you with everything and the kitchen sink. On the contrary, React tries hard to remain light and as flexible as possible. Not only that, but it is also much less opinionated than some other solutions.

As a matter of fact, React is incredibly malleable, as demonstrated by the many satellite projects that have emerged around it over the last couple of years. React can be used in many scenarios, including web, mobile, desktop, AR, and VR. For example, the React 360 (`https://facebook.github.io/react-360`) project allows you to use React to create immersive 360° experiences.

It is also possible to do SSR using the `react-dom` renderer or libraries such as NextJS (`https://nextjs.org`).

We can also create static websites with React using tools such as Gatsby (`https://www.gatsbyjs.org`) or NextJS. As a matter of fact, NextJS is actually a framework built on top of React that supports other use cases as well.

> While exploring React, we will draw many parallels with what we have seen so far with Angular and Vue.js. As we'll see, Vue is actually the closest in philosophy to React. Our goal is not to spend too much energy comparing frameworks/libraries. If you're looking for such a side-by-side comparison, then you can take a look at this great article by Jens Neuhaus:
> `https://medium.com/unicorn-supplies/angular-vs-react-vs-vue-a-2017-comparison-c5c52d620176`.

The React community is huge, very active, and prolific. There are tons of resources available online to help you out and a lot of innovation going on.

With this quick introduction, the message that we want to convey is that React might be *just a library*, but it is actually a large ecosystem composed of many pieces that can be combined to provide great experiences to end users!

History

React was created at Facebook by Jordan Walke (`https://twitter.com/jordwalke`) in 2011. It was used on Facebook's News Feed and it was later added to Instagram as well. Hence, since its infancy, React has been used on some of the most heavily used websites in the world.

React was kept proprietary until 2013, when it was made available under an open source license (initially with a variant of the BSD license). After quite a long history of criticism around the chosen license, Facebook finally changed it to MIT in 2017.

React has been used in production by hundreds of large companies around the globe for quite some time now and it is really mature, stable, and robust.

At the time of writing, the last release of React is 16.10.2.

Application architecture

A key thing to understand about React is that its rendering engine is kept separate from the core library. Thanks to that separation of concerns, many different *renderers* have been created.

For example, `react-dom` is the default renderer for the web platform; it takes care of rendering components to HTML DOM elements. To do that, React DOM uses a virtual DOM, a technique that we have discussed in the previous chapters and that React has made popular.

When targeting mobile platforms, there is a more adequate solution that you can use: `react-native`. Check out the resources listed at the end of this chapter to discover other ones.

 Don't confuse React and React Native (`https://facebook.github.io/react-native`) as they are not one and the same. React Native is a solution for building *native* mobile applications for Android and iOS using JavaScript and React. We won't cover it in this book.

React applications *may* be made up of *components* (for example, dumb components) and *pages* (that is, smart/presentational components), so we'll remain in a familiar environment since we will keep decomposing the user interface of our applications in the same way as we did so far: with encapsulated and reusable components.

 Note that React is actually not imposing one way of doing things, so if the preceding metaphor does not suit you, then you can use other ones as you see fit. For the rest of this chapter though, we will continue using our simple dichotomy between dumb and smart components as it is easy to comprehend and works as well with React as with Angular and Vue.

One major difference between React components and Angular ones is that *React has chosen to mix markup and logic together in the same files*. This shouldn't be too shocking as we have seen a sort of similar idea being applied with single-file Vue.js components.

Here's the unavoidable `Hello world` with React, assuming that both React and `ReactDOM` have been loaded on the page beforehand:

```
ReactDOM.render(
  <h1>Hello, world!</h1>,
  document.getElementById('root')
);
```

This code uses the `render` function of `ReactDOM` to render a `heading` tag. The result is added to the DOM of the element that has the `root` identifier (this name is arbitrary, it must just be part of the actual DOM of the page!)

You might be surprised by the syntax. In the preceding `render` function, we *did* mix HTML markup and JavaScript code together; that was no mistake. This indeed goes further than what Vue.js does with SFCs.

This code snippet is actually written in JSX, a syntax extension for JavaScript initially created for React, but also supported by other libraries (for example, Vue.js!). We will discuss JSX soon, so don't worry about it for now.

Here's a second example that defines and renders a custom React component:

```
function DisplayMessage(props) {
  return <div>Welcome to React {props.name}!</div>;
}

ReactDOM.render(
  <DisplayMessage name="foo" />,
  document.getElementById('container')
);
```

The `DisplayMessage` function is a very basic example of React component: a simple function that accepts a `props` object as input and returns elements defined with JSX. Props are indeed the properties of the component (we'll come back to this later). To render our component, we do the same as before, this time using our custom `DisplayMessage` component.

We'll explore other ways to create React components in the next sections, but keep in mind that *defining components using functions is considered to be the idiomatic React way.* We'll explore why this approach is preferred later on.

 Microsoft has created React-Native-Windows (`https://github.com/microsoft/react-native-windows`), a solution to create native Windows applications using React.

Let's continue.

Numbers, numbers, numbers

As we have said before in this book, it is almost pointless to try and compare the performance characteristics of the different modern web frameworks and libraries, as they are constantly evolving. Another point that is kind of futile to compare is the size of the libraries, as that is also a moving target.

If you really want to see numbers, then check out this great benchmark: `https://krausest.github.io/js-framework-benchmark/current.html`, but take it with a grain of salt.

 If you're looking for a really lightweight solution, take a look at Preact (`https://preactjs.com/`). It provides almost the same basic API as React, with minor differences (`https://preactjs.com/guide/differences-to-react`) and only weighs 3 KB!

But what about support and maintenance?

Evolution and support

Another great point about React is its long-term support policy and the stability of its API. Stability is actually part of the core design principles (`https://reactjs.org/docs/design-principles.html`) of React. As stated on that page, Facebook itself has more than 50,000 components that use React. Because of that, Facebook tries really hard to keep the public API surface of React as stable as possible.

This does not mean that things are frozen though—far from it. What usually happens is that deprecation warnings are issued and remain until the next major release. At that point, `codemod` scripts are often provided to automate the bulk of the modifications needed to upgrade from a previous release to the latest and greatest. We won't cover codemods any further in this book, but you can check out the `react-codemod` repository (`https://github.com/reactjs/react-codemod`) to learn more. To summarize, upgrades are rarely a source of headaches with React because the necessary changes are automated through upgrade scripts.

 To be fair, Angular also assists with the upgrade process: `https://update.angular.io`.

Another element to keep in mind about React is that it is backed by a large corporation, just like Angular is. This can be perceived as good or bad depending on the point of view, but it certainly helps React to quickly evolve. Given the importance of React for Facebook, it is unlikely for it to be abandoned any time soon. If that happens at some point though, React will certainly continue to live on given the size of its developer community.

Let's get to know to React a little better now.

Understanding JSX

If you want to understand React, then you need to know about JSX.

Introduction

As we mentioned in the introduction of this chapter, JSX is an extension to JavaScript. It expands the syntax of the language to allow writing XML-like code in JavaScript.

In reality, JSX is *only* syntactic sugar; it is never executed as is at runtime. *A build step is required to transform JSX code into JavaScript.* The default choice for handling this transformation is *Babel* but as we'll see later, TypeScript can also take care of it for us.

Here's a basic example of JSX code:

```
const element = <h1>Hello, world!</h1>;
```

Here, we created a simple React element (we'll explain what those are in the next section).

JSX elements such as the preceding one actually get converted into calls like these: `React.createElement(component, props, ...children)`, which are API calls used to create React elements.

Here's what the preceding code becomes once transpiled into JavaScript:

```
const element = React.createElement('h1', null, 'Hello, world!');
```

One goal of React with JSX is to keep state away from the DOM. If you think about it, what Angular and Vue.js do is introduce a fairly limited JavaScript-like syntax into HTML templates. React does the opposite; it uses HTML-like syntax in JavaScript code.

If you want to follow along and try out the examples, then you can use the **Read-Eval-Print Loop** (**REPL**) of Babel over at `https://babeljs.io/repl`.

An important benefit of React's approach with JSX is that *if you know JavaScript, then you know most of the syntax needed to write React applications*. Getting better at React mostly means getting better at JavaScript. Obviously, this is an advantage compared to the framework-specific syntaxes that we learned about for Angular and Vue.js, which takes a bit of time to master.

Developers that are used to the MVC design pattern often have the feeling that mixing HTML with JavaScript (and CSS) goes against the separation of concerns principle. That criticism is valid when considering the technological point of view, but the idea of React components is that the concern is the component as a whole. As a matter of fact, the model, view, and controller of a component are deeply tied together, whether we isolate them in separate files or not.

Here's another JSX example taken from the official documentation:

```
class Hello extends React.Component {
  render() {
    return <div>Hello {this.props.toWhat}</div>;
  }
}

ReactDOM.render(
```

```
    <Hello toWhat="World" />,
    document.getElementById('root')
);
```

And here's the transpiled version:

```
class Hello extends React.Component {
  render() {
    return React.createElement('div', null, "Hello",
    this.props.toWhat);
  }
}

ReactDOM.render(
  React.createElement(Hello, {toWhat: 'World'}),
  document.getElementById('root')
);
```

Don't worry about the class for now; we'll explore the different ways to create React components in the next section.

As you can guess from the preceding code, it is actually not mandatory to use JSX with React when writing components, but it is the default and recommended choice. The official documentation provides instructions on how to use React without JSX: `https://reactjs.org/docs/react-without-jsx.html`.

JSX makes the code of components more readable. Also, as stated in the official documentation, it allows React to show useful error messages.

JSX is not HTML

One thing to be aware of is that JSX is not HTML.

It mimics HTML but has some (minor) differences:

- Inline styles are defined using plain objects that describe patches to apply to the DOM element's `style` property: `<div style={{ color: "green" }}></div>`.
- `htmlFor` is used instead of `for`.
- `className` is used instead of `class`.

- Comments are written using the JavaScript syntax and not with standard HTML comments. Moreover, they don't end up in the rendered HTML.
- ReactDOM uses camelCase for property names; for example, `tabindex` becomes `tabIndex` in JSX.

Those differences are explained by the incompatibility of the original HTML syntax with JavaScript. For example, `class` is a reserved keyword in JavaScript. These differences are quite limited, so it's not much of an issue in practice.

Expressions

Within JSX, we can embed expressions using curly braces.

Here's an example:

```
const name = 'Foo';
const element = <h1>Hello, {name}</h1>; // we use JSX to create a
React element

ReactDOM.render(
  element, // then we render it
  document.getElementById('root')
);
```

In this example, we have defined a constant and have embedded it inside of our JSX code. JSX supports all valid JavaScript expressions within curly braces.

For example, we could also call a function:

```
function getName() { return 'foo'; }

const element = <h1>Hello, {getName()}</h1>;
```

Moreover, since JSX code is transpiled into standard JavaScript function calls, it can be used and passed around just like any JavaScript function can (for example, passed as a function argument, used in conditional statements or within loops, or returned from functions).

Here's another example taken from the official documentation:

```
function getGreeting(user) {
  if (user) {
    return <h1>Hello, {formatName(user)}!</h1>;
  }
  return <h1>Hello, Stranger.</h1>;
}

function formatName(name) { return `Mr/Mrs ${name}`; }
```

In this example, we return a different React element if `user` has been passed into the function.

Attributes

To define attributes in JSX code, you can use quotes:

```
const element = <div id="someDiv"></div>;
```

Or you can use curly braces if you need to define the value dynamically:

```
function getActiveClass() {
    return 'active';
}
const anotherElement = <div class={getActiveClass()} />;
```

Element trees

JSX code can also create `element` trees:

```
function FullName(props) {
    return (
      <span>{props.givenName} {props.lastName}</span>
    )
}

const element = (
  <div id="root">
    <FullName givenName="Sebastien" lastName="Dubois" />
    <FullName givenName="Alexis" lastName="Georges" />
  </div>
)
```

The preceding React element has multiple children.

 In the last example, we spread our JSX expression over multiple lines to keep the code readable. Notice that the JSX is surrounded by parentheses to avoid issues with **Automatic Semicolon Insertion (ASI)**: `http://www.bradoncode.com/blog/2015/08/26/javascript-semi-colon-insertion`.

As you can see, JSX is quite clean and powerful!

 For the security-concerned developers (you should be one!), it is important to know that *values embedded in JSX code are automatically escaped*, providing a good level of protection against injection attacks.

You can find the sources of this example in the code samples of this book, under `Chapter11/02-react-element`. Open it up in your web browser, go to the developer tools, and take a look at the React element.

 We'll see this in practice in the next chapter but, for the transpiled JSX code to work, React must be imported and in scope for the JSX code. This is explained here: `https://reactjs.org/docs/jsx-in-depth.html#react-must-be-in-scope`.

We will learn some more about JSX throughout this chapter, but this should be enough to get you started!

React elements

In the previous section, we mentioned that JSX code is transpiled into `React.createElement` function calls. As its name implies, the `createElement` function of React creates React elements. But what are those?

> *"Elements are the smallest building blocks of React apps."*

> *- React website*

To understand, let's take a look at the JavaScript code that the last JSX example transpiles into:

```javascript
function FullName(props) {
    render(React.createElement('span', null, props.givenName, ' ',
    props.lastName));
}

const element = React.createElement('div', {
    id: 'root'
}, React.createElement(FullName, {
    givenName: 'Sebastien',
    lastName: 'Dubois'
}), React.createElement(FullName, {
    givenName: 'Alexis',
    lastName: 'Georges'
}));
```

The properties defined on the `FullName` tag have been converted into an object literal after transpilation. That object represents `props` of the element.

The `createElement` function accepts three parameters:

- The type of element
- A set of `props` passed as an object (we'll discuss those in detail soon)
- Children (optional)

When executed, `createElement` will actually create an object literal that has the following basic structure:

```javascript
const element = {
    type: 'div',
    props: {
        id: 'root',
        children: [
            {
                type: 'FullName',
                props: {
                    givenName: 'Sebastien',
                    lastName: 'Dubois',
                },
            },
            { ... }
        ]
    }
};
```

This structure is really interesting and deserves some attention. The important takeaway is that *a React element is a descriptor*—a sort of recipe to create a component hierarchy with a specific state. *Each React element describes a part of the user interface.* The React elements contain all the information needed for the renderer to do its job: the type of each element is known as well as its inputs, children, and so on.

However, a React element doesn't prescribe *how* it should be rendered; that is the role of the renderer! React elements are, hence, not tied to a *host element* directly. They merely describe something that we *might* want to render at some later point in time.

To render elements, we can use the `render` function of a renderer. For example, here's how to render the preceding element to the DOM using `ReactDOM`:

```
ReactDOM.render(element, document.getElementById('root'));
```

Indeed, this was part of the very first example that we looked at in this chapter! Again, the second argument of the `render` function is the DOM node that will be the *host* for what `ReactDOM` renders for us.

When `ReactDOM` renders the element, it will instantiate it (depending on its type), then it will set its `props` and trigger its lifecycle methods (more on those later).

An important point is that *React elements are immutable*. Updating the user interface really means creating new elements to replace the previous ones. Because of this, *React elements are disposable*; they are not recycled after use.

> *"I like to think of React elements as being like frames in a movie. They capture what the UI should look like at a specific point in time. They don't change."*

> *-Dan Abramov*

Here's an example from the official documentation:

```
function tick() {
  const element = (
    <div>
      <h1>Hello, world!</h1>
      <h2>It is {new Date().toLocaleTimeString()}.</h2>
    </div>
  );
  ReactDOM.render(element, document.getElementById('root'));
}

setInterval(tick, 1000);
```

As you can see, each time we want to render a new value (that is, each second when the `tick` function is called), we need to create a new React element before we pass it to the `render` function of `ReactDOM`.

You can find the sources of the last example in the code samples of this book, under `Chapter11/03-react-element-immutable`.

Thanks to the fact that React uses a virtual DOM, it will actually only change the minimal amount of DOM elements possible, leading to better performance. In this specific case, only the time will be updated (not even the whole h2 tag!).

Components and props

Now that you know about React elements, we can go one level higher and finally look at how to write components.

React components, like Vue.js or Angular ones, are all about composing user interfaces from small and reusable pieces. Of course, components are meant to be composed together. To compose components, you can simply refer to those in JSX code or using `React.createElement(...)` calls.

Interestingly, in React, there is no need to register components as we need to with Angular. Components that are used just need to be *in scope* where they are used (that is, they either need to be imported or declared before they are used).

Conceptually, React components are really straightforward: they accept a single (immutable!) `props` object as input. As output, they return JSX (or `React.createElement(...)` calls) and, hence, React elements.

 As we just learned in the previous section, React elements are simply immutable descriptors for a part of the user interface.

With React, we never instantiate components ourselves. Instead, React takes care of this for us. The reason for this is that React can optimize things much further by keeping control over the base lifecycle of components. It can actually render components lazily.

This also means that React has the same issues as Vue.js with dependency injection libraries such as Inversify. The solution that we applied in the previous chapter actually works with React as well.

React's name comes from its reactivity. When component inputs change (that is, its props), then its output changes as well; a new React element is created and passed to the renderer, which takes care of efficiently updating the target (for example, the DOM).

With React, components can be defined as follows:

- Using pure functions: These are called **function components** (heavily recommended).
- Using classes: These are called **class components**.

 Whether you use pure functions or class components, it is important to keep in mind that the `props` object (that is, the component inputs) must never be mutated by the component.

We'll quickly explore both approaches in the following sections.

Class components

Class components should be the exception rather than the norm in your React applications. Still, let's explore these a bit to see how they are written.

To create a class component, you need to extend the `React.Component` class and implement the `render` method. That method will be the one creating/returning a React element.

Here is an example of a `component` class using ES2015 (that is, not TypeScript yet!):

```
const createElement = React.createElement;

class SayHiButton extends React.Component {
    constructor(props) {
        super(props);
        this.state = {
            buttonClicked: false,
        };
    }
```

```
    render() {
        console.log('Rendering');
        if (this.state.buttonClicked) {
            console.log('The buttonClicked property of the state is
            true; showing the message');
            return 'Hello from React!';
        }

        return createElement(
            'button',
            {
                onClick: () => {
                    console.log("The button's click handler was
                    clicked. Changing the state of the component");
                    this.setState({
                        buttonClicked: true,
                    }, null)
                }
            },
            'Say hi!' // button's text
        );
    }
}

const domContainer = document.querySelector('#hello-react-container');
ReactDOM.render(createElement(SayHiButton), domContainer);
```

In this example, we created a `SayHiButton` component, which simply displays a different message based on its internal state. Don't worry about the state management logic; we'll come back to that a bit later.

Class components, like function components, receive their inputs as a single `props` object. In the case of class components, those properties are passed to the constructor function.

In the constructor function of this example, we passed the `props` object to the parent class, then we initialized the `state` object of the component (more on this later).

In the `render` method, we used the `React.createElement(...)` function to create and return a React element.

Finally, notice that, in this example, we reused the standard `button` HTML element. Also, we used the second parameter of `createElement` to define an event handler.

Here's another example, this time using JSX:

```
export class Foo extends React.Component {
  constructor(props) {
    super(props);
  }

  render() {
    return (
      <div>Bar</div>
    );
  }
}
```

From these two examples, what we mentioned earlier should become much more obvious: using the class-based approach for defining components is quite verbose.

As time passes and as React evolves, class components become less and less appealing. In the most recent releases, Functional Components have grown to be a lot more powerful than before. Let's take a look at those now.

 There might actually be value in (sometimes) choosing class components (for example, for performance reasons with the `PureComponent` base class and custom `shouldComponentUpdate` methods), but covering those (few?) cases is out of the scope of this book. Moreover, as we've stated many times already, performance is a moving target. Check out the references in the *Further reading* section at the end of this chapter if you want to dig deeper.

Let's look at function components next.

Function components

Idiomatic React components are written using pure functions. There are multiple reasons for this:

- Functions are simpler to write and to read/understand.
- Functions require less code than classes.
- Pure functions are *stable, deterministic, predictable* and have *no side-effects*.
- Pure functions are easily testable.

Function components are powerful enough for most use cases and should be preferred whenever possible.

In versions of React prior to 16.8 (`https://reactjs.org/blog/2019/02/06/react-v16.8.0.html`), class components were needed to be able to use features such as component state, lifecycle methods, and refs (concepts that we will cover later on), so their use was usually justifiable. Since then, with the introduction of React hooks, we can now leverage those features with function components as well. This is why we said earlier that Functional Components are now mostly on par with class components and should be preferred.

We will also explore React hooks later in this chapter.

Let's look again at the first example that we showed at the beginning of this chapter:

```
function DisplayMessage(props) {
  return <div>Welcome to React {props.name}!</div>;
}
```

This was indeed a Functional Component. As you can see, defining a React component using a function is really as simple as it gets and is much terser than its class-based counterpart!

You can find more details about the naming conventions of React here: `https://reactjs.org/docs/jsx-in-depth.html#user-define d-components-must-be-capitalized`.

Have you heard about object destructuring yet? Well, we mentioned it a few times in the previous chapters, but let's take some time to properly introduce that feature of JavaScript/TypeScript.

Object destructuring

In this section, we'll explain object destructuring, a JavaScript syntax that can be used to easily extract parts of other objects. Knowing about this feature will prove useful for writing React components, but you can also leverage it in many more situations.

Destructuring is often useful when you are only interested in a subset of the properties of an object returned by a function call.

Object destructuring was introduced by ES2015 and is, of course, supported by TypeScript.

Here's a simple example:

```
const myObject = {
    firstName: 'Sebastien',
    age: 36,
    country: 'Belgium',
};

const {firstName, age} = myObject;

console.log(`Firstname: ${firstName}`);
```

Here, we first defined an object with multiple properties. Then, using the destructuring syntax with curly braces, we *extracted* some of the object properties into new constants.

Without destructuring, we would have had to extract everything ourselves one property at a time:

```
const firstName = myObject.firstName;
const age = myObject.age;
```

Object destructuring is also useful for React components that have a single input. All React components receive a `props` object as an argument, but when there is a single input, it is cumbersome to have to type `props.myPropertyName` to get access to it.

To make things simpler, we can use destructuring directly on the function argument, as follows:

```
function DisplayMessage({name}) {
  return <div>Welcome to React {name}!</div>;
}
```

In the preceding example, notice the brackets around the function argument. We extracted the `name` property of the `props` object received as input by the component. Thanks to this, we don't need to type `props.` anymore.

Let's go back to React.

Component state

Creating stateless components is ideal for simplicity and testability (among other benefits), but of course, it isn't always possible. React allows components to maintain their own internal state as an object with arbitrary keys.

Whenever the state or props of a component change, a rendering cycle is triggered for that component and its children.

Unlike props, the component state is mutable by the component itself (since it owns its state), but mutations have to be done in a specific way; otherwise, React will not detect the changes and won't re-render the component sub-tree. Don't worry though: defining and managing the internal state of a React component is really simple to do.

Let's see how it works!

 For now, we'll only show you how to manage state inside of class components. We will explain how to do the same with function components when we introduce *React hooks*.

For class components, we do the following:

1. First, we need to initialize the internal state object, either through the constructor function or using a property initialized at creation time. This is the *only* place where you are allowed to mutate the state directly.
2. After the object has been constructed, we must use the `this.setState(...)` function whenever we want to mutate the state.

Here is an example:

```
import React from 'react';

export class Calculator extends React.Component {
    constructor(props) {
        super(props);
        this.state = {
            currentResult: this.props.initialValue,
        };
    }

    render() {
        return (
            <div>
                <span>Current result:
```

```
{this.state.currentResult}</span>
                    <br/>
                    <br/>
                    <button onClick={() => this.add(1)}>+1</button>
            </div>
        );
    }

    add(value) {
        this.setState((state, props) => {
            return {currentResult: state.currentResult + value}
        });
    }
}
```

In the `add(...)` function of this example, you can see how the state of the
component is updated. It is not the only way to do it, but it is the safest, and the
recommended, approach.

 You can find the source code of this example in the code samples of
this book, under `Chapter11/04-react-component-state`.

As stated before, *the class constructor and initializers are the only places that are allowed to
directly set the state of a class component.* After construction time, the
`this.setState({...})` method needs to be called instead. Otherwise, React won't
know about the change and won't re-render the component.

State updates made through calls to `setState(...)` are *merged shallowly* into the
current state (that is, only what you define in the new object is replaced in the
previous one).

One thing to be careful about is that *props and state updates can happen asynchronously*
(for example, for performance reasons, React might decide to regroup some updates
and perform them all at once). For this reason, we had to use the second form of the
`setState` method, which accepts a function as an argument. As you can see in the
preceding example, that function receives `state` (the first argument) and `props` (the
second argument).

Components can pass their own state to children components (for example, as props), but they remain in charge of those values. *By default, React will re-render a component and its children anytime state or props change*, even if those changes don't impact what should be rendered! You can avoid wasteful re-renders using the `shouldComponentUpdate` method:

`https://reactjs.org/docs/react-component.html#shouldcomponentupdate.`

Just like with Angular and Vue.js, you should try to maximize the number of *dumb* components in your applications so as to favor code reuse. The official documentation of React provides specific guidance for this:

`https://reactjs.org/docs/lifting-state-up.html.` You should also take a look at the following page, which shares great ideas about how to develop modern component-based web applications:

`https://reactjs.org/docs/thinking-in-react.html.`

There's more to know, but we can't cover all of the details here; check out the resources in the *Further reading* section of this chapter if you want to learn more.

To conclude, defining and managing state in a class component is dead simple.

We will soon take a look at React hooks and the `useState` one in particular, which will allow us to create stateful function components. But first, let's learn about something else: lifecycle hooks!

Bonus: Improving rendering performance

In the last example, we actually used a naive function binding on the following line:

```
<button onClick={() => this.add(1)}>+1</button>
```

The issue with this line is that, by defining our handler function inline, a new function will actually get created each time the component is re-rendered. This doesn't cause much harm in the examples in this book, but applying this approach for actual applications will certainly cause performance issues.

A better approach consists of defining the function once and binding it instead:

```
function onClickHandler() { ... }
...
<button onClick={this.onClickHandler}>+1</button>
```

With the preceding code, the same `onClickHandler` function will be reused when the component gets re-rendered.

Lifecycle hooks

React components have a specific lifecycle, just like Angular and Vue.js ones.

In the case of class components, hooking into this lifecycle is, once again, simply a matter of implementing specific methods in your components.

Here's an example:

```
import React from 'react';
import ReactDOM from 'react-dom';
...
export class LifecycleAwareComponent extends React.Component {
    constructor(props) {
        super(props);
        ...
    }

    render() {
        ...
    }

    componentDidMount() {
        console.log('componentDidMount lifecycle hook called');
    }
    ...
}
```

In this example, we used the `componentDidMount` lifecycle hook, which is called as soon as the component's initialization is completed.

There are many other lifecycle hooks in React. Wojciech Maj (a member of the React community) created a great interactive diagram to visualize those. You can find it here: `http://projects.wojtekmaj.pl/react-lifecycle-methods-diagram`.

Here is the light version, listing only the most commonly used lifecycle hooks:

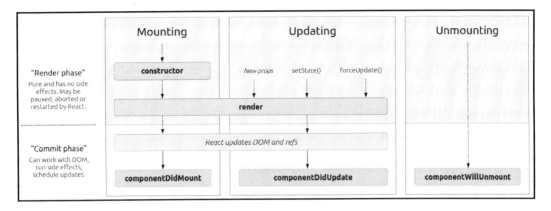

React lifecycle methods diagram

And here's a brief explanation of each of these:

Lifecycle hook function	Description
componentDidMount	This lifecycle hook is invoked when the component has been instantiated and when its props and state have been initialized and rendered (usually in the DOM). Here, you can safely initiate network requests to load data, connect to a store (for example, Redux), and so on.
componentDidUpdate	With this lifecycle hook, you can react as soon as an update has been completed (for example, props or state have changed). Here, you can implement side-effects that should occur depending on the new values of your component. For example, you could initiate a new network request to fetch new data. This hook receives the previous props and state as an argument, which allows you to identify the exact changes that have occurred
componentWillUnmount	This hook is invoked when the component is about to be destroyed. Through this hook, you can clean things up. For example, you can use it to remove store subscriptions, cancel ongoing network requests, and so on.

You can also find a more comprehensive example in the code samples of this chapter, under `Chapter11/05-react-lifecycle-hook-class`. To try it out, you need to install the required dependencies using `yarn install` (or `npm install`) and then run the application using `yarn start` (or `npm start`). Once started, take a look at the console while you click on the different buttons. You should see how and when each hook is invoked.

Let's look at event handling now.

Emitting and handling events

Communication between React components is of course not limited to components passing props to their children. Child components can also emit events for their ancestors to handle.

In the previous examples, we have already seen how to define callback functions to react to events.

Let's look again at the code of the `Calculator` component:

```
render() {
    return (
        ...
        <button onClick={() => this.add(1)}>+1</button>
        ...
    );
}

add(value) {
    this.setState((state, props) => {
        return {currentResult: state.currentResult + value}
    });
}
```

In this example, the component associates the click event of the `button` child component to a local function. So, we already know how a parent can listen and react to events emitted by its children. Now, let's see how those children can emit custom events.

The solution is actually really simple: since a parent can pass props to its children, it can also pass a callback function as one of those props. In the React world, these are referred to as **render props**. They work like other props, but simply expect to receive a function and to return a React element; render props are therefore used for composition.

Here's an example with a parent component:

```
import React from 'react';
import {ChildComponent} from "./ChildComponent";

export class ParentComponent extends React.Component {
    render() {
        return (
            <ChildComponent onAdd={this.add}/>
        );
    }

    add(value) { console.log(`Parent has received the following value:
    ${value}`);
    }
}
```

And the following is its child:

```
import React from 'react';

export class ChildComponent extends React.Component {
    render() {
        return (
            <button onClick={() => this.props.onAdd(1)}>+1</button>
        );
    }
}
```

In this simple example, `ParentComponent` defines an `add` method that it passes down to `ChildComponent` through an `onAdd` prop. As you can see, `ChildComponent` receives it and simply calls it when the button is clicked upon.

 You can find the source of the preceding example in the code samples of this book, under `Chapter11/07-render-props`.

There are traps that you could easily fall into regarding the usage of the `this` keyword within this kind of callback function. You can learn about these here: `https://reactjs.org/docs/handling-events.html`. Actually, we have already learned how to avoid such issues using TypeScript.

If you want to fix the issue, then you need to change this:

```
add(value) {
    console.log(`Parent has received the following value: ${value}`);
}
```

The following is what it should be changed into:

```
add = (value) => {
    console.log(`Parent has received the following value: ${value}`);
}
```

With this change applied, calling `this.add` will work as expected. With the first form, `this` would, in fact, be pointing to the `props` object passed to `ChildComponent` when invoked in the click event handler of `ChildComponent`!

Render props are simple props, but they serve a particular purpose. They are useful since they allow us to reuse logic across components. As an added benefit, as we've just seen, they also enable simple communication between components.

Communication between distant components

We have shown a few examples of how to pass props from a component down to its children, but what happens when components that need to exchange data are further away from each other in the component tree?

In these cases, you have different choices.

First one is simply to keep passing the values through props, but you can only do that until the point where it becomes too cumbersome and creates strong coupling between otherwise unrelated components.

At that point, you can consider using a feature of React called **context** (`https://reactjs.org/docs/context.html`), which we won't be covering in this book. *The Context API is useful, but it can limit the reusability of your components, so it should be used consciously and sparingly.*

Yet another possibility is to use a state management solution such as Redux (which we briefly introduced in `Chapter 9`, *Introducing Vue.js*) or MobX (`https://github.com/mobxjs/mobx`), which is more and more popular.

You can find more patterns here:
`https://itnext.io/four-patterns-for-global-state-with-react-hooks-context-or-redux-cbc2dc787380`.

Controlling rendering

With Vue.js and Angular, a specific template syntax must be used to determine whether some elements should be rendered, visible, and so on.

With React, since we write and manipulate our components mainly using JavaScript (or TypeScript) code, it is actually very simple and intuitive to programmatically control rendering. Having all of the power of JavaScript constructs at our disposal, we can, for example, assign components to variables, use `if-else` constructs to decide what to render and how, and so on.

Here's an example taken from the official documentation demonstrating this:

```
class LoginControl extends React.Component {
  ...
  render() {
    const isLoggedIn = this.state.isLoggedIn;
    let button;

    if (isLoggedIn) {
      button = <LogoutButton onClick={this.handleLogoutClick} />;
    } else {
      button = <LoginButton onClick={this.handleLoginClick} />;
    }

    return (
      <div>
        <Greeting isLoggedIn={isLoggedIn} />
        {button}
      </div>
    );
  }
}
...
```

In this example, an `if-else` expression is used to decide whether a login or logout button needs to be rendered.

Since we can use any valid expression within JSX code, we can also embed logical expressions directly inside of the JSX code.

For example, it is possible to use a ternary operator (that is, `condition? true: false`):

```
render() {
  const isLoggedIn = this.state.isLoggedIn;
  return (
    <div>
      The user is <b>{isLoggedIn ? 'currently' : 'not'}</b> logged in.
    </div>
  );
}
```

You can learn more tricks in the official documentation of React:
`https://reactjs.org/docs/conditional-rendering.html`.

Rendering lists

If you still remember, with Angular and Vue.JS, rendering lists also required the use of a specific syntax. In addition, to improve the rendering efficiency, we could assign a unique *key* to each element in the rendered lists so that Angular and Vue could easily recognize those and only re-render what had really changed. React also has the same concepts.

Rendering lists is really easy with React. Once again, since we can use standard JavaScript code and assign React elements to variables/constants, nothing prevents us from simply iterating over array elements using a `map` operation to construct our components.

Here's an example:

```
const membersList = [
  {id: 1, name: 'Sébastien'},
  {id: 2, name: 'Alexis'},
  {id: 3, name: 'John'},
  {id: 4, name: 'Doe'}
];
const memberElements = membersList.map((member) =>
  <li key={member.id}>{member.name}</li>
);
```

This example clearly illustrates how straightforward it is. Once again, if you're good at JavaScript/TypeScript, then React is simple to learn!

 Did you notice the `key` attribute? This is what allows React to recognize specific elements of the list in the DOM tree. The values associated with the `key` should be *stable* and *unique*. Note that those values are only used by React; they're not added to the `props` object! You can learn more about those keys here: `https://medium.com/@adhithiravi/why-do-i-need-keys-in-react-lists-dbb522188bbb`.

Let's see how we could create a React component that renders a list (provided as input) through `props`:

```
function MembersList(props) {
  const members = props.members.map((member) =>
    <li key={member.id}>{member.name}</li>
  );
  return (
    <ul>{members}</ul>
  );
}

const membersList = ... // same as before
ReactDOM.render(
  <MembersList members={membersList} />,
  document.getElementById('root')
);
```

Here, the `MembersList` component expects an array of members to be passed in as `prop` and then renders it. Rendering that list to the DOM is just a matter of calling `ReactDOM.render(...)`, as explained previously.

 React gives a lot of freedom to components. For instance, a component's `render` function is not limited to returning a single element.

We should now look at templating.

Content projection/templating

With Vue and Angular, components can let other ones provide them with child components to render. With Vue, that feature is called *slots* and Angular refers to that principle as *content projection* or *transclusion* (a term inherited from AngularJS). React also has a similar feature.

In React, if a single slot (also called a **hole**) can be used to project content, then the convention is to use a prop called `children`. If you need to define multiple slots, then you can invent your own nomenclature (for example, header, content, footer, or anything that makes sense for your use case).

Let's see how this works with a single slot:

```jsx
import React from 'react';
import './App.css';
import {Gruyere} from "./Gruyere";

function App() {
  return (
    <div className="App">
      <Gruyere>
        <h1>Hello</h1>
        <span>World</span>
      </Gruyere>
    </div>
  );
}

export default App;
import React from 'react';

export class Gruyere extends React.Component {
    constructor(props) {
        super(props);
    }

    render() {
        return (
            <div>
                {this.props.children}
            </div>
        );
    }
}
```

Once more, this is really intuitive: the `Gruyere` component simply renders the passed children elements as part of its template.

You can learn more about this here: `https://reactjs.org/docs/composition-vs-inheritance.html#containment`.

Exploring React hooks

"Hooks embrace JavaScript closures and avoid introducing React-specific APIs where JavaScript already provides a solution."

- React website

In the previous sections, we covered different concepts of React, but we only provided examples for class components. While doing so, we kept repeating that **hooks** are *enablers* for the same functionality in function components. But what exactly are hooks and what is their purpose? Let's find out!

In the past, React class components were comparatively more powerful than function components: they could have an internal state, could hook into the lifecycle, and so on. Function components on the other hand, did not have equivalent APIs. The only way to use some features was to convert the concerned function components into class-based ones. This was clearly not ideal.

React hooks were introduced to fill that gap. They *provide a simple API allowing Functional Components to handle state, tap into the component's lifecycle, and much more!*

Hooks not only empower function components, but they also facilitate code reuse across components, and in particular, the reuse of stateful logic. By using hooks, it becomes possible to split components into smaller (but coherent/cohesive) functions and to avoid one of the pitfalls of class components, where related logic ends up being split into different lifecycle methods.

 To eliminate any doubt that you may have: no, React hooks cannot be used within class components.

By making function components more potent, the React team also aims to lower the barrier to entry for new React developers. They consider (rightfully so) classes to be more complex to understand. Oftentimes, developers can get over-enthusiastic about object orientation and create complex code bases, which isn't the best idea.

As we'll see, hooks can also be combined and it is possible to create custom ones.

Now you have an understanding of why hooks came to be, but you still don't know what they are and how they work. Let's find out by taking a look together at some of the hooks provided out of the box with React.

 You can find the sources of all of the following examples in the code samples of this book, under `Chapter11/06-react-hooks`.

Let's look at some of the built-in hooks now.

Defining state with the useState hook

The first React hook that we'll discover together is probably also the one that you'll use most: `useState`. As its name suggests, it **enables function components to have/use internal state**. React will maintain that internal state in-between the re-renders of the concerned components.

You can invoke the `useState` hook within a function component to define a *single* state variable, along with a function to update it.

 You can also call `useState` multiple times in a single component to define multiple state variables.

Take a look at a simple example:

```
import React, {useState} from 'react';

export function Switch(props) {
    const [currentSwitchStatus, switchStatus] = useState(false);

    return (
        <div>
            <span>The switch is currently: {currentSwitchStatus? 'ON':
            'OFF'} </span>
```

```
            <button onClick={() =>
            switchStatus(!currentSwitchStatus)}>Change the value!
            </button>
        </div>
    );
}
```

Here, we have created a `Switch` component. By default, the switch is disabled, but we can change its state by clicking on the button.

The most important line is this one: `const [currentSwitchStatus, switchStatus] = useState(false);`.

The value that we pass to the `useState` function (that is, to the hook) is the *initial value* for our new state variable.

The `useState` function returns a **tuple** composed of the following:

- There's the current state, which we assigned in the preceding code to a constant called `currentSwitchStatus`.
- It has a function that must be used to update the state. In this example, we have assigned it to a constant called `switchStatus`.

> The `[ ]` characters around our constants are an ES2015 feature called **array destructuring**. We'll explain how it works in the next section.

In the JSX code of the component, we have simply used the current state constant to display either **ON** or **OFF**. Finally, in the `onClick` event handler of the button, we called the state update function to switch the value.

> The state update function does not merge the new value into the previous one; it simply replaces it. Again, immutability is favored and that's a good thing!

That's it—you're now hooked on hooks, right?

For reference, see the following: `https://reactjs.org/docs/hooks-state.html`.

Array destructuring

Earlier in this chapter, we discovered object destructuring. **Array destructuring** is another useful ES2015 feature (also supported by TypeScript). It works in a similar way to object destructuring, but with arrays instead.

We have all written code like this at some point:

```
const values = ['A', 'B', 'C'];

const first = values[0];
const second = values[1];
const third = values[2];
```

It works fine, but it is also verbose. With array destructuring, we can easily extract elements of an array into other variables/constants.

Here's another version of the previous example, this time using array destructuring:

```
const values = ['A', 'B', 'C'];
const [first,second,third] = values;
```

The variables that we are destructuring the array elements into can be defined sooner as well.

It is also possible to define default values, in case some of the values we extract from the array are undefined:

```
const [first = 0, second = 1, third = 3] = ['A', undefined, 'B', 'C'];
console.log(second); // 1
```

Another cool trick that we can do with array destructuring is to swap elements in an array without relying on a temporary variable:

```
let x = 13;
let y = 37;
[x, y] = [y, x];

console.log(`${x} - ${y}`); // 37 - 13
```

Isn't this cool? Here's one more:

```
const [x, , y] = [1, 2, 3]; // x === 1, y === 3
```

With the preceding example, you can skip any array elements when **destructuring**.

Here's one last tip before we move on—it is possible to extract a subset of the values into variables, then extract all of the remaining ones in another one:

```
const values = ['A', 'B', 'C', 'D'];
const [first, ...allTheRest] = values;

console.log(allTheRest); // 'B', 'C', 'D'
```

Isn't that nice? Think about these tricks the next time you need to take elements out of an array!

Handling side-effects with the useEffect hook

This hook is the functional counterpart to the React lifecycle methods of class components. *The* useEffect *hook enables Functional Components to define logic that should execute after the component has been rendered/re-rendered.*

Before we explain further, let's look at an example:

```
import React, {useState, useEffect} from 'react';

export function Switch(props) {
    const [currentSwitchStatus, switchStatus] = useState(false);

    useEffect(() => {
        alert('The switch has been activated. Hopefully, this was not
        by mistake :)');
    });

    return (
        <div>
            <span>The switch is currently: {currentSwitchStatus? 'ON':
            'OFF'} </span>
            <button onClick={() =>
            switchStatus(!currentSwitchStatus)}>Change the value!
            </button>
        </div>
    );
}
```

In this example, notice that we call the useEffect hook and that we pass a function to it. This function will be called whenever React updates the DOM for this component (that is, after each render). As such, it is effectively a sort of combination of the componentDidMount, componentDidUpdate and componentWillUnmount lifecycle hooks that we saw previously.

A nice characteristic of `useEffect` is that, since it is within the scope of the component, it has access to its props and state; React hooks take full advantage of JavaScript closures.

 In practice, each time that your component is rendered, a *new function* will be passed to the `useEffect` hook. You can learn more about that here: `https://reactjs.org/docs/hooks-effect.html#explanation-why-effects-run-on-each-update`.

`useState` and `useEffect` are great and will definitely be used heavily, but React hooks hide a lot more power under the hood. You can use many other built-in hooks, but can also create custom ones and compose them to create higher-level abstractions: `https://reactjs.org/docs/hooks-custom.html`

There is more to know, but we have to stop here. Check out the *Further reading* section at the end of this chapter to learn more.

The React developer tools

We have now explored the most important features of React to be aware of when starting out. Before we take a look at how to use TypeScript with React, we're going to learn about some of the tools that can assist us while developing React applications.

First of all, the React team maintains an official web browser plugin called the **React developer tools**, allowing users to inspect running React applications.

Similar to the Vue developer tools, it allows users to take a look at the component tree, the state of each component, and much more:

React developer tools in Google Chrome

> Did you notice the **Profiler** tab? Here's a guide explaining how to
> use that feature to diagnose performance issues in React
> applications:
> `https://www.netlify.com/blog/2018/08/29/using-the-react-dev`
> `tools-profiler-to-diagnose-react-app-performance-issues`.

You can download and install the React developer tools for Google Chrome and
Mozilla Firefox:

- Google Chrome:
  `https://chrome.google.com/webstore/detail/react-developer-tools/f`
  `mkadmapgofadopljbjfkapdkoienihi`
- Mozilla Firefox:
  `https://addons.mozilla.org/en-US/firefox/addon/react-devtools`

Go ahead and install the React developer tools now; they'll prove useful later on. It
feels a bit unfair to stop here, but we have to move on. Don't hesitate to read the
official documentation to learn more: `https://github.com/facebook/react/tree/`
`master/packages/react-devtools`.

Taking advantage of the Create React App (CRA) tool

In the early days of React, a common complaint in the community was that the lack of
tooling was detrimental to the developer experience. Fortunately, an officially
supported **boilerplate** has been created since then and is now provided with a CLI to
allow customizations. By boilerplate, we mean a default project structure, with
configuration, build scripts, and so on.

CRA is React's tool of choice. With it, you can easily scaffold new React applications.
In essence, it is similar to the Vue and Angular CLIs, but doesn't go the extra mile like
the Angular CLI does (for example, it doesn't support scaffolding UI components).

The official website of CRA can be found here: `https://create-react-app.dev`.

Applications created with CRA come with *batteries included*. They incorporate a
modern build system that uses Webpack, Babel, and other tools underneath the
covers. Usually, you won't even need to look at the build; it just works out of the box
and lets you concentrate on what matters most: the application itself. If, at some
point, you need to adapt the configuration, note that you can customize anything you
fancy: `https://auth0.com/blog/how-to-configure-create-react-app`.

All projects created using CRA include a set of pre-defined scripts such as `start`, `build`, and `test`:

- The `build` script bundles your application.
- The `start` script builds and serves it.
- The `test` script launches the test runner.

You can find out more here:
`https://facebook.github.io/create-react-app/docs/available-scripts`.

CRA includes a whole lot more than just a build and some scripts. For example, it has support for automated tests, transpilation, bundling, linting, live reloading, and source maps.

Also, projects created using CRA can be updated to use the latest and greatest build/scripts:
`https://facebook.github.io/create-react-app/docs/updating-to-new-releases`.

Creating a project using create-react-app

Using CRA to create a new React application is as simple as executing the following command:

```
npx create-react-app my-app
```

Or you can use `yarn`:

```
yarn create react-app my-app
```

Once done, the project will be ready to use in the chosen folder. CRA uses `yarn` by default, but you can also use `npm` if you prefer. After having created the file and folder structure, CRA will automatically start the installation of the dependencies.

You can find an example project in the assets of this book, under `Chapter11/09-create-react-app-example`.

File and folder structure

Here is an overview of the created file/folder structure taken from the official documentation:

```
my-app
├── README.md
├── node_modules
├── package.json
├── .gitignore
├── public
│   ├── favicon.ico
│   ├── index.html
│   └── manifest.json
└── src
    ├── App.css
    ├── App.js
    ├── App.test.js
    ├── index.css
    ├── index.js
    ├── logo.svg
    └── serviceWorker.js
```

The first thing to notice is the simplicity of the structure.

In the `public` folder, you can find the `index.html` page, along with the favicon (that is, the icon that goes at the top left of the web browser tab) and a `manifest.json` file.

If you open the `index.html` file, you won't see any direct mention of React. Don't worry though—it really is there. The build system provided by CRA will take care of bundling your code and third-party dependencies (including React) and injecting these in the `index.html` file.

 The `manifest.json` file is one of the elements necessary to create **Progressive Web Applications (PWAs)**. Specifically, this manifest allows mobile and desktop devices to **install** and use your web application as if it was a native one. For instance, users will get an icon to launch the application. You can learn more about that manifest here: https://developer.mozilla.org/en-US/docs/Mozilla/Add-ons/WebExtensions/manifest.json.

In the `src` folder, you'll find `index.js`, which is the entry point of the application that loads React:

```
import React from 'react';
import ReactDOM from 'react-dom';
import './index.css';
import App from './App';
import * as serviceWorker from './serviceWorker';

ReactDOM.render(<App />, document.getElementById('root'));

// If you want your app to work offline and load faster, you can
change
// unregister() to register() below. Note this comes with some
// pitfalls.
// Learn more about service workers: https://bit.ly/CRA-PWA
serviceWorker.unregister();
```

We already covered `ReactDOM.render(...)` earlier. Here, the code simply renders an instance of the `App` React component inside of the `root` div.

 Service Workers (SW) are something new in this book. We cannot really cover these here, but you should at least know that they are a key piece in the PWA puzzle. Thanks to service workers, we can create web experiences that continue to work even when the user is offline. Check out the following Mozilla Developer Network article to learn more:
https://developer.mozilla.org/en-US/docs/Web/API/Service_Wo
rker_API/Using_Service_Workers.

In the generated application, the last important element is, of course, the `App` component.

CRA is not very opinionated about the project structure, so you have a lot of freedom in choosing how to organize everything.

Generating a TypeScript project

At this point in the chapter, you might be worried (or sad) about not seeing TypeScript code for so long. Don't panic just yet though; we're just getting started! We first wanted to present **vanilla** React code before adding TypeScript to the mix.

The first good news that we can give you is that CRA supports generating TypeScript-enabled React applications.

It is as simple as adding the `--typescript` flag to the `create-react-app` command:

```
npx create-react-app my-app --typescript
```

React applications created in this way exhibit some differences from what we've shown before.

First of all, they have a `tsconfig.json` file that looks as follows:

```json
{
  "compilerOptions": {
    "target": "es5",
    "lib": [
      "dom",
      "dom.iterable",
      "esnext"
    ],
    "allowJs": true,
    "skipLibCheck": true,
    "esModuleInterop": true,
    "allowSyntheticDefaultImports": true,
    "strict": true,
    "forceConsistentCasingInFileNames": true,
    "module": "esnext",
    "moduleResolution": "node",
    "resolveJsonModule": true,
    "isolatedModules": true,
    "noEmit": true,
    "jsx": "react"
  },
  "include": [
    "src"
  ]
}
```

In this configuration file, there is an interesting option that we haven't encountered so far: `jsx`. Its name should give you a hint about what is coming next!

Also, note that the file containing the `App` component now has a `.tsx` extension. Indeed, as we'll see right after, TypeScript has built-in support for JSX! We'll explore the code in a jiffy.

Finally, if you take a look at the `package.json` file, you'll see that TypeScript typings have been added for `react`, `react-dom`, and `jest`.

With Visual Studio Code and IntelliJ/WebStorm, you can debug your code directly in the editor: `https://facebook.github.io/create-react-app/docs/setting-up-your-editor#debugging-in-the-editor`.

You can find an example project in the assets of this book, under `Chapter11/10-create-react-app-typescript`.

For further reference, check out the following: `https://create-react-app.dev/docs/adding-typescript`.

Leveraging TypeScript with React

Even if it is not a real surprise, we can finally say it out loud: **yes, TypeScript also works great with React**.

As we mentioned in the previous section, TypeScript actually has built-in support for JSX and there are typings available for React and many of the surrounding libraries.

In this section, we'll explore how we can leverage TypeScript to write awesome React applications.

And let's reassure you already: we will, of course, use TypeScript and React while rewriting the LyricsFinder application together in the next chapter.

Many of the TypeScript patterns and best practices for React that we will present in the following sections are heavily inspired by Martin Hochel's article: `https://medium.com/@martin_hotell/10-typescript-pro-tips-patterns-with-or-without-react-5799488d6680`. Martin is a great TypeScript and React developer, so make sure to read his excellent articles and to subscribe to his blog updates!

You will find the sources of the examples in this section within the code samples of this book, under `Chapter11/11-react-typescript-basics`.

JSX support through TSX files

TypeScript has built-in support for JSX, through the `.tsx` file extension. Writing JSX code in TypeScript grants all of the type safety benefits that we are used to.

To enable JSX support in TypeScript, the first step is to enable the `jsx` option in the compiler configuration file (that is, `tsconfig.json`). The value associated with that option determines what TypeScript does with the JSX code when it transpiles the files. The different values allowed are `preserve`, `react`, and `react-native`.

By default, projects created using the latest versions of the Create React App tool use the `react` mode. In that mode, TypeScript will replace JSX code with `React.createElement()` calls, generating pure JavaScript code.

Not so long ago, CRA was using the `preserve` mode instead, which kept the JSX code intact in the output of the TypeScript compiler. At the time, a second transpilation step was necessary to finally get JavaScript code that could actually be understood by web browsers.

In `.tsx` files, the React naming conventions still apply: components should generally start with an uppercase letter, to distinguish them from built-in elements, which are always in lowercase and are referred to as *intrinsic elements*. It is important to respect this rule, as both TypeScript and React treat these differently.

We'll keep the usual file naming convention for TS and TSX files: **dash-case** (also known as **kebab-case**).

When the TypeScript compiler encounters JSX elements, it needs to determine whether it is an intrinsic element (for example, `div`, `h1`, and so on) or a *value-based* one (that is, a custom component defined in the application).

As we have said before, React treats these differently. As stated in the official React and TypeScript documentation, built-in elements such as `div` are created using `React.createElement("div")`, while application components such as `App` are created using `React.createElement(App)`. You can read more about the distinction and differences in treatment here: `https://reactjs.org/docs/jsx-in-depth.html#user-defined-components-must-be-capitalized`.

Just like with standard JSX code, you will only be able to use a custom application component if it is *in scope* (that is, either declared in the same file or imported).

As we saw earlier, we can create React components using either a functional style or an object-oriented style. TypeScript will first check whether the component uses a functional style (as it is React's default recommendation). If it doesn't, then TypeScript will try to resolve that component as a class. If that also fails, then the compiler will bail out. You should not mix this up with what React checks at runtime.

Whether you use one style or the other, TypeScript ensures that the component returns a valid `JSX.Element` (or `null`, `false`, or an array of elements).

We'll show you how to write components using both approaches but, while rewriting LyricsFinder, we will focus on the functional style, which is more in line with React's philosophy and guidelines.

Take a look at the JSX page in TypeScript's reference documentation to learn more: `https://www.typescriptlang.org/docs/handbook/jsx.html`.

Class components with TypeScript

Here is what a React class component looks like with TypeScript:

```
import React, {Component} from 'react';

type Props = {};
type State = {};

export class HelloWorld extends Component<Props, State> {
    render() {
        return <span>Hello World!</span>
    }
}
```

Now that we can use TypeScript, we can, of course, start adding types—great! The first thing that we did in the preceding example was define the shape of the `props` object and the state. In this basic example, these are empty though.

 We have used a custom `type` rather than `interface` mainly for conciseness (there is simply less code to type). Type aliases are a good fit with React thanks to their composability.

Our component extends the `Component` class and uses its generic type arguments to pass our `Props` and `State` types, allowing TypeScript to give us autocompletion and type checking within the class.

One thing that you should notice is that we did not use a constructor to define the initial state/props. There is already a constructor in the superclass and, usually, we won't need to create a constructor ourselves. React handles the instantiation of the components so we don't need to take care of that ourselves.

Great—let's continue.

Class components with internal state

Let's now see what a component with internal state looks like:

```
import React, {Component} from 'react';

type Props = {};

const initialState = Object.freeze({
    currentSwitchStatus: false,
});

type State = typeof initialState;

export class Switch extends Component<Props, State> {
    readonly state = initialState;

    render() {
        const {currentSwitchStatus} = this.state;

        return <div>
            <span>The switch is currently: {currentSwitchStatus ? 'ON'
            : 'OFF'} </span>
            <button onClick={() => this.switchStatus()}>Change the
            value!</button>
        </div>
    }

    switchStatus = () => {
        this.setState((state: State, _: Props) => {
            return {currentSwitchStatus: !state.currentSwitchStatus};
        });
    }
}
```

Here, there are multiple interesting points to understand:

- To define the initial internal state of the component, we have simply created a constant outside of the class.
- We have made the `initialState` object immutable by using `Object.freeze`. This ensures that we will not mutate it by mistake. You can learn more about that API here: `https://developer.mozilla.org/en-US/docs/Web/JavaScript/Reference /Global_Objects/Object/freeze`.
- The `State` type is defined by using type inference from `initialState`; this allows us to avoid duplicating type information.
- The `state` field has been marked as `readonly`. This ensures that we won't re-assign it by mistake and that we will instead call the `this.setState(...)` method as required. Of course, this protection completely disappears at runtime since this only exists before the code is transpiled.
- We have used **object destructuring** to get a hold of the `currentSwitchStatus` value in the state. This is not mandatory but is usually more readable (especially when a prop or state element is used multiple times).

We have already discussed the benefits of immutability on multiple occasions so far, but we'll reiterate, as immutability is also heavily recommended with React. *Immutability helps us to avoid silly mistakes and makes our applications more robust and more predictable.*

 If you need some logic to initialize the state of your component (for example, based on the props it has received), then take a look at the pattern proposed by Martin Hochel: `https://medium.com/@martin_hotell/10-typescript-pro-tips-pa tterns-with-or-without-react-5799488d6680#6912`.

You can already see that TypeScript improves the type safety of our code. We could have added other types here and there, but those would have only added unnecessary noise. For example, the return type of the `render()` function is actually `ReactNode`, but specifying it would just hinder readability without helping us in any meaningful way.

Types provided by React typings

Here are some of the types defined by `@types/react` that it might be useful to know about:

- `Component`: This is the base class for class components.
- `FunctionComponent` or `FC` (shorthand): This is the base interface for Functional Components.
- `ReactNode`: This is any React element that can be rendered. This type is often useful for child components.
- `JSX.Element`: This is the type used for all JSX expressions. Note that JSX expressions are black boxes.
- `JSX.IntrinsicElements`: These are all built-in components (for example, `div`, `span`, and so on).

Components written using TypeScript can, of course, accept props—let's see how.

Class components accepting props

Let's now take a look at an example component that accepts some props:

```
import React, {Component} from 'react';

const defaultProps = Object.freeze({
    buttonText: "DEFAULT BUTTON TEXT",
    messageToDisplay: "DEFAULT MESSAGE",
});

type Props = typeof defaultProps;

type State = {};

export class CustomizableButton extends Component<Props, State> {
    readonly state = {};
    static readonly defaultProps = defaultProps;

    render() {
        const {buttonText} = this.props;
        const {messageToDisplay} = this.props;

        return <div>
            <input type="button" value={buttonText} onClick={() =>
            window.alert(messageToDisplay)} />
```

```
          </div>
      }
  }
```

In this example, the `CustomizableButton` component accepts two props to be defined: `buttonText` and `messageToDisplay`. Both of these have default values, allowing users of the component not to specify them. Also, as proposed by Martin Hochel, we use `Object.freeze` as a best practice to make sure that we don't mutate anything by mistake.

As we did with the state earlier on, we have used type inference with the `typeof` operator to avoid having to write additional boilerplate.

Within the class, there are a few details to pay attention to.

First of all, notice `static readonly defaultProps = defaultProps`. This is actually a feature of TypeScript 3.0 at work. This syntax allows us to define the default value for our props in a type-safe manner.

Before TypeScript 3.0, workarounds were required to achieve this. These involved declaring properties as optional and using definite assignment assertions within the `render` function. You can learn more about this feature here: https://www.typescriptlang.org/docs/handbook/release-notes/typescript-3-0.html#support-for-defaultprops-in-jsx.

On the usage side, the important difference to notice is the type: we now get autocompletion when using the component, thanks to TypeScript and `Props`.

We'll stop here with class components because our goal was simply to give you an idea about how to write them using TypeScript. Make sure to take a look at Martin Hochel's article; as mentioned before, it is a great reference for writing *idiomatic* React/TypeScript code, in line with the JavaScript philosophy.

 React has a *strict* mode that you can enable by wrapping the JSX of your App with a `<React.StrictMode>` component. When the strict mode is enabled, React can detect some issues early on and give you warnings. You can learn more about React's strict mode here: https://reactjs.org/docs/strict-mode.html.

The preceding syntax is quite nice and bearable, but let's now look at Functional Components instead. Hopefully, you'll see that we can further reduce the amount of boilerplate thanks to these.

Functional Components with TypeScript

Let's initiate our discussion with a basic example:

```
import React from 'react';

export const HelloWorldTSFunctionalComponent = () => (
    <span>Hello world from our TS Functional Component</span>
);
```

This is the simplest TypeScript-based Functional Component that you can imagine. As you can see, there's really nothing visible to distinguish it from what we saw earlier in this chapter in pure JS.

As with class components, we could add types here and there, such as : FC<Props> (that is, Functional Component) for the component type or : JSX.Element for the component function's return type, but it would not help us *at all*; it would just hinder the readability.

Compare the previous example with the following:

```
import React, {FC} from 'react';

type Props = {};

export const HelloWorldTSFunctionalComponent: FC<Props> = ():
JSX.Element => (
    <span>Hello world from our TS Functional Component</span>
);
```

Which form is better in your opinion? Indeed, the component is a Functional Component (hence the FC type), but we don't have props or anything else here, so what's the point? Also, the component's function indeed returns a JSX Element, but the TypeScript compiler is smart enough to infer that for us.

Regularly throughout this book, we have added types all around to make the examples clearer to beginners' eyes, but in practice, you should try to leverage type inference as much as possible to improve readability while maintaining maximal type safety.

Let's now look at a more involved example:

```
import React, {useEffect, useState} from 'react';

const defaultProps = Object.freeze({
    alertMessage: 'The switch has been activated. Hopefully, this was
```

```
        not by mistake :)', // 1
});

type Props = {aMandatoryProp: string} & Partial<typeof defaultProps>;
// 2, 3

export const SwitchWithAlert = (props: Props) => { // 4, 5
    const [currentSwitchStatus, switchStatus] = useState(false); // 6

    console.log(`Mandatory prop provided: ${props.aMandatoryProp}`);

    useEffect(() => {
        alert('SwitchWithAlert Functional Component rendered');
        if(currentSwitchStatus) {
            alert(props.alertMessage);
        }
    });

    return (
        <div>
            <span>The switch is currently: {currentSwitchStatus? 'ON':
            'OFF'}</span>
            <button onClick={() => switchStatus
            (!currentSwitchStatus)}>Change the value!</button>
        </div>
    );
};

SwitchWithAlert.defaultProps = defaultProps; // 7
```

This example is more elaborate, but it demonstrates how to define props (including optional ones) and state with Functional Components in TypeScript.

Here are some things that you should observe:

1. We have defined a default value for the `alertMessage` property within the `defaultProps` constant.

2. The `Props` type has only one mandatory property: `aMandatoryProperty`.

3. The properties that have a default value have been added to the `Props` type with a *type intersection* and have been marked as optional using `Partial<typeof defaultProps>`. This syntax might not be the most intuitive to take in, but it is really helpful to master it.

4. Our `SwitchWithAlert` component receives a `Props` object as input.

5. You could use object destructuring there.

2. We have used the `useState` hook as before and, here, TypeScript infers the type of the `switchStatus` function correctly:
   - For more complex data types, you can help TypeScript by using the generic type of `useState` as follows: `useState<SomeComplexStateType>(...)`.

3. The last important detail to pay attention to is the way that we have passed the default props: `SwitchWithAlert.defaultProps = defaultProps;`. This syntax is supported since TypeScript 3.1, as explained here: https://www.typescriptlang.org/docs/handbook/release-notes/typescript-3-1.html#properties-declarations-on-functions.

 At the time of writing, there are still some issues around this last point in TypeScript. There are also discussions in the React community to deprecate `defaultProps` on function components: https://github.com/reactjs/rfcs/blob/createelement-rfc/text/0000-create-element-changes.md#deprecate-defaultprops-on-function-components.

Let's continue.

Introducing the prop-types library

One thing that we haven't mentioned so far about React is that it provides an additional library called **prop-types** (https://www.npmjs.com/package/prop-types), which you can use to define the types of props. That library only performs runtime checks though. It will be of interest to you if you share your components with the outside world (for example, as an `npm` package).

If you only use your components within your own TypeScript-based project, then they don't bring any added value, since TypeScript does compile-time checks.

You can learn more about `PropTypes` here:

- https://reactjs.org/docs/typechecking-with-proptypes.html
- https://stackoverflow.com/questions/41746028/proptypes-in-a-typescript-react-application

Going further with Functional Components

Let's look at an example with a `TodoList` component that renders a set of `TodoItem` components:

```
import React from 'react';

export interface TodoItem {
    id: string;
    description: string;
    done: boolean;
}

type Props = {
    todo: TodoItem;
    itemClicked: (id: string) => void;
};

export const TodoItem = (props: Props) => {
    const {todo} = props;

    return <li id={todo.id} onClick={() => props.itemClicked(todo.id)}
style={{backgroundColor: 'gray', cursor: 'pointer'}}>
    {todo.description}</li>;
};
```

Our `TodoItem` component accepts two inputs:

- It accepts a `TodoItem` object.
- It accepts a function that will be called when the `todo` item is clicked upon. Notice that the shape of the required function is clearly defined.

In the component, we have added some simple inline styles. Inline styles are not recommended though; we have just added those to show you the syntax. To define CSS styles, we pass a plain old JavaScript object where the keys are the CSS property names. The advantage with TypeScript is that we also get autocompletion for all of those properties. You can learn more about how to style React components here:
`https://codeburst.io/4-four-ways-to-style-react-components-ac6f323da822.`

Here's the code:

```
import React from 'react';
import {TodoItem} from './todo-item';

type Props = {
    todos: readonly TodoItem[];
};

export const TodoList = ({todos}: Props) => {
    const items: JSX.Element[] = todos.map(todo => <TodoItem todo=
    {todo} itemClicked={(id) => alert
    (`Todo item clicked: ${id}`)} />);

    return <div>{items}</div>
};
```

The preceding `TodoList` component accepts a single prop: an array of `TodoItem` objects.

 Did you notice that we used the `readonly` keyword next to the array type? Earlier in this book, we achieved the same goal using `ReadonlyArray`. Support for using the `readonly` keyword for arrays was introduced in TypeScript 3.4: https://www.typescriptlang.org/docs/handbook/release-notes/typescript-3-4.html.

In the function definition, we use object destructuring to avoid having to write `props`. Then, we construct an array of JSX elements simply by mapping the `todos` array, creating a `TodoItem` component for each element in the array.

Finally, we return `div` containing our JSX elements, which will render them all.

This component can be used as follows:

```
<TodoList todos={[{id: '1', description: 'First', done: false}, {id:
'2', description: 'Second', done: false}, {id: '3', description:
'Third', done: false}]}/>
```

To end this series of examples, let's look at a component that accepts child components to be passed in through props (that is, using content projection):

```
import React, {ReactNode} from 'react';

type Props = {
    children: ReactNode;
}

export const Header = ({children}: Props) => <div>{children}</div>;
```

As you can see, there's not much to it; this component just wraps whatever elements have been passed in through props into div.

As a matter of fact, the children prop exists on *all* React components, but it is optional by default. By defining it in our Props type, we have made it mandatory.

Notice the ReactNode type that we have used for the children prop. If you open up the typings of React (which can be found under node_modules/@types/react/index.d.ts), then you'll find the following definitions related to ReactNode:

```
type ReactNode = ReactChild | ReactFragment | ReactPortal | boolean |
null | undefined;
type ReactChild = ReactElement | ReactText;
type ReactText = string | number;
interface ReactNodeArray extends Array<ReactNode> {}
type ReactFragment = {} | ReactNodeArray;
...
```

These type definitions are interesting to discover, as they shed some more light on what can be passed to our children property. For example, a simple string or number would be valid, as well as a single React element, or an array of any of those. Using those types, you can more precisely control what can be passed to the children prop.

You can find a few more advanced composition patterns for React children in the following article:
https://medium.com/@martin_hotell/react-children-composition-patterns-with
-typescript-56dfc8923c64.

Here, we have shown the very basics to get you started. We'll leverage this knowledge in our project. Feel free to go through the references in the *Further reading* section at the end of this chapter if you want to learn more.

Take some time to digest all this information about React before you continue with the next section because we'll be looking at something completely different. Take the opportunity to try out the samples and code some components of your own.

Discovering NestJS in a jiffy

As we said in the introduction of this chapter, we will be using **NestJS** as the base building block for the backend of the new version of LyricsFinder.

Let's quickly introduce NestJS and explain why we have chosen it over the numerous alternatives:

The official NestJS logo

There are many ways to create backend applications based on Node.js. Of course, our goal is to leverage TypeScript wherever possible in the context of this book.

For instance, we could have used the standard Node.js SDK or the Express library (`https://expressjs.com`) to get higher-level abstractions. The first option would've been too involved and would have required us to explain many lower-level **primitives**. The second was more approachable, but we saw a great opportunity to introduce a modern and really appealing solution: **NestJS**.

NestJS (`https://nestjs.com`) is an open source (MIT licensed) framework that can be used to build server-side applications on top of Node.js. *NestJS fully supports TypeScript (it is actually written in TypeScript itself), functional programming, and functional reactive programming styles.*

It provides everything that you would expect from a framework: abstractions, reusable building blocks, patterns, tools, guidance, and so on. Also, NestJS is extensible and already has quite a lot of plugins, including an official one for GraphQL (which we will cover later in this chapter).

Architecture

Architecture is actually the key difference between NestJS and **bare-bones** Express. Comparing NestJS and Express is a bit like comparing Angular to React; one is a framework and the other one is a library. Neither is better or worse, but they clearly have a different philosophy.

At its core, Express is a routing library: it allows you to associate URLs to functions and request elements to function arguments, define interceptors (that is, middleware) and it has an extension layer to plug in additional middleware. And that's about it!

As a matter of fact, *NestJS is built on top of Express and provides many additional features heavily inspired by Angular*. As you will soon discover, many features of NestJS purposefully work and look almost exactly the same as their Angular counterpart! Developers already used to Angular will feel right at home with NestJS.

 We could've introduced NestJS together with Angular, but we didn't want to risk confusing you about the two. Nevertheless, if you are working on a full-stack project, then combining NestJS on the backend with Angular on the frontend makes a lot of sense!

First of all, NestJS actually aims to provide a *platform* for backend development. As such, it not only provides reusable libraries, but also tooling, patterns, best practices, and so on.

CLI

The main tool provided by NestJS is its CLI, which mimics the Angular CLI in many ways.

For instance, creating a NestJS project is as simple as this:

```
npx @nestjs/cli new-project-name
```

It **supports schematics** and can be used to generate starting code for services, controllers, pipes, guards, and so on. We will use this CLI on multiple occasions while developing our backend application.

Modules

The first thing that NestJS borrows from Angular is its *abstractions*, such as **modules** that allow us to decompose our applications and properly isolate features/concerns.

NestJS modules are almost exactly the same as Angular modules.

They can also be created using the NestJS CLI:

```
npx @nestjs/cli generate module helloworld
```

Once again, this is the same command as we could use with the Angular CLI.

Let's look at the generated module file, which you can find in the code samples of this book, under Chapter11/12-NestJS/src/helloworld/helloworld.module.ts:

```
import { Module } from '@nestjs/common';

@Module({})
export class HelloworldModule {}
```

Do you see anything surprising? No? Exactly! There are no surprises here!

Now you probably wonder whether there is also an App module as with Angular. And yes, there is!

Here's what it looks like in our hello world NestJS example:

```
import { Module } from '@nestjs/common';
import { AppController } from './app.controller';
import { AppService } from './app.service';
import { HelloworldModule } from './helloworld/helloworld.module';

@Module({
  imports: [HelloworldModule],
  controllers: [AppController],
  providers: [AppService],
})
export class AppModule {}
```

Notice again the familiar `@Module` decorator. Its properties are also similar: we can see an array of `imports` and an array of `providers`, exactly like Angular's.

Dependency injection

This brings us to the feature that NestJS **borrows** from Angular: **DI**. Once again, it works exactly like with Angular.

In reality, the whole API of NestJS is very close to the Angular API. Kamil Mysliwiec, the author of NestJS, did this on purpose, to limit the mental overhead of learning another framework with its own specific universe. Thanks to this, **NestJS is really easy to learn for anyone already familiar with Angular**.

Just like with Angular, we can use an `@Injectable` decorator to declare injectable elements, define `providers`, and easily inject instances where required.

 One (important) difference between NestJS and Angular providers is the fact that **NestJS providers are private by default.** This means that they have to be exported to be made publicly available. Angular works in the opposite way; providers are public by default and are globally accessible unless otherwise specified.

Let's look at controllers and routing.

Controllers and routing

One thing that NestJS has that Angular does not is **controllers**. Controllers are used to define endpoints in NestJS and to associate requests/parameters to functions/arguments, shown as follows:

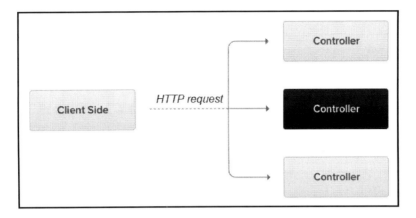

How Controllers are used in NestJS

NestJS's *routing* mechanism is responsible for identifying which controller should receive and process incoming requests. Indeed, NestJS's routing system is built upon Express or, optionally, Fastify (`https://www.fastify.io`).

A controller's purpose is to handle the requests targeting specific *routes* of the application. The routing mechanism controls which controllers/methods receive which requests.

Usually, controllers are associated with multiple routes, each of which implements different operations. For instance, in a `Customer` controller, we could define routes to handle the different CRUD operations.

NestJS controllers are created using TypeScript classes and dedicated decorators such as `@Get()`, `@Post()`, and `@Body`. These decorators associate the classes/methods with the metadata allowing NestJS to define its internal **routing table**.

Let's take a look at an example created using the CLI:

```
npx @nestjs/cli generate controller hello
```

Here is an example controller:

```
import {Controller, Get, Query} from '@nestjs/common';

@Controller('/')
export class HelloController {
    @Get('hello')
    hello(@Query('name') name?: string) {
        const personName = name? name: 'stranger';
        return `Hello ${personName}`;
    }
}
```

Unsurprisingly, controllers are declared using the `@Controller` decorator. Within that decorator, we can set an optional base path associated with this controller. Here, we have set it to `/` to match the root route of the backend, but it isn't mandatory in this case.

The `@Get('hello')` decorator associates our `hello` method with the `/hello` route, which means our method will be invoked whenever a GET request is sent toward `/hello`. The method name actually doesn't matter. All that matters is the combination of the base path defined on the `@Controller` and/or the one defined on the method's decorator.

Also notice the `@Query` decorator, which we have used to retrieve the value of a query parameter (if present). In the method, we use the associated value (or lack thereof) to determine what message to return.

Accessing the URL `http://localhost:3000/hello` results in the following response: `Hello stranger`. If you provide the query parameter in the URL `http://localhost:3000/hello?name=world`, then the response becomes `Hello world`. Neat!

Of course, you can also access other parts of the request objects:

- Their body using `@Body`
- Path parameters using `@Param`
- Headers using `@Headers`
- Or even the whole request using `@Request`

Check out the official controller documentation to learn about how NestJS handles routing, method parameters, and return values.

And everything else

As frustrating as it is, we have to stop here, even if there is a ton more to learn about NestJS.

For example, NestJS supports the following:

- Middleware
- Exception handlers
- Pipes
- Guards
- Interceptors
- Lifecycle hooks

But also authentication, validation, caching, logging, serialization, security, compression, configuration, databases/ORM, and lots more!

The official website's documentation is top-notch, so dive into it if you want to know more.

 Don't forget to check the *Further reading* section at the end of this chapter to find useful references.

Let's learn about GraphQL now!

Introducing GraphQL

Let's now quickly try to understand what GraphQL is and why it is all the rage these days:

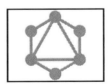

The official GraphQL logo

We'll start with a quick refresher about REST.

Introduction

GraphQL (`https://graphql.org`) is a query language created at Facebook around 2012. Facebook's goal with GraphQL was to create an efficient querying and data fetching API, able to simply and efficiently query/retrieve anything from Facebook's enormous data graph.

The first thing to understand about GraphQL is that there are two parts to it:

- A server-side runtime that listens for **GraphQL requests**, interprets them and executes them, optionally returning requested data
- A set of client-side libraries that you can use to create/send GraphQL queries to pull/push data

 Some see GraphQL as the future of APIs while others criticize it and prefer to stick with REST (or even SOAP). We don't want to pick a side. Try each and choose the right tool for the right job. It is up to you and your teams to decide which is best in your specific situation! Don't let the hype guide your choices.

As stated in the official documentation, the server-side GraphQL runtime is not tied to any specific database or storage engine, which means that you can add it on top of anything you'd like (for example, MySQL, MongoDB, a filesystem, and so on). This is one of the key strengths of GraphQL. For instance, in our case, we will plug GraphQL on top of the MusixMatch web API.

GraphQL libraries exist for many programming languages, including JavaScript/TypeScript, Java/Kotlin, Python, and so on.

Compared to REST, GraphQL is much more *prescriptive*. There is a clear specification detailing how queries work, how to filter datasets, how to mutate data, pass variables, and so on. In that regard, GraphQL is great because it doesn't leave too much room for **bikeshedding**.

In the following section, we'll briefly introduce some GraphQL concepts. Once again, consider this a really condensed and basic introduction; we do not intend to go in-depth here.

Queries

Let's look at what GraphQL queries look like.

The query language of GraphQL is another of its strong points. It allows clients to define both the data to retrieve and the required shape of that data. This means that **a GraphQL *client* can not only be selective about the data to retrieve, but also dictate how the response should be structured!**

Compared to REST, this is incredibly powerful and is standardized by the GraphQL specification. With RESTful APIs, since there is no standard, each and every API can implement (or not) features such as include/exclude, pagination, search, and filtering. With GraphQL, there is one well-defined method for many concepts.

A complete learning guide is available on the GraphQL website: `https://graphql.org/learn`.

For the following examples, we will use the Star Wars GraphQL API, which you can find here: `https://github.com/graphql/swapi-graphql`. You can try all of the examples through the playground available here: `https://graphql.github.io/swapi-graphql`.

We'll start with a basic example where a client wants to retrieve the titles of all of the Star Wars movies:

```
{
   allFilms {
     films {
       title
     }
   }
}
```

In this example, we have used the `allFilms` query of the Star Wars API and we have asked to retrieve the `title` property of each item in the `films` collection.

The GraphQL queries are *not JSON*, even if they're a bit similar.

Here's an extract of the response that the GraphQL server would return:

```
{
  "data": {
    "allFilms": {
      "films": [
        {
          "title": "A New Hope"
        },
        {
          "title": "The Empire Strikes Back"
        },
        {
          "title": "Return of the Jedi"
        },
        ...
      ]
    }
  }
}
```

As requested by our GraphQL client, the server has only provided the `title` property. This feature of GraphQL is incredibly powerful and can greatly improve the network friendliness of your applications.

 As you can see, contrary to the queries, **the GraphQL responses are using JSON**, which means that they can easily be parsed. Not that it is the only possibility, but it is the default one.

Let's look at a second example. This time, our client wants to retrieve the ID, name, and species name of each character in the Star Wars movies:

```
{
  characters: allPeople {
    people {
      id
      name
      species {
        name
      }
    }
  }
}
```

The syntax is quite straightforward.

> Notice the `characters:` prefix in front of `allPeople`. This notation allows us to define an **alias**. Aliases are useful to further customize the shape of responses.

In return, the server might respond with the following:

```
{
  "data": {
    "characters": {
      "people": [
        {
          "id": "cGVvcGxlOjE=",
          "name": "Luke Skywalker",
          "species": {
            "name": "Human"
          }
        },
        {
          "id": "cGVvcGxlOjI=",
          "name": "C-3PO",
          "species": {
            "name": "Droid"
          }
        },
        ...
      ]
    }
  }
}
```

Again, the server has responded with the data that we asked for (no more, no less) and using the shape and structure that we requested.

This is quite simple, isn't it?

> One thing to know about GraphQL is that requests are always sent to the same endpoint URL, using either GET or POST. This is in stark contrast with RESTful APIs, where each resource has its own base URL. Some see this as a major weakness of GraphQL and prefer REST's approach with resource-specific URLs.

Some queries allow or require parameters to be passed in.

Here's how our client can retrieve the name and birth year of `Luke Skywalker` (knowing its identifier):

```
{
  person(id: "cGVvcGxlOjE=") {
    name
    birthYear
  }
}
```

Query parameters are simply passed as key-value pairs.

Here is the corresponding response:

```
{
  "data": {
    "person": {
      "name": "Luke Skywalker",
      "birthYear": "19BBY"
    }
  }
}
```

GraphQL can do a whole lot more. For instance, clients can use parameters to request specific/alternative data formats, content translations, and so on. Such transformations can spare client-side applications the hassle of doing it themselves and much more still.

Schema, validation, and resolvers

On the server side, a **GraphQL schema** is used by the GraphQL runtime to figure out what is being requested and how to retrieve it.

We won't be able to cover schemas in detail but know that they are central to GraphQL. They describe the different objects, their types (we won't be able to cover `String`, `Int`, `Float`, `Boolean`, `ID`, and so on), as well as all supported **queries** and **mutations**, with their required/optional arguments.

Whenever a request comes in, it is validated against the schema (which can, for example, force some fields to be present). If the validation passes, then the query is analyzed and **GraphQL resolvers** take care of getting the requested data.

As a matter of fact, responses can (optionally) also be validated against the schema.

As we will see with our application, the schema can also be used to generate classes/types/interfaces that correspond to it. We'll also see that it is a mature ecosystem of tools to assist us with that process.

Apollo

Apollo GraphQL is a very popular open source *platform* for developing GraphQL APIs and API clients.

The main elements of Apollo are the following:

- The Apollo GraphQL server
- The Apollo GraphQL client
- The Apollo GraphQL CLI

In the next chapter, we will see how to integrate all of these into our application. For now, suffice to say that the different Apollo modules make it really easy to develop GraphQL-enabled applications:

The official Apollo logo

In addition, Apollo also provides client-side integration with many popular web frameworks, such as Angular, Vue, React, Meteor, and Ember, and even mobile platforms such as Android and iOS. This integration makes it a breeze to use GraphQL for different kinds of projects.

Nothing forces us to use everything provided by Apollo. In our case, we will make use of the server, client, and CLI for simplicity's sake, but since Apollo respects the GraphQL specifications, we could also use any other client implementation. There's no vendor lock-in to be afraid of. The main building blocks of Apollo are all open source, so the developer community can contribute and improve those.

Apollo's popularity comes from its simplicity. It is something that you'll probably notice once we get started with it.

The NestJS GraphQL plugin

As we mentioned earlier, NestJS supports plugins and some of those are officially supported. The **GraphQL plugin for NestJS** is one of those.

This plugin provides a NestJS module called `GraphQLModule`. It is nothing more than a wrapper around the Apollo server. Its goal is mainly to facilitate its integration within NestJS applications, and it does a great job of that.

The GraphQL plugin for NestJS supports two different approaches.

With the **schema-first** approach, you start by defining the GraphQL schema, which becomes the single source of truth for the application. The alternative way is to use a **code-first** approach. In that case, the source of truth is the application code, which we need to decorate in order for the NestJS plugin to be able to generate the GraphQL schema on the fly for us.

Both approaches have their pros and cons. In this book, we will be using the *code-first* approach, but it doesn't mean that it is any better.

We will learn more about how to use this plugin while developing our backend in the next chapter.

Summary

In this chapter, we discovered many new things.

First of all, React, one more hugely popular solution for creating modern web applications. We saw that even though it looked kind of intimidating at first, we could really quickly get started using CRA and no configuration at all, and with a minimal amount of code.

We learned about JSX and how enabling it can leverage the power of JavaScript while defining components. Of course, the syntax feels a bit alien at first for anyone used to separating templates and logic, but on the other hand, we showed that JSX helps to really take advantage of our JavaScript/TypeScript skills instead of having to learn a lot of new syntax!

We saw how to write React components using classes but quickly switched to the more idiomatic functional style that the React community loves. While doing so, we saw that it enabled us to write very concise components, while retaining all the power of React, thanks to React hooks such as `useState` and `useEffect`.

We also saw how to pass properties to components, how to manage internal state, both with class and Functional Components, how to hook into the lifecycle of our components, and a ton more!

On the backend side, we saw that we could leverage our knowledge of Angular to quickly be proficient with NestJS, which reuses many concepts of Angular, mimics its APIs, and even provides a similar CLI tool.

Then, we discovered GraphQL, a novel and popular way to create powerful web APIs. We saw that, combined with Apollo GraphQL, we could easily create awesome web APIs.

Aside from all of that, we, of course, continued to learn about TypeScript features as part of this chapter. We discovered what object and array destructuring are, how well TypeScript supports React and JSX, and more!

In the next chapter, we will revisit the LyricsFinder application using all of the things that we have learned about in this chapter! It's going to be really cool!

Further reading

Here are some useful resources related to the subjects covered in this chapter.

React

The following sections cover all of the links related to React.

General

Here are some useful links about React:

- Official website: `https://reactjs.org`
- Official documentation: `https://reactjs.org/docs`
- Official blog: `https://reactjs.org/blog`

- **Sources:** `https://github.com/facebook/react`
- **API documentation:** `https://reactjs.org/docs/react-api.html`
- **React renderers:** `https://github.com/chentsulin/awesome-react-renderer`
- **react-codemod:** `https://github.com/reactjs/react-codemod`
- **Preact:** `https://preactjs.com`
- **NextJS:** `https://nextjs.org`
- **Gatsby:** `https://www.gatsbyjs.org`
- **React Native:** `https://facebook.github.io/react-native`
- **React 360:** `https://facebook.github.io/react-360`
- **React Router:** `https://reacttraining.com/react-router`
- **Thinking in React:** `https://reactjs.org/docs/thinking-in-react.html`
- **Deep dive:** `https://overreacted.io/react-as-a-ui-runtime`

JSX

Here are some links about JSX:

- **JSX:** `https://reactjs.org/docs/introducing-jsx.html`
- **In-depth guide:** `https://reactjs.org/docs/jsx-in-depth.html`

CreateElement

Here are some useful links about this subject:

- **React** `createElement`: `https://reactjs.org/docs/react-api.html#createelement`
- **React element:** `https://reactjs.org/docs/rendering-elements.html`
- **ReactDOM render function:** `https://reactjs.org/docs/react-dom.html#render`

Components

Check out the following references:

- Components API: https://reactjs.org/docs/react-component.html
- PureComponent base
  class: https://reactjs.org/docs/react-api.html#reactpurecomponent
- How to choose between Functional
  Components, Component, and PureComponent: https://stackoverflow.
  com/questions/40703675/react-functional-stateless-component-
  purecomponent-component-what-are-the-dif

Function components

Check out the following references:

- Function
  components: https://reactjs.org/docs/components-and-props.html#fu
  nction-and-class-components
- JSX and
  props: https://reactjs.org/docs/jsx-in-depth.html#props-in-jsx
- Passing props to
  components: https://www.robinwieruch.de/react-pass-props-to-compo
  nent

State management

The following are some references:

- State and
  lifecycle: https://reactjs.org/docs/state-and-lifecycle.html
- Using setState: https://medium.freecodecamp.org/get-pro-with-reac
  t-setstate-in-10-minutes-d38251d1c781
- Using shouldComponentUpdate: https://developmentarc.gitbooks.io/
  react-
  indepth/content/life_cycle/update/using_should_component_update.h
  tml
- Controlling when to
  re-render: https://lucybain.com/blog/2017/react-js-when-to-rerender

- **State updates may be asynchronous:** `https://reactjs.org/docs/state-and-lifecycle.html#state-updates-may-be-asynchronous`
- **State updates are merged:** `https://reactjs.org/docs/state-and-lifecycle.html#state-updates-are-merged`

Component lifecycle

The following are some references:

- **Complete component lifecycle:** `https://reactjs.org/docs/react-component.html#the-component-lifecycle`
- **Diagram of the lifecycle hooks:** `http://projects.wojtekmaj.pl/react-lifecycle-methods-diagram`
- **An interesting article about the React lifecycle:** `https://css-tricks.com/the-circle-of-a-react-lifecycle`

Context

The following are some references:

- **Context:** `https://reactjs.org/docs/context.html`
- **Context article:** `https://daveceddia.com/context-api-vs-redux`
- **Props drilling:** `https://kentcdodds.com/blog/prop-drilling`

Hooks

Check out the following references if you want to learn more:

- **Hooks introduction:** `https://reactjs.org/docs/hooks-intro.html`
- **Video introduction by Kathryn Middleton:** `https://developers.facebook.com/videos/2019/intro-to-react-hooks`
- **Introductory guide** `https://medium.com/@dan_abramov/making-sense-of-react-hooks-fdbde8803889`

- **Reference:** https://reactjs.org/docs/hooks-reference.html
- **Rules:** https://reactjs.org/docs/hooks-rules.html
- **Official FAQ:** https://reactjs.org/docs/hooks-faq.html
- **Implementing lifecycle hooks using React hooks:** https://dev.to/elanandkumar/react-component-lifecycle-with-hook-6lo
- **Design patterns:** https://itnext.io/essential-react-hooks-design-patterns-a04309cc0404
- **Deep dive:** https://www.netlify.com/blog/2019/03/11/deep-dive-how-do-react-hooks-really-work
- **Gotchas and how to avoid them:** https://medium.com/@pshrmn/react-hook-gotchas-e6ca52f49328
- **Creating a custom hook:** https://scotch.io/tutorials/create-a-custom-usefetch-react-hook
- **Effect hook:**
    - https://reactjs.org/docs/hooks-effect.html
    - https://reactjs.org/docs/hooks-effect.html#tips-for-using-effects

Create React App

Check out the following references:

- **Official documentation:** https://create-react-app.dev
- **Changelog:** https://github.com/facebook/create-react-app/blob/master/CHANGELOG.md
- **List of resources:** https://github.com/tuchk4/awesome-create-react-app
- **Alternatives to CRA:** https://reactjs.org/community/starter-kits.html

TypeScript and React

Here are some very useful guides for using TypeScript with React:

- Martin Hochel's
  tips: https://medium.com/@martin_hotell/10-typescript-pro-tips-patterns-with-or-without-react-5799488d6680
- https://fettblog.eu/typescript-react/components
- Great
  cheatsheet: https://github.com/sw-yx/react-typescript-cheatsheet
- Hooks in TypeScript: https://medium.com/@jrwebdev/react-hooks-in-typescript-88fce7001d0d
- Children composition
  patterns: https://medium.com/@martin_hotell/react-children-composition-patterns-with-typescript-56dfc8923c64
- Most common
  types: https://medium.com/@tiago.souto/most-common-react-app-types-using-typescript-99f4d5d4c4f8

NestJS

The following are some references:

- NestJS official website: https://nestjs.com
- NestJS Sources: https://github.com/nestjs/nest
- Express API: https://expressjs.com/en/4x/api.html
- CLI overview: https://docs.nestjs.com/cli/overview
- CLI usage: https://docs.nestjs.com/cli/usages
- Modules: https://docs.nestjs.com/modules
- Providers: https://docs.nestjs.com/providers
- Controllers: https://docs.nestjs.com/controllers

GraphQL

Here are some resources for you to explore:

- **Official documentation:** `https://graphql.org/learn`
- **Beginner guide:** `https://medium.freecodecamp.org/a-beginners-guide-to-graphql-60e43b0a41f5`
- **Comparison with REST:** `https://blog.apollographql.com/graphql-vs-rest-5d425123e34b`
- **Queries:** `https://graphql.org/learn/queries`
- **Schemas and types:** `https://graphql.org/learn/schema`

Apollo

The following are some references:

- **Documentation:** `https://www.apollographql.com/docs`
- **Sources:** `https://github.com/apollographql`
- **Interesting article:** `https://medium.com/airbnb-engineering/how-airbnb-is-moving-10x-faster-at-scale-with-graphql-and-apollo-aa4ec92d69e2`

NestJS support for GraphQL

Check out these references:

- **Quick start guide:** `https://docs.nestjs.com/graphql/quick-start`
- **Sources:** `https://github.com/nestjs/graphql`

TypeScript

The following sections state all of the links related to TypeScript.

Object destructuring

The following are some references:

- http://exploringjs.com/es6/ch_destructuring.html#_object-destruct uring
- https://dev.to/sarah_chima/object-destructuring-in-es6-3fm

Array destructuring

Check out these references:

- https://developer.mozilla.org/en-US/docs/Web/JavaScript/Reference /Operators/Destructuring_assignment#Array_destructuring
- https://codeburst.io/es6-destructuring-the-complete-guide-7f842d0 8b98f

12
Revisiting LyricsFinder

In this chapter, we will take advantage of everything that we learned about in the previous chapter to revisit the LyricsFinder application.

We will leverage React, NestJS, GraphQL, and Apollo to create an awesome version of our application.

Let's see what topics are in store for us in this chapter:

- Building our application with React
- High-level design and technical stack
- Getting started with the project
- Backend – adding the necessary dependencies
- Backend – implementing the GraphQL API with a first resolver
- Backend – importing and configuring the GraphQL NestJS module
- Backend – testing the API using the GraphQL playground
- Backend – adding support for artists and lyrics
- Frontend – installing React Bootstrap
- Frontend – installing React Router
- Frontend – creating the home view skeleton
- Frontend – creating the search component
- Frontend – integrating with the backend API
- Frontend – creating and using the songs list component
- Loading lyrics and redirecting to the lyrics page
- Implementing the lyrics page

By going through this chapter, you will have a better understanding of how to use these frameworks and libraries to create great modern web applications.

Let's not waste a minute and get started!

What will you build?

It's time to get our hands dirty one more time! Now that you have the basics of React in mind, you can start building applications with it.

Earlier in this book, we built the first version of LyricsFinder using Vue.js. For this chapter, we plan to help you to rewrite LyricsFinder using React, **Bootstrap**, and **React Bootstrap**.

Since you seem to like learning new things (otherwise you would not still be here with us, right?), we thought that you'd like to explore additional areas where TypeScript can also bring value.

In the first iteration of LyricsFinder, our Vue.js application directly made use of the MusixMatch API. That was a very reasonable choice but, this time, we'll create our own backend API. Of course, this won't become the next worldwide source of song lyrics, but let's pretend.

In practice, LyricsFinder V2 will keep the same basic functionality, but its user interface and API layer will change drastically.

With LyricsFinder V2, you'll not only create a frontend React SPA, but you'll also implement a backend **GraphQL** API using **Apollo** with the help of the **NestJS** framework, right on top of the **Node.js** runtime. This is quite a mouthful and might sound like gibberish for now but, hopefully, it'll all be clearer in your mind by the end of this chapter!

High-level design and technical stack

Let's take a look at the high-level design for our new version, as well as the technical stack that we will use.

Schema

Here is a visualization of what we are going to create together:

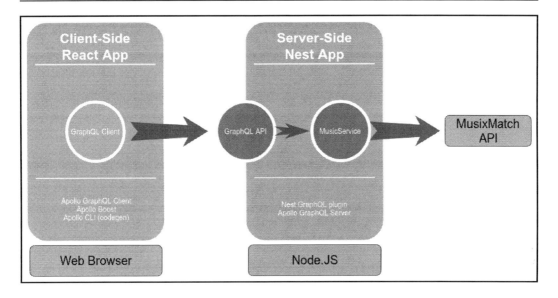

Let's zoom in on the different parts.

Frontend – user interface with React Bootstrap

To create the user interface of LyricsFinder V2, we will install and use React Bootstrap (`https://react-bootstrap.github.io`), a React UI components library created on top of the hugely popular Bootstrap (`https://getbootstrap.com`) CSS library.

With nearly 30 components at our disposal, we should have more than enough to construct our new user interface.

Again, just like with Angular and Vue.js, there are many alternative UI toolkits available for React. We didn't do a thorough evaluation for LyricsFinder V2 though. We simply chose a popular library different from what we have used so far in this book (namely, Angular Material and Element). That way, you get to see one more way of assembling an interface.

Here are some other React UI toolkits that you might want to take a look at:

- `https://dev.to/kayis/react-ui-kits-3fm2`
- `https://www.codeinwp.com/blog/react-ui-component-libraries-framew orks`
- `https://hackernoon.com/23-best-react-ui-component-libraries-and-f rameworks-250a81b2ac42`

To handle the navigation between our pages, we will use React Router (`https://reacttraining.com/react-router`), a popular open source router for React.

We will see later how to install and use all of these tools.

Check out the following references:

- React Bootstrap: `https://react-bootstrap.github.io`
- Bootstrap: `https://getbootstrap.com`

Frontend – API calls

To fetch information about artists, songs, and lyrics, our frontend application will use the Apollo GraphQL client with React Apollo (`https://github.com/apollographql/react-apollo`) and Apollo Boost (`https://github.com/apollographql/apollo-client/tree/master/packages/apollo-boost`). For now, just keep in mind that we will be using a GraphQL client to send GraphQL queries and fetch the data that we need. We'll cover the details as we progress through this chapter.

Backend

To implement our backend application, we will combine different things:

- A platform/runtime: Node.js
- A framework: **NestJS** (`https://nestjs.com`)
- A query language/API: **GraphQL** with **Apollo GraphQL**

Using these, we will create a backend system able to expose information about artists, songs, and lyrics through a GraphQL API.

The GraphQL API that we will create will actually fetch the data from the MusixMatch API using `MusicService` that we already developed in the previous version of the application. As such, our GraphQL API will be a sort of **API gateway layer**. Don't sweat over this—it is just an excuse to learn about GraphQL!

Check out these references:

- GraphQL: `https://graphql.org/learn`
- NestJS: `https://nestjs.com`
- Node.js: `https://nodejs.org/en`
- Apollo: `https://www.apollographql.com`
- GraphQL plugin for NestJS: `https://github.com/nestjs/graphql`

TypeScript

Let's reassure you right away: we will use TypeScript everywhere—in the frontend, but also in the backend.

Hopefully, we shall be able to convince you (if you still need to be) that TypeScript is not limited to frontend application development, but is really a programming language that you can learn once and use at all levels of the technical stack.

Let's get started!

Getting started

We will start the implementation with the backend NestJS application. We'll integrate our MusixMatch service and expose it through a GraphQL API.

Once our backend is ready, we will create the client-side React application on top of it. Our React application will use the Apollo GraphQL client to fetch information about artists, songs, and song lyrics.

Before we start though, we need to create the project and see how we are going to organize the different parts.

Creating the project

We've prepared a skeleton for this new version of the project, which you can find in this book's assets under `Chapter12/lyricsfinder-v2-initial`.

Once again, the goal of the skeleton is to allow us to focus on new elements rather than on the grunt work needed to integrate code/logic that we've already seen before.

In the `frontend` folder, you'll find the React application, created using `create-react-app` with TypeScript enabled. In the `backend` folder, you'll find the NestJS application, created using the NestJS CLI and already including our previous `MusicService` class and the related code.

 Since React uses `yarn` by default, we will use it in this chapter. You can use `npm` instead (for example, using the `npm ci` command), but be aware that it might require some tweaks because we didn't include a lock file along with the initial project, which means that you might end up with different versions of the dependencies, leading to unpredictable behavior.

If you haven't installed `yarn` yet, then please do it now. To do so, you can use different methods. The simplest, since you already have `npm` installed, is to leverage it to install `yarn` globally:

```
npm install --global yarn
```

Alternatively, you can use any of the methods listed here: `https://yarnpkg.com/lang/en/docs/install`.

If you have `yarn`, then go ahead and do the following:

1. Copy the `Chapter12/lyricsfinder-v2-initial` folder into your workspace.
2. Install the project dependencies using `yarn install` in the `frontend` folder as well as in the `backend` folder.

Project structure and conventions

As noted previously, the project has *two main folders* at the top level: `backend` and `frontend`. Of course, this is to clearly separate the applications in our solution.

In a real-world project, we would probably introduce and use a tool such as **Nrwl NX** (`https://github.com/nrwl/nx`) to manage our whole workspace, as it would allow us to easily share code and optimize builds (among other benefits), but we won't have the opportunity to cover that in this book. Take a look at the resources provided in the next and final chapter to learn more.

In both the frontend and the backend projects, we will put our source code under the `src` folder. We will also continue to use lower-kebab-case for the filenames, including for React components. The only exception that we will make is for the default files created by `create-react-app`, but you could of course also rename these if you wish to keep the structure uniform.

The components of the frontend React application will be created under `src/components`, just like with Vue.js. In that folder, we will only put **dumb components**. For **smart components** (that is, pages), we will create a `pages` folder, just like with our Angular app.

As we have mentioned in the previous chapter, this is an opinionated choice that we make for our application; it certainly isn't the only way to write React applications.

Backend – creating and configuring the application

If you open the `backend` folder, you'll see that it already contains a starting point. We created it beforehand to simplify the explanations and provide you with some default content.

To create the initial backend project, we have simply used the NestJS CLI, as follows: `npx @nestjs/cli new backend`.

To be able to build our backend easily, the `MusicService` class that we have used in the previous chapters has been copied, refactored a bit for NestJS, and put within the `backend/src/musixmatch` directory. You can take a look at it now if you're curious, but we haven't changed much.

Now that you know about what we've already included, it's your turn to roll up your sleeves.

Starting the development servers

In this application, we will have **two** separate servers running at the same time:

- One with the backend Node/NestJS application, exposing the GraphQL API
- One with the frontend React application, consuming the GraphQL API

Following are the commands:

1. To start the backend server, you will use `yarn start:dev` from the `backend` folder.
2. To start the frontend server, you will use `yarn start` from the `frontend` folder.

 Be aware that the backend application will **NOT** be functional at first. We will fix that in the very next section together!

From now on, you should keep two Terminal windows open: one for the backend application and another one for the frontend application. As soon as our frontend starts making calls to the backend, both will have to be started in parallel for the application to be functional.

 As usual, look at the console to find the port number that each server is listening on. Normally, the frontend should listen on port `3000` and the backend on port `4000`.

Let's create and configure the backend application.

Backend – adding the necessary dependencies

Since we will be using GraphQL, we need to add some dependencies to the backend:

1. Go to the `backend` folder.
2. Execute this command: `yarn add @nestjs/graphql apollo-server-express graphql-tools graphql type-graphql`.

We will use these packages soon to implement our GraphQL API. Notice that we have also installed the GraphQL plugin for NestJS, which will ease our task.

Backend – implementing the GraphQL API with a first resolver

Let's implement our first GraphQL resolver on the backend.

Adding your MusixMatch API key

Before we get to the code, the first thing that you need to do is to add your MusixMatch API key (the same that you've used in Chapter 9, *Introducing Vue.js*) into the `backend/src/api-key.ts` file. If you don't, then your code won't be able to fetch any data from MusixMatch.

 If you don't have a MusixMatch API key yet, go back to the Vue chapter (that is, Chapter 9, *Introducing Vue.js*) to find out how to obtain one.

Do not skip this step, as it is mandatory for the application to function.

Creating the song module

Go into the `backend` folder with your Terminal and execute the following command using the NestJS CLI:

```
npx @nestjs/cli generate module song
```

This will create the `song` NestJS module in the project. As we saw earlier, NestJS modules are very similar in shape and form to Angular modules. As with Angular modules, we can use NestJS modules to cleanly separate the different parts of our application.

Creating the song GraphQL resolver

Next up, execute the following command (made available by the GraphQL plugin for NestJS):

```
npx @nestjs/cli g resolver song
```

This command generates an empty **GraphQL resolver** for us; we'll adapt it later on.

This command will also register this resolver in the module for us.

Creating the song DTO and decorating it for GraphQL

Now that we have our first module and our resolver, we need to create a **Data Transfer Object (DTO)** for songs. Create a `song.dto.ts` file under `src/song`.

Add the following contents to that file:

```
import { Field, ID, ObjectType } from 'type-graphql';

@ObjectType()
export class SongDto {
  @Field(() => ID)
  id: string;

  @Field()
  name: string;

  @Field()
  artistId: string;

  @Field(() => Boolean)
  hasLyrics: boolean;

  @Field(() => [String])
  genres: string[];
}
```

This is the basic definition of a song. Notice that we have decorated our class with the `@ObjectType()` decorator from the `type-graphql` library to configure this class as a type that GraphQL should consider.

Also, each field has been decorated with @Field to let GraphQL take those into account as well.

 When no value is passed to @Field(), the property is considered a string.

With that done, we're ready to implement the song resolver.

Implementing the song resolver and leverage NestJS features

Now we can finally complete the implementation of our GraphQL resolver for songs.

This resolver will be responsible for fetching and returning Song objects. To do so, it'll make use of MusicService, which is already available in the project. We have simply ported the existing code.

Create then open the backend/src/song/song.resolver.ts file and adapt it as follows:

```
import { Args, Query, Resolver } from '@nestjs/graphql';
import { MusicService } from '../musixmatch/services';
import { Inject } from '@nestjs/common';
import { TYPES } from '../musixmatch/ioc/types';
import { SongDto } from './song.dto';
import { Observable } from 'rxjs';

@Resolver('Song')
export class SongResolver {
  constructor(
    @Inject(TYPES.MUSIC_SERVICE)
    private readonly musicService: MusicService,
  ) {}

  @Query(() => [SongDto])
  songs(@Args('value') value: string): Observable<SongDto[]> {
    return this.musicService.findSongs(value);
  }
}
```

As you can see, we have injected `MusicService` using the `@Inject()` decorator of NestJS. As we explained in the previous chapter, NestJS has great support for DI. Notice that we have also passed the *injection token* so that the correct implementation can be identified and injected for us by NestJS.

Also, we have implemented a method called `songs` that accepts an argument and returns `Observable`.

 As shown in the official documentation of the plugin, it is also possible to write `async` functions that return `Promise` but we prefer to deal with RxJS observables instead.

There are additional things to notice in that code:

- The `@Resolver` decorator indicates that this class is a resolver.
- The `@Query` decorator describes what kind of objects this resolver resolves; in this case an array of `SongDto` objects.
- `@Args` links the query argument and the resolver function argument.

The different decorators listed in the preceding are all part of the NestJS GraphQL plugin, but ultimately, they rely on other libraries such as `type-graphql` (`https://github.com/MichalLytek/type-graphql`). The GraphQL plugin of NestJS mainly gives us syntactic sugar/easy-to-use abstractions, but we could also achieve the same results without it.

What matters here is that our resolver simply takes the search text value from the query and passes it to the `MusicService`, which in turn contacts the MusixMatch API to fetch the results. All of this, of course, happens asynchronously.

 This idea is kind of interesting: we can easily use GraphQL to expose an API that in fact serves as a gateway/facade in front of other APIs.

We could go further and fetch only the exact dataset that we are interested in, but we'll skip that to keep this tutorial simple.

Backend – importing and configuring the GraphQL NestJS module

Before we continue and start using GraphQL, you should take a look at AppModule.

Open backend/src/app.module.ts. It should look as follows:

```
@Module({
  imports: [
    GraphQLModule.forRoot({
      debug: true,
      playground: true,
      autoSchemaFile: 'schema.gql',
    }),
    // ...
  ],
  // ...
}
export class AppModule {}
```

If you've followed the Angular chapter (that is, Chapter 8, *Discovering Angular, Angular Material, and RxJS*), then this whole file should make you feel right at home. NestJS uses the same decorators/properties that we are now used to. In this case, we load GraphQLModule and configure it as required.

 We have enabled the debug mode and playground to be able to debug and play with our GraphQL API through the web browser. The playground is a web application that we can use to easily interact with the GraphQL API and write/validate/test queries.

For this exercise, we have decided to follow the **Code First** approach, as proposed by the NestJS GraphQL plugin authors. This is the reason why we have defined the autoSchemaFile: 'schema.gql' option.

The GraphQL **schema** file will be generated automatically for us by the NestJS GraphQL plugin, thanks to the decorators that we have defined in the DTO as well as in the resolver.

Backend – testing the API using the GraphQL playground

`SongModule` is now correctly defined and `GraphQLModule` is loaded in the NestJS application's app module. We are ready to give the API a try.

Execute the following command to start the backend server (if you haven't done so already):

```
yarn start:dev
```

Now, open up your web browser and go to `http://localhost:4000/graphql`.

You should see the following:

This is the playground that we enabled a bit earlier. You can learn more about it here: `https://github.com/prisma/graphql-playground`.

Through the playground, we can easily write and test queries. Given that our API is already functional (albeit limited), we can already write our first GraphQL query together.

Remove everything on the left-hand pane, then type in the following query:

```
{
    songs(value: "never gonna give you up") {
        id,
        name,
        hasLyrics
    }
}
```

This query is rather straightforward: we request
the id, name, and hasLyrics properties for songs that match the provided song title,
in this case, a famous song by Rick Astley.

 You can use *Ctrl* + spacebar (or *cmd* + spacebar if you are on macOS)
in the GraphQL playground to get auto-completion.

If you execute that query, then you should see some results appear on the right,
proving that our API actually works:

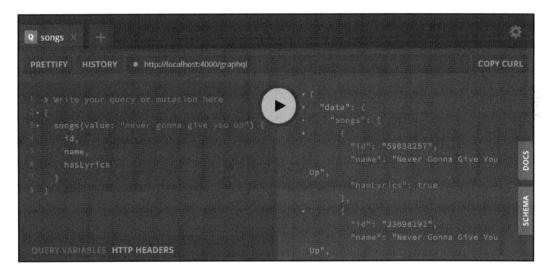

This editor is quite user-friendly, so it doesn't need much explanation.

Backend – adding support for artists and lyrics

Next, we want our GraphQL API to also support finding artists and loading song lyrics. Let's proceed with the creation of their respective modules and GraphQL resolvers.

Execute the following commands from the `backend` folder:

- `npx @nestjs/cli g mo artist`
- `npx @nestjs/cli g r artist`
- `npx @nestjs/cli g mo song-lyrics`
- `npx @nestjs/cli g r song-lyrics`

 Notice the shorthand versions for **module** (that is, `mo`) and for **resolver** (that is, `r`).

Next, we have to create the DTOs for artists and song lyrics. As we did for `song` before, we'll add a field for each property declared in `backend/src/musixmatch/domain/artist.ts` and `backend/src/musixmatch/domain/song-lyrics.ts`. Since our `MusicService` class will return objects based on those classes, we have to be sure that our DTOs contain the same fields. On a real project, you would need to spend more time thinking about the differences between entities, DTOs, and view models.

Go ahead and create a DTO and a resolver for both artists and lyrics using the NestJS CLI.

Our artist DTO file should be located in `backend/src/artist/artist.dto.ts` and should look as follows:

```
import { Field, ID, ObjectType } from 'type-graphql';

@ObjectType()
export class ArtistDto {
  @Field(() => ID)
  id: string;
  @Field()
  name: string;
}
```

Its corresponding resolver should be located in
`backend/src/artist/artist.resolver.ts` and should contain the following
code:

```
import { Query, Resolver, Args } from '@nestjs/graphql';
import { TYPES } from '../musixmatch/ioc/types';
import { MusicService } from '../musixmatch/services';
import { ArtistDto } from './artist.dto';
import { Inject } from '@nestjs/common';

@Resolver('Artist')
export class ArtistResolver {
  constructor(
    @Inject(TYPES.MUSIC_SERVICE)
    private readonly musicService: MusicService,
  ) {}

  @Query(() => [ArtistDto])
  async artists(@Args('name') name: string): Promise<ArtistDto[]> {
    return this.musicService.findArtists(name).toPromise();
  }
}
```

As we did before, we simply inject and use an instance of `MusicService`. In this case
(just for a change), we have used an `async` function and returned `Promise`. The end
result is the same, but as we saw before, this isn't needed since NestJS also supports
RxJS observables.

To finish up, let's do the same for song lyrics.

The DTO for song lyrics should be placed in `src/song-lyrics/song-
lyrics.dto.ts` and should contain the following code:

```
import { Field, ID, ObjectType } from 'type-graphql';

@ObjectType()
export class SongLyricsDto {
  @Field(() => ID)
  id: string;

  @Field()
  copyright: string;

  @Field(() => Boolean)
  explicit: boolean;

  @Field()
```

```
    lyrics: string;
}
```

Its resolver should be under `src/song-lyrics/song-lyrics.resolver.ts` and should look like this:

```typescript
import { Query, Resolver, Args } from '@nestjs/graphql';
import { SongLyricsDto } from './song-lyrics.dto';
import { MusicService } from '../musixmatch/services';
import { Inject } from '@nestjs/common';
import { TYPES } from '../musixmatch/ioc/types';

@Resolver('SongLyrics')
export class SongLyricsResolver {
  constructor(
    @Inject(TYPES.MUSIC_SERVICE)
    private readonly musicService: MusicService,
  ) {}

  @Query(() => SongLyricsDto)
  songLyrics(@Args('id') id: string) {
    return this.musicService.findLyrics(id);
  }
}
```

That's it: our backend is now implemented. Of course, it is really basic/trivial, but it does what we wanted it to.

 Before you switch to the implementation of the frontend, you should play a bit with the GraphQL playground to get more familiar with how to write GraphQL queries.

Let's work on the frontend side now.

Frontend – installing React Bootstrap

Now that our backend is implemented, we can turn our attention to the frontend React application.

Since we will be creating our user interface using the React Bootstrap UI toolkit, we need to add it to our project.

First of all, we will need to install the `react-bootstrap` library as well as the `bootstrap` package:

1. Go to the `frontend` folder.
2. Execute `yarn add react-bootstrap bootstrap`.

The `bootstrap` package is the official Bootstrap CSS library. We need to install it because the stylesheet of Bootstrap is not included in `react-bootstrap`. We should be able to use the most recent version.

Next, we need to load the stylesheet of Bootstrap, so that components can later be styled correctly.

Open the `frontend/src/index.tsx` file and add the following import on top:

```
import 'bootstrap/dist/css/bootstrap.min.css';
```

The installation is now complete!

To use `react-bootstrap` components, we need to import them one by one, just like Angular Material components with Angular Material. This limits the impact on the size of application code bundles.

To verify that we have correctly installed the library, let's try to use some `react-bootstrap` components. We'll add the title of the application to the `App` component.

Go ahead and open the `frontend/src/App.tsx` file. Then, replace its current content with the following:

```
import React from 'react';
import './App.css';
import Jumbotron from 'react-bootstrap/Jumbotron';
import Button from 'react-bootstrap/Button';

const App: React.FC = () => {
  return (
    <Jumbotron>
      <h1>LyricsFinder v2</h1>
      <p>
        This will become the number one source of lyrics on the
        Interwebs.
      </p>
      <p>
        <Button variant="primary">Learn more</Button>
      </p>
    </Jumbotron>
```

```
    );
};

export default App;
```

Notice that we have imported two components from `react-bootstrap`:

- `Jumbotron` is used to display some content that can take up the entire viewport.
- `Button` supports different variants (for example, primary, secondary, success, danger, and so on).

After doing this, you can also do the following:

1. Clear the current contents of the `frontend/src/App.css` and `frontend/src/index.css` files as we won't use those styles at all.
2. Remove the `frontend/src/logo.svg` file as we won't be using it either. This might prove difficult as the animation is mesmerizing!

If everything goes according to plan, then the home page of the application should now look like this:

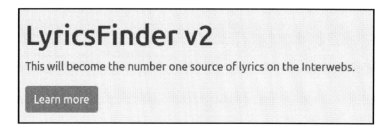

As you can see, using the Bootstrap components in our application is quite easy with `react-bootstrap`. As an added benefit, we now have auto-completion for the different properties. The `react-bootstrap` package even includes TypeScript type definitions!

Let's move on!

Check out these references:

- **Jumbotron:** `https://react-bootstrap.github.io/components/jumbotron`
- **Buttons:** `https://react-bootstrap.github.io/components/buttons`

Frontend – installing React Router

As with the previous version of LyricsFinder, we will use a router to go from the home page to the lyrics page. Let's start by installing the router.

Once again, you should see a lot of similarities between what we did before and what we'll do in a minute with the router; the concepts are the same. As we said at the beginning, we are going to use `react-router`.

Let's install the library and its typings by executing the following command:

```
yarn add react-router-dom @types/react-router-dom
```

 If you want to easily find/add missing type definitions for your dependencies, then you can give this utility a try: `https://github.com/jeffijoe/typesync`.

Now, we're going to add the router outlet (that is, define the place where the router will render the active route) in our `App` component.

Open the `frontend/src/App.tsx` file and adapt it as follows:

```
const App: React.FC = () => {
  return (
    <React.Fragment>
      <Jumbotron>
        ...
      </Jumbotron>
      <BrowserRouter>
        ...
      </BrowserRouter>
    </React.Fragment>
  );
};
```

 The `React.Fragment` component reacts like `<ng-container>` in Angular. It gives the ability to group multiple HTML elements without adding an extra node in the DOM. It is really useful here because `App` can only return a single HTML element. Check the official documentation for more information: `https://reactjs.org/docs/fragments.html`.

Don't forget to add the corresponding import:

```
import { BrowserRouter } from 'react-router-dom';
```

As with the Vue Router, the contents of the router outlet will be replaced by the contents of the **active** route.

Check out this link for further reference: `https://reacttraining.com/react-router`.

Frontend – creating the home view skeleton

Now that the router is in place, let's create our initial views. We'll start with the `Home` view, which will be displayed by default. This view will be similar to the one in LyricsFinder V1. We will later add the search component to it.

Go ahead and do the following:

1. Create a `pages` folder under `frontend/src`.
2. Create a `home.tsx` file in the newly created `pages` folder.

For now, just add this within the `home.tsx` file:

```
import React from 'react';

export const Home = () => {
    return <h2>Home</h2>;
};
```

Now, adapt `frontend/src/App.tsx` and add the following inside of the `BrowserRouter` component:

```
<Route exact path='/' component={Home} />
```

With this, we have instructed the router to render the `Home` page when the URL is exactly `/`. This means that the `Home` page will not be rendered if we are at `/something` or anywhere else but `/`.

Before continuing, add the following imports in `App.tsx`:

```
import { BrowserRouter, Route } from 'react-router-dom';
import { Home } from './pages/home';
```

Let's continue with the implementation.

Creating the lyrics view skeleton

While you're at it, you can already create the `Lyrics` page.

Create a `lyrics.tsx` file under `frontend/src/pages` and add the following code to it:

```
import React from 'react';

export const Lyrics = () => {
    return <h2>Lyrics</h2>;
};
```

Now that the page is created, you can add one more `Route` to the router.

Edit `frontend/src/App.tsx` again and add the following line within the `BrowserRouter` tag:

```
<Route path='/lyrics' component={Lyrics} />
```

This new route will activate when the URL is set to `/lyrics`. Go ahead and give it a try. If you go to `http://localhost:3000/lyrics` now, you should see the `Lyrics` component.

 Here, we've shown you how to install and use `react-router`, a really popular routing library for React. If you're curious about alternatives, then you should check out `reach-router`, which is a new router created by the authors of `react-router`. It will probably become the default choice for React applications over the coming months. Check out the official website to learn more about it: `https://reach.tech/router`.

Once again, if your editor didn't automatically import `Lyrics`, don't forget to add the following import:

```
import { Lyrics } from './pages/lyrics';
```

Let's now work on the search component.

Frontend – creating the search component

The first component that we can implement is `Search`, which we will use in our `Home` page.

Functionally, this component will remain the same as in the first version, with text input, a way to clear it, and a search button. We will simply implement it as a React component using JSX and `react-bootstrap`.

Let's get started.

First of all, we'll create a home for our (dumb) components, as described in the project structure and conventions section. Create the following folder: `frontend/src/components`.

 As applications grow larger, you might want to structure your code around the features at the first level, just like we would do with Angular modules.

Next, continue with the search component's skeleton.

Creating the search component skeleton

Now, create the component's file. Again, following our conventions, we will use lower-kebab-case. Create a file called `search.tsx` under `frontend/src/components`.

Next, add the following basic structure for the component:

```
import React, { useEffect } from 'react';

import Container from 'react-bootstrap/Container';

type Props = {
};

export const Search = (props: Props) => {
    useEffect(() => {
        console.log('Search component rendered');
    });
```

```
    return (
        <Container className='lf-search'>
            TODO add content here
        </Container>
    );
};
```

For now, the component is just an empty shell, but you can already add it to the `Home` page.

Open the `frontend/src/pages/home.tsx` file and do the following:

1. Import the `Search` component using `import { Search } from '../components/search';`.
2. Replace the JSX code in the page with `<Search />`.

In the next subsections, we will wrap our search `input` and `button` within the React Bootstrap `Container` element.

We will proceed in multiple steps:

1. First, we will add the components we need inside of the container.
2. Then, we'll define the state of our component and **bind** our input to it.
3. After that, we will define handlers for the different events.
4. Finally, we will define some `props` so that our component can communicate with its **clients**.

This process is roughly inspired by the following article: https://reactjs.org/docs/thinking-in-react.html.

Defining the component hierarchy

Let's add our components. We will make use of multiple `react-bootstrap` components:

- `FormControl`: This component renders form elements and applies Bootstrap's styling to them.
- `FormGroup`: This component wraps a form control (or set of controls), applying spacing. It is also possible to define a label and display the validation state of `FormGroup`.

- `InputGroup`: This component allows to put other elements before or after an input, using `InputGroup.Prepend` or `InputGroup.Append`, respectively.

Replace the `Container` component with the following code:

```
<Container className='lf-search'>
    <FormGroup id='searchForm'>
        <InputGroup size='lg'>
            <FormControl id='searchText' type='text'
                         placeholder='Artist or song to search for'
                         aria-label='Artist or song to search for'/>
            <InputGroup.Append>
                <Button variant='secondary' aria-label='Clear the
                search text'>X</Button>
                <Button variant='primary' aria-
                label='Search'>Search</Button>
            </InputGroup.Append>
        </InputGroup>
    </FormGroup>
</Container>
```

Following are some remarks about this code:

- `InputGroup` has been made larger using `size='lg'`.
- `FormControl` is our text input and it has an `aria-label` property.

 We have added a section about accessibility and ARIA in the next chapter. Don't miss that topic if you want to build applications for humans (that is, great applications), whether that is with Angular, Vue, React, or anything else!

Before you continue, don't forget to add the necessary imports:

```
import Button from 'react-bootstrap/Button';
import FormGroup from 'react-bootstrap/FormGroup';
import FormControl from 'react-bootstrap/FormControl';
import InputGroup from 'react-bootstrap/InputGroup';
```

Here's how the component should look at this point:

Bootstrap and `react-bootstrap` are sparing us a lot of effort, including in non-obvious ways.

 We won't cover this in this book, but both React and `react-bootstrap` have great support for forms. In our case, there is only a single input so we don't really need more than the few components we have used. There are multiple third-party libraries such as **Formik** (`https://github.com/jaredpalmer/formik`), which you can use to go further. For React, check out the following page: `https://reactjs.org/docs/forms.html`.

Check out the following references:

- Forms support in `react-bootstrap`: `https://react-bootstrap.netlify.com/components/forms`
- The `InputGroup` component: `https://react-bootstrap.netlify.com/components/input-group`
- Formik: `https://github.com/jaredpalmer/formik`

Adding state and binding our input to it

Now that we have the base structure of our component, we can add its state. Internally, our `Search` component will only keep one data point: the current search input text.

First of all, add the following line at the beginning of the component function, just before the `useEffect` function call:

```
const [searchText, updateSearchText] = useState('');
```

Then adapt the following import:

```
import React, { useEffect, useState } from 'react';
```

As we saw earlier in this chapter, `useState` allows us to define both a state variable and a function to modify it. If you remember what we've explained before, the empty string passed to `useState` is the initial value.

Our component now has a piece of state called `searchText`. To bind it with the component, you need to add the following to the `FormControl` component:

```
value={searchText}
```

Once done, it should look as follows:

```
<FormControl id='searchText' type='text'
    placeholder='Artist or song to search for'
    aria-label='Artist or song to search for'
    value={searchText}
/>
```

With that done, the value of the text input `FormControl` is now bound to the `searchText` state variable of our `Search` component. That is a one-way binding from the component to `FormControl`.

What we're missing here is a binding in the other direction. We want our component's state to be updated whenever the text in the input is changed (for example, when the user types or pastes something). To achieve this, we need to attach an **event handler** to the `onChange` event.

Modify `FormControl` as follows:

```
<FormControl id='searchText' type='text'
    placeholder='Artist or song to search for'
    aria-label='Artist or song to search for'
    value={searchText}
    onChange={handleSearchTextInputChange}
/>
```

Next, you need to add an implementation for the `handleSearchTextInputChange` function.

Add the following inside of the component, under the `useEffect` function call:

```
const handleSearchTextInputChange = (event:
FormEvent<FormControlProps>): void => {
    const searchInputNewValue: string = event.currentTarget.value ||
"";
    updateSearchText(searchInputNewValue);
    console.log(`Search: search text changed to
[${searchInputNewValue}]`);
};
```

For this code to compile, you will also need to add the following imports:

- `import { FormEvent } from 'react';`
- `import { FormControlProps } from 'react-bootstrap/FormControl';`

As noted earlier, React has support for forms. In this case, we are relying on its `FormEvent` interface. Inside the function, we extract the value of the event and call our `updateSearchText(...)` function to update the state of our component.

 Notice that we must handle the case where the value is `undefined`. This could happen when the input gets cleared. You can learn more about that here: `https://github.com/DefinitelyTyped/DefinitelyTyped/issues/16208`.

Having added that, we now have a two-way binding in place for our text input.

Clearing the input

With our two-way binding in place, we can now easily clear the input by adding the following constant to the component, under the previous one:

```
const clearHandler = () => {
    updateSearchText('');
};
```

Then, modify the first button of `InputGroup`, as follows:

```
<Button variant='secondary' aria-label='Clear the search text'
onClick={clearHandler}>X</Button>
```

Clicking on this button will now call the `clearHandler` function, which will reset the `searchText` state variable. In turn, the value change will modify `FormControl`.

Adding the search handler

When the user presses *Enter* or clicks on the `Search` button, we want to initiate the search.

To achieve this, the first thing that we need to do it to create a handler function within the component:

```
const searchHandler: VoidFunction = () => {
  console.log('Search: search handler called. Search text: ',
  searchText);
  if (searchText === '') {
    clearHandler();
  }
}
```

For now, we only log to the console, but we will revisit this very soon.

Now, attach that function to the `onClick` event of the search `Button`:

```
onClick={searchHandler}
```

With that done, you should be able to validate that the message is displayed in the console when you click on the button.

Next up, attach the same function to the `onKeyUp` event of `FormControl`, which should now look as follows:

```
<FormControl id='searchText' type='text'
  placeholder='Artist or song to search for'
  aria-label='Artist or song to search for'
  value={searchText}
  onChange={handleSearchTextInputChange}
  onKeyUp={(e: React.KeyboardEvent) => e.key === 'Enter' ?
  searchHandler() : null}
/>
```

Here, we have simply checked the `key` property of the React `KeyboardEvent` event to determine whether the *Enter* key was pressed. Notice there is a bit less magic involved here compared to Angular and Vue.js.

Adding props to communicate with the outside world

Our component is now almost complete. The last thing that we need to do is to let the outside world know whenever a search action is requested and whenever the search text gets cleared.

To do this, we will add two entries to our props, so that users of this component can pass in functions for us to call when the respective events occur.

Go ahead and modify the Props interface as follows:

```
type Props = {
    searchTriggered: (searchText: string) => void;
    searchCleared: VoidFunction;
};
```

We have defined two functions that we expect to receive through props:

- The first one is called searchTriggered, which we will call whenever a search has been requested. We will pass the current searchText value to it.
- The second one is called searchCleared, which we will call whenever the input has been cleared.

Now, adapt the searchHandler function as follows:

```
const searchHandler: VoidFunction = () => {
  console.log('Search: search handler called. Search text: ',
   searchText);
  if (searchText === '') {
    clearHandler();
  } else {
    props.searchTriggered(searchText);
  }
}
```

Let's continue.

As we saw before, if you don't want to prefix that with props., you could declare a constant before using object destructuring.

Next, add the following line to the clearHandler function:

```
props.searchCleared();
```

Our component is now ready!

Open the Home page (that is, frontend/src/pages/home.tsx) and make the following modifications.

First off, add the two functions that we will pass to the Search component through props within the component:

```
const search = (text: string) => {
    console.log(`Home: searching for ${text}`);
};

const searchInputCleared = () => {
    console.log('Home: search cleared');
};
```

Then, pass these to the component:

```
<Search searchCleared={searchInputCleared} searchTriggered={search}/>
```

That's it!

Now, if you test the application and manipulate the Search component while looking at the console, you'll see that our events get triggered and that our Home page's handler functions are indeed invoked as a result.

Frontend – integrating with the backend API

Now that our search component is implemented, functional, and added to the Home page, we can finally start integrating our React application with the backend GraphQL API to fetch data. To do so, we will use the Apollo GraphQL client libraries and the Apollo CLI to perform some code generation.

From now on, you will need to start both servers in parallel for the application to work properly.

Adding the required dependencies

First of all, you need to install a few dependencies:

1. Go to the frontend folder.
2. Execute this command: yarn add apollo apollo-client apollo-boost react-apollo graphql.

Here is why we need each of these:

- `apollo`: This package includes the Apollo CLI (among other things), which we will use to generate client-side code for GraphQL queries, based on the server-side GraphQL schema and validated against it. This process will ensure that our queries are valid (that is, match the server-side schema) and that we have type safety and auto-completion.
- `apollo-client`: This contains the base required to create an Apollo Client and interact with the backend server.
- `apollo-boost`: This contains utilities to start using Apollo easily (for example, the `ApolloClient` utility class that we'll use soon).
- `react-apollo`: This integrates Apollo with React and provides utility React components for GraphQL.
- `graphql`: This is the library that does the actual work (for example, parsing the GraphQL queries).

Here, we're using Apollo Boost only to quickly get started. As soon as you develop serious applications with Apollo, you'll rapidly feel the need to let go of `apollo-boost` and switch to the `raw` Apollo library. If you reach that conclusion at some point, then follow this guide: `https://www.apollographql.com/docs/react/advanced/boost-migration`.

Let's define some queries now!

Defining GraphQL queries and generating code using Apollo

As we will soon see, the code generation feature of Apollo GraphQL is one of its big advantages. Thanks to this, we will be able to ensure that the queries we write on the client-side are valid. They will be checked against the server-side GraphQL schema. Also, TypeScript interfaces will be generated for the queries and their parameters, allowing us to write type-safe code while interacting with the backend GraphQL API.

We will make our code evolve one step at a time:

1. First, we're going to prepare our GraphQL queries.
2. Then, we will use the Apollo CLI to generate TypeScript code.

3. After that, we will create an Apollo Client inside of the `Home` page.
4. Finally, we will use the client to search for artists and songs when the search component calls our search handler function.

Let's get to it. First of all, do the following:

1. Create a new folder called `graphql` under `frontend/src`.
2. Create a `queries.ts` file under `frontend/src/graphql`.

Then, add the following contents to the `queries.ts` file:

```
import gql from 'graphql-tag';

export const FindArtistsQuery = gql`
  query FindArtists($value: String!) {
    artists(name: $value) {
      id,
      name
    }
  }
`;

export const FindSongsQuery =  gql`
  query FindSongs($value: String!) {
    songs(value: $value) {
      id,
      name,
      hasLyrics
    }
  }
`;

export const FindLyricsQuery = gql`
  query FindLyrics($id: String!) {
    songLyrics(id: $id) {
      id,
      lyrics,
      explicit,
      copyright
    }
  }
`;
```

These are the only three queries that we will use. For all of these, a `String` parameter is made mandatory with the `!` character. For the `FindArtistsQuery` and `FindSongs` queries, this parameter respectively corresponds to the artist and song name to look for. For the `FindLyrics` query, it is the identifier of the song to retrieve the lyrics for.

Each query also specifies the fields it wants to retrieve. In the case of `FindSongsQuery`, we ask for the `hasLyrics` flag to know whether there are lyrics available. We will use that information, later on, to filter out the songs for which no lyrics are available.

At this point, we don't know for sure whether our queries are valid as these are just plain strings. Let's fix that with the help of Apollo!

Open the `frontend/package.json` file and add the following scripts to it:

```
"apollo:download": "apollo schema:download --
endpoint=http://localhost:4000/graphql graphql-schema.json",
"apollo:generate": "apollo codegen:generate --
includes=src/graphql/queries.ts --endpoint
http://localhost:4000/graphql --addTypename --target typescript --
globalTypesFile build/ignoreMe.txt --tagName gql --outputFlat
src/generated --customScalarsPrefix lyricsFinder"
```

The first script, `apollo:download`, is a small utility that will download the GraphQL schema in JSON form from the backend server. You can run this script if you're curious about what the final schema looks like. We won't be using this file in our project though.

 In a real project, you might want to keep a copy of the schema in your client-side project (assuming the backend API is correctly versioned) to avoid being dependent on the backend server's availability for building your frontend application.

The second script, `apollo:generate`, uses the `codegen:generate` command of the Apollo CLI. As you can guess, its goal is to generate code for our queries, based on the GraphQL schema.

Here's an explanation of the different parameters that we make use of in the `apollo:generate` script:

- The `includes` parameter is a **glob pattern** that points the CLI toward the files to use as input. The CLI will read these files and identify all of the queries that it contains. Then, for each of these, it will generate code.

- The `endpoint` parameter points to the backend GraphQL API. Instead of this parameter, we could've used the `localSchemaFile` option to point to a local GraphQL schema JSON file.
- The `addTypename` parameter adds a `typename` property to the queries. Adding this instructs GraphQL to add the name of the data types in the responses (as the value of the `typename` property). You can learn more about this meta field here: `https://graphql.org/learn/schema`.
- The `target` flag simply defines the target language—in our case, TypeScript, of course!
- `globalTypesFile` is the path to a file in which global types are placed:
  - Don't pay attention to the value we have used here—it is simply a workaround for the following issue: `https://github.com/apollographql/apollo-tooling /issues/1179#issuecomment-501555846`.
- `tagName` is the name of the tag we use to delimit our GraphQL queries (we will see how this works later on).
- `outputFlat` is an option that allows us to flatten the output. In our case, we simply put all of the generated code into the `src/generated` folder.
- Finally, the `customScalarsPrefix` option prefixes scalars. This is useful to avoid name clashes.

You can find the complete CLI reference here: `https://github.com/apollographql/apollo-tooling#apollo-clientcodegen- output`.

 Generally speaking, the generated code should be kept out of your source code repository. In this case, you could add the `frontend/src/generated` folder to the `.gitignore` file.

Now that you have added the code generation script, you can execute it:

```
yarn apollo:generate
```

Once done, you should find the generated code under `frontend/src/generated`.

Let's take a look at the `FindArtists.ts` file:

```
/* tslint:disable */
/* eslint-disable */
// This file was automatically generated and should not be edited.
```

```
// ========================================================
// GraphQL query operation: FindArtists
// ========================================================

export interface FindArtists_artists {
  __typename: "ArtistDto";
  id: string;
  name: string;
}

export interface FindArtists {
  artists: FindArtists_artists[];
}

export interface FindArtistsVariables {
  value: string;
}
```

Inside of it, you'll find three different interfaces, each serving a specific purpose:

- The FindArtists_artists interface represents the datatype of each object that we will receive back in response to our GraphQL query. As you can see, we expect to receive the id and name fields. Moreover, we know for a fact that we should receive what is known as ArtistDto on the backend side.
- The FindArtists interface corresponds to the result type of the query—in this case, an array of FindArtists_artists objects (that is, the list of results).
- The FindArtistsVariables interface describes the variables that should be passed to the query.

If you look at the other generated files, you'll see that they have the same base structure.

Of course, this example is trivial, but it clearly shows that we can easily generate TypeScript code based on GraphQL queries and validated against a schema. We will later see how these interfaces can be used to increase the safety of our code.

Bonus: Tagged template literals

In the previous section, you might have noticed the weird gql prefix before the GraphQL queries. This was no mistake.

That is actually called a **tagged template literal**. It is a feature of ECMAScript introduced with ES2015 and (of course) supported by TypeScript.

By now, you are used to template strings that allow us to embed expressions using `${...}`. You have seen these on many occasions throughout this book.

Tagged template literals build upon template strings. They allow us to **tag** a template string with the name of a function. When a template string has been tagged, the tagged function will be executed and it will have a chance to parse/transform the expression.

The tagged function can actually transform the **template literal** into another string or anything else it fancies.

In the case of GraphQL, the `gql` function transforms the readable query into a properly formatted string that can be sent over to the GraphQL API over HTTP.

Check out these references:

- MDN: `https://developer.mozilla.org/en-US/docs/Web/JavaScript/Reference/Template_literals#Tagged_templates`
- Wes Bos's article: `https://wesbos.com/tagged-template-literals`

Creating, configuring, and using an Apollo GraphQL client

Now that we have defined our queries and that we have generated code for those using Apollo, we can start using them.

We will now create and use an Apollo Client with the help of Apollo-Boost. Apollo-Boost isn't strictly necessary, but it will heavily simplify our implementation.

We will use the Apollo Client within our `Home` component.

When the `search` function gets invoked by the `Search` component, we will use the Apollo Client to search for artists and songs. Also, when the user selects a song, we will use it again to retrieve its lyrics.

First of all, let's create our Apollo Client instance.

Let's get started:

1. Open the `frontend/src/pages/home.tsx` file.
2. Then, add the following declaration right after the `import` statements:

```
import ApolloClient from 'apollo-boost';

const apolloClient = new ApolloClient({
    uri: 'http://localhost:4000/graphql'
});
```

As you can see, we simply had to instantiate the `ApolloClient` class provided by Apollo-Boost and point it to the GraphQL endpoint that we want to send our queries to.

Before we start sending our queries, we need to add some states using the `useState` hook. We will use that state to store the search results.

Add the following declarations at the beginning of the `Home` page (within the function's body):

```
const [foundArtists, updateFoundArtists] =
useState<FindArtists_artists[]>([]);
const [foundSongs, updateFoundSongs] =
useState<FindSongs_songs[]>([]);
```

Notice that we have specified the type of our state using the generic argument of `useState`. In the case of the `foundArtists` state, we know that we will get back an array of `FindArtists_artists` objects. For the `foundSongs` state, we will store an array of `FindSongs_songs` objects.

Then, add the following imports to make it work:

```
import { useState } from 'react';
import { FindArtists_artists } from '../generated/FindArtists';
import { FindSongs_songs } from '../generated/FindSongs';
```

Now that we have our state, we can finally execute our queries and store the results that we get back.

We have covered this syntax in the previous chapter, but here's a quick reminder just in case. When we call `useState`, we pass it the initial state—in this case, an empty array. In return, we receive a *tuple* back, out of which we extract (using array destructuring) two things that we need to treat as constants. The first one is the current value of this piece of state and the second is the function that we can use to safely update it.

Modify the `search` function in the `Home` view, as follows:

```
const search = (searchText: string) => {
    console.log(`Home: searching for ${searchText}`);

    apolloClient.query<FindArtists, FindArtistsVariables>({
        query: FindArtistsQuery,
        variables: {value: searchText}
    }).then((result: ApolloQueryResult<FindArtists>) => {
        console.log('Home: found artists: ', result.data);
        updateFoundArtists(result.data.artists);
    });

    apolloClient.query<FindSongs, FindSongsVariables>({
        query: FindSongsQuery,
        variables: {value: searchText}
    }).then((result: ApolloQueryResult<FindSongs>) => {
        console.log('Home: found songs: ', result.data);
        updateFoundSongs(result.data.songs);
    });
};
```

And add the following imports at the top of the file:

```
import { FindArtists, FindArtistsVariables } from
'../generated/FindArtists';
import { FindSongs, FindSongsVariables } from
'../generated/FindSongs';
import { FindArtistsQuery, FindLyricsQuery, FindSongsQuery } from
'../graphql/queries';
import { ApolloQueryResult } from 'apollo-boost';
```

Here, we execute two different GraphQL queries one after another using our Apollo Client: the first to find artists and the second to find songs. This mimics what we did in the first version of the application. Note that the responses to each query will be received asynchronously, hence the `.then(...)` function that we define.

The responses could also be received out of order, but it doesn't matter in our case.

As you can see from the preceding, the `query` method of the Apollo Client accepts some generic parameters:

- The first one corresponds to the shape of the response.
- The second one corresponds to the shape of the variables that we need to provide along with our query.

Also, notice that we pass an object to the `query` method, containing the following:

- It contains a key called `query` whose value is the GraphQL query that we have defined earlier as a tagged template literal in our `queries.ts` file.
- It also contains a key called `variables` that defines the different query parameters along with their respective values. Note that this object must respect the type specified as the `variables` generic argument.

In our case, we have a single variable to provide: the search term, which we have received from our `Search` component when the search operation was triggered.

In the case of the query to find songs and assuming that the happy path is followed, when the response is received, our `.then` function will be called with the result of the query. In this case, it should receive an object of the `ApolloQueryResult<FindSongs>` type.

Finally, within the callback, we extract the `data` property of the query result and pass the `Song` objects that it contains to our `updateFoundSongs` state update function to update our component accordingly.

The query to retrieve artists works in the exact same way.

From that point on, our template can use the updated state. Since we have used the state update function (which is mandatory!), then our component and its children get re-rendered.

If you want to give it a try right away, then you can replace the code right after the `searchInputCleared` function with the following:

```
const foundArtistsList = foundArtists.map(item => <li
key={item.id}>{item.name}</li>);
const foundSongsList = foundSongs
    .filter(item => item.hasLyrics)
    .map(item => <li key={item.id}>{item.name}</li>);

return (
    <Container className='lf-home'>
        <Search searchCleared={searchInputCleared} searchTriggered=
        {search}/>
        <ul>
            {foundArtistsList}
        </ul>
        <ul>
            {foundSongsList}
        </ul>
    </Container>
);
```

And import `Container` from `react-bootstrap`:

```
import { Container } from 'react-bootstrap';
```

Here, we have constructed a list of `li` HTML elements by looping over the list of found artists as well as another one for the list of songs. We then simply render those insides of a `ul` element within the template.

In the case of the songs list, we have added a filter to ignore songs for which no lyrics are available. In a real-world scenario, you should directly filter the result set in the backend (to avoid unnecessary network traffic).

Alternatively, you could instead adapt the user interface to either visually make the distinction between songs that do have lyrics and those that don't, or provide a toggle to show/hide songs without lyrics. These are important UI/UX considerations but this is out of the scope of this book.

At this point, you have seen the whole process, from defining the backend GraphQL type using a code-first approach to writing queries, generating code, sending actual queries from the client-side, and handling the results.

This indeed eludes many important design questions, such as what happens when the backend is unavailable or how to deal with errors in general, but it at least gives you a good overview of how you can create and use a GraphQL API to integrate a frontend application to a backend system.

We won't go any further with GraphQL and Apollo here, but rest assured that there is a whole lot more to learn. For instance, here we have only performed read operations, but GraphQL also supports modifications through mutations.

 The React integration of Apollo also allows us to write queries directly as part of the JSX code, using the `<Query>` element. We won't cover it here as we have chosen a more generic/programmatic approach, but in real-world applications, you would certainly prefer to use the React way. You can find more information about that here: `https://www.apollographql.com/docs/react/integrations` and

here: `https://medium.com/open-graphql/react-hooks-for-graphql-3fa8ebdd6c62`. As you'll see, there are equivalent integrations for Angular and Vue.

GraphQL APIs are getting really popular lately, so make sure to check out the following references if you want to continue learning about those.

Check out these references:

- Apollo GraphQL client: `https://www.apollographql.com/docs/react`
- React Apollo: `https://www.apollographql.com/docs/react`
- Great GraphQL tutorial: `https://www.howtographql.com`
- Official GraphQL documentation: `https://graphql.org/learn`
- Generating types with Apollo: `https://www.leighhalliday.com/generating-types-apollo`
- Relay: `https://relay.dev`

Frontend – creating and using the songs list component

Just like we did with our Vue version, let's now implement a `SongsList` component.

Creating the skeleton

Go ahead and create a `songs-list.tsx` file under `frontend/src/components`.

Then, add the following skeleton to this file:

```
import React, {useEffect} from 'react';

import Container from 'react-bootstrap/Container';

type Props = {
};

export const SongsList = (props: Props) => {
    useEffect(() => {
        console.log('Songs List: component rendered');
    });

    return (
        <Container className='lf-songs'>
        </Container>
    );
};
```

So far, there's not much to it.

Still, you can already add it to the `Home` view:

1. Open the `frontend/src/pages/home.tsx` file.
2. Add `<SongsList />` at the end of the JSX content (and don't forget to import it on top).

Defining the props

Our `SongsList` component will be a dumb component. We now need to define and use its `props`.

We will pass two things to that component:

- A list of songs to render
- A callback function that should be invoked whenever an element in the list gets selected

Go back to the `songs-list.tsx` file.

Change the `Props` interface to the following:

```
type Props = {
    songs: FindSongs_songs[];
    songSelected: (song: FindSongs_songs) => void;
};
```

And add the import:

```
import { FindSongs_songs } from '../generated/FindSongs';
```

Now that we have clearly stated our requirements, we can code assuming that we will get the expected inputs. Let's use the `songs` array to build the JSX elements to render.

 We will go back to the `Home` view a bit later to adapt it.

Let's render the list of songs now.

Rendering the list of songs

For this part of the user interface, we will use two more UI components of `react-bootstrap`:

- `ListGroup`: Renders a list of elements
- `ListGroup.Item`: Renders an element in the list

As we will see, these will make it easy for us to highlight the fact that the list items are actionable and can be clicked upon. Having this for free will also remove the need for some of the styling code that we had with the Vue.js version.

Still in `songs-list.tsx`, add the following code inside of the `SongsList` component:

```
const songElements = props.songs
    .filter((song: FindSongs_songs) => song.hasLyrics)
    .map((song: FindSongs_songs) =>
        <ListGroup.Item key={song.id} className='lf-song' action
    style=
```

```
                {{cursor: 'pointer'}}
                    onClick={() => props.songSelected(song)}>{song.name}
                    </ListGroup.Item>
        );
```

And add the import for `ListGroup`:

```
    import { ListGroup } from 'react-bootstrap';
```

Here, we simply filter the list of songs to ignore those that don't have lyrics. Then, we create `ListGroup.Item` JSX elements out of the remaining ones.

Following are some points to notice:

- We have set `key` on each element to optimize the re-rendering operations.
- We have set `action` property to mark the items as actionable. You can learn more about that here: `https://react-bootstrap.github.io/components/list-group/#list-group-item-props`.
- We have added an `onClick` event handler that calls the provided `songSelected` callback function.

 The `filter` operation doesn't really belong in our presentational (that is, dumb) component, so you may choose to move it to the `Home` component instead.

Finally, update the return expression of the component, as follows:

```
    return (
      <Container className='lf-songs'>
          <h3>Songs</h3>
          <ListGroup>
              {songElements}
          </ListGroup>
      </Container>
    );
```

Here, we simply display the section's title and render our `ListGroup.Item` elements inside of `ListGroup`.

With this done, all that's left is to update the `Home` view.

Open the `frontend/src/views/home.tsx` file and add the following constant within the `Home` component:

```
const songSelected = (selectedSong: FindSongs_songs) => {
    console.log('Home: song selected: ', selectedSong);
};
```

Once bound to the `SongsList` component, this function will be called each time a song is selected in the list. We will later update it to fetch the song lyrics and redirect to the `Lyrics` view.

Now, update the `SongsList` element in the `Home` view as follows to bind the songs list and pass the `songSeleted` function to `SongsList`:

```
<SongsList songs={foundSongs} songSelected={songSelected} />
```

Finally, you should also remove our previous `foundSongsList` constant as well as the corresponding `ul` tag in the JSX code.

That's it. You can now go ahead and give it a try. If you search for a song, then the view should be updated. Moreover, selecting an item in the list should trigger the call to the preceding `songSelected` function. Take a look at the console to see the message.

Frontend – loading lyrics and redirecting to the lyrics page

Let's now handle the song selection event. When a user selects a song, we want to show the (yet to be completed) `Lyrics` page and have it render the lyrics.

To do this, there are many possible solutions. Typically, we would pass the song ID as a route parameter to the route and use it in the `Lyrics` page to fetch the lyrics. In our case, since we already have our GraphQL client configured, we will directly fetch the lyrics in the `Home` page and pass them along with the song through the **route parameters**.

The first thing to know is that since our `Home` page is rendered by `react-router`, it automatically receives several routing-related `props`. Let's start by making that more obvious.

Open the `frontend/src/pages/home.tsx` file and do the following:

1. Add the following import: `import { RouteComponentProps } 'from react-router';`.
2. Declare the props argument: `export const Home = (props: RouteComponentProps)` and others.

The `RouteComponentProps` interface is part of the `react-router` type definitions. It is defined as follows:

```
export interface RouteComponentProps<Params extends { [K in keyof
Params]?: string } = {}, C extends StaticContext = StaticContext, S =
H.LocationState> {
  history: H.History;
  location: H.Location<S>;
  match: match<Params>;
  staticContext?: C;
}
```

The details are not that important here. What matters is that our `props` include the following:

- `History`: This is a prop that we can use to redirect the user to another page and pass parameters while doing so. Under the hood, it uses the `History` `API` provided by modern web browsers.
- `Location`: This is a prop that we can use to retrieve the current route and its parameters.

Now that we have defined our `props`, we can use these.

Adapt the `songSelected` function as follows:

```
import { FindLyricsQuery } from '../graphql/queries'
import { FindLyrics, FindLyricsVariables } from
'../generated/FindLyrics';

...

const songSelected = (selectedSong: FindSongs_songs) => {
    console.log('Home: song selected: ', selectedSong);

    apolloClient.query<FindLyrics, FindLyricsVariables>({
        query: FindLyricsQuery,
        variables: {
            id: selectedSong.id,
```

```
        },
    }).then((result: ApolloQueryResult<FindLyrics>) => {
        const songLyrics = result.data.songLyrics;
        console.log(`Home: lyrics loaded for [${selectedSong.name}]:
        ${songLyrics.lyrics}`);

        props.history.push('/lyrics', {
            song: selectedSong,
            songLyrics,
        });
    }).catch((error: any) => {
        console.log('Home: error while loading lyrics: ', error);
    });
};
```

First of all, we use our Apollo Client to send the `FindLyrics` query, which calls our backend and receives the lyrics in return. In the `then` callback function, we use the `history.push(...)` function of the history prop to push a new state using the History API.

The `push` function accepts multiple parameters. In this case, we have passed the following:

- The URL of the route we want to redirect to (that is, `/lyrics`)
- The parameters to pass along, hence the selected song as well as the song lyrics, which we have associated with the `songLyrics` key

 We have added a `catch` block to handle any errors returned by `Promise`. In this case, we simply log the error, but in a real-world application, you would rather show a notification to the end user to warn about the failure. If you want to improve the error handling, then you should look into the `Toast` component of `react-bootstrap`: `https://react-bootstrap.github.io/components/toasts`.

We are almost done!

Frontend – implementing the lyrics page

The last thing that we need to do to complete our V2 is to update our `Lyrics` page so that it renders the song lyrics.

Open the `frontend/src/pages/lyrics.tsx` file and modify it as follows:

```
import React, { ReactElement } from "react";
import { RouteComponentProps } from 'react-router';
import Container from 'react-bootstrap/Container';
import { Link } from 'react-router-dom';
import { FindLyrics_songLyrics } from '../generated/FindLyrics';
import { FindSongs_songs } from '../generated/FindSongs';
import Card from 'react-bootstrap/Card';

type LyricsLocationState = {
    song: FindSongs_songs;
    songLyrics: FindLyrics_songLyrics;
};

interface LyricsProps extends RouteComponentProps<any, any,
LyricsLocationState> {
}

export const Lyrics = (props: LyricsProps) => {
  const songLyrics = props.location.state.songLyrics;
  const songLyricsLines: ReactElement[] = [];

  if (songLyrics.lyrics) {
    songLyrics.lyrics.split("\n").forEach((line, i) => {
      songLyricsLines.push(
        <span key={i}>
          {line}
          <br />
        </span>
      );
    });
  }

    const song = props.location.state.song;
    return (
        <Container className='lf-lyrics'>
            <Card>
                <Card.Header>{song.name} (<Link to='/' title='Go
                back'>Go back</Link>)</Card.Header>
                <Card.Body>
                    <Card.Text>
```

```
                    <span>{songLyricsLines}</span>
                </Card.Text>
                <h4>Copyright:</h4>
                <span>{songLyrics.copyright}</span>
            </Card.Body>
        </Card>
    </Container>
    );
};
```

Let's explore this code bit by bit.

First of all, we have defined `type` as well as `interface` for our `props` with the following:

```
type LyricsLocationState = {
    song: FindSongs_songs;
    songLyrics: FindLyrics_songLyrics;
}

interface LyricsProps extends RouteComponentProps<any, any,
LyricsLocationState> {
}
```

Here, we have leveraged the generic types of the `RouteComponentProps` interface. We did this to clearly specify the type of state associated with the location.

Thanks to this, the following lines can be strongly typed:

```
const songLyrics = props.location.state.songLyrics;
const song = props.location.state.song;
```

Without the previous declaration, we would not get any help from TypeScript.

To be honest, this is an *optimistic* type declaration, since we have no guarantee that the location state will contain what we expect. If you want to write safer code, then you should mark the location state properties as optional and check for their presence in the component's code. In the future, you will also be able to use **optional chaining** in TypeScript to simplify code like that: `https://devblogs.microsoft.com/typescript/announcing-typescript-3-7-beta`.

After having retrieved the song and song lyrics, we split the lyrics into multiple rows:

```
const songLyricsLines: ReactElement[] = [];

if (songLyrics.lyrics) {
  songLyrics.lyrics.split("\n").forEach((line, i) => {
    songLyricsLines.push(
      <span key={i}>
        {line}
        <br />
      </span>
    );
  });
}
```

If you remember from the Vue chapter (that is, `Chapter 9`, *Introducing Vue.js*), we need to do this because MusixMatch and our backend give us back the lyrics as a single string with newline characters (that is, `\n`). In this version of the application, we could also handle this transformation in the backend side of the application and shield the frontend from this implementation detail.

So the preceding code transforms the string with newline characters into an array of `ReactElement`. To do so, we simply use the `split` function and loop over the lines, generating `span` for each line.

Finally, our JSX code can then simply render these:

```
<Container className='lf-lyrics'>
    <Card>
        <Card.Header>{song.name} (<Link to='/' title='Go back'>Go
        back</Link>)</Card.Header>
        <Card.Body>
            <Card.Text>
                <span>{songLyricsLines}</span>
            </Card.Text>
            <h4>Copyright:</h4>
            <span>{songLyrics.copyright}</span>
        </Card.Body>
    </Card>
</Container>
```

To render the lyrics nicely, we have used the `Card` component of `react-bootstrap`, which can have a header, a body, and some text.

In the header of the card, we have used the `Link` component of `react-router-dom` to generate and display a link allowing the user to go back to the `Home` page.

In the preceding code, notice that we could have directly bound the song lyrics without splitting the lines ourselves, by using the `dangerouslySetInnerHTML` **attribute of React** (`https://en.reactjs.org/docs/dom-elements.html#dangerouslysetinnerhtml`). Truth be told, we actually did this in the first iteration of the application, as a way to move forward more quickly. The thing is that doing so would introduce a big security risk in our application since the source of the content (that is, a third party) cannot be fully trusted. By avoiding directly binding the value in the browser's DOM, we avoid exposing the users of our application to **cross-site scripting** (**XSS**) attacks!

That's it! The first alpha of LyricsFinder V2 is now completed! Congratulations!

You can find the completed example in the code samples of this book, under `Chapter12/lyricsfinder-v2`.

Check out the following references:

- Card component:
  `https://react-bootstrap.github.io/components/cards`
- DOMPurify: `https://github.com/cure53/DOMPurify`

Adding icons

For starters, you could introduce icons just like we had in the previous version of LyricsFinder.

These icons were previously provided to our application by the Element UI library. In contrast, `react-bootstrap` is not opinionated about iconography, so we may pick and use any icon collection we fancy.

If you want to have some fun, why don't you add the popular **FontAwesome** (`https://origin.fontawesome.com`) icons library to the project? You can add its `npm` package easily and then import it as we did with `react-bootstrap`.

Once installed and loaded, you should be able to easily add icons to the different pages/components.

Creating an ArtistsList component

Another improvement could be to implement an `ArtistsList` component and to then render both lists side by side in the `Home` page like we did with the Vue version of the application. To do so, you could, for example, wrap the two lists of the `Home` page inside of an accordion or in a tabbed panel.

Here's an example taken from the final version of the code, which you can find under `Chapter12/lyricsfinder-v2` in the code samples of this book:

```
<Accordion>
    <Card>
        <Accordion.Toggle as={Card.Header} variant="link"
         eventKey="0">
            <h3>Artists</h3>
        </Accordion.Toggle>
        <Accordion.Collapse eventKey="0">
            <Card.Body>
                <ul>
                    {foundArtistsList}
                </ul>
            </Card.Body>
        </Accordion.Collapse>
        <Accordion.Toggle as={Card.Header} variant="link"
         eventKey="1">
            <h3>Songs</h3>
        </Accordion.Toggle>
        <Accordion.Collapse eventKey="1">
            <Card.Body>
                <SongsList songs={foundSongs} songSelected=
                {songSelected}/>
            </Card.Body>
        </Accordion.Collapse>
    </Card>
</Accordion>
```

With this done, you would get a nicer visual result.

Showing a message when there are no songs or no artists

You could also use conditional rendering in the `SongsList` and `ArtistsList` components to display a message when there are no elements to display.

Here's how we've done this for songs in the final version of the code:

```
<Container className='lf-songs'>
    {songElements.length > 0? (
    <ListGroup>
        {songElements}
    </ListGroup>
    ) : (
      <span>No songs</span>
    )}
</Container>
```

This approach uses a ternary operator to either render the `ListGroup` element or `span`. There are many other ways to do conditional rendering with React; check out the following references for more details:

- Accordion
  component: `https://react-bootstrap.github.io/components/accordion`
- Tab component: `https://react-bootstrap.github.io/components/tabs`

Adding loading indicators

One more improvement that you could make is to add loading indicators as we did with the Vue version.

Doing so is rather easy with React and `react-bootstrap`. One way to do so is to add two state variables to hold the loading state for artists and songs.

Here's an example with artists:

```
const [artistsLoading, setArtistsLoading] = useState(false);
```

With this defined, you could set the state to `true` within the `search` function just before sending the GraphQL query and back to `false` once `Promise` has settled.

Here's an example taken from the final code of LyricsFinder V2:

```
setArtistsLoading(true);
apolloClient.query<FindArtists, FindArtistsVariables>({
    ...
}).then((result: ApolloQueryResult<FindArtists>) => {
    ...
}).finally(() => setArtistsLoading(false));
```

With this logic in place, displaying and hiding the loading indicator is simply a matter of using conditional rendering again in the JSX code.

Here is how you can implement this:

```
<Accordion.Toggle as={Card.Header} variant="link" eventKey="0">
    <h3>Artists</h3>
    { artistsLoading &&
        <Spinner animation="border" role="status">
            <span className="sr-only">Loading...</span>
        </Spinner>
    }
</Accordion.Toggle>
```

As you can see, we have used the `Spinner` component of `react-bootstrap` and wrapped it into a conditional expression.

 This is the recommended way to write conditional expressions in JSX. The idea is that if `artistsLoading` is *truthy*, then `Spinner` will render.

You can, of course, apply the same logic for the songs list, as we did in the final version of the code:

```
{ songsLoading ? (
    <Spinner animation="border" role="status">
        <span className="sr-only">Loading...</span>
    </Spinner>
) : null}
```

In this case, just to show an alternative way, we've used a ternary expression. This other way of writing conditional expressions in JSX is more useful when you actually have two alternatives to render.

These are all just baby steps; there are many more things to improve. That is the whole difference between a small prototype like those in this book and real-world applications!

Following are some references:

- Spinner
  component: `https://react-bootstrap.github.io/components/spinners`
- React conditional rendering
  approaches: `https://blog.logrocket.com/conditional-rendering-in-react-c6b0e5af381e`

Summary

In this last big chapter, you have achieved something quite memorable; you have learned about and used some of the coolest web technology around today. You have now learned about Angular, Vue.js, and React. Not only that, but you have also discovered NestJS, a great framework to build backend systems, which keeps gaining traction.

You have even learned the basics of GraphQL, a modern and more standardized alternative to REST for exposing and consuming data/services on the web.

By building a new version of LyricsFinder using all of these, you have seen how they actually work, which is much more valuable than only understanding the theory behind them.

We saw together that, by introducing Apollo GraphQL and the GraphQL plugin for NestJS into LyricsFinder, we could really quickly create our API, acting as a gateway to the MusixMatch API. This has demonstrated how GraphQL can be used to create a **facade** in front of various existing services.

Finally, we have continued leveraging the incredible power of TypeScript to ease the development of our application, this time both on the backend and frontend sides!

This chapter concludes our introduction to modern web development. We sure hope that you have enjoyed discovering those subjects together with us.

In the next and final chapter, we will take a look back and do a retrospective of what we have learned together in this book.

Then, we will give you some pointers about what to look at next on your journey to master modern software development.

What's Next?

What a journey this has been!

In this book, we covered quite a large spectrum of subjects and technology, both theoretical and practical. TypeScript was, of course, the center of our attention throughout this book. Hopefully, we have been able to demonstrate how powerful this programming language is and how useful it can be, independently of the frameworks or libraries being used and whether you are developing frontend or backend applications.

Unfortunately, a single book is far from enough to go in depth into all of the subjects that we have touched on.

In this closing chapter, we will do a small retrospective of the most important things that we have learned along the way and we'll then conclude by pointing you towards some ideas about what to learn next.

This final chapter consists of the following topics:

- Retrospective – first half
- Retrospective – second half
- Where to go next and what to learn

Retrospective – first half

We started our journey by looking at how the frontend software development ecosystem has evolved over the last couple of years. We highlighted the positive impact of the new yearly release cadence of the ECMAScript specification, pushing the language forward much faster and empowering developers.

We introduced the minimum amount of tooling necessary to get started and we covered how to install Visual Studio Code, Git, Node.js, NPM, and, of course, TypeScript.

We then introduced the foundational concepts of TypeScript, along with its basic types, and then explained how to write functions with it.

After going through the inevitable `Hello World` program, we introduced many more TypeScript features, such as lambdas, iterators and loops, type declarations, type inference, arrays, the `null` special type, and the `as` (cast) operator.

While developing the first version of the `TodoIt` application, we had the opportunity to explain how npm works, how to write and execute scripts, manage dependencies, and much more. We also saw how to configure the TypeScript compiler and how to build in watch mode from the command line as well as through Visual Studio Code. Finally, we learned how to leverage the powerful developer tooling inside of modern web browsers to debug our applications. To improve the debugging experience, we learned about source maps and saw how to generate those with TypeScript.

In `Chapter 3`, *Improving TodoIt with Classes and Interfaces*, we took a detour to the world of **object-oriented programming** (**OOP**) and reviewed its main concepts, namely, the following:

- Encapsulation
- Abstraction
- Inheritance
- Polymorphism
- Interfaces
- Classes

We also explained some important idioms, such as why composition should generally be favored instead of inheritance, and we covered important design principles such as the SRP, the **Law of Demeter** (**LoD**), the open/closed principle, the SOLID design concepts, and more! Also, we reviewed the basics of the **Unified Modeling Language** (**UML**).

After this, we continued introducing some important features of TypeScript, namely, the following:

- Classes and inheritance
- Fields and visibility
- Constructors and accessors
- Interfaces
- Type annotations
- Custom types
- Structural typings

- The readonly keyword
- Optional arguments
- Default values

In the second half of that chapter, we leveraged this newly acquired (or refreshed) knowledge to build a new version of the TodoIt application and saw how it helped us to better structure our code, clearly showing the benefits of applying OOP to define the domain model of our applications.

In Chapter 4, *Leveraging Generics and Enums to Build a Media Management Web Application*, we developed a new application called MediaMan, which made use of generics, enums, promises, and IndexedDB.

While programming it, we learned about some more TypeScript features, namely, the following:

- Generics
- Enums
- String literal types
- Union and intersection types
- Type definitions and @types
- Decorators
- The any and never special types
- The keyof keyword
- Mapped types

We also learned about the storage APIs that are part of all modern web browsers, such as LocalStorage, SessionStorage, and IndexedDB. Interacting with IndexedDB was also the occasion for us to introduce and use the Promises API. Also, we used libraries such as localForage and class-transformer.

In Chapter 5, *Coding WorldExplorer to Explore the Population of the World*, we focused our attention on modularity. This led us to introduce TypeScript concepts, allowing us to better structure our applications by splitting different logical parts into separate modules: imports and exports, modules, re-exports and barrels, namespaces, module resolution, and many others.

To understand those concepts, we also looked at how modularity has evolved in JavaScript over the years, going from the Revealing Module pattern to AMD/CommonJS, UMD, and TypeScript modules.

We explained the concept of module loaders and module bundlers as well as the difference between them. We saw that they help us to package our applications efficiently but can do so much more for us.

To put those concepts to good use, we created the `WorldExplorer` application. This application interacted with the World Bank's RESTful APIs using the Fetch API and `async`/`await` and allowed us to write asynchronous code as if it was synchronous. We took some time to explain what REST is all about as well as how the Fetch API and `async`/`await` work.

In that chapter, we also spent some time looking at runtime type safety, which we can achieve using the `io-ts` library. That library helped us to ensure that the API responses matched our expectations and didn't require us to duplicate type information, which is great.

Finally, in Chapter 6, *Introduction to Testing*, we also discussed testing by describing different types of tests and testing concepts such as the difference between unit and integration tests, BDD, and many others. After listing some testing tools, we saw how to install, configure, and use Jest, one of the most popular testing libraries.

Retrospective – second half

From Chapter 7, *Discovering Angular, Angular Material, and RxJS* to Chapter 12, *Revisiting LyricsFinder*, we created new applications using Angular, Vue.js, and React, three of the most popular frontend frameworks/libraries out there. We covered many important concepts for each of these and explained their main similarities and differences.

Our goal was certainly not to try and show you the best solution (hint: there isn't one), but rather to show you different ways of creating modern web applications, all while seeing how TypeScript can be leveraged to improve the developer experience and the quality of our code.

While exploring Angular and creating the second version of MediaMan in Chapter 7, *Discovering Angular, Angular Material, and RxJS*, and Chapter 8, *Rewriting MediaMan Using Angular and Angular Material*, we learned about TypeScript decorators, a feature that is used extensively by Angular. We also clarified what the **SPA**, **RWD**, **PWA**, and **SSR** acronyms stand for (that is, **Single Page Application**, **Responsive Web Design**, **Progressive Web Application**, and **Server-Side Rendering** respectively).

We also covered **Reactive Programming** and **Functional Reactive Programming** (FRP), as well as the RxJS library, which is so crucial in the architecture of Angular applications but is actually a great alternative to promises.

In `Chapter 9`, *Introducing Vue.js*, and `Chapter 10`, *Creating LyricsFinder with Vue.js*, we presented Vue.js and discussed many surrounding topics, such as routing and state management (including Redux and its one-way data flow) as well as DI, which we used in our application with InversifyJS.

Finally, in `Chapter 11`, *Diving into React, Nest, GraphQL, and Apollo*, and `Chapter 12`, *Revisiting LyricsFinder*, we went the extra mile and introduced React, Nest, Apollo, and GraphQL. We saw that Nest borrows many concepts from Angular and that it is really easy to learn it once you know Angular, making it a great fit for full-stack JavaScript/TypeScript-based projects when combined with Angular.

While explaining the basics of GraphQL, we tried to draw some parallels with RESTful APIs and gave some examples of powerful built-in GraphQL features, such as the possibility to customize the contents and shape of the API responses.

While quickly exploring the basics of React, we saw that function components are great and that they are now on par with the class-based alternative. We also saw that React is quite different from Angular and Vue.js, but still shares many of the same ideas. Also, we discovered JSX and saw how powerful and enabling it is, allowing us to really take advantage of our JavaScript and TypeScript skills instead of forcing us to learn a lot of new syntax.

We used all of those to create an entirely new version of LyricsFinder. Doing so was also a great opportunity for us to teach you about a few more TypeScript features, such as its support for JSX and object/array destructuring.

The second half of this book should have given you confidence that TypeScript is a great choice irrespective of the chosen framework or library as it really improves the quality of the code and the developer experience.

Where to go next and what to learn

This is a fair question to ask and, honestly, it all depends on you and what you want to learn next.

Whether you are a junior or seasoned software developer, there is always something to learn. This is why our field of work is so fun and motivating!

There are many things that we had to leave out of the book. Not by lack of motivation, but really because of the lack of space. For instance, we could've said a whole lot more about testing and quality assurance, a ton more about user experience, and infinitely more about CSS and web design in general. The same is true for code quality, error handling, security, internationalization, localization, performance, state management, Angular, Vue.js, Angular, Nest, GraphQL, and oh so many other subjects!

Initially, this chapter was intended to be a source of inspiration for you by providing many links towards different resources and things to learn to go further. Unfortunately, the page count of the book was really too high, so we had to leave this part out. But don't be too disappointed; we have decided to publish the list on our blog. You can find it here, with the original content: `https://medium.com/ @dSebastien/typescript-3-projects-whats-next-c22c38293788`.

Summary

You probably realize it by now, but this book was just the beginning of your very own journey! The only constant in our field of work is change. To cope with the pace at which technology evolves, we need to keep learning and sharing. There is no alternative if you want to stay relevant.

But this is also a great time to be doing IT because each new day is full of things to learn and tinker with, which is tons of fun and really entertaining.

We sincerely hope that you've had as much pleasure reading this book as we've had while researching and preparing its content.

More importantly, we hope that you have learned at least a few things from us and that you'll pass it on to the people around you!

Other Books You May Enjoy

If you enjoyed this book, you may be interested in these other books by Packt:

Advanced TypeScript Programming Projects
Peter O'Hanlon

ISBN: 978-1-78913-304-2

- Discover how to use TypeScript to write code using common patterns
- Get to grips with using popular frameworks and libraries with TypeScript
- Leverage the power of both server and client using TypeScript
- Learn how to apply exciting new paradigms such as GraphQL and TensorFlow
- Use popular cloud-based authenticated services
- Combine TypeScript with C# to create ASP.NET Core applications

Mastering TypeScript 3 - Third Edition
Nathan Rozentals

ISBN: 978-1-78953-670-6

- Gain insights into core and advanced TypeScript language features
- Integrate existing JavaScript libraries and third-party frameworks using declaration files
- Target popular JavaScript frameworks, such as Angular, React, and more
- Create test suites for your application with Jasmine and Selenium
- Organize your application code using modules, AMD loaders, and SystemJS
- Explore advanced object-oriented design principles
- Compare the various MVC implementations in Aurelia, Angular, React, and more

Leave a review - let other readers know what you think

Please share your thoughts on this book with others by leaving a review on the site that you bought it from. If you purchased the book from Amazon, please leave us an honest review on this book's Amazon page. This is vital so that other potential readers can see and use your unbiased opinion to make purchasing decisions, we can understand what our customers think about our products, and our authors can see your feedback on the title that they have worked with Packt to create. It will only take a few minutes of your time, but is valuable to other potential customers, our authors, and Packt. Thank you!

Index

P

URL 193, 426, 577

S

SASS
  URL 445
Scala
  URL 425
schematics
  about 383, 384
  reference link 385
SCSS (.scss)
  URL 444
search component
  creating 714
  creating, with Vue slots 590, 592, 593, 594, 595
  hierarchy, defining 715, 716
  input, binding 717, 718
  input, clearing 719
  props, adding to communicate 720, 722
  search handler, adding 719, 720
  skeleton, creating 714, 715
  state, adding 717, 718
search engine optimization (SEO) 375
searchTriggered 721
semantic versioning
  URL 63
semver
  about 60
  URL 60
Server-Sent Events (SSE)
  reference link 371
server-side rendering (SSR) 369, 370
service layer design pattern
  about 180
  reference link 180
Service Locator (SL)
  about 540
  with InversifyJS 540, 542, 544, 545, 546, 547
  with reflect-metadata 540, 542, 544, 545, 546, 547
Service Worker API
  reference link 371
Service Workers (SW) 654

service-oriented design 180
services
  reference link 412
SessionStorage
  about 188, 189
  reference link 190, 371
shared logic
  integrating 448, 449, 450
shouldComponentUpdate() method
  URL 635
simple store pattern
  about 556, 557
  reference link 556
Single File Components (SFCs)
  reference link 504
single responsibility principle (SRP) 135, 136, 504
Single-Page Applications (SPA) 370, 372
SL design pattern 539, 540
slots 592
smart component 404, 456, 697
SOLID design principles
  reference link 111
songs list component
  creating 600, 601, 602, 603, 604, 605, 733
  props, defining 734, 735
  rendering 735, 736, 737
  skeleton, creating 734
  using 600, 601, 602, 603, 604, 605, 733
source maps
  about 102
  obtaining, for easier debugging 101, 102, 103
Spinner component
  reference link 747
splice
  reference link 94
state management, for modern web applications
  about 553, 554
  simple store pattern 556, 557
  state changes, broadcasting 555
  state changes, propagating with custom events and props 554
static fields 110
static methods 110

Made in the USA
Las Vegas, NV
18 October 2022

57624647R00442